Mastering

Photoshop 6

Mastering™

Photoshop® 6

Steve Romaniello

SYBEX®

San Francisco • Paris • Düsseldorf • Soest • London

Associate Publisher: Cheryl Applewood
Contracts and Licensing Manager: Kristine O'Callaghan
Acquisitions and Development Editor: Mariann Barsolo
Editor: Pete Gaughan
Production Editor: Dennis Fitzgerald
Technical Editor: Susan Glinert
Book Designer: Maureen Forys, Happenstance Type-O-Rama
Graphic Illustrator: Tony Jonick
Electronic Publishing Specialist: Maureen Forys, Happenstance Type-O-Rama
Proofreaders: Nanette Duffy, Laurie O'Connell, Yariv Rabinovitch, Nancy Riddiough
Indexer: Ted Laux
CD Technicians: Keith McNeil, Kara Eve Schwartz, Kevin Ly
Permissions and Licensing Specialist: Dan Mummert
Cover Designer: Design Site
Cover Illustrator/Photographer: Jack D. Myers

Library of Congress Card Number: 00-109112

ISBN: 0-7821-2841-6

Software License Agreement: Terms and Conditions

For my daughter, Leah

Foreword

When I think of the best way to learn something—and I mean really learn it—I know I can do that most successfully with the support of an experienced and compassionate teacher. Such teachers takes the time to explain the broad vision behind a lesson as well as its specific parts. They use analogies to make the learning personal, and also put the learning into the broader spectrum of life rather than just an individual application. This way, I can take the lessons to mind as well as heart, and they stay with me forever.

I first met Steve Romaniello when he was chairman of the Communication Graphics program at Pima Community College. I was a new adjunct instructor, hired to develop and teach classes about Web design. Many of my students had taken Steve's Photoshop classes and not only were well-prepared technically to use Photoshop, but also possessed a broad vision of how this software application played into the field of graphic design. I'd overhear students talking about what an inspiration he was, what an energetic and careful instructor.

Though our initial relationship was as professional colleagues, Steve's interest in everything that was happening within the department soon led to us having many a conversation about art, design, and the growing interest in the Web. Out of these conversations a natural friendship grew, and we soon not only found ourselves working together at the college itself, but exploring ways to bring unique graphic design instruction to other arenas. Out of our friendship and these goals, we ended up as co-authors of a Sybex book about GoLive, Adobe's Web authoring tool.

Writing a book alone is no easy task. Writing a book with someone else demands excellent communication skills as well as a strong vision that—even when perspectives are not exactly shared—respects and uses those differing perspectives. What's more, deadlines are very intense in the computer book business. But Steve and I wrote that book without once encountering any problems between us—an awesome accomplishment! Part of the success of that project, I am sure, had to do with the fact that we are both dedicated teachers who are more concerned about our students and readers than our own selves. See, we love this stuff.

That Steve loves design, art, and how these things can be brought to elegant fruition via a powerful application such as Photoshop is a very strong reason that he is not only the best person to have written this book, but one of the very best people to teach you—the reader—how to use Photoshop in both the specific and broad sense. Whether you are using Photoshop in its classic application for print design and photo correction and enhancement, or tapping into its growing collection of awesome Web-based tools, I am absolutely confident that you will benefit from and thoroughly enjoy Steve Romaniello's *Mastering Photoshop 6*.

Molly E. Holzschlag
Tucson, Arizona
November 12, 2000

Acknowledgments

Writing a book of this kind is by no means a solitary venture. It would have been impossible to produce *Mastering Photoshop 6* without the efforts and support of many friends who gave freely of their time and expertise.

First of all, thanks is owed to my agent, David Fugate at Waterside Productions Inc., for representing me with integrity and finesse. Much gratitude to the editorial and production team at Sybex, particularly acquisitions and development editor Mariann Barsolo, who planted the seed and nursed the germination of this book; Dennis Fitzgerald, production editor, who carefully inventoried and organized its contents; and Pete Gaughan, senior editor, whose vast experience helped me craft its ideas and images into a real manuscript. My thanks to the technical editor, Susan Glinert, for her insistence on precision and attention to detail. I'm grateful to Maureen Forys, the electronic publishing specialist, for her aesthetic vision in designing this book and laying out its pages, and to Keith McNeil, Kara Schwartz, and Kevin Ly for helping to compile the CD. Thanks to Dan Mummert, permissions and licensing specialist, who researched the acquisition of materials for the book.

I am extremely grateful to those who contributed material towards the book, including Photoshop master Imo Baird, internationally respected color specialist Brian Lawler, pre-eminent author and web designer Molly Holzschlag, writer Marilyn Smith, and scanning specialist and author Erica Sadun—all shared their experience and expertise in several of the chapters. Thanks to my artist friends—David Adix, Liisa Phillips, Boyd Nicholl, Andrew Rush, and Margo Burwell—who provided images and inspiration for several of the step-by-step exercises and the Hands-On modules. Thanks to Terry Etherton of Etherton Gallery for his insights into the history of photography. My gratitude to Chris Mooney of Balfour Walker/Chris Mooney Photography; Francis Morgan of Morgan, Cain, and Associates; and Margo Burwell for their contributions to the digital gallery.

Thanks to all of my colleagues at Pima Community College, but particularly Kathy Assar, who helped me get the flex time to write this book; Mary Leffler, who provided technical support; and Dennis Landry for his moral support. I also want to thank the many students I've taught over the years. I'm sure that I have learned as much or more from them as they have from me.

My gratitude to Adobe Systems' Christie Evans and the beta support team, who helped me leap over some of the hurdles by providing the Windows and Macintosh beta versions of the software early in the process. Thanks to Alps, Corel, Photo Disk, Corbis, CMCD, and ImageVault for providing images from their CD libraries. And thanks to Alien Skin Software for providing the cool Eye Candy plug-ins on the CD.

Thanks especially to my daughter, Leah, for helping me with many of the screen shots, and to my wife, Rebecca, for her unwavering patience and support throughout this process.

Contents at a Glance

Contents

Introduction

Photoshop 6:
The Image Transformed

Since the early part of the nineteenth century, the photographer has been the primary recorder of events: the magician who captures rays of light and commits to glass, metal, film, or paper, fleeting moments of time. At one time, the credibility of these images could not be challenged. Whether it was a picture of a crime scene in the back alleys of New York snapped by WeeGee in the 1930s, an image of five Marines raising a flag on a war-ravaged Pacific island in the 1940s, or an astronaut making the first footprints on the moon's virgin surface in the 1960s, the photograph was considered the undisputed visual representation of the truth. The thousands of images published in popular picture magazines like *Life* or *Look* have become an integral part of the pictorial legacy of America and the world.

Artists such as Oscar Gustave Rejlander and Henry Peach Robertson performed experiments in altering and compositing images as early as the 1850s. They both used double exposure, printing from multiple negatives, and cut-and-paste assemblage to produce elaborate photo-compositions. These chemical and mechanical processes were quite labor intensive, required great skill on the part of the artist/technician, and were often detectable by the close scrutiny of a trained eye.

Historically, photographic images have been altered for many reasons: to conceal or fabricate evidence, to discredit or accuse, to promote a political agenda. Let's not forget that images have also been altered for less sinister ends. Like the cosmetic surgeon, the airbrush artist routinely removed unwanted wrinkles and hair, photos were optically enhanced in the darkroom in the process of preparing them for publication, and of course, artists have found the photograph fertile ground for fantasy and experimentation.

Here we are at the beginning of a new millennium. Adobe Photoshop has been around for 10 years, and in the decade of its existence, it has had a profound effect not only on the methods we use to manipulate images but also on the very way in which we view them. From the introduction of computer graphics in the 1960s and the evolution of imaging software in the '70s and '80s, to the release of a powerful, personal, mainstream image editing package called Photoshop in the early '90s, the credibility of the photograph has been shattered. With a personal computer, a trained eye, and a bit of practice, anyone can alter the reality of an image from the familiar confines of their desktop.

The tools that a culture has at its disposal define that culture's potential. Photoshop, being the ultimate imaging tool, affords you a direct pathway to unlimited, creative possibilities. Photoshop is more than software; it is a process unto itself. From the initial scan to the final output, Photoshop gives you access to a complete set of controls that can create, manipulate, edit, or correct digital images for use in any publishing media, including print, multimedia, video, and the World Wide Web.

Mastering Photoshop: Who Should Use This Book

The immense popularity of Adobe Photoshop is in part attributable to the fact that it enables us to alter the reality of images. And who, after all, can resist the temptation to change the nature of what we see? *Mastering Photoshop 6* is for anyone who has ever unconsciously scribbled a moustache on a face in a magazine while talking on the telephone. It's for those of us who take photographs, draw, paint, and cut and paste pictures. It's for computer artists, graphic designers, and printers. It is intended to help master the software, at whatever level you may be in the learning curve. The book covers the basics of Photoshop but also delves into the intermediate and advanced levels of the program.

A Systematic, Comprehensive Approach

The focus of *Mastering Photoshop 6* is to present a complete and organized guide to the tools and operations of Adobe's amazing image editing software. It is intended to offer descriptions, explanations, and techniques that will make all aspects of the software more accessible and familiar to you without oversimplifying or "dumbizing" the information. How you work in Photoshop will be defined by your specific output goals. The book explores the basic concepts that are fundamental to your understanding of the digital image. Each chapter contains information to help you master the Photoshop skills you need. Most chapters contain step-by-step modules, and many conclude with Hands-On projects, which will further enhance your capabilities so that you can ultimately apply the techniques to your own images.

Photoshop is an enormous software package with the capability to perform almost any imaging operation. When you consider the number of operations that Photoshop can execute, and how they might be combined, the image editing possibilities become infinite. Making this information understandable and, above all, interesting to you, is the intent of *Mastering Photoshop 6*.

How to Master Adobe Photoshop 6

The Master in the art of living makes little distinction between work and play, labor and leisure, mind and body, education and recreation, love and religion. He simply pursues his vision of excellence in whatever he does, leaving others to decide whether he is working or playing. To him he is always doing both.

—Zen aphorism

Mastering Photoshop is much like mastering any discipline. Learning where the tools and operations are and how to use them is only the beginning, which is why this book goes beyond mere inventory and directions to philosophy, practice, and experimentation. The real mastery comes from being able to creatively apply what you know. Although Photoshop is used by scientists and engineers for image manipulation and color correction, the majority of end users are interested in expressing visual ideas. Photoshop gives them the power to paint, color, synthesize, collage, composite, manipulate, and distort the reality of their pictures and fulfill the potential of their artistic vision.

Photoshop is like all visual art forms, in that the best work is created with love, passion, focus, and skill. The fundamentals of design, composition, and color apply to digital images just as they do to traditional drawings, paintings, and graphics. The basic principles of design are balance, proportion, unity, direction, and emphasis. Great images are *balanced* in that they carry an appropriate weight within a given space. The viewer's eye can move from one element to another with fluid ease. The *proportional* relations of elements create an optical rhythm throughout the composition that the viewer can sense, which effectively communicates the content of the image. The image is *unified* by a strong cohesive force that holds it together. The eye moves in a determined *direction* and does not wander aimlessly around looking for a place to rest. Elements are structured in a visual hierarchy, which *emphasizes* them in the order of their importance. The mood, color scheme, and ambiance are relevant to the content and message of the image.

Along with a cognizance of the importance of design, the Photoshop master is innately sensitive to the formal elements of the image—color, light, shadow, form, and perspective—and knows the potential and the limitations of the tools that are needed to produce the desired results. The master pays attention to the minutest of details with the realization that the photographic image is relentless in its seamless portrayal of reality.

Finally, the Photoshop master is committed to the attainment of absolute perfection but is well aware of its elusiveness. Each new project presents a fresh opportunity to apply his or her knowledge, skills, and insights to the fulfillment of this exalted goal.

Whether the path to mastery is strewn with broken glass or freshly cut flowers depends on your route. *Mastering Photoshop 6* is intended to take the sting out of learning the program and make the experience pleasant and interesting. It will be your tour guide and point out some of the remarkable landmarks and points of interest along the way, helping to make your journey absorbing and entertaining. Of course, merely reading this book is not enough. You must work through the step-by-step operations and Hands-On exercises until you understand the concepts and then apply what you've learned to your images. From time to time you will need specific questions answered, and I hope *Mastering Photoshop 6* will provide all the answers you need.

Making the Most of *Mastering Photoshop 6*: What's Inside

The primary content of *Mastering Photoshop 6* is distributed into several parts. There is also a special color insert and a support CD-ROM, containing the documents and images used in this book.

Part I: Back to Basics

To put the phenomenon of Adobe Photoshop into an historical perspective, the introductory chapter presents the artistic foundations and technical innovations that have lead to its emergence as the leading image editing methodology in the world today. The sources are as diverse as the impressionist movement and the development of the World Wide Web. In Chapter 2, I cover all of the new features that make version 6 a most spectacular upgrade.

The rest of Part I, which is by far the largest section of the book, explores the nuts and bolts of Photoshop. The fundamentals of digital imaging are explained to provide insight as to how Photoshop documents are created and structured. With this basic information under your belt, you will gain a working, hands-on knowledge of Photoshop's basic tools and operations, knowledge enough to begin to apply them to real-world projects.

Part II: Color Adjustment and Photo Retouching

Part II presents techniques for managing and manipulating color. This is the section where you will learn how to manage color throughout the entire imaging process to assure predictable results. Part II delves into color tonal adjustment and correction. A variety of creative color-mapping and correction possibilities are explored, along with techniques for image enhancement and photo retouching.

Part III: Mastering Techniques

You'll really flex your Photoshop muscles in Part III. Featured are advanced techniques to manage layers, make complex selections, apply creative and enhancement filters, superimpose images, and automate the program.

Part IV: Photoshop 6 for the Web

The Internet, being a fundamental aspect of communication in the twenty-first century, deserves an exclusive section of the book. Photoshop is universally used to create and edit images for the web. We will explore techniques for Web page design in Photoshop and methods for optimizing and saving images for use on the Internet. You'll explore ImageReady, Adobe's Web image preparation software that is bundled with Photoshop, and you'll learn to create spliced images, rollovers, and animations.

Appendices

The appendices provide lists of relevant information that pertain to specific aspects of the program. They include a description of Photoshop 6's tools, file format information, explanations of blending modes, and a list of key commands.

Glossary

The focus of *Mastering Photoshop 6* is to demystify the software and make it more user friendly and understandable to you. I have deliberately taken pains to avoid computer-ese wherever possible; however, in many instances it is not possible to explain certain concepts without using a specialized vocabulary. For this reason, I have included a comprehensive glossary for common (and uncommon) terminology that you may not be familiar with or that is needed to clarify a concept.

Conventions Used in This Book

These features will accelerate your ability to learn Photoshop and find specific information when you need it.

Tips and Warnings

Tips are helpful hints that demonstrate efficient, effective procedures to accomplish your task. Warnings alert you to potential problems or areas where you need to proceed with caution.

This is a Tip. Tips contain specific helpful suggestions.

This is a Warning. Warnings call attention to bugs, hazards, and other trouble spots.

CD and New Materials

Throughout the book, we've flagged the places where you can take advantage of files on the CD-ROM. Look for the CD margin icon to quickly spot hands-on practice and demo files.

I've also identified features that are new to Photoshop 6 with a "New" margin flag. If you're familiar with previous versions of Photoshop and want to skim a topic for the latest changes, look for this marker. Photoshop's new features and operations are also summarized in Chapter 2.

Sidebars

Sidebars develop specific ideas and expand upon information that is related to the chapter's primary information. Sidebars also present related troubleshooting techniques and sources for additional information.

Color Gallery

The 32-page color section displays many relevant examples of information demonstrated within the chapters.

What's on the CD

The CD-ROM contains the images and documents used to perform the step-by-step operations and Hands-On modules. Images are contained within labeled folders for each chapter. The images are copyright-free except where noted, so you can freely edit and print them. There is also a gallery section and live demos and plug-ins.

How to Reach the Author

It gives me great pleasure to make the information I've gathered over the past ten years available to you. I truly hope that *Mastering Photoshop 6* serves your needs and answers your questions. When I co-authored *Mastering Adobe GoLive 4* with Molly Holzschlag, I was amazed at the incredible feedback to the book we received from all over the world. I appreciate your feedback and would like to hear from you. You can reach me at `www.globaleyesystems.com`.

Steve Romaniello
Tucson, Arizona

Part I
Back to Basics

In This Part

The Foundations of Photoshop

PHOTOSHOP

Chapter 1

To understand how Photoshop works, it's helpful to have a perspective of the artistic and technical traditions from which it evolved. Techniques that have been in general use for centuries are the source of most of what we can do on a computer today; software is merely the tool to apply the techniques. These tasks have been performed manually or optically to achieve similar results throughout the ages. Putting Photoshop into an historical context will give you a perspective of its potential and how its many features are related to traditional methods of working with images. This chapter covers these topics:

- What is image technology?

- The history of imaging, from ancient Rome to today

- Painting, printing, and photography

- The world of Photoshop and the Web

Image Technology

Image technology is the method in which pictures are produced. Since the first images were painted on the stone walls of caves with pigment extracted from natural materials, humans have invented new image technologies to visually express their ideas and experiences. The process of technical evolution was slow in preindustrial societies. For thousands of years, the techniques of creating images were primarily done by the skilled hands of artists and artisans. During and after the industrial revolution however, image technology accelerated to the point where today we see new innovations on almost a daily basis.

The evolution of the visual image is, in part, due to the methods available to the artist. Artistic styles are an expression of the zeitgeist (literally, spirit of the time) of the periods that produce them. As technology evolves, new ideas and visual idioms emerge that reflect the cultural ambiance of their times. This idea is quite apparent in the twentieth century from the speed in which new technologies emerged. The obvious changes in aesthetic values can be observed decade by decade as cultural, political, and technological influences affected visual expression. Each decade of the twentieth century can be associated with distinct aesthetic styles that are part of the ongoing development of culture.

The Romans

One significant milestone in the history of visual art was the ability to portray tonality. Tonality is the effect of changing light or color on an image. In the real world, we see a seamless continuum of blended color that defines our visual world in light and shadow, and produces a tangible, three-dimensional reality of color and form. Primitive artists made no attempt to express tonality, in part because the technology was unavailable to them.

If you think that digital images are a new phenomenon, however, think again. One of the first methods of simulating the effect of tonal variation was to place tiny individual units of slightly varied color next to each other. We see this technique commonly employed in mosaics from Imperial Rome, like the one in Figure 1.1. Each element of color is a separate glass or ceramic tile. The tiles, placed next to each other in a graduated sequence, produce the effect of varied tonality.

Figure 1.1 *A mosaic from first century B.C.E. Pompeii.* The Defeated Persians under Darius *(detail).*

The mosaics of two thousand years ago are the predecessors of today's Photoshop images. Instead of glass, the digital artist uses tiles of light called *pixels* (see Figure 1.2). Today's scanners can "see" and interpret color information from a continuous-tone image into these tiny units. When the image has been captured, we can, in Adobe Photoshop, select and change the color of pixels individually or in groups.

Painting

Creating images by applying color to a surface is one of the most basic forms of artistic expression; indeed, the history of the world can be viewed in the legacy of paintings that have been left behind by our talented predecessors. Throughout history, the technical and aesthetic qualities of painting have changed, various styles have emerged, and pictorial content has evolved.

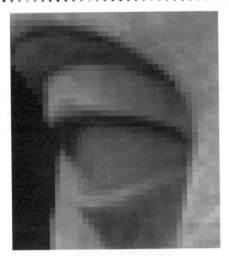

Figure 1.2 Photoshop's pixels

Representational painting dominated the world for centuries. Paintings contained content that could be easily recognized, whether the subject matter was religious, historical, or descriptive. In the late nineteenth century, artists begun to abstract the tangible realities that they observed to produce art filtered through their personal experiences. Within 50 years, abstraction led to the creation of a totally nonobjective idiom in styles like the Abstract Expressionism of the 1950s and the Minimalism of the 1960s.

Still, the tradition of representation coexisted with abstract painterly forms, but it was reinvented time and again as it reflected the zeitgeist in which it created. Pop Art of the 1960s, for example, introduced us to the idea that the objects and icons of popular culture could be assimilated and even elevated into the realm of "pure art." This concept was revolutionary, because it changed the way we viewed the commonplace.

Though the imagery has changed, the painter's tools have remained pretty much the same over the centuries. Paint, palette, knife, brushes, solvent, paper, canvas or panel, and easel have been around for quite some time, having seen few refinements throughout history. Even the airbrush evolved from an air-driven breath atomizer that has been in use since the eighteenth century. The concept remains the same: mix colors on the palette, adding solvent if desired, and apply them to the painting surface with a brush or knife. Only recently have methods of applying color to a surface been substantially transformed.

Photoshop is a virtual art studio. Through Photoshop's graphic user interface (GUI), you can apply color to an image as if you were painting. Instead of pigment, however, you are mixing colors and painting with light. Photoshop has numerous tools, operations, and filters that enable you to make a photographic image appear as if it had been painted in virtually any style and with any paint medium. You have 16,777,216 colors to choose from and a brush of any size or shape with which to apply the color.

Printing

Another significant change in the ability to produce images came about a thousand years ago, with the emergence of woodcuts, which were used to print textiles. In the early fifteenth century, the use of woodcuts and wood engraving began to take hold in Europe as a method of producing pictures (see Figure 1.3). At about the same time, Gutenberg introduced the concept of movable type technology. Printing gave us the capability of producing multiples of the same image—the first big step in mass communication.

Figure 1.3 *Detail of a woodcut from Torquemada's* Meditations on the Passions of Our Lord, *a book published in 1473.*

Of course, the printed image has evolved over the past 500 years; we've invented numerous methods of imprinting ink on paper, monochromatically or in full color.

In the case of traditional offset printing, the process involves separating colors into their ink components, transferring the information to a piece of film and then to a metal plate. Ink is applied to the plate, and the color is imprinted onto paper.

Photoshop software is used to prepare images for almost any commercial printing technique, including offset lithography, silk screen, and digital press. Artists even use Photoshop to create and transfer images for traditional copper or zinc intaglio printing.

Of course, the most direct method of printing a Photoshop image is to a laser or ink-jet printer. Photoshop files can also be output to film recorders (to generate color slides) and imagesetters (to produce high-resolution color separations). Exciting new output technologies have appeared within the last few years to print super-sized ink-jet images and continuous-tone photographic prints.

The Impressionists

In the nineteenth century, in an attempt to revive what was perceived to be the glories of the classical civilization of the Greeks and Romans, much of what was being produced in the art world consisted of the representational, idealized images of the Neoclassic style. In the latter part of the century, the nature of European art shifted. The Impressionist movement emerged with a fresh new approach to painting. Artists like Claude Monet, Paul Cézanne, and Mary Cassatt produced paintings that were explorations of the quality and nature of light and color.

The importance of the Impressionist's contribution to the way we perceive color can not be overstated. One particular group of Impressionists, the Pointillists, and particularly Georges Seurat (see Figure 1.4; a color version of this image is in the color section), were most influential to the digital art we practice today. The Pointillists worked extensively with color theory and how one color affects the colors around it. They applied paint to the canvas in units, or little dots, not unlike the pixels on a Photoshop document or the halftone dots on a color separation. They experimented with how the eye mixes adjacent colors. Placing dots of two opposite colors—red and green, for example—next to each other will produce gray when seen from a distance. The relative density of the dots affects the darkness and lightness of the perceived color and its tint.

Figure 1.4 *Detail from Georges Seurat's* The Models, *painted in 1883*

Pointillism influenced the development of process printing, which uses four colors to produce full-color images. Figure 1.5 presents a close-up view of such a four-color picture (for a color view of this image, check the color insert section). In process printing, each color plate contains tiny dots of cyan, magenta, yellow, or black (CMYK). Like Pointillist painting, the densities of the colored dots on each plate influence the surrounding colors when the eye mixes them together.

Figure 1.5 *Detail of a four-color process image*

Photoshop is the ultimate color separator. It can configure and generate process-color separations and separate duotones, tritones, and quadtones. In addition. Photoshop has filters that allow you to simulate Impressionist and other painterly effects.

Photographers

When you think of how many centuries passed in which images were created exclusively by hand, you can appreciate how revolutionary the photograph was. A crude type of camera called a camera obscura was developed in the beginning of the fourteenth century that captured and projected light on a surface. However, it wasn't until 1826 that the first true photograph was taken. Early photographers needed special equipment and a broad knowledge of chemistry to produce photographs. As a result of the scientific and technical discoveries of the nineteenth and twentieth centuries, cameras became more efficient and easier to operate, so that today millions of still photographs are taken and processed every day.

A camera is very much like the human eye. Light rays enter a camera and are focused on a surface into an image. Film rests on the surface and is exposed, causing a chemical reaction. The exposed film is then bathed in certain chemicals in a process called developing. If the film is a negative, light is passed through it onto a piece of photosensitive paper. The paper is developed, stopped, and fixed which produces a positive photographic image.

Several tools, filters, and operations are designed to make the photographer feel right at home in the digital Photoshop environment. In fact, Photoshop is a virtual darkroom that includes tools to dodge, burn, saturate, enlarge, and of course, correct and adjust color. New digital printers are available that shine laser light on photosensitive paper to produce beautiful, continuous-tone color prints.

As a result of the popularity of computer programs like Adobe Photoshop, digital cameras have become a recent addition to photo technology. Digital cameras create pictures that can be transferred to a computer or television set. The digital camera's lens focuses light on a light-sensitive mechanism called a charge-coupled device (CCD), which changes the light into electrical signals. The electronic pictures can then be stored on disks or opened in a computer graphics program. With additional equipment, electronic images can also be sent over telephone lines or printed on paper.

Surrealism

In the early part of the twentieth century, the artistic revolution in Europe was shocking the world with images that had never been seen before. Instead of representational content, the pictorial sources came from an abstraction of physical reality or the realization of a personal, inner reality. Cubists, Dadaists, and Surrealists changed the face and meaning of art.

Before World War I, the Dada movement produced works of anti-art that deliberately defied reason. Growing principally out of Dada, Surrealism flourished in Europe between the World Wars as a visual art and literary movement. Surrealist images have a dream-like quality where time, space, and matter are completely malleable. Compelled by the idea that rational thought and behavior had brought the world close to the brink of annihilation, the Surrealists created images that were anti-rational and anti-bourgeois. Surrealist painters like Jean Arp, Max Ernst, Salvador Dalí, Paul Delvaux, René Magritte, André Masson, Joan Miró, and Yves Tanguy created new worlds where the nature of reality depended only on the artist's unlimited imagination.

Hand in hand with this new aesthetic freedom came new image technologies. For artists concerned with the free association of images and the meaningful relation of unrelated objects, collage was the technique of choice. The recycling of printed graphics and text in the form of collage was developed to accommodate the Surrealists' need to create the visual non sequitur. For the first time, printed images from multiple sources were combined to produce a new pictorial reality. The Surrealist Max Ernst created an entire book called *Une semaine de bonte* (*A Week of Kindness*), a pictorial novel consisting entirely of recycled engravings from newspapers, magazines, and catalogs (see Figure 1.6). This novel was a technical and aesthetic tour de force when it was published in 1933. It epitomized and refined the absurdist viewpoint of the Surrealists and the freedom and creativity in which they pursued their artistic vision.

Figure 1.6 *An engraving from Max Ernst's* Une semaine de bonte

Photomontage

New movements in art and graphic design blossomed in Europe in the 1920s and 1930s as a result of the instability brought about by aftermath of World War I, the Great Depression, and the Russian Revolution. Constructivism, New Typography, Streamline, and Dada recycled photographic images, typography, and graphics as collage elements in a new process called photomontage.

Radical magazines and newspapers from the period, like *Simplicicity* and *Arbeiter-Illustrierte-Zeitung (AIZ, or Worker's Illustrated Times)*, published photomontage images as satirical cartoons to promote a socialist or anti-fascist political agenda. Photomontage is a collage of photographs that are carefully cut and pasted together to create a new visual reality. Often, type and other graphic elements are incorporated into the composition. These images synthesized the seamless pictorial realities of multiple photographic images into biting political metaphors (as in Figure 1.7) and clever visual puns. Traditional cut-and-paste photomontage was an art form derived from the Cubist, Dadaist, and Surrealist movements but was displayed in the commercial venue of magazine publications. It was the predecessor of the digital composite images we see in many of today's advertisements.

The ability to combine photographs, text, and graphics from multiple sources is one of Photoshop's strongest features. Images can be collected from a scanner, digital camera, or PhotoCD and be composited, superimposed, positioned, scaled, flipped, rotated, and distorted. In Photoshop almost any effect is possible; the only limitation is your imagination.

The Web

Recently, the world has been transformed by a powerful new invention. This new communication technology is as revolutionary as the telephone and as ubiquitous as the automobile. Within a few years, it has imbedded itself deeply in our lives and has affected how we communicate and how we do business. The World Wide Web (Figure 1.8) is by far the most accessible communication medium in which to publish images or text. As a research tool, the Web gives us instant access to every conceivable form of information. The Web is the ultimate technical manifestation of democracy in that it embodies the essence of free speech and freedom of the press. Being the most unregulated of all publishing mediums, anyone can publish anything at any time.

Figure 1.7 *A montage by John Heartfield, published in AIZ in 1934. Reproduced with permission of Artist Rights Society (ARS), New York.*

The Web has changed the nature of how we handle pictures. Images can be transmitted electronically and downloaded, making access to them almost instantaneous even at a distance. Many art museums and libraries have placed digital files of their entire archives online, making them accessible to everyone. If you need a picture of a particular subject, the first and last place to look is now the Web.

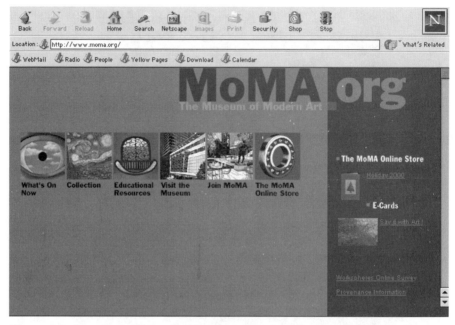

Figure 1.8 *Reproduced from the Museum of Modern Art, New York, Web site: www.moma.org. Copyright © 1999 The Museum of Modern Art, New York.*

The tools and functions introduced with Photoshop 5.5 have been almost exclusively devoted to Web publishing. Methods for choosing, optimizing, and saving files in the appropriate format have been seamlessly integrated into the program, eliminating all guesswork. A new color picker offers the choice of Web-compatible hexadecimal colors. ImageReady, software used for creating slices, animations, and rollovers, has been bundled with Photoshop to further extend Photoshop's capabilities and to work in a fully integrated environment.

Photoshop

The introduction of new artistic idioms into our culture not only affects the world of art galleries and museums, it influences advertising, architecture, industrial design, and fashion. As new styles appear on the scene through commercial vehicles, they become an integral part of our everyday lives. The same is true of new image technologies: as new ones are introduced, they become embedded into the production cycle of our economy.

In our contemporary culture, images are everywhere. Pick up a book, magazine, or newspaper, and images dominate the layout. Take a walk or drive, and you'll see images on billboards, signs, and the sides of buildings. These pictures are the result of the work performed by artists, designers, illustrators, and photographers. The legacy of image technology is the primary influence on the images we see today. Its evolution has given us the foundation to create and manipulate images to visually communicate ideas in personal, commercial, or artistic venues.

Never in the history of art have we seen anything quite like Adobe Photoshop. Never has one single tool, studio, or machine combined so many powerful methods of working with images. Photoshop is the culmination of the development of image technology over thousands of years. It is a revolutionary new way of visually communicating ideas. It unites the vision of the artist with the technology of the moment. Since its first release, it has been the world's most popular imaging software, because it endows its users with so many possibilities for the creation and development of images for any form of publication. Photoshop presents those possibilities in the elegant, user-friendly environment of the virtual art studio, darkroom, or print shop, where images can be created and edited in any conceivable size, content, or configuration.

Up Next

Now that you've seen the origins of the image technologies that inspired Adobe Photoshop, let's take a peek at the new features in version 6. Each time Adobe releases a new version of the software, your capabilities are further enhanced and extended. Sometimes the interface is improved, sometimes new tools and operations are added.

If you are familiar with earlier versions of the software, you'll see major improvements. If Photoshop 6 is your first version, the next chapter will define the latest tools and operations that will complete your image-editing arsenal.

What's New Briefly

PHOTOSHOP

Chapter 2

Photoshop 6 has a lot of new features that, I think you'll agree, have greatly improved the program. In addition to an ingenious interface that improves the accessibility of your tool options, a multitude of new features are designed to streamline your workflow. Exciting, new, cutting-edge tools and operations increase Photoshop's power to generate and transform images.

When you purchase Photoshop 6, you receive ImageReady 3, Adobe's Web graphics software that is neatly integrated with Photoshop. There are substantial improvements in ImageReady for processing and preparing images for the Web. It includes many of Photoshop's new enhancements plus additional Web-specific upgrades. If you're familiar with Photoshop 5.5, then these new features will be recognizable improvements. If you're new to Photoshop, you'll get an idea of the extent of its potential. I'll go through the new features in categories so that you can get a general idea of what to expect.

Interface and Navigation

New features enable you to access and save files more efficiently. There have been big improvements over the management of the desktop environment and handling of palettes and presets.

Accessing and Viewing

Photoshop provides even more ways to open and view your documents, including these:

- Favorites and Recent buttons in the Open dialog box let you quickly access recent files.

- A Find button in the Open dialog box, which launches Sherlock, the Macintosh search command (Mac only).

- The Open dialog box offers Thumbnail browsing.

- The File menu has an Open Recent command.

- A simplified Twain lets you access scanning and other input devices more easily.

- You can undo a step backwards or redo a step forward from the Edit menu or with key commands. Step Backward: Command+Option+Z/Ctrl+Alt+Z; Step Forward: Shift+Cmd/Ctrl+Z.

- View ➜ New Guide creates a guide in a designated location.

- Preferences and Color Settings submenus are now found under the Edit menu.

- Holding down Shift+Cmd+Option or Shift+Ctrl+Alt while launching deletes the preferences file, allowing you to quickly return to Photoshop's factory settings.

Palettes

Vast improvements have been made to palette operations making them more accessible and easier to handle, including:

- The Brush and Swatches palettes are resizable vertically as well as horizontally.

- The Brush palette is attached to the Options bar and is accessible when any tool requiring a brush is selected. You can rapidly create temporary brushes.

- The Swatches palette displays the names of its colors when you hover the mouse over them.

- You can attach individual palettes vertically and move them as a unit.

- There is a new Styles palette, which lets you apply layer styles to the contents of a layer.

- Pressing the Tab key hides all palettes as in former versions. Shift+Tab now hides all palettes except the Tool palette and Options bar.

- The Ignore Palettes check box, in the Zoom tool Options bar, lets you increase the size of the window past the palette boundaries as you zoom in.

- Descriptive labels called *tool tips*, formerly only accessible when hovering over the Tool palette, have been added to many of the menu items and dialog boxes.

Presets

The new Preset Manager lets you save and load libraries of brushes, swatches, gradients, styles, patterns, contours, and custom shapes, making them readily accessible.

Tools

The Tool palette has been reorganized. An Options bar replaces the Options palettes. A few tools have been added to the list, including the Slice, Path Component Selection, Shape, and Notes tools. The tool menus in the Tool palette contain the icon, name, and shortcut key.

Toolbar

Access to your tool options has been overhauled. I think the new Options bar, which replaces the Tool Options palettes of former versions, is the one upgrade that will increase efficiency more than any other. When you click a tool, its options appear at the top of the screen (always in the same location, although you can move it). You no longer have to dig through piles of palettes to find the one you're looking for. The Options bar has a Palette Well where you can dock seldom-used palettes, so you can keep the desktop free of stuff that interferes with your view of the image.

The Options bar also features:

- Choice of Boolean options—Add, Subtract, Intersect, and Exclude—when drawing or selecting

- Access to numeric Free Transform operations

- A new Show Bounding Box check box that lets you display and transform selected areas and layer contents quickly when using the Move or Path Component Selection tools

- An improved Brush Dynamics pull-down menu, giving you more control over faded and pressure-based brush strokes

Crop Tool

The Crop tool has been significantly improved for better display and more flexible performance.

- The Perspective crop option in the Options bar lets you make non-rectangular crops. It distorts the image to fit within the new rectangular shape.

- Shield Cropped Area dims the portion of the image outside the crop marquee for more precise cropping.

- Image → Crop works on any selection, including feathered ones.

- A new command, Image → Trim, removes the transparency or a color from an image.

- The new Image → Reveal All enlarges the document to encompass all of the image—even data on layers outside the image area.

Shape Tools

The new Shape tools provide a method of quickly drawing vector or raster shapes. The shape tools include the Rectangle, Ellipse, Polygon, Star, and Custom Shape. You can create extensive custom shape libraries. You can make Actions from shape drawing.

Path Component Selection Tool

Use the new Path Component Selection tool to select and modify shapes and paths.

Annotation Tools

The new annotation tools (Notes tool and Audio Annotation tool) let you attach written or audio notes to your document for later reference.

Patterns and Gradients

Patterns and gradients are powerful fill operations that have been greatly improved.

- You can name patterns and save them to a list so you can access more than just as single pattern.

- You can make a pattern out of the entire document, if you don't make a selection prior to defining the pattern.

- You can move or scale patterns.

- The Fill command lets you choose patterns from a list.

- The Gradient Editor has been improved, with color and transparency stops for determining the distribution.

- You can create new noise-based gradients.

- The new Gradient Map feature in the Image ➜ Adjust submenu maps gradients to the brightness values of your image.

Slice Tools

The new Slice tool and the Slice Select tool are used to cut an image into smaller components for efficient downloading on the Web.

Text

Numerous modifications to the Type tool are some of the most dramatic changes to the program.

- Direct entry and on-screen editing of type are now possible.

- You can take advantage of point and box text entry and word wrapping.

- New type styles options include case, ligatures, and old-style figures.

- The new Character and Paragraph palettes (similar to Adobe Illustrator's) give extensive control of text generation.

- New Asian text options include Japanese formatting controls.

- The Create Outlines feature in the Layers palette pull-down menu will create outlines from a text layer if font outline data is available.

- A Warp Text option lets you bend and flex type into a large variety of shapes.

- You can color individual text characters.

Layer Management

Layers are one of the best methods of organizing your documents into accessible dynamic components. The Layers palette has been improved for efficiency of operation.

- Layer sets have been added to cluster contiguous layers so that they can be repositioned in the stack and transformed simultaneously.

- Version 6 lets you lock the transparency, editing, and position of a layer. (In 5.5 you could only lock transparency.)

- You can color-code layers and layer sets for easy recognition.

- The new Layer Styles (formerly Layer Effects) dialog box is accessible by double-clicking a layer. Many new styles have been added to the list.

- To name a layer, press Option/Alt and double-click the layer to display the Layer Properties dialog box.

- Blending and advanced blending options have been included in the Layer Styles dialog box.

- Prior versions limited the number of layers to 99. You can now create an unlimited number of layers.

Mini Programs

Photoshop has several built-in features that I like to call "mini programs" because they act as complete software programs unto themselves. They are nicely integrated into Photoshop and have similar, elegant interfaces. The existing ones have been improved and a new one has been added.

Save For Web

The File ➜ Save For Web option has been improved from the 5.5 version to offer some new features.

- Save For Web supports the selection of slices created in ImageReady or Photoshop.

- You can create, change, or slice characteristics from within the dialog box.

- The slice number, type, and links are displayed from within the dialog box.

- You can turn on and off the visibility of the slices with the Slice Display button.

- An Output Settings control lets you determine document-specific settings for your HTML code when saving Web graphics.

Extract

Image ➜ Extract has seen improvements, including:

- Smart Highlighting that determines the most appropriate edges of an extracted area

- Touch-up tools for cleaning up edges

- An OK button that lets you quickly exit the dialog box without having to preview the extract

Liquify

The Image ➜ Liquify command is the centerpiece of this upgrade and its most fun feature. Using it is like sculpting with pixels.

- Move, shrink, stretch, twist, and enlarge areas of the image with a complete set of interactive brushes.

- Freeze areas of an image to prevent them from being distorted.

- Fine tune adjustments with the mesh option.

- Reconstruct all or part of the image.

Increased Settings

- For several operations, the range of settings has been extended.

Function	New Limit	Old Limit
Select ➔ Modify ➔ Contract	100	16
Select ➔ Modify ➔ Expand	100	16
Select ➔ Modify ➔ Smooth	100	16
Select ➔ Modify ➔ Border	100	16
Image ➔ Matting ➔ Defringe	200	64
Filter ➔ Stylize ➔ Emboss	100	10
Filter ➔ Stylize ➔ Mosaic	200	64
Filter ➔ Other ➔ Maximum	100	10
Filter ➔ Other ➔ Minimum	100	10
Filter ➔ Other ➔ Median	100	10
Filter ➔ Noise ➔ Dust & Scratches	100	10

- Most layer effects have increased their size capabilities to apply the effect to up to a 250-pixel size.
- Shadows can be offset by as much as 30,000 pixels.
- Edit ➔ Stroke now supports units other than pixels.
- Filter ➔ Add has been changed to work with percentages rather than pixels.

Saving and File Formats

New modifications to saving options and file formats have been added.

- Save As and Save A Copy have been consolidated into one menu.
- TIFF and Photoshop PDF formats now support layers.

- TIFF format now offers LZW, JPEG, and ZIP compression schemes.

- PBM, Wavefront RLA, and Alias PIX formats are now supported.

- Improvements have been made to the PhotoCD import dialog box.

- Resolution-independent vector output can be produced from files saved in PDF format.

- PDF supports Duotones and spot colors.

Actions and Automations

Several features have been added to Actions and Automations that are designed to streamline your workflow and make it easier to batch process files.

- A new upgraded Contact Sheet dialog box lets you specify fonts and sizes for your labels.

- The Web Photo Gallery command instantly creates a Web site from the images contained within a folder. Introduced in Photoshop 5.5, it has been improved to contain specific templates of predefined layouts and an HTML frames option.

- The Picture Package is now template-driven. It no longer adds extra margins around the image.

- The Droplets command in the Automate menu lets you generate an Actions droplet that performs the operation when you drag an image file or folder onto it.

- Brush selection options are scriptable.

Color Management

Photoshop's color management features have been revamped. Edit ➜ Color Settings, which have always been confusing to the novice at first look, present a formidable learning curve because they are so extensive. The new interface actually makes color settings more understandable.

- RGB, CMYK, Grayscale, and Profile Setups have been merged into a single dialog box.

- Extensive descriptions have been built into the dialog box to help you understand the complexities of color management.

- There is better support for cross-program color management.

- The color management interface is similar to Illustrator 9.

- Select from preset settings or create your own.

ImageReady 3

Adobe ImageReady3 is bundled with Photoshop 6 and has been upgraded to offer even better controls for Web documents. Many of the Photoshop's commands, tools, and menu items are also available in ImageReady. The major improvements have taken place in the following areas.

- Better integration with Adobe GoLive, Adobe's Web authoring software, lets you save ImageReady files to GoLive-compatible code.

- Better integration with Photoshop lets slices generated in Photoshop be edited in ImageReady and vice versa.

- Improved code generation lets you determine case and naming conventions for HTML code.

- Variable file compression settings can be based on slices or alpha channels.

- Enhanced slice controls let you create slices from layers.

- The creation of rollovers has been simplified.

- A new Image Map tool that lets you define an area as a rectangle, ellipse, or polygon.

- The Jump To command has been simplified. It is no longer necessary to save a document before Jumping to Photoshop.

Up Next

Major improvements have made Photoshop even more powerful. As you read through *Mastering Photoshop 6,* the new features will be indicated by the New icon. Take special note of these items to learn these powerful new features.

Next we'll look at some of the fundamental processes that aid you in working on your images. We'll talk about the basic structure of a digital image so that you can understand how Photoshop processes files. I'll teach you ways to streamline your work-flow by implementing simple production strategies. You'll learn how to open and save files, and I'll talk about platform and compatibility issues.

The Nature
of the Beast

PHOTOSHOP

Chapter 3

Photoshop is indeed a beast. It's big, wild, and colorful. In fact, version 4.0 of Photoshop was actually code-named the Big Electric Cat. The 6.0 version was code-named Venus in Furs; a secret splash screen portrays a sleek, female cat as a dominatrix in high, black, leather boots, holding a whip (no doubt the midnight whim of a sleep-deprived programmer). Indeed, Photoshop 6 is a sleeker, smarter beast that will do your bidding if you ask it nicely.

Photoshop has dominated the world as the most popular image-editing software because it is so big and friendly and it does so much. It has the combined attributes of all of its competitors wrapped into a powerful, elegant, user-friendly package that empowers you to alter the reality of digital images.

Before you can tame the beast, you need to understand its temperament. In this chapter, you'll learn about:

- The anatomy of a digital image: vector and raster images

- Color channels

- Working in Photoshop

- Opening, saving, and duplicating documents

- File formats, platforms, and other software

The Anatomy of a Digital Image

There are two fundamentally different methods in which software constructs images. Vector graphics consist of objects constructed by mathematically defined points and curves. Raster images use a grid of squares, or *pixels,* to determine color variations.

Understanding Vector Graphics

Vector graphics are composed of lines and objects that define their shapes. On a computer, you can draw hard-edged graphics that, when printed, produce clean, sharp lines and edges. This is particularly valuable for illustrators who want to create crisp, well-defined artwork. Vector software is also ideal for graphic designers who work with type, because type characters need razor-sharp edges with no "jaggies" (stair-step edges caused by a series of right angles trying to represent a curve).

Vector-based illustration software like Adobe Illustrator, Macromedia FreeHand, and CorelDRAW, or page-layout programs like QuarkXPress, Adobe PageMaker, and Adobe InDesign, are sometimes referred to as *object-oriented* software, because the primary technique requires building independent graphic lines or shapes ("objects") point by point, segment by segment, and stacking and arranging them until your drawing or page is complete.

To draw these objects, the artist uses a method of clicking and dragging the mouse, which deposits points, line segments, or shapes. The objects created in vector-based software are made from *Bezier curves,* like the ones in Figure 3.1. Bezier curves can even be straight lines, but what makes them different from the pixels used by raster images is that that they are composed of mathematically defined points and segments.

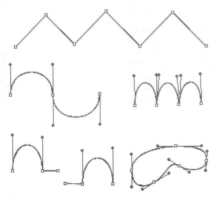

Figure 3.1 *Bezier curves*

One advantage of using vectors to create images is that the images are *resolution-independent*, which means that they automatically conform to the highest resolution of the output device on which they are printed, whether it's a desktop ink-jet, a laser printer, or a high-resolution imagesetter.

Because the data of vector-based images are mathematical equations, a printer can read the formulas of each object transmitted in a printer language and convert the information into tiny dots. An image that is created at the size of a postage stamp can be resized and printed at the size of a billboard with no loss of quality. The complexity of a vector image, not its size, is what determines the file size; therefore, vector images take up much less space on a disk than raster images of comparable dimensions. Figure 3.2 shows raster and vector versions of the same image. The image on the left is composed of pixels; the image on the right is composed of objects surrounded by anchor points and line segments that define Bezier curves. The Bezier curves do not print. (This image is also presented in the color section.)

Figure 3.2 *(left) A raster image (composed of pixels) and (right) a vector version of the same image, composed of shapes constructed from Bezier curves*

Object-oriented software extends your capability to produce high-impact color graphics. Vector-based illustration software is appropriate for the creation of traditional logos, charts, graphs maps, cartoons, highly detailed technical and architectural plans, and illustrations and images that require hard edges, smooth blends, and sumptuous color. Vector-based page-layout software is ideal for the creation of documents where images and text are combined, as in books, pamphlets, brochures, and flyers.

Understanding Raster Images

Although Photoshop uses vector-based graphics in a few of its operations (see the sidebar, "Vector Tools in Photoshop"), it is primarily designed to edit *raster images*. Raster images, sometimes called *bitmaps*, are fundamentally different than vector images in that they consist of a grid of little squares called *pixels* (short for *picture elements*). A pixel is an individual square of colored light and is the smallest editable unit in a digital image. The pixels in a digital image are usually so small that, when seen, the colors blend into what appears to be a continuous-tone image. Figure 3.3 is enlarged so you see the individual pixels that make up the image's overall effect.

Figure 3.3 *A close-up detail of an image composed of pixels*

Vector Tools in Photoshop

Although Photoshop's capabilities are primarily designed to select and edit pixels, a few tools are vector-like in their performance. The Pen tool uses Bezier curves to make accurate selections. Its operation is similar to the Pen tool in Adobe Illustrator. Once you've created a curve or path, you can stroke or fill it, convert it into a selection for raster editing, or export it to a vector-based program. (The Pen tool is discussed in detail in Chapter 9, "Drawing Paths.")

The Type tool creates type generated from your installed fonts. The type remains editable until you rasterize it or "flatten" the image. The Photoshop Type tool is extremely powerful for creating display text and special text effects, but it does not handle body copy (usually text 12 points or smaller) very well because of the anti-aliased nature of raster images. It is best to import your Photoshop image into a vector-based illustration or layout program and generate the body copy there. When printed, the image will conform to its specific image resolution, and the text will print at the resolution of your printer. (See Chapter 8, "Working with Type," for more on the Type tool.)

Photoshop 6's Shape tool (described in Chapter 9) is an another vector generator. You can choose from a list of standard shapes, such as rectangles, ellipses, and polygons, and you can construct, edit, and store entirely unique vector-based shapes.

The distinction between Photoshop and vector-based illustration software, like Illustrator, FreeHand, or CorelDRAW, is that Photoshop does not print object-oriented graphics as vectors. Instead it depends on the resolution information of the document to automatically rasterize them before they are sent to the printer. The vector operations in Photoshop are designed to make the interface more powerful and user-friendly but do not affect the image when it is output.

The quality of a raster image and how it prints depend on the number of pixels the image contains, or its *resolution*. If you think of a pixel as the basic building block of an image, you can envision how a larger number of smaller blocks will more precisely define an edge or an area than fewer, larger blocks. The file sizes of raster images are usually quite large compared to other types of computer-generated documents, because information needs to be stored for every pixel in the entire document.

Raster-based software is best suited for editing, manipulating, and compositing scanned images, images from digital cameras and Photo CDs, continuous-tone photographs, realistic illustrations, and hyper-real artwork including logos with subtle blends, soft edges, or shadow effects and artistic filter effects like impressionist or watercolor.

Color Channels

When an image is scanned, the color information the scanner "sees" is separated into red, green, and blue components. Photoshop configures this information into three color channels plus a composite RGB channel, which displays the entire image in full color. Think of each color channel as a separate, transparent color overlay consisting of red, green, or blue pixels. The combination of the three color values, when superimposed over each other, produces full color. When an image is scanned, each channel can potentially contain a total of 256 possible shades each of red, green, or blue, because each pixel on the channel contains eight bits of tonal information (see the sidebar, "Bit Depth").

The computer processes the information in each channel as an independent grayscale image. Each pixel is assigned a specific numerical gray value, where black equals 0 and white equals 255.

By default, individual color channels are displayed in grayscale, because it is easier to see the subtle variations in contrast when looking at the channel in black and white. You can, however, see the independent components of an RGB image in color. Follow these steps:

1. Choose Window → Show Channels.

2. Choose File → Preferences → Display & Cursors.

3. Check the Color Channels In Color option, shown in Figure 3.4. Click OK.

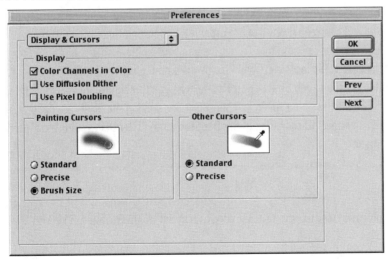

Figure 3.4 *Check the Color Channels In Color option in the Display & Cursors preferences.*

Bit Depth

A computer uses the binary number system to describe pixels. The simplest graphic images are one bit "deep." In these files, only one binary digit of information describes the pixel: 0 for off, 1 for on. Each pixel is one of two colors, either black or white.

Grayscale and Indexed color images use an 8-bit system, in which any pixel can be one of 256 shades of gray or colors, respectively. Each pixel contains eight bits of information. Each bit can either be on (black) or off (white), which produces 256 possible combinations ($2^8 = 256$).

Full-color images are 24-bit color, using three 8-bit primary color channels—for red, green, and blue—each containing 256 colors. These three channels produce a potential of 16.7 million colors ($256^3 = 16,777,216$). Photorealistic images that consist of smooth gradations and subtle tonal variations require 24-bit color to be properly displayed.

Some scanners will produce images of 32-bit color. In this system, the information is actually being distributed into four 8-bit channels that produce more than four billion colors (256^4). The extra channel extends the dynamic range of the scanner so that it can produce more subtle tonal variations. Once the image has been scanned, however, it is usually resampled down to decrease its file size. Photoshop can read images with 16 bits of information per channel, like a 48-bit RGB or a 64-bit CMYK color image, but the file sizes of these images are much larger and the operations and filters that are available for them are limited.

Even though images with higher bit depths contain more color information, they are displayed on the monitor at the bit depth capability of your video card, which in most cases is 24 bits. To see an image in 24-bit color depth, on a Macintosh, the monitor should be set to Millions Of Colors; in Windows, the setting should be Full Color.

The information from the image that you create in Photoshop is transmitted from the computer to the monitor. A color monitor consists of a grid of screen pixels that are capable of displaying three values of color simultaneously. There are three electron guns inside the monitor—a red, a green, and a blue—that scan the surface of the screen and fire streams of electrons at it. The more electrons that hit the screen pixel, the brighter it glows. When all three guns are firing at full intensity, the screen pixel appears white; when all three guns are not firing, the pixel appears black. The variation of the intensities of red, green and blue electrons striking the pixels is what produces the full range of color that we see on screen. Of course, all of this happens much faster than your eye can perceive, so you see a stable image on your monitor.

In the Channels palette (Figure 3.5), click the thumbnail of the red, green, or blue color channel to display that color component of the image on screen.

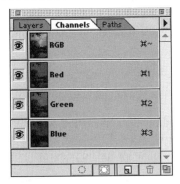

Figure 3.5 *The Channels palette*

If you think about it, the computer is really a mega calculator that sits on your desktop and crunches numbers at lightning speed. Although the graphics user interface, or GUI (pronounced "gooey"), of a raster software program like Photoshop lets you perform virtual operations that mimic real-world tasks like painting, compositing, or filtering, what is actually happening behind the scenes is that the numeric color values of the red, green, and blue pixels in each color channel are being changed.

Working in Photoshop

Photoshop works as an image editor, color corrector, or photo compositor, but by no means is it limited to these tasks. Its primary purpose is to alter reality, and that is the ultimate reason for its popularity. There is something very compelling and empowering about changing the color of the sky in a landscape or replacing Uncle Herman's scowl with a smile from another photograph.

No matter how you alter an image, the sequence of procedures you employ is quite similar:

1. Capture the image using a device like a scanner or digital camera. These devices "see" the continuous-tone image and divide the information into pixels, which Photoshop can display and edit.

2. Save the image to a disk. The image is stored on your disk media as a sequence of numbers that represent its pixel information.

3. Open the image in Photoshop and use one of Photoshop's selection techniques to isolate the part of the image you want to affect. When you make a selection, you are telling Photoshop in advance where you would like to apply an operation.

4. Apply one of Photoshop's numerous tools or operations to the image to implement an edit.

Of course, this sequence can vary and can become extremely complex by the application's specialized selection techniques, multiple operations, or sophisticated layer methods, but generally speaking, this is how you work in the program.

Strategies

Because high-resolution images require large amounts of memory and processing time, the digital artist or designer should develop a strategy for each job. A good production strategy should focus on four areas:

- Configuring and optimizing your system so that it runs smoothly

- Working wisely and efficiently in Photoshop

- Using shortcuts

- Communicating clearly with your client

Optimizing Your System

These items are discussed in detail in Chapters 5 and 15, but here are some basics for optimizing your system:

- Increase the application memory.

- Assign the scratch disk to your fastest hard drive with the most disk space. From the size of the largest open file, Photoshop requires three to five times that much disk space for the scratch disk. You can choose additional scratch disks to increase the amount of virtual memory.

- Keep the clipboard clear of large amounts of data.

- Keep your disks optimized, using a utilities program regularly.

- Install as much RAM as possible.

- Turn Virtual Memory off (Macintosh users).

- Work on a calibrated system.

- Compress files whenever possible.

Working Wisely

These items are discussed in more detail throughout the book. You'll want to keep these in mind when you are working in Photoshop:

- Create a low-resolution version of the document. Lay out the image and experiment with operations and effects. Then apply those same operations to a high-resolution version.

- Save your settings when adjusting color.

- Work on a duplicate of your image (Image ➜ Duplicate) so that you can experiment freely.

- Save selections as paths or alpha channels whenever possible.

- Use layers to segregate parts of the image in order to keep the editing process dynamic.

- Apply filters to each channel individually when necessary.

- Learn and use keyboard shortcuts, Actions, and the History palette.

- Save your document often, and back up your work.

- Archive your images to CD or other media in order to free up hard disk space.

Using Shortcuts

While a good production strategy will smooth your workflow, numerous key commands and shortcut techniques can enhance your performance. In Photoshop, there are several ways to execute almost every operation, which can be confusing at first. Many of the same operations can be performed from a menu, by a key command, or from a palette, field, or button. As you develop knowledge of the program, however, you will begin to fashion a way of working that is unique to your personal style, and it will be only a matter of deciding which method suits you.

The quick-key list in Appendix D gives you a list of Photoshop's key commands. It pays to learn as many of them as possible, particularly the ones that you use most frequently. Not only will this save you work time, it can be physically beneficial to try a new style of operating your computer. Finally, if you work on more than one operating system, be sure to read the section on "Platform Compatibility" later in this chapter for more on keyboard shortcuts.

Taking Advantage of Actions

You can write a Photoshop script, called an Action, that you play by pressing a function key. Actions automate one or a sequence of operations. Actions enable you to perform multiple tasks quickly. One nice perk is that you can save Actions to a file. When you need a particular Action or Action sequence, you can play it and apply its operations to any image. Photoshop ships with some tasty default Actions that are really convenient to use. You can even run a Batch Action that will be applied to all of the images in a folder while you are sleeping, watching television, or eating a grilled cheese sandwich. For more about Actions, read Chapter 21, "Automating the Process."

Accessing Tools

Photoshop's numerous tools are accessible by simply touching a letter key on the keyboard. Of course, you have to remember what tool each letter represents. Sometimes it's quite obvious—for example, M for the Marquee tool—but sometimes it's not, as in K for the Paint Bucket tool. Don't worry if you if you forget a tool's keyboard equivalent. Simply hold your cursor over any tool, and a little label, called a tool tip, will tell you the name of the tool and the key that represents it. As you can see, the shortcut key for the Paintbrush tool is B.

Saving Adjustments, Colors, and Brushes

Color adjustment settings can be saved as a separate file and loaded for application to other documents. You can make a brush of virtually any shape, size, hardness, or angle and save it for use in any Photoshop document. You can create and save special Color palettes and apply the colors to any Photoshop image. These techniques are covered in detail in Chapter 10, "Creating and Applying Color," and Chapter 16, "Adjusting Tonality and Color."

Photoshop's interface is so well designed that the processes of saving and loading adjustments, colors, brushes, or Actions are all the same. When you've learned to save or load one, you've learned to save or load them all.

Communicating with Your Clients

Whether you're a professional designing for commercial customers, or a volunteer producing images for nonprofits, many of you are using Photoshop to create images for clients. When you're working for a client, the creative process becomes a collaboration. Clear and open communication with your client is essential to maintaining a smooth workflow. Here are some keys to keeping your client satisfied:

- Make sure that you and your client have agreed on the job's objectives and specifications. Show your client your work in stages. Start with thumbnails and develop the project over time, getting your client's approval for each iteration before proceeding with the next. Determine how the finished image will be used. If you are going to output to print, determine film and print specifications like paper, ink, and halftone screens. If it's going to be output to CD-ROM or the Web, be sure find out what the size and format specifications are. Put all the job specifications in writing.

- Determine the nature of the job, what work is to be done, and what third-party vendors will be involved. Will you need to purchase high-end scans, or will desktop scans suffice? Are you responsible for output, or will your clients deal directly with the service bureaus, printers, or Internet providers?

- Define each component of the project and build a realistic schedule around this information. You will then be able to structure your time and make consistent progress on the project.

Opening Documents

Most of your work in Photoshop will be performed on images that have been acquired using some piece of digital technology that converts color information into pixels. After you've captured an image with a scanner or digital camera and stored it to a disk, you can open these files by choosing File ➜ Open, which brings up the dialog box shown in Figure 3.6.

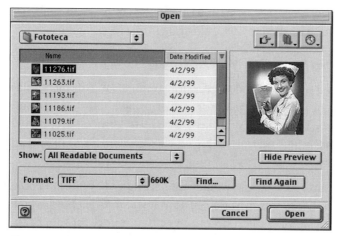

Figure 3.6 *The Open dialog box*

You are presented with a list of files on your disk. Highlight one by clicking it with your mouse. If the Show Preview button is clicked (it then becomes the Hide Preview button), the dialog box displays a thumbnail of the image.

You swear that you saved an image to a particular disk, but it does not appear in the list. Well, the Photoshop Open window may not display certain files when it doesn't recognize the file's type. On the Macintosh, a file's type code is four characters long and can be seen in its Get Info box. On Windows, the file type is represented by the file-name extension, which is three characters long. For example, TIFF in MacOS equates to .tif in Windows.

To display those files regardless of their type code or extension, Macintosh users should select All Documents from the Show options pop-up list; Windows users click the down arrow in File Of Type and select All Formats. Photoshop attempts to guess at the format in which it thinks the file has been saved. If you think Photoshop has guessed incorrectly, then click the Format options list and choose the correct format (as shown in Figure 3.7). If you get an error message, keep trying. If you've tried all of the formats and can't open the image, it is either corrupt or incompatible with Photoshop.

Figure 3.7 *The Open dialog with the Format list*

Finding Files

In Photoshop for MacOS, the Open command has a Find function built into it. If you can't find the file you're looking for, click the Find button. In the next dialog box, enter all or part of the file name, click Find, and the program will take you to the first item on your disk with the same name. If the Find function displays the wrong file, click Find Again until you locate what you're looking for.

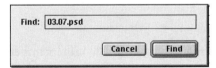

Importing a Scanned Image

Scanner software often has a plug-in module that will work directly within Photoshop to scan an image. The module must be placed in the Plug-Ins folder in the Photoshop folder when the scanner software is installed. In most instances, the plug-in will be automatically placed in the Plug-Ins folder when it is installed. Choose File ➜ Import to access the module. When the image is scanned, it will automatically appear in a new Photoshop window.

Creating New Documents

You can generate a new, empty document in Photoshop. The new document can be used as a blank canvas on which to paint or to paste images from other sources.

To create a new document, follow these steps:

1. Choose File ➜ New. The New Document window (shown in Figure 3.8) appears.

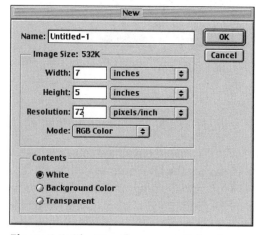

Figure 3.8 *The New Document dialog box*

2. In the Name field, enter a name for the document, but remember that naming the document is not the same as saving it. Eventually you will need to save it to your disk.

3. Just under the Name field, the file size in bytes is displayed. This will change depending on the height, width, and resolution you choose for the document. Enter a width and a height in the appropriate units.

4. Enter the resolution of the document. This will depend on how the document will be output. (See Chapter 13, "Scanning and Resolution.")

5. Choose a mode from the Mode list, which indicates how the color information of the new document will be configured. Use Bitmap for line art and Grayscale for black and white images with tonality. RGB (red, green, blue), CMYK (cyan, magenta, yellow, and black), and Lab (Lightness, A, and B) modes will produce full-color images. (See Chapter 10 for more on color modes.)

6. In the Contents field, indicate what the color of the background will be. You can choose white or choose the current background color in the Tool palette; these will produce a flattened image. If you choose Transparent, the Background will become a regular layer (with a checkerboard pattern to indicate transparency), because the Background cannot be transparent (see Chapter 7).

7. Click OK.

Creating a Document from the Clipboard

You can create a document window from an image that has been copied to the clipboard. To perform this operation, follow these steps:

1. Choose Select ➜ All.

2. Choose Edit ➜ Copy to copy an image or the contents of a selection in Photoshop, or a raster image from another software program, to the clipboard.

3. Choose File ➜ New; Photoshop automatically displays a New Document dialog box with the dimensions of the copied image.

4. Click OK. The new, empty image window appears.

5. Choose Edit ➜ Paste, and the image is copied into the new document.

Saving Files

There are five different methods for saving a Photoshop document to a disk, including the Export functions; all are found in the File menu. They are affected by the options set under File ➜ Preferences ➜ Saving Files (see Chapter 5). What follows is a description of each method.

Save As

Use File ➔ Save As to save your document to a designated location on your disk. You can name the document and choose a format for it. The newly named document will replace the image in the document window. Version 6 provides new options in the Save As dialog box (Figure 3.9).

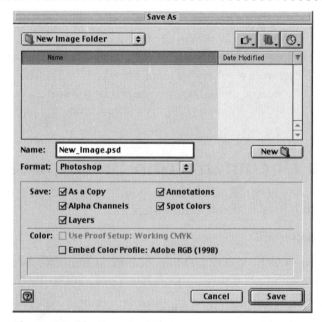

Figure 3.9 *The Save As dialog*

Checking or unchecking the boxes in the Save field of the Save As dialog box allows you to choose options that configure the document to your particular needs.

As A Copy   In previous versions of Photoshop, Save A Copy was a separate menu item; it is now an option in the Save As dialog box. When you check Save As A Copy, the document is saved to a designated location on your disk but does not appear in the image window. Be sure to rename it so as not to replace the current image.

Save As A Copy creates a new, identical document that is automatically renamed with the current document's name plus the word copy—*for example,* mydocumentcopy.psd. *If you Save As A Copy with the same name to the same location, you replace the original file, defeating the make-two-versions purpose of the command and essentially just performing a plain Save. Proceed with caution, because it is possible to lose the previous document.*

Alpha Channels   If you're saving an image that contains alpha channels to a format that supports alpha channels, this box will be active. Formats that support alpha channels are: Photoshop (PSD), Photoshop 2.0, Photoshop PDF, PICT, Pict Resource, Pixar, Raw, Targa, TIFF, and Photoshop DCS 2.0. (See Chapter 12, "Using Channels and Quick Mask.")

Layers   If you're saving an image that contains layers to a format that supports layers—Advanced TIFF or Phothsop (PSD)—this box will be active. (See Chapter 7, "Using Layers.")

Annotations   If you've attached notes to your document with Photoshop 6's new Notes tool, you can include them in the saved version by checking the Annotation box. Photoshop (PSD), Photoshop PDF, and TIFF are the only formats that support annotations. (See Chapter 4, "Navigation: Know Where to Go.")

Spot Colors   Spot color channels can be saved by checking this box. Formats that support spot color are: Photoshop (PSD), Photoshop PDF, TIFF, and Photoshop DCS 2.0. (See Chapter 23, "Duotones and Spot Color.")

The boxes in the Color field of the Save As dialog box determine whether color management information will be saved with the document. (See Chapter 15, "Color Management and Printing.")

Use Proof Setup   A soft proof is an on-screen document that appears as close as possible to what the image will look like if printed to a specific device. If you are saving the image as a Photoshop EPS, Photoshop PDF, or Photoshop DCS 1.0 or 2.0, you can embed in the document the soft proof profile, which you choose from the View ➜ Proof Setup menu. (See Chapter 15.)

Embed Color Profile   Checking this box embeds the CMYK profile chosen in the Edit ➜ Color Settings dialog box under the Working Spaces field. You can select this option if you're saving to any format except Photoshop 2.0. (See Chapter 15.)

Save

Saving a document (File ➜ Save) updates the file that you are working on and saves it to the current document. When working in Photoshop—or any software, for that matter—it is always a good idea to save frequently so you won't lose valuable time and effort should your system crash.

Save For Web

This option (File ➜ Save For Web) was introduced in the 5.5 version and serves as a convenient tool for preparing files for Web publication. On the Web, as in life, there is always a compromise between quality and speed. When you choose Save For Web, you choose the best combination of format characteristics for Web images (Figure 3.10). You can compare the appearance and download times of up to four possible configurations for your image at a time. The Save For Web option is covered in detail in Chapter 24.

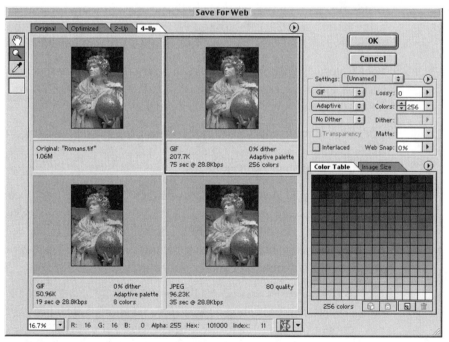

Figure 3.10 *The Save For Web dialog box*

Paths To Illustrator

The File ➔ Export ➔ Paths To Illustrator command lets you save paths created with Photoshop's Pen tool as an Adobe Illustrator file. You can align and trace paths on an image in Photoshop and export Paths To Illustrator; when you open them in Illustrator, they will be fully editable as Bezier curves. (See Chapter 8 for more about paths.)

Duplicating a Photoshop Document

You can duplicate a document on the fly. The Image ➔ Duplicate function will produce an exact copy of the document along with its layers and alpha channels. It is useful for quick experimentation when you don't want to affect the original image. The new file, which by default is given the name of the original plus the word *copy*, is unsaved and exists only in memory. If you plan to keep the duplicate file, it is wise to save it immediately. Check the Duplicate Merged Layers Only box if you want to combine the visible layers into one merged layer in the new document.

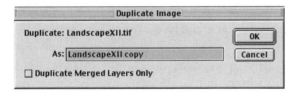

File Formats

Different file formats serve different purposes. Some formats are used to compress data to make the file size smaller on the disk, while others are used to make a file compatible with another software program or the World Wide Web. The format you choose will depend on how the image will ultimately be used. It is important to know what saving an image to a specific format will do. At worst, saving a file to the wrong format can actually damage it; at the very least, it will inconvenience you by losing the ability to place the document into another program.

Photoshop 6 can open 26 and save to 20 different file formats. With the addition of plug-ins that attach to the Import and Export submenus, Photoshop supports even more, which means it is a great program for converting files to make them compatible with other software programs. A complete list of file formats, what they do, and how they operate can be found in Appendix C.

Platform Compatibility

In ancient computer times (less than a decade ago), a battle raged between Macintosh and Windows users. Amazingly, the passion and prejudice generated by proponents of one platform or the other bordered on religious fervor. The Mac was vilified by Windows users as "the OS for people who can't read." Windows 95 was besmirched by Mac disciples as "Macintosh 89." Ugly remarks were hurled, and fisticuffs broke out at a Seybold conference. Macintosh fanatics booed Bill Gates and Steve Jobs at a Macworld convention when they announced a partnership between Microsoft and Apple.

What is it about a computer platform that generates such divisiveness in its adherents? I think it has to do with the fact that a personal computer is, in essence, an auxiliary brain. It stores information and ideas that can't fit into the limited storage capacity of our own gray matter and extends our ability to make calculations and perform complex tasks. A platform simulates the way we think and organize our reality. We can personalize the way each interface behaves and how it looks, to a certain extent, which increases our attachment to it.

The phenomenon of platform prejudice will, I'm sure, be a topic for social theorists to thoroughly investigate in the future. The battle has died down, to some extent, because of the ability of the different computers to read each other's data. MacOS 7.0 and later versions have a program called PC Exchange bundled into the system, which gives the computer the ability to read Windows disks. If you install a program like MacOpener by DataViz (`www.dataviz.com`) on your Windows PC, it will read Macintosh disks. With the same data now readily accessible by both platforms, the barriers have come down some.

The platform issue has also diminished because of programs like Photoshop that, for the most part, ignore platform differences. Photoshop is designed to be cross-platform-compatible and to perform comparably in Windows and Macintosh environments. Photoshop will open documents from either platform, providing they have been saved in a format that supports cross-platform compatibility. The native Photoshop format is probably your best bet, because it supports layers. TIFF (which in version 6 also supports layers), PICT, and EPS are good alternatives for flattened images, providing they are saved with cross-compatibility in mind. You can use JPEG format with its efficient compression scheme to archive images to CD and open them in either platform.

Photoshop performs equally well on Macintosh and Windows computers. For the most part, the Photoshop interface is similar for both versions of the software, with minor differences in appearance. Because Macintosh and Windows keyboards differ slightly, keyboard commands are different; Table 3.1 lists the parallel command keys on the two systems. In this book, whenever I list a keyboard shortcut for a platform, it's safe to assume that the keys listed here will work on the alternative platform.

Table 3.1 Macintosh and Windows Keyboard Equivalents

MACINTOSH	WINDOWS
Command*	Ctrl
Option	Alt
Delete	Backspace
Return	Enter

*The key with the apple and/or four-loop icons on it

Software Compatibility

In the age of information, publishing is indeed a universe unto itself. The process of creating an image for print, multimedia, video, or the Web may involve many steps that require specific tools. It is the task of the designer, image editor, desktop publisher, or computer artist to assemble the tools that best perform the necessary tasks. Photoshop does not exist in a vacuum but works in concert with other computer programs to integrate the images, text, graphics, animations, etc., that compose the final publication.

Interestingly, as the platform battle mentioned earlier in this chapter raged in the early nineties, so did the Software Wars. What was the better program? Illustrator or FreeHand? QuarkXPress or PageMaker?

Today, the battle rages over Web-authoring programs like FrontPage, Dreamweaver, and GoLive. As absurd as it sounds, individuals are as passionately attached to their computer programs as they are to their political ideologies.

In that publishing programs are designed to capture the market, they continually leapfrog each other in their capabilities from version to version. The bottom line is that they are really quite comparable. Which publishing software you choose is, of course, a matter of personal preference, and it's claimed that the Romans used to say *de gustibus non est disputandum*—there is no disputing about taste. If you can learn how to use a program in a reasonable amount of time, if you like the way it is organized, if you enjoy its look and feel, and if you can perform the required tasks easily and efficiently with a minimum of bombs and errors, then you've chosen the right software.

Images created in Photoshop integrate into all mainstream desktop-publishing, illustration, Web-authoring, and video-editing programs. Because of its ability to open and save in so many different file formats, Photoshop is preferred by most design professionals as the essential image-editing software and is the mainstay in a suite of powerful publishing tools.

Up Next

Now that we've looked into the eyes of the beast and seen that it's not particularly ferocious, but not exactly warm and cuddly either, we're going to jump inside its mouth and examine its teeth, so to speak. We'll look inside Photoshop at the many tools, menus, and palettes that make it operational, and you'll learn a few tricks to help navigate around its interface.

Chapter 4 will give you a handle on how Photoshop displays images and where to find the things you need. We will also discuss some of the basic tools and how they work.

Navigation:
Know Where to Go

PHOTOSHOP

Chapter 4

When you think about it, a computer-generated image is not really that complex. In fact, the image really exists as a series of positive and negative charges on a piece of magnetic media. Quite unlike a drawing, painting, or photograph—for which you only need your eyes and a half-decent light source to see—viewing a digital image requires some very fancy electronic equipment, like a computer and a monitor. To edit or manipulate the image, you need a mega-software program like Adobe Photoshop. Photoshop is big all right—so big that it's quite possible to get confused or lost trying to determine where all the stuff is and what it means. Use this chapter as your road map, because it explains Photoshop's numerous navigation features that enable you to find your way around the program. We will look at Photoshop's workspace, menus, and palettes, and learn how to view images.

In this chapter, you'll learn about:

- Launching the program

- Photoshop's GUI

- Accessing menus

- Working with palettes

- Displaying the image

- Using rulers, guides, and grids

Launching the Program

When you install Photoshop 6, you can access the program files from your Macintosh or Windows desktop. The Adobe Photoshop 6.0 folder (see Figure 4.1) contains icons that make Photoshop functional, plug-ins that extend its capabilities, and settings that contain Photoshop's preferences. Also included are additional folders that contain extras like stock art, additional color palettes, custom brushes, and other freebies.

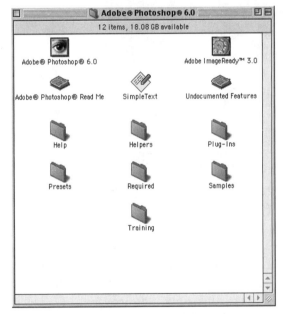

Figure 4.1 *The Photoshop folder (Macintosh version)*

The Adobe Photoshop 6.0 folder contains the Photoshop application. To launch the program, double-click the program icon.

The Splash Screens

When you double-click the Photoshop 6 icon, the splash screen (Figure 4.2) appears, telling you what components of the program are loading. It also displays some of the data you entered when you loaded the program onto your computer, such as your name and the program's serial number. The splash screen contains a few amusing features worth mentioning. It is the signature piece of the designers and software engineers who contributed to the program's development.

Figure 4.2 *Photoshop's splash screen*

As soon as the program finishes loading, the splash screen disappears. You can display it again by choosing About Photoshop from the Apple menu on a Macintosh or from the Help menu in Windows. Wait a moment, and the text starts to scroll. Hold down the Option key (Mac) or the Alt key (Win) to accelerate the scroll rate. If you wait for one complete scrolling cycle and then hover or Ctrl-click your cursor just above the large Adobe Photoshop 6 title, you will see Photoshop Transient Witticisms, a series of one-liners created by Photoshop's program developers and engineers. To make the splash screen disappear, click it.

If you press Command (Mac) or Ctrl (Win) while pulling down the menu command to display the splash screen, you see the secret splash screen. The dominatrix cat (a take-off on an earlier Photoshop feline theme) is called Venus in Furs.

The eye icon at the top of the Tool palette accesses the Adobe Online splash screen, which launches your browser and takes you to the Adobe Web site at www.adobe.com for online help.

When the program is fully loaded, the splash screen disappears and your interface looks like Figure 4.3. The Tool palette is displayed on the left, and four palette clusters are displayed on the right side of the screen. At the top of the screen are the menus. From these three areas, you will access all of Photoshop's image editing tools and operations.

Figure 4.3 *The Photoshop workspace (Windows version)*

Photoshop's GUI

A graphical user interface (GUI) is a software program's way of communicating with you. The computer is really not much more than a machine that does really fast math. Each operation is a series of mathematical calculations. Imagine how labor-intensive it would be if you had to perform that math yourself. For example, suppose you had to change the RGB values of one square inch of an image to be printed in a magazine. You would have to perform 90,000 calculations by hand. Talk about mathaphobia! Fortunately, software designers have set up an environment—the GUI—that makes it easy for you to perform complex calculations quickly and without even having to add 2 + 2. In fact, when you work in a program like Photoshop, the GUI is so seamless that it feels as though you're painting or drawing to change the color of pixels.

Photoshop's GUI is very easy to use once you learn what the tool icons and menu items represent and how they perform. This can take a while, because Photoshop can do so much. The Photoshop GUI provides tools and operations that are used by many image-related professionals, including designers, architects, photographers, artists, printers, and scientists. These virtual tools simulate the processes and operations performed by their real-life counterparts and furnish a comfortable, familiar working environment.

The Image Window

When you open or create an image, it is displayed in the image window (shown in Figure 4.4). To change the window's size, place your cursor on the lower-right corner, click the mouse button, and drag while holding the mouse button. To move the window, click the bar at the top of the window and drag. The scroll bars to the right and at the bottom allow you to scroll around images that appear larger than the size of the window.

The image window contains information about the document. The title bar gives the document's name, the percentage (of the image's full size) in which you are viewing it, and its color mode. In the lower-left of the image window (on the Macintosh) or the Photoshop application window (in Windows) is the status bar. The left-most field of the status bar shows, again, the view size as a percentage of the image. This, however, is the magnification box, where you can enter a specific percentage, to the hundredth of a percent, in which to view the image.

Calculating a File's Size

A document's file size is calculated by multiplying its height and width in pixels by its bit depth, or the amount of memory each pixel consumes. For example, a full-color document that is 7" wide by 5" tall and has a resolution of 72 ppi (pixels per inch) is 504 pixels by 360 pixels.

Since the image is in full color, each pixel consumes 24 bits of space on the disk. For this information to be of use to us, we must convert it into bytes; since there are 8 bits in a byte, we divide 24 by 8 and get a factor of 3. We multiply the height by the width by the bit-depth factor, or $504 \times 360 \times 3 = 544{,}320$ bytes. Since there are 1024 bytes in a kilobyte, we divide 544,320 by 1024 = 531.56, or 532 kilobytes rounded off to the nearest whole number.

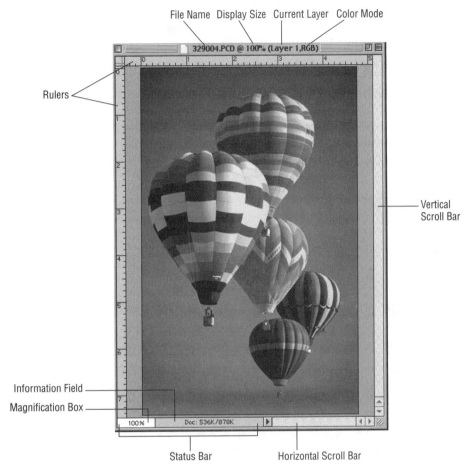

File Name Display Size Current Layer Color Mode

329004.PCD @ 100% (Layer 1,RGB)

Rulers

Vertical
Scroll Bar

Information Field

Magnification Box

100%   Doc: 536K/878K

Status Bar   Horizontal Scroll Bar

Figure 4.4 *The image window*

In the second field at the bottom of the window, by default, are two numbers divided by a slash, representing the document file size. The number to the left of the slash indicates the base amount of space the file consumes on your disk, or the size of a flattened Photoshop image. When you save the image in another format, the file size may shrink, because many formats use a compression scheme to consolidate data.

The number to the right of the slash indicates the size of the image with the addition of any alpha channels, paths, spot color channels, or layers you may have created. The second number, of course, better represents the actual size of the image.

Getting Information about Your Documents

Photoshop has options to show you important information about your document, your computer, and the program's current state of operation. All this information is useful in determining how efficiently your file will be processed and printed.

Clicking the Information Field

Image Position   Clicking the information field itself displays a diagram of the image as it will appear on the paper specified in File ➜ Page Setup (see Figure 4.5). Use this to assure that the image will fit on your paper before you print it.

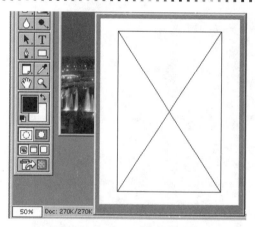

Figure 4.5 *Clicking the information field shows you the position of your image in the page layout.*

Size and Mode Info   Option-click (Mac) or Alt-click (Win) the field, and the image's size, resolution, color mode, and number of channels are displayed.

Tile Info   Command-clicking (Mac) or Ctrl-clicking (Win) displays the tile sizes of the document. Photoshop uses tiles to display and process images. When you display an image or when the image refreshes, you can sometimes see the image appear progressively, as it tiles on screen. This window tells you how many tiles the image is composed of and is of little practical use.

Clicking the Status Bar Pop-Up Menu

Document Size   The status bar, by default, displays the current size of your document. But if you click the small black arrow at the right end of the bar, a pop-up menu allows you to select other information to be displayed.

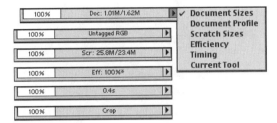

Scratch Size   The number to the left of the slash indicates the amount of memory needed to hold the current image open in RAM. The number to the right indicates the amount of memory Photoshop has been allocated (see the section "Allocating Memory" in Chapter 5). Because of Photoshop's ability to record events in its History palette, the number on the left grows every time you perform an operation, because RAM is being consumed. (See Chapter 11 to learn more about Photoshop's History features).

Document Profile   This option displays the name of the color profile with which the image was saved. The color profile affects how the image appears on screen (see Chapter 15).

Efficiency   This option indicates what percentage of the last operation was performed in RAM. If this percentage drops below 80%, you may want to consider allocating more memory to Photoshop (see "Allocating Memory" in Chapter 5).

Timing   If you select Timing, the information field tells you how long the last operation took to perform to the tenth of a second.

Current Tool   This option displays the name of the currently selected tool.

Accessing Menus

The majority of Photoshop's most powerful operations are accessed through its nine pull-down menus at the top of the screen (illustrated in Figure 4.6). The menus are quite logical and user-friendly, with related operations accessible from the same menu.

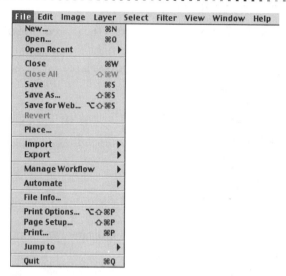

Figure 4.6 *Photoshop's menus, with the File menu selected*

Commands on the menus can apply various filters, effects, or operations to an image, directly or through dialog boxes. Some of the menus, such as the View menu or Window menu, are used to display additional tools or palettes and to change how the image appears on screen.

When applying an operation like an image adjustment, for example, you will see a dialog box (Figure 4.7) that displays the items for that particular operation. You usually cannot perform any other operations until you implement or cancel the dialog. There are a couple of exceptions: You can still access the Zoom tool while a dialog box is open (see "Navigation Shortcuts" later in this chapter), and you can hide the edges of selection marquee (see Chapter 6).

The dialog boxes are all similar to each other in the way that they perform. To access options that are in a dialog box, follow these general steps:

1. Choose the desired operation from the menu. The dialog box appears.

2. Choose from the options or enter the values in the dialog box.

3. If there is a preview box, make sure it's checked to preview the result of the operation before closing the dialog box.

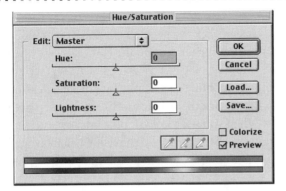

Figure 4.7 *A dialog box (in this case, the Hue/Saturation settings)*

4. Make your changes, or abandon them, using these methods:

- To undo the last operation inside a dialog box, press Command+Z or Ctrl+Z.

- If you've entered values and wish to cancel the operation but keep the dialog box open, press the Option key (Mac) or the Alt key (Win) and the word *Cancel* changes to *Reset*. Click the Reset button.

- Click Cancel to abort the operation and close the dialog without making any changes.

- Click OK to implement the operation.

Working with Palettes

Many of Photoshop's tools and operations are displayed in a system of floating palettes. These palettes are displayed on the desktop when you launch the program. The palettes let you efficiently apply operations directly to the image, thereby saving the time and hassle of following a sequence of windows to accomplish a task. All the palettes can be displayed or hidden from the Window menu.

Palette Clusters

By default, palettes appear in clusters, which can be separated or reconfigured according to how you may want to use them. To separate a palette from a cluster, click its tab and drag it away from the cluster. Wherever you release the mouse, the palette will be positioned.

To place a palette into a cluster, click the palette's tab and drag it into the cluster. When you see a heavy black outline appear around the cluster, release the mouse button.

Open palettes can be joined and moved as a unit. To join a palette to another palette while keeping both visible, click the palette's tab, drag it, and place it on the bottom of the target palette. When you see a bold double line, release the mouse; the palette should snap to the bottom of the target. To move the palettes together, click the bar of the topmost palette and drag them into position.

Organizing Palettes

You can organize your palettes to use the desktop space more efficiently. You can move a palette or a cluster by mouse-dragging the bar at the top of the palette. You can reduce the size of a palette by clicking the Minimize button on the bar at the top of the palette. This method unfortunately conceals the tabs that identify the palette, and you will have to maximize the palette to see its contents. A more efficient method of decreasing a palette's size is to double-click the tab; the palette will collapse, but the name tab will remain visible.

Photoshop 6's new Palette Well is a space saver, allowing you to consolidate all of your palettes to a small area on screen. The Palette Well is an extension of the new tool-bar. To deposit a palette onto the Palette Well, drag its tab and position it within the well until you see a heavy black outline, then release the mouse.

You can reveal or conceal all of your palettes simultaneously by pressing the Tab key. Once you've moved or separated the palettes, or changed the way they function, you may want to reset them back to their original positions and their values to the original defaults of the program. You can accomplish this quickly and easily by choosing Window ➔ Reset Palette Locations.

The Tool Palette

Photoshop's Tool palette displays the icons for 22 different tools. Some of the tool icons expand to access tools that are not visible, bringing the entire number of tools to 50, plus paint swatches, Quick Mask icons, view modes, and the Jump To command.

Figures 4.8 and 4.9 show the Tool palette with all of its pop-up tools and their shortcut keys. If you see a small black arrow next to the tool, click it with your mouse and hold down the mouse button, and the additional related tools will pop up.

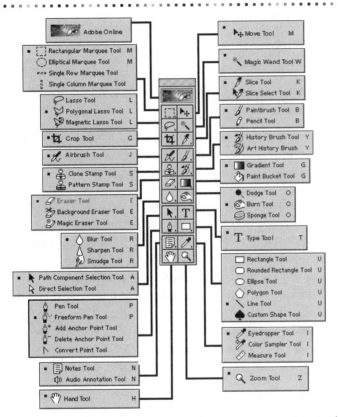

Figure 4.8 *The Tool palette (selection, editing, painting, and display tool sections), showing the expanded tools and tool tips*

Don't be intimidated by the Tool palette! When you place your cursor over a tool, a helpful label, or "tool tip," that identifies the tool and its shortcut key appears within a few seconds. Photoshop 6 has extended the use of tool tips to describe the function of many of its operations inside the palettes, tool bar, and dialog boxes, which can be an asset to obtaining a quick understanding of the program. To activate a tool tip, "hover" your cursor on the function or operation and wait a few seconds.

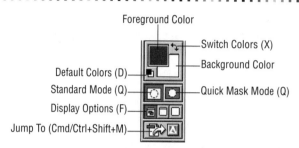

Foreground Color

Switch Colors (X)

Default Colors (D)

Background Color

Standard Mode (Q)

Quick Mask Mode (Q)

Display Options (F)

Jump To (Cmd/Ctrl+Shift+M)

Figure 4.9 *The Tool palette (color, Quick Mask, display option, and Jump To sections)*

To access a tool through its shortcut key, press the shortcut letter or Shift plus the letter (depending on your preference settings). For grouped sets of tools (like the three Lassos, or Blur/Sharpen/Smudge), typing the shortcut repeatedly cycles through the tools in the group.

The Tool palette is divided into seven general sections. From top to bottom, as very broad categories, are the selection tools, painting tools, editing tools, and display tools. Below that are the color swatches, Quick Mask options, display options, and (at the very bottom of the palette) the Jump To command.

The Tool palette is designed to place all of the manual operations of the program in full view on the desktop for easy access. Each tool is represented by a different cursor icon. To choose a tool, click its button on the Tool palette. Then place the cursor where you want to affect the image. Click the mouse, or click and drag (depending on the tool), to apply the tool's function to the image.

The Options Bar

Photoshop 6, by default, displays an Options bar at the top of the screen when you launch the program. This element is similar to the Options palette in earlier versions of the program but more convenient as it is easier to locate. When you select a tool, its options become visible in the Options bar and you can determine the behavior characteristics of the tool. Figure 4.10 shows the Options bar with the Clone Stamp tool selected. A tool's performance can vary considerably with different options, so it's a good idea to check out the settings before you apply the tool to the image.

Figure 4.10 *The Options bar (with the Clone Stamp tool selected)*

Quite a few new tools have been added to Photoshop 6. See Appendix B for a complete list of tools and descriptions of what they do and how they operate.

The Notes Tool

Two new tools in Photoshop 6 lets you conveniently attach reminder notes to the image. You can create an annotation as either as a sticky note or a recording.

To create a written annotation:

1. Click the Notes tool in the Tool palette, or press N on the keyboard.

2. Click the image, and a yellow sticky note appears.

3. Enter the information and click the Close box.

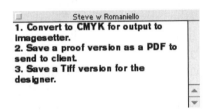

4. To access the information on the note, click the note icon on the image.

To record an audio annotation, you'll need a microphone and audio input capabilities.

1. Click the Notes tool and hold down the mouse to expand the palette. Choose the Audio Annotation tool.

2. Click the image, and the Record dialog box appears.

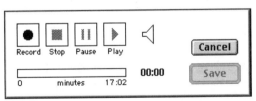

3. Click the Record button to record; click the Stop button when you've completed recording.

4. To play the annotation, click the audio icon on the image.

Displaying the Image

When you open an image in Photoshop, it is displayed to fit in the image window so that you can see the entire image regardless of its size. When working on an image, it's often necessary to vary the view size so that you can see changes to the document as a whole, concentrate on specific areas of the image, or work closely on details. Varying the size of the image display does not effect the physical size of the image. You can choose from several alternative viewing methods in Photoshop 6.

The Zoom Tool

The Zoom tool is a fast way take a closer look at the image and probably the technique you'll use most frequently for changing the view. Choose the Zoom tool from the Tool palette by clicking it or by typing the letter Z on the keyboard. Place your cursor on the area of the image that you want to see close up; you will see the Zoom tool cursor (a magnifying glass) with a plus sign to indicate that the Zoom tool will enlarge the view. Click your mouse. Continue to click until the image appears at the desired view. Each time you click, the image appears larger, to a maximum view size of 1600 percent.

You can reduce the size of the displayed image by pressing the Option key (Mac) or the Alt key (Win). The Zoom tool displays a minus sign to indicate that it will reduce the view. Each time you click the mouse with the Option or Alt key held down, the image diminishes in size, all the way down to one screen pixel.

Display Size and Image Resolution

The percentage size in which you see an image in Photoshop depends on the ratio of the image resolution to the monitor's screen resolution. Macintosh monitors have a screen resolution of 72 pixels per inch (ppi), while Windows monitors use 96 ppi to display an image.

A document with an image resolution of 72 ppi, when viewed at 100%, will display at a ratio of 1:1 of its actual height and width dimensions on a Mac and 33% larger on Windows. A resolution of 144 ppi will display an image at twice its print size on a Mac and, again, larger on a Windows machine, when displayed at 100% viewing size. (See Chapter 13 for more on monitor and image resolution.)

Scrolling in Photoshop

Scrolling tools and techniques let you move the image around the window when the image is larger than the image window.

The Hand Tool   Choose the Hand tool from the Tool palette. Click the image and drag to move the image around.

Scroll Bars   Like most software, the scroll bars are to the right and bottom of the image. Click and drag a scroll handle, or click an arrow at the end of a scroll bar, to scroll in the desired direction.

Keyboard   You can use either a keyboard or an extended keyboard to scroll the image up, down, left, or right. Table 4.1 lists the commands.

Table 4.1 Keyboard Commands for Scrolling

SCROLL ACTION	MACINTOSH KEYBOARD	MAC EXTENDED KEYBOARD	WINDOWS KEYBOARD
Up	Control+K	PgUp	PgUp
Up slightly	Shift+Control+K	Shift+PgUp	Shift+PgUp
Down	Control+L	PgDn	PgDn
Down slightly	Shift+Control+L	Shift+PgDn	Shift+PgDn
Left	Cmd+Control+K	Cmd+Control+PgUp	Ctrl+PgUp
Left slightly	Shift+Cmd+Control+K	Shift+Cmd+Control+PgUp	Shift+Ctrl+PgUp
Right	Cmd+Control+L	Cmd+Control+PgDn	Ctrl+PgDn
Right slightly	Shift+Cmd+Control+L	Shift+Cmd+Control+PgDn	Shift+Ctrl+PgDn

Navigation Shortcuts

Clicking over and over again to display the image can get to be tiresome and consume precious time. As you become more proficient in Photoshop, you will want to consider alternative methods to speed up the process of viewing your image at the right size. What follows are a few techniques that will enhance your ability to see the image on screen.

Centering an Image   This technique centers and zooms an area of the image on screen. It is the fastest way to get a close view of a detail of the image you are working on. Choose the Zoom tool. Click in the image, drag a marquee around the portion of the image you wish to enlarge, and release the mouse. The selected area enlarges to fill the window.

Restoring the Display to a 100% View   Double-click the Zoom tool icon in the Tool palette.

Toggling to the Zoom Tool   To toggle directly from any tool or dialog box to the Zoom tool, use one of these shortcuts:

- Hold down the Command or Ctrl key and the space bar, and click the mouse to zoom in. Release the keys to resume using the tool.

- Hold down the Option or Alt key and the space bar, and click the mouse to zoom out. Release the keys to resume using the tool.

Toggling to the Hand Tool   To quickly access the Hand tool from any tool or dialog box, press the space bar. Click and drag your mouse to scroll. The Hand tool lets you scroll around the image when it exceeds the size of the image window. Release the space bar to resume using the tool.

The Navigator

When you are viewing an image close up, it can be difficult to tell exactly what you are looking at and where it is, especially if the image contains large areas of similar texture. The Navigator (Figure 4.11) is a map of the image displayed as a thumbnail, showing the exact location of what appears in the image window relative to the entire image.

When you launch Photoshop, the Navigator is displayed by default and offers the following navigational features:

View Box   The red rectangle on the thumbnail indicates what is currently displayed in the image window. Place your cursor on the rectangle, click your mouse, and drag to scroll around the image. You can change the color of the View box by clicking the arrow in the upper-right corner of the palette and choosing Palette Options. You can then choose a color from the pull-down menu or click the swatch to choose a color from the Color Picker.

Zoom Slider   You can zoom in on the image by moving the slider to the right, or zoom out by moving the slider to the left.

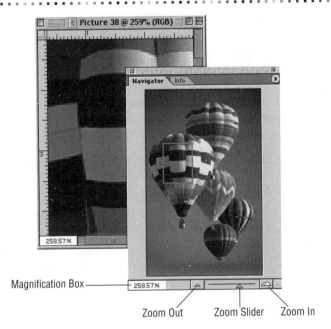

Magnification Box — 258.57%

Zoom Out   Zoom Slider   Zoom In

Figure 4.11 *The Navigator palette*

Zoom In and Zoom Out Buttons   The button with the small mountains on the left of the slider zooms out, and the button with the large mountains to the right of the slider zooms in. The buttons use the same predefined increments as the Zoom tool.

Magnification Box   At the bottom-left of the Navigator palette, you can enter a specific percentage at which to view your image.

Sizing the Navigate Palette   You drag the lower-right corner of the Navigator box to increase or decrease the size of the Navigator palette and its image thumbnail.

The View Menu

When you get to know the program a little better, you will discover that many of its operations seem to be redundant, and working effectively becomes a matter of choosing your favorite method in which to achieve identical end results. For example, the View ➔ Zoom In command achieves the same results as the keyboard shortcut Command/Ctrl+plus sign; the Zoom Out command is the same as typing Command/Ctrl+minus sign. These techniques are identical to the Zoom tool and, of course, all of these commands are similar to the function of the Navigator and the magnification box, with slight variations.

The other options in the View menu are

Fit on Screen　displays the image at the maximum horizontal or vertical size the monitor screen will accommodate.

Actual Pixels　displays the image in a 1:1 ratio with the monitor's screen resolution.

Print Size　accurately displays the height and width dimensions of the image.

New View　The View ➔ New View command displays multiple windows of the same document. Multiple windows give you the ability to observe two or more views of your image simultaneously, so that you can see the close-up detail in which you are working and the global effect on the entire image. When you edit the image, you will see the changes on both views.

Display Modes

Three icons on the Tool palette determine how the image is seen on screen. These modes act like electronic mats. There are three options:

Standard Background　The default view displays the image up against the operating system's desktop.

Full Screen with Menu Bars　The image takes up almost the entire surface of the monitor screen and displays menu bars across the top. When you zoom to a smaller display size, the image appears centered against a gray background.

Full Screen　The image takes up the entire surface of the monitor screen (as shown in Figure 4.12). When you zoom to a smaller display size, the image appears centered against a black background.

The Full Screen display modes are ideal for displaying a view of your work unobstructed by other windows. It can be even more helpful to see an image in the Full Screen modes without any distracting palettes. To conceal or reveal all currently visible palettes, press the Tab key.

Figure 4.12 *Full Screen display mode*

Using Rulers, Guides, and Grids

Rulers, guides, and grids are used to align image content. Alignment of visual elements is critical to maintaining a cohesive structure to the composition. A good composition gently guides the viewer's eye across its surface so that important elements are emphasized. Rulers, guides, and grids are also used to assure the precision measurement and placement of image components.

Setting Preferences for Rulers and Guides

Photoshop can display a horizontal ruler across the top of the screen and a vertical ruler along the left side of the screen; to display them, choose View ➜ Show Rulers.

Rulers give you a visual reminder of the physical size of your image, which you may forget from time to time as you zoom in or out. Ruler units can be changed by choosing Edit ➜ Preferences ➜ Units & Rulers (see Chapter 5 for more on setting preferences).

The zero point, or point of origin for all measurements, is in the upper-left corner of the image, where the rulers intersect. The point of origin can be changed by placing your cursor on the cross hairs, clicking and dragging down and to the right, positioning to the desired location, and releasing the mouse.

Graphic designers use grids and guides to align elements within a layout. Aligning visual elements creates a compositional structure, which helps to control the viewer's eye. The importance of good composition in a Photoshop document cannot be stressed enough. The View menu contains the commands that let you create guides and display a grid, which are superimposed over the image to help you align elements within the composition. Neither guides nor grids print. The color and properties of guides or grids can be changed by choosing Edit ➜ Preferences ➜ Guides & Grid.

Chapter 5, "Setting Up Photoshop," goes into more detail on preference settings.

Using Guides

Guides are horizontal or vertical lines that can be positioned anywhere on the image's surface. To create a horizontal or vertical guide, choose View ➜ Show Rulers. Place your cursor on the ruler, click your mouse, and drag down or to the right, releasing the mouse wherever you want to place a guide (see Figure 4.13).

Display or Conceal Guides   You can hide or reveal guides. The operation is under the new Show command in version 6. Choose View ➜ Show ➜ Guides to toggle them on and off; if the option is checked, they'll be visible, and if it's unchecked they'll be hidden.

Snap To Guides   When moving a portion of a layer or a selected area of the image, you can snap it to a guide to assure the accuracy of its position. The operation is under the new Snap To command in version 6. Choose View ➜ Snap To ➜ Guides to toggle snapping on and off.

Move a Guide   With the Move tool currently selected, click the guide and drag. If another tool is selected, Command-click (Mac) or the Ctrl-click (Win) the guide and drag.

The Move a Guide Cmd/Ctrl-click shortcut does not work with the Slice tool or the Hand tool.

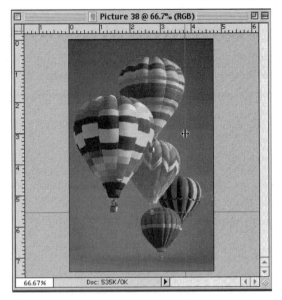

Figure 4.13 *Dragging out a guide*

Delete a Guide   Select the guide as if you were going to move it and drag it out of the image window.

Delete All Guides   Choose View ➔ Clear Guides.

Lock a Guide   Choose View ➔ Lock Guides. This prevents accidentally moving a guide while you work.

New Guide   Another method of generating a new guide is to choose View ➔ New Guide. This has the advantage of enabling you to enter a value for the guide's exact location. A dialog box appears where you can determine whether the guide is horizontal or vertical.

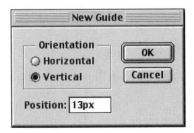

Change the Orientation of a Guide   You can change a guide from horizontal to vertical or vertical to horizontal. While in the Move tool, place your cursor on the Guide. Hold down the Option key (Mac) or the Alt key (Win) and click the guide.

Change Guide Characteristics   The color and style of your guides can be modified by choosing Edit ➜ Preferences ➜ Guides & Grid. Choose a color from the pull-down menu, or click the swatch to display the Color Picker. From the Style pull-down menu, choose either a dashed or solid line.

Using a Grid

A grid helps you see the global relationships between aligned elements on a page (as shown in Figure 4.14). A grid is a series of equally spaced horizontal and vertical lines that create a visual matrix. Like guides, grids do not print.

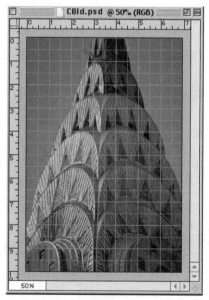

Figure 4.14 *A grid*

Display or Conceal the Grid   Choose View ➜ Show ➜ Grid.

Snap To Grid   When moving a portion of a layer or a selected area of the image, you can snap it to a horizontal or vertical grid line. The operation is under the new Snap To command in version 6. Choose View ➜ Snap To ➜ Grid.

Grid Characteristics   The color and style of the grid can be modified by choosing Edit ➜ Preferences ➜ Guides & Grid. Choose a grid color from the pull-down menu, or click the swatch to display the Color Picker. From the Style pull-down menu, choose either a dashed line, a solid line, or dots. You can also change the grid size by entering values in the Gridline and Subdivisions boxes.

Up Next

This tour of Photoshop's interface has given you an overview of how its features are accessed and how they work. Photoshop's interface is extremely practical and logical. After you've used it for a while, you should have no trouble finding the tools and operations that you need.

In Chapter 5, I'll show you how to set up the program to perform most efficiently. You'll learn to modify the interface, customize its appearance, and enhance its performance to best suit the requirements of your particular job.

Setting Up Photoshop

PHOTOSHOP

Chapter 5

Before any job, there is always preparation. Let's say you are going to change the oil in your car. Before you crawl under it and loosen the plug, you'll need to move the car to an appropriate location—certainly not near your newly planted front lawn, and not on the side of a hill. You'll need to find a level spot and gather an oil filter, pan, pouring spout, and rag. A simple job, yes. But consider how difficult the task would be if any of the elements were missing. If you choose the wrong location, you might kill your grass; or if you park on a hill, some of the old, dirty oil will stay in the crankcase. The pan is essential, because without it, the oil will spill onto the ground. You get the idea.

At this point, you may be thinking, "What does a messy job like changing the engine oil in my car have to do with working in a sophisticated, state of the art, image-editing program like Adobe Photoshop 6?" Well, not really very much, but it does make a couple of important points: Choose the right workspace and prepare it with all of the things you need before you begin the job. In the case of Photoshop 6, that means setting up the program to run at its optimal level, customizing the interface to best suit your needs, and choosing the best color environment.

This chapter will describe:

- Photoshop's settings

- Allocating memory

- Setting preferences: how and why

- The Preset Manager

- Basic color management: monitor calibration, gamma, and choosing a color space

Photoshop's Settings

The settings control how Photoshop appears and behaves. Many settings are stored in files in folders and directories with names like Settings or Preferences or in the Windows Registry. When you modify any setting and quit the program, the information is saved to these files.

When you launch Photoshop for the first time, a set of *preferences* is created. These are the factory default settings. Any changes you make in the appearance or the behavior of the program is recorded in the preferences file. After a work session, when you quit the program, these preferences are stored, so that the next time you launch the program the position of the palettes, the tool settings, the color of the guides or grid, or any other changes you made remain the same.

If Photoshop starts behaving unpredictably or bombing frequently, it could indicate that the preferences are damaged. You should restore your preferences to the originally installed default settings. Re-creating your preferences file resets Photoshop to its defaults and may troubleshoot problems.

The disadvantage to restoring your preferences file is that you lose any and all customization you've done in Photoshop, everything from brush definitions to function keys. If you want to try a clean set of "prefs"—either to debug troublesome Photoshop behavior, or to attempt a new technique uncomplicated by settings you've already chosen—you can "hide" your preferences temporarily. Quit Photoshop and drag the preferences file from its current location to an unrelated folder or directory (named something like temppref or hideit). (The next two sections tell you where to find the prefs file in MacOS or Windows.) When you restart Photoshop, you'll have a clean program, but if you want your old settings back you can always reverse the process, closing the program and dragging the old preferences file back to where Photoshop can find it.

I recommend that, as you begin each of the Hands-On projects in this book, you hide your "prefs" file and restart Photoshop to create a clean set of options. This will make working the exercises easier.

Restoring Preferences on the Macintosh

To restore your preferences on the Macintosh:

1. Quit Photoshop.

2. Locate and open the Adobe Photoshop 6 Settings folder (Figure 5.1). It's in the Preferences folder inside the System folder.

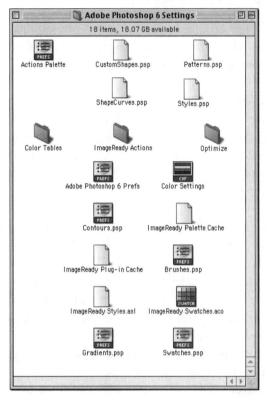

Figure 5.1 *The Photoshop settings folder on the Macintosh*

3. Select the file named Adobe Photoshop 6 Prefs and drag it to a location outside any Photoshop or System folder. If you might want to recover these preferences, create a folder named something like OldPrefs; if you won't need the
   current settings again, you can drag the file to the Trash (or Control-click it
   and choose Move To Trash from the shortcut menu).

4. Launch Photoshop.

Restoring Preferences in Windows

1. Quit Photoshop.

2. Locate and open the *directory* with the preferences file, which should be the PSP file at the end of this path:

   ```
   C:\WINDOWS\Application Data\Adobe\Photoshop\6.0\Adobe
   Photoshop 6.0 Settings\Adobe Photoshop 6.0 Prefs.psp
   ```

3. Drag the `Adobe Photoshop 6.0 Prefs.psp` file to a location outside the `WINDOWS` directory. If you might want to recover these preferences, create a directory named something like `OldPrefs`; if you won't need the current settings again, you can drag the file to the Recycle Bin (or right-click it and choose Delete from the shortcut menu).

4. Launch Photoshop.

As an alternative to this drag-and-kill procedure, there's another way you can completely reset your preferences to Photoshop's factory defaults. Immediately after launching Photoshop, press and hold the Alt+Ctrl+Shift keys. In the dialog box that appears (Figure 5.2), click Yes to restore preferences.

Figure 5.2 *When launching Photoshop for Windows, hold down Alt+Ctrl+Shift to display the Reset Preferences dialog.*

Allocating Memory

Large amounts of memory are required to process graphics files. Photoshop is a memory hog, so the often-asked question, "How much memory do you need to best operate Photoshop?" is easily answered with another question: "How much memory can you afford?" Adobe's minimum requirement of 64 MB of RAM is only barely enough to launch and run the program. Purchase and install as much memory as you can. Once you've installed the memory, be sure to allocate it to Photoshop, using one of the following procedures.

Allocating Memory in the Macintosh

1. Launch Photoshop and all other programs that you need to run while using Photoshop.

2. Switch to the Finder and, under the Apple menu, choose About This Computer (see Figure 5.3). Add the Largest Unused Block and the memory Photoshop is currently using; this is your available memory.

Figure 5.3 *This Mac has 140.6 MB (48.9 + 91.7) available for Photoshop.*

3. Quit all programs.

4. Highlight the Photoshop application icon and choose File ➜ Get Info ➜ Memory.

5. Suggested Size is the amount of memory Photoshop wants to operate. In the Preferred Size field, specify the memory dedicated to Photoshop. Allocate as much as possible but never more than 90% of available memory (see Figure 5.4).

6. Close the Get Info window and relaunch Photoshop.

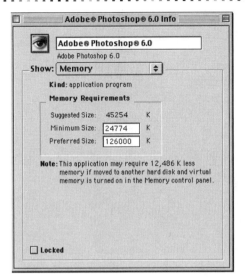

Figure 5.4 *You could give Photoshop as much as 126 MB (90% of 140.6) under Preferred Size.*

Allocating Memory in Windows

1. With Photoshop running, choose Edit ➜ Preferences ➜ Memory & Image Cache (bringing up the dialog shown in Figure 5.5).

2. In the Used By Photoshop field, enter the proportion of available memory you want to dedicate to Photoshop. The 50% default setting is a good beginning to operating the software.

3. During a Photoshop work session, if the Efficiency setting (in the information field at bottom of the window) ever drops below 100%, increase the percentage of memory by 10% increments until the Efficiency remains at the maximum 100%.

4. After you reset the memory allocation, you must quit and relaunch the program for the change to take effect.

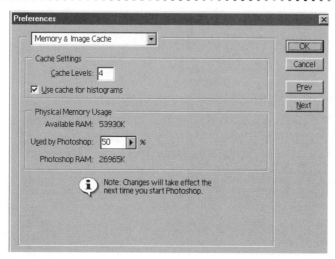

Figure 5.5 *The Memory & Image Cache preferences in Windows*

Setting Preferences

When you change Photoshop's preferences, you affect the behavior or the appearance of the program. By so doing, you can customize the interface to best suit your style of working. In the descriptions throughout this chapter, I have recommended (in parentheses in text) the preference configuration that is most suitable for the majority of working situations.

There are two main methods for accessing Photoshop's preferences, which have moved in version 6. Instead of the File menu, as in previous versions, they are now found under the Edit menu. In either platform, you can choose Edit → Preferences → General, or type Command+K (Mac) or Ctrl+K (Win), to display Photoshop's Preferences dialog box. You also have the option of going directly to the preference category you want under the Edit → Preferences submenu.

From the dialog, you can navigate to any of the preference categories by clicking the pop-up list at the top of the dialog box. You can also jump from preference category to category by clicking the Next or Prev buttons.

General Preferences

When you first open the Preferences dialog, you see Photoshop's General preference settings (Figure 5.6), which are global settings that affect most of your working environment.

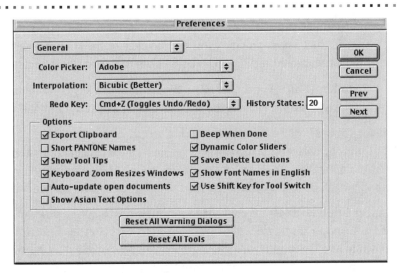

Figure 5.6 *The General preferences*

Color Picker (Adobe)   You can specify which color picker to use when choosing a foreground or background color. The color picker you select is also used throughout the program to define preferences, like the color of your guides and grids for example. In both Macintosh and Windows, you can choose between the Adobe Color Picker and the operating system's color picker.

Interpolation (Bicubic)   This sets the global default for how Photoshop resamples, or sizes, images. When you resize an image, pixels are either added (if you increase the image size or resolution) or subtracted (if you reduce the image size or resolution). When adding pixels, the Nearest Neighbor setting, which is the fastest, makes an exact copy of the adjacent pixel. Bilinear uses an average of the two pixels above and below and the two pixels on either side to create gradations for smoother transitions. Bicubic produces the best results by averaging the eight closest neighbors and adding a sharpening effect to increase the contrast.

The only reason to use any method other than Bicubic is to increase the size of a Bitmap or line art image where all the pixels are either black or white. Nearest Neighbor will preserve the absolute values without producing intermediate gray transitions or anti-aliasing. Otherwise, choose Bicubic for best results.

Redo Key (default)   You can specify which key command will undo or redo an operation. The defaults are:

Undo Key (Cmd/Ctrl+Z)   By pressing this key combination, you go back one state in the History palette. (You have to click in the History palette or use the Step Backward command to go back more than one step.)

Redo Key (Shift+Cmd/Ctrl+Z)   By pressing this key combination, you go forward to the last state in the History palette from the next-to-last.

History States (20)   You can determine the maximum number of states that will appear in the History palette before the earliest one is discarded. History requires RAM to remember stages or "states" in the process of developing an image. Limit the number of states to the default so as not to compromise the efficiency of program.

Export Clipboard (off)   If you are running more than one program, the content of Photoshop's clipboard will be transferred to the system's clipboard. When you switch to another program, those contents can be pasted into a document there. If you only copy and paste images within Photoshop, turn this option off to reduce the amount of time it takes to activate another program.

Short PANTONE Names (off)   Photoshop supports spot color. PANTONE is a brand name of spot color inks that is used throughout the world. Some older publishing programs don't support the more recent long-name PANTONE conventions. If you have trouble printing Photoshop spot color separations that have been placed in a desktop publishing program, turn this option on and resave the document. Otherwise, leave the box unchecked.

Show Tool Tips (on)   The small, yellow identification tags on the Tool palette that display each tool's name and keyboard shortcut are turned on and off from here. The Tool palette in version 6 also displays the same information when the palette is expanded. So the information is somewhat redundant; however, it's not a bad idea to get a double hit of this information until you learn what the tools are and how to access them with shortcut key commands. Another reason to keep this box checked is that the tool tips in version 6 also appear as short descriptions on many of Photoshop's commands, giving you a clear idea of their purpose.

Keyboard Zoom Resizes Windows (off)   This preference lets you resize the image window when you use the key commands for zooming in (Cmd/Ctrl+plus sign) and zooming out (Cmd/Ctrl+minus sign). The window will increase in size until it fills the screen vertically or horizontally.

Auto-Update Open Documents (off)   If an image is updated by another program outside of Photoshop, Photoshop will automatically reread and replace the open document with the updated version.

Show Asian Text Options (off)   Checking this box displays Chinese, Japanese, and Korean text options in the paragraph palettes. You need this option only if you are working with Asian characters.

Beep When Done (off)   You can instruct Photoshop to emit a warning signal after it has performed an operation that displays a progress window. This can be helpful if you are away from your computer, waiting for a long process, like a rotation or resize of a high-resolution image, to be completed.

Dynamic Color Sliders (on)   When this box is checked, the sliders on the Color palette preview the range of potential colors that can be designated, so that you know exactly where to move them to designate a specific foreground or background color. Leave this box checked to speed up the process of determining your colors.

Save Palette Locations (on)   If you choose this option, Photoshop will remember the position of your palettes when you quit and then relaunch the program. If the box is unchecked, Photoshop restores the palette locations to the default positions.

Show Font Names In English (on)   If you have any fonts on your system that do not use Roman characters, such as Asian fonts, their names will be displayed in English in the font list.

Use Shift Key For Tool Switch (off)   With this preference off, in order to switch to a tool or switch among grouped tools, simply type the shortcut key for that group (L for the Lassos, E for the Erasers, etc.). Checking this option adds the Shift key to the process, to prevent you from inadvertently switching while using a tool.

Reset All Warning Dialogs   This button resets all warnings that have Don't Show Again options, unchecking that option.

Reset All Tools   Clicking this button resets all of the tool settings in the Options bar to their original defaults.

Saving Files

The Saving Files preferences (Figure 5.7) let you designate whether your saved files will have previews or extensions attached.

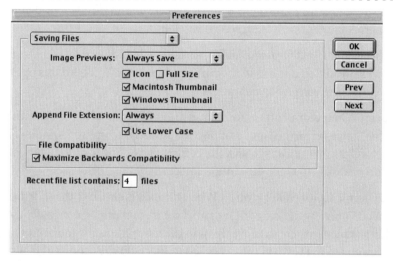

Figure 5.7 *The Saving Files preferences*

Image Previews (all on, Ask When Saving)   The Macintosh Thumbnail and Windows Thumbnail options create previews that will be displayed in the dialog box that you see when you open the image using File ➜ Open. There are two more options on Photoshop for MacOS: Icon creates a tiny picture that you can view from the desktop for the purpose of identifying an image before you open it, and Full Size creates a preview that can be placed in a desktop publishing program. The problem with previews is that they produce larger file sizes, so you need to decide whether the convenience of seeing the image prior to opening is worth the memory used.

(Append) File Extension (Ask When Saving, Use Lower Case)   In Windows, which automatically adds a three-character extension (like .tif, .psd, or .eps) to the filename, the File Extension option allows you to select whether the extension is upper- or lowercase. (Whichever way you choose here, you have the option to switch the extension's case for each given file as you use the Save dialog boxes.) On the Macintosh version of the program, Append File Extension determines when to add an extension to the filename. These extensions are used by Microsoft Windows, Web browsers, and other programs to identify a particular file format. I recommend that you choose the Use Lower Case option when saving files to the Web because of Unix servers' preference for lowercase extensions.

Both Image Previews and Append File Extension give you the option to save or use them Always, Never, or Ask When Saving. Since circumstances may vary from image to image, choose the Ask When Saving option so you can make your decision based on the specific application of the image.

Maximize Backwards Compatibility (In Photoshop Format) (off)   This preference gives backward compatibility to your Photoshop 6 documents so that you can open them in 2.0 and 2.5 versions of the program. Choosing this option creates a flattened version of the image, which is stored with each file. This greatly increases its file size. If you save a document with this option selected, your files will be larger, so turn it off unless you are sure you need it.

Enable Advanced TIFF Options (on)   This option allows you to compress TIFF files using JPEG and ZIP compression and to designate TIFF support for layers and annotations.

Recent File List Contains (4)   You can find a list of the most recent files that have been opened under File ➜ Open Recent. Enter a value for how many of the latest documents you would like to see displayed.

Display & Cursors

Use the Display & Cursors preferences (Figure 5.8) to configure the way cursor icons and colors appear on screen. These preferences do not affect the image data, but they do affect how you see the image.

Color Channels In Color (off)   By default, color channels appear in black and white. Each color channel is actually an 8-bit grayscale image that supports 256 shades of gray. Photoshop will display a channel in red, green, or blue, depending on the color information it represents, if this box is checked. The black and white information of the default is displayed more clearly and is probably more useful to you, so leave the box unchecked.

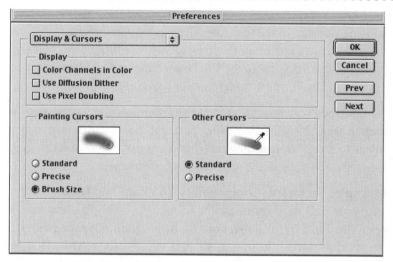

Figure 5.8 *The Display & Cursors preferences*

Use Diffusion Dither (on)   This option is used to control the pattern of pixel blending on low-resolution color monitors, or if you're displaying anything less then Millions Of Colors (Mac) or True Color (Win). Dithering is a method of distributing pixels to extend the visual range of color on screen.

Use Pixel Doubling (on)   When moving an image from one file to another, you can speed up the process by reducing the resolution display. With this box checked, when you move an image, it will appear jagged and unrefined until it is in position and the operation is complete.

Painting Cursors (Brush Size)   To change the display of the painting cursor, click the desired radio button. Standard displays the tool icon as the cursor. Precise displays crosshairs. Brush Size, the default, displays an cursor that is the size and shape of the brush for the currently selected tool.

Other Cursors (Standard)   To change the display of tool cursors that do not use brushes, choose either Standard (the tool icon as the cursor) or Precise (a crosshair icon).

If you use Standard or Brush Size cursors, you can toggle back and forth to Precise with your Caps Lock key.

Transparency & Gamut

This is where you control the appearance of transparency on the Layers palette and the color of the CMYK gamut warning (Figure 5.9).

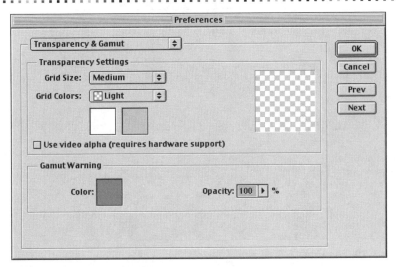

Figure 5.9 *The Transparency & Gamut preferences*

Transparency Settings (default)   This is where you can set the default preferences for the transparency display on your layers. Sometimes the default, gray checkerboard is not visible due to similar colors within the image. Under Grid Size, choose from a small, medium, or large grid. Grid Colors lets you select from a predefined list of color checkerboards. To choose specific grid colors, click either of the color swatches to display the Color Picker.

Gamut Warning (default)   When working on images intended for four-color process printing, you'll want to preview the files before converting. To see which colors are out of the CMYK gamut, choose View → Gamut Warning. The Gamut Warning displays a colored mask over the areas that are out of range. The Gamut Warning preferences let you determine the color of the mask. Click the Color swatch to display the Color Picker. Choose an Opacity percentage between 1 and 100 to affect the transparency of the mask.

Units & Rulers

You can establish settings for all measurement systems in Photoshop (Figure 5.10).

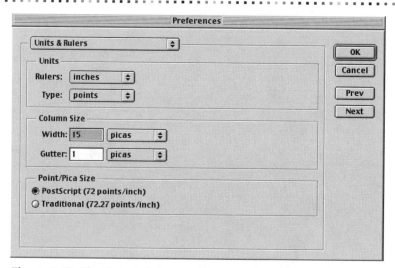

Figure 5.10 *The Units & Rulers preferences*

Rulers (inches)   The Rulers setting allows you to determine which measurement system will appear on the rulers when they are displayed. You can choose among pixels, inches, centimeters, points, picas, and percent.

Column Size (default)   If you're importing your image to a desktop publishing program for publication to a newspaper, newsletter, or magazine, you may want to configure it to a specific column size. You can choose a width of a column and a gutter size so that your image will conform to the column size of the intended publication. You can determine the number of columns on the document when choosing File → New or Image → Image Size.

Points/Pica Size (PostScript)   This preference determines the size of your type characters. In PostScript type, there are 72 points per inch; in Traditional type, there are 72.27 points per inch. PostScript has clearly become the convention with the advent of desktop publishing and computer typography. Some purists still may prefer the Traditional type option, so it remains available.

Guides & Grid

Graphic designers use guides and grids to align visual elements on a page (as described in Chapter 4). The Guides & Grid preferences (Figure 5.11) allow you to determine the color and style of your ruler guides and your grid. Under Color, choose from the options list or click the large swatch on the right side of the dialog to select a specific color from the Color Picker. You can determine the matrix of your grid by entering a value in the Gridline Every field, and the number of subdivisions in the grid by entering a value in the Subdivisions field.

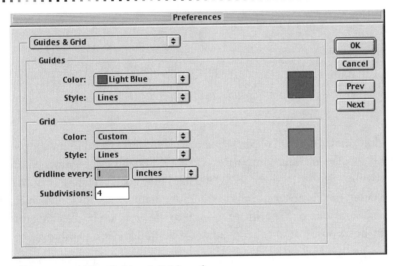

Figure 5.11 *The Guides & Grid preferences*

Plug-Ins & Scratch Disks

Plug-ins are modular mini programs or filters that add functions to Photoshop. You can activate or deactivate third-party plug-ins from Plug-Ins & Scratch Disks preferences dialog (Figure 5.12). A scratch disk is hard disk space used as memory. You can designate one or more hard disks in which to process images to increase the processing capabilities of your computer.

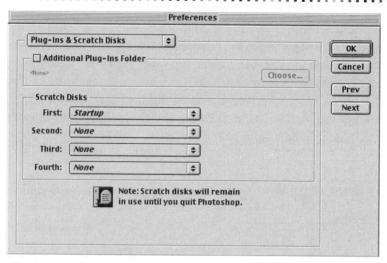

Figure 5.12 *The Plug-Ins & Scratch Disks preferences*

Additional Plug-Ins Folder/Directory   Plug-ins extend Photoshop's capabilities; they include the filters, import/export modules, displacement maps, and third-party programs like Kai's Power Tools. You load or unload preferences from the Plug-Ins folder in the Photoshop application folder or any other folder on your disk. You can reorganize and load specific plug-ins into the program by checking this option, clicking the Choose button, and locating the desired folder on your disk.

Scratch Disks   When Photoshop exceeds the amount of allocated memory, it uses a scratch disk as a source of virtual memory to processes images. In the Scratch Disks field, assign the First scratch disk to your fastest hard drive with the most unused disk space. If you have additional hard drives, you can choose Second, Third, and Fourth disks on which to allocate space. When the primary scratch disk is maxed out, the second one will kick in, then the third, and so on. Built-in memory is considerably faster than virtual memory, so you will experience a significant change in Photoshop's performance when you exceed the RAM allocation. Photoshop requires at least three to five times the file size for the amount of empty hard disk space, so be sure to keep a block of space on your scratch disk(s) free of data. The disk should be defragmented and optimized regularly using a utility program.

Adobe recommends that you avoid working on removable media such as Jaz or Zip disks, because they are less stable and much slower than hard drives.

A warning may appear at the bottom of the dialog that says changes to the Plug-Ins & Scratch Disks options kick in only after you've quit and relaunched the program. If you anticipate the need to change the plug-ins, hold down the Cmd+Opt (Mac) or Ctrl+Alt (Win) keys while the program is launching. The Plug-Ins *folder will appear, where you can designate the plug-ins for the your work session without having to quit and restart the program.*

· ·

Purge Memory

Let's say you've been working on a file for the past 20 minutes, and you're about to apply the Unsharp Mask filter to give the image that final sparkle before sending it to the printer. You tweak the filter settings to perfection and click the OK button. A dialog box appears that tells you the filter cannot be applied because the scratch disk is full. Before you throw your shoe at the monitor in frustration, try purging the data stored on the scratch disks.

Choose Edit ➡ Purge and choose data you would like to delete from the submenu. You can free up the Undo, Clipboard, and History memories individually, or choose All, which dumps everything. Be careful, though; you cannot undo this operation.

· ·

Image Cache / Memory & Image Cache

Image caching accelerates the screen redraw during the editing process. Control your use of this feature in the Image Cache (Mac; Figure 5.13) or Memory & Image Cache (Win; Figure 5.5) preferences.

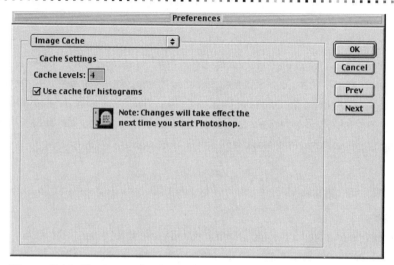

Figure 5.13 *The Image Cache preferences in Macintosh*

Cache Levels (8) The specified number of copies of your image are stored in memory to update the screen more quickly at reduced view sizes. For example, if you do a color adjustment to an image at 50% view, it happens much faster because the program only has to change 25% of the pixels. Experiment with the settings for images larger than 15 MB. Eight is the maximum setting, but high settings will deplete your system resources, because the smaller previews are stored in memory. If you are working on large images and have sufficient RAM, as most computers do today, set the image cache to 8 levels. For smaller images with less RAM, use lower settings.

Use Cache For Histograms (off) A histogram is a graph of the brightness values of an image. Histograms are displayed in the Levels or Threshold dialog boxes (see Chapter 16, "Adjusting Tonality and Color"). Uncheck the Use Cache For Histograms option. This preference defines the histogram based on the zoom ratio and the cumulative display of histograms throughout the work session, which compiles a histogram faster but with less accuracy.

(The Memory portion of this dialog box in the Windows platform is discussed earlier in this chapter, in the section "Allocating Memory in Windows.")

The Preset Manager

Photoshop 6 now gives you the ability to manage several libraries from a single palette. The Preset Manager is the storage unit for all of the elements that you may want to apply to the image. It's a library of palettes that can be utilized by the program. As you add or delete items from the palettes, the currently loaded palette in the Preset Manager displays the changes. You can save the new palette and load any of the palettes on the system.

Choose Edit ➜ Preset Manager to access its dialog box (Figure 5.14). From the Preset Type option list, choose the type of palette you wish to affect. You can pick from Brushes, Swatches, Gradients, Styles, Patterns, Contours, and Custom Shapes.

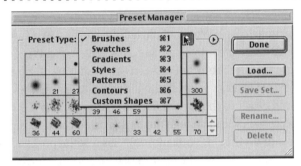

Figure 5.14 *The Preset Manager*

The small arrow to the right of the Preset Type list displays a pop-up menu that is divided into three groups of commands. The top field lets you restore the current palette to the default or replace it with a previously saved palette. In the second group is a list of display options for the items within the palette, which let you display the items as thumbnails or by their names. The third group lists additional palettes that can be readily accessed.

Adobe provides several different palettes with Photoshop 6. If, for example, you are working on a document that will be used exclusively on the Web, you may want to load the Web Safe Swatches palette.

Calibrating Your Monitor

Part of the initial setup in Photoshop is assuring that your colors look right on screen. A calibrated monitor is the foundation from which all other color settings are determined. A calibrated monitor is the initial stage of color management that will ultimately provide consistency during each work session and predictable results from your printer. You can use a calibration device that sticks on the surface of your monitor's glass and measures the temperature of the phosphors (for more on this, see Chapter 15, "Color Management and Printing"). These devices are more accurate than the Adobe Gamma utility software that is bundled with Photoshop. If you have a monitor calibration device, generate a profile with it. Do not use the Adobe Gamma utility from the 4.0 version of Photoshop, as it is obsolete.

The Adobe Gamma calibration package—which includes Adobe Gamma software, the Gamma Wizard, and ICC (International Color Consortium) color profiles for some RGB devices—is simple to use. When you install Photoshop, the Gamma software is automatically loaded into a control panel on Macintosh and Windows systems. Before calibrating, be sure that the monitor has been on for at least 30 minutes and that the ambient light in the room is set as you will use it during your work sessions. Your monitor's bit depth should be set to thousands of colors or more. Turn off any background patterns or screen images, and change the background color to neutral gray. (Read the sidebar for how to do this.) If your monitor has a white point adjustment, use the monitor's utility and later set Adobe Gamma's white point control to match the monitor's settings.

Using Adobe Gamma

A monitor's gamma is actually a measurement of the contrast of the midtones of images displayed on screen. You can learn about gamma in the Photoshop Help: choose Help ➜ Help Contents ➜ Search, and in the Search field, type Adobe Gamma. Windows systems default to a higher gamma (2.2) than Macs (1.8), meaning that images will look slightly darker and have more contrast on a Windows computer than on a Mac.

To calibrate your monitor on the Macintosh, choose the Adobe Gamma utility (Figure 5.15) from the Control Panels. On Windows, choose Start ➜ Settings ➜ Control Panel ➜ Adobe Gamma.

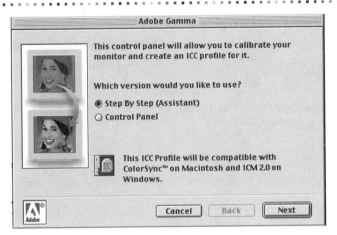

Figure 5.15 *The Adobe Gamma utility*

The first time you calibrate, choose Step By Step (called Assistant in MacOS and Wizard in Windows) by checking its radio button and clicking Next. The Gamma Wizard takes you by the hand and walks you through the calibration process, with explanations of hows and whys of brightness and contrast, gamma, white point, and black point. (Once you are familiar with its components, you can access the Control Panel version of Adobe Gamma.) As a starting point, click the Load button and select as an ICC profile, Adobe Monitor. Choose Next and follow the instructions and explanations as detailed by the Gamma Wizard. At the end of the session, compare the results by clicking the Before and After radio buttons. Save the new profile.

The gamma settings that you specify will automatically load each time your computer is started. Monitors deteriorate over time, so recalibrate periodically. If you find it impossible to calibrate your monitor to the standard settings, then it may be too old and faded and should be replaced.

Choosing a Color Working Space

The next step in setting up the program is to choose a *color working space*, to compensate for variables that occur as a result of different output devices. For example, an image intended for four-color process printing needs to look different on screen than an image intended for the Web. Photoshop 6 lets you work in RGB spaces other than those defined by your monitor.

Creating a Neutral Gray Desktop

Basic color theory teaches us that your perception of a color is affected by the colors surrounding it. To assure that your perception of color is unaltered by any ambient color or patterns, it's best to work with a completely neutral desktop.

In the Macintosh interface, the background needs to be created and applied. In Windows, a neutral background can be specified from the Display applet in Control Panel.

Macintosh

1. Choose File ➔ New. In the dialog box that appears, enter the filename `Gray Background.psd` and the following specifications:

Width	640 pixels (choose Pixels from the pull-down menu)
Height	480 pixels
Contents	White

2. Click the foreground color swatch in the Tool palette to display the Color Picker.

3. Enter these values in the Hue, Saturation, and Brightness fields: H = 0, S = 0, and B = 50. Click OK. Notice that the foreground color swatch has turned gray.

4. Choose Select ➔ Select All, or type Command+A, to select the entire image.

5. Press Option+Delete to fill the selection with the gray color.

6. Choose File ➔ Save As and save the file to a folder on your hard disk as `Gray Background.psd`.

7. From the Apple menu, choose Control Panels ➔ Appearance ➔ Desktop.

8. Choose Place Picture and locate the `Gray Background.psd` image.

9. Click the Set Desktop button.

Windows

1. Choose Start ➔ Settings ➔ Control Panel. Launch the Display applet.

2. Click the Appearance tab.

3. From the Item list, choose Desktop.

4. From the color swatch pop-up list, choose Medium Gray (the color on the far right in the first row).

5. Click Apply to see the result or OK to implement the operation.

Choose Edit ➜ Color Settings. In the Settings pop-up list, choose Web Graphics Defaults if you're preparing images for the Web, or U.S. Prepress Defaults if you're prepping files for four-color printing (see Figure 5.16).

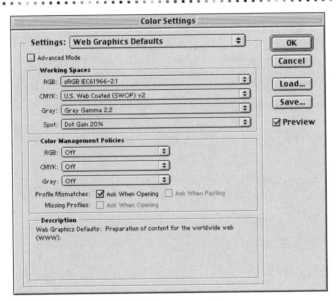

Figure 5.16 *Photoshop 6 Color Settings*

Photoshop setup is now complete. In Chapter 15, "Color Management and Printing," we'll look at other methods of calibration and ways of predicting accurate color from your printing devices.

Up Next

Customizing the interface lets you work in an environment that is especially suitable to your specific image-editing goals. The initial setup of Photoshop 6 is important so that you can feel completely comfortable in your work space and to assure that the color fidelity of the image displayed on screen has been maximized. Next, we'll look closely at some of Photoshop's more labor-intensive tasks: isolating areas of the image to edit.

Making Selections

PHOTOSHOP

Chapter 6

Basic to image editing is the ability to isolate an area of the image so that an effect can be applied exclusively to that area. A selection serves two contradictory purposes: it affects and it protects. When a Photoshop tool or operation is applied, the area within the bounds of the selection marquee will be altered and the area outside the selection marquee will remain unaffected. Think of a selection simply as a hole through which you can alter the reality of your image.

This chapter will introduce you to:

- The power of masking

- Using selection tools

- Applying selection techniques

The Power of Masking

Masking, or the process of protecting portions of an image, used to be an entirely manual process. In ancient times—that is, the 1980s—one of the most the most common methods of altering a photograph was to paint it with a cylindrical air-driven tool called an airbrush. To affect a photograph with an airbrush required a person with a steady hand and a razor-sharp knife. A piece of transparent frisket film was placed over the entire image. The artist slowly, carefully, and gently (so as not to damage the photo) cut a hole in the film to expose the area of the photograph to be painted. The artist saved every scrap of frisket to place over areas that later needed masking. Paint was then sprayed on the image, and the exposed area received the color, while the areas where the frisket remained were protected. The frisket was then peeled back to reveal the colored shape of the hole.

Photoshop's selection tools are similar in principle, but quite different in application, to the traditional mask. Masking techniques in Photoshop 6 afford even more control and are even more user-friendly than in previous versions. The selection tools range from purely manual, like the Lasso, to semi-manual, like the Marquee, to semi-automatic, like the Magnetic Lasso, to fully automatic, like the Magic Wand. Each selection tool is designed to hasten the masking process, depending on the characteristics of the image. Since images vary in contrast, tonality, color, and content, Photoshop provides tools that attempt to cover every possible situation.

This being said, however, making selections is undoubtedly the most labor-intensive and time-consuming of all Photoshop operations. There are many situations where one selection tool is insufficient and several must be combined to surround the target area. Often, other selection techniques will be employed in combination with the tools for greater accuracy or to isolate a tricky area.

Using Selection Tools

When you make a selection in Photoshop, an animated marquee defines the boundaries of the selected area. This moving dash-lined border is sometimes referred to as the "marching ants" because of its resemblance to a column of tiny insects on the move.

Three of Photoshop's selection tools are located at the top of the Tool palette (see Figure 6.1). When you press and hold the mouse on the Rectangular Marquee tool, the palette expands to reveal three additional tools. When you expand the Lasso tool, two more tools are revealed, for a total of eight different selection tools.

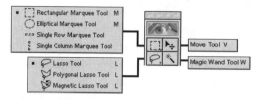

Figure 6.1 *Photoshop's selection tools*

Other methods can enhance the speed or accuracy of the selection process. The Pen tool, covered Chapter 8, uses Bezier curves to define edges; Quick Mask (Chapter 12) uses paint tools to select areas; and Color Range (Chapter 9) is an industrial-strength Magic Wand tool.

The Selection Tool Options Bar

Photoshop 6's Options bar (Figure 6.2) replaces the Tool Options palettes of prior versions. Choosing a tool displays its options automatically in the Options bar. Each tool has specific options, but some options are universal to all of the selection tools.

Figure 6.2 *The Options bar replaces the old Tool Options palette (here, the Options for the Rectangular Marquee tool).*

When you choose a selection tool, the icon that represents it appears on the left end of the Options bar. The next four icons represent selection options that in former versions were performed only by key commands.

New Selection   Click this button to create a new selection with the chosen selection tool.

Add To Selection   Click this button to add to an existing selection with the chosen selection tool. You can perform the same function by holding down the Shift key as you drag with the selection tool.

Subtract From Selection   Click this button to omit from an existing selection with the chosen selection tool. You can perform the same function by holding down the Option or Alt key as you drag with the selection tool.

Intersect Selection   After the first selection is made, you draw another selection that overlaps it. Photoshop makes a selection from only the overlapping area of the two selections. You can perform the same operation by pressing Shift+Option or Shift+Alt as you use the second selection tool.

Feather   Prior to drawing a selection, you can program a tool to produce a soft-edged selection by specifying a numerical value in the Feather field in the tool's Options bar.

Feathering creates a gradual transition between the inside and the outside of the border. When you apply an effect to a feathered selection, it diminishes and becomes more transparent, producing a softening or blurring effect as shown in Figure 6.3. Feathering a selection gives you the power to increase the credibility of your image by gradually blending colored pixels into each other and eliminating any evidence of a hard edge. When you choose Select ➜ Feather, a dialog box appears; enter a value for a Feather Radius. The Feather Radius extends the specified number of pixels into the selection outline (becoming increasingly more opaque) and outside the selection border (becoming increasingly more transparent). For example, if you enter a value of 10, the distance of the feather will be 20 pixels from the opaque pixels inside the selection border to absolute transparency outside the selection border.

Figure 6.3 *The Feather command softens the edge of a selection border.*

A feather differs from anti-alias in that you can determine the size of the soft edge in pixels that the marquee will affect. The width of an anti-alias is determined by the resolution of the image; you have no control over its size.

When you apply a feather to an existing selection border, sometimes you will see it decrease in size or slightly change shape. This is because Photoshop only displays selection borders around areas that represent 50% transparency or more. Areas less than 50% are selected, and you will notice a change when you apply an effect, but you do not see an outline around them. Feathering can be pre-programmed into a selection by entering a value here, in the Options bar, or applied to an existing selection outline by choosing Select ➜ Feather.

Anti-Aliased　An anti-alias is a two- or three-pixel border around an edge that blends into the adjacent color to create a small transition zone. It is intended to simulate depth of field in a photograph. Without the anti-alias, an image would look "aliased" or stair-stepped, without smooth transitions between colors. Anti-aliasing is slightly different than feathering, because the size of the transition of a feather can be controlled, whereas an anti-aliased edge is automatically applied when the option is chosen and is usually just a few pixels wide, depending on the resolution of the document (see Figure 6.4).

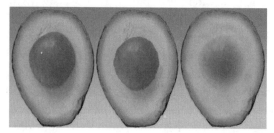

Figure 6.4　*(left) Anti-aliased, (center) aliased, and (right) feathered edges*

Shape Selection Tools

The Rectangular Marquee tool and its fly-out, the Elliptical Marquee tool, are useful when you need to select a fairly standard shape within your image—a rectangle, square, circle, or ellipse.

From the Tool palette (but for some reason not included in the Shift+M key shortcut when you cycle through them), you have two more options for these "predefined" selections: the Single Column Marquee and the Single Row Marquee.

Rectangular Marquee

The Rectangular Marquee tool is used to select rectangular or square portions of the image. Click in the image and drag in any direction to select a rectangular area of the image.

The Style menu in the Marquee tools' Options bar enables you to choose from three methods for sizing the Rectangular and Elliptical Marquees.

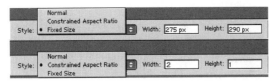

Normal   I wish they would rename this "Manual" because that's precisely what it is—the setting for hands-on control of these Marquee tools. By choosing Normal, you determine the size and proportion of the marquee by dragging.

Constrained Aspect Ratio   Enter numerical values for the proportion of the marquee in the Height and Width fields. Although you can change the *size* of the marquee by dragging, its *proportions* will remain constant.

Fixed Size   The size of the marquee is determined by the values, in pixels, that you enter in the Height and Width fields. A marquee size is defined by pixels because it can't select anything smaller. If you want Photoshop to accept values in units other than pixels—inches, for example—then right-click (Win) or Control-click (Mac) on the Width and Height fields and drag to your preferred units. Photoshop will create a marquee to the nearest pixel that you specify.

Table 6.1 describes the keyboard modifiers you can use with the Rectangular and Elliptical Marquee tools—a few neat tricks to control the behavior of marquees as you draw them.

Table 6.1 Moving and Constraining Marquees

TECHNIQUE	HOW TO DO IT
Constrain to Square or Circle	Shift-dragging constrains the Rectangular Marquee selection to a square, or the Elliptical Marquee to a circle.
Draw from Center	By default, a marquee originates from a corner point. To originate the marquee from its center, place your cursor in the center of the area and Option-drag or Alt-drag.

Table 6.1 Moving and Constraining Marquees (*continued*)

TECHNIQUE	HOW TO DO IT
Reposition While Dragging	While dragging out a marquee, hold down the space bar and drag at any time to reposition it.
Reposition After Drawing	While in the marquee tool, place the cursor inside the marquee and drag to reposition it.
Combination Techniques	You can combine any of these key command techniques. For example, press the Shift key and the mouse button and drag to constrain the image to a circle or square. Then while dragging, add the Option or Alt key to radiate it from its center point.

Elliptical Marquee

Use this tool to create ellipses or circles. Its performance is identical to the Rectangular Marquee: Click and drag in any direction to produce an elliptical or circular selection.

The Elliptical Marquee tool has the same Style options as the Rectangular Marquee (described in the previous section). Table 6.1, also in the previous section, describes the keyboard modifiers you can use to constrain or move the Elliptical Marquee tool.

Single Column Marquee

The Single Column Marquee tool selects a single vertical column of pixels. Click anywhere in the image, and a selection marquee appears around single column of adjacent pixels that runs vertically across the entire image.

One way you can use this feature is to create stripes that can later be colorized to produce wood-grain effects. Here's how:

1. Open an RGB document with a white background.

2. Select a single column of pixels.

3. Choose Filter ➔ Noise ➔ Add Noise ➔ 400, and click OK.

4. Choose Edit ➔ Transform ➔ Scale. Drag the center handle of the left or right edge to the left or right.

5. Press the Return/Enter key to initiate the transformation (or the Esc key to cancel it).

Single Row Marquee

The Single Row Marquee tool selects a single horizontal row of pixels. Click anywhere on the image, and a selection marquee appears around single, continuous row of adjacent pixels that runs horizontally across the entire image.

Free-Form Selection Tools

Photoshop offers three main ways to make irregular-shaped selections. The Lasso tool (and its fly-outs, the Polygonal Lasso and Magnetic Lasso) draw selections based on your mouse movements, in varying degrees of freedom. Cycle through these tools by pressing Shift+L.

The Magic Wand tool (shortcut key Shift+W) allows you to select without regard for position, but instead based on the brightness of the pixels in your image.

Lasso

The Lasso tool draws free-form selections. Click the edge of the area you want to select and drag to surround the area with the selection border. Close the marquee by placing the cursor on the starting point, or release the mouse to close the selection with a straight line.

Polygonal Lasso

The Polygonal Lasso tool is used to create straight-edged selection borders. Click and release the mouse. Reposition the mouse to the next corner of the polygon, and click and release again. Repeat the process until the area is surrounded. Close the marquee by clicking the starting point again.

Once you've begun making a new selection with the Lasso tool, you can toggle between the Lasso and the Polygonal Lasso by pressing the Option or Alt key.

Magnetic Lasso

The Magnetic Lasso tool intuitively makes selections based on the contrast values of pixels. As you click and drag, the Magnetic Lasso deposits a path that is attracted to areas of the most contrast. When the mouse is released, the path becomes a selection.

The Magnetic Lasso selection tool takes a while to get used to. If you find that you've lost control over the path, double-click the mouse to complete the selection, deselect (using Select ➜ Deselect or Cmd/Ctrl+D), and begin again. The Magnetic Lasso tool rarely makes perfect selections, but it's a time-saver if combined with other selection tools.

The tool has three settings in the Options bar that affect its behavior:

Width (in pixels) This setting determines the distance from the path of the mouse within which pixels will be evaluated for contrast by the Magnetic Lasso.

Edge Contrast This is the minimum percentage of pixel contrast that the Magnetic Lasso will be attracted to. The higher the number, the smaller the range of contrast, hence the more selective the tool will be.

Frequency Enter a value for the frequency with which points are automatically deposited. The points create segments along the path that fix the previous segments and better control its behavior. You can always deposit a point manually by clicking your mouse as you drag along the edge to be defined.

Magic Wand

The Magic Wand tool selects areas of an image that are similar in brightness. To use the Magic Wand, place your cursor on the area to be selected and click your mouse. Adjacent pixels of similar color will be included in the selection.

You can affect the range of pixels that are selected by adjusting the Tolerance in the tool's Options bar. Higher Tolerance values include in the selection more pixels of greater color and brightness range. Lower values include fewer pixels in the selection.

The numerical Tolerance value that you enter determines the range of the brightness values—higher *and* lower than the clicked pixel—that will be included in the selection. In the middle example in Figure 6.5, I entered a Tolerance of 32 and clicked a pixel with a brightness value of 128. The Magic Wand then included all the pixels that are 32 steps lighter and all the pixels that are 32 steps darker than the original pixel—that is, all adjacent pixels whose brightness is between 96 and 160. When selecting RGB color images with the Magic Wand tool, the range is determined by the each of the red, green, and blue values of the sampled pixel.

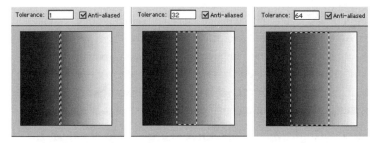

Figure 6.5 *Tolerance determines the range of pixels that the Magic Wand selects.*

Other values in the Options bar enhance your ability to control the operation of the Magic Wand tool:

Contiguous   By default, the Contiguous box is checked, which limits the selection to adjacent pixels. Uncheck this box to select all the pixels in the image within the same Tolerance range.

Use All Layers   If this box is unchecked, you will limit the selection to only pixels within the same Tolerance range on the same layer. Checking this box also includes pixels within the same Tolerance range on other layers. (Layers are covered in Chapter 7.)

Applying Selection Techniques

There are several ways to modify a selection outline; among them, you can conceal it, transform it, add to it, subtract from it, soften its edges, and eliminate it. These commands are important because they facilitate the process of masking. For example, if you draw a selection incorrectly, then instead of redrawing it from scratch, it might be more efficient to make a few alterations to it. What follows are some outline-altering techniques that you will find indispensable.

The Select Menu

Some selection adjustments can be automatically applied by accessing them from the Select menu or applying a shortcut key command. You will find that you use these commands quite frequently, so in the interest of working efficiently, I recommend that you learn to use the shortcuts.

Select All   (Cmd+A on Macintosh, Ctrl+A in Windows) This command selects the entire content of an image or a targeted layer. Because you can perform virtually any operation to the entire image in Photoshop when no specific area has been defined by a selection border, this command is somewhat redundant and is used primarily to select the image prior to copying and pasting.

Deselect   (Cmd/Ctrl+D) Use Select ➜ Deselect to deactivate the selection. Another method is to click off the selection, anywhere on the image.

Reselect   (Shift+Cmd/Ctrl+D) Choose this command to reactivate the last deselected selection border.

Inverse   (Shift+Cmd/Ctrl+I) To deselect the selected portion of the image and select the masked portion, choose Select ➜ Inverse. This technique can save time when an image has been photographed on a single colored background. The background can be selected quickly with the Magic Wand and inverted to select the desired content, as in Figure 6.6.

Figure 6.6 *After selecting the background (left), the Inverse command deselects that portion of the image and selects the masked portion (right).*

Hide Edges   (Cmd/Ctrl+H) Use Select ➜ Hide Edges to conceal and reveal the marching ants from view while the selection remains active. This command is useful to be able to see changes to the image without the distracting selection border.

 With the border invisible, you may forget that an area on the image is selected. Photoshop will not perform operations anywhere else on the image until the selection border is deactivated. If you find that the Paintbrush tool is not painting or the Smudge tool not smudging, press Cmd/Ctrl+D to deactivate the invisible selection.

Feather   After you've made a selection, you can soften its edges by applying a feather radius to it. For an explanation on feathering, see the previous section "The Selection Tool Options Bar."

Modify   Once a selection has been made, you can alter its dimensions by choosing one of the Select ➜ Modify subcommands. Each command changes the selection marquee and alters its dimensions:

> **Border**   frames the selection and deselects the inside area of the outline, producing a selected "border" of specific thickness (see Figure 6.7). When you choose Select ➜ Modify ➜ Border, you are presented with a window. You determine the thickness of the border by entering a value in pixels into the Width field.

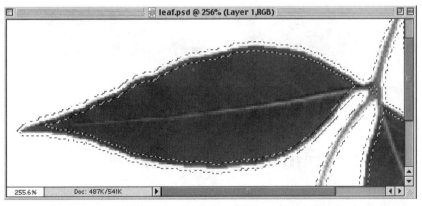

Figure 6.7 *The Border command selects only the outermost portion of your selection (here, the pixels immediately inward and outward from the edge of the plant).*

> **Smooth**   rounds sharp corners of a selection, eliminating protrusions and stairstepped areas of the selection border. When you choose Select ➜ Modify ➜ Smooth, you are asked to put in a Sample Radius value. Enter larger values to increase the effect. In Figure 6.8, the Sample Radius results in "cutting off" the left tip of the triangle.

> **Expand and Contract**   both perform in the same way to enlarge or reduce the size of the selection by a specified number of pixels. This command is quite useful for trimming off stubborn, unwanted edge pixels (see the section on

matting in Chapter 16, "Advanced Layer Techniques") or tightening up your selection a bit. Choose Select ➜ Modify ➜ Expand or Contract. and enter a value between 1 and 16 pixels. Click OK to implement the operation.

Grow   The value entered in the Tolerance field of the Magic Wand's Options bar determines how much the selection will grow. When you choose Select ➜ Grow, the selection marquee expands to include adjacent pixels that are lighter or darker by no more than the Tolerance range.

Similar   In order to use this operation, a selection must be active. When you choose Select ➜ Similar, Photoshop selects all pixels within the image that are the same colors as the pixels within the selected area.

Figure 6.8 *The Smooth command rounds off jagged corners, like the tip of this triangle.*

Transforming a Selection

Once you have made a selection, you may want to alter its shape before applying one of Photoshop's many powerful operations to its content. Photoshop gives you the ability to scale, rotate, or move a selection border. To transform a selection, choose Select ➜ Transform Selection. A rectangular transformation box appears around the selection border. You can then transform the size, angle, or position of the selection border with the following procedures:

▶

Move   To move the selection, place your cursor within the rectangular transformation box; the Move cursor appears. Press your mouse button and drag the selection into position, then release the mouse.

The icon in the center of the transformation box represents the point of origin. The icon can be moved prior to scaling or rotating the selection, to change the point from which the selection will transform. When you want to move the box, however, place your cursor anywhere in the selection except on the icon.

Scale   To scale a selection border, place your cursor on one of the square handles on the corners or sides of the box. The Scale cursor appears. Press your mouse button and drag. To constrain the selection border to its current proportion, press your Shift key while dragging.

Rotate   To rotate a selection, place your cursor outside the box. The Rotate cursor appears. Press your mouse button and drag to rotate the selection.

Scale and Rotate are demonstrated in Figure 6.9. To implement the transformation, press the Return key (Mac) or the Enter key (Win); the transformation box will disappear. To cancel the transformation, press the Escape key.

Figure 6.9 *Transform Selection techniques: Scale (left) and Rotate (right)*

After you've chosen Select ➜ Transform Selection and the transformation box is displayed, you can also apply many more transformations to the selection by choosing Edit ➜ Transform. A list of options appears, including Skew, Distort, Perspective, and various precise Rotate commands. These additional functions are performed by repositioning the anchor points of the transformation box. The Flip Horizontal or Flip Vertical commands will mirror the marquee across a horizontal or vertical axis passing through its point of origin icon.

See Chapter 13 for more on sizing and transforming images.

Other Selection Techniques

Once a selection has been made, you can reposition the marquee with or without its contents using the following techniques:

Move Selection Outline   While in any selection tool, click inside the marquee and drag. When you've relocated the outline, release the mouse.

Nudge Selection Outline   While in any selection tool, press the right, left, up, or down arrow keys to move a selection in increments of one pixel. Press the Shift key plus any of the arrow keys to move the selection outline 10 pixels at a time.

Move Selection Contents   Choose the Move tool; click inside the marquee and drag. When you've relocated the marquee, release the mouse. You can also move the contents while in any selection tool: Cmd-click or Ctrl-click inside the marquee and drag. When you've relocated the selection, release the mouse and then the key.

After you've selected an area and moved it once, it "floats." That is, it can be moved again by placing a selection tool inside the marquee, pressing the mouse button, and dragging. You no longer need to press Cmd/Ctrl. The selection will remain floating until you deselect it.

Nudge Selection Contents   You can nudge the selection contents in one-pixel increments: With the Move tool active, press the left, right, up, or down arrow keys. Press the Shift key and any of the arrow keys to move the selection contents 10 pixels at a time.

Duplicate Selection Contents   Position the cursor inside the marquee; hold down Option+Command (Mac) or Alt+Ctrl (Win) while you click and drag. (Or get the Move tool and hold down Option or Alt while you drag.) When you've relocated the copy to the desired position, release the mouse.

Up Next

Next, I'll present the first of several Hands-On projects that will appear regularly throughout this book. These sections will give you real Photoshop files and step-by-step directions on how to use them to produce a wide variety of art and effects. You'll see suggestions for ways to experiment beyond the pictures shown here, and extra instruction on the myriad possibilities of Photoshop.

This first Hands-On work will give you the chance to practice the tools and techniques described so far, but especially the selection methods described here in Chapter 6.

Hands-On
Selection

Making accurate selections is fundamental to maintaining the credibility of your image. Poorly drawn selections that are rough, inaccurate, stair-stepped, or that contain unwanted edge pixels are sure to destroy the illusion of a seamless reality. It's important, then, to familiarize yourself with the masking process and hone your selection-making skills. That is what I hope this step-by-step section will accomplish.

My good friend, David Adix, is a folk artist who lives in Tucson, Arizona. He has a particular genius for assembling the most charming and interesting sculptures (Figure 1 is one example and can be seen in color in the color section) from stuff that most people would throw away. He kindly sifted through his "trash stash" to find the items needed for this tutorial.

Figure 1 *An assemblage by David Adix*

While David assembles his 3-D sculptures using real bits of old metal, wood, and other "treasures," we are going use Photoshop to build a virtual assemblage from digital images of the materials that David uses. To further emphasize the versatility of Photoshop, we will use the digital assemblage as an interesting graphic of a king for a playing card. This module will take you through a broad range of selection tools and techniques used to isolate and edit portions of the image.

Getting Started

Hide your preferences file before beginning this Hands-On exercise, then restart Photoshop to create a clean version. The "Photoshop's Settings" section in Chapter 5 details how to temporarily reset your preferences to Photoshop's defaults. You can restore your customized, personal settings when you're done.

Once you have launched Photoshop with default preferences, here's how to begin the Hands-On project:

1. Insert the *Mastering Photoshop 6* CD in your CD-ROM drive.

2. Choose File ➜ Open. Look for `Rex_start.psd` (shown in Figure 2) in the `Ch06` folder on the CD and open it.

Figure 2 *The pieces for the virtual assemblage*

3. Choose File ➜ Save As and save the document to your disk.

 A color version of Rex_start.psd *is in the color section of the book. You can also preview the color version of the finished digital assemblage by viewing the file* Rex_end.tif *(Figure 3) on the CD or in the color section.*

Figure 3 *This is what we'll make out of the virtual elements.*

Building the Background

Selecting the Red Rectangle

1. Choose the Rectangular Marquee tool. Place your cursor on the upper-left corner of the red rectangle. Click and drag to the lower-right corner to make your selection, as shown in Figure 4. (Yes, you could use the Magic Wand here for the solid red shape. Like most work in Photoshop, there are several ways to do everything. We'll use a variety of tools in these tutorials to help you become familiar with each.)

Figure 4 *Selecting the rectangle*

2. From the View menu, choose Show Rulers. Drag a guide from the vertical ruler and place it along the right side of the rectangle.

3. Choose View ➔ Snap To ➔ Guide.

4. Place your cursor inside the marching ants. First click the mouse button, and then press the Shift key to constrain the horizontal movement of the marquee

as you drag to the right. Align the marquee's left border with the right side of the red rectangle (it will snap into place).

5. Choose View ➔ Clear Guides.

6. Choose Window ➔ Show Swatches and click a light blue color swatch. Notice that the chosen color appears as the foreground color in the Tool palette.

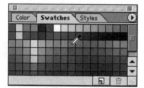

7. Press Option+Delete (Mac) or Alt+Backspace (Win) to fill the rectangle with the foreground color.

8. Save the document (File ➔ Save, or Cmd/Ctrl+S).

Selecting the Lattice

Since the lattice that will make up the king's crown is all black, we can select it with the Magic Wand tool set at a relatively low range of brightnesses.

1. Choose the Magic Wand tool (click its icon in the Tool palette or press the W key). In the Options bar, be sure the Tolerance is set to 32.

2. Click the lattice to select it.

3. Choose the Move tool. Place the cursor inside the selection, on a black area of the lattice. Drag the lattice, centering it on the two colored rectangles (as in Figure 5), and release the mouse.

4. Save the document.

Selecting the Board

1. Choose the Elliptical Marquee. In the Options bar, from the Style pop-up list, choose Constrained Aspect Ratio. Enter 2 for the Width and 1 for the Height.

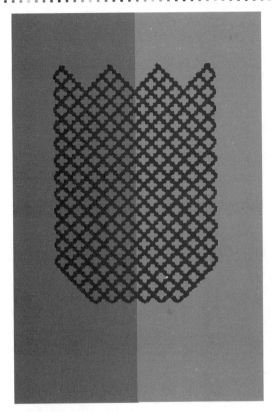

Figure 5 *Placing the lattice*

2. Place your cursor on the rectangular wooden board with various shapes down its middle. Drag out until the oval is about the same width as the board. Keep the mouse button down while sizing the image and press the space bar, which will allow you to reposition the marquee by dragging it; move the marquee so that it spans the board. Release the space bar to resize until your selection looks like Figure 6.

3. Choose the Rectangular Marquee. Click the Add To Selection icon in the Options bar. Under Style, choose Fixed Size. Enter 138 pixels wide by 145 pixels high. Press the space bar to position the rectangle so that its two top corners are aligned with the widest part of the ellipse. Release the mouse; your selection should resemble Figure 7.

Figure 6 *Board selected with the Elliptical Marquee tool*

Figure 7 *The rectangle added to the ellipse*

4. Choose the Move tool. Drag the selected part of the board and center it on the lattice.

5. Deselect everything (Select ➔ Deselect, or Cmd/Ctrl+D).

Building the Face

Building the Eyes

1. Select the Elliptical Marquee. Shift+Option-click or Shift+Alt-click the center of the aluminum dial and drag to radiate a circle from its center point. Drag to 4 or 5 pixels from the outermost edge of the dial, as in Figure 8.

Figure 8 *The dial selected*

2. Choose Select ➜ Feather. Enter 3 for the pixel radius to produce a feathered edge on the selection.

3. Choose the Move tool. Drag the dial and place it on the left side of the board. Notice the effect of the feathered edge: The dial's edges blend into the background.

4. Select the Elliptical Marquee. In the Options bar, set a Feather Radius of 3 pixels. This will pre-program the selection tool to produce a feathered selection when you draw with it. Place your cursor in the center of the rusty circle. Shift+Option-click or Shift+Alt-click and drag to radiate the circle. Drag to 4 or 5 pixels from the outermost edge.

5. Choose the Move tool. Drag the rusty circle and place it on the right side of the board. Its edges also blend into the background.

6. Select the Elliptical Marquee. In the Options bar, set the Feather to zero. Place your cursor in the center of the small blue bead. Shift+Option/Alt-click and drag to radiate a circle from its center point to select the bead.

7. Choose the Move tool. Drag the bead and place it in the center of the oval-shaped wooden bowl, so it looks like Figure 9.

Figure 9 *The bead placed on the oval*

8. Choose the Elliptical Marquee. Option-click or Alt-click and drag to radiate an ellipse, selecting the stacked bead and the oval-shaped bowl from their center point.

9. Choose the Move tool. Drag the selection, place it on the aluminum dial, and release the mouse to create the king's right eye.

10. With the selection still active, place the cursor in its center. Hold down the Option or Alt key while dragging to duplicate the image. Drag and position the duplicate eye to the right of the original eye, onto the rusty circle, and release the mouse (see Figure 10).

Figure 10 *The eyes placed on the board*

11. Save the document.

Selecting the Nose

We will use the dark railroad spike for the nose. Because the spike consists of mottled colors of approximately the same values, we can select it with the Magic Wand tool. Finding the right tolerance is often a matter of trial and error. We should be cautious to avoid too low a tolerance, which would select too little of the surface, or too high a tolerance to select unwanted white, edge pixels.

1. Use the Navigator palette to zoom in on the spike.

2. Choose the Magic Wand tool. In the Options bar, set the Tolerance to 32.

3. Click the spike. You see a partial selection of its surface.

4. Hold down the Shift key to add to the selection. Click an unselected area, and a little more of the spike is selected. You can see that it might take a while to select the entire spike.

5. Deselect (Select → Deselect, or Cmd/Ctrl+D).

6. Reset the Tolerance to 60 and click the spike. This time, much more of the spike is selected.

7. Press the Shift key and continue to click the unselected areas until the entire spike is selected (see Figure 11).

Figure 11 *Selecting the spike with the Magic Wand tool*

8. Choose the Move tool. Place the cursor inside the selection marquee. Drag the spike and position it between the eyes, as shown in Figure 12, then release the mouse.

9. Save the document.

Figure 12 *The spike becomes the nose.*

Selecting the Mustache

The easiest way to select the wing nut that will be used as the mustache is to combine two selection techniques.

1. Choose the Rectangular Marquee and drag a rectangle around the wing nut.

2. Choose the Magic Wand tool. In the Options bar, set the Tolerance to 32. Choose the Subtract From Selection icon.

3. Place the Magic Wand cursor on the white area of the selection (it should have a minus sign, representing the Subtract operation) and click.

4. Choose the Move tool. Place the cursor inside the selection marquee. Drag the wing nut and position it under the nose. Release the mouse (see Figure 13).

5. Save the document.

Figure 13 *The wing nut placed as the mustache*

Selecting the Arm

Combining the Magic Wand and the Grow command is a quick way to select areas with a lot of tonal variations distributed over a large area.

1. Zoom in on the wooden arm shape.

2. Choose the Magic Wand, and set the Tolerance to 32.

3. Click the wooden surface of the arm to partially select it.

4. Choose Select ➜ Grow. More of the arm is selected.

5. Continue to choose Select ➜ Grow until the entire arm is selected.

6. Choose the Move tool. Click inside the selection marquee and drag to position the arm at the bottom of the "face" board. Release the mouse.

7. Save the document.

Selecting the Beard

When you need to make a complex selection with a contrasted edge, the Magnetic Lasso tool can be a real time saver. The Magnetic Lasso often produces imperfect results, so be sure to scrutinize the marquee carefully and make corrections or changes manually with the Lasso tool.

1. Zoom in on the U-shaped molding.

2. Choose the Magnetic Lasso tool. Use the default settings in the Options bar to control its performance.

3. Carefully drag along the edge of the molding. Click your mouse frequently to deposit anchors.

4. When you've entirely surrounded the edges with the magnetic selection outline, place your cursor on the original point and click your mouse to implement the selection (Figure 14).

Figure 14 *Selecting the molding with the Magnetic Lasso tool*

5. Choose the Move tool. Click inside the selection marquee, drag the beard, and position it on the chin (Figure 15). Release the mouse.

6. Save the document.

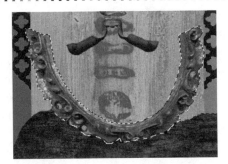

Figure 15 *Moving the beard into place*

Selecting the Hair

When confronting an area that needs to be selected, you can evaluate its shape and then choose the appropriate combination of selection tools and techniques.

1. Choose the Elliptical Marquee. Place the cursor in the *middle* of the circular area of the curly blue shape. Option-click or Alt-click to radiate a circle from its center point. Release the mouse when your selection looks like the one in Figure 16.

Figure 16 *Start with the Elliptical Marquee.*

2. Choose the Polygonal Lasso tool (hold down on the Lasso tool icon to get it from the fly-out, or type Shift+L until you have the right cursor). Click the Add To Selection icon in the Options bar.

3. Click the top-right corner of the shape. Release, and move to the bottom of the straight right edge. Click again to place an anchor point, release the mouse, and move across the top of the circle. Click again and go to the top of the right edge, clicking to form a triangle. Your selection should resemble Figure 17.

Figure 17 *Add to the selection with the Polygonal Lasso tool.*

4. Type Shift+L twice to toggle to the regular Lasso. (Make sure the Add To Selection option is still clicked.) Drag to select the curved edge. Drag inside the triangular portion of the selection and release the mouse to complete the selection.

5. Choose the Move tool. Drag the selection marquee and position it on the left side of the head, as in Figure 18. Release the mouse.

An alternative method to quickly add the rest of the hair to the selection is to choose the Magnetic Selection tool. Choose the Add To Selection icon. Start within the top point of the existing selection and drag to follow the edge of the curve, then place your cursor just inside the diagonal line of the existing selection and release your mouse. The selection will close with a straight line.

Figure 18 *Position the curl of the hair on the board.*

Building the Props

Selecting the Sword

1. Choose the Polygonal Lasso.

2. Hold down the Shift key to constrain the selection to vertical, horizontal, and 45-degree directions. Start at the top-right of the pointed wooden stick; click and release the mouse. Keep Shift-clicking to create anchor points at the bottom-right corner, the bottom-left corner, and up the left side even with the top-right point.

3. Move the cursor up at a slight angle to the horizontal middle of the molding. The line will constrain to 45 degrees to create the left side of the sword's point. Now, move the cursor down to where the selection was begun. When you've

surrounded the wooden molding, double-click the mouse to close the selection (see Figure 19).

Figure 19 *The Polygonal Lasso tool constrained to 45-degree directions*

4. Choose the Move tool and drag your selection into position above the hand.

5. Save the document.

Creating the Hilt

1. Scroll down to the king's arm. Choose the Rectangular Marquee. Drag a small, narrow rectangle anywhere on the arm.

2. Choose the Elliptical Marquee (from the Marquee tool fly-out or by typing Shift+M).

3. Click the Add To Selection icon. Shift-drag a small circle on either end of the rectangle, as I've done in Figure 20. We'll copy this selection to serve as the hilt of the sword.

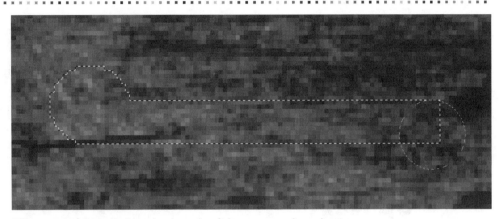

Figure 20 *Add a circle to both ends of the rectangular selection.*

4. Choose the Move tool. Option-drag or Alt-drag the hilt into place (Figure 21) to duplicate it.

Figure 21 *Duplicate the hilt.*

Selecting the Letter

1. Choose the Rectangular Marquee and drag a rectangle around the gold letter K.

2. Choose the Magic Wand tool. In the Options bar, set the Tolerance to 32. Choose the Subtract From Selection icon.

3. Click in the white area of the selection.

4. Choose the Move tool. Click inside the selection marquee and drag the K to the upper-left corner of the image. Release the mouse.

5. Place the cursor on the active selection again. Press Option/Alt while clicking and dragging the K away to duplicate it. Drag the copy into the lower-right corner. Your image should now look like the file Rex_end.tif (shown back in Figure 3).

6. Deselect (Cmd/Ctrl+D) and save the document (File ➜ Save, or Cmd/Ctrl+S).

Up Next

Making selections can be the most labor-intensive of all of Photoshop's operations. Accurate selections are critical to the credibility of an altered image. Perfect perform-ance is achieved by practicing the techniques presented here and carefully scrutinizing the results. I hope that this project has shown you some of the many selection tech-niques and has you thinking about creatively combining them to isolate those difficult areas on the image. Read Chapters 12 and 19 to learn how to tighten up your selections using the paint tools and how to select really tough areas.

Chapter 7 looks at another fundamental method Photoshop uses to isolate areas of the images—layers. We will discover how to use layers to our best advantage so that the image remains dynamic throughout the editing process. We'll look at some of the new layer techniques Photoshop 6 has to offer, like layer sets, layer locks, and layer styles.

Layering Your Image

PHOTOSHOP

Chapter 7

All digital images are completely flat; even the most three-dimensional-looking images only *look* as if they have depth. Photoshop images appear on flat screens, but they can look three-dimensional in part because of the power of layers to help create the illusion.

Layers are critical to working dynamically in Photoshop. Images on individual layers can be edited separately and moved independently of each other. The stacking order of layers can help determine the position of visual elements within the picture plane. In short, working with layers gives you tremendous control over the image during the process of creating it.

This chapter will help you learn about:

- Understanding the Layers palette

- Creating new layers

- Blending layers

- Using layer styles

- Consolidating layers

- Working with Type layers

The Illusion of Depth

The illusion of three-dimensionality is really quite remarkable, but because we see it so often, we take it for granted. The visual effect of depth on a flat surface is created by the use of techniques that mimic what we see in the world.

One technique, called one-point perspective, achieves the effect by the use of converging lines that intersect at a vanishing point. An object whose contours align with the perspective lines will appear to recede in space.

Another method of producing the effect of depth is to adjust the relative scale of visual elements in an image. Larger objects appear closer to the viewer than smaller ones. Because this visual phenomenon is a naturally occurring characteristic of sight in the 3-D world, when we see it in a picture we subconsciously draw the conclusion that the objects exist in space when, in fact, the picture is two-dimensional.

The position of an object in an image also contributes to the illusion of depth. If one element blocks out a portion of another element, the obstructing element will appear to be in front of the obstructed one. Another common device, atmospheric perspective, uses tonality to simulate distance. As objects recede in space, they appear lighter and less distinct due to the presence of dust and haze in the air.

The fact remains, however, that no matter how many devices are used to produce three-dimensionality, and no matter how deep the image appears, unless its surface is textured, it is as flat as a pancake.

Photoshop images are close to being an exception to the flat-as-a-pancake rule. They appear on screen as flat images of colored light, and they have a specific height and width. They can also have depth in the form of *layers*. A Photoshop layer is like a piece of clear glass (see Figure 7.1). Parts of the image can be pasted to the glass. If you have different parts of the image separated onto multiple layers, you can shuffle their position in the stack, allowing one part of the image to appear in front of another. Because the layers isolate each part of the image, you have the added advantage of being able to individually control the contents of each layer separately.

When a part of the image is isolated on an individual layer, it can be singled out and affected at any time. A layer can be moved horizontally or vertically, or repositioned anywhere in the stack, to help produce the illusion of depth. The color relations of pixels on superimposed layers can be modified, and their level of opacity can be adjusted. Special layer styles can be applied to produce realistic shadows, embosses, textures, patterns, and glowing effects.

Figure 7.1 *Layers in a Photoshop document*

Looking at the Layers Palette

At the heart of all this power is the Layers palette (shown in Figure 7.2). It is the control center from which most layer operations are performed. By default, the Layers palette is clustered with the Channels and the Paths palettes. If the Layers palette is not displayed, you can access it by choosing Window ➜ Show Layers or by pressing the F7 key on an extended keyboard.

Each layer in the palette is separated from the one directly below or above it by a thin line. Each layer's row includes a thumbnail of the layer's contents, the layer's name, and any layer styles, masks, or locks applied to that layer. In the far left column is an eye icon which, when displayed, indicates that the contents of the layer are visible. Immediately to the right of this visibility indicator is another column that displays a brush icon if the layer is the target layer, a small chain icon if the layer is linked, or a mask icon if the layer is a Fill or Adjustment layer.

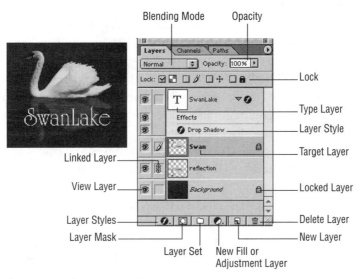

Blending Mode — Opacity

Lock

Type Layer

Layer Style

Linked Layer — Target Layer

View Layer — Locked Layer

Layer Styles — Delete Layer

Layer Mask — New Layer

Layer Set — New Fill or Adjustment Layer

Figure 7.2 *The Layers palette*

Above the layer stack are Lock check boxes, which enable you to lock the transparency, editing, and movement of layer contents. At the top-left of the Layers palette is a list of blending modes that can alter the color relations of layers in the stack. And to the right of the blending modes is the Opacity slider that controls the level of transparency of a targeted layer's contents.

Many layer actions can be accessed from the palette pull-down menu (shown in Figure 7.3). Clicking the small triangular icon on the top-right of the palette reveals these options.

Figure 7.3 *The Layers palette pull-down menu*

The Background Layer

When you scan or import an image from another program and open it in Photoshop, the Layers palette displays one thumbnail, labeled *Background*. You can think of the Background as an image mounted to a board. If you were to cut away a portion of the image with an X-ACTO knife, you would see the board underneath—in this case, the background color behind the Background contents. The contents of all of the layers float on top of the Background. Unlike a layer, the Background is opaque and cannot support transparency. If the document contains more than one layer, the Background is always at the bottom of the stack and cannot be moved and placed in a higher position. When new layers are added to the document, their content always appears in front of the Background.

By default, the Background is locked. If you want to move its contents, adjust its opacity, or reposition it in the Layers stack, you need to convert it to a layer. Like many of Photoshop's operations, there is more than one way to perform this task. To convert the Background into a layer from the menu, choose Layer ➜ New ➜ Layer From Background. To convert the Background from the Layers palette, follow these steps:

Macintosh   Option-click the Background's name or thumbnail to display the New Layer dialog box. Enter a name for the new layer in the Name field and click OK.

Windows   Alt-click the Background's *name* to automatically change it into a layer named Layer 0. Alternatively, Alt-click the Background's *thumbnail* to display the New Layer dialog box, then enter a name for the new layer in the Name field and click OK.

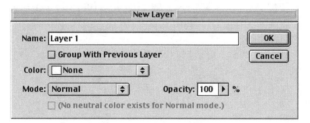

By default, Photoshop names the converted layer Layer 0, but I recommend that you give it a name that readily identifies it. The New Layer dialog box also lets you color-code your layer and adjust its opacity. You can also group it with other layers if, for example, you're using it to make a clipping group. (Chapter 20, "Advanced Layer Techniques," describes clipping groups.)

If your image is composed entirely of layers, you can convert one of your layers into a Background. Target a layer and choose Layer ➜ New ➜ Background From Layer.

Naming your layers is essential to establishing an efficient workflow. The default numbers that Photoshop assigns to new layers become quite anonymous when their content is too small to be recognized on the thumbnail or there are 30 or 40 of them in the document. Naming each layer with a descriptive title is a fast way to organize the components of your image for easy identification.

Naming Layers

To change the name of a layer, use one of these methods to bring up the Layer Properties dialog box:

- Option-click (Mac) or Alt-double-click (Win) the layer name in the Layers palette.

- Control-click (Mac) or right-click (Win) a layer and choose Layer Properties from the context-sensitive shortcut menu.

- From the Layers palette pop-up menu, choose Layer Properties.

In the dialog box, type a name in the Name field and click OK.

Viewing and Targeting Layers

The content of a layer can be concealed or revealed by clicking the eye icon in the first column of the Layers palette. To reveal or conceal the contents of more than one layer at a time, click the eye next to each of the desired layers. To conceal all but one layer, press the Option or Alt key while clicking its eye icon. With the same key held down, click the icon again to reveal all layers.

Choosing Your Thumbnail Size

The thumbnails that represent each layer display the content in miniature. You can choose from three different sizes of thumbnails, or you can choose to display no thumbnail at all. To specify a thumbnail display, pull down the palette menu and choose Palette Options. In the dialog box that opens (Figure 7.4), click the desired thumbnail size and then click OK.

Figure 7.4 *Options for Layers palette thumbnails*

Targeting a Layer

You can apply virtually any Photoshop operation to affect the contents of a layer, but first you must target the layer you want. A *targeted* layer is active and ready to be edited. To target a layer, click its name, which appears to the right of the thumbnail. You will see a colored highlight in the text field and a brush symbol in the second column to the left of the layer's thumbnail (as in Figure 7.5). Only one layer can be targeted at a time; a targeted layer must be visible to be affected. Certain effects can be applied to multiple layers simultaneously by linking them (see "Linking Layers" below) or grouping them (see Chapter 20).

Figure 7.5 *The swan's* reflection *is the targeted layer.*

Understanding Transparency and Opacity

Since transparency is invisible, it's difficult to display. If a color like white represents transparency, how is the viewer to know what is transparent, what is translucent, and what is opaque? Photoshop solves this problem by displaying transparency using two colors in the form of a checkerboard.

If you see an area on a layer that is displayed as a gray checkerboard, then the area is totally transparent. This means that either it is void of pixels or the pixels are completely transparent. If it's displayed as a combination of image and checkerboard, then it is semitransparent; and if it's displayed totally as image, then it's opaque. Figure 7.6 illustrates the difference between opaque and semitransparent images.

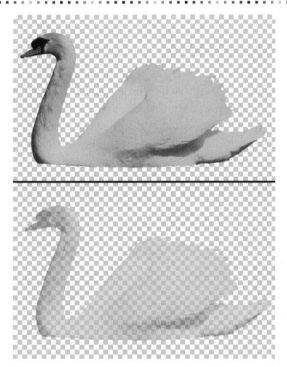

Figure 7.6 *The swan at the top is displayed at 100% opacity; the swan at the bottom is displayed at 50% opacity.*

If only one layer is displayed and its content is surrounded by areas of transparency, the image will appear against a gray checkerboard. If the color of the image is predominantly gray and the checkerboard becomes difficult to see, the color and size of the checkerboard can be changed in the Transparency & Gamut Preferences to better reveal the image.

Controlling Opacity

The Opacity slider enables you to adjust the level of transparency of all the pixels on a targeted layer, so that you can see through the image to the underlying layers in the stack. Click the arrow next to the Opacity field on the Layers palette; a slider pops up, which you can drag right to increase or left to decrease opacity. Or enter a value from 0 to 100 percent directly in the box.

If any tool is active other than the painting and editing tools, you can press any number between 1 and 100 to change the Opacity value of the targeted layer.

Changing Layer Order

The stacking order in the Layers palette determines the plane of depth where the visual elements appear. The content of the topmost layer in the Layers palette appears in the front of the image. The further down in the stack a layer is, the farther back its content appears, all the way back to the bottommost layer or the Background.

You can change a layer's position in the stack, and consequently its visual plane of depth in the image. In the Layers palette, click and drag the thumbnail or name of the layer you wish to move. As you drag up or down, you will see the division line between layers become bold (as in Figure 7.7). The bold line indicates the new location where the layer will appear when the mouse is released.

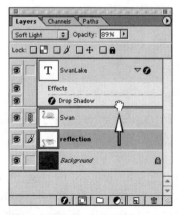

Figure 7.7 *You can change a layer's position in the stacking order.*

Another method of changing the position of the layer in the stack is to choose an option under Layer ➜ Arrange, or use the equivalent key command. In the Arrange submenu, you are presented with four options, as shown in Table 7.1.

Table 7.1 Shortcuts for Positioning Layers

POSITION	MACINTOSH SHORTCUT	WINDOWS SHORTCUT	RESULT
Bring To Front	Shift+Cmd+]	Shift+Ctrl+]	Moves the layer to the top of the stack
Bring Forward	Cmd+]	Ctrl+]	Moves the layer on top of the layer immediately above it
Send Backward	Cmd+[	Ctrl+[	Moves the layer under the layer immediately below it
Send To Back	Shift+Cmd+[	Shift+Ctrl+[	Moves the layer to the bottom of the stack but in front of the Background

Linking Layers

Let's say you've positioned two elements of a logo on separate layers, and you are quite content with their visual relation to each other, except that they are a little too large and they need to be moved a half inch to the left. You can transform or move two layers simultaneously by *linking* them.

To link one or more layers, target one of the layers. Click in the column to the immediate left of the thumbnail on the layers that you want to include in the link. A chain icon appears, like the one next to the reflection layer in Figure 7.8, indicating that the layers are linked. You can then choose the Move tool or any transformation function (Edit ➜ Transform), and the layers will scale, rotate, distort, etc., all together. (See Chapter 13 for more on transformations.)

When you apply a transformation operation to linked layers, the transformation marquee will surround only the content of the targeted layer. If you proceed with the operation, all of the linked elements will transform.

Figure 7.8 *Linked layers are indicated with a chain icon.
Here the reflection is linked to the Type layer.*

Linked layers are used for the purpose of transforming and moving multiple layers simultaneously. To apply other effects to multiple layers, there are specific layer-based operations like the following. (These effects are described in more detail in later sections of this chapter and later chapters in the book.)

Adjustment Layers   for color, brightness, and contrast adjustments and color mapping functions (see Chapter 16).

Layer Masking   to conceal and reveal portions of two sequential layers in the stack (see Chapter 20).

Blending Modes   to apply a preprogrammed color formula to affect the relation between the pixels on a layer and the layer immediately below it in the stack (see Appendix C).

Layer Sets   for grouping, opacity control, positioning of multiple layers in the stack, and transforming or moving layers (see the following section).

Fill Layers   to apply a solid color, gradient, or pattern to an independent layer. When the opacity is adjusted, the Fill layer affects the underlying layer. A Fill layer also contains a layer mask, so that the color, gradient, or pattern can be superimposed onto a specific area of the image (see Chapter 10).

Clipping Groups   for using the content of one layer to clip portions of another (see Chapter 20).

Grouping Layers in Layer Sets

Earlier versions of Photoshop supported a mere 99 layers; Photoshop 6 now supports an unlimited number. The potential to produce enormous quantities of layers made a layer-management tool an absolute necessity. *Layer sets* have been introduced to let you consolidate contiguous layers into a folder on the Layers palette. By highlighting the folder, you can apply certain operations to the layers as a group. The layers in a layer set, like Swan and Reflection in Figure 7.9, can be can simultaneously revealed or concealed by clicking the eye icon for the set in the Layers palette; the whole set can be repositioned in the stack, moved, and—like linked layers—transformed using any of the transformation tools.

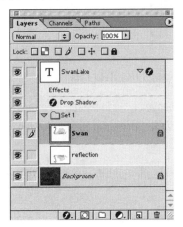

Figure 7.9 *The Swan and Reflection layers make up a layer set.*

Although you can perform transformations and repositioning to both layer sets and linked layers, layer sets differ from linked layers in that they contain contiguous layers—that is, layers that are sequenced immediately above or below each other in the stack. Layers that are linked can be anywhere in the stack.

You can also determine which color channels will be affected. To reveal the layers within the set, click the triangle to the left of the folder so that it points down. To conceal the contents of the layer set to eliminate clutter, click the triangle so that it points to the right.

There are a few different ways to create a new layer set:

- From the Layer menu, choose Layer ➜ New ➜ Layer Set.

- From the Layers palette menu, choose New Layer Set.

- Click the Layer Set icon in the Layers palette. By default, the first layer set will be named Set 1.

With the first two commands, the Layer Set dialog box appears. You can name the layer set, color-code it, and specify the color channels of which the images will be composed.

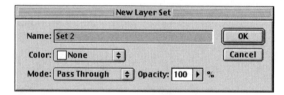

To add a layer to a set, drag the layer name to the layer set.

A fast way to create a layer set is to link the layers that you want in the set. Then choose Layer ➜ New ➜ Layer Set From Linked. All of the linked layers will be consolidated into one set.

However, when you convert linked layers into a layer set, they will all become contiguous and their position in the stack may change.

Locking Layers

Photoshop 6 offers four controls in the Layers palette that prevent a layer from being modified. Each lock is represented by an icon at the top of the palette; to lock a layer, target the layer and check the box for the lock type you want.

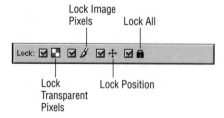

Lock Transparent Pixels   This function is comparable to Preserve Transparency in earlier versions of the software. It protects the areas of the targeted layer that don't contain pixels from being edited. If you attempt to paint on a transparent area, for example, the tool will not respond, so in a sense, Lock Transparency works like a mask. The areas that do contain pixels will still respond to any Photoshop operation. Locking transparency does not protect transparent areas from the effect of transformations like scaling, rotating, or moving.

Lock Image Pixels   The entire targeted layer is protected from editing functions like painting, color adjustments, or filters. You can, however, transform or move the content of a layer. Menu operations that you can't perform are grayed out. If you attempt to apply a tool function, you will be greeted with a circle with a line through it.

Lock Position   Checking this option prevents you from moving a targeted layer or applying Edit ➜ Free Transform or any of the Edit ➜ Transform operations such as Scale and Distort. When the Lock Position box is checked, these menu items are grayed out.

Lock All   You can protect a targeted layer from all editing functions by checking the Lock All box.

Creating New Layers

It is often necessary to create a new layer, either to add new content to the image or to isolate an existing element. When a new layer is added, the file size of the document increases commensurate with the quantity of information on the new layer. Adding several new layers can significantly increase the amount of space the image consumes on your disk. This however, is a small inconvenience for the power that layers deliver. As part of your workflow, though, you'll no doubt want to consolidate layers during the imaging process to decrease the file size (see "Consolidating Layers" later in the chapter).

Creating a New Empty Layer

Here is an another example of redundant Photoshop operations. Two of these operations produce identical results, and one produces similar results with a slight variation. All three create a new layer; let's try them:

- From the Layers menu, choose Layer ➜ New ➜ Layer. The New Layer dialog box appears. Name the layer and click OK.

- From the Layers palette pop-up menu, choose New Layer. The New Layer dialog box appears. Name the Layer and click OK.

- Click the New Layer icon (next to the trash icon at the bottom of the Layers palette). A new layer, named Layer 1, appears in the stack immediately above the targeted layer. To rename the new layer, Option-click or Alt-double-click its name, or Option/Alt-click the New Layer icon itself. The Layer Properties box appears; enter the name and click OK.

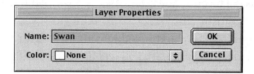

 You can also access the Layer Properties dialog box from the Layer menu or from the Layers palette pull-down menu.

Creating a New Layer with Content

There are two potential sources for the content of new layers; elements cut or copied from another layer or Background, and elements dragged and dropped from another document. Whatever their source, the end result isolates the content onto a separate layer so that it can be moved, edited, or rotated in the stack.

Copying an Image to a New Layer

When you choose Layer ➜ New ➜ Layer Via Copy, the selected portion of the image is duplicated and moved to the same position on a new layer. By default, the first new layer you copy or cut is assigned a number that hasn't been used.

 The name that Photoshop assigns to a new layer depends on the technique you choose to create the new layer and the existing content of the Layers palette. It will appear as Layer 0, Layer 1, or some other number. To avoid the confusion of inconsistent labels, rename your new layer immediately upon creating it.

To copy the contents of a layer to a new layer:

1. Target the layer or Background that you intend to copy.

2. Make an accurate selection of the area on the layer or Background using one of the selection tools or techniques.

3. Choose Layer ➜ New ➜ Layer Via Copy, or press Cmd/Ctrl+J. The content within the selection marquee is copied to a new layer and is placed immediately above the layer from which it was copied. The new layer automatically becomes the target layer. In Figure 7.10, I selected just the swan on the Background and copied it to a new layer.

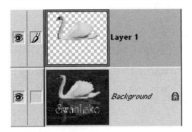

Figure 7.10 *Layer* ➜ *New* ➜ *Layer Via Copy*

4. Option-click (Mac) or Alt-double-click (Win) the name of the layer to display the Layer Properties dialog box, and rename the Layer.

5. Click OK.

Cutting an Image to a New Layer

When you cut a selected portion of an image to a new layer, the contents of the selection is either filled with the current background color (if it's on the Background) or replaced by transparency (if it's on a layer). It is transferred to the same position on a new layer.

1. Target the layer or Background with the element(s) that you intend to cut.

2. Make an accurate selection of the area using one of the selection tools or techniques.

3. Choose Layer ➜ New ➜ Layer Via Cut, or press Shift+Cmd/Ctrl+J. The content is cut to a new layer, leaving a transparent hole in the original layer or an area filled with the background color (if it was cut from the Background). The new layer is placed immediately above the targeted layer. In Figure 7.11, I again selected the swan on the Background, but this time I *cut* it to a new layer.

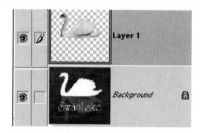

Figure 7.11 *Layer* ➜ *New* ➜ *Layer Via Cut*

4. Option-click or Alt-double-click its name to display the Layer Properties dialog box.

5. Name the layer and click OK.

Dragging a Layer from Another Document

A layer from an open document (and all that layer's contents) can be copied to another open document simply by dragging and dropping it. The layer will appear immediately above the targeted layer in the stack.

The source *document is the document you will get the layer from. The* destination *document is where you will put the layer.*

1. Open the source document and the destination document so that they both appear on screen.

2. Target the layer or Background on the Layers palette of the source document.

3. Drag the layer name or thumbnail from the source to the destination document until you see an outline of the layer. Release your mouse.

4. Option-click or Alt-double-click the layer's name to display the Layer Properties dialog box to rename the layer.

5. Name the layer and click OK.

Dragging a Selection from Another Document

The contents of a selection can be copied from an open document and placed in another open document by dragging and dropping. When you drag and drop a selection, a new layer is automatically created in the destination document and will appear immediately above the targeted layer in the stack. Let's try it:

1. Open the source document and the destination document so that they both appear on screen.

2. Target the layer or Background on the Layers palette of the source document.

3. Make an accurate selection of the area to be moved.

4. Choose the Move tool. Drag the selection from the source to the destination document until you see a rectangular outline. Release your mouse when the outline appears where you want the selection to be placed.

5. Option-click or Alt-double-click the layer's name to display the Layer Properties dialog box to rename the Layer. Click OK.

Duplicating Layers

Two techniques produce identical results for creating an exact copy of a layer. The copy will be placed directly above the original layer; the name of the copy will be the name of the original plus the word *copy*. The new layer will have the same opacity, styles, and blending mode settings as the original. To duplicate a layer, do *one* of the following:

-   Target the layer to be copied. Choose Duplicate Layer from the Layer menu or from the Layers palette pop-up menu.

-   Drag the layer's name or thumbnail to the New Layer icon in the Layers palette. If you Option/Alt-drag, you'll be able to name the new layer from the Layer Properties dialog box that automatically appears.

Removing Layers

Layers can be eliminated from the Layers palette (deleting the contents of that layer in the process). To discard a layer, do *one* of the following:

-   Target the layer to be deleted. Choose Delete Layer from the Layer menu or from the Layers palette pop-up menu.

-   Drag the layer's thumbnail or name to the trash icon in the Layers palette.

Blending Layers

Imagine having two color slides on a light table. Let's say you sandwich a red transparent gel between the two slides. The image you see would be a combination of the bottom slide and the top slide affected by the tint of the gel. But suppose instead of just the tinted image, you had the ability to slide in more complex, specific effects, such as color saturation, color inversion, or color bleaching.

That's how *blending modes* perform. They are preprogrammed effects that determine the color relations between aligned pixels on two consecutive layers in the stack. Figure 7.12 demonstrates many applications of blending. (A color version of this illustration is presented in the color section.)

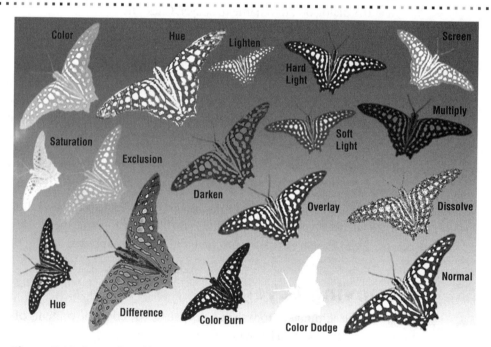

Figure 7.12 *Examples of blending modes applied to an image*

 For a complete description of the each of the blending modes, see Appendix C.

A blending mode can be assigned to a layer a couple of different ways.

- Target the layer, then use the Mode pop-up list at the top of the Layers palette (directly under the palette title tab) to choose the desired blending option.

- Double-click the layer name or thumbnail to display the Layer Style dialog box. From the list on the left, choose Blending Options: Default. In the General Blending area, choose your blending mode and opacity level.

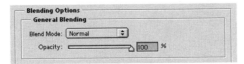

The options in the General Blending area are identical to those at the top of the Layers palette: a pop-up menu for choosing a blending mode and an opacity control. But by using the General Blending area of the Layer Style dialog, you have the additional ability to save the settings as a style and apply them to a different layer. (See "Using Layer Styles" later in the chapter.) When you adjust opacity and apply a blending mode from within the dialog box, the mode and opacity setting in the Layers palette change to reflect the adjustment.

Advanced Blending

The Advanced Blending area (Figure 7.13) lets you control several different characteristics of the color relations between the targeted and the underlying layer.

Fill Opacity   This value controls the interior opacity of the pixels in the layer. However, if the image has a style applied to it, such as Drop Shadow, Fill Opacity does not affect the style. Move the slider to select a percentage between 0 and 100, or enter a value in the field.

Channels   You can choose which channel to blend. Choosing any one or two of the channels excludes the color information from the others; consequently, the pixels on the layer will change color depending on their color content.

Knockout   You can use this option to cut a hole through the content of the layer. Knockout works hand in hand with the Fill Opacity and Blend If sliders. As you move the sliders, Shallow knocks out the image to the layer underneath it; Deep punches a hole clear through all layers to the background.

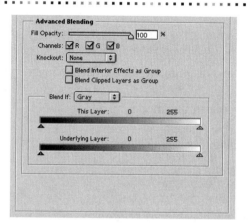

Figure 7.13 *The Advanced Blending options*

Blend Interior Effects As A Group   If you check this box, the Fill Opacity and Blend If sliders affect any interior effects applied to the layer, like Inner Shadow or Inner Glow. If unchecked, the effects are excluded from blending.

Blend Clipped Layers As A Group   If you check this box, the Fill Opacity and Blend If sliders affect layers that are included in a clipping group. (Clipping groups are described in Chapter 20.)

Blend If   You choose the specific color components to be affected by the blend. Choose Blend If Gray to affect all of the colors, or pick a specific color channel to affect. The Blend If color sliders let you accurately adjust the highlight, midtone, and shadow areas to be blended.

Layer Styles

When introduced in Photoshop 5, they were called layer effects. Now they are referred to as *layer styles*, and they jazz up your images with dazzling realistic enhancements like drop shadows, neon glowing edges, and deep embossing. Layer styles are really efficient, canned effects that simplify operations that used to require tedious channel juggling and layer manipulation.

Layer styles apply their effects to the edges of the layer; they are translucent or soft-edged, through which the colors of the underlying layer can be seen, so the content on the target layer should be surrounded by transparency.

When a layer has been affected by a style, an italic *f* icon appears to the right of its name in the Layers palette (like the one next to Layer 1 in Figure 7.14). In Photoshop 6, the Layers palette can be expanded to reveal a list of the layer styles that have been applied, by clicking the small arrow to the left of the *f* icon. Clicking any one of these effects will display its controls so that you can modify it.

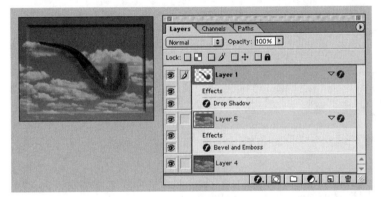

Figure 7.14 *Image with a Drop Shadow and a Bevel and Emboss effect*

Using Layer Styles

If you want to create, define, or edit a layer style, access the Layer Style dialog box (Figure 7.15) by doing *one* of the following. If a layer is targeted when you open this dialog, the style you choose will be applied when you click OK.

- Choose Layer ➜ Layer Style.
- Double-click the layer's thumbnail or title.
- Double-click the Layer Style icon at the bottom-left of the Layers palette.

From the Layer Style dialog box, you can choose an effect. To display the extensive controls for each effect, click its name. Many of the controls have similarities, and experimentation with a live preview is the best way to see the result of your efforts. Under the Preview button is a swatch that demonstrates the effect on a square. This is very helpful to see the result of combination effects.

Figure 7.16 demonstrates several samples of the layer styles effects. (This comparison is also available in the color section.)

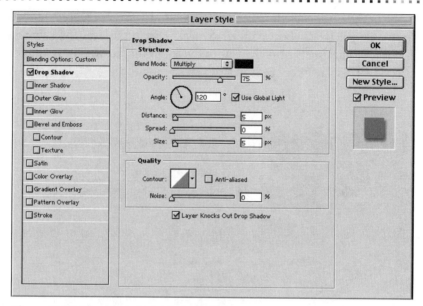

Figure 7.15 *The Layer Style dialog window*

Each layer style provides a unique and potentially complex set of options. Experimentation with the controls and with combinations of styles is the key to producing the best possible effect for your particular image.

Drop Shadow   Every object casts a shadow if placed in the path of a light source (except vampires). Drop shadows are a key element in creating credible, realistic images. The Drop Shadow will be the same shape as the pixels on the target layer. This is a fast way to give your image a realistic look. There are two sets of controls:

Structure   determines the opacity, size, and position of the shadow.

Quality   determines the contour of its edges and its texture.

Inner Shadow   As a drop shadow is cast outward, away from the layer content, an inner shadow is cast from the edge inward toward its center. Use this style to model your image or to create inner depth. The settings are similar to Drop Shadow for controlling the Structure and Quality of the effect, except that Choke, a term used in the printing industry to indicate an inward expansion, replaces Spread, a term for outward expansion.

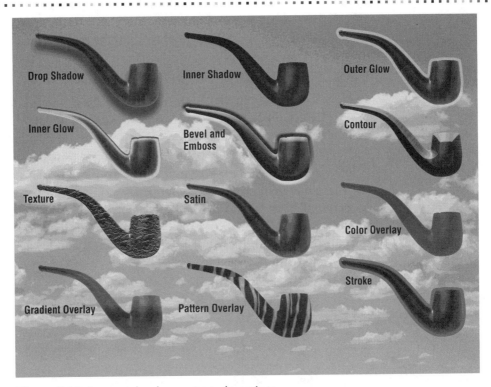

Figure 7.16 *Layer styles demonstrated on pipes*

Outer Glow   This style is perfect for a neon look. It creates a halo of a light color around the outside edge of the layer's content that can be as soft- or hard-edged as you like, depending on the settings you choose.

Inner Glow   The best way to describe this effect is a soft-edged, light-colored stroke. Use Inner Glow to create a halo from the edge of the layer's content inward.

Bevel and Emboss   The Bevel and Emboss style applies a highlight and a shadow to the layer content to create the illusion of three-dimensional relief. You can choose from five styles of embossing, each of which applies a different kind of sculptured surface. Twelve separate options let you minutely control structure and shading of the effect.

Contour   You can control the shape of the edge of your Bevel and Emboss effect by editing its contour. Double-click the name Contour on the Styles list. Choose a contour from the pop-up list. Adjust the range of the contour with the Range slider. A smaller percentage decreases the range of the contour relative to the bevel; a larger percentage increases the range.

To create a new contour, click the icon to display the Contour Editor (Figure 7.17). Click the New button and name the contour. A dotted line on the graph displays the profile of the current contour. Edit the position of the anchor points by dragging them, or click the dotted line to place new anchor points. Check the Corner box if you want a corner point, or uncheck it if you want a smooth point. Drag the anchor points to modify the curve to the profile of the edge you want. The Input value represents the percentage of the horizontal position of an anchor point. Output represents the percentage of the vertical position of an anchor point. Click OK when you're satisfied with your settings to save the new contour.

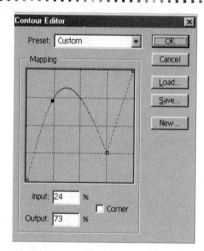

Figure 7.17 *The Contour Editor*

As you create a contour, a live preview in the image window will display the results on your image.

Texture   The Bevel and Emboss Texture option lets you map a textural surface to your layer's content. Display the texture controls by clicking the word Texture in the styles list. Choose a pattern from the pop-up list. The Texture controls use the Pattern presets as a source for textures (see Chapter 10, "Creating and Applying Color," for more on patterns). Essentially, it applies the colorless texture of the pattern to the content of the layer. You can move the sliders to adjust the scale and depth of the texture. Checking the Invert box changes the appearance of the texture from emboss to relief.

You can reposition the texture while in the Texture dialog box by clicking the texture in the image window and dragging.

Link the textural style to the layer by checking the Link With Layer box. If you move the layer, the texture moves along with it. If the box is unchecked, the texture will remain in place while the layer moves.

Satin   To produce the effect of light and shadow bouncing off a satiny surface, Photoshop applies a soft-edged shadow across the middle of the layer's content. Controls let you determine its size, position, opacity, and contour.

Color Overlay   This style is a no-brainer. It simply fills the layer's content with a color that you select by clicking the swatch. You can control its opacity.

Gradient Overlay   Similar to Color Overlay, Gradient Overlay applies a gradient to the pixels on the layer. You can choose a gradient from the current Gradient palette, or create one on the fly by clicking Gradient to display the Gradient Editor. (See Chapter 10 for more on gradients.) From the menu, you can control the opacity, style, angle, and scale of the gradient.

Pattern Overlay   If you have one or more patterns stored in the current Patterns presets, you can overlay a pattern on the layer content as an effect. This is similar to the Bevel and Emboss Texture option. The difference is that Pattern overlay applies the colors as well as the texture of the pattern. You can control the opacity and scale of the pattern, and you can link the pattern to the layer so that it will accompany the layer if the layer is moved horizontally or vertically.

Stroke   To apply an outline as an effect to the edge of the image, choose Stroke. You can determine the color and size of the stroke and whether it's placed on the inside, middle, or outside of the edge of the layer content. The best new feature of this effect is Fill Type, which applies a gradient or pattern to the stroke; this is excellent incentive to use the Stroke layer style instead of the similar Edit ➜ Stroke.

Applying Layer Styles

There are several ways to apply a layer style. If you have a style defined and wish to simply apply it, target the layer, then click the Layer Style icon at the bottom-left of the Layers palette and choose the style from the list that pops up.

The Layer Style dialog box can be used to apply a style, by following one of these methods:

- Target the layer, choose Layer ➜ Layer Style, select a style by checking its box from the Layer Style dialog box, and click OK.

- Double-click the layer's thumbnail or title; select a style and click OK.

- Target the layer, double-click the Layer Style icon at the bottom-left of the Layers palette, select a style, and click OK.

Checking the style's box in the Layer Styles dialog box applies the style to the layer. To view the controls of a particular layer style, however, you must click the style's name.

Saving Layer Styles

If you've applied one or more styles or blending options to a layer, and you're satisfied with the result, you may want to save the style to later apply it to a separate layer. To save a style, click the New Style button in the Layer Style dialog window. You'll be prompted to name your new style.

Working with Type Layers

When you enter type in Photoshop using the Type tool, a new layer is automatically created. The layer is conveniently named with the text. Type layers are pretty much like any other layer in that they can be edited, transformed, reordered in the stack, and modified by applying effects to them. The thumbnail of a Type layer is identified by a capital *T*. If you've entered type and want to edit it, double-click the thumbnail to automatically highlight it.

Several Photoshop operations cannot be applied to Type layers, including color adjustments or filters that only affect pixels. Before a text layer can be affected by these operations, it must first be *rasterized*. Rasterization converts the vector information of the type fonts into pixel-based information. Once you've rasterized the type, you can no longer edit it with the Type tool. To rasterize a type layer, target the layer and choose Layer ➜ Rasterize ➜ Type.

For the big picture on generating and editing type, read Chapter 8.

Consolidating Layers

At some point during the process of creating a brilliant digital image, you will have accumulated more layers than you can shake a mouse at. This can present problems, because with the addition of each new layer, the size of your file will increase depending on how much information the layer contains. Too many layers also presents an organization problem. It can become quite time-consuming to have to scroll through dozens of layers in order to find one. For these reasons—I can't stress it enough—*name your layers*.

But even with a multitude of named layers, you may still have trouble locating the one you need. Therefore, in the interest of streamlining your workflow, you should, from time to time, *merge* your layers.

Merging layers combines the content of two or more layers into one. You can merge visible layers, linked layers, and you can merge down from a targeted layer. You can flatten the image so that all of the layers are consolidated into one Background.

Before you flatten the image, be sure that you are done editing the layer's content and no longer need the layer operations. It is wise to flatten a duplicate version of the image instead of the original, because once the image has been saved and closed, it cannot be unflattened.

A fast way to merge layers without losing them is to hold down the Option/Alt key and select a Merge function from the palette menu. This merges the layers into a new one, but doesn't delete the original layers. You can then check the merged layers before duplicating the image for flattening. To quickly flatten the duplicate image, conceal all layers from view except the merged layer. Then choose Layer ➜ Flatten Image ➜ Discard Hidden Layers.

Merge Visible Layers

This operation merges the content of all of the visible layers into one layer. You will probably use this method more than any of the others, because you can see in the image window exactly what the new merged layer will look like. Let's merge visible layers:

1. Only the layers you want to merge should be visible. In the Layers palette, click the eye icon next to any visible layer that you don't want to merge, to conceal it from view.

2. Target one of the visible layers.

3. From either the Layer menu or the Layers palette pop-up menu, choose Merge Visible.

The contents of the visible layers will be merged into the targeted layer. That layer will retain its previous name.

Merge Linked Layers

This operation merges the content of all of the linked layers into one layer.

1. In the Layers palette, click the second column to link the layers that you want to merge. Only the layers you want to merge should be linked.

2. Target one of the linked layers.

3. From either the Layer menu or the Layers palette pop-up menu, choose Merge Linked.

The images on the linked layers will be merged into the targeted layer, which keeps its previous name.

Merge Down

This operation merges the content of the targeted layer and the layer immediately below it into one layer.

1. In the Layer palette, target a layer.

2. From either the Layer menu or the Layers palette pop-up menu, choose Merge Down.

The layer retains the name of the bottommost layer.

Flatten Image

Flattening your image eliminates all layers and places all of the content onto one Background. Because many other programs aren't able to read Photoshop's native layers format, you must usually flatten the image when you are saving your image to a format such as EPS for use in a desktop publishing program or to GIF or JPEG for use on the Web.

TIFF format now supports Photoshop layers. Even so, when saving your file as a TIFF to be imported to another program, remember that layered documents have much larger file sizes and will consequently take longer to print. It's a good idea to flatten a duplicate version of the document before saving it as a TIFF that will be imported elsewhere.

1. Be sure all of your layers are visible. Photoshop will discard layers that are not visible.

2. Choose Flatten Image from either the Layer menu or the Layers palette pop-up menu.

Up Next

Layers are one of Photoshop's most powerful attributes. It takes a little while to get the hang of them, but once you've mastered Photoshop layers you can work more efficiently and with more confidence, because the imaging process becomes dynamic from beginning to end.

The next chapter focuses on type. We'll play with the new, improved Photoshop 6 type tools and operations. Those of you Photoshoppers who have experienced the type upgrades in the 5.0 and 5.5 versions will be tickled to see vast improvements, including a new type interface and an amazing arsenal of cool type effects.

The Hands-On Layers and Type project that follows the next chapter wraps up the content of Chapter 7 and 8 into a step-by-step module, so that you can apply these techniques to an actual image.

Working with Type

PHOTOSHOP

Chapter 8

Photoshop 6 offers more power over text than ever before, including much tighter control over hyphenation, justification, and line breaks, and a complete set of tools for working with Asian fonts.

These type functions resemble page layout programs, and you may be tempted to use Photoshop to create text documents. But don't try to drive a nail with a screwdriver! Use the right tool for the job. When generating body copy, it's better to import your image into a page-layout program and generate or manipulate the text there.

Where Photoshop really shines is in its ability to produce cool text effects and large display type for headlines, subheads, and graphic text. This chapter will introduce you to:

- Typography 101

- Using the Type tools

- Applying character and paragraph specifications

- Working with Chinese, Japanese, and Korean type

- Warping text

- Rasterizing type

Type in Photoshop

New features have been added to Photoshop 6 that greatly improve its type-creating capabilities. The Type tool has been improved. In addition to the ability to generate fully editable type, you can now enter and edit type directly on the image without a cumbersome type window. All of the type functions, including orientation, font, style, size, anti-aliasing, alignment, and color, are displayed on the Options bar when the Type tool is selected.

Additional type-specific specifications, like leading, tracking, horizontal and vertical scale, and baseline shift, are accessed from buttons and pull-down menus on the Type tool Options bar. You can set type attributes before you enter text, or edit selected characters after they're entered. And you now have a complete set of tools that allow you to work precisely with Chinese, Japanese, and Korean characters.

Don't be fooled by all these features into trying to use Photoshop for page layout. You'll find it easier to import your image into a page-layout program, like InDesign, QuarkXPress, or PageMaker, and generate the body copy there. For one thing, the file size of your page-layout documents will be a much smaller than equivalent documents in Photoshop. For another, Photoshop's performance in managing large amounts of text is pretty clunky even on the fastest computers. It's best to concentrate Photoshop's type features where they'll do the most good: on spot text, headlines, and other display copy—any text where graphic enhancements are needed.

You now have the ability to enter text in a bounding box. The bounding box is a boon to visual type alignment because it acts as a container that controls the shape and flow of the text. But the best new feature in the Photoshop 6 arsenal is the Warp Text palette, which gives you precise control over the bending and curving of type. For joy, for joy! You no longer have to import curved type from Illustrator or FreeHand—you can now bend and twist it in Photoshop.

Typography 101

If you are going to create type on any software program, it's quite helpful, if not absolutely essential, to understand the nature of type and the terminology used to express its characteristics. Type is more than just words. It is a powerful but often neglected visual element, capable of expressing ideas. Type is a silent voice that delivers its message in words without sound. Your eye perceives the character forms, and your brain freely associates what it sees with what it knows—it translates the unique visual relationships of the text symbols into a voice. That voice can have a gender; it can convey a particular time in history. It may have an accent from another language or culture. It can be humorous, serious, fluid, mechanical, or any other description. It can have a specific tempo and pitch.

Figure 8.1 identifies the traditional names for the key type features and dimensions that help define your type's voice. These characteristics, and many others, are explained in the following sections.

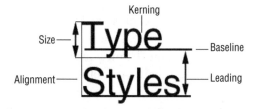

Figure 8.1 *Anatomy of type characters*

Font

Font is the name for the style or appearance of a complete set of characters. The choice of a font can greatly influence the quality of the publication. There are four categories of fonts.

Serif   fonts have a horizontal linear element on their extremities that guides the eye across the page.

San Serif   fonts don't have the horizontal linear element.

Cursive   fonts are typographic versions of handwritten script.

Display   characters are usually embellished with shapes or ornaments that endow them with a unique illustrative character.

Size

In traditional typography, the *type size* of a character is determined by the distance from the top of a capital letter to the bottom of a descender. Size is traditionally measured in *points,* with 72 points in an inch.

Style

By controlling the *style* of a character, you place a visual emphasis on its meaning. In Photoshop, style is chiefly a function of font *weight* (thickness or heaviness) and *obliqueness* (whether it leans). You can specify either of these two type characteristics by choosing a bold or italic typeface from a type family on your system, or applying faux styles from the Character palette pull-down menu. The weight or obliqueness of type creates emphasis or meaning when used in headlines, subheads, and character-based logos. A bold character headline, for example, may be used to indicate power or to simply ensure that it is the first thing seen by a viewer.

Alignment

Aligning text is an important step to maintaining readability. The alignment choices in traditional page layout are flush left, flush right, centered, and justified. Photoshop lets you apply these alignment options to horizontally or vertically oriented type. Alignment of text within an image reacts directly with the composition. It is a way to stabilize the viewer's eye movement by creating visible margins around the text blocks that establish clean, fluid lines and spaces. Aligning text to other visual elements frames the contents of the page so that there is ample, consistent space between the edge of the page and the content.

Leading

Leading is the typographic term to describe vertical spacing between lines; the word originated when typesetters hand-set wooden or metal type. The space between lines was filled with lead slugs, which controlled the spacing. This term has been adopted throughout the industry as a way to describe the distance, in points from baseline to baseline, of rows of type characters. Type conventions apply auto leading for body copy to traditional type at 120% of the type's size.

Tracking and Kerning

These terms refer to the space between characters. *Tracking* is the global space between selected groups of characters, and *kerning* is the space between two individual characters (Figure 8.2). Type characters are rarely of equal distance from each other. Because each letterform has its own specific visual characteristics, characters are optically spaced. For example, in the top line of type in Figure 8.2, the capital *T* next to the lowercase *y* needs less space than the capital *H* next to the lowercase *i* to appear the same distance apart. Sometimes even Photoshop-generated text needs manual kerning.

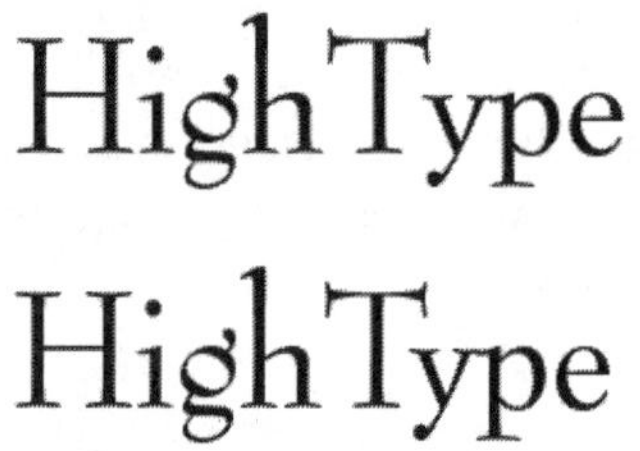

High Type

High Type

Figure 8.2 *The characters in the top row, set using Photoshop's default tracking, seem to isolate the capital* T. *The text in the bottom row has been manually kerned to accommodate the optical spacing and connect the capital* T *with the rest of the word* Type.

Horizontal and Vertical Scale

The horizontal and vertical *scale* of type radically changes its appearance, as seen in Figure 8.3. When you reduce the horizontal scale of a letterform (as in the second row of the example), you squeeze it from side to side. When you scale it "up" horizontally (to a percentage higher than 100), all of the vertical strokes appear fatter and the characters appear extended, as in the third row of type in the figure.

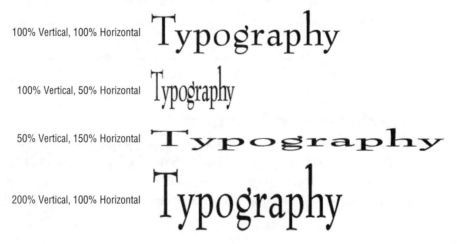

100% Vertical, 100% Horizontal   Typography

100% Vertical, 50% Horizontal   Typography

50% Vertical, 150% Horizontal   Typography

200% Vertical, 100% Horizontal   Typography

Figure 8.3 *Horizontal and vertical scale*

When you vertically scale a letterform (as in the fourth row of Figure 8.3), you stretch it from top to bottom. With scaling greater than 100%, the vertical strokes appear thinner and elongated relative to their size. The character appears condensed, even though it's at the normal horizontal width.

Baseline Shift

Shifting the *baseline* of a character, as in Figure 8.4, moves it horizontally or vertically from its default starting position or baseline. Unlike leading, which affects all of the characters in a paragraph, baseline shift targets individual characters and moves them up or down.

Typography

Figure 8.4 *Baseline shift*

Type Conventions

Typography is an art that has developed over thousands of years and, like any art form, it has its common sense or rules of thumb. Type conventions act as guides to help the artist/designer achieve readable, well-emphasized character combinations. The conventions emphasize certain visual elements so that the viewer's eye is gently guided through the text.

For the sake of continuity and clarity, I mention these conventions here, because when designing with type they are a good place to begin. Remember, however, that you can ignore the conventions, break the rules, and get wild and crazy in the anything-goes world of graphic design, providing you don't lose sight of your goal: to clearly and efficiently communicate your ideas visually.

Less is More   Don't use more than two fonts, three sizes, or three styles in a design field. As a complicated example, a headline might be 36-point Gill Sans Bold, the subhead might be 20-point Gill Sans Demi, and the body text might be 12-point Garamond Medium.

Stick with Standard Leading   Normal leading equals 120 percent of the type size; if a character is 10 points, its normal leading is 12 points. If your leading is too small—the lines too tight together—you lose readability; if your leading is too loose, the reader's eye will wander instead of flowing smoothly from the end of one line to the beginning of the next.

No Faux Styles   Whenever possible, avoid using faux styles—that is, styles applied by a software program to the text. If you want to use a boldface style, use the bold style from that font's family, because there are subtle differences in the characters.

Kern and Track Your Text   Pay attention to the kerning and tracking of type. This is an area that is painfully neglected by many desktop publishers. Be sure the spacing looks natural. Although Photoshop auto-kerns its characters, it's wise to tweak the character spacing, *especially* when you apply warping or styles to the type. Look for consistent spacing of text by squinting your eyes. Correct gaps where the characters are too far apart or bunching where they are too close together.

Use Ligatures   Use *ligatures* whenever possible. A ligature is a set of two characters that are designed to replace certain character combinations, such as fl and fi, to avoid spacing conflicts.

Using the Type Tools

To generate text, choose the Type tool, click the point in the image where you want the text to appear, and enter the text from the keyboard. You can pre-program the Type tool with specific characteristics prior to entering the text, or you can highlight the text after it has been entered and modify its specifications.

- To highlight text so that it can be edited, click in front of it and drag.

- To select a word, double-click it.

- To select a line of text, triple-click it.

- To select all characters in a bounding box, quadruple-click anywhere in the box, or press Command/Ctrl+A (Select All)

When you select or format text on a Type layer, the Type tool shifts into edit mode. Before you can perform other operations, you must commit the changes by clicking the check mark, or cancel by clicking the X, at the right end of the Options bar or by pressing Return (Mac) or Enter (Win) on the keyboard.

You have two variations of the Type tool to choose from the Type tool Options bar. At the far left is the basic Type tool, which you'll use most of the time; it generates a Type layer. The other variation is the Type Mask tool, which generates a selection marquee in the shape of the specified character. It can be used for generating type on existing layers or for pasting visual elements into the type to produce interesting type/image combinations.

The icons to the right of the two Type tools control the horizontal or vertical orientation of the text. The Type tool Options bar also displays type characteristics:

Font   Choose a font and weight from the menus.

Size   Choose a size in points from the list, or enter a numeric value.

Anti-Alias   This setting will determine how the type blends into its background in varying degrees. None produces a jagged character, while Strong makes a heavier character, Crisp a sharper character, and Smooth a smoother character.

Alignment   You can align either flush left, centered, or flush right. The type aligns to the insertion point. When the type is vertically oriented, the top, center, or bottom of the text aligns to the insertion point.

Color   Click the swatch and select a fill color for the type from the Color Picker.

Warp Text   You can place your text on a path, twist it, or bend it using this function (see "Warping Text" later in this chapter).

 Commit/Cancel   After you've input your type specs, click one of these buttons to commit the edit or to cancel it.

Entering Type in a Bounding Box

There are two ways of entering type in Photoshop: from a point or within a bounding box. The bounding box lets you control the shape and flow of text (see Figure 8.5). Once the bounding box has been drawn and entered, you can size the box to re-flow the text.

To enter text in a bounding box, follow these steps.

1. Choose the Type tool.

2. Click in your image and drag to the approximate size you want the bounding box to be. Release the mouse and the bounding box appears.

3. Set your type specifications in the toolbar and enter the text.

4. Readjust the size of the bounding box by dragging any of the corner or side points.

The master
of the art of
living makes
little distic-
tion between

Figure 8.5 *A bounding box around paragraph text*

You can convert point text to paragraph text and vice versa. Target the Type layer and choose Layer → *Type* → *Convert To Point Text or Convert To Paragraph Text.*

Applying Character and Paragraph Specifications

Photoshop gives you two palettes that expand your capabilities for generating text, above and beyond those readily available in the Tool palette. To access the palettes, select the Type tool and click the Palettes button in the Options bar. The Character and Paragraph palettes appear.

The Character Palette

This palette consolidates all of the character attributes into one floating palette. To access the Character palette, you can either choose Window → Show Character, or with the Type tool selected, click the Palettes button in the Options bar.

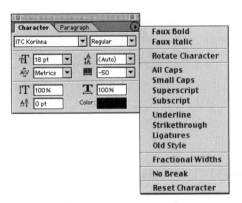

You can designate the following characteristics on the Character palette. For most changes to these settings, you can click the Commit (checkmark) button at the right end of the Options bar to apply your edits, or click the Cancel (X) button to change your mind. For most settings, pressing Enter (Win) or Return (Mac), or choosing another tool, or targeting another layer, will commit your changes.

Size To change size in points, highlight the text, then enter a value or choose a size from the list.

If you need to work with other units when setting type, enter the number and then the unit abbreviation or name—in inches (in), millimeters (mm), pixels (px), etc. Photoshop will automatically convert the value into the current type units specified in the preferences.

Kerning is measured in thousandths of an em space. (An em space is a standard for type measurement. The width of an em space depends on the size of the text; it's usually about the width of the letter *m*.) The Metrics setting uses the font's default spacing; to kern manually, place your insertion point between the two characters and enter a value or choose a width from the list. Negative values decrease the spacing between characters; positive values increase the spacing.

Tracking (akin to kerning) is also measured in thousandths of an em space. Tracking is the space between groups of characters. To change tracking, highlight the text, then enter a value or choose a width from the list. Like kerning, negative values decrease the size of the space between characters, and positive values increase the size of the space.

Leading is measured in points from baseline to baseline. To change the leading, highlight the text, then enter a value or choose one from the list.

Baseline Shift   is measured in points. To change the Baseline Shift, highlight the text, then enter a value or choose one from the list.

Vertical/Horizontal Scale   is measured as a percentage of normal scale. To change the horizontal or vertical scale, highlight the text and enter a value.

Color   To change the color, click the swatch and choose a color from the Color Picker.

The Character Palette Menu

Click the arrow in the upper-right corner of the Character palette to access more commands and options for your type characters.

Style   If you don't have a bold or italic type font, you can apply a faux style by choosing Faux Bold or Faux Italic.

Rotate Character   Select this option to rotate vertical type by 90 degrees so that the characters flow parallel to the text line.

Case   You can select a case option before typing to enter text as All Caps or Small Caps, or format it after it has been entered by highlighting all or part of the text on a Type layer and choosing the case you want from the palette menu.

Selecting Small Caps will have no effect on text that was originally typed as capital letters.

Superscript, Subscript, Underline, and Strikethrough   These traditional type aspects should be familiar. Superscript and subscript characters are smaller and shifted above or below the text baseline.

Ligatures and Old Style Numerals   If your font provides them you can use ligatures and old style typographic numerals. Choose Ligatures or Old Style from the Character palette menu.

Fractional Widths   The spacing between characters varies, with fractions of whole pixels between certain characters. Most of the time, fractional character widths provide the best spacing. Fractional widths can cause small type to run together, making it difficult to read. To turn fractional widths off so that the type is displayed in whole-pixel increments, choose Fractional Widths from the palette menu and uncheck the option.

The Paragraph Palette

The Paragraph palette specifies options for an entire paragraph, which is defined by Photoshop as one or more characters followed by a hard return. Each line of text entered at a point is a separate paragraph because it's separated by a return—Photoshop won't wrap multiple lines in one paragraph unless you resize it with a bounding box.

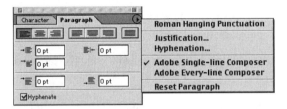

You can access the Paragraph palette by choosing Window ➜ Show Paragraph. Or, with the Type tool selected, click the Palettes button on the Options bar, then click the Paragraph tab.

Selecting Paragraphs

You can format a single paragraph, multiple paragraphs, or all paragraphs in a Type layer.

To Format This:	Do This:
A single paragraph	Choose the Type tool and click between any two characters in a paragraph.
Multiple paragraphs	Select the Type tool and drag to highlight the text range of the paragraphs you want to select.
A Type layer	Target the Type layer that you want to affect in the Layers palette.

Aligning and Justifying Type

You can *align* text to one edge or *justify* text to both edges. You can align point text and paragraph text; you can justify paragraph text but not point text.

To specify alignment for horizontally oriented text, click the Left Align, Center, or Right Align icons at the top of the Paragraph palette. For vertically aligned type, these become Top Align, Center, and Bottom Align.

In order to justify type, it will have to be "paragraph text"—that is, be in a bounding box. When you choose a justification icon, the text is spread out so the left and right edges of the text both align. The icons offer four options for aligning the last line of horizontally oriented type (Justify Last Left, Center, or Right, or Justify All) and, again, four options for vertically oriented type (Top, Center, Right, and Justify All).

Indenting Paragraphs

An indent is the space between the text and the insertion point or the edge of the bounding box. You specify a paragraph indent by entering a value in the indention fields. You can specify a left, right, or first-line indent:

Indent Left Margin   indents the whole paragraph from the left edge of the bounding box.

Indent Right Margin   indents the whole paragraph from the right edge of the bounding box.

Indent First Line   indents the first line of text in the paragraph relative to the left indent.

To create a first-line "hanging" indent, enter a negative value for Indent First Line.

Space Before and After

Enter a value in the Add Space Before Paragraph or Add Space After Paragraph fields in order to add space between paragraphs. The values entered will be the units specified in the Units & Rulers preferences (described in Chapter 4).

The Paragraph Palette Menu

Click the arrow in the upper-right corner of the Paragraph palette to access commands that affect justification, hyphenation, and flow of the text.

Hanging Punctuation

The Roman Hanging Punctuation option enhances the alignment of text by placing punctuation marks outside the margin. When this option is active, the following punctuation marks will be affected: periods, commas, single and double quotation marks, apostrophes, hyphens, en and em dashes, colons, and semicolons.

To hang punctuation marks, choose Roman Hanging Punctuation from the Paragraph palette pull-down menu.

Justifying Text

Justification determines word- and letter-spacing defaults on justified text. To set justification options, choose Justification from the Paragraph palette menu.

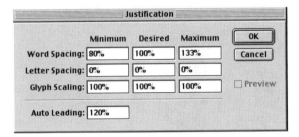

 Justification options are applied to the entire paragraph. If you want to increase or decrease space for a few characters, use the Kerning or Tracking functions.

For the options with three columns of settings, Photoshop will space text in order to stay between the Minimum and Maximum values, and will try to come as close to the Desired value as possible while balancing all the settings. The values you end up with are chosen not only by the spacing options, but by things like the hyphenation settings and font size.

Word Spacing   specifies the amount of space between words when the space bar is pressed. Values range from 0 to 1000%; at 100% no additional space is added to the default spacing of the specified font.

Letter Spacing   determines the normal distance between letters, which includes kerning and tracking values. Values range from 0 to 500%; at 100% no additional space is added to the default spacing of the specified font.

Glyph Scaling   scales the actual width of characters to justify them. Input a Minimum value, a Desired value, and a Maximum value to fit characters into a justified line of text.

Auto Leading   is the normal distance between baselines of text—120% of the font size by default.

Preview   lets you see the result of your specification in selected text before closing the window.

Hyphenating Text

Hyphenation options determine where a word breaks to be hyphenated. To activate automatic hyphenation, click the Hyphenate box in the Paragraph palette. To set hyphenation options, choose Hyphenation from the palette pull-down menu.

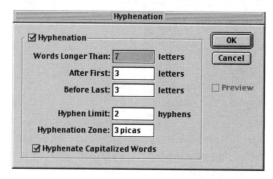

Words Longer Than specifies the minimum length, in letters, of a word to be hyphenated.

After First specifies the minimum number of letters at the beginning of a word before a hyphen.

Before Last specifies the minimum number of letters at the end of a word after a hyphen.

Hyphenation Limit is the number of consecutive lines that can contain hyphens.

Hyphenation Zone is the distance at the end of a line of unjustified text that will cause a word break.

Capitalized Words will hyphenate capitalized words. Turn this option off to be sure headlines are not hyphenated. This only works with the Single-Line Composer.

Preview lets you see the result of your specifications on selected paragraphs before closing the window.

Composing Text Lines

Composing methods determine possible line breaks, based on the hyphenation and justification settings. There are two composition methods to choose from:

The Every-Line Composer looks ahead five lines to determine the line breaks. The result is more consistent spacing and less hyphenation. The every-line composer is selected by default.

The Single-Line Composer composes text one line at a time. The result is more consistent spacing within a line but less consistent spacing and hyphenation among multiple lines. This option is preferable if you want to manually compose your type.

Reset Paragraph This option sets the paragraph to its previously formatted state before attributes from the Paragraph palette were recently applied.

Working with Asian Characters

If you have the proper fonts installed, Photoshop can manage Chinese, Japanese, and Korean (CJK) text. To access the CJK options in the Character and Paragraph palettes, choose Edit ➜ Preferences ➜ General ➜ Show CJK Features. The CJK features will appear in the Character and Paragraph palettes.

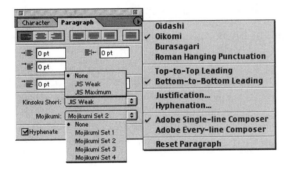

Tsume

The majority of Asian characters are *monospaced,* meaning that all of the characters are the same width when using horizontal text and the same height when using vertical text. You can enter a percentage in the Tsume field in the Character palette to specify a character width for selected text. This will decrease the size of each character but increase the proportional spacing between characters.

Tate-chuu-yoko

The *tate-chuu-yoko* system (also called *kumimoji* and *renmoji*) "flips" certain nontextual items. You can improve the readability of vertical text by rotating numerals and acronyms so that they are horizontally oriented. To do this, highlight the characters that you want to rotate and choose Tate-chuu-yoko from the Character palette pulldown menu.

Japanese Composition

Mojikumi

Mojikumi determines the composition of Japanese text, including character spacing between punctuation, symbols, and numbers, based on composition rules set forth in the Japanese Industrial Standards (JIS #4051).

Photoshop includes several mojikumi sets from which you can choose. They are accessible from the Paragraph palette Mojikumi pop-up list.

Kinsoku Shori

You can choose different methods for processing line breaks. *Kinsoku shori* are characters that cannot begin or end a line based on composition rules set forth as Japanese industrial standards. Choose JIS Weak or JIS Maximum from the Kinsoku Shori pop-up list.

Oidashi and oikomi are line-break rules as applied to kinsoku shori:

Oidashi　　is push-out line breaking, which increases the number of characters on a line by reducing the space between letters.

Oikomi　　is push-in line breaking, which decreases the number of characters on a line by increasing the space between letters.

You can choose either of these options from the Paragraph palette pull-down menu. A check mark indicates which option is selected.

Hanging CJK Punctuation

You can specify hanging punctuation on CJK text. Using hanging punctuation (called *burasagari*) forces punctuation marks to be placed outside the indent margins and evens the edges of the paragraph. Choose Burasagari from the Paragraph palette menu. If the option is checked, it is active.

Warping Text

The new Warp Text option in Photoshop is the designer's dream tool. Type can now be bent to conform to almost any type of curve. The Warp Text option is accessible from the Type tool Options bar. When you click the icon, the Warp Text dialog window appears (Figure 8.6). You can choose from fifteen different styles (all demonstrated in Figure 8.7), each with its own precision set of controls.

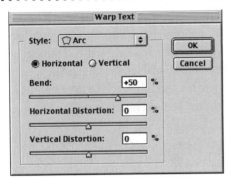

Figure 8.6 *The Warp Text dialog box*

Figure 8.7 *The 15 Warp Text styles*

There are so many combinations of style and settings that it's impossible to list them all here. I'll show you how to warp a few lines of text in the Hands-On project that follows this chapter, but play with these controls. Experiment with settings, sizes, and fonts so you'll be familiar with some of the wild, twisted type effects you can create.

Rasterizing Type

Photoshop text is generated using vector-based fonts, which preserve the ability to edit the text throughout the imaging process. Once you've generated the text, you can scale it and apply any layer style to it. You can also warp it or change its color.

There are, however, Photoshop filters and color adjustment operations that do not work on vector-based type. If you want to apply those effects, you'll have to *rasterize* the type, or convert it into pixels. Pixel-based type has its advantages and disadvantages. The main disadvantage is that once you render your type, it will appear at the same resolution as the document. This is particularly problematic for small type on low-resolution documents, because there may not be enough pixels to do a decent job of smoothing the type's edges (as seen in the sample in Figure 8.8).

Res
Res

Figure 8.8 *(top) Crisp, vector-based type, and (bottom) jagged, rasterized type*

The advantage of pixel-based type is the ability to do pretty much anything to the image you please, such as pasting images into the type or applying artistic filters to it.

To render your type, target the Type layer and choose Layer ➜ Rasterize ➜ Type.

Up Next

Type has come a long way since Photoshop's first release. Now that Photoshop can support vector-based operations, a multitude of new features have sprung up that extend its text-generating and -editing features. Live text entry makes entering type much more user-friendly. The Character and Paragraph palettes put all of the type attributes at your fingertips, and I'm sure you will have a ball bending and warping your headlines and display text.

Next is a Hands-On project that will give you practice with the features described in Chapters 7 and 8: manipulating layers and taking advantage of Photoshop's incredible type powers.

Hands-On
Layers and Type

Layers greatly increase your power to manage your work. In this Hands-On session, I'll put you through the moves of layers and type so that you can apply some of the powerful techniques from Chapters 7 and 8 to an actual project.

Liisa Phillips is a surrealist painter who inspired this poster with her amazing paintings of flying women. (I've included her work in the color section.) While she delicately applies layer upon layer of thin oil glazes to her canvases to achieve brilliant color blending and a mysterious atmospheric ambiance, you will apply layer upon layer of digital images to produce a phantasmagoric poster. You will see the advantage of organizing your layers into sets. We will also take a crack at generating type, applying layer styles, and warping text.

Getting Started

Hide your preferences file before beginning this Hands-On exercise, then restart Photoshop to create a clean version. The "Photoshop's Settings" section in Chapter 5 details how to temporarily reset your preferences to Photoshop's defaults. You can restore your customized, personal settings when you're done.

Once you have launched Photoshop with default preferences, here's how to begin the Hands-On project:

1. Insert the *Mastering Photoshop 6* CD in the CD-ROM drive.

2. Choose File ➡ Open; select and open `Flying_Women_start.psd` (Figure 1) in the Ch08 folder on the CD.

3. Save the file to your disk as `Flying_Women.psd`.

Figure 1 *The original Flying Women file*

The book's color section includes color versions of the beginning and finished (Figure 2) stages of the Amazing Flying Women poster.

Figure 2 *The completed Flying Women poster*

Arranging Layers

Viewing Layers

1. When you open the file Flying_Women_start.psd, you see only the transparency checkerboard. The Layers palette, however, reveals that the image contains 2 layer sets (containing 2 layers each), 8 additional layers, and a Background. To reveal the contents of the Background, click the first column next to its thumbnail. An eye icon appears, and the Background image appears in the image window (Figure 3).

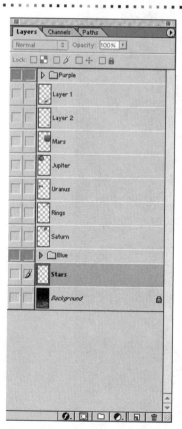

Figure 3 *The Layers palette of the Flying Women file*

2. Reveal the contents of all layers. Option-click or Alt-click the eye icon of the Background. Figure 4 shows the image with all the layers visible. The two layer set folders are closed, but their contents are visible in the image window.

Figure 4 *Option/Alt-click the Background to display the entire content of the image.*

3. Then conceal the layers that we don't need right now. Click the eye icon next to the following layers or layer sets to conceal their content: Purple, Layer 1, Layer 2, Blue. (Your image should look like Figure 5.)

Figure 5 *The image and Layers palette with the Purple and Blue layer sets, Layer 1, and Layer 2 no longer visible.*

Moving Layers

The contents of layers can be repositioned. We will move the planets into their vertical and horizontal positions on the image.

1. Be sure the rulers are visible (choose View ➜ Show Rulers if they're not).

2. Target the Mars layer by clicking its thumbnail or its name.

3. Select the Move tool. Place your cursor in the approximate center of Mars, click, and drag until Mars aligns with the 12″ vertical and 8″ horizontal marks on the rulers (as in Figure 6). Release the mouse.

Figure 6 *Mars and ruler marks*

4. Target the Jupiter layer. Using the same technique, place the center of Jupiter on the 2″ vertical and the 8″ horizontal ruler marks.

5. Save your work (press Cmd/Ctrl+S or use File ➜ Save).

Moving Linked Layers

When items are linked, they can be moved or transformed simultaneously.

1. Target the Saturn layer.

2. Click in the second column next to the Rings layer. The link icon appears.

3. With the Move tool, drag and place the center of Saturn and its rings at the 7.25″ vertical and 3″ horizontal marks. Check your image against Figure 7.

Figure 7 *The planets have been moved. Two layers (Saturn and Rings) are linked so that they can be moved as a unit.*

Naming Layers

To keep your document organized, name your layers.

1.   Display Layer 1 and 2; target Layer 1. From the Layers palette pull-down menu, choose Layer Properties. The Layer Properties dialog box appears.

2.   Name the layer Yellow Woman.

3.   Press the Option or Alt key and double-click Layer 2 to get the Layer Properties dialog again.

4.   Rename Layer 2 as Yellow Costume.

Making a Layer Set

Layer sets organize your layers so that they can be easily managed.

1.   Target the Yellow Woman layer. Click the Create A New Set icon on the Layers palette. A new layer set folder appears above the targeted layer.

2. Double-click the layer set. The Layer Set dialog box appears. Rename the layer set Yellow. For Color, choose yellow.

3. Click the Yellow Costume layer and drag it on top of the Yellow layer set icon. The layer becomes part of the set.

4. Drag the Yellow Woman layer on top of the Yellow layer set. Notice that the layers inside the folder have been automatically color-coded yellow.

5. Save your work.

Moving Items within a Layer Set

The costume is not on the yellow woman. She might be getting cold, flying around in deep space in her underwear. We need to dress her. You can reposition the contents of a layer and change its stacking order within the layer set.

1 Target the Yellow Costume layer, choose the Move tool, and drag the yellow costume onto the yellow woman.

2. The costume is behind the yellow woman. In the Layers palette, drag the Yellow Costume layer above the Yellow Woman layer within the layer set.

3. With the Move tool, on the image window, reposition the costume so that it aligns with the yellow woman.

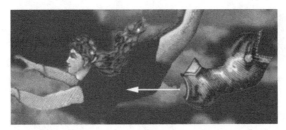

Changing the Order of Layers

You can change the position in the stacking order of a layer or of a group of layers in a layer set. Use the order, from top to bottom in the Layers palette, to control which content lays "on top of" other image elements. Note that you can restack all of the layers within a set simultaneously—no other function does this.

1. Option-click or Alt-click the first column of the Layers palette to make the content of all layers visible. Notice that the Blue Woman is behind Mars.

2. To bring all the layers in the layer set forward, they must be moved up in the stacking order. Place your cursor on the Blue layer set folder or name. Click and drag the layer set to the top of the stack. The woman and her costume appear in front of Mars.

Using Layers to Create and Edit

Cutting and Copying Images to a New Layer

New layers can be made from the contents of existing layers. This can make it easier to apply effects to specific pieces of your image.

1. Target the Uranus layer.

2. Option-click or Alt-click the eye icon of the Uranus layer to reveal only its contents against a transparent checkerboard.

3. Choose the Rectangular Marquee. Draw a marquee around the blue planet.

4. Choose Layer ➜ New Via Copy or press Cmd/Ctrl+J. The selected planet is copied onto a new layer. Name the layer Galaxy.

5. Target the Uranus layer again. Draw a rectangular marquee around the green planet.

6. Choose Layer ➜ New Via Cut or press Shift+Cmd/Ctrl+J. The selected planet is cut to a new layer. Name the layer Mercury. (Yes, I know Mercury isn't really green. Call it a little artistic license.)

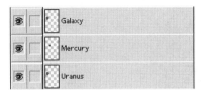

Editing the Contents of a Layer

1. Target the Galaxy layer.

2. Option/Alt-click the eye icon of the Galaxy layer to reveal only its contents against a transparent checkerboard.

3. Choose the Move tool. In the Options bar, choose Show Bounding Box.

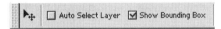

4. Click the top-middle handle of the bounding box and drag downward to squash the circular planet into an oval. Press Return (Mac) or Enter (Win) to implement the transformation.

5. Choose Filter ➜ Blur ➜ Gaussian Blur ➜ 10 to blur the edges of the oval.

6. Draw a Rectangular Marquee around the oval.

7. Choose Filter ➜ Distort ➜ Twirl, and set a value of –999 to twirl the oval into a galaxy.

8. Press Cmd/Ctrl+D to deselect.

9. With the Galaxy layer still targeted, choose the Move tool and drag the galaxy into the upper-left corner of the document so that its approximate center aligns with the 1″ vertical and 2″ horizontal marks on the rulers.

10. View and target the Mercury layer. Press the Shift key as you drag Mercury to constrain its horizontal movement; reposition the planet so that its center aligns with the 6.5″ vertical and 8.75″ horizontal marks on the rulers.

11. View and target the Uranus layer. Move Uranus so that its center aligns with the 14″ vertical, 2.25″ horizontal marks on the rulers.

12. Save the document.

Moving Layers from Another Document

You can easily move layers from one document to another. Here we will move two linked layers.

1. In the Flying_Women.psd file, click the eye icon next to the Background and the Saturn and Ring layers to make them visible. Target the Saturn layer.

2. Open the file Red_Woman.psd from the Chapter 8 folder on the CD, and target the Red Costume layer.

3. In Red_Woman.psd, click in the second column next to the Red Woman layer to link it with Red Costume.

4. Place your cursor on the Red_Woman.psd image. Press your mouse, drag the image, and place it on the Flying_Women.psd document. Release the mouse and a new layer appears between the Saturn layer and the Ring layer.

5. Choose the Move tool and position the Red Woman and the Red Costume between Saturn and its rings.

There are three different ways to drag layers and place them on another image. Make sure you use the right one:

- You can drag an individual layer from the Layers palette or from the image window to another image.

- To drag linked layers and maintain the linked relationship, you must target one of them and drag from the image window.

- To drag a layer set from an image, drag from the *name* or *folder* of the layer set in the Layers palette.

Apply a Style to a Layer

A drop shadow adds realism and depth to an image. Creating the drop shadow as a layer style is easy.

1. With the Red Woman layer targeted, double-click the layer to bring up the Layer Style dialog box.

2. Click the Drop Shadow option to display its controls (see Figure 8).

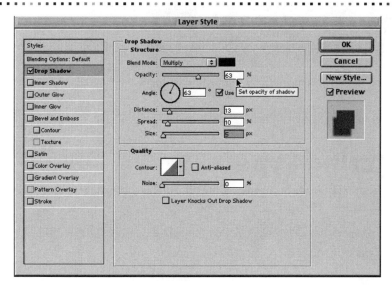

Figure 8 *Drop Shadow controls*

3. Set the following specifications, then click OK. Your image should look like Figure 9.

Opacity   63%

Distance   13 px

Spread   10%

Size   5 px

Figure 9 *The Red Woman flying through the rings*

Entering Type

Photoshop 6's Type tool is powerful for producing sophisticated text effects. Combined with Photoshop's layer styles, the graphic possibilities are endless.

1. Display all of the layers in the document by pressing the Option/Alt key and clicking the eye icon next to the Background.

2. Choose the Type tool and enter the following specifications in the Options bar:

Font	Helvetica
Size	100 pt
Anti-Alias	Smooth
Alignment	Centered
Color	Red

3. Display the Character palette (Window ➔ Character, or click the Palettes button on the Options bar); in the palette, set Leading at 100 pt.

4. Click the image, somewhere between the galaxy and Saturn. (If necessary, you can reposition the type after you've entered it.) You see a blinking insertion point. Type this: Amazing <return> Flying Women. When you're finished typing, click the check mark on the Options bar. This will create a new Type layer named Amazing Flying Women.

5. Change the settings on the Options bar to Font: Helvetica Bold, Size: 45, and Color: Yellow. From the Character palette pull-down menu, choose All Caps.

6. Type the words: From Outer Space. Click the check mark in the Options bar to create a new Type layer. Your text should resemble Figure 10.

Figure 10 *The basic title for our poster*

Warping Text

Photoshop 6 lets you bend and twist type to any shape.

1. Target the Amazing Flying Women layer and choose the Text tool.

2. Click the Create Warped Text button in the Options bar.

3. Choose Style ➔ Flag.

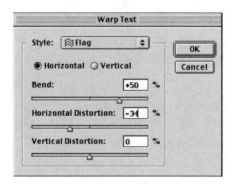

4. Enter the following values and click OK.

Bend	50%
Horizontal Distortion	−34%
Vertical Distortion	0%

5. Target the From Outer Space layer.

6. From the Style list, again choose Flag.

7. Enter the following values and click OK.

Bend	66%
Horizontal Distortion	−24%
Vertical Distortion	0%

8. In the Layers palette, adjust the Opacity of the From Outer Space layer to 55%. Your text should now look like Figure 11.

Figure 11 *Warped text*

Applying Multiple Effects to Layer

We've seen how you can apply a Drop Shadow layer style to a layer. We'll now apply several different effects to a Type layer.

1. Target the Amazing Flying Women layer.

2. Double-click the layer to display the Layer Style dialog box.

When working in the Layer Style dialog, you must click the name of the style in order to display the individual layer style controls. Checking the box next to the name doesn't display the controls; it's an indicator that the effect has been applied to the current layer.

3. From the Style list on the left, click the name Inner Shadow. The check box is automatically checked, and the Inner Shadow controls are displayed (see Figure 12).

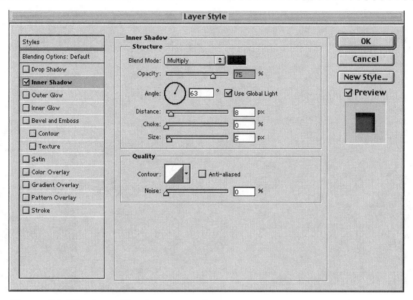

Figure 12 *The Inner Shadow controls*

4. Set the following specifications (use the default values for settings that aren't listed here):

Angle	63°
Distance	8 px
Choke	0%
Size	5 px

5. Click the Bevel and Emboss style. Set the following specifications (use the defaults for the remaining options):

Style	Outer Bevel
Technique	Smooth
Depth	201%
Direction	Up
Size	5 px
Soften	5 px

6. Click the Satin style.

7. Click the Color Overlay style.

8. Click the Stroke style. Set the Color to Yellow, and use the defaults for the other settings.

Your text should now look something like Figure 2. Better, isn't it?

It makes no difference in what order you apply the multiple layer styles.

As I said in the earlier in the chapter, type is more than just words. By applying the type-twisting techniques and multiple effects that you learned in this chapter, you've transformed your type into a strong visual element that resonates with form, texture, and color. With such a multitude of controls, the choices are infinite.

Adjusting Opacity of a Layer Set

Now that all of the poster elements are in place, you can subdue the color of the planets so that the flying women stand out more.

1. Link all of the planet layers except Saturn and Rings. That includes Jupiter, Mars, Uranus, Mercury, and Galaxy.

2. Make a new layer set by choosing, from the Layers palette pull-down menu, New Set from Linked.

3. Name the layer set Planets.

4. In the Layers palette, adjust the Opacity of the Planets layer set to 75%.

Merging Layers

In order to reduce the file size and more efficiently manage your document, you can merge layers.

1. Click off the eye icons next to all the layers but the Blue, Purple, and Yellow layer sets. Target one of the layer sets.

2. Choose Merge Visible from the Layers palette pull-down menu. The content of all three of the layers sets is merged into one layer. (Name that layer Purple.)

Notice the reduction in the file size in the information field in the lower-left corner of the image window.

3. Choose Image → Duplicate. Name the new image Flying_Women_flat.psd.

4. Be sure all layers are visible, and make a note of the file size in the information field in the lower-left corner of the image window. From the Layers palette pull-down menu, choose Flatten Image. Notice the dramatic reduction of the file size.

5. Save the image.

Up Next

Photoshop used to be exclusively a pixel-based program. Now you can create vector objects in Photoshop. I wouldn't toss my copy of Illustrator, FreeHand, or CorelDRAW just yet, because the interface is still a little clunky. But Chapter 9 walks us down the vector path. You'll learn how to draw Bezier curves and how to create shapes using Photoshop's new Shape tool.

Drawing Paths

PHOTOSHOP

Chapter 9

Photoshop provides several methods for isolating areas on the image, as you saw in Chapter 6. Still, making accurate selections can be difficult or time-consuming, because each image presents different problems. The Pen tools and the Paths palette add more capabilities to further enhance the accuracy and speed of making selections and defining the smooth edges. Once you've learned to draw with the Pen tool, you'll find it indispensable because it can be the easiest and fastest way to select images with long, smooth curves.

This chapter covers topics that include:

- The path tools and the Paths palette

- Drawing and editing paths

- Using paths to apply color

- Paths and selections

- Exporting paths

- Paths and the Shape tools

The Path Tools

If you are familiar with vector illustration programs, then the Paths function in Photoshop will be familiar to you. Paths are *vector objects* that mathematically define specific areas on an image by virtue of their shape and position. Vector objects are composed of anchor points and line segments known as *Bezier curves,* like the ones shown in Figure 9.1. (See Chapter 3 for more information on these terms.)

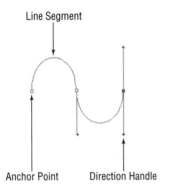

Figure 9.1 *Components of Bezier curves*

Paths enable you to create straight lines and curves with more precision than the selection tools. If the path is left open-ended, it can be stroked with a color to form a curved line. If its two end points are joined, it encloses a *shape*. The path can be filled with color, stroked with an outline, or stored in the Paths palette or the Shape library for later use. Most importantly, it can be converted into a selection where a Photoshop operation can be implemented.

The primary path maker is the Pen tool, which has three variations, located in the Tool palette. To pick a Pen tool, click its icon or type P. If you hold down the mouse button, you can expand the Tool palette to display all of the other Path tools (Shift+P cycles through these). Photoshop 6 has two tools for drawing paths and four tools for editing paths. There are also two tools designed specifically to move a path or a portion of a path.

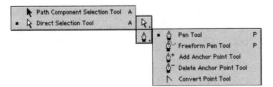

Path-Drawing Tools

The Pen tool   draws paths by clicking and dragging.

The Freeform Pen tool   draws a freeform line that converts itself to a path when the mouse is released.

The Freeform Pen tool with the Magnetic option   (sometimes simply called the Magnetic Pen) intuitively defines edges based on contrasting colors.

Path-Editing Tools

The Add Anchor Point tool   adds anchor points to existing paths.

The Delete Anchor Point tool   removes anchor points from existing paths.

The Convert Point tool   changes a corner point to a curve or a curve to a corner point.

The Path Component Selection tool   selects and moves the path as a unit.

The Direct Selection tool   selects and moves individual anchor points and segments.

Drawing Paths

Each of the path-drawing tools has a unique method of creating a path outline; choose the one that is most comfortable for your situation. Learning to draw accurately with the Pen tools can be challenging at first, because Bezier curves are unlike any other form of traditional drawing. With a little practice, however, as you become familiar with the process, your speed and accuracy will increase.

The Pen Tool

The Pen tool enables you to draw straight lines and smooth curves with more control and precision. The basic techniques for drawing paths in Adobe Photoshop are similar to the techniques used in Adobe Illustrator. Usually, a path is drawn to follow the form of the area to be isolated, and then the path is edited and refined to a considerable degree of accuracy.

The Pen tool Options bar displays options that let you control its behavior. Before you draw the shape, specify in the Options bar (Figure 9.2) whether to make a new Shape layer or a new work path. This will affect how the shape can later be edited. If you choose the Shape Layer icon, Photoshop generates an independent Shape layer (see "Creating Lines and Shapes" at the end of this chapter). If you choose the Work Path icon, Photoshop draws an independent path on the current layer or Background. Check the Auto Add/Delete feature to automatically add anchor points when one of the Pen tools is placed on a segment or delete a point when a Pen tool is placed over an anchor point. If you check Rubber Band, you can preview the path as you draw.

Using the Zoom tool or the Navigator to view the image more closely greatly enhances your ability to draw with precision.

Creates a work path   Shows path before drawing

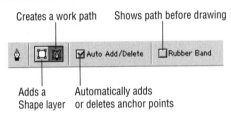

Adds a   Automatically adds
Shape layer   or deletes anchor points

Figure 9.2 *The Pen tool Options bar*

Straight Paths

A straight path consists of two anchor points joined by a straight line segment. You add additional segments to the straight path by moving the cursor and clicking the mouse. The segments can abruptly change direction as the corners zigzag their way across the document.

Drawing a Straight Path

1. Select the Pen tool and click the image where you want to begin the path. An anchor point appears; release the mouse button.

2   Click (and release) your mouse at the next point on the image. A line segment with another anchor point appears.

3   Continue to click and move your mouse to produce a series of straight line segments connected by corner anchor points.

Curved Paths

A curved path consists of two anchor points connected by a curved segment. Direction handles determine the position and shape of the line segment.

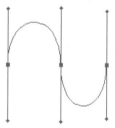

Drawing a Curved Path

1. Select the Pen tool and place the cursor on the image where you want the path to begin.

2. Click your mouse *and drag*. An anchor point with a direction handle appears. Without releasing the mouse button, drag the handle in the direction you want the curve to be placed.

3. Release the mouse and move the cursor to the next point on the image.

4. Click your mouse and drag. A curved segment with another anchor point and direction handle appears. Drag in the opposite direction of the curve.

5. With the mouse button still depressed, adjust the direction handle until the curved line segment is in the desired position and release the mouse.

Tips for Drawing Curved Paths

- Drag the first point in the direction of the peak of the curve and drag the second point in the opposite direction. Dragging the first and second point in the same direction produces an S curve, which is undesirable because its shape is difficult to control.

- Use as few anchor points as possible to assure a smooth path.

- Place the anchor points on the sides of the curve and not on the peaks or valleys, to maintain better control and smooth transitions.

- A path is a continuous series of segments connected by anchor points. You can add anchor points to the middle of a segment, but you can only add segments to the end points of an open path.

- An anchor point can only connect two segments.

- If you should stop drawing and want to add a new segment to a path, resume drawing by first clicking one of the end points with a Pen tool.

- If you are drawing an open path and want to begin a second path that is not connected to the first, click the Pen tool icon on the Tool palette before starting the new path.

Changing the Direction of a Curved Path

You can draw a scalloped path by changing the direction of the curve. When performing this operation, it helps to think of the Option or Alt key as a turn signal. In the following example, the segments will curve upward.

1. Select the Pen tool. Click the image where you want to begin the path and drag up. An anchor point with a direction handle appears. Without releasing the mouse button, drag to adjust the direction handle; then release.

2. Click where you want the next part of the curve. Click your mouse and drag down. A curved segment with another anchor point and direction line appears; release the mouse.

3. Place your cursor on the last anchor point and press Option or Alt (the turn signal!). Click and drag the direction handle up and release the mouse.

4. Move your cursor to the next location, click your mouse, and drag down. Adjust the segment so that the curve is the desired length and position.

5. Repeat step 3.

6. Repeat steps 2 through 4 until the desired number of curves are drawn.

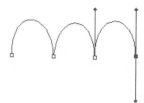

Adding a Curved Path to a Straight Path

Usually, paths you draw are combinations of straight and curved paths. These techniques combine the two into one continuous path.

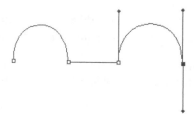

1. Select the Pen tool and click the image where you want to path to begin. An anchor point appears; release the mouse button.

2. Click the next point on the image. A straight segment with another anchor point appears.

3. To add a curved segment, place your cursor on the last anchor point, and press Option or Alt while holding down the mouse button and dragging up.

4. Release your mouse button and move your cursor to the next location.

5. Click your mouse and drag down to finish the curve. Release the mouse when the size and position of the curve is achieved.

Adding a Straight Path to a Curved Path

1. Select the Pen tool, click the image where you want to begin the path, and drag up. An anchor point with a direction handle appears. Without releasing the mouse button, drag the direction handle in the direction of the curve.

2. Release the mouse and move the cursor to the next point.

3. Click your mouse and drag down. A curved segment with another anchor point and direction line appears. Release the mouse.

4. Place your cursor on the last anchor point, press Option or Alt, and click your mouse once.

5. Move your cursor to the next location and click your mouse to complete the segment.

Closing a Path

By closing a path, you create a shape. To close a series of straight paths, draw at least two paths, then place your cursor on the first anchor point. A little circle appears beside the cursor to indicate that the path is ready to be closed. Click the mouse. To close one or more curved paths, draw at least *one* path and click the first anchor point.

The Freeform Pen Tool

Drawing with the Freeform Pen tool is similar to drawing with the Lasso tool. If you place your cursor on the image, click, and drag your mouse, the Freeform Pen will be followed by a trail that, when the mouse is released, produces a path (see Figure 9.3). The Freeform Pen tool is a fast way to draw a curve but doesn't offer the same control as the Pen tool. You can't control the number or placement of anchor points. Paths created by the Freeform Pen usually require editing or removal of excess anchor points after the path has been completed.

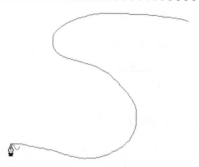

Figure 9.3 *The Freeform Pen tool draws an unrestricted path.*

When you select the Freeform Pen, the Options bar provides new settings: Curve Fit and Magnetic. You can specify the Curve Fit between 0.5 and 10.0 pixels to determine the sensitivity of the tool to the movement of your mouse. A lower tolerance produces a finer curve with more anchor points; a higher tolerance produces a simpler path with fewer anchor points.

The Magnetic Pen Option

The performance of the Freeform Pen tool with Magnetic checked (also called "the Magnetic Pen tool") is similar to the Magnetic Lasso (see Chapter 6). It intuitively snaps to defined areas of contrast within an image as you drag. Where the Magnetic Lasso converts to a selection, the Magnetic Pen converts to a path.

To access the Magnetic Pen, select the Freeform Pen tool (click and hold the cursor on the Pen tool in the Tool palette, and choose the Freeform Pen from the fly-out; or type Shift+P once or twice to select the tool) and check the Magnetic box in the Options bar. Then click the magnet icon to display the Magnetic Options:

Width   Enter a distance in pixels from the edge that the tool will be active. Higher values mean the tool is "attracted" at a greater distance.

Contrast   Enter a value between 1% and 100% to determine the tool's sensitivity in detecting contrasting borders. Higher values detect edges of greater contrast, while lower values increase the tool's sensitivity to low-contrast edges.

You can increase the detection width in one-pixel increments while drawing by pressing the [key. You can decrease the width by pressing the] key.

Frequency   Enter a value between 1 and 100 to establish the rate at which the Magnetic Pen places anchor points. Higher values place more anchor points over a shorter distance.

Stylus Pressure   If you are working with a stylus tablet, check Stylus Pressure. As you drag, the pressure of the stylus will correspond to the Width setting. An increase of pressure on the stylus will narrow the pen width.

Drawing with the Magnetic Pen

1. Click the image to set the first point.

2. Release the mouse button and drag. A path will follow along the most distinct edge within the Pen width. Periodically, the Pen places anchor points along the specified border, while the most recent segment remains active (see Figure 9.4).

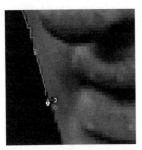

Figure 9.4 *A path made with the Magnetic Pen "snaps" to a line of contrasting pixels.*

3. Press Return (Mac) or Enter (Win) to end an open path. You can resume drawing the open path by clicking the last anchor point and dragging.

4. If you stop dragging and double-click, you create a segment that connects the last anchor point with the first one and closes the path. You can also close the path by hovering over the first anchor point. The little circle appears. Click once.

You can temporarily turn off the Magnetic option by holding down the Option (Mac) or Alt (Win) key with the mouse button depressed to draw a straight path, or with the mouse button released to draw a freeform path.

Editing Paths

Once a path has been drawn, all or part of it can be moved or reshaped. Anchor points can be added or omitted, and corners can be converted into curves or curves into corners.

The path-editing tools include the Path Component Selection tool, the Direct Selection tool, the Add Anchor Point tool, the Delete Anchor Point tool, and the Convert Point tool.

The Path Component Selection Tool

The black arrow, the Path Component Selection tool, selects all of the anchor points and segments of a path. The path can then be repositioned anywhere on the image by dragging with this tool.

Another method of selecting a path is to use the Path Component Selection tool to click and drag a marquee that touches any part of the path. All the anchor points will appear solid, indicating that the entire path is selected.

A path can be duplicated by dragging and dropping it with the Path Component Selection tool and the Option or Alt key depressed, as seen in Figure 9.5.

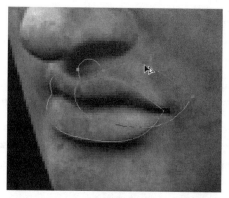

Figure 9.5 *Option/Alt-drag to duplicate a path.*

Aligning Paths

The Path Component Selection tool enables you to automatically align and distribute paths and vector objects such as lines and shapes. You cannot align or distribute shapes on separate layers. To align multiple paths, select two or more paths with the Path Component Selection tool by dragging a marquee that touches the objects, or by Shift-clicking the paths. From the Options bar, choose one of the alignment options shown in Figure 9.6.

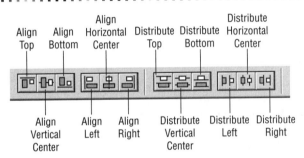

Figure 9.6 *Alignment features of the Path Component Selection tool*

The Align choices match up the edges or centers of paths and objects, as follows:

Top	Aligns the top edges of the path or vector object
Vertical Center	Aligns the vertical midpoints
Bottom	Aligns the bottom edges
Left	Aligns the left edges
Horizontal Center	Aligns the horizontal midpoints
Right	Aligns the right edges

The Distribute choices position the edges or centers of paths and objects over equal distances, in these ways:

Top	Distributes the top edges of the path or vector object
Vertical Center	Distributes the vertical midpoints
Bottom	Distributes the bottom edges
Left	Distributes the left edges
Horizontal Center	Distributes the horizontal midpoints
Right	Distributes the right edges

The Direct Selection Tool

The Direct Selection tool selects or modifies a segment or the position of an anchor point on a path. It is essential for reshaping the path once it has been drawn.

To select, move, or edit a segment or anchor point, choose the Direct Selection tool. Click a segment or anchor point to select it. Click and drag an anchor point to reposition it or a segment to reshape it. To deselect a path, click anywhere on the image.

You can toggle from any of the Pen tools or path-editing tools to the Direct Selection tool by pressing the Command (Mac) or Ctrl (Win) key.

Reshaping Paths

To alter the shape of a path once it has been drawn, follow these steps:

1. Choose the Direct Selection tool.

2. Click an anchor point to select it.

3. Click and drag one of the anchor point's *direction handles* until the desired shape of the curve is achieved (as in Figure 9.7).

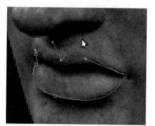

Figure 9.7 *Reshaping a path*

Editing Anchor Points

After you have drawn a path around an area on the image, you may need to refine it by adding or deleting anchor points. When you do, you increase your ability to edit the path.

It might be tempting to add dozens of anchor points, to facilitate the drawing of a path. Extra points are not recommended, because they increase the path's complexity and compromise the smoothness of the shape.

Adding and Deleting Anchor Points

To add an anchor point, choose the Add Anchor Point tool and click the path. A new anchor point will appear. To delete an anchor point, choose the Delete Anchor Point tool. Click an anchor point, and the two segments connected by the point join into one.

Converting Anchor Points

There are two types of anchor points. Smooth points connect curved or straight lines that flow into each other. Corner points connect lines that change direction. An anchor point can be converted from corner to smooth or smooth to corner (see Figure 9.8) by clicking the point with the Convert Point tool. Click a smooth point and it converts to a corner point; to convert a corner point, click it and drag out the direction handles until the desired curve is achieved, and release the mouse.

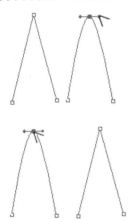

Figure 9.8 *Converting (top) a corner to a smooth point and (bottom) a smooth to a corner point*

Transforming Paths

Like selection outlines and selection contents, paths can be modified with the Transformation tools. Once the path has been drawn, you must select it with one of the arrow tools. If you select it with the Path Component Selection tool, you can employ any of the transformation operations in the Edit menu, including Free Transform, Scale,

Rotate, Skew, Distort, Perspective, or Flip, to edit the entire path. If you select one or more points or segments with the Direct Selection tool, you can apply any of the transformation operations to the selected part of the path.

To learn how to use Photoshop's transformation features, see Chapter 13.

Combining Paths

If you have drawn two or more paths that intersect, you can combine them into one path. Select both paths with the Path Component Selection tool by pressing your mouse button and dragging a marquee that touches both of them, or by clicking them in sequence while pressing the Shift key. On the Options bar, click the Combine button. The elements of both paths combine into one continuous path.

The Paths Palette

The Paths palette is the central control for all path operations. Like a layer or a channel, a path can be stored to a palette so it can later be edited or converted into a selection. The Paths palette (Figure 9.9) can be accessed by choosing Window → Show Paths. (If you still have the Paths palette in the default cluster—grouped with the Layers palette— then pressing the F7 function key will also bring it up.)

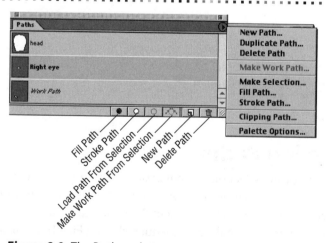

Figure 9.9 *The Paths palette*

Work Paths

When you begin drawing a path with the Pen tool, it appears as a thumbnail in the Paths palette, named Work Path. The work path is a temporary element that records changes as you draw new sections of the path. If you complete a path on an image, click the Pen tool, and draw another path. It will appear on the same Work Path thumbnail as the first path. If you wish to create separate additional paths, it is necessary to save the work path to the Paths palette.

You can increase or decrease the size of the Paths palette thumbnails, or turn them off, by choosing Palette Options from the palette pull-down menu and clicking the radio button next to the desired thumbnail size.

Saving Paths

Saving a path to the Paths palette has a distinct advantage over saving selections as alpha channels (which are described in Chapter 12): The file size of a document does not substantially increase with each saved path.

Once your path has been drawn and appears as a Work Path thumbnail, you can save it by choosing Save Path from the palette menu. A dialog box appears where you can name the path; if no name is entered, the path name defaults to Path 1. You can also save a path by dragging the Work Path to the New Path icon at the bottom of the palette.

The Paths palette lists saved paths from top to bottom in the order in which they were created. The paths can be reorganized within the list by clicking the path's name or thumbnail and dragging it to the desired location.

Displaying Paths

To display a path, click the path's name or thumbnail in the Paths palette. Photoshop allows only one path to be displayed at a time. When displayed, it will appear on the image. You can edit it, move it, add other paths to it, or delete portions of the path. To conceal a work path or saved path from view in the image window, click the empty portion of the Paths palette.

Deleting Paths from the Image Window

To delete a path from the image, do one of the following:

- Select an entire path with the Path Component Selection tool. Press the Delete or Backspace key. If it's a work path, the path and its icon are deleted. If it's a saved path, the path is deleted from the image window, but its empty thumbnail remains in the Paths palette.

- Select a part of the path with the Direct Selection tool. Press the Delete or Backspace key once to delete the selected part of the path or twice to delete the entire path.

Deleting Paths from the Palette

You may want to discard a path from the Paths palette. To do so, target the path's name in the palette and perform one of the following operations.

- Drag the path thumbnail to the trash icon at the bottom of the palette.
- Choose Delete Path from the Paths palette pull-down menu.
- Click the trash icon in the Paths palette. In the dialog box that appears, click Yes.
- Target the path in the Paths palette. Press the Delete or Backspace key.

Using Paths to Apply Color

You can apply color to an area of an image within a closed path or to the edge of a path.

Filling a Path

To fill the area within a path, draw an open or closed path or display an existing path from the Paths palette by clicking its thumbnail. Choose a foreground color. Choose Fill Path from the Paths palette pull-down menu.

The Fill Path dialog box appears (Figure 9.10), the top two fields of which are identical to the Fill dialog box in the Edit menu (see Chapter 10). In the additional Rendering field, you can enter a Feather Radius for the edges of the path and check the Anti-Aliased option. Click OK when you have the settings you want.

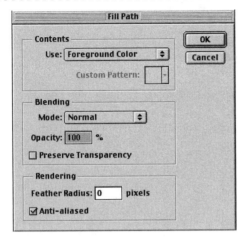

Figure 9.10 *The Fill Path dialog box*

You can fill a path with the current Fill Path dialog box settings by clicking the Fill Path icon at the bottom of the Paths palette.

Stroking a Path

A path can be stroked with a line of a specific color and width. This is an important operation in Photoshop because it is really the only way to precisely create smooth curved lines. Try drawing one with the Paintbrush or Pencil; it's quite difficult to achieve satisfactory results. Drawing an open path, editing it to your exact specifications, and then stroking it with a color produces perfect results every time.

To color the line of a path, draw a path or load one from the Paths palette. Choose a foreground color; then, from the Paths palette pull-down menu, choose Stroke Path. The Stroke Path (Figure 9.11) dialog box appears; pick a tool from the pop-up list. When you click OK, the stroke will be painted with the current characteristics of the chosen tool as defined in the Options bar.

You can quickly stroke a path with the current tool characteristics set in the Stroke Path dialog box by clicking the Stroke Path icon at the bottom of the Paths palette.

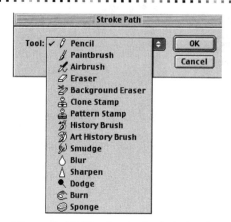

Figure 9.11 *The Stroke Path dialog box*

Converting Paths

The primary reason to use paths is the ease and facility with which you can precisely define regions of an image. While some of the new selection tools offer unique selection techniques, there is nothing quite like the paths operations to quickly and precisely surround an area.

Paths are easy to edit and require less real estate on your disk to store. Eventually, though, you are going to need to convert your path into a selection to be able to apply a Photoshop operation to the area it surrounds.

Converting a Selection to a Path

You can determine the characteristics of a new selection and its relation to active selections on the image. Target the path in the Paths palette, and choose Make Selection from the Paths palette pull-down menu. A dialog box is displayed that enables you to choose the characteristics of the new selection (Figure 9.12).

Feather Radius	Sets distance in pixels for feathering of the selection outline.
Anti-Aliased	Determines whether the selection will possess an anti-aliased edge.

New Selection	Makes a selection from the path.
Add To Selection	Adds the area defined by the path to the active selection.
Subtract From Selection	Omits the area defined by the path from the active selection.
Intersect With Selection	Makes a selection from the overlap of the path and the active selection.

Click OK to convert the path into a selection.

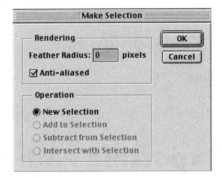

Figure 9.12 *The Make Selection dialog*

 You can convert a path into a new selection by clicking the Load Path As Selection icon at the bottom of the Paths palette.

Converting a Selection into a Path

To convert a selection into a path, draw a marquee with one of the selection tools. Choose Make Work Path from the Paths palette menu. A dialog box is displayed that enables you to set the tolerance of the path in pixels. Tolerances with low values produce more complex paths with greater numbers of anchor points, while tolerances with higher values produce simpler paths. Click OK to convert the selection into a path.

You can also convert a selection into a path by clicking the Make Work Path From Selection icon at the bottom of the Paths palette.

You might use the ability to make selections from paths to modify a typeface, as in Figure 9.13. To modify type, first create it with the Type Outline tool, then click the Make Work Path From Selection icon. Modify the path outlines as desired, then click the Load Path As Selection icon. The selection can be either filled, or an image can be pasted into it.

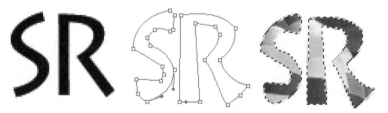

Figure 9.13 *Modifying type by using paths*

Importing and Exporting Paths

Photoshop paths can be utilized by other programs, where they can be modified. You can transfer a path directly from Photoshop to popular vector-based drawing programs like Illustrator or FreeHand, or vice versa, to take advantage of either program's unique path-editing features.

Copy and Paste

If you're moving the path from Photoshop to a vector-based drawing program, select the entire path with the Path Component Selection tool and copy it to the clipboard (by choosing Edit ➔ Copy or pressing Cmd/Ctrl+C). Open a document in the other program and paste the path into it. The paths remain fully editable in either program.

When you paste a path into Photoshop, a dialog box appears that asks you to choose to place the path as a rasterized image (Pixels), a vector path, or a Shape layer.

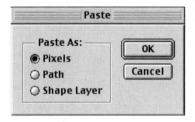

Drag and Drop

You can drag and drop a path from Photoshop to Illustrator. With both programs running, select the path with the Path Component Selection tool. Drag the path onto the Illustrator pasteboard. The new Illustrator path is fully editable.

Paths to Illustrator

If you can't run Photoshop and Illustrator simultaneously, you can export the file as an Illustrator EPS file using the File ➔ Export ➔ Paths to Illustrator command. In the dialog box that appears, for Write, choose Work Path. When you quit Photoshop, launch Illustrator, and open the document, the exported path will be fully editable in Illustrator.

Clipping Paths

When saving Photoshop documents into vector drawing applications or to desktop publishing programs, it is sometimes necessary to "knock out" portions of the image—that is, make them invisible. The Clipping Paths option in the Paths palette pull-down menu enables you to create a path that will knock out the area outside the path when it is opened in another program. The interior portion of the path will be displayed, and the area outside the path will be completely transparent.

To create a clipping path:

1. Draw a path around an area on the image (see Figure 9.14).

Figure 9.14 *Selecting the area with the Pen tool*

2. From the Paths palette pull-down menu, choose Save Path.

3. Choose Clipping Path from the palette menu.

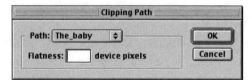

4. Select the name of the path from the pull-down submenu. Click OK.

5. For most paths, leave the Flatness setting blank. When you print the image, the printer's default flatness setting will be used to define the shape. However, if you experience printing problems, then save the path with new settings (see sidebar).

The path name is outlined (Mac) or boldfaced (Win) in the Paths palette, indicating that it is a clipping path.

Images containing clipping paths must be saved in EPS format, and therefore can only be imported into programs that support EPS images. It's best to save a copy of the image so that the original image retains Photoshop's attributes.

To save a clipping path as an EPS:

1. Choose File ➜ Save As. Check the As A Copy option.

2. From the Format list, choose Photoshop EPS. A dialog box appears.

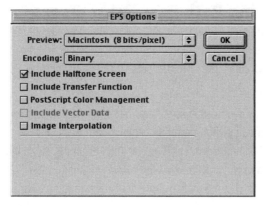

3. Choose a preview option, depending on the type of computer and the platform you are using: Macintosh or Windows, 1 bit or 8 bit (see Appendix B, "File Formats," for a detailed explanation of the EPS dialog box).

4. Choose Binary for Encoding.

5. Click OK.

6. Open a document in a desktop publishing program or vector drawing program, and place the EPS image (see Figure 9.15).

Figure 9.15 *The image clipped by the path*

Troubleshooting Clipping Path PostScript Errors

A raster image processor (RIP) is software on a computer or a device inside an imagesetter or PostScript printer that interprets a vector curve by connecting a series of straight line segments together. The *flatness* of a clipping path determines the fidelity of the lines to the curve. The lower the setting, the more lines are produced and so, the more accurate the curve.

If a clipping path is too complex for the printer's capabilities, it cannot print the path and will produce a limitcheck or PostScript error. Any printer can be jammed up with a complex clipping path, although you may find that a clipping path may print perfectly well on a low-resolution printer (300–600 dpi) because it uses a higher flatness value to define the curve. The same clipping path may not print on a high-resolution imagesetter (1200–2400 dpi). If you run into printing problems on an image with a clipping path, troubleshoot them in the following ways.

- Increase the Flatness settings and resave the file. Flatness values range from 0.2 to 100. Enter a flatness setting from 1 to 3 for low-resolution printers and 8 to 10 for high-resolution printers.

- Reduce the number of anchor points in the curve by manually eliminating them with the Delete Anchor Point tool.

- Re-create the path with lower Tolerance settings:

  1. Target the path in the Paths palette.

  2. Click the Load Path As Selection icon at the bottom of the palette.

  3. Click the trash icon to delete the path but leave the selection.

  4. Choose Make Work Path from the palette's pull-down menu. In the dialog box, decrease the Tolerance to 5 pixels (a good place to start).

  5. Name and save the new work path.

  6. Choose Clipping Path from the palette pull-down menu.

  7. Save the file in EPS format.

Creating Lines and Shapes

Photoshop 6 handles lines and shapes quite differently than its predecessors did. In fact, it has an entirely new interface for creating and managing shapes that is more like Illustrator's. Like type, lines and shapes are vector objects. You draw a predefined shape using one of the Shape tools or a custom shape using the Pen tool. Once drawn, shapes can be edited by adjusting their anchor points with the path-editing tools. When you create a shape, it appears on an independent layer with a Layer Clipping Path thumbnail next to a Color Fill Layer thumbnail.

The shape also appears as a separate path in the Paths palette. To apply any filter to a shape, it must first be *rasterized* or turned into pixels. If you flatten the image, shapes are automatically converted to pixels.

Like paths, shapes are vector objects. The Shape tool can instantly create rectangles, rounded rectangles, ellipses, polygons, lines, and custom shapes that are editable using the path-editing tools. The Shape tool icon in the Tool palette, when clicked, expands to reveal all of the available tools. Once you've chosen a shape from this fly-out, click in the image and drag to size the shape.

The Shape Tool Options Bar

As you choose a different shape from the Tool palette or from the Shape list in the Options bar, the Options bar changes to accommodate specific characteristics of the shape. Figure 9.16 illustrates the differences in the Options bar when the three different drawing options are selected.

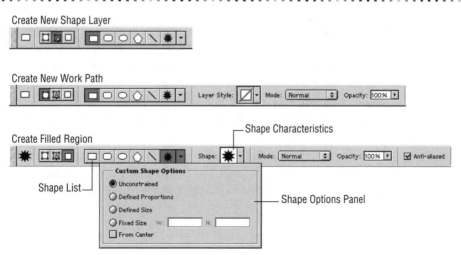

Figure 9.16 *The Options bar of the Shape tools*

Options Bar Feature	Function
Create New Shape Layer	Makes a shape and a path on a new layer.
Create New Work Path	Makes the path outline of the shape on an existing layer or Background.
Create Filled Region	Fills an area with the foreground color in the form of the shape.
Shape List	Lets you choose a shape.
Shape Options Panel	Enter specifications for the size and proportion of the shape.
Layer Style	Attach a layer style to the Shape layer (available with New Shape Layer).
Shape Characteristics	Assign values for the characteristics of a particular shape, or choose a custom shape.
Mode	Select a blending mode for the shape (available only with New Shape Layer or Filled Region).
Opacity	Opacity slider for the shape (available only with New Shape Layer or Filled Region).
Anti-Alias	Applies an anti-alias to the shape (available only with Filled Region).

Drawing Shapes

To draw a shape, first choose a foreground color. Click the Shape tool in the Tool palette and choose a tool type from the expanded palette or from the Options bar. Click in the image and drag to form the shape.

Since shapes are vector objects, you use the Path Component Selection tool, Direct Selection tool, or path-editing tools to move or edit a shape or to add and delete anchor points.

Each shape performs slightly differently. The Options bar of each shape lets you adjust its individual characteristics. For example, you can enter a value for the radius of the corners on the Rounded Rectangle tool, or for the number of sides on the Polygon tool.

The Rectangles and Ellipse Tools

As with the selection Marquee tools, icons on the Shape tool Options bars let you add, subtract, intersect, or exclude areas from a shape as you draw. Clicking the arrow to the right of the Shape tool icons on the Options bar offers additional controls on a pop-up panel. When you choose the Rectangle, Rounded Rectangle, or Ellipse tool, the down-arrow on the Options bar offers you these choices:

Unconstrained	Checking this button sizes and proportions the shape as you draw.
Square (or Circle)	Checking this button constrains the shape.
Fixed Size	Input values for the shape's Width and Height.
Proportional	Enter values in the Width and Height fields to define the shape's proportion.
From Center	Check this box to radiate the shape from a center point.
Snap To Pixels	Aligns the shape to the on-screen pixels (Rectangle and Round-Cornered Rectangle only).

 To constrain the Rectangle or Round-Cornered Rectangle to a square or the Ellipse to a circle, hold down the Shift key as you drag.

The Polygon Tool

When the Polygon tool is selected, a Size field in the Options bar allows you to set the number of the shape's sides. The Polygon Options panel choices differ from those of the other shapes. Figure 9.17 illustrates the wide variety of shapes you can create by adjusting these settings.

Radius	Enter a corner radius for a round-cornered polygon.
Smooth Corners	Rounds the corners of the polygon.
Indent Sides By	Enter a percentage value to curve the sides inward.
Smooth Indents	Rounds the indents.

Figure 9.17 *Polygon examples*

The Line Tool

When the Line tool is selected, you can enter a value in the Options bar for the Weight of the line in pixels. Choices in the Line Options panel determine what type of arrow will appear at either end of the line. Check the Start or End boxes, or both, to produce an arrowhead at the beginning and/or end of the line. Enter values in Width, Length, and Concavity for these characteristics of the arrowhead. (Figure 9.18 demonstrates the wide variety of possibilities in these settings.)

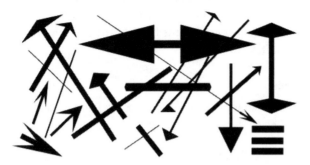

Figure 9.18 *Examples of lines, with and without arrowheads*

The Custom Shape Tool

You can generate custom shapes with the Shape tool. With the Custom Shape tool selected, the Options panel displays these options:

Unconstrained	Manually determines the proportion of the shape as you draw.
Defined Proportions	Drag to constrain the proportion of the shape.
Defined Size	Draws the shape at the size it was created.
Fixed Size	Enter a values for the shape in the height and width fields.
From Center	Radiates the shape from a center point.

The Options bar Shape menu lets you choose from fourteen pre-defined custom shapes. You can create additional shapes with the Pen tool and save them to this list.

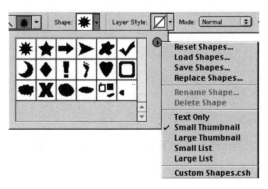

The pull-down submenu on the panel provides a list of commands that let you Save, Load, Reset, Delete, and Replace custom shapes, plus several palette viewing options. The Custom Shapes.csh option at the bottom rung of the submenu replaces the default list with 63 additional shapes.

Drawing Custom Shapes

To practice applying custom shapes, open the file `Empty_Face.psd` in the Ch09 folder on the *Mastering Photoshop 6* CD.

1. Choose a foreground color.

2. Make a new empty layer by clicking the New Layer icon in the Layers palette. Name the layer `Watch Shapes`.

3. Click the Shape tool in the Tool palette.

4. In the Options bar, click the Custom Shape icon to display the Shape Options panel. Click the Unconstrained radio button.

5. In the Options bar, click the Shape menu arrow to display the default custom shapes. Click the arrow on the panel to display the list of commands in the pull-down submenu; choose Custom Shapes.csh to load the additional 63 shapes.

6. Click a shape in the Shape menu. Place your cursor on the watch face at the 12 o'clock mark, click, and drag until the shape is the size and proportion you want. To reposition the shape, press the space bar while dragging. Then release the mouse.

7. Choose additional shapes from the Shape menu and repeat step 6 for all of the hours on the clock, as in Figure 9.19. (There's a color version of this image in the color section.)

Defining Custom Shapes

To create a custom shape:

1. Use one of the Pen tools and draw a shape outline.

2. Choose Edit ➜ Define Custom Shape.

3. Choose the Custom Shape tool. The new shape will appear in the Shape menu in the Shape tool Options bar.

Figure 9.19 *The watch face adorned with custom shapes*

Up Next

Paths are yet another method in the Photoshop tool box that endow you with faster, more accurate performance. Someday, you'll confront that long, smooth edge on an image, and you'll know exactly where to go to make selecting it a breeze. Paths serve multiple purposes. Not only do they delineate edges and make selections, but they also fill, stroke, and knock out backgrounds. The new Shape tool creates vector objects that are fully editable with the path-editing tools.

Chapter 10 shows you how create and apply digital color to an image. We'll learn how to use Photoshop as a powerful paint program to produce beautiful painterly effects. You'll make your own brushes and apply color with the paint tools. You'll learn to use several new features, such as Fill layers and the new Pattern interface. In the Hands-On project that follows Chapter 11, you'll use paths combined with the painting tools and the History palette to produce a colorful digital painting.

Creating and
Applying Color

PHOTOSHOP

Chapter 10

Photoshop's painting functions are designed to simulate the real-life studio environment, with their ability to apply color with a variety of virtual tools. Photoshop draws and paints with light, yet has the ability to simulate almost any effect that can be created on paper or canvas. These same capabilities can be greatly extended by applying artistic, textural, and brush stroke filters that can convert a photograph into anything from a Rembrandt to a Picasso instantaneously.

In this chapter, I'll talk about:

- Understanding digital color

- Color modes

- Choosing colors

- Creating brushes

- Using the painting and editing tools

- Making and applying gradients

- Filling and stroking

Painting, with Paint and Pixels

Applying color to a surface is one of the most common forms of self-expression. From the meticulous application of thinned glazes to render exacting detail on photorealistic paintings, to pigment splashed on by the gallon on abstract expressionist canvases, the application of color is the artist's way of whispering, speaking, or shouting.

Paint is indeed a versatile medium. Colors are made from minerals or organic substances, ground and mixed with either an oil- or water-based vehicle that forms a liquid or paste to make them fluid enough to apply. It can brushed, troweled, rolled, sprayed, poured, spattered, or thrown onto a surface. It can be mixed, blended, glazed, or smeared, thin or thick, to produce an infinite variety of colors and surface effects.

Photoshop's drawing and painting functions simulate the real-life studio environment but use light instead of physical compounds on paper or canvas. Specifying digital color and applying it with one of the painting tools is fundamental to digital imaging. The painting tools go far beyond just the ability to apply color in an artistic capacity. They are essential for spot editing and photo retouching, creating textural surfaces, and image compositing.

Understanding Digital Color

Every pixel in each color channel of your document is assigned a numeric value. These values can be translated into specific color systems that distribute the information depending on your needs. For example, the three-channel RGB system is used to display images on screen, but the four-channel CMYK color system is designed to organize the information into color separations so that it can be printed on a printing press.

In Photoshop, you can choose a specific color system. Some of these systems are called color *modes,* like RGB, CMYK, Lab, and Grayscale, in which the information is organized into color *channels* with specific characteristics. Others, such as HSB, are called color *models* and are supported for your convenience, so that you can easily pick the exact color you want by determining its basic characteristics.

Color Models and Modes

A color mode or model is a system of displaying or printing color. Photoshop supports the HSB color model and RGB, CMYK, Lab, Indexed, Duotone, Grayscale, Multichannel, and Bitmap color modes. To convert an image from one color mode to another, choose Image ➜ Mode and select a color mode.

Because the gamut, or range of possible colors, of one color mode may be different from that of another, converting your document can sometimes present problems in the form of color shifts. See Chapter 15 for more on this and how to avoid it.

Digital Imaging and Fine Art

Since the introduction of computer painting and imaging software like Adobe Photoshop, there has been an ongoing debate in art circles about whether painting will be replaced by its digital counterpart. The controversy embraces many aspects of the meaning and purpose of art and especially its commercial value to collectors, museums, and galleries.

When it was first introduced, graphic designers and commercial illustrators immediately gravitated to photo manipulation and desktop publishing software to replace traditional graphic arts techniques performed with paste-up, technical pens, and process cameras. It took almost a decade, however, for digital art to be taken seriously as a "real" art form by the art establishment of universities, galleries, and museums. This was due, in part, to reluctance by the institutions to accept a new medium, and to the limitations of hardware to produce archival-quality output. (*Archival* simply means that the ink won't fade and paper won't deteriorate over time.)

These days, however, many images we see hanging on the walls of museums and galleries are produced by computers. The recent introduction of direct, high-end printing to archival-quality paper with archival ink, as with Iris printers, or photographic output devices, like Light-Jet RGB printers, has made museum-quality computer art possible. Some of these direct-to-print digital images are photographic, and some are painterly. Because they can be systematically reproduced, they acquire the status of limited edition prints or photographs.

Owing to the unique differences of the processes of painting and computer art, one can hardly replace the other. Painting is a much more physical process than computer art. It requires broader movement of the body and direct contact with wet media, which intrinsically presents entirely different visual, tactile, and olfactory sensations. On a computer, most operations can be performed using the fingers, hand, and wrist in an environment that is free of the odors of solvents and the feel of the brush against a surface.

Just as the traditional visual arts have continued to thrive in our society as a means of self expression, the computer has emerged as another dynamic art form. In addition, the computer has become an aid to the artist. With the capability of quickly creating multiple versions, it helps some artists visualize and refine the style, composition, and color relations of their work.

HSB Color Model

The HSB model uses the basic characteristics of color to define each color; HSB is the Color Picker's default. Each color consists of the following characteristics:

Hue   is the color of light that is reflected from an opaque object or transmitted through a transparent one. Hue in Photoshop is measured by its position on a color wheel, from 0 to 360 degrees.

Saturation   or *chroma* is the intensity of a color as determined by the percentage of the hue in proportion to gray from 0 to 100 percent. Zero percent saturation means that the color is entirely gray.

Brightness   or *value* is the relative lightness or darkness of a color, measured from 0 to 100 percent.

RGB Color Mode

The RGB mode represents the three colors—red, green, and blue—used by devices such as scanners or monitors to display color. Each range of color is separated into three separate entities called *color channels*. Each color channel can produce 256 different values, for a total of 256^3, or 16,777,216, possible colors in the entire RGB gamut. Photoshop can display all of these colors providing you have a monitor and video card that support 24-bit color.

Because RGB produces color with light, the more light that is added, the brighter the color becomes; hence, RGB is referred to as an *additive* color model (see Figure 10.1; although this illustration is printed here for reference, you'll find a more useful copy in the color section). Each pixel contains three brightness values—a red, a green, and a blue—ranging from 0 (black) to 255. When all three values are at the maximum, the color is pure white. Colors with low brightness values are dark, and colors with high brightness values are light.

CMYK Color Mode

The CMYK (cyan, magenta, yellow, black) color mode produces a full range of color by printing tiny dots of cyan, magenta, yellow, and black ink. Because the colored dots are so small, the eye mixes them together. The relative densities of groups of colored dots produce variations in color and tonality. Because the more ink you add to a CMYK image, the darker it becomes, CMYK is referred to as a *subtractive* color system (see Figure 10.1, and its color view in the color section). You specify CMYK colors to ultimately segregate colors onto film negatives called color separations. The separations are used to burn plates, which are used in the offset lithography printing process.

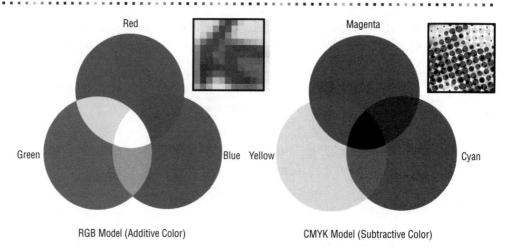

Figure 10.1 *The (left) RGB and (right) CMYK color models*

Lab Color Mode

The CIE Lab color mode is an international color measurement system developed in 1931 by the International Commission on Illumination (Commission Internacionale de l'Éclairage, or CIE). Lab color is device-independent, meaning that the color model is based on the perception of the human eye rather than a mechanical ink or light system. Lab color consists of three channels: a luminance or lightness channel (L), a green–red component (a), and a blue–yellow component (b) (see Figure 10.2, especially the version in the color section). In the Color Picker, entering a value from 0 to 100 in the L channel controls the brightness information, and values from +127 to –128 in the a and b channels control the color information.

As a color model, Lab can be used to adjust the luminance and color of an image independently of each other. Photoshop uses Lab as an interim color space when converting files from one color mode to another.

Grayscale Mode

Grayscale is a mode that displays black and white images. A Grayscale image is composed of one channel with 256 possible shades of gray. Each pixel has a brightness value between 0 (black) to 255 (white). (However, sometimes Grayscale pixels are measured in percentages of black ink from 0 percent (white) to 100 percent (black).) When color images are converted to Grayscale, their hue and saturation information is discarded and their brightness or *luminosity* values remain.

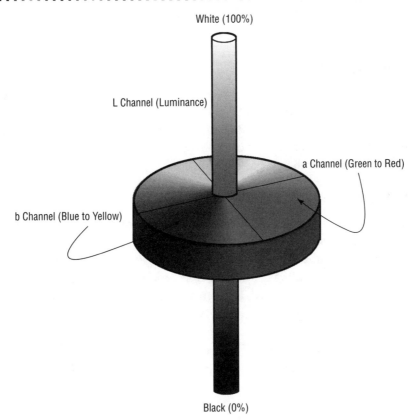

Figure 10.2 The CIE Lab color model

Bitmap Mode

Bitmap images are the simplest form of graphic image. They contain either black or white pixels and are used to create line art and digital halftones. Bitmap images contain only one bit of information per pixel, so their file sizes are much smaller than grayscale images, which contain eight bits per pixel, or color images, which contain 24 bits per pixel.

Indexed Color Mode

Indexed color mode uses a maximum of 256 colors to display full-color images. When you convert an image color to the Indexed mode, Photoshop stores the color information as a color lookup table (CLUT). You can then use a specific palette to display the image to match the colors as closely as possible to the original. Because it contains fewer colors, Indexed color creates smaller file sizes, which is why it is often used when publishing files to the Web or to multimedia applications.

Duotone Mode

Duotones are images that have been separated into two spot colors. Duotone modes supports Tritones (images with three colors) and Quadtones (four colors). The Duotone color information is contained on one color channel. Photoshop displays a preview that is an RGB simulation of the ink combinations. Duotones and spot color are covered in more depth in Chapter 23.

Multichannel Mode

The number of channels in a Multichannel document depends on the number of channels in the source image before it was converted. Each channel in a Multichannel document contains 256 levels of gray. This mode is useful for converting a Duotone image into separate color channels for the purpose of analyzing the color information. Multichannel will convert RGB to cyan, magenta, and yellow spot color channels and CMYK into CMYK spot color channels.

You cannot print a color composite from Multichannel mode. Most export file formats do not support Multichannel. However you can save a Multichannel file in DCS 2.0 file format. See Appendix B, "File Formats."

Choosing Colors

Picking a color in Photoshop 6 is as simple as squeezing paint from a tube. It is a matter of choosing a color from one of Photoshop's three color interfaces. In addition, you can sample colors directly from an image.

    There are two color swatches near the bottom of the tool palette, representing the current foreground and background colors. The swatch on the left is the foreground color, which is applied by any of the painting tools. The default foreground color is black. The background color on the right is applied with the Eraser tool or if you cut a selected portion of an image on the Background. The default background color is white.

You can reverse the foreground and background colors by clicking the curved arrow to the upper-right of the swatches. To restore the colors to the default black and white, click the icon at the lower-left of the swatches.

Note: When you cut a portion of an image on a layer, the area becomes transparent.

The Color Picker

To choose a foreground or background color, click its swatch; the Color Picker appears (Figure 10.3; this image is also presented in the color section). The Color Picker lets you choose from four methods of defining your colors: HSB, RGB, Lab, and CMYK. Your main tools in the Color Picker are a vertical slider and a large color field.

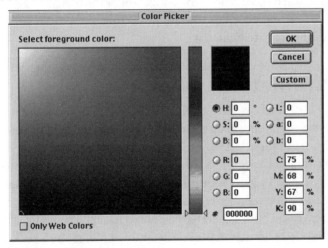

Figure 10.3 *The Color Picker*

Hue This is the position of the color on a color wheel. When the H radio button is selected in the Color Picker, the vertical slider displays the spectrum of all of the available hues, and the color field presents that hue's saturation and brightness variations. Notice that the top and bottom of the spectrum slider are both red. If you drag the slider to the top or bottom of the color bar, the values in the Hue box are the same: 0 degrees. No, we are not taking the hue's temperature; we're determining its position on a color wheel. The vertical bar is actually a color wheel that has been cut and straightened at the 0 degree, or red, position. Drag the slider any-where on the bar, and notice that the hue value changes to a number between 0 and 360 degrees. As you move the slider, the field to the left changes color.

Saturation   The color field on the left determines the saturation and brightness of the hue. Saturation is the intensity of a particular hue. There are two ways to determine the saturation of a color in the Color Picker: Enter a value in the Satura-tion box, or click or drag within the color field. If the value in the Saturation box is 100 percent, or if the circle on the color field is to the far right, the color will be as intense as it can possibly be. If a 0 is entered in the Saturation box, or if the circle is placed at the far left of the field, the color will be gray.

Brightness   The value of a color is controlled in a similar manner. Brightness is the lightness or darkness of a color. Lower values produce darker colors, with zero percent equaling black. Higher values produce lighter colors, with 100 percent equaling white when there is no color saturation or the lightest possible combina-tion of hue and saturation. Click toward the bottom of the color field to darken the color or toward the top to lighten it.

Active Parameters of Color

By default, the Color Picker opens in HSB mode with Hue as the active parameter. The slider represents the colors (hues) on the color wheel, and the field represents the satu-ration and brightness of the selected hue. The Color Picker can be changed to display several different configurations; the color section of this book includes a side-by-side comparison of the Color Picker's appearance when using each of the value fields.

The color picker can be configured for HSB, RGB, Lab, and CMYK active para-meters by clicking a radio button next to the desired model. The vertical bar then rep-resents the selected characteristic in the selected model. When the S radio button is active, for instance, the active parameter of the Color Picker shifts to Saturation mode and the vertical bar becomes a saturation slider. The color field now displays hue and brightness variations. If you click or drag in the field, to the left or right, you affect the hue; if you click or drag up or down, you affect the brightness.

When the B radio button is checked, the active parameter of the Color Picker shifts to Brightness, and the vertical bar becomes a brightness slider. The color field now dis-plays hue and saturation variations; clicking in the field or dragging the circle to the left or right affects the hue and dragging it up or down affects the saturation.

In the case of RGB (red, green, or blue) and Lab (lightness, a, or b), when a color channel's radio button is selected, the vertical slider displays the variations of color within that channel, and the color field becomes the other two color channels, one represented horizontally and the other represented vertically.

The color swatch at the top of the Color Picker has two parts. The bottom of the swatch shows the current color setting; the top shows the color you've selected in the Color Picker.

Specifying CMYK Colors

Let's say a client walks into your office and wants you to add a logo to an image with specific CMYK color values to correspond to the official corporate colors of her business. Once you've scanned the logo, you can define the colors in the Color Picker and fill the logo with the exact tint values of cyan, magenta, yellow, and black needed to produce the corporate color.

To define and apply CMYK colors:

1. Click the foreground swatch to display the Color Picker.

2. Enter the CMYK percentage values in their boxes.

3. Click OK. The color appears as the foreground color.

4. Select the area to be filled.

5. Press Option+Delete (Mac) or Alt+Backspace (Win) to fill the selected area.

The CMYK Gamut Warning

You would think that, because CMYK is represented by four color channels instead of three, there would be more colors available in this color mode. But in fact, a high percentage of black plus any combination of cyan, yellow, and magenta usually yields black. This greatly limits the possibilities of CMYK. In fact, the CMYK gamut is so small that some colors cannot be produced at all, especially highly saturated ones. The color section includes a schematic comparison of the gamut of visible, RGB, and CMYK colors.

If you choose a color in HSB or RGB that is outside the printable range or gamut of CMYK, you will see the percentage values in the CMYK boxes. However, you will also see a CMYK Gamut Warning next to the color swatch in the Color Picker. The small swatch below the warning is a representation of how the color will print. Some CMYK colors, especially highly saturated colors, can vary significantly from their RGB counterpart. If you get a warning, you may want to specify a different color for a closer match, or be prepared to accept considerable variation of the color on the printed piece.

Specifying Web Colors

In HTML code, colors are coded with a combination of six hexadecimal digits so that World Wide Web browsers can read and display them. Not all browsers can display all colors. You can use the Color Picker to assure that the colors you use are browser-safe.

To specify a Web color, check the Only Web Color box at the bottom of the Color Picker. The color bar and color field then limit themselves to 216 Web-compatible colors; note the banding in Figure 10.4, indicating that the color field no longer has a continuous, nearly infinite color set. When you click any variation, the color's six-digit hexadecimal number appears in the # box. If you know the Web color's number, you can select that color simply by entering the number in the # box.

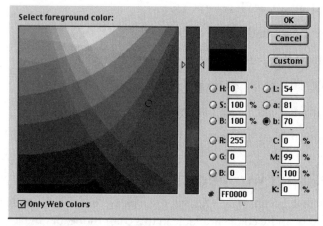

Figure 10.4 *When Only Web Colors is checked, the Color Picker restricts itself to browser-safe possibilities.*

Like CMYK colors, Web colors have a very limited gamut compared to RGB. When the Only Web Colors box is unchecked, the Color Picker displays a Web Color Gamut Warning next to the large swatch in the Color Picker. The small swatch below the warning shows how the color will be seen on Web browsers.

It is very hard to control exactly how even Web-safe colors are seen on browsers. A lot depends on the quality and age of the viewer's monitor, what system palette they are using, and how the brightness and contrast controls are set. The Web-safe colors feature lets you choose colors that will not radically change when viewed on other monitors of the same quality and calibration as the one you are working on.

Specifying Custom Colors

The PANTONE Matching System is a group of inks used to print spot colors. Where CMYK mixes only four colors to produce a full color spectrum, PANTONE inks are solid colors used to print rich solid or tinted areas. The PANTONE system is recognized all over the world; a PANTONE ink can be specified in the U.S. and printed in Japan, for example, simply by telling the printer its number. Photoshop also supports other matching systems, such as ANPA DIC, Toyo, Focoltone, HKS, and TRUMATCH (a CMYK computer color-matching system).

To specify a custom color:

1. Click a color swatch to display the Color Picker.

2. Click the Custom button to display the Custom Color dialog box (Figure 10.5).

3. From the Book pop-up list, choose the desired matching system.

4. Enter the color's number using the keypad. You can, instead, scroll through the color list using the slider; when you find the color you want, click it.

5. Click OK.

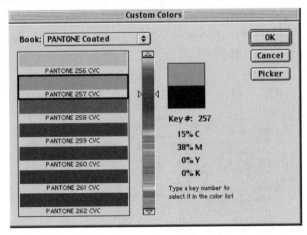

Figure 10.5 *Choosing custom colors*

Using Color Palettes

While the Color Picker displays all of the color characteristics and models in one integrated field, it is sometimes cumbersome to use because it is not *context-sensitive*. A context-sensitive palette will respond immediately to your commands without having to click an OK button. But the Color Picker must be displayed by clicking the foreground or background swatch. You must then choose a color model and a color. Finally, you must click OK. This process can be time-consuming because of the many steps involved. Instead, you may want to use the context-sensitive Color and Swatches palettes that conveniently float on the desktop.

The Color Palette

The Color palette (Figure 10.6) is in the same default palette cluster as the Swatches and Styles palettes. You can access it by choosing Window ➔ Show Color Palette (or by pressing the F6 function key). By default, the RGB color model is displayed, but you can choose HSB, Grayscale, CMYK, Lab, or Web Color sliders from the palette pull-down menu. Click a swatch in the upper-left corner of the palette to designate whether you want to affect the foreground or background color. The position of the sliders determines the color. By default, the sliders are *dynamic,* meaning that a gradient bar displays the selected color that corresponds to the position of the sliders. The Tool and Color palette swatches simultaneously change to indicate the color as you drag the slider. You can also enter specific values for each component of any color model in boxes to the right of the sliders.

Figure 10.6 *The Color palette*

The fastest way to select a color is to click or drag in the spectrum bar at the bottom of the Color palette to designate an approximate color. Release the mouse and the color will appear as the foreground color. Then move the sliders to tweak the color until you get exactly the color you want.

The Swatches Palette

To display individual swatches of color, choose the Swatches palette (Figure 10.7) from the palette cluster. Predefined colors can be chosen, or new colors can be added and saved.

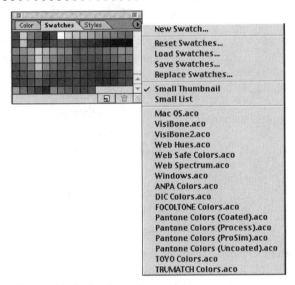

Figure 10.7 *The Swatches palette*

Swatches Technique	How to Do It
To Select a Foreground Color	Click it; the color will appear as the foreground swatch on the Tool palette.
To Select a Background Color	Press the Option (Mac) or Alt (Win) key while clicking the color.
To Add a Color	Place your cursor in the blank space below the color swatches. The cursor changes to a paint can. Click your mouse, name the color, and the foreground color will appear in the palette as a new swatch.

Swatches Technique	How to Do It
To Delete a Color	Press the Command (Mac) or Ctrl (Win) key and click the swatch. Or, Control-click (Mac) or right-click (Win) and select Delete Swatch from the shortcut menu.
To Save a Swatch Palette	Once you've added colors to the swatches, you may want to save the palette for use in other documents. From the Swatches palette menu, choose Save Swatches. Designate a folder in which to store your palette.
To Load Swatches	To access a saved palette, choose Load Swatches from the Swatches palette menu. (New Swatches palettes can also be loaded from the Preset Manager found in the Edit menu.) You can then access the swatch from the folder in which you saved it, or choose a specific palette like PANTONE, Focoltone, ANPA, or Web Safe Colors from the list.
To Reset Swatches	The Reset Swatches command on the palette menu restores the swatches to the Photoshop default palette.
To Name a Swatch	Color swatches can be named for identification. To name a swatch, double-click it and enter the name in the Swatch Name dialog box. Or Control-click (Mac) or right-click (Win) and select Name Swatch.

Sampling Colors

Foreground and background colors can be specified by sampling directly from the image. This is quite helpful if you want to match a color on the image. To sample a color, choose the Eyedropper from the Tool palette and click or drag across the image. As you drag, notice that the foreground swatch changes to the color the eyedropper is touching. To sample a background color, hold down the Option or Alt key as you click.

You can toggle from any painting tool, like the Paintbrush or Pencil, to the Eyedropper tool by pressing the Option or Alt key. As you drag, you will sample a foreground color.

Choose the Sample Size menu in the Eyedropper tool's Options bar to modify it to Point Sample (which picks up color from one pixel), a 3 By 3 Average (the average color of a square of nine pixels), or 5 By 5 Average (the average of a square of 25 pixels).

Creating Brushes

Photoshop provides you with many brushes that apply color to your image in a variety of ways. In addition, you can create new brushes and control their size, hardness, spacing, roundness, and angle. You can also make custom brushes in virtually any shape.

In Photoshop 6, the brushes are displayed on the left side of the Options bar of all of the painting and editing tools. To choose a brush, choose a painting tool, click the small arrow to the right of the Brush icon in the Options bar to expand the panel (Figure 10.8), and then click the desired icon. The currently loaded brushes are displayed as icons in a grid. The default brushes are ordered, with smallest and hardest on top to the largest and softest on the bottom. Each brush is displayed at actual size unless it is too big to fit in a grid, in which case it is displayed with a number that indicates its diameter in pixels.

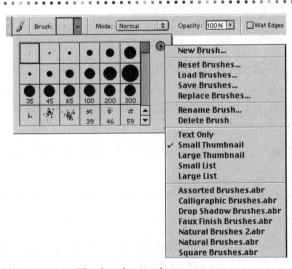

Figure 10.8 *The Brush panel*

From a pull-down menu on the expanded Brush panel, you can add new brushes to the palette, change the characteristics of existing brushes, and name brushes. As with Swatches, you can save and load brushes as well.

Make a New Brush

From the Brush pull-down menu, choose New Brush and a dialog appears (Figure 10.9). Adjust the following characteristics.

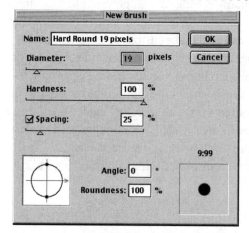

Figure 10.9 *The New Brush dialog box*

Diameter   determines the size of the brush, from 1 to 999 pixels. Higher resolution documents need larger brushes; for example, a 72 ppi brush on a 72 ppi document will paint a stroke 1 inch in diameter. The same brush will paint a half-inch stroke on a 144 ppi document.

Hardness   specifies the gradient transition of the edges of the brush, from 0% to 100%.

Spacing   affects how frequently the color is deposited as you drag, from 0% to 100%.

Roundness   affects the shape of the brush, from 0% (a line) to 100% (a full circle).

Angle   determines the angle of the brush stroke if you've modified its roundness so that it is elliptical. Angle values range from +180 degrees counterclockwise from horizontal to –180 degrees clockwise from horizontal.

You can enter a value in the Roundness or Angle fields or adjust the interactive icon at the bottom-left of the dialog. The field at the bottom-right displays an illustration of the brush. If the brush is larger than the field, the numbers displayed underneath indicate the zoom ratio at which the brush icon is displayed. The numbers displayed on the palette, however, indicate the brush diameter in pixels.

Modify an Existing Brush

If you wish to change the characteristics of an existing brush, click it in the Brush palette; its icon will appear in the Options bar. Now, click the Options bar icon to display the Brush Characteristics dialog box, which is similar to the New Brush dialog. Make the desired adjustments to the brush, then close the dialog by clicking the icon in the upper-left corner.

Create a Custom Brush

A brush of virtually any shape can be made from a selected piece of your image and later be used to clone an area of the image or paint it with a texture. The process of creating a custom brush has changed significantly in Photoshop 6 in that the brush shape now needs to be isolated on a separate layer.

To create a custom brush, follow these steps:

1. Select an area of an image. Choose Layer ➜ New ➜ Via Copy to isolate it to a transparent layer. (You can also paint on a new layer or copy and paste an image to a new layer.)

2. Choose Edit ➜ Define Brush. The Brush Name dialog box appears.

3. Name the brush and click OK. The New Brush dialog box appears. (No, you're not confused—naming the brush brings up the New Brush dialog, which also has a Name field. These could have been combined into one dialog box.)

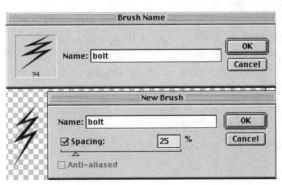

4.   Choose a desired spacing and click OK. The brush appears on the Brush palette.

5.   Choose a painting tool. Choose the custom brush from the Brush palette, choose a color, and paint with the brush. The brush image is the content of the entire layer.

Using the Painting and Editing Tools

The painting and editing tools are used to manually apply color or to modify an area of the image. With the exception of the Gradient and Paint Bucket tools, the painting tools rely on the motion of your hand to distribute the color or apply an effect. Each tool has its own unique set of characteristics. You can access the painting and editing tools by clicking them in the Tool palette or by pressing the appropriate letter key on the keyboard.

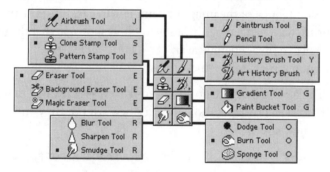

The Painting Tools

The painting tools include the Airbrush, Paintbrush, and Pencil; these tools are designed to simulate real studio painting techniques. In the color section, I've included finished examples of images using each technique for a side-by-side comparison— check those out, but to quickly compare the strokes made by the Paintbrush, Airbrush, and Pencil, look at Figure 10.10.

In Photoshop 6, you change the behavior of the painting tools by adjusting their characteristics in the Options bar. What follows is a description of each tool that uses a brush to manually affect the image.

Airbrush   Pencil

Paintbrush   Paintbrush with
                  Wet Edges

Figure 10.10 *Comparison of various painting-tool strokes*

Airbrush (shortcut key J)

Use the Airbrush to spray color. By placing your cursor on the image, clicking your mouse, and dragging, you can spray a pattern of color. If you drag slowly or stop dragging, the color will build up just like a real airbrush. You can adjust the pressure of the airbrush in the Options bar, which controls the amount of color that is deposited.

Paintbrush (B)

You apply color to the image with the Paintbrush by clicking your mouse button and dragging. By default, the stroke is a solid color. You can adjust the characteristics of the tool to alter the quality of the paint stroke.

Opacity   The transparency of the stroke is controlled with the opacity slider from 0% to 100%. When painted on a colored surface, the transparent or translucent stroke will reveal the pixels underneath it.

Wet Edges   This adjustment produces a watercolor stroke that looks as though the color is concentrated along its edges and translucent in its center.

Pencil (B)

The Pencil is the only tool that produces an aliased or hard-edged stroke. Use the Pencil to draw crisp horizontal or vertical lines or stair-stepped diagonals. Like the Paintbrush, you can adjust the opacity or assign a color mode to the stroke.

You can use the Pencil as an eraser by checking the Auto Erase box. If you start painting on an area containing the foreground color, the Auto Erase function replaces it with background color. If you start painting on an area containing any color other than the foreground color, the Pencil paints with the foreground color.

The Editing Tools

The editing tools include the Clone Stamp, Pattern Stamp, History Brush, Art History Brush, Eraser, Background Eraser, Magic Eraser, Blur, Sharpen, Smudge, Dodge, Burn, and Saturate tools. While the editing tools don't apply color directly to the image, they are essential for manipulating small regions within the image and modifying existing colors. Many of the editing tools have filter counterparts that produce the effect over larger areas, but the tools offer the dexterity and control of a hands-on operation. (For a demonstration of how some of the editing tools affect an image, see the Cardinal image in the color section).

Clone Stamp (shortcut key S)

Use the Clone Stamp to copy an area of the image and paint it elsewhere with a brush. The Clone Stamp is perfect for cloning textures from one small area of the image to another.

To clone an area, you must first sample it:

1. Choose the Clone Stamp from the Tool palette.

2. Choose an appropriate brush from the Brush menu on the Options bar.

3. Press the Option (Mac) or Alt (Win) key and click your mouse on the point that you want to copy.

4. Release your mouse and reposition the cursor where you want the sample to be painted.

5. Click your mouse and begin painting. As you paint, the tool will begin copying the point of the image that was sampled. A small cross will indicate the area that is being copied as you drag the brush across the image.

Check the Aligned option to maintain the alignment of the Clone Stamp brush with the original sampled area. Each time you release the mouse, move the brush, and resume cloning, the alignment will persist depending on where the brush is in relationship to the original sampled point (as seen in the middle image in Figure 10.11). If Aligned is unchecked, each time you click, you restart cloning from the original sample point as the source of the image.

Figure 10.11 *(left) An original image, with (center) aligned and (right) non-aligned clones*

If the Use All Layers option is checked, the Clone Stamp image is sampled from all of the visible layers. If it is unchecked, the image is sampled from only the targeted layer.

Pattern Stamp (S)

Use the Pattern Stamp to paint an area with a repeating pattern that you choose from the Pattern pull-down menu on the Options bar. Photoshop provides you with several default patterns in the list, or you can define your own (see "Creating Custom Patterns" later in the chapter.)

Check the Aligned option to maintain the alignment of the brush with the pattern. Each time you release the mouse, move the brush, and resume painting, the alignment of the pattern continues (Figure 10.12). If Aligned is unchecked, then each time you click, the center of the pattern tile will again be the source of the new image.

History Brush (Y)

The History Brush restores a portion of the image to a former state. Choose the History Brush and target a state in the History palette, choose a brush size, press the mouse and drag across the image. For more information about the History Brush, see Chapter 11.

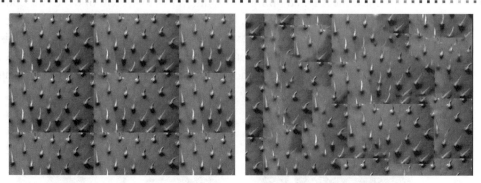

Figure 10.12 *The Pattern Stamp, with the Aligned option (left) checked and (right) unchecked*

Art History Brush (Y)

 This tool is quite handy for creating instant Impressionist effects (see the full-color copy of Figure 10.13 in the color section). Its behavior is really wild—like an industrial-strength smudge tool, paintbrush, and blur tool all in one. It paints with stroke clusters that vary in color depending on the color of the area you are painting on. When you paint with the Art History Brush, color is deposited rapidly in several directions. Choose from a list of characteristics in the Options bar that affect the style of the stroke and the rapidity in which it is deposited.

Style determines the size and shape of the strokes that are deposited. Choose from a list that includes Tight, Loose, Short, Long, Dabs, and Curls.

Fidelity is a percentage (from 0% to 100%) that affects the color of the stroke and how close it will be to the color on which you are painting. Higher values produce more monochromatic effects, and lower values produce more color variation.

Area determines how wide a region the strokes will be deposited over, from 0 to 500 pixels. Higher-resolution files need higher values.

Spacing controls the frequency (from 0% to 100%) at which the stroke is deposited as you drag. Dragging faster produces wider gaps between stroke clusters.

Figure 10.13 *The version on the right has been altered with the Art History Brush—Style: Tight Short, Fidelity: 100%, Area: 50 px, Spacing: 0.*

Eraser (E)

The Eraser performs differently depending on whether you're working on the Background or a layer. When working on the Background, the Eraser replaces the area with the background color in the Tool palette. When erasing to a layer, it replaces the layer content with transparency. If the transparency option on the layer is locked, then the pixels are replaced with the background color.

The Eraser offers four modes in which to work: Airbrush, Paintbrush, Pencil, or Block. The characteristics of each tool are inherent in the erasure. For example, if you choose the Wet Edges option in Paintbrush mode, the Eraser erases to a watercolor effect.

You can erase the image back to a History state by clicking the first column in the History palette to set a source and choosing the Erase To History option from the Options bar.

Background Eraser (E)

The Background Eraser tool is a combination of the Magic Wand tool and the Eraser, in that it lets you sample and set a tolerance to determine what range of color will be erased. You can also determine the sharpness of the remaining edges. The Background Eraser erases to transparency on a layer, or automatically converts the Background into a layer when applied there.

Erasing Modes   control what pixels will be erased. Choose:

Discontiguous   to erase all of the pixels within the Tolerance range on the entire layer.

Contiguous   to erase pixels of the sampled color that are adjacent to each other.

Find Edges   to erase pixels of the sampled color that are adjacent to each other but better preserve the sharpness of the edge pixels of the remaining image.

Tolerance   controls the range of colors to be erased. Low Tolerance erases colors that are similar to the sampled colors; high Tolerance erases to colors that are more diverse in range.

Sampling Option   determines the method in which the colors will be chosen:

Continuous   samples colors continuously as you drag, erasing areas of different colors.

Once   samples a color when you first click and then continues to erase only that color. Use this option to erase areas of solid color.

Background Swatch   erases areas that are the current background color.

Check the Protect Foreground box to ensure that areas of the foreground color are not erased.

Magic Eraser (E)

The Magic Eraser erases all pixels of similar color within the Tolerance range when you click the color you want to erase. It allows you isolate the erasure to specific colors.

Tolerance   in the Options bar controls the range of colors to be erased. Low Tolerance erases colors that are similar to the sampled colors; high Tolerance erases to colors that are more diverse in range.

Opacity   determines the strength of the erasure.

Contiguous   determines what pixels will be erased. When checked, you erase only *adjacent* pixels of the color. With Contiguous unchecked, the Magic Eraser erases all pixels of the color on the layer.

Use All Layers   determines where the information will be erased. With this option checked, the Magic Eraser erases through all of the visible layers; without this option, it erases only the pixels on the target layer.

Blur (R)

The Blur tool softens the region as you apply it by decreasing the relative contrast of adjacent pixels. Use it to blend colors and soften edges, or to reduce the focus of a background. Increase the Pressure setting in the Options bar to strengthen the effect.

Sharpen (R)

The Sharpen tool increases the relative contrast values of adjacent pixels. As you drag over an area, the pixels randomly change color. The more you drag, the more diverse the colors of the adjacent pixels become. Increase the Pressure setting in the Options bar to increase the intensity of the effect. Sharpening fools your eye into thinking an image is in focus. This tool can be used to enhance portions of an image that you want to emphasize, or as a quick fix for photographs that are slightly out of focus.

Smudge (R)

Use the Smudge tool to simulate charcoal or pastel effects. As you drag with the Smudge tool, you move one area of color into another while blending and mixing the colors as you move them.

Checking the Use All Layers option smudges areas of colors on different layers (otherwise, the Smudge tool only blends only areas on the targeted layer). If you check the Finger Painting box, you mix the current foreground color into the smudged area.

Dodge (O)

Dodging is a technique used by photographers in the darkroom to overexpose or lighten specific areas of an image. In Photoshop, the Dodge tool performs a similar function by increasing the brightness values of pixels as you paint with it. The Dodge tool's Options bar lets you concentrate the effect on a specific range of tonality by choosing Highlights, Midtones, or Shadows from the Range pull-down menu. Adjusting the Exposure will weaken or strengthen the effect.

Burn (O)

Photographers burn an image in the darkroom to underexpose or darken areas of an image. Photoshop's Burn tool darkens by lowering the brightness values of pixels as you move it over the image. As with the Dodge tool, the Options bar lets you pick a range of pixels to affect by choosing Highlights, Midtones, or Shadows from the menu. Again, adjusting the Exposure will weaken or strengthen the effect.

Sponge (O)

The Sponge tool changes the intensity as it touches pixels. From the Options bar, choose either Saturate to enhance a color or Desaturate to diminish the color and push it toward gray.

Using the Dodge, Burn, or Sponge tool at full strength can often be overpowering. When you use these tools, try lowering the Exposure or Pressure to between 5% and 20% and make multiple passes to gradually build up the effect.

Brush Dynamics

The behavior of all of the painting tools can be controlled from the Brush Dynamics menu on the right side of the Options bar. This control lets you fade, taper, or change the color of a stroke over a specified distance .

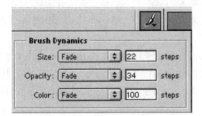

Choose from the following characteristics:

Size Specify a number of steps to gradually taper the thickness of the brush stroke until it disappears.

Opacity Set a number of steps to gradually fade the brush until it completely disappears.

Color Enter a number of steps to gradually fade the foreground color into the background color.

Color Blending Modes

Blending modes control the relation of the color that is being applied to the existing colors on the image. The Normal blending mode, at 100% opacity, applies the color as if it were painted straight out of a tube (subject to the settings of the particular brush being used, of course). Other blending modes produce less predictable results and require a bit of experimentation. For a complete list of blending mode characteristics, see Appendix C.

If the color that is painted with a brush tool looks peculiar, one of the first places to look to correct the problem is the Modes list in the tool's Options bar (also shown at the top of the Layers palette). Any mode other than Normal may affect the paint stroke with variety of unusual color combinations.

Painting Tool Shortcuts

Here are a couple of shortcuts that will increase your dexterity in handling the painting tools and performing tasks that would be otherwise impossible. For horizontal and vertical lines, press the Shift key as you drag up or down, left or right. For a straight line in any other direction, click and release your mouse, then move the cursor to a new location and Shift-click.

Making and Applying Gradients

In nature, we see countless variations of color that subtly blend into one another as light and shadow intermingle into dimensional forms. The ability to gradually blend colors is essential to the credibility of a realistic image. Photoshop gradients blend multiple colors into each other or into transparency over a specified distance.

Choosing Gradients

 Choose the Gradient tool from the Tool palette and notice how the Options bar configures itself. At the far left is a preview bar, or *gradient swatch,* with a down-arrow; clicking in this swatch calls up the Gradient Editor, while clicking the arrow pops up a simpler Gradient Picker panel. Both display all saved gradients, beginning with the several pre-installed gradients. The default gradient creates a fill that blends from the foreground color to the background color. Another gradient, called Foreground to Transparent, fills from the current foreground color to transparency. Use it to gradually fade a single color or multiple colors. You can choose from the gradients on the default list that comes with Photoshop, and you can create new ones.

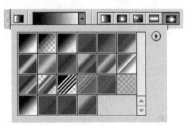

If you click the arrow at the upper-right of the Gradient Picker pop-up panel, you will display the Gradient Options pull-down menu. The first group of commands on this menu let you reset, load, save, or replace gradients. The second group displays different ways of viewing the gradients in the menu, either by thumbnail or by name. At the bottom of the menu is a list of additional pre-made Photoshop gradients.

On the Options bar, to the right of the gradient swatch, are icons for the five gradient types, which blend the color in unique ways (demonstrated in Figure 10.14). Choose one to indicate in what direction you want your gradient built.

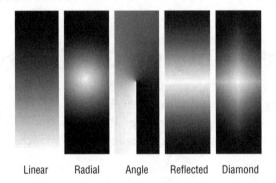

| Linear | Radial | Angle | Reflected | Diamond |

Figure 10.14 *The gradient types*

Gradient Type	Effect
Linear	Applies a continual gradient over a specified distance from beginning point to end point.
Radial	Radiates around a center point to its end point.

Gradient Type	Effect
Angle	Radiates counterclockwise around a center point.
Reflected	Creates two linear gradients on each side of a center point.
Diamond	Radiates from a center point into a diamond blend.

Making Custom Gradients

Use the Gradient Editor to edit existing gradients or make new custom gradients and add them to the list. You can also save and load entire gradient palettes from the Gradient Editor or from the Preset Manager.

Call up the Gradient Editor (Figure 10.15) by clicking the gradient swatch in the Options bar. Click a gradient in the Presets list to select it. The gradient preview bar shows the gradient's colors, their proportional distribution, and the position of any transparency. These characteristics can be edited.

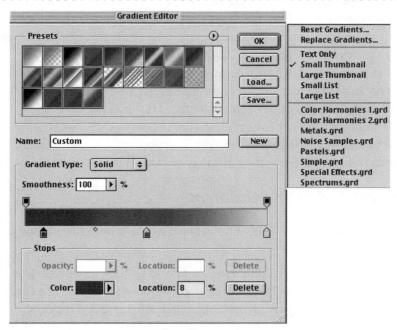

Figure 10.15 *The Gradient Editor*

Editing Gradient Color

The house-shaped markers along the *bottom* of the color bar are *color stops,* used to determine where a solid color ends and where a gradient begins. You can assign a color to a color stop by clicking it to highlight it. Move the cursor off the Gradient Editor and onto the image, the Color palette, or the Swatches palette to sample a color. Another method of choosing a color is to double-click the Color swatch in the Stops area; the Color Picker will be displayed. To redefine a stop's location, drag it left or right or set a value in the Location field as a percentage of the gradient's length.

The small diamond under the preview bar marks the *midpoint* of the transition between the two colors that are being blended. Move it to redistribute the relative color proportions of the gradient.

To add a color to a gradient, click underneath the preview bar and a new color stop will appear. Determine a color for the color stop, drag the stop into position, and adjust the color's midpoint. To delete a color, drag its color stop off the Gradient Editor.

Editing Gradient Transparency

The house-shaped markers along the *top* of the gradient preview bar determine where transparency ends and where it begins. To blend transparency into the gradient, click a transparency stop and enter a percentage value in the Opacity field. Drag a stop to determine its location, or enter a number in the Stops area.

If transparency is set anywhere along the gradient, a diamond on top of the pre-view bar marks the center point of the transparency range. Move the midpoint to redistribute the proportion of transparency in the gradient.

To add transparency to a gradient, click above the color bar. Determine an opacity value in the Opacity field, move the stop into position, and adjust its midpoint. To delete a transparency, drag the transparency stop off the Gradient Editor.

Editing an Existing Gradient

1. Choose the Gradient tool and click the gradient swatch on the Options bar to display the Gradient Editor.

2. At the top of the Editor is a list of Presets—the gradients that have already been saved. Double-click the gradient you want to edit. The Gradient Name dialog box appears. If desired, enter a new name and click OK.

3. On the preview bar in the Gradient Editor, you see the configuration of color and transparency of the selected gradient as determined by the number and

position of the color and transparency stops and the midpoint diamonds. Slide the stops to the left or right to adjust the color or transparency proportions. Slide the midpoint diamonds to adjust the centers of the blend.

4. Add a color by clicking under the preview bar to create a new stop.

5. Double-click the stop to display the Color Picker. Choose a color for the stop and click OK.

6. When satisfied with the edited gradient, click OK to leave the Gradient Editor. The edited gradient now appears in the Options bar.

7. Choose a Gradient tool, click in the image, and drag. Release the mouse to apply the gradient.

Making a Noise Gradient

The Noise option under Gradient Type in the Gradient Editor adds random colors to a gradient depending on the predefined colors you choose. The results can be somewhat unpredictable, so experiment to achieve the best results. To create a noise gradient:

1. In the Gradient Editor, under Gradient Type, choose Noise.

2. For Roughness, choose or enter a percentage. This will determine the strength of the noise.

3. Choose a color mode or model—RGB, HSB, or Lab. The effect will vary significantly with each system.

4. Check Restrict Colors to prevent oversaturation.

5. Check Add Transparency to create a transparent gradient.

6. Click Randomize to preview variations of the effect.

Creating a New Gradient

1. Click the gradient swatch on the Options bar to display the Gradient Editor.

2. Click the New button. The Name field displays the name of the currently selected gradient, and the preview bar displays its properties.

3. Enter a name for the new gradient.

It's easy to be thrown by the fact that the name and properties of the of new gradient are the same as the current gradient. It's important to change the name immediately to avoid confusion.

4. Target each of the color or transparency stops and change their colors and locations as described under "Editing an Existing Gradient."

5. Add color or transparency stops if desired by clicking under or over the preview bar.

6. Click OK to finalize the gradient and to select it into the gradient swatch.

Applying Gradients

All gradients are applied over a specified distance (see Figure 10.16). You choose the Gradient tool, click the image where you want the gradient to start, and drag in the desired direction. Release the mouse where you want the gradient to end. You will fill a selection if one is active, or the entire Background or layer if no selection is active. The distribution of the gradient depends on its color content and the position of the stops, but just as important are the placement of the cursor and the length and direction you drag on the image.

Figure 10.16 *Applying a gradient includes choosing its direction.*

Press the Shift key while dragging to constrain the gradient to a vertical, horizontal, or 45-degree angle.

Creating Patterns

A selection can be filled with a repeating pattern. A pattern can be any image contained within a rectangle, or *tile*, that defines its top, bottom, left, and right edges.

To create a pattern in Photoshop:

1. Select an area on an image using the rectangular marquee.

2. Choose Edit ➜ Define Pattern.

 The rectangular marquee must have a feather radius of zero pixels. In other words, it cannot have a feathered edge. It can, however have an anti-aliased edge. If you select an area on the image and you find that the Define Pattern command is grayed out in the Edit menu, check the Rectangular Marquee's Options bar to be sure that the Feather Radius reads 0px.

3. If you look in Edit ➜ Preset Manager ➜ Preset Type ➜ Pattern, you'll see that the pattern has been added to the list.

Patterns are applied to the image with the Pattern Stamp, with the Fill command, with the Paint Bucket, or as a Pattern Fill layer (see the sections on these features elsewhere in this chapter).

Filling and Stroking

You may find it difficult or time-consuming to paint large areas of the image, and impossible to paint the outline of a shape. Photoshop provides several alternatives that automatically perform these tasks.

The Fill Command

Filling an area changes its pixels to a designated color.

1. Before an area can be filled, it must first be selected. Make an accurate selection with any of the selection tools to define the area. If the selection is feathered, the area that is filled will have a soft edge.

2. Choose Edit ➜ Fill. The Fill dialog box is displayed (Figure 10.17).

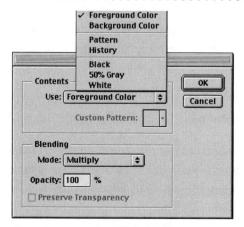

Figure 10.17 *The Fill dialog box*

3. From the Use pop-up list, choose a color or method to fill your selection:

Color or Method	Effect
Foreground Color	Fills the selected area with 100% of the current foreground color
Background Color	Fills the selected area with 100% of the current background color.
Pattern	Fills the selected area with a pattern chosen from the Pattern menu.
History	Fills the selected area with a selected state in the History palette (see Chapter 11).
Black	Fills the selected area with 100% black or an RGB value of 0 red, 0 green, 0 blue.
50% Gray	Fills the selected area with 50% black or an RGB value of 127 red, 127 green, 127 blue.
White	Fills the selected area with 0% black or an RGB value of 255 red, 255 green, 255 blue.

4. Choose a Blending Mode and Opacity. (See Appendix C for details on blending modes.)

5. If you are filling a layer, you can choose to preserve the transparent areas and fill only the areas that contain pixels.

6. Click OK.

A fast method of filling an area with 100% of the foreground color is to press Option+Delete (Mac) or Alt+Backspace (Win).

To fill an area selected on the Background with 100% of the background color, press Delete or Backspace.

The Paint Bucket (shortcut key G)

The Paint Bucket tool is a combination of the Magic Wand tool and the Fill command, in that it will fill an area with color based on the tolerance, or range of color, of the target pixels.

To fill with the Paint Bucket:

1. Expand the Gradient tool in the Tool palette and choose the Paint Bucket.

2. In the Options bar, choose the type of fill, either the foreground color or a pattern. If filling with a color, choose a foreground color from the Color palette, Swatches palette, or Color Picker.

3. Set the Blending Mode and Opacity for the fill.

4. Set the Tolerance to determine the range of adjacent pixels to be colored. Higher tolerances color a wider range of pixels.

5. If you only want adjacent pixels to be colored, check the Contiguous box. If the box is unchecked, all of the pixels within the tolerance on a targeted layer will be affected.

6. Check the Anti-Aliased box if you want the fill to extend into the edge pixels of the selection or image.

7. Check the All Layers box if you want the tolerance measured and the fill applied through multiple layers.

8. Place your cursor on the area you want to affect and click your mouse.

Fill Layers

New to Photoshop 6 is another unique method filling an area, called a Fill layer. Fill layers are more dynamic than the traditional methods of filling large areas of color, because they combine potential of the Fill command with the flexibility of layers. You can create Fill layers with colors, gradients, or patterns (Figure 10.18).

Figure 10.18 *(left to right) Color, Gradient, and Pattern Fill layers*

Creating a Solid Color Fill Layer

1. Choose Layer ➜ New Fill Layer ➜ Solid Color.

2. The New Layer dialog box appears, with the layer named Color Fill 1 by default. Enter a name for the layer to better identify it and click OK. As with any layer, you can group the Fill layer with the one immediately above it, forming a clipping group. Choose a color from the list if you want to color-code it, an opacity, and a blending mode.

3. The Color Picker is displayed. Choose a color and click OK.

4. The new layer that appears in the Layers palette has a layer mask linked to it, represented by the thumbnail to the left of the layer name (as seen in Figure 10.18). A layer mask enables you to conceal portions of the image by painting on it.

If you make a selection prior to creating a Fill layer, the new Fill layer will fill only the selected area and create a layer mask that conceals the unselected areas. The layer mask thumbnail that appears in the Layers palette displays the revealed area as a white shape and the masked area as a black border.

See Chapter 7, "Layering Your Image," and Chapter 20, "Advanced Layer Techniques," for more on how to manipulate Fill layers.

Creating a Gradient Fill Layer

1. Choose Layer ➜ New Fill Layer ➜ Gradient.

2. The New Layer dialog box appears. The name of the new layer defaults to Gradient Fill 1. Enter a name for the layer to better identify it. Click OK; the Gradient Fill dialog box appears.

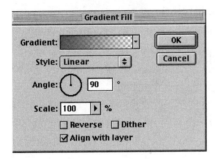

3. The colors of the gradient default to the last gradient chosen. If you want a gradient other than the one presented, click the down-arrow to the right of the Gradient swatch to choose a saved gradient, or click the swatch itself to display the Gradient Editor and create a new one. In the Gradient Fill dialog, set the following specifications:

   Style Choose a gradient type from the Style pop-up list.

   Angle Enter a number, or click the diagram, to choose an angle to control the direction of the gradient.

   Scale Choose a scale by clicking on the arrow and moving the slider or entering a value, to control the gradient's relative distribution over an area.

   Reverse Check Reverse to flip the gradient's direction over the entire layer.

   Dither Check Dither to soften the blending of the gradient. Dithering may help prevent banding that sometimes occurs when the Gradient is printed.

Align With Layer   If the gradient is contained within a selection, check Align With Layer to distribute the gradient over the entire layer but reveal only the selected portion.

4. Click OK to fill the layer.

Creating a Pattern Fill Layer

1. Choose Layer ➜ New Fill Layer ➜ Pattern.

2. The New Layer dialog box appears, with the layer named Pattern Fill 1 by default. Enter a name for the layer to better identify it and click OK; the Pattern Fill dialog box appears.

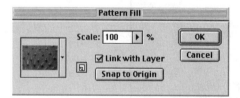

3. Click the down-arrow to choose a pattern, and set the following options:

Scale   Choose a scale to determine the size of the pattern.

Snap To Origin   You can move the pattern by placing your cursor on it on the image window, or you can snap it back to its origin by clicking the Snap To Origin button.

Link With Layer   Checking this box aligns the pattern's layer mask to the layer.

Create A New Preset From This Pattern   Click the small document icon to save the pattern to the Presets.

Once they have been created, Color Fill, Gradient Fill, and Pattern Fill layers can be edited by double-clicking their thumbnails in the Layers palette to reveal the Color Picker, the Gradient Fill dialog, or the Pattern Fill dialog, respectively.

Stroking

The Stroke command in Photoshop outlines a selection border with a color. Strokes can vary in width and relative position on the selection border, as you can see in Figure 10.19. A feathered selection will soften the edge of the stroke.

Stroke Inside

Stroke Outside

Stroke Center

Feathered

Figure 10.19 *You can position your stroke in different places relative to the selection.*

To apply a stroke to a selection:

1. Make a selection with any of the selection tools.

2. Choose a foreground color.

3. Choose Edit ➜ Stroke. The Stroke dialog box appears (Figure 10.20).

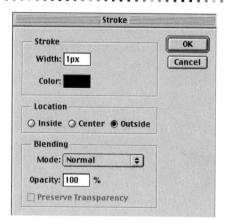

Figure 10.20 *The Stroke dialog box*

4. Set the following attributes:

    Width   Enter a value in pixels for the stroke width between 1 and 250 pixels.

    Color   Click the swatch to reveal the Color Picker. Choose a stroke color and click OK.

    Location   Inside places the stroke on the inside of the selection outline. The Center option centers the stroke between the inside and the outside of the selection outline. Outside places the stroke on the outside of the selection outline.

    Blending Mode   Choose a blending mode from the pop-up list to affect the relationship of the color that is being applied to the existing colors on the image. (See Appendix C, "Blending Modes.")

    Opacity   Set the Opacity from 1% to 100%.

    Preserve Transparency   If the image is on a layer surrounded by transparency, checking the Preserve Transparency option will prevent the transparent area from being stroked.

5. Click OK to apply the stroke.

Up Next

As you can see, Photoshop 6 can do more with color than ever before. You can paint with up to almost 17 million different colors and apply color with any conceivable size or shaped brush. The addition of Fill layers, the new Pattern interface, and the Shape tools have increased Photoshop's capabilities as a paint program.

In the next chapter, we'll work with Photoshop's built-in time machine—the History palette—and see how it facilitates the creative process. In essence, you'll learn to move back and forth in time, stop at any point, and develop your image into multiple versions. The Hands-On project following Chapter 11 combines the painting features you read about in this chapter, and the path features covered previously, with the History operations as you push the artistic envelope to create a digital work of art.

Altered States: History

PHOTOSHOP

Chapter 11

I like to call Photoshop the "bachelor's software." Why? Because as we've seen, using layers and saving selections to alpha channels during the editing process keeps the image dynamic. As you continue to work, you can make changes to the image at any time. In other words, you *never have to make a commitment*—that is, until you finally settle down and publish your work.

Photoshop takes the concept of the bachelor's software to the max with the extreme flexibility of its History palette. The History palette is Photoshop's answer to the concept of multiple undos. Where some programs provide a system of undoing operations backwards in sequence, Photoshop's interactive History palette features sequential and nonlinear editing.

This chapter explores Photoshop's undo and history features. In addition, the Hands-On section that follows will put you through the moves on the information covered in Chapters 9 and 10 on history, paths, and painting.

In this chapter, you'll learn about:

- Undoing what you've done

- Photoshop's Time Machine

- Working with snapshots

- Editing history

Undoing What You've Done

It's almost impossible to make a mistake in Photoshop, because Photoshop can instantly undo errors. You don't have to ever compromise, because you can reverse any operation. With this in mind, you can feel confident to experiment freely with your images.

The Undo Commands

There are several techniques that reverse unwanted edits. Let's say you are carefully cloning out the blemishes on Uncle Herman's portrait. You've drunk too many double espressos, and your hand is a bit jittery. You slip, you drag a little too far, and you place a big wart on the tip of his nose.

An easily corrected mistake? Yes! The first course of action is to head straight to the top of the Edit menu and select Undo, which will instantly revert the image to the moment before you made the fateful clone stroke. When you order Undo, you get a new command on the Edit menu, Redo, which restores the undone action. You can toggle back and forth between the previous artwork (Undo) and the later look (Redo) by selecting the command again, or better yet, use the key commands in the list below.

Photoshop 6 takes the Undo command a step further than previous versions by adding two additional commands to the Undo operations:

Step Backward   This undoes the last command and then continues in a backward sequence through the operations you've performed, undoing them one at a time. As the operations are undone, you see them disappear one by one in the image window.

Step Forward   If you've applied the Step Backward command more than once, you can restore the undone operations by choosing Edit ➜ Step Forward. As the operations are redone, you see them appear one by one in the image window.

You'll use these operations so frequently that it's worth remembering their corresponding key commands:

Command	Windows	Macintosh
Undo	Ctrl+Z	Command+Z
Step Backward	Ctrl+Alt+Z	Command+Option+Z
Step Forward	Shift+Ctrl+Z	Shift+Command+Z

New

As you apply them, the Step Backward and Step Forward commands move one by one through the state list in the History palette. See "The History Palette" later in this chapter.

Begin Again

Another lifesaving operation reverts the image to the last time you saved it. Suppose you've been working on an image for ten minutes since your last Save, and you decide that somewhere along the line you went astray and the image is not going in the direction you want it to. You have gone too far to make corrections, so you decide you want to begin again. Choose File ➜ Revert, and the image will be reopened to the last saved version.

Photoshop's Time Machine

The *history* of a Photoshop image is simply a record of work that has been performed on it. Photoshop automatically records every edit, operation, or technique that you apply to an image. As you work, each event, called a *state*—whether it's a paint stroke, filter, color correction, or any other operation—is listed in the History palette (Figure 11.1). You can target a specific state on the list and display its contents in the image window. Like riding in a H.G. Wells time machine, you can freely move through the history of the document, alter states, and in so doing affect the outcome of the final image.

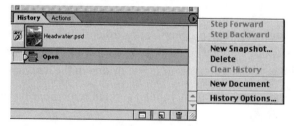

Figure 11.1 *The opening History palette: nothing has been done yet.*

The History states are not layers. They don't contain isolated parts of the image per se. Rather, each state is a record of how the image looked after a specific tool or operation was applied to it. The history is exclusively a record of the changes to the image during the current work session. Once the image is closed, the history is wiped clean, and when you reopen the document, the history begins again. The history cannot be saved or transferred to another image. Program changes to preferences, palettes, color settings, and Actions are not recorded.

The History Palette

The recorder for all of the states is the History palette, which you access by choosing Window ➜ Show History. By default, when the image is opened, the History palette displays a snapshot. The opening snapshot is a picture of the image as it appeared when it was last saved. It is from this point on where you will make changes to the image. Each time you perform an operation, the History palette produces a state with the name of the operation or tool that was used—for example, Paintbrush, Levels, Smudge Tool, etc. The most recent state is at the bottom of the History stack; note that in Figure 11.2, opening the document is at the top. The higher the state appears in the stack, the earlier in the process the state was made.

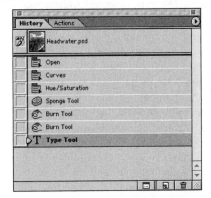

Figure 11.2 *The History palette after a few operations*

Changing History

They say you can't change history, but in fact, you can. If you want to move backward in time and see a previous state, click it in the History palette. The image window will display the image as it was during the targeted state. All states below it in the History palette are grayed out.

Be careful! If you work on the image with a state targeted earlier than the most recent, all states below it will be deleted.

For example, if you paint a brushstroke with the Paintbrush on an early state, all states below it will be replaced by one state called Paintbrush. Later I'll show you how to avoid this by using the Non-Linear History option.

Increasing History States

What allows Photoshop to remember all of the History states is, of course, memory. Each state is stored in your computer's RAM or on the scratch disk. When you exceed the current limit on states, the oldest state is deleted to make room for the most recent state. The number of History states is limited to 20 by default. You can increase or decrease the default number of History states by selecting Edit ➜ Preferences ➜ General ➜ History States and entering a number from 1 to 100.

Specifying an excessive number of History states earmarks memory for the History cache and takes the allocation away from Photoshop's other operations. This could compromise Photoshop's performance. Whenever possible, keep the number of states at the default.

Looking at History Options

You can change the behavior of the history by checking options in the History Options window. In the History palette pull-down menu, choose History Options to view or change these settings:

Automatically Create First Snapshot   preserves a snapshot of the original image upon opening it and places its thumbnail at the top of the History palette (see the next section, "Working with Snapshots").

Automatically Create New Snapshot When Saving   generates a snapshot of the current state when saving and adds its thumbnail to the top of the History palette.

Allow Non-Linear History   allows you to discard or edit a previous History state without deleting more recent states.

Show New Snapshot Dialog By Default   automatically displays the Snapshot dialog box when a new snapshot is created.

Working with Snapshots

At any point in time, you can save the current image to a snapshot (see Figure 11.3). By saving a snapshot, you can explicitly preserve various states of the image. Snapshots don't count toward the History state limit; they're saved, period, and you don't have to worry about that state being discarded when the limit is exceeded. But of course, they use up memory and, like the rest of the history, are discarded when the file is closed.

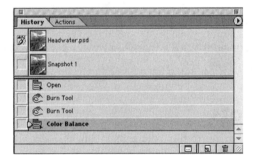

Figure 11.3 *History palette with a snapshot*

Saving Snapshots

Click the History palette pull-down menu and choose New Snapshot. The dialog box that appears allows you to name the snapshot and determine which combination of layers the snapshot will be made from.

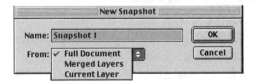

Full Document   makes a snapshot of all the visible layers and the Background.

Merged Layers   makes a snapshot of all the layers and merges them into one layer.

Current Layer   makes a snapshot of the currently targeted layer.

 A fast way to make a snapshot is to target a history state and click the Create New Snapshot icon at the bottom of the History palette.

Saving a Snapshot as a New Document

If you want to work on multiple versions of the image or preserve it in a particular state, you can save a snapshot as a new document.

1. Save the History state as a snapshot.

2   Target the snapshot in the History palette and choose New Document from the pull-down menu.

3. Choose File ➜ Save As and save the document to a location on your disk.

You can quickly make a new document from a snapshot by dragging the state to the Create New Document From Current State icon.

Deleting Snapshots

When you no longer need them, you can discard your snapshots. Here are several ways to do it.

*   Drag the snapshot to the trash icon in the lower-right corner of the History palette.

*   Click the snapshot and choose Delete from the History palette pull-down menu.

*   Click the snapshot and then click the trash icon.

Editing History States

The primary purpose of Photoshop's history is to keep the editing process dynamic. There are several ways to use the History palette to keep the workflow flexible so that you can experiment freely and confidently.

For all history operations, to target a state, click it in the History palette.

Deleting History States

Sometimes you'll want to delete a state. Try any of these commands.

- Drag the state to the trash icon at the bottom of the History palette.
- Target the state, then choose Delete from the palette pull-down menu or click the trash icon.
- Target a state. All states beneath it will be grayed out. Perform an edit to the state and the grayed out states will be purged.
- Choose Clear History from the palette menu to clear all of the states. Clearing the history retains the snapshots.
- Choose Edit ➜ Purge ➜ Histories. All the states but the one at the bottom of the list will be deleted. The snapshots are retained.

Non-Linear History

If you do delete a state, then by default, you'll also eliminate all of the states underneath it. You can, however, change the default. From the History palette pull-down menu, choose History Options and check Allow Non-Linear History.

The Allow Non-Linear History option gives you the ability to eliminate or edit a state in the History palette and still preserve all of the states below it in the stack. For example, you can target a state, make changes to it, save the altered state as a snapshot, target the most recent state and continue working on the image. Experiment carefully with this option, because you can produce strange and unexpected results.

The History Brush

The History Brush tool enables you to delete portions of a state. You use the History Brush to restore parts of the image back to a prior event. You can erase portions of a state even if you've edited them later on or painted over them. The Source column at the far left of the History palette tells Photoshop which state you want to return to.

For example, suppose you paint a brush stroke on an image. As you continue to work, each time you perform an operation, a new state is added. If you later decide that you only want to retain half of a brush stroke, here's how to do it:

1. Open the History palette.

2. Click the states from bottom to top in sequence, until you determine the state where you made the brushstroke. (As you click through the history, the brush stroke will suddenly appear within the image.)

3. Click the Source column to the left of the *previous* state, just above the state with the brush stroke. A History Brush icon appears in that column.

By choosing the previous state as the Source, you are telling the History palette that this is what you want the erased portions of the image to look like. You are actually painting with the previous state in order to eliminate the portion of the brushstroke.

4. Choose the History Brush from the Tool palette and retarget the most recent state.

If the Allow Non-Linear History option is not selected, you must target the last state in the history if you want to avoid losing the intervening states.

5. Paint on the portion of the brush stroke you want to eliminate.

The Art History Brush

It's called the Art History Brush because it's quite handy for creating instant Impressionist effects (Impressionism being an important movement in the history of art). And I mention it here only because it is in the History Brush flyout on the Tool palette. But it does *not* use the history to alter the image as the History Brush does, except, like any other tool or operation, its effects are recorded as a state each time you apply it. (See Chapter 10 for a complete description of the Art History Brush tool, and see Figure 10.13 for a demonstration of what it can do.)

Painting with a Snapshot

You can use a snapshot in a similar manner as using the History Brush. Suppose you take a snapshot of an edit you made with a filter. After undoing the filter or eliminating its state, you can selectively apply the snapshot to specific portions of the image. If you save the snapshot as the full document or a single layer, the History Brush will paint from one layer to the corresponding layer on the targeted state. (The color section of the book includes a demonstration of painting with the History Brush.)

To paint with a snapshot:

1. Apply a filter, brush stroke, color adjustment, or any other effect to the image.

2. Choose Make Snapshot from the History palette pull-down menu.

3. Choose Edit ➜ Undo to undo the effect.

4. Click the Source column next to the new snapshot.

5. Choose the History Brush from the Tool palette. Choose a brush size and specify opacity and other brush characteristics in the Options bar.

6. Paint on the areas of the image that you want to affect.

Other History-Editing Features

There are a couple of history-editing features scattered throughout the program that you should be aware of.

The Eraser Tool   With the Erase to History option selected, the Eraser tool erases to a designated History state. You must designate the History state by clicking the Source column in the History palette next to the state you wish to erase to.

Fill From History   Choose Edit ➜ Fill ➜ Use History to fill a selected area with a designated state. You must designate the History state by clicking the Source column in the History palette next to the state you wish to fill with.

Up Next

You're ready for a Hands-On exercise that involves several skills. The following project will provide practice on everything covered in Chapters 9, 10, and 11: making and editing paths and shapes, using the painting tools, and taking advantage of Photoshop's history features. You'll work on an illustration for a children's book and discover how easy it is to apply color, patterns, and shapes to an image.

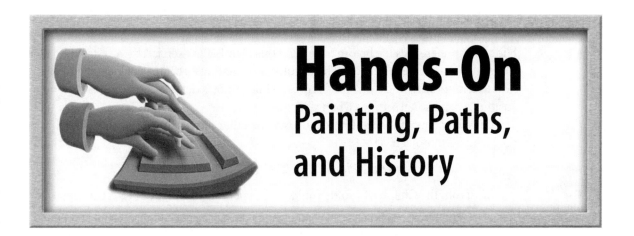

Hands-On
Painting, Paths, and History

It is rare, when working on any Photoshop document, that you exclusively use one particular tool or technique to accomplish a task. Even images that are painted work best if you separate parts of the image to layers, use paths, and make and save selections to alpha channels. If you make a mistake or want to experiment, you can use the History palette to revert to an earlier state or a saved snapshot.

This is a lesson on combining these Photoshop techniques. You will use a variety of techniques covered in Chapters 9, 10, and 11 to color an illustration for a children's book.

Getting Started

Hide your preferences file before beginning this Hands-On exercise, then restart Photoshop to create a clean version. The "Photoshop's Settings" section in Chapter 5 details how to temporarily reset your preferences to Photoshop's defaults. You can restore your customized, personal settings when you're done.

Once you have launched Photoshop with default preferences, here's how to begin the Hands-On project:

1. Insert the *Mastering Photoshop 6* CD in your CD-ROM drive.

2. From the Chapter 11 folder on the CD, open the file `Headville_start.psd` (see Figure 1).

To preview the completed image (Figure 2), see the picture presented in the color section, or in the `Ch11` *folder on the CD as* `Headville_end1.tif`.

3. Choose File ➜ Save As and save the file to your disk.

Figure 1 *The beginning Headville children's book project; you should have the Outline layer visible and the Painting layer targeted.*

Figure 2 *A painted version of Headville*

The Layers palette consists of a Background and two layers. The Outline layer contains a black outline of the image; the Painting layer is empty.

You will be performing most of your painting tasks on the Painting layer. The Outline layer will remain mostly unchanged throughout the editing process. It is important that the Outline layer remains higher in the layer stack than the Painting layer, because you will use Outline to determine where to apply color. The Painting layer will be the target layer, so be sure it is highlighted in the Layers palette.

Painting the Landscape

Painting the Roadway

1. Conceal the Background by clicking its eye icon in the Layers palette.

2. Target the Painting layer.

3. Choose Window ➜ Show Swatches and choose a light beige or pink color.

4. Choose the Paintbrush, and a small brush from the Options bar. Paint the top part of the road. As you paint wider areas, choose larger brushes from the Options bar. Stay loose and don't worry too much about going outside the lines.

5. If you make a major mistake, choose Window ➜ Show History and click a state higher in the stack to undo it, as in Figure 3.

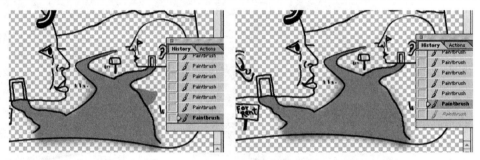

Figure 3 *Correcting a mistake with the History palette*

6. Choose a lighter color of pink, yellow, or beige, and scribble some broad lines with a fairly wide brush on the road.

7. Choose the Smudge tool and smudge the colors together.

8. From the Swatches palette, choose a dark blue color. Choose the Airbrush and a medium brush. Set the Pressure to 15 and spray a light mist along the left edges of the roads and paths to create a shadow (see Figure 4).

Any time you make a mistake or don't like the result of an operation, click a step back in the History palette to restore the image to a previous state.

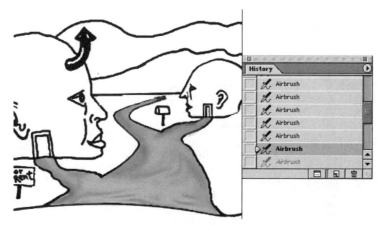

Figure 4 *The road painted with the Airbrush and a correction in the History palette*

Defining and Applying a Brick Pattern

1. Open the document Brick_Pattern.psd on the CD.

2. Choose Select → All.

3. Choose Edit → Define Pattern. The Pattern window appears.

4. Name the pattern Brick.

5. Click the Headville image to activate it.

6. Target the Outline layer by clicking its name in the Layers palette.

7. Choose the Magic Wand tool. In the Options bar, set the Tolerance to 20. Click inside the large head to select it. Press the Shift key and click inside the lips to add them to the selection.

8. Target the Painting layer.

9. Choose Edit → Fill → Pattern (Figure 5). Choose the Brick pattern from the list.

10. Click OK to fill the head with the pattern. Your image should look like Figure 6.

11. Press Cmd/Ctrl+D to deselect and Cmd/Ctrl+S to save the file.

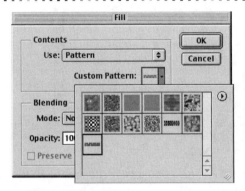

Figure 5 *Choose the brick pattern to Fill with.*

Figure 6 *The filled head*

Creating a Pattern Fill Layer

Because we want to proportionately reduce the size of the pattern when we fill the small head, we will use a pattern fill layer.

1. Target the Outline layer.

2. Choose the Magic Wand. In the Options bar, set the Tolerance to 20. Click inside the small head to select it.

3. Choose Layer → New Fill Layer → Pattern. The New Layer window appears.

4. In the New Layer window, name the layer Brick. Click OK.

5. In the Pattern Fill dialog box, enter a Scale of 50%. Click OK.

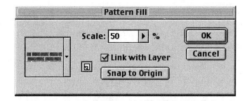

6. Press Cmd/Ctrl+D to deselect.

7. Target the Painting layer. Link the Brick layer and the Painting layer by clicking the second column in the Layers palette next to each of their thumbnails. From the Layers pull-down menu, choose Merge Layers.

Modeling the Heads

To give the heads a little more presence, add a shadow to their left sides.

1. Target the Painting layer.

2. Choose the Burn tool in the Tool palette, and set the Exposure to 15. Choose a large, soft brush and drag over the left side of the large head until it darkens. Don't darken it too much—just enough to give it a rounded look. Do the same to the left side of the small head.

3. Choose the Paintbrush from the Tool palette. Paint the details of the image— the window, doors, For Rent sign, and mailbox. Choose whatever colors appeal to you.

Painting the Horizon Line with the Pencil

1. Target the Outline layer.

2. Press the D key to restore the color swatches in the Tool palette to their black and white defaults.

3. Choose the Pencil tool. Place your cursor on the end of the left horizon line where it is broken and click once.

4. Place your cursor on the right horizon line. Press the Shift key and click once to connect the line, as in Figure 7.

5. Save the file.

Figure 7 *The horizon line*

Painting the Hills and Mountains

1. Choose the Paintbrush and a fairly large brush from Brush menu. On the Options bar, check Wet Edges.

2. Choose a light color from the Swatches palette, like yellow, tan, or green, and paint the front hills loosely to produce a watercolor effect. Choose a darker blue color and paint the mountains in the same manner. Multiple passes enhance the effect (you can look ahead to Figure 8 to see how I've done it).

 Remember, any time you make a mistake or don't like the result of an operation, click a few steps back in the History palette to restore the image to a previous state.

Filling the Tree with Color

1. Choose the Magic Wand tool. Set the Tolerance to 20 in the Options bar.

2. Target the Outline layer.

3. Click inside the tree trunk.

4. Choose a brown color from the Swatches palette.

5. Display the Color palette (Window ➜ Color, or click the title tab of the Color palette wherever it is).

6. Move the sliders to get the exact shade of brown you want.

7. Target the Painting layer.

8. Press Option+Delete or Alt+Backspace to fill the selected area with color.

9. Press Cmd/Ctrl+D to deselect.

10. Repeat steps 2 through 8, this time using green for the leaves of the tree.

11. When the top part of the tree is filled, make several passes on the tree with the Airbrush at a low pressure, using a dark shade of green to create shadows.

12. Deselect (Cmd/Ctrl+D) and save (Cmd/Ctrl+S).

Filling the Grass

1. Choose the Magic Wand tool. Set the Tolerance to 20 in the Options bar.

2. Target the Outline layer.

3. Click inside one of the areas that define the grass. Shift-click to add the additional areas of grass to the selection.

4. Choose a light green color from the Swatches palette.

5. Move the sliders to get the exact shade of green you want.

6. Target the Painting layer.

7. Press Option+Delete or Alt+Backspace to fill the selected area with color.

8. Choose Filter ➜ Noise ➜ Add Noise and set the noise slider to 5.26. For Distribution, choose Gaussian. Click OK.

9. Deselect all and save your document. Figure 8 shows the image at this stage.

Figure 8 *After painting the tree, grass, and hills*

Working the Sky

Applying a Gradient to the Sun

1. Target the Painting layer.

2. Choose the Elliptical Marquee. In the Options bar, specify a 5-pixel Feather Radius. Press the Shift key to constrain the marquee to a circle and the Option or Alt key to radiate the circle from a center point. Click the approximate center of the sun and drag outward slightly beyond the edge of the outline.

3. Click the Gradient tool in the Tool palette.

4. Click the Radial Gradient icon in the Options bar.

5. Click the gradient swatch in the Options bar to display the Gradient Editor (Figure 9).

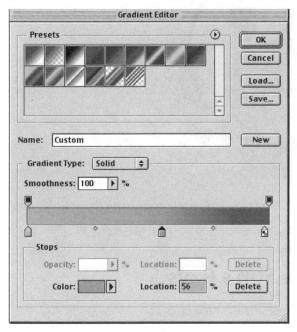

Figure 9 *The Gradient Editor*

6. Create a custom gradient for the sun and name it Sun.

7. Double-click the color stops at the bottom of the gradient bar to display the Color Picker to change colors; I suggest a warm orange at the left to a bright red at the right. Add stops by clicking under the Gradient bar (you might insert a magenta stop in the middle). Slide the stops into position to change the proportion of the gradient's colors, keeping the sun mostly orange. When you're satisfied with the gradient, click OK.

8. Click the right eye of the sun and drag at about a 45-degree angle down and to the left, to apply the gradient. It should look something like Figure 10.

9. Deselect.

Figure 10 *The sun, with the feathered selection and with the gradient applied*

Painting the Sun's Rays

1. Continue to target the Painting layer.

2. Choose the Paintbrush and the fourth brush from the left in the top row of the brush menu.

3. From the Brush Dynamics menu in the Options bar, enter Size:Fade 15 and Opacity:Fade 15.

4. Choose a reddish foreground color from the Swatches palette.

5. Place the cursor a short distance away from the outer circle of the sun. Click and drag a ray away from the center, as in Figure 11.

6. Repeat step 5 for each ray.

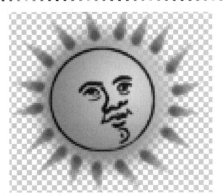

Figure 11 *Painting the sun's rays*

Creating the Fill Layer for the Sky

1. Target the Outline layer.

2. Choose the Magic Wand tool; set the Tolerance to 20.

3. Click the sky area. Press the Shift key and click between the branches of the tree to select those areas.

4. From the Swatches palette, choose a sky blue as a foreground color and white as a background color.

5. Choose Layer ➜ New Fill Layer ➜ Gradient.

6. Name the Gradient layer Sky. Click OK; the Gradient Fill dialog appears.

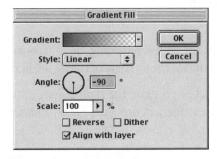

7. Set the Angle to –90 degrees. Click OK.

Creating a Custom Shape for the Clouds

You're going to use the Pen tool to draw the clouds. We'll use the technique you learned in Chapter 9 for drawing a scalloped curve by changing the direction of the curve. When performing this operation, it helps to think of the Option or Alt key as a "turn signal."

1. Choose the Pen tool. Click the image to deposit your first anchor point and, without releasing the mouse, drag up to establish the direction of the curve. Release the mouse.

2. Move the cursor over, click again, and drag down to draw the first curve.

3. Press your Option or Alt key (the turn signal) and click the second point and drag up again to create a direction handle. Release the mouse. Move the cursor over again, click and drag down to create a scalloped curve (see Figure 12).

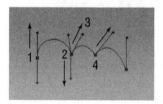

1. Click, drag up, release the mouse.
2. Move cursor, click, drag down, release the mouse.
3. Press Option/Alt, click the anchor point, drag up.
4. Move cursor, click, drag up.

Figure 12 *Beginning the cloud path*

4. Continue to create anchor points, repeating the process as you work your way to the right, until you've drawn the top part of the cloud, like the one in Figure 12.

5. Click to deposit an anchor point on the right corner of the cloud. Drag downward. Move the cursor to the left, deposit a point, and drag upward to create a gentle S curve.

6. When the curve is completed, click on the starting anchor point to close the curve. The cloud should look like Figure 13.

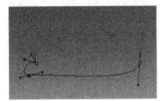

Figure 13 *The completed cloud*

7. Choose Edit ➜ Define Shape; the Shape Name dialog box appears. Name the shape Cloud.

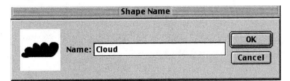

Applying the Cloud Shape to the Image

1. Choose the Custom Shape tool from the Tool palette.

2. Click the arrow next to Shapes in the Options bar to display the shape list; choose the Cloud shape.

3. Choose light gray as a foreground color from the Swatches palette.

4. Check the Create Filled Region icon on the Options bar.

5. Target the Painting layer.

6. Position the cursor on the image and drag the cloud into place. You can move it as you drag by pressing the space bar. Release the mouse.

7. Repeat the previous section and this one to make clouds of different sizes in the sky.

Applying the Art History Brush to a Snapshot

You can create a snapshot of the image in a specific state, and later apply parts of it to a previous snapshot. Ultimately, you'll duplicate the altered snapshot and end up with three completely different versions of the image. Let's start by making a separate document of the image we now have, so as not to lose it.

1. Choose Window ➜ Show History to display the History palette.

2. Click the last state in the History palette.

3. Click the Create Document From Current State icon, and a document of the Art History image will appear. Save and name the document.

4. Make a snapshot of the image by choosing New Snapshot from the pull-down menu. Name the snapshot Original.

5. Choose the Art History Brush from the Tool palette. Place your cursor on the image and start to paint. As you paint, experiment with techniques on various parts of the image. Vary the Style, Fidelity, Area, and Spacing. The Art History brush is wild; it rapidly spits out painterly effects wherever you drag. I've found in using this tool that less is more—smaller, tighter strokes made with smaller brushes produce more cohesive designs—but I encourage you to experiment. In the case of Figure 14, I used a Tight Short style with a 34-point brush and 10 px spacing. You can see that I have destroyed most of the detail in the image.

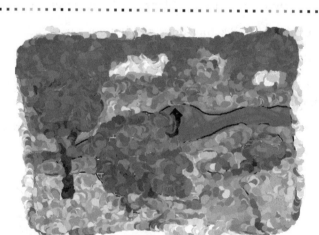

Figure 14 *The image obliterated with the Art History brush*

6. In the History palette, make a snapshot of the image with the Art History brush applied. Name it Art History 1.

Painting from an Art History Snapshot

1. Choose the History brush. Click the Source column next to the Art History snapshot. Target the Original snapshot.

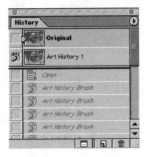

2. Carefully paint portions of the Art History 1 snapshot onto the original. You have much more control than painting with the Art History Brush. I painted the grass and the leaves on the tree, as in Figure 15. (This version is also available in the Ch11 folder on the CD as Headville_end2.tif.)

And finally: any time you make a mistake or don't like the result of an operation, you know what to do...

Up Next

To err is human. I find that when working in Photoshop, I can often be a little too human. Fortunately, the history features let me cover my trail when I have to. You'll find that you'll use it frequently, not only to undo mistakes, but to experiment with wild effects like the Art History Brush without having to commit until you're absolutely satisfied with the results.

Making selections with the selection tools can be the most labor-intensive of all of Photoshop's operations. In order to store your selections, you save them as alpha channels. Chapter 12 looks at the Channels palette, alpha channels, and Quick Mask to help you make and save precise selections. The Hands-On section will show you how to apply what you learn to an image. You'll see that the processes of masking in Photoshop, whether it be alpha channels, Quick Mask, or layer masks (covered in Chapter 20), are similar and that learning to use one makes learning the others a piece of cake.

Figure 15 *The completed version of the Headville image, with the Art History brush applied selectively*

Using Channels and Quick Mask

PHOTOSHOP

Chapter 12

I t's raining outside. You're dry and warm in front of your computer working on an assignment to colorize a black and white group photograph of 34 mariachis. You've spent the last hour and fifteen minutes carefully selecting their pants, tunics, and sombreros, and you're about to apply the Hue and Saturation command to simultaneously color all of their costumes a brilliant turquoise. You hear thunder in the distance! The lights flicker! Your screen goes dead.

Fortunately, you've been regularly saving your work. You restart your computer, launch Photoshop, and open the image. The 34 mariachis are there, but without the precious selection marquee over which you lovingly labored for so long.

If you haven't saved the selection, more than an hour of work has just gone down the tubes. However, before you utter a stream of unprintable obscenities, remember, you've learned a valuable lesson: Save your selections as alpha channels.

- What are channels?

- Looking at the Channels palette

- Editing alpha channels

- Using Quick Mask

- Performing channel operations

Channel Your Energy

There are two types of channels in a Photoshop document. *Color channels* are graphic representations of color information. Having access to this information enables you to perform powerful modifications and corrections to the appearance and color values of the image. *Alpha channels* are selections that have been made with the selection tools and stored for later use.

Color channels are composed of information segregated by color. Each color channel is actually a separate grayscale image. When you view the color channels superimposed on each other in an image, you see the full-color composite image. For a detailed description of color channels, see Chapter 3.

An alpha channel is also a grayscale image. Like a color channel, it can support 256 shades of gray. Unlike a color channel, however, an alpha channel does not contain information that contributes to the image's appearance. Instead of the values of gray representing tonality or color, they represent the areas of opacity, semitransparency, or transparency of a mask.

Photoshop provides many features that help you isolate parts of the image so that you can perform edits and adjustments to them. It's helpful to think of an alpha channel as a tool that you create, store, and later use to isolate a region so that a tool or command can ultimately be applied to it.

Alpha Channels and File Size

Bear in mind that although alpha channels are stored selections and do not affect the way the image appears, they are perceived by Photoshop as part of the image and therefore increase the file size of the image proportionally each time you save a selection. Photoshop supports up to 24 total channels (except in bitmap images and 16-bit images, which don't support alpha channels) in a document. Images with alpha channels can become quite large and consume a great deal of disk space, so it is best to delete your alpha channels when you are absolutely sure you are done with them.

Looking at the Channels Palette

Channels are displayed in the Channels palette (Figure 12.1). (To access the Channels palette, choose Window ➜ Show Channels. Or you can press the F7 key to display the Layers/Channels/Paths cluster.)

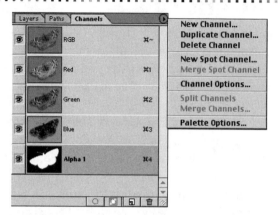

Figure 12.1 *The Channels palette*

The composite channel appears at the top of the palette. The individual color channels appear underneath, each labeled with the name of the color that they represent and a key command that displays them in the image window. As in the Layers and History palettes, the first column, to the left of the thumbnail, displays or conceals an eye icon that tells you what you can see—in this case, it indicates what channels are displayed. Clicking to turn off the eye next to the Red channel, for example, reveals the content of the Green and the Blue channels. Clicking the composite channel eye reveals or conceals the full-color image.

If you save a selection to an alpha channel, it is placed underneath the color channels in the stack in the order in which it was created.

Saving Selections as Alpha Channels

Because making an intricate selection can sometimes be difficult or time-consuming, Photoshop enables you to store selections to the Channels palette so that they can be used when you need them. It is wise to save a selection as an alpha channel if the selection is complex, if you need to refine it, or if you are going to use it more than once.

To save a selection:

1. Make a selection with one of the selection tools.

2. Choose Select ➜ Save Selection.

3. In the dialog that appears (Figure 12.2), designate the document where the selection will be saved.

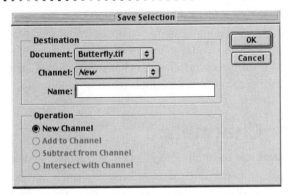

Figure 12.2 *The Save Selection dialog box*

Document   You can save a selection as an alpha channel to the document where the selection was made, or to any open document that is the exact same height, width, and resolution. Their names will appear in the Document pop-up list. Choosing New creates a new document with no color channels and one alpha channel in the Channels palette.

Channel   Choosing New here makes a new channel. You can name the new channel in the Name field. If you don't name it, the saved selection will appear on the Channels palette titled Alpha 1, 2, etc. Selecting a channel name in the Channel pop-up list writes over an existing channel.

Layer Mask   You can save a selection as a layer mask from the channels dialog box. The name of the layer mask defaults to Layer Mask 1. It appears in the Layers palette and the Channels palette. (See Chapter 20, "Advanced Layer Techniques.")

4. If you have an active selection on the image and you choose a channel name to write over, the Operation area presents you with four options. To choose, click the radio button next to the operation.

Replace Selection   discards the original mask channel and replaces it with an entirely new alpha channel.

Add To Selection   has the effect of adding the new selected area to the alpha channel.

Subtract From Selection   omits the new selected area from the alpha channel.

Intersect With Selection   creates an alpha channel of the area where the original channel and the new selection overlap.

5.   Click OK to save the selection.

You can quickly save a selection as a new alpha channel by clicking the Save Selection As Channel icon at the bottom of the Channels palette.

Viewing Color Channels

It is often necessary to examine a color channel in black and white to better observe the brightness relationships of its pixels. By default, color channels are displayed in the Channels palette as black and white thumbnails and in the image window as grayscale images. You can display color channels as color overlays by choosing Edit ➤ Preferences ➤ Display & Cursors ➤ Color Channels In Color.

Viewing Alpha Channels

Once an alpha channel has been saved, you can display it or conceal it in the Channels palette. As with viewing color channels, you view or conceal alpha channels by clicking the eye icon to the left of the channel's thumbnail.

Once a selection has been saved as an alpha channel, it can be viewed in the image window: click the channel's name or thumbnail (see Figure 12.3). By default, black represents masked areas, and white represents selected areas. Areas represented by gray are semitransparent.

Figure 12.3 *An alpha channel displayed in the image window*

When color channels and alpha channels are both visible, you see the alpha channels as superimposed translucent color overlays. By default, the overlays are 50% red, which is designed to resemble Rubylith, a traditional masking film used in the graphic arts industry.

The Channel Options

You may need to change the color of an alpha channel overlay if you are looking at more than one channel at a time, or if the content of the image closely resembles the color of the overlay. If you double-click the thumbnail of the alpha channel, the Channel Options dialog box appears (Figure 12.4). You can then set display options for that channel. The radio buttons in the Color Indicates area let you choose Masked Areas or Selected Areas to be displayed as color overlays, or if you are working with spot colors, you can designate a spot color channel (described in Chapter 23).

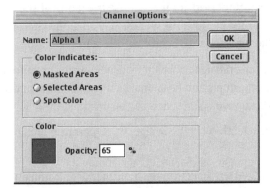

Figure 12.4 *The Channel Options dialog box*

Always check the Channel Options dialog to see if Masked Areas or Selected Areas are represented by color. Look at the alpha channel in the image window by its thumbnail. When masked areas are represented by color, the masked area will appear black and the selected area will appear white. The reverse is true when color represents selected areas.

To change the color of a mask:

1. Double-click the channel thumbnail to display the Channel Options dialog.

2. Click the swatch to bring up the Color Picker.

3. Choose a color and click OK.

You can specify the opacity of the mask from 0% to 100%, which affects only the way you see the mask and not its masking characteristics. Reducing the opacity helps you see the image more clearly through the mask.

Loading Selections

Once saved to the Channels palette, the alpha channel can be loaded as a selection. Loading a selection surrounds the area with a selection marquee just as if you outlined it with a selection tool.

To load a selection:

1. Choose Select ➜ Load Selection.

2. In the Load Selection dialog box, the options are similar to the Save Selection dialog. From the Document pop-up list, choose the name of the document where the channel was made. This list will display all alpha channels from all open documents that are the same height, width, and resolution.

3. From the Channel pop-up list, choose the source channel to be loaded. This list displays all alpha channels and layer masks from the current document. The Invert box loads an inverse selection of the mask.

4. If you have an active selection on the image, the Operation area presents four options:

   New Selection loads a new selection on the image, replacing any currently selected area, if there is one.

   Add To Selection adds the loaded selection area to an active selection marquee.

   Subtract From Selection omits the loaded selection area from an active selection marquee.

   Intersect With Selection loads the area where the loaded selection and an active selection marquee intersect.

5. Click OK to load the selection.

You can quickly load a selection by dragging its icon to the Load Channel As Selection icon at the bottom of the Channels palette.

Editing Channels

It is sometimes desirable to change portions of the channel using the painting or editing functions. If, for example, you missed a small part of the selection while using the Lasso tool, you can alter the contents of the mask channel with the Paintbrush to include the areas that were excluded from the original selection. Any painting or editing function that can be applied to a grayscale image can be applied to an alpha channel.

Fine-Tuning Alpha Channels by Painting

Suppose that after having saved a selection there are inaccuracies visible on the mask that weren't visible on selection marquee. You can fine-tune these and other flaws by painting directly on the alpha channel.

Here's a practice exercise on how to alter the contents of an alpha channel:

1. Open the file `Alpha_Head.psd` from the `Ch12` folder on the *Mastering Photoshop 6* CD (Figure 12.5).

Figure 12.5 *The open document Alpha Head*

2. View and target the alpha channel in the Channels palette by clicking its name or thumbnail. The channel will appear in the image window.

3. Notice that the foreground and background color swatches in the Tool palette have changed to black and white and the Swatches palette only displays black,

white, and gray. This is because a channel is a grayscale image and does not support color.

4. Choose the Paintbrush, Airbrush, Pencil, or any tool that deposits foreground color.

5. Choose a brush and paint out the eyes of the head with the foreground color (black) as in Figure 12.6. The resulting painting will, by default, alter the selection to mask the newly painted areas when the selection is loaded.

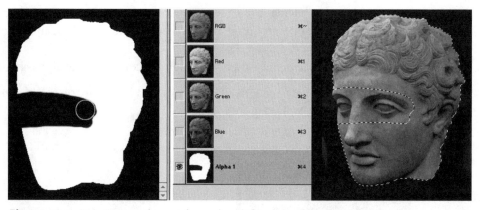

Figure 12.6 *Painting on the mask overlay (left) alters the selection when the channel is loaded (right).*

 In order to produce a more precise selection, it is often necessary to see the image while you are altering the mask channel. You can view both the alpha channel and the composite channel by clicking the eye icons next to them in the Channels palette. Target the alpha channel and apply the paint.

6. Target the RGB channel to view the full-color image.

7. Use Select ➜ Load Selection and choose Alpha 1 from the Channel pop-up list, to see the result.

 If you paint with white, you will erase the masked areas. Painting with a shade of gray will create a partially masked area, the degree of masking depending on how light or dark the paint is. The darker the shade of gray, the more an area will be masked; black will produce areas that are entirely protected.

Performing Channel Operations

You can perform several operations within the Channels palette that change the structure of the document. Some of these operations produce shifts in the color mode, and some disperse the channels into several documents.

Because of the radical changes to the color information, it is always a good idea to make a copy of the document before implementing most of these channel operations. To duplicate the document, choose Image ➜ Duplicate.

Duplicating Channels

When you duplicate a targeted channel, you get an exact copy of it in the Channels palette. You should duplicate the channel if you want to experiment with modifying it by painting, applying a filter effect, or any other editing function. Also duplicate the channel if you want to convert a copy of the channel into a mask. Click the arrow in upper-right corner of the Channels palette and scroll down to the Duplicate Channel command (see Figure 12.1).

The Duplicate Channel option will be dimmed if the composite channel is targeted, because you can only duplicate one channel at a time.

A fast way to duplicate a channel is to drag it to the New Channel icon at the bottom of the Channels palette.

Deleting Channels

You can delete a targeted channel from the document by choosing Delete Channel from the palette pull-down menu. You can delete alpha channels and maintain the integrity of the image. If you delete color channels, however, the color mode of the image will change to Multichannel (see "Using Multichannel" in this chapter). If you delete the Red channel of an RGB image, for example, the remaining color channels will convert to Magenta and Yellow (Multichannel documents always default to CMYK descriptions). You cannot delete the composite channel.

A fast way to delete a channel is to drag it to the Delete Current Channel icon (the trash icon) at the bottom of the Channels palette.

Splitting Channels

Photoshop can split a document's channels into independent Grayscale documents. The title of each window is automatically appended to the channel's color name as a suffix in the image title bar at the top of the window. For example, a CMYK document named Box will be divided into 4 channels: Box Cyan, Box Magenta, Box Yellow, and Box Black. Alpha channels will be converted to separate Grayscale documents. This option is useful as a first step in redistributing channels or for making a single document out of the channels information. This is not a process you'll use everyday unless you're a printer who needs to isolate the color information to a single document, or if you have very specialized needs to analyze the channel information. The new documents are not automatically saved, so you should save them to your hard disk.

To split a channel, first flatten the image. Choose Split Channels from the Channels palette pull-down menu. When you perform this operation, the original document is automatically closed.

Merging Channels

Separate channels can be merged into a single Multichannel document by choosing Merge Channels from the Channels palette pull-down menu. The images must be open, grayscale, and the exact same height, width, and resolution. A dialog box appears that allows you to assign a color mode to the image based on the number of images open. Three open images will produce an RGB, Lab, or Multichannel image; four open images will produce a CMYK or Multichannel image. Click OK and another dialog enables you to determine the distribution of the color channels. You can create some rather surprising color distortions by switching color information between channels.

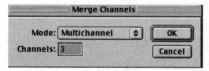 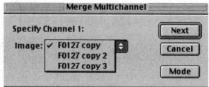

Using Multichannel

An image's channels can be divided into an individual series of channels. When you choose Image ➜ Mode ➜ Multichannel, the new channels lose their color relation to each other and appear as individual grayscale channels within a single document so there is no composite channel. This is useful if you want to separate the color information of a composite channel like a Duotone, Tritone, or Quadtone and view the color information of each ink color separately. (Chapter 23 goes into more detail on image features like Duotones and spot colors.) The Multichannel operation converts the Red, Green, and Blue channels on RGB images into separate Magenta, Cyan, and Yellow channels, within the same the same document.

Mixing Channels

Channel Mixer is a Photoshop feature that enables you to adjust the color information of each channel from one control window. You can establish color values on a specific channel as a mixture of any or all of the color channels' brightness values. The Channel Mixer can be used for a variety of purposes, including:

- Creating an optimal grayscale image from an RGB or CMYK file

- Making a high-quality sepia tone from a CMYK or RGB file

- Converting images into alternative color spaces

- Swapping color information from one channel to another

- Making creative color adjustments to images by altering the color information in a specific channel

To learn how to use the Channel Mixer, see Chapter 16.

About Spot Color Channels

The spot channel features in the Channels palette pull-down menu are used to create images that are output to film for printing on printing presses. Their most frequent application is used on grayscale images for two- and three-color print jobs. They are also used on four-color process (CMYK) images when additional areas of solid rich color, varnishes, and special inks are specified. Spot colors are usually printed with PANTONE or other custom color inks. See Chapter 23 to learn how to work with spot colors.

Using Quick Mask Mode

As you become more proficient in Photoshop, the speed of performing tasks will become more crucial to your particular style of work. As you understand the relations of tool functions and begin to recognize the logic and similarity of the various windows, palettes, and toolbars, you'll want to explore shortcuts that accelerate your work. Selecting areas on a Photoshop image can be the most time-consuming part of the image-editing process; Quick Mask mode can accelerate the selection making and enhance the precision.

You can toggle directly into Quick Mask mode on the Tool palette by pressing the letter Q or clicking the Quick Mask icon.

Quick Mask mode is an efficient method of making a temporary mask using the paint tools. Quick Masks can quickly be converted into selections or be stored as mask channels in the Channels palette for later use. By default, the Quick Mask interface is similar to the channels interface in that Photoshop displays a colored overlay to represent the masked areas.

Quick Mask is versatile way of making or editing selections using many of Photoshop's painting and editing tools. You can even use the selection tools to define areas of the Quick Mask to edit.

When you choose Quick Mask mode from the Tool palette, a temporary thumbnail labeled Quick Mask, in italics, appears in the Channels palette. The thumbnail will change appearance as you apply color to the Quick Mask (see Figure 12.7).

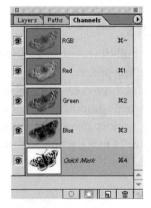

Figure 12.7 *A Quick Mask thumbnail in the Channels palette*

Quick Mask Options Window

The Quick Mask Options dialog is identical to the Channels Options dialog and can be accessed by double-clicking the Quick Mask icon. To practice creating a mask in Quick Mask mode, follow these steps:

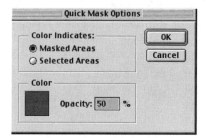

1. Open the file Guitar.psd from the Ch12 folder on the CD.

2. Click the Quick Mask icon in the Tool palette. Notice that the foreground and background swatch colors in the Tool palette become black and white.

3. Choose the Paintbrush from the Tool palette. Set Brush options in the Options bar.

If you want to be sure that the area is completely masked, set the Opacity slider in the Paintbrush Options bar to 100%. Setting the opacity to 50%, for example, will paint with translucent color; the result will be that the painted area will be only partially masked.

4. Choose a brush from the Brush menu and paint over the guitar. Painting on a Quick Mask is similar to painting on an alpha channel with the composite channel visible. By default, as you paint, if the foreground color is black, the paint tool will deposit a red color. If the foreground color is white, the paint tool will erase the mask color.

5. When you have completed painting the guitar, click the Normal mode icon from the Tool palette. The masked area is outlined by a selection outline. By default, the areas that were painted are now excluded from the selection. You've selected the background. If you want to select the guitar, choose Select → Invert to invert the selection.

6. After all that work, you should save the selection to an alpha channel. Click the Save Selection As Alpha Channel icon at the bottom of the Channels palette.

Once a Quick Mask has been made, I recommend that you carefully examine it for missed areas and pin-holes. It is quite easy to make mistakes because it can be difficult to see omissions and errors on the image. The best way to examine the Quick Mask is to view it as a grayscale image. You can see the Quick Mask as a grayscale by turning off the eye icon on all the other channels in the Channels palette except for the one to the left of the Quick Mask. Examine it carefully to assure that the masked areas are solid and opaque. If necessary, apply more paint to deficient areas. (See the Hands-On section that follows for a demonstration.)

Quick Mask is ideal for cleaning up selections that you have made with one of the selection or marquee tools. You can paint a few pixels at a time with a small brush or the Pencil, greatly enhancing the precision of making selections.

Up Next

I have found that Quick Mask is the most efficient way to ensure the accuracy of your selections. Nonetheless, Quick Masks may require time and precision on your part when making complex selections. You'll therefore want to save the selection that the Quick Mask produced as an alpha channel as soon as you exit the mode. The Hands-On exercise that follows will help you get familiar with these tools and operations.

Hands-On
Channels

The goal of this project is to make a selection of part of an image—some chickens—using the Quick Mask technique. You will save the selection as an alpha channel, duplicate it, and make it into a gradient mask. A filter will then be applied to the background through the gradient mask to give the chickens movement and life.

Getting Started

Hide your preferences file before beginning this Hands-On exercise, then restart Photoshop to create a clean version. The "Photoshop's Settings" section in Chapter 5 details how to temporarily reset your preferences to Photoshop's defaults. You can restore your customized, personal settings when you're done.

Once you have launched Photoshop with default preferences, open the file Chickens_in_Motion_start.psd (Figure 1) in the Ch12 folder on the *Mastering Photoshop 6* CD. To see a color preview of the before and after (Figure 2) versions of the image, check the color section. Save the file to your disk.

Figure 1 *The original chickens, standing around*

Figure 2 *The Chickens in Motion*

Selecting the Chickens

1. With the Magic Wand tool, try to select the chickens. Click them once; press the Shift key and click again. You'll see that, because the colors of the chickens are close to the background, it is impossible to isolate them.

2. Click the lightest area of a chicken with the Magic Wand tool. Click the Add to Selection icon in the toolbar and continue to select the lightest areas. Select as much as you can but not too much (see Figure 3).

3. Go to Quick Mask mode (click the Quick Mask icon in the Tool palette or type Q). What you've selected so far becomes your Quick Mask.

Figure 3 *Selecting chicken parts: Select the lightest areas of the chickens first.*

4. Choose the Paintbrush. Click the Reverse Colors icon in the Tool palette so that white is the foreground color. Choose a brush and begin to erase the red transparent color on the chickens. Carefully paint to the edges. If you make a mistake and paint outside the edge, reverse the colors so that black is the foreground color and paint out the mistake.

5. When you get to the chickens' red combs, it becomes difficult to see where to erase the red color. Change the color of the mask by double-clicking the Quick Mask thumbnail in the Channels palette. In the Quick Mask Options dialog, click the swatch, choose a green color from the Color Picker, and click OK. (The color section includes a comparison of a red and a green mask.)

6. Reduce the opacity of the Quick Mask to 30% for a better view of the background.

7. Erase the mask from the chickens and their legs with the Paintbrush tool, using white as a foreground color.

8. Once you've completed that selection, choose the Lasso tool and select the wall they are standing on (as in Figure 4) and the parts of their feet that extend upward slightly from the wall.

Figure 4 *Selecting the wall*

9. Be sure white is the foreground color. Press Option+Delete (Mac) or Alt+Backspace (Win) to delete the green mask from the wall area. Press Cmd+D (Mac) or Ctrl+D (Win) to deselect.

10. When the Quick Mask of the chickens is complete, click the Normal mode icon to convert the mask into a selection.

11. Save the document.

Saving and Cleaning Up the Alpha Channel

1. Click the Save Selection As Channel icon in the Channels palette to quickly save the selection. A thumbnail labeled Alpha 1 appears in the palette. Deselect.

2. Click the thumbnail to display the alpha channel in the image window. Notice that there are some flaws, areas that you missed or edges that are not sharp (see Figure 5). Choose the Paintbrush, choose white as a foreground color, and paint out the flaws in the white area of the alpha channel.

Figure 5 *The flaws in the alpha channel*

3. While making repairs to the edges, you may want to see the image. Click the eye next to the RGB composite channel to reveal the image and the alpha channel at the same time.

4. When the alpha channel is complete, save the document (File ➔ Save or Cmd/Ctrl+S).

Duplicating and Modifying the Channel

1. Drag the Alpha 1 channel to the New Channel icon at the bottom of the Channels palette to duplicate it. The new channel is named Alpha 1 Copy.

2. Choose Image ➔ Adjust ➔ Invert to reverse the colors of the channel, making the black areas of the channel white and the white areas black (Figure 6).

3. Double-click the channel thumbnail. In the Channel Options dialog box, name it Gradient Mask.

4. Click the Gradient Mask channel to target it. Drag Alpha 1 to the Load Selection icon at the bottom of the Channels palette.

Figure 6 *The inverted alpha channel*

5. Press your D key to make the foreground color black and the background color white (or click the Switch Colors double-arrow icon on the Tool palette swatches). Choose the Gradient tool and click the Radial option in the Options bar. Click and drag from the center outward towards the edge of the document to modify the areas surrounding the chickens with a gradient, as in Figure 7. Your alpha channel should then look like Figure 8.

Figure 7 *Drag the gradient on the inverted alpha channel.*

Figure 8 *The completed Gradient Mask channel*

Filtering and Adjusting the Selection

1. Click the RGB composite channel to target it.

2. Load the Gradient Mask channel by dragging it to the Load Selection icon at the bottom of the Channels palette. Your image should look something like Figure 9.

Figure 9 *The loaded selection*

3. Choose Filter ➜ Blur ➜ Radial Blur, and set these options: Amount: 100, Blur Method: Zoom, and Quality: Best.

4. Click OK.

You may want to further enhance the image by adjusting its brightness through the Gradient Mask channel. Target the RGB composite channel. With the channel still loaded, choose Image ➜ Adjust ➜ Auto Levels. Deselect (Cmd/Ctrl+D) and save (Cmd/Ctrl+S).

Up Next

Color channels determine the color structure of an image; alpha channels are stored selections. Learning to work with both types of channels is fundamental to mastering Photoshop. In earlier versions of Photoshop, alpha channels were the only way to produce gradients, drop shadows, and other special effects. It was a challenge to learn to use them. Photoshop 6 has so many built-in features that alpha channels are used much less often for building sophisticated masks. Still, there are certain operations in which they are still extremely important, if not essential, particularly the ability to save and store selections.

The next two chapters address very important subjects: resolution and scanning. What is the best resolution for your particular purposes? What is the relation between size and resolution? How do you achieve the best possible results at the scanner? What is the difference between dpi, ppi, and lpi? How does the resolution of your monitor affect what you see on the screen? These questions and more will be answered.

Sizing and Transforming Images

PHOTOSHOP

Chapter 13

Photoshop provides a wide assortment of tools that offer you full control over image size and orientation. These tools offer you precise handling of your picture's dimensions and resolution, and they will allow you to adjust image elements using the best transformation algorithms available. When you need to change your image's pixels in any way, Photoshop's built-in features and dialogs will provide you with precise and accurate results.

This chapter will help you understand:

- Image size

- The Crop tool

- Canvas size

- The Resize Image Assistant

- Transformation operations

Image Size and Resolution

Image size and image resolution refer to two of the most important concepts in Photoshop. They help define both underlying image composition and how an image will display and print. The *size* of an image specifies the exact number of pixels that compose a picture. The *resolution* of an image determines at how large that picture will appear and how that number of pixels is distributed over length and width.

Several terms relate to these two key concepts and may crop up as you read through this chapter. Before you jump into the discussion that follows—on how to control and manipulate image size and resolution—take some time to review the following terms. This will help you better navigate your way through the rest of this chapter.

Image resolution	The number of pixels that occupy a linear inch of a image, measured in pixels per inch (ppi).
Monitor resolution	The number of pixels that occupy a linear inch of your monitor screen (72 ppi for most Macintosh RGB monitors, 96 ppi for Windows VGA monitors). This resolution never changes, as it represents the physical matrix of the monitor.
Image size	The physical size and resolution of an image.
Printer resolution	The number of dots that can be printed per linear inch, measured in dots per inch (dpi). These dots compose larger halftone dots on a halftone screen or stochastic (random pattern) dots on an ink-jet printer.
Halftone screen	Also called screen frequency, this refers to the dot density of a printed image, measured in lines per inch (lpi). A halftone screen is a grid of dots. The tonality of a printed image is determined by the size of the dot within the specific matrix. Table 13.1 lists some standard values.

DPI Versus PPI Versus LPI

Dots per inch (dpi) and pixels per inch (ppi): The two terms sometimes get mixed up and confused. Manufacturers often refer to the resolution capabilities of their scanners in dpi. A scanner creates pixels and a printer prints dots. In this book, I use ppi when referring to pixel resolution from a scanned image or on a monitor. I use dpi when I refer to the output of a printer and lpi for the screen frequency of a halftone screen.

Table 13.1 Typical Halftone Screen Values

Value	Definition
65 lpi	The lowest quality, suggested for screen printing.
85 lpi	This value works well for newsprint.
133 lpi	This value produces a glossier result, suggested for things like web (not "Web"!) printing and weekly magazines.
150 lpi	This produces good quality results, suitable for brochures, pamphlets, and commercial printing applications.
200 lpi	This value produces the best quality prints. You might use this option when creating annual reports, art books, and the like.

Image Resolution and Monitor Resolution

Size can deceive—at least it may seem to when you work with Photoshop images. The picture you see on your screen may differ (in apparent dimension) from the same picture shown on a friend's monitor. It may look larger; it may look smaller. So why isn't this a problem for Photoshop users? The answer lies in *resolution*. Resolution assures that no matter how big or small your image appears on the screen, it always prints at an exact size.

Zoom or Change Res?

Many people ask which is better: zooming in on a lower-resolution display (such as older or less-expensive 13-inch monitors that are limited to displaying 640×480 pixels), or viewing the image at a display of 1024×786 or greater on a high-resolution or multi-resolution monitor? The answer is that your choice should lie in your own preference. A lower-resolution display allows menus, palettes, and other screen elements to display larger, using more screen space and placing less demand on your eyes. At the same time, you cannot display as much of a picture at once. You may have to scroll tediously through your image or zoom in and out to work on different sections.

Higher-resolution screens, in contrast, allow you to see and work on more of an image at once. On the other hand, everything displays "smaller," occupying fewer inches on each screen. Pick the solution that you are most comfortable with.

Each Photoshop image is composed of a specific number of pixels, which determine its resolution. You might work on one picture with 72 pixels per inch (a common resolution for pictures intended for the Web) or another at 300 pixels per inch (a fairly typical print resolution). Both images may take up similar space on your screen while containing quite different amounts of picture data.

Consider Figure 13.1, containing two identical images. Everything about these images matches—the number of pixels, the size displayed, the picture itself, and so forth. Even the display scaling—33.3% in this example, as you can see in the title bar of each image—is the same. However, the resolutions differ, the left at 300 dpi and the right at 72 dpi. You can see this because I turned on the ruler feature for each image. The left picture, if printed, would produce a compact print just over 3×4 inches, while the right picture would occupy more than 12×16 inches!

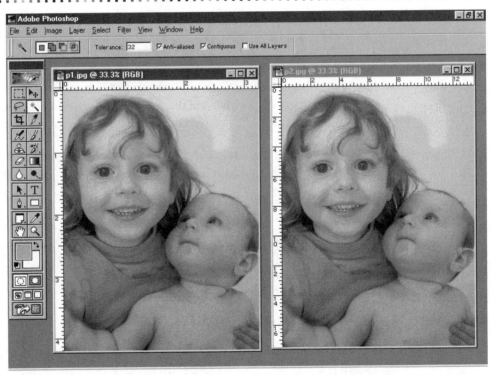

Figure 13.1 *Identical images at different resolutions. Notice the difference in the rulers.*

Image quality for prints increases as resolution increases. The more detail you include per printed inch, the finer your results. You'll see more features and pictures look smoother and clearer. However, as you increase resolution, you place a higher demand on your computer in terms of memory, image size, and so forth. The bigger the picture, the more memory you'll need to work on it. Photoshop allows you precise control over resolution so you can balance the rewards of high definition with your own system's limitations.

Scanning Resolution

To acquire sufficient information to produce good quality images from your high-resolution imagesetter or laser printer, scan your images at 1.5 to 2 times the screen frequency of the halftone screen you're going to print to. That means if your image is going to be printed in a newspaper or in a newsletter, scan it anywhere from 128 to 170 pixels per inch (1.5 or 2×85) If your image is going to be printed to a glossy magazine, scan your image at 225 to 300 ppi (1.5 or 2×150). Remember, the image size should be scanned at 100% of the size it will be printed.

If you're going to print only to desktop ink-jet printers, I recommend that you scan your images at 150 ppi at 100%. Or even better, scan the same image at resolutions of 72, 150, 225, and 300 pixels per inch and then print each image to determine which is the best option for your specific printer. I cover scanning in detail in the next chapter.

Scanning at high resolutions allows you to "magnify" your pictures. If you scan a picture at 600 dpi and print it at 300 dpi, you can essentially zoom in by a factor of two in height and width, creating an overall magnification (or scaling) of four times.

To get a clear idea of the size that your image will print, choose View ➜ Print Size. The image will be displayed at the size that it will print no matter what its resolution. Alternatively, you can turn on your rulers whenever you want to visualize resolution. Simply choose View ➜ Show Rulers to reveal the rulers around your picture.

Changing Image Resolution

Changing the resolution for your image lets you determine the number of pixels in the image. When you resample down, you discard pixels. When you resample up, you create new pixels. Usually the results are okay when you decrease the size of an image, but I don't recommend that you increase the size or resolution of an image by a large amount. Photoshop manufactures pixels from predefined interpolation algorithms that produce a loss of sharpness and dulling of color. If you need a larger image, rescan it properly, taking into account its output size.

Exceeding the optical resolution of a scanner is essentially the same as resampling up in Photoshop. It will produce less than desirable results. For best results, don't exceed the scanner's optical resolution.

Two third-party plug-ins do a fairly descent job of resampling images up with a minimum of loss of quality. They are both from Altimira: Print Pro ($259), which is used in enlarging CMYK images, and Genuine Fractals ($139), used to increase the size of RGB images and for output to large-format printers.

To change an image's size or resolution without resampling:

1. Choose Image ➜ Image Size. The Image Size dialog box will appear, as you can see in Figure 13.2.

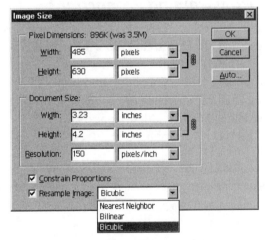

Figure 13.2 *The Image Size dialog box*

2. Make sure that the Resample Image box is *unchecked*, which causes the Constrain Proportions box to be checked and grayed out.

3. Enter a new value into the Resolution field. In this example, you might change the resolution from 300 pixels/inch to 150, decreasing the resolution of the image by half but doubling its physical size.

4. Click OK to apply the changes.

Disallowing and Allowing Resampling

When you disallow resampling, as in the above example, your image retains its original pixels, while changing only its print size. In contrast, resampling allows you to change image resolution or physical size. This occurs by adding pixels to increase an image's physical size or resolution, or removing pixels for a smaller size or lower resolution.

To use this feature, check the Resample Image box and pick from one of the three algorithms listed: Nearest Neighbor, Bilinear, and Bicubic. Each of these choices determines how Photoshop decides how to add or remove pixels from your image. The Nearest Neighbor setting evaluates an adjacent pixel. Bilinear averages the four pixels above, below, and on either side for smoother transitions. Bicubic produces the best results by averaging the eight closest neighbors and adding a sharpening effect to increase the contrast. As a rule of thumb, I suggest you select Bicubic and stick with it. This algorithm produces excellent results for nearly every circumstance you might run across.

Constraining and Unconstraining Proportions

When you enable the Resample Image feature, you have the option to constrain the image's proportions. When selected, the Constrain Proportions check box ensures that image height will vary proportionately with image width. Change one, and the other will automatically update to preserve proportionality. For example, increase the height by 50%, and the width will automatically increase by 50% as well. But when you turn this feature off, the link between height and width disappears. You will increase the height without affecting the width at all. Your image, in this example, will stretch vertically and disproportionately.

You can only turn off Constrain Proportions when you allow image resampling. Without resampling, proportions remain automatically constrained, as shown by the link icon.

The Crop Tool

With Photoshop 6, Adobe has moved an old tool to a new slot, directly onto its default Tool palette. The Crop tool, found by default on the left column in the third row, allows you to trim down your images. This tool offers fine control and feedback for one of Photoshop's most common operations. You can also select an area with the Rectangular Marquee tool and then choose Image ➜ Crop, but you sacrifice the flexibility and versatility of the Crop tool and all of its neat features.

To perform a basic crop with the Crop tool, open the Mandrill.psd file from the Ch13 folder of the *Mastering Photoshop 6* CD:

1. Choose the Crop tool from the Tool palette.

2. We want to crop the black border out of the picture. Drag the mouse to define the bounding box. As you can see in Figure 13.3, the area outside your crop will darken, highlighting your selection.

You can turn the dark area on and off by checking or unchecking the Shield Cropped Area box in the Crop tool Options bar. Choose a color for the shielded area by clicking the swatch, or an opacity by choosing or entering a value.

Figure 13.3 *After making your initial cropping selection, areas outside the crop will darken. Use the handles to fine-tune your selection.*

3. Fine-tune your crop interactively. Use the handles to encompass more or less of the image. and move the bounding box by placing the cursor inside its boundaries and dragging.

4. To crop, click the Commit (check mark) button in the Options bar or press the Enter (Win) or Return (Mac) key. You can also double-click inside the cropping area to commit your crop. (If you wish, instead, to cancel the crop, press the Esc key or click the Cancel (X) button.)

5. Photoshop will crop your image, removing all areas outside the crop selection and shrinking the picture to the new boundaries, as you can see in Figure 13.4. If you're satisfied with this crop, continue with your other tasks. Otherwise, choose Edit ➜ Undo Crop.

Figure 13.4 *Applying a crop removes all areas outside your selection from the image.*

Rotating a Crop

One of the Crop tool's most helpful features allows you to crop down to a *rotated* area. To rotate a cropped image, start, as above, by opening the Mandrill.psd file on your CD.

1. Choose the Crop tool from the Tool palette and highlight your initial crop area, just as in Figure 13.3.

2. Move your mouse just outside any of the corner selection handles until the cursor changes to the curved rotation icon.

3. Drag the mouse to rotate the selection, as in Figure 13.5. Further adjust your selection using any of the handles until you're satisfied with the new, rotated crop.

Figure 13.5 *The Crop tool allows you to rotate your selection to choose an angled crop area.*

4. As before, click the Commit (check mark) icon in the Options bar. Photoshop will crop the image, rotating it as needed, as you can see in Figure 13.6.

Figure 13.6 *The results from Figure 13.5, after rotation and cropping.*

When you rotate during a cropping operation, expect Photoshop to take longer to complete the operation than it would for a normal crop. Rotations are memory-intensive and may take several seconds to complete.

Cropping to Size

The Crop tool allows you to trim your image to fixed sizes. This is an important feature to keep in mind when you intend to print your picture to a particular paper size or if you plan to upload your final image to an online photo-finishing site. By selecting heights and widths, you constrain your selections to fixed proportions. The fixed proportion assures a proper match to a fixed-size printing medium.

Here's how you can set sizes for your own images. Start by opening the Chana.psd file from the Ch13 folder on your CD.

1. Choose the Crop tool from the Tool palette.

2. Locate the Width and Height fields in the Options bar. For this example, enter **6 in** for the width and **4 in** for the height. This will mimic the most common photo print size.

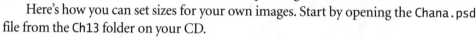

3. Drag out your selection within your picture. Notice that Photoshop automatically retains the 6:4 aspect ratio for you. You can still rotate your selection as described above.

4. Commit your change (click the check mark icon in the Options bar or press Enter or Return) to finish cropping your image.

Cropping Perspective

After you've drawn your crop marquee, the Options bar changes to display several options. Check the Perspective box to be able to independently adjust the corner anchor points of the bounding box. The Perspective option is useful if you want to distort an image as you crop it or to fit image content into a specific area. When you implement the crop, the image area will distort to conform to the new rectangle (see the example in Figure 13.7).

Figure 13.7 *The new Perspective crop option lets you crop an irregular shape into a rectangle.*

Sizing Your Canvas

The canvas is the surface on which your image resides. You can use Image ➜ Canvas Size as a cropping tool to eliminate canvas, but you are better off using the Crop tool for this because it allows you to visualize the crop. The Canvas Size command is most proficient at adding more space and more pixels to work with.

When you apply this operation, the new canvas is filled with the background color. First choose a background color from the Color Picker, Color palette, or Swatches palette.

Choose Image ➜ Canvas Size to access the dialog box that allows you to expand or shrink your canvas. Enter a new value for the width and/or the height, select an anchor, and click OK.

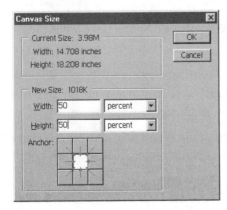

The Current Size indicates your file size for the current canvas size. The New Size indicates the file size of the image with the new height and width you've entered.

The Anchor buttons allow you to control where the new canvas will be added. Click the center button, and the canvas will trim grow equally on all sides. Click the bottom-right button, and size adjustments affect the left and top sides only. Your choice of anchor controls how Photoshop makes its adjustments.

When using the Canvas Size dialog box, you can work in any of seven units: percent, pixels, inches, centimeters, points, picas, and columns. For example, you may want to increase your canvas width to 150 percent. This allows your canvas to expand by 50%. To do this, choose Percent from the pull-down list to the right of the Width field and enter **150** into that field. The Height and Width fields operate independently.

In the following example, you will first shrink, then expand, your canvas. Figure 13.8 shows the original picture we'll work on: open Leah.psd from the Ch13 folder on your CD.

Figure 13.8 *I'll use this picture to demonstrate how you can change the size of your canvas.*

1. Start by shrinking the canvas. The current size of the image is 5.38″ by 9″; you'll crop it to 4″ by 7″. Choose Image ➜ Canvas Size.

2. To shrink the canvas, enter 4 in the Width field and 7 in the Height field. Notice how we've chosen the default center anchor for this task. To finish the operation, click OK.

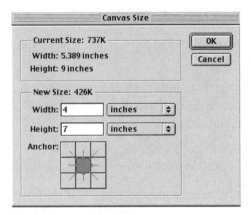

3. Whenever you shrink the canvas, Photoshop will demand confirmation before proceeding with this destructive action. To continue, you must click Proceed in the warning box.

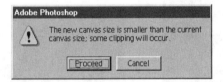

4. After you've confirmed the operation, Photoshop will proceed. In this case, it shrinks the canvas anchored at the center of the image. As you can see in Figure 13.9, the image is clipped evenly around all sides.

Figure 13.9 *The center-anchored clipping produces a shrunken canvas, anchored symmetrically at the middle of the image.*

Next, let's expand the canvas:

1. Choose Black as a background color. Once again choose the Image ➔ Canvas Size menu option.

2. Expand the canvas size to 8″×11″ by entering those values in the Height and Width fields. Anchor the image to the center. Click OK. The expansion of the canvas is seen in Figure 13.10a.

3. As an alternative, you can anchor the image to the bottom-left corner. This time enter values of 7″ × 10″. The results are shown in Figure 13.10b.

Notice how the canvas has expanded around all four sides of the image in Figure 13.10a but to the top and right of the original image in Figure 13.10b, due to our anchoring.

Figure 13.10 *Expanding the canvas produces new areas around the image: (a) anchored in the center and (b) anchored at the bottom-left corner.*

Rotating the Canvas

When you wish to rotate the entire image, rather than a single layer or selection, use the Rotate Canvas commands. These menu options, which you can find under Image ➜ Rotate Canvas, will reorient your entire document in various ways.

180°   This command tells Photoshop to turn your canvas until it is upside down. Unlike Flip Horizontal, your image will retain its left-right features, as you can see by comparing Figures 13.11a and 13.11b. If you look at the rotated image upside down, it will appear identical to the original: Facial features are not reversed, and if there were any text in the image it would still be readable.

90° CW   This command allows you to rotate your canvas by 90 degrees in a clockwise direction.

90° CCW   Like the clockwise rotation, this command allows you to rotate your canvas by 90 degrees—in this case, in a counterclockwise direction.

Arbitrary   This command opens the Rotate Canvas dialog box, which allows you to specify an exact angle to rotate. Enter a number in the Angle field, choose CW or CCW (clockwise or counterclockwise), and click OK.

Flip Horizontal   Choose this option to precisely mirror your image across the vertical axis. Each picture element will mirror horizontally, so items from the right will appear on the left and vice versa (compare Figures 13.11a and 13.11c). Writing and other features will appear reversed.

Flip Vertical   As with Flip Horizontal, this option precisely mirrors your image, in this case across the horizontal axis with vertical mirroring. Do not confuse this menu option with 180-degree rotation. This command will alter picture elements through mirroring, whereas the standard rotation will not (as seen by Figures 13.11b and 13.11d).

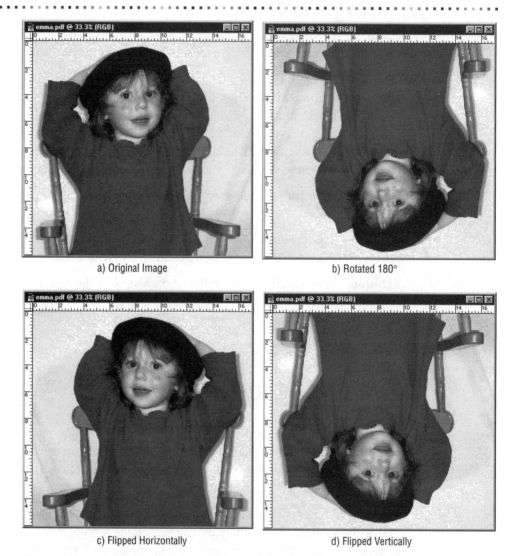

a) Original Image

b) Rotated 180°

c) Flipped Horizontally

d) Flipped Vertically

Figure 13.11 *The Rotate Canvas menu provides quick control over image orientation.*

Although some menu options appear similar, each option produces a unique result. Try these transformations yourself—you'll find the Emma.psd file that these images were made from in the Ch13 folder on the CD.

Getting Help with Resizing Images

Photoshop provides a handy little helper called the Resize Image Assistant (Macintosh) or Wizard (Windows). This interactive tool guides you through the entire process of changing your image size. Here's how you can take advantage of this feature.

1. Choose Help ➜ Resize Image and wait for the Resize Image Wizard window to appear.

When you use the Resize Image Wizard, Photoshop duplicates your document. The operation has no effect on the original.

2. Will you use the image for online, that is Web-based, use or do you plan to print it? Choose the appropriate option and click Next. In this sequence, let's assume we're preparing an image for print, which is slightly more complicated than preparing one for the Web.

3. Set the new image height and width. These values are linked and vary proportionately; if you choose a new, larger height, the width will automatically update to a proportionately larger value. You can choose from any of five units from the pull-down lists to the right of each text field: inches, centimeters, points, picas, and columns. Pick the unit that works best for your project, and type a value into either the Height or Width fields. After you've entered the new value or values, click Next.

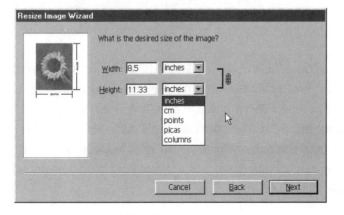

When preparing an image for the Web, rather than for print, you need only enter a new pixel count (the unit pull-down list does not appear in this case) and allow Photoshop to resize the image for you. The Web resize process ends after this step.

4. Choose a halftone screen value and click Next. This value refers to the lines per inch (lpi) for your image. The higher the number, the higher the print quality— and, similarly, the higher the memory load needed for Photoshop.

The proper term for "halftone screen value" is screen frequency. *It refers to the number of printer dots (or* halftone cells*) that a printer can create per inch.*

5. Next, set the image quality level for your picture. Do this by moving the slider between 1× and 2×. The higher the number, the better the image quality and the larger the file. Similarly, the lower the number, the smaller the file. In the Results area, found below the slide bar, you can see the size of the original image, the new image and the pixels per inch that will be produced. After selecting an image quality, click Next.

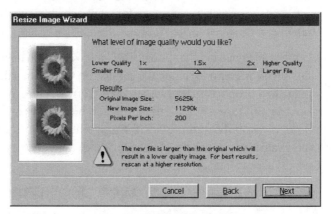

"Image quality level" refers to the proportion between the final image resolution and the screen frequency you picked in the previous step. When you pick a value between 1.5 and 2 times the screen frequency, you're assured of creating images at the highest quality the printer can produce. Because you include more information, the printer can create smoother and more realistic transitions. However, some imagesetting devices and laser printers use screening technology alternatives rather than traditional halftoning. If you're unsure how to set image quality and screen frequency values, consult the manual that came with your printer.

6. Wait for Photoshop to complete your transformation. When the confirmation box appears, click Finish.

Transformation Operations

Photoshop offers a wide range of transformation operations that allow you to stretch, squeeze, rotate, and otherwise alter your image selections. These tools provide you with hands-on image control and should form the basis of many of your day-to-day Photoshop operations.

Each of these operations can be found in the Edit ➜ Transform submenu (Figure 13.12). To use any of them, you can make a selection, choose the tool you wish to use, and then interactively apply it to the selection or to an independent layer.

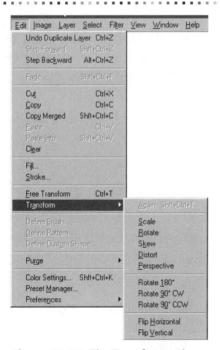

Figure 13.12 *The Transform submenu*

You'll save time and effort if you isolate the item to be transformed to its own layer before performing a transformation. The advantage is that Photoshop lets you apply the transformation to the contents of layer without having to make a selection.

Many of these transformations act very much like the canvas operations discussed above. However, they differ in some ways. They only affect your current selection or the active layer (and any layers linked to it). They also simultaneously affect all the layers in a layer set.

Scaling a Selection

Scaling refers to how you change the size of a portion of the image by stretching or squeezing it along one or both dimensions. For example, you might stretch your selection along one axis to lengthen it and create an excessively tall, fun-house-mirror look. Similarly, you might shrink your selection symmetrically along both axes to create an identical, but smaller, image. You can also constrain the transformation to maintain its proportions. Choose Edit ➜ Transform ➜ Scale. This menu command turns your selection marquee into an interactive bounding box (like the one in Figure 13.13) that allows you to apply a variety of scaling operations to your selection.

Figure 13.13 *An Elliptical selection with the rectangular bounding box*

Resize along Both Axes Drag one of the bounding box corners. The new bounding box will follow your mouse movement. Release the mouse and the selection will resize to the box you've chosen.

Resize Proportionately along Both Axes Hold the Shift key down while you drag a bounding box corner. The new bounding box will increase or decrease in size as you move the mouse, but it will retain the proportions of the original selection. Release the mouse to finish the resize task. The short step-by-step that follows demonstrates this operation.

This operation may prove to be one of the most important and useful transformations you can learn in Photoshop: Shift-drag a bounding box to change the size without changing the proportions.

Resize along One Axis   Drag one of the four handles that appear at the midpoint of each bounding box side. This allows you to stretch your selection along one axis while retaining the dimension of the other axis. The bounding box will stretch or shrink as you move the mouse. Release the mouse and the selection resizes to the new dimension.

1. To practice resizing proportionately, open the Clown.psd file, found in the Ch13 folder on your CD.

2. Choose the Elliptical Marquee tool from the Tool palette and select the clown's nose.

3. Choose Edit → Transform → Scale.

4. Press the Shift key while dragging a corner handle to enlarge your selection.

Rotating a Selection

Photoshop allows you to *rotate* a selection or the content of a layer by turning it around a point. You can rotate as much or as little you need. Rotation allows you to change a selection's orientation, choosing a new direction for it. You can use rotation to slant text, image elements, or turn a feature on its side. To rotate, choose Edit → Transform → Rotate.

In rotation, it's important to understand the concept of the *center point*. You find it whenever you create an interactive bounding box. It looks like a tiny little compass rose and appears initially in the exact center of your bounding box.

The center point defines the fulcrum around which the rotation occurs. I'll rotate Figure 13.14. In the first rotated example, the center point remains in the middle and I've manually rotated the image counterclockwise to align its edges with the edge of the canvas. In the second example, I've moved the center point to the upper-right and rotated the image around it.

Original Image

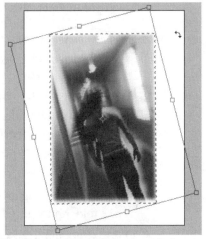

Rotated manually to align its edges with the canvas sides

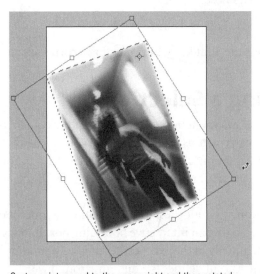

Center point moved to the upper-right and then rotated.

Figure 13.14 *(a) The original image, (b) rotated manually to align its edges with the canvas sides, and (c) with the center point moved to the upper-right and then rotated*

To move your center point, simply drag it to its new location. Here are several tips that will help you place your center point.

- Your center point's location need not lie within the selection's bounding box. Select any spot on your image to place your point. You can use this feature to rotate around your picture's corners or around an important design feature.

- When dragging the center point, as you approach the original central location of your selection, the point will automatically bounce back to this default. This snap effect allows you to return the center point to its initial position after you've experimented with moving it.

- Hold the Shift key down when moving the center point to constrain the point to several key axes: horizontal, vertical, and 45-degree diagonals.

- The center point location is shown in the first fields of the Options bar, *x* and *y*.

Performing the Rotation

Once you've set your center point, you're ready to rotate your selection. To perform your rotation, move your mouse to just outside of the bounding box. The cursor will change, becoming a small arc with arrows at each end. When you see this cursor, you're ready to rotate. Simply drag the mouse and the selection's bounding box will rotate along with your mouse movements. Release the mouse and the image will update, the selection rotating to match the new border.

The following tips might help you while rotating:

- Hold down the Shift key while rotating to limit your rotation to increments of 15 degrees. This allows you easy access to such important and common angles as 30, 45, and 60 degrees.

- Sometimes your hand slips when making an important rotation. Choose Edit ➜ Undo (or Cmd/Ctrl+Z) to reverse any rotation by one manipulation. This option leaves you within the rotation but undoes your last movement.

- Press the Esc key to completely cancel all rotation operations.

- Press Enter (Win) or Return (Mac), or double-click inside the boundary, to commit your rotation.

- The Options bar will show you the exact degree of rotation you've selected in the fifth field, the one marked by an angle symbol. To determine an exact angle of rotation, type the value into this field. Remember to use negative numbers for counterclockwise rotation and positive numbers for clockwise rotation.

Other Rotations and Flipping

The Edit ➜ Transform submenu offers five standardized transformations. These options work the same as their Image ➜ Rotate Canvas counterparts, but only on the active selection, and offer you one-click access to some of the most common image modifications.

Command	Action
Rotate 180°	Rotates your selection by 180 degrees, turning it upside down.
Rotate 90° CW	Rotates your selection clockwise by 90 degrees.
Rotate 90° CCW	Rotates your selection counterclockwise by 90 degrees.
Flip Horizontal	Mirrors your selection across the vertical axis, creating a horizontal reflection.
Flip Vertical	Mirrors your selection across the horizontal axis, creating a vertical reflection.

Skewing, Distorting, and Applying Perspective

These three functions—skewing, distorting, and applying perspective—all share a common basis: Each allows you to alter your selection by slanting image elements. Open the Clown.psd image on the CD and try these out. They work as follows.

Skew   Skewing slants your selection along one axis, either vertical or horizontal. The degree of slant affects how pitched your final image will become. To skew, simply drag one of the handles of the bounding box. The border will update after each drag. When skewing, you can move each corner independently (affecting only one border side), or you can drag the handle at the center of an edge to skew parallel borders symmetrically, as shown in Figure 13.15.

Distort   When you distort a selection, you can stretch either of its axes. Unlike skewing, slanting is not restricted to a single border at a time. Simply drag a corner and both adjacent edges will stretch along that corner (as in Figure 13.16). If you drag a border midpoint, you will stretch or shrink your selection along that edge. You can also drag the selection from any point in the middle to relocate it.

Figure 13.15 *Slant your selection with the Skew command.*

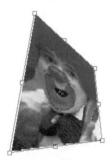

Figure 13.16 *Distort your selection by adjusting the handles on the bounding box.*

Perspective   The Perspective transformation will squeeze or stretch one edge of a selection, slanting the two adjacent sides either in or out, as shown in Figure 13.17. This produces an image that mimics the way you perceive a picture slanted at a distance. To create a perspective, you drag a corner in only one direction, either horizontally or vertically. As you drag, you either pinch together one end of the picture or pull it out.

Create skewed perspectives as easily as simple perspectives. Simply drag any border midpoint to slant your results.

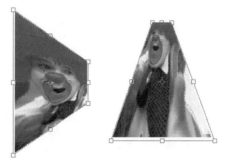

Figure 13.17 *Applying perspective to your selection makes it appear to fade off into the distance or zoom into the foreground. You can produce some wacky effects with this transformation. (left) Top-right perspective handle moved downward; (right) top perspective handles moved toward the center.*

These three transformations share some common traits. Here are some tips that apply to all three operations.

- Enter an angle into the fifth (angle) field in the Options bar, and you can rotate your selection at the same time that you skew, distort, or change perspective.

- Choose Edit ➜ Undo to reverse your last manipulation without leaving the interactive mode that allows you to skew, distort, or change perspective.

- To finish your transformations, click the check mark in the Options bar or press Enter (Win) or Return (Mac). You can instead double-click inside the boundary.

- To cancel your transformation, press Esc or click the Cancel (X) button in the Options bar.

Free Transformation

Photoshop provides an interactive bounding box that allows you to scale, rotate, or move the selection or layer contents. This combines the features of several of the tools described above in a handy, Swiss-Army sort of transformation. You can access this command in several ways.

- Choose Edit ➜ Free Transform.

- Press Ctrl+T (Win) or Command+T (Mac).

- When using the Move tool, click Show Bounding Box in the Options bar.

Once you've activated free transformation, here are the ways you can directly access its features from the bounding box.

- Drag the center point as needed. It works exactly as described in the "Rotating a Selection" section above.

- Move your mouse just outside of any of the eight squares on the bounding box, and your cursor will change to a quarter-circle with arrows on each end. You are now in Rotate mode. You can use all the rotation techniques described above.

- Move your mouse over any of the borders and you can Scale them horizontally or vertically.

- Move your mouse over any of the corners to Scale them by dragging. You can use all the scaling techniques described previously.

- Hold the Cmd/Ctrl key while dragging a corner and you enter Distort mode. The corner will drag independently of the rest of the selection.

- To duplicate the selection you wish to transform, hold down Alt (Win) or Option (Mac) while you transform it.

- If the cursor is inside the selection but not on the center point, you can move the selection.

Transforming with the Move Tool

The Move tool has become the transformation shortcut in Photoshop 6 that lets you transform your images on the fly. No more fishing around in the Edit menu for transformation features—you simply choose it and use it. When you choose the Move tool, the Options bar displays the Show Bounding Box check box. When you check the box, a bounding box surrounds the content areas of a layer. You can then move, rotate, or scale the bounding box as you would with the Free Transform feature.

Up Next

In this chapter, you learned quite a bit about the way you can transform all or part of an image. We covered the basics of image size and resolution. You learned how to adjust your image resolution and how to apply different techniques. You also studied how to crop images and how to move and resize Photoshop canvases. Finally, you learned how to apply transformations to scale, rotate, distort, or apply perspective to a selection or layer.

With the knowledge you gained in this chapter, you should feel comfortable varying the size, angle, and shape of your image. Take advantage of all these commands that empower you to manipulate specific elements within your image and to control its composition.

In the next chapter, I'll show you how to build a very important set of Photoshop skills: scanning and digital image capture. You will use some of the skills from this chapter and from the next in the Hands-On exercise that follows Chapter 14.

Scanning and
Image Capture

PHOTOSHOP

Chapter 14

Scanning and image capture can prove a very important part of your repertoire of Photoshop skills. Unless you learn how to scan or otherwise capture your own photographs, you're limited in the digital images you can use. Master the skills covered in this chapter, and you become independent, free to explore and enjoy your own photos in your own Photoshop projects.

This chapter will introduce you to:

- Scanners, cameras, and other sources

- Preparing scanned images

- Fixing scanning flaws

- Adjusting digital photographs

Scanners, Cameras, and Other Sources

A variety of technical solutions now allow you to capture image data in a form that your computer and, particularly, Photoshop 6 can understand. These technologies transform visual information into digital data. They work by translating analog values from light into digital levels that you can store and manipulate on your computer. Here's a sampling of today's most common digital imaging solutions.

Scanners

Think of your scanner as the Photoshop workhorse, providing the simplest and most direct way to convert a photographic print, transparency, or negative into digital form. A scanner sees color and tonality and converts what it sees into pixels.

Flatbed Scanners

A scanner transforms a line at a time, recording it as a series of samples, or pixels, by bouncing light off the area it needs to digitize. The scanner directs the bounced light to a series of detectors that convert color and intensity into digital levels. After recording one line, it proceeds to the next. Flatbed scanners provide good-quality images with a reasonable quantity of picture data. Compare flatbed scanners by evaluating the samples or dots produced per inch (dpi)—the higher the value, the better the scanner. Be wary, however, of advertised "interpolated" values. Interpolation means that your scanner simply guesses at the values between real samples. Keep an eye out, instead, for *optical resolution*. Reasonable-quality scanners often cost less than $100.

Transparency Scanners

Instead of bouncing light off of a piece of opaque art, a transparency scanner passes light through the emulsions on a piece of negative film or a color slide. In general, the quality of this light is better and less distorted because it is stronger than reflected light. A transparency scanner's *dynamic range* determines its ability to distinguish color variations. If you're going to purchase a transparency scanner, look for one with a high dynamic range (3.0–3.4) and a high optical resolution (2700–8000 dpi). Good transparency scanners for 35mm slides range in price from $400 to $2000. Transparency scanners are available for 120mm and 4×5 film and these are significantly more expensive.

Transparency adapters are available for flatbed scanners, but these devices don't produce the quality scan that a dedicated transparency scanner can produce, because they use reflected light instead of direct light.

Drum Scanners

Drum scanners are analog devices and have been used in the graphics industry for years. The opaque art or transparency is taped to a drum that spins very rapidly while the scanner's sensors record its color and tonality information. Older drum scanners output to process color film separations, converting the information directly into halftone dots. Newer drum scanners convert the information to pixels first. The advantage of using a drum scanner is the precision control it offers over color balance and contrast, and its ability to scan large reflective art. Drum scanners can produce outstanding quality color separations; however, they are gradually being replaced by high-end flatbed and transparency scanners.

Digital Cameras and Digital Video Cameras

Both still and video digital cameras work along the same principle. Each contains a two-dimensional array of detectors that convert an entire scene of light into digital values. Light enters the camera and is focussed onto the detectors, and the entire picture is produced at once. Two types of detectors dominate the digital camera market, the higher-quality charge-coupled devices (CCDs) and the less-expensive complementary metal-oxide semiconductor (CMOS) chips. CMOS solutions are much more prone to noise and distortion.

The size and quality of your detector limits the data you can create with your digital camera. Inexpensive digital cameras produce ever larger and more detailed images, but cannot yet come close to the level of picture information provided by the most common, inexpensive scanners. The appeal of digital cameras, however, is immediately apparent. You cannot, at last look, carry a scanner around in your pocket to snap family pictures.

Fair-quality digital cameras now cost somewhere around $500. Professional, single lens reflex, 35mm digital cameras with interchangeable lens systems are available that can produce digital images at high speeds comparable to any 35mm slide. These are significantly more expensive, ranging from $4000 to $30,000. Digital backs that attach to 120mm and 4×5 film cameras are also available and quite pricey.

Many photo processors now offer low-cost digital solutions for traditional film processing. For a few dollars, they will digitize your film and either ship them to you on a CD, upload them to a World Wide Web site, or both. This opportunity now allows more and more people to enter the world of digital imaging without laying out money for either a digital camera or a scanner.

Digitizer Boards

These special-purpose computer cards easily transform video signals into image data. Image sources for this technology include television signals and the output from VCRs and traditional (non-digital) video cameras. Such sources produce a picture screen (or *frame*) by sending out a long series of image information. Digitizer video boards, sometimes called "frame grabbers," wait until an entire screen has been received and then display it. Select the Capture function for your board, and you can grab a screen at a time.

Be aware that this method of image capture produces the noisiest and lowest-quality pictures. Most video systems depend on motion to allow your brain to interpolate between successive pictures, providing the illusion of greater image quality than really exists. As I'm sure you've seen, when you hit the Pause button on your VCR, the actual images are quite raw and low-grade. You can probably pick up a digitizing board for about $80.

Digitizing Issues

No matter which technology you use to capture your images, you should always keep a few issues in mind relating to the quality of the image you produce. For some of these topics, you have little control—the problems derive from the nature of the digitizer. For others, you can use preemptive measures to ensure that you create the highest-quality image possible.

Noise   refers to random, unintended image values added to and distributed across a digital picture. Noise is primarily a result of digitizing technology. Video capture boards create the most noise, scanners the least. To help limit noise, shoot your pictures or video with as much ambient light as possible. Photoshop can only correct noise to a limited extent.

Artifacts   are unintentional image elements produced in error by an imaging device. Artifacts usually derive from dirty optics. Make sure to clean your lenses and dust both your scanner bed and lid to help avoid artifacts in your pictures.

Resolution   is the pixel count produced by a digitizing device: the higher the pixel count, the better the image quality. Keep this in mind when purchasing a scanner or digital camera. In general, when capturing your image, always err on the side of using a higher resolution where possible. You can always use Photoshop to reduce resolution to a more manageable picture size, but you can never increase pixel count without resorting crude guesswork (called *interpolation*). Try to start at higher qualities and then work down. Keep in mind the memory and disk limitations of your computer; as you increase image resolution, you place a higher computational burden on your system.

Color Depth   refers to the number of shades you can capture at once. The more bits there are per pixel, the more hues you can represent. The most common color depth, 8 bits per color, can produce 256 shades of each hue. This may not sound like a lot of colors, but all three hues in combination (red, green, and blue) can produce almost seventeen million different colors. Color depth is particularly important in choosing a digital camera, where many manufacturers "cheat" on the blue color depth.

Color and bit depth is discussed in more detail in Chapter 10.

Preparing Scanned Images

Photoshop provides direct integration with most scanner control software. And, although you can simply open a previously scanned image, you can also scan your picture while working directly in Photoshop. The File ➜ Import submenu offers direct access to any installed scanners. As you can see in Figure 14.1, I've installed a Visioneer OneTouch on my computer. Of course, this menu will vary with the hardware currently installed.

After selecting a scanner from the submenu, its controlling dialog box will appear, as seen in Figure 14.2. Once again, this illustration represents the software and hardware installed on my personal computer, and your results will vary. However, the control panel does reflect the standards in the field in the following ways:

Quality   Most scanners offer you the opportunity to choose between Better Quality and Faster results. Better Quality means that your scanner will enable higher resolutions, providing a higher pixel count and a finer grain to your images. Faster means that your scanner will trade off resolution for time; it will scan at a lower resolution, providing a smaller, more compact image in a shorter time.

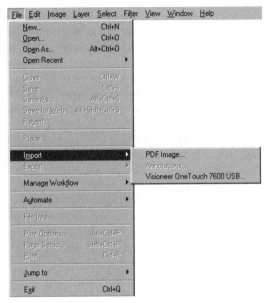

Figure 14.1 *The Import menu offers direct control of installed scanners.*

Figure 14.2 *A typical scanning dialog box*

Preview   Many scanners offer a Preview feature, which allows you to perform a very quick, low-quality scan. This scan appears in the dialog box (in this case, in the rectangle on the right). You can adjust the border of the area to be scanned in order to scan just the area you want. This allows you to reduce the memory load when performing a high quality scan.

B&W or Color   Most scanners allow you to select between a grayscale or color scan. Grayscale images typically use about a third of the memory of color images.

Scan   Every scanner provides a Scan button to initiate the scanning process. As the scan proceeds, you will generally see a progress bar indicating what percentage of the document has been scanned.

Try it yourself: See if you can use your scanner to capture a digital image to use with Photoshop. Don't have a scanner? You can open the Cover.psd file found in the Ch14 folder on the *Mastering Photoshop 6* CD (and shown in Figure 14.3). This image shows a scan made of a book cover. Either way, you will need to open a scanned image so you can follow the directions found throughout the upcoming sections. Once your scanner finishes digitizing your image, the picture opens automatically in Photoshop.

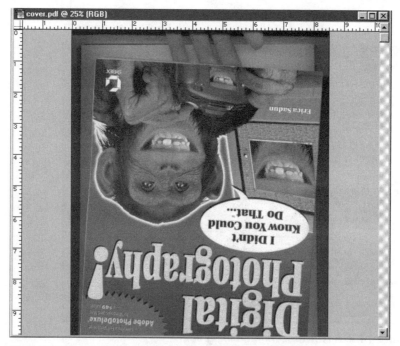

Figure 14.3 *This image shows many flaws typical of the scanning process.*

Don't scan copyrighted material without permission! I had specific approval to use this book cover from the folks at Sybex.

The scan in Figure 14.3 demonstrates several problems associated with scanning. Try to identify and note these problems. They will better allow you to assess, and later correct, the results of your scans.

Orientation　The image has scanned upside down. My scanner, and many others, counterintuitively scans from bottom to top rather than top to bottom. Whenever I forget, orienting my material with the normal lay of the machine, my picture appears topsy-turvy.

Skew　Some people find the task of precisely aligning their material with the scan-lines nearly impossible—especially if they do not line their source material exactly along the sides of the scanner. Pictures often scan at a slight angle that must be fixed. Ideally, a perfect alignment allows you avoid later rotation, a task that can degrade image quality.

Extra Bits　When scanning, extra things tend to appear around your main image. These things might include bits of the scanner bay, sticky notes, or even fingers, as you can see in Figure 14.3.

Using your hand to hold down a book, as I did in the illustration, is a terrible habit. Hands can leave fingerprints on your glass, and heavy scanner lids can cause injury. I've provided this example to demonstrate scanning problems, not to promote bad scanning technique!

Artifacts　Although not shown in Figure 14.3, unintended streaks, fingerprints, scratches, and stray pen marks may pop up in your scanned images. Be on the alert for these flaws, and always make sure to clean your scanner glass each time you use it.

The key to preparing a scanned image is to do as little correction and embellishment as possible. Recall that each time you manipulate an image in Photoshop, you might erode its quality. Your goal in this stage of image preparation should be creating a usable, well-detailed source photo that you can use for other tasks.

You should always make a backup of your raw, original scan as well as your corrected "original."

The scanning flaws detailed above motivate the way you must approach preparing your image. First, you correct orientation. Second, you align the image. Third, you crop. After performing these three steps, you'll have transformed the scanned photo into a usable and useful digital image.

Correcting Orientation

You might come across a variety of orientation problems in scanned images. In addition to finding pictures upside-down, you might also scan pictures whose widths exceeds their heights, enough that you must scan them sideways. The Image → Rotate Canvas submenu (described in Chapter 13) allows you to select between rotating your image completely around, turning it to the left (a 90-degree counterclockwise rotation), or turning to the right (a 90-degree clockwise rotation). Select the option that best suits your scanned image. If your image is upside-down, choose Image → Rotate Canvas → 180°. You can observe the results of this rotation on the book cover in Figure 14.4.

You may note that the two steps, orienting and aligning your images, seem similar. I separate these steps, orienting the image before aligning it, simply because my perception works far better when pictures look "right side up" to me.

Figure 14.4 *After rotation, the scanned image returns to its proper orientation.*

Aligning the Image

After correcting the orientation, your next challenge lies in removing its skew. As you can see in Figure 14.4 (the Cover.psd file after Image ➔ Rotate Canvas ➔ 180°), the book cover lies at a decided slant. Let's align the image.

1. Zoom in so that you can clearly see the top edge of the cover including both the left and right corners.

2. Display the rulers (View ➔ Show Rulers) and pull a guide down to the left corner of your scanned image's top edge. Watch out for shadows and place the guide exactly.

3. Next, pull a guide from the left ruler to the top-left corner of the scan. Again, take care to place the guide precisely. (Figure 14.5 shows the Cover.psd image with guides in place.) You will be using the intersection of these two guides to place your axis of rotation.

Figure 14.5 *I've zoomed in and placed guides that intersect precisely at the corner of the book.*

4. Repeat the previous two steps to place guides crossing at the top-right corner of the cover.

5. Select the Measure tool from the Eyedropper tool flyout.

6. Draw a line from the top-left corner to the top-right corner of the cover. The guides will assure that the Measure tool snaps to the two corners.

7. Select Image → Rotate Canvas → Arbitrary. Note that the Measure tool has automatically placed the angle into the dialog.

8. Click OK and wait for Photoshop to rotate your image so that it is level.

In the Hands-On project that follows this chapter, I'll show you a slightly different method for precisely rotating your image, using guides exclusively.

Cropping the Image

Once you've aligned the image, it's time to crop it. This will remove all the extraneous material, returning your picture to its original state. Follow these steps to perform your crop.

1. If you continue from the last step, you will need to clear the guides from your image. To do so, select View → Clear Guides.

2. Carefully place guides along each edge of your image. Drag each guide Figure 14.6 shows the book cover image with all four guides in place.

3. Select the Crop tool from the Tool palette.

4. Drag out the cropping area, allowing the Crop tool to snap to each guide as in Figure 14.7.

5. Press the Enter (Win) or Return (Mac) key to complete the crop.

6. Select View → Clear Guides to clean up your image by removing the guides.

Figure 14.8 shows the final result of this procedure. Make sure to save a copy of your correct images before proceeding with additional Photoshop operations! (You will find a copy of this aligned and cropped image in the Cover_crop.psd file in the Ch14 folder on the CD.)

Figure 14.6 *Guides will ensure a perfect crop.*

Figure 14.7 *Dragging the Crop tool from one guide corner to the opposite corner makes a perfect crop marquee.*

Figure 14.8 *After orienting, aligning, and cropping, a final image is produced.*

Fixing Scanning Flaws

Scanning, particularly from print material, often produces the kind of moiré pattern seen in Figure 14.9. This flaw appears as a series of ridges and is an artifact of both the scanning and rotating process. Fortunately, Photoshop provides tools that can help minimize this effect.

Filters like Despeckle and Gaussian Blur are the topic of Chapter 18, "Filtering Your Image."

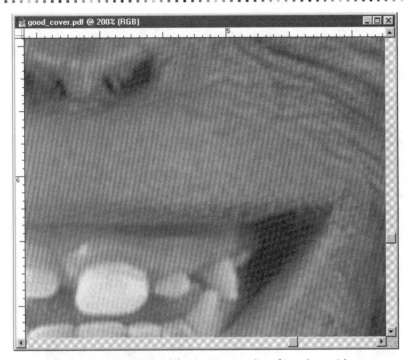

Figure 14.9 Images scanned from print media often show ridges.

Using Despeckle

Often, I first turn to Despeckle to fix these ridges. This filter detects the edges in your image. It then blurs all the selection *except* for those edges. It works by removing noise yet preserving detail and is intended specifically for flaws of this type. Some Photoshop users automatically use Gaussian Blur to fix all kinds of noise, often overlooking small treasures like Despeckle. Let's fix some of those flaws. Start by opening Cover_crop.psd from the Ch14 folder on the CD.

1. Select the Zoom tool from the Tool palette and zoom in on the monkey's mouth and teeth to 200%, as shown in Figure 14.9.

2. Choose Filter ➜ Noise ➜ Despeckle to detect the edges in your image.

3. Go ahead and apply Despeckle again. Figure 14.10 shows the result of applying Despeckle twice to Figure 14.9.

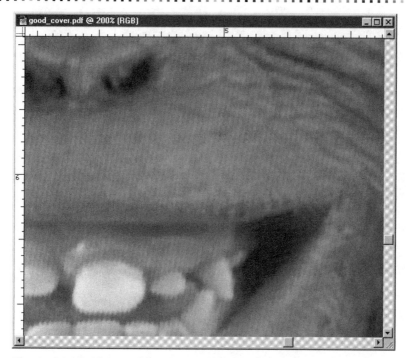

Figure 14.10 *After applying Despeckle twice, image flaws are noticeably reduced.*

Using Gaussian Blur

Don't rule out using Gaussian Blur. It provides excellent results for many circumstances. In this case, where you're aiming to process the image without eroding general quality, Gaussian Blur works far better when applied solely to the Blue channel. One of the great secrets of scanner and digital camera technology is that the human eye responds less to blue than it does to red or green. This allows manufacturers to "cheat" by including less information and more noise in the Blue channel and focus quality on the better-perceived Red and Green channels. Because of this, you'll often greatly improve your image by adjusting its Blue channel.

To review the Channels interface and functions, read Chapter 12.

1. Open the Channels palette (Window ➜ Show Channels) and hide all the channels except Blue. Figure 14.11 shows the Blue channel of the book-cover image. Notice the coarseness and blobby artifacts found throughout this channel.

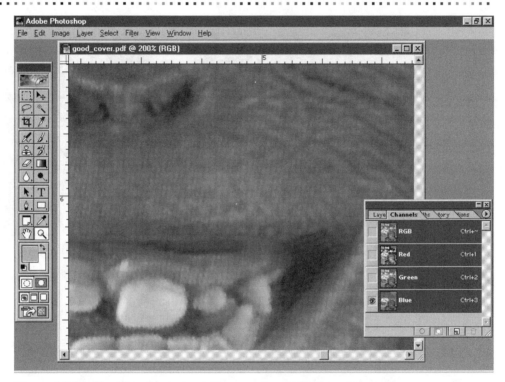

Figure 14.11 *The Blue channel reveals many image flaws.*

2. Select the entire image by choosing Edit ➜ Select All or pressing Cmd/Ctrl+A.

3. Choose Filter ➜ Blur ➜ Gaussian Blur. Use small Radius values, under 3.0. (I used 2.0 in this example.) It's best to take this in steps: If you're not satisfied with the blurring effect, you can undo the filter or apply it again to increase the blur. Also, do not overlook the preview feature that allows you to see the results

before you commit the filter. By applying the Gaussian Blur filter to the Blue channel, you allow Photoshop to smooth out many image flaws while retaining crispness in both the Red and Green channels. Contrast the before and after images in Figure 14.12 to see how effectively this filter blurs the Blue channel. Notice how this filter differs from Despeckle in that even the features and edges blur to a smooth finish.

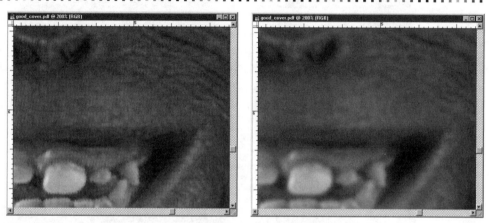

Figure 14.12 *Use the Gaussian Blur filter to smooth out the rough edges found in your Blue channel: (left) before and (right) after.*

4. Make the Red and Green channels visible again.

5. Zoom back out to a macroscopic level, using the Zoom tool or the View menu. Figure 14.13 shows your image at 66.7%.

Notice that we've retained excellent image detail throughout the transformation while ridding ourselves of the more unfortunate side effects of the scanning process. The fine creases and skin textures remain around the monkey's nose and fingers. The camera looks smooth and finished. You can still detect the fine structure of individual hairs. If you look carefully, particularly on the "pinky" of the monkey's hand, you can still see remnants of the original flaws. All in all, however, you can declare this repair process a success and move on to using this image in other projects.

Figure 14.13 *You've successfully removed most of the scanning artifacts while retaining excellent image detail.*

Adjusting Digital Photographs

Digital photographs share many traits with scanned images while retaining a few quirks of their own. Here are some ways in which they differ:

Size   Digital photographs are limited in size to the resolution of their image-capture chip and produce, in general, much smaller images than scanners do.

Functionality   Digital cameras work best when used in the same way you'd use a traditional camera. Many do not capture pages or printed photographs particularly well, although they can be used in a pinch to create relatively low-resolution copies of printed material.

Blue Channel   The "Blue channel" effect discussed in the previous section tends to be far more pronounced in digital photography than in scanned images. The solution for this—blurring the Blue channel—proves just as effective with digital photos, if not more so. (See Chapter 12, "Using Channels and Quick Mask.")

Noise   Noise in digital photographs tends to be the product of low light conditions (a different problem than the systematic and regular patterns of scanning that you saw in the previous section). One of the best ways to avoid noise in digital snapshots is to increase ambient light. Of course, an even better method is to purchase better-quality equipment with high-end sensors.

Lens Flaws   Digital cameras are much more subject to systematic flaws from lens distortion than scanners are, especially for images taken at close range. While this is something to keep in mind, lens flaws rarely affect your day-to-day camera operations or the way you process them in Photoshop.

Cropping and Rotation   Although you can choose to crop your digital snapshots—after all, photos frequently need cropping—you might not have to. Fill your viewfinder, keep your finger off the lens, and you will often not have to deal with equivalents to the hand and scanner-lid artifacts seen in the preceding book-cover example. Similarly, when shooting a photo rather than scanning one, you rarely (if ever) need to make the fine alignment adjustment that you do for scanned images.

Preparing Digital Photographs

As with scanned imagery, it helps to prepare your photographs before using them in Photoshop projects. However, the steps commonly taken vary slightly. Instead of placing your emphasis on rotation and alignment, you'll focus on fixing your Blue channel and bringing out hidden features. The steps you'll take include orientation, blue correction, and adjusting levels. Again, be sure to save a copy of your "digital negative" before proceeding with these steps.

Correcting Orientation

Because you can, and often do, hold a camera in nearly any orientation, the first step in preparing a digital photograph involves restoring the intended bearings. To practice, open Outdoors.psd (Figure 14.14) in the Ch14 folder on the CD, in Photoshop. Although this isn't the most intriguing composition in the world, it does serve to demonstrate some common problems with capture, color, and contrast.

Figure 14.14 *A digital photograph, opened in Photoshop*

Select a command from the Image ➜ Rotate Canvas submenu to turn your image around. You can choose between turning it 90 degrees clockwise or counterclockwise. For the Outdoors.psd image, rotate 90 degrees counterclockwise. Zoom as needed before moving on to the next series of steps.

Smoothing the Blue Channel

You can improve nearly any digital photograph by smoothing its Blue channel. Digital snapshots cheat much more in blue than scanned images do. I make it a regular step when preparing a digital photograph to give a nice little blur to the blue. Be aware that you sacrifice detail by using this process. Take special care when your image contains a lot of blue detail that you do want to retain—for example, a close-up shot of denim.

1. Choose Window ➜ Show Channels.

2. Click the Blue channel thumbnail to target it.

3. Turn off the other channels to show the Blue channel only.

4. Choose Filter ➜ Blur ➜ Gaussian Blur.

5. Blur your image with a Radius of 2.0.

6. Click the RGB channel to restore the visibility of the Red and Green channels.

Adjusting Levels

My third automatic step when processing a digital snapshot involves taking advantage of Photoshop's wonderful Auto Levels feature. This command, found at Image ➜ Adjust ➜ Auto Levels, instantly corrects many digital photographs; using it can quickly provide you with a first stab at enhancing colors, brightness, and contrast to create a more pleasing and usable image. Notice, however, that I said "many." The Auto Levels command does fail, particularly in well-illuminated outdoor shots where important image detail can be lost in shadows.

Watch your previewed image carefully, and be ready to Undo, because Auto Levels can potentially intro-duce color casts that you will need to eliminate.

Improving your image by adjusting levels and curves is covered in more detail in Chapter 16, "Adjusting Tonality and Color."

Up Next

In this chapter, you've been introduced to the technologies and methodologies used for bringing digital images into Photoshop. You've learned about the various ways you can capture digital pictures, how to prepare and fix some basic problems with scanned images, and how you can quickly adjust photos from digital cameras before using them in other projects.

You learned about several digitizing techniques: scanners, digital cameras, and frame grabbers. I covered how to prepare a scanned image, and the ways that system-atic scanning errors could appear in a scan. You explored images produced by digital cameras and compared the ways that digital photography differs from scanned images.

The following Hands-On project provides practice for some of the tasks you learned in Chapters 13 and 14.

Hands-On
Digital Photograph Prep

Now that you've learned all about sizing, transforming, and capturing digital images, let's get your hands dirty! Here's the scenario. You're a pro, doing advertising design. But your father has just shown up on your doorstep. He says: "I cannot find the negative *anywhere,* and I need copies of this picture right away for my holiday cards! Can you scan this picture?"

Your father wants to upload a copy of the snapshot to a digital photo-processing site, so he can order a huge number of inexpensive copies. And now he needs you. Here's how you can make him happy.

Getting Started

Quit Photoshop and hide your preferences file before beginning this Hands-On exercise. Then relaunch Photoshop to create a clean version. The "Photoshop's Settings" section in Chapter 5 details how to temporarily reset your preferences to Photoshop defaults. You can restore your customized personal settings when you're done.

Before aligning or correcting your image, start by orienting it correctly. The following steps guide you through this process.

1. Open the scanned original, `Family_start.psd` (Figure 1), from the `Ch14` folder of the CD accompanying this book.

2. As you can see, the image has scanned completely upside down. Select Image ➜ Rotate Canvas ➜ 180°. This step rotates your picture completely around, righting its orientation.

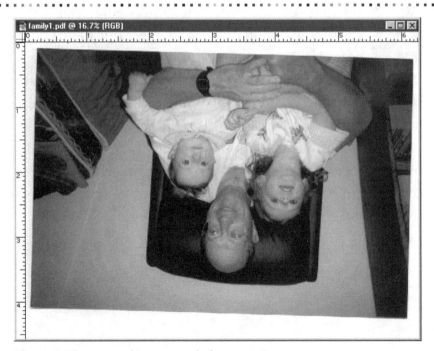

Figure 1 *The scanned image, ready for correction*

Aligning Your Image

Your next task is to select a good alignment so the main subjects will not appear to "lean" on the print. You'll do this by orienting along the top edge of the black chair. This will provide your rotation reference point. This "all-guides" technique provides an alternative to the Measure tool procedure discussed in Chapter 14.

1. If they are not already turned on, turn on your image rulers by selecting View ➜ Show Rulers.

2. Move your mouse onto the top ruler and drag down a guide until it touches the indentation on the top left of the black chair.

3. Move your mouse onto the left ruler and drag across another guide, again touching the indentation on the top left of the black chair. These two guides will help set the rotation point for your picture.

4. Select the entire image with Cmd/Ctrl+A.

5. Choose Edit ➜ Transform ➜ Rotate.

6. Move the center point of the rotation to the intersection of the two guides. By doing so, you'll rotate around the top-left indentation of the black chair.

7. Move the mouse near the border of your selection, until it turns into the "quarter-circle with two-arrows" Rotate cursor. Always make sure you see this cursor before you attempt to rotate!

8. Carefully rotate your image until the indentation on the top right of the black chair touches the top guide. I suggest you perform this rotation in a series of small incremental adjustments.

9. When the top-right indentation exactly touches the top guide, press Enter (PC) or Return (Mac). Wait for Photoshop to complete the rotation.

10. Select View ➔ Clear Guides to remove your guides from the picture.

After performing this series of steps, you'll have added a much-needed, more natural alignment to the picture.

Cropping Your Picture

Now that you've aligned the picture, you can crop it down to a 4×6 rectangle, suitable for printing.

1. Click the Crop tool on the Tool palette.

2. Click the Width field in the Options bar and enter **6 in**.

3. Click the Height field in the Options bar and enter **4 in**. When you set these fields, you constrain your crop to a 6:4 aspect ratio and create a perfectly sized result.

4. Drag out a cropping rectangle from just above and to the left of the black chair to just below and to the right of the baby's elbow.

5. Press Enter (Win) or Return (Mac) to perform the crop.

Now that you've finished cropping, you've created a well-composed, balanced and presentable image. And because you used precise proportions for a 4×6 image, you know the picture will print perfectly at the finishers.

Checking Your Resolution

Now that you have cropped your image, we'll confirm that you've retained enough resolution to create a good-quality print—if you have not, you'll probably want to undo the previous step and try again. In general, do not attempt to create a silver-halide print of any image with a resolution below 100 pixels per inch (ppi). 200 ppi provides much better quality. Any resolution above that—say, 300 ppi or higher—will produce excellent, 35mm-quality prints.

To check your resolution, select Image → Image Size. Do this and you will confirm that this sample image retains a resolution of more than 400 ppi, even after cropping down to a 4×6 print size. This assures you that your image will produce a silver-halide print at the very highest quality. In fact, the quality is almost too high. The current size of your document is well over 10 megabytes. You are going to have lower the resolution in order to limit the time it will take to upload your image to the World Wide Web. However, reducing resolution should always come as your last step. Perform this resolution check after your crop, but wait to resize your canvas until *after* you have finished all your Photoshop corrections. This ensures that you work with the greatest number of the pixels and the highest quality data before committing yourself to a drastic loss of image information.

Correcting Image Levels

It's now time to improve the way your picture looks. Don't settle for drab, washed-out photos. Often, we'd start by allowing Auto Levels to do its job. However, when you do so here (just choose Image → Adjust → Auto Levels), little improvement occurs. The flash photography employed in taking this snapshot has resulted in a flat, overexposed image. Instead, we'll use Levels to improve our picture.

1. Choose Image → Adjust → Levels to bring up the Levels dialog box. Take note of the three eyedropper buttons found in the lower-right corner of the dialog, just above the Preview option. You will use this dialog to set the levels for the darkest, lightest, and midpoint for your photo and allow Photoshop to set the levels in between.

2. Click the Black Eyedropper icon, the first and leftmost of the three. Your cursor will change, reflecting this option. Move the eyedropper to the darkest part of the black chair and click.

3. Click the White Eyedropper icon, the third of the three choices. Use the eyedropper to click the whitest part of the man's shirt.

4. Now we'll set the midtone. Click the Gray Eyedropper icon and click the wall to the left of the subjects. Click fairly low down—say, a quarter of the way from the bottom. You may wish to experiment here, clicking at several locations until arriving at one that pleases you. You can always compare "before" and "after" by selecting and deselecting the Preview box.

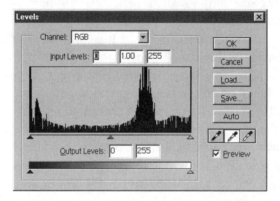

Downsizing

After you have finished all image corrections—if you've read ahead in the book, I imagine that you might spend some time fixing the baby's red-eye and the glare on the man's glasses—you're ready to downsize your image. Waiting until the end to do this allows you to proceed without hampering the corrective process with irreversible data loss. This also permits you to retain an "original" fixed image and a copy, saved for printing, at a lower resolution.

1. Select Image ➔ Image Size.

2. Turn on the Resample Image option, retaining Bicubic interpolation selection from the pull-down list to its right (Figure 14.2).

3. Enter 200 in the Resolution field and click OK. Wait for Photoshop to finish resampling the image.

4. Once again, select Image ➜ Image Size and note that the image now occupies only about 3 megabytes, much more suitable for uploading to the Internet. (To save time, click Cancel, as we have only reopened this dialog for information purposes.)

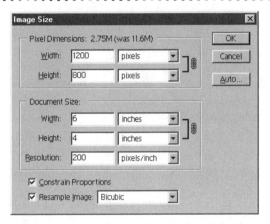

Figure 14.2 *Be sure the Resample method is Bicubic.*

Up Next

So congratulations. You've done it all! You're ready to save the picture, upload it to your father's favorite photofinisher, and order prints for him. You can get on to some paying work now. (But don't forget to call Dad, okay?)

Part II of this book, "Color Adjustment and Image Retouching," begins next. In Chapter 15, you'll be introduced to color management systems, and you'll see how important it is to control your color space and hardware. I'll also discuss converting and printing color files.

Part II
Color Adjustment and Image Retouching

In This Part

Color Management and Printing

![PHOTOSHOP]

Chapter 15

You labored long and hard to get the color exactly right. You used all the tricks—Levels, Curves, Selective Color, Color Balance, Adjustment layers, the Unsharp Mask filter—and the image looked perfect on the monitor. Unfortunately, what your printer spit out looks quite different. Those beautiful sky blues and brilliant magentas turned to gloomy grays and muddy maroons. Furthermore, the image looks quite different from monitor to monitor.

If you're a digital artist or graphic designer using Photoshop to print color images, you probably frequently ask yourself two very important questions: How can I be confident that the color on my monitor will be matched by the color of the printer? And how can I trust that the color on *my* monitor will look like the color on *your* monitor? These questions are about how you *manage* color from one device to another, and that's what this chapter is about.

In this chapter, you'll read about:

- Why we need to manage color

- Managing color between monitors

- Converting colors

- Printing images

Why Manage Color?

In the years before the desktop publishing revolution, professional color systems were used in the creation and modification of high-quality printing and publishing. These, methods of color management relied on what is called "closed-loop" color, the idea being that nothing ever escaped the system. No outside files were accepted, and no files were ever allowed to leave the system except in the form of separated film, ready for printing. Looking back, those were the "good ol' days" when the reliability of color was—mostly—under control. The systems were expensive, and compared to today's computers, very slow. But they worked.

Desktop technologies created a *distributed* model for color production. Some of the work was done on a computer not connected to a prepress color system. It was the differences between systems—different monitors, different viewing conditions, and different software applications—that created the need for color management.

Scientists went to work on the problem in the late 1980s, developing a model for color management that would eventually provide software tools to ensure that color would match, location-to-location and device-to-device. The first practical color management system, Apple ColorSync, arrived in 1991, and has undergone improvements since. Over the years, the idea of color management has migrated to most professional software applications—including Adobe Photoshop. Today most computers and operating systems have a facility for color management, and most applications have built-in support for color management. The challenge is getting it to work.

The Color Working Space

In the fall of 1998, the Photoshop development team rocked the design and printing community with a completely new outlook on color. The release of Photoshop 5.0 got the attention of all color practitioners in the digital imaging world by introducing the concept of the *color working space*. Prior to Photoshop 5, "color" was only the color available on the computer monitor. The curious thing about that philosophy is, there are so many different types of monitors that the color of a document on one computer may very well appear dissimilar to the same document on another monitor. It was impossible to maintain color accuracy, or to display an image correctly on any other machine.

The color working space changed all that by creating an environment for handling the color that is separate from the monitor. Under this model, it is possible to scan, save, work, and store an image with a color space other than that of the monitor. The image is embedded with an ICC (International Color Consortium) profile that describes the color working space (sometimes simply called color space or working space). The image can then move from one computer to another with its profile and can appear the same on two different monitors.

The color working space concept created the opportunity for Photoshop to accommodate images from scanners and other sources whose color gamuts exceed the available colors on monitor. The color working space allows for color to be captured, modified, stored, and output without harming the color gamut of the original.

A Window into a Window

To grasp the concept of color working space, imagine that the image you see on your monitor exists on a separate, parallel plane, just behind your monitor, and that your monitor acts like a window into the image. The image you see may be the entire image, but it might not be. It might be distorted by the window's characteristics or size. Perhaps the window is not perfectly transparent, perhaps it is slightly tinted, or perhaps light is reflecting off of its surface causing the image to appear different than the image that exists in the color working space.

In fact, computer monitors really behave like windows into our images, modifying the "reality" of the actual image and displaying something that is appropriate to the monitor's abilities, but not always appropriate to the qualities of the image itself.

For professional graphic artists, the monitor is an excellent window into the image. This is true because we spend considerable sums of money on quality monitors that have good color gamuts and a range of brightness that will allow us to see *almost* all the qualities of the image in Photoshop. But lesser monitors don't provide such an undistorted view.

Monitor Quality

To better understand this, consider the monitor. Monitors are light emitters: they create light from electrical energy. A cathode ray tube monitor like the one on your computer is a television-like picture tube. As illustrated in Figure 15.1, it uses electrons beamed at the monitor's face from the back of the picture tube to stimulate mineral phosphors that are coated on the inside of the face of the tube, creating light of a single color on the face. The electrons are invisible to the human eye, but when they strike the coating, the phosphors react, emitting visible light in a spectrum that is within the color gamut of human vision. Activating those phosphors in combination with others causes "color" to be created on the face of the picture tube.

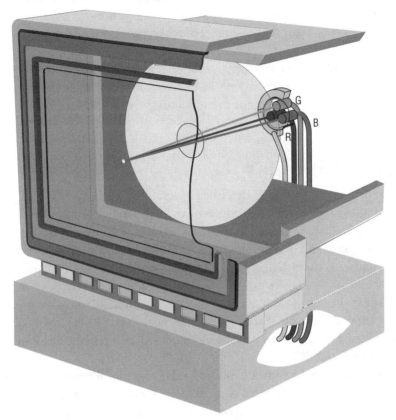

Figure 15.1 *A cross-section of a cathode-ray tube showing the separate high-voltage amplifiers for the red, green, and blue signals.*

As with many electromechanical devices, there is considerable variability in the manufacture of picture tubes and in the quality of minerals used to coat the inside of the tube. Some computer monitors sell for less than $100, while others sell for more than $1500. In addition to the size of the monitor, there are quality issues to take into account when evaluating a monitor's color. Is the color quality of a sub-$100 monitor likely to be very good? How will it compare to the color quality of a graphic arts–quality monitor designed for critical color decisions? Cost-cutting measures taken by the makers of low-cost monitors include coating the monitor with phosphors of inconsistent quality or low purity. It might be possible to reduce manufacturing costs by reducing the quality control checks that are made in manufacture to ensure that each monitor meets the company's standards. By contrast, a graphic arts–quality monitor will be made from components that cost more to make, more to test, and more to deliver to the end user.

The Photoshop team's challenge with version 5, then, was to make it possible to create an image on a computer with a $1500 monitor, that could be viewed on a monitor of lesser quality, and continue in production—without damaging the color of the image in the process.

Monitor Profiles

A monitor's characteristics are described by its ability to display pure red, green, and blue colors as bright, clear components of an image. In the visual arts we use such colors, and the millions of color permutations possible when mixing them together, to make our photos and illustrations. In order for Photoshop to display an image correctly, it must know the characteristics of the monitor you are using. To do this, we provide Photoshop with a piece of software called a *monitor profile*.

The monitor profile is made by one of several means. The easiest method is to make a visual calibration of your monitor using version 5 or later of Adobe Gamma to test and adjust the appearance of the monitor, and then save the resulting information as a *color profile* (see Chapter 5, "Setting Up Photoshop").

Adobe Gamma is a software monitor calibrator that allows the artist to build and save a monitor profile without having to spend money on more costly measurement instruments and software that serve this purpose. Gamma is installed when Photoshop is installed. To use it, follow the on-screen instructions.

The Viewing Environment

Professionals in the printing and publishing industries have known for years that good color on a computer monitor is accomplished partly by putting the monitor into a "proper" viewing environment. The International Organization for Standardization (ISO) and its partner national organizations recently adopted a new color standard for viewing color for the photographic and graphic arts industries worldwide. Called ISO 3664, the standard dictates, among other things, that a proper viewing environment is a workspace without windows or skylights—no natural light at all. They also specify that the color of the walls should be neutral gray (the ISO committee specifies the color

Munsell N5 through N7 for the walls). The walls should be absent of colorful artwork, and the artist in front of the computer should be wearing neutral clothing, preferably gray or black. Room lighting recommendations in the ISO standard are for very low, preferably diffuse lighting of the proper 5000 K temperature.

Is this a happy place to work? It's pretty dull, but it's a workplace where color can be viewed most accurately. Some design studios and professional prepress operations have such a workplace, but reserve it for "soft proofing" visits, which provide an opportunity for workers to go into the "cave" only long enough to approve color on-screen.

Determining a Monitor Profile

Just having the monitor profile and a proper viewing environment are not enough. You must first tell your operating system about the profile, setting it as the system profile, and then, when you launch Photoshop, it will use your monitor profile for some of its color display calculations.

There are two ways to tell your system about the monitor profile you have created on a Macintosh. Under the Apple menu, choose Control Panels ➜ Monitors and click the Color icon; from the ColorSync menu, choose a profile. Or choose Control Panels ➜ ColorSync directly from the Apple menu to display the dialog box. Click the Set Profile button and choose a profile from the list.

On Windows 98 or 2000, choose Start ➜ Settings ➜ Control Panel ➜ Display ➜ Color Management. (Windows 95 and NT do not support color management.)

 The Windows path will depend on the video board you have installed. For some boards, you may have to choose Control Panel ➜ Display ➜ Settings ➜ Advanced ➜ Color Management.

Choose the system profile or the profile you created with Adobe Gamma or another monitor-profiling application. The computer will know how to correct the color displayed on your monitor through the profile, making adjustments on the fly to all images displayed on screen.

Photoshop automatically looks to the operating system to get the name of the current monitor profile, and you cannot change that setting from within the latest version of Photoshop. But it is possible to "turn color management off" in the Color Settings control panel. This has the effect of returning Photoshop 6 approximately to the functionality of Photoshop 4, limiting the color gamut to that of the monitor and disabling all color-space conversions.

The Yin/Yang of Color

When we discuss the *gamuts* of color working spaces, we must understand that the gamut of a monitor is a triangular space with its corners in the red, green, and blue areas of an industry-standard color chart. The gamut chart in Figure 15.2 (please refer to the full-color version in the color section) plots the available colors of a device (a monitor, for example) compared to the gamut of colors humans can see—and the differences are extreme.

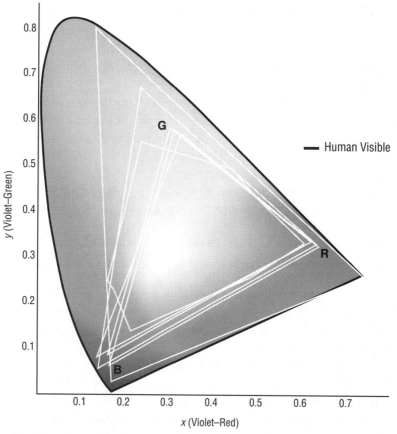

Figure 15.2 *The color gamuts of various color working spaces*

All of the color spaces of the world of graphic arts and photography converge inside a large triangle that falls well within the colors of human vision. With Photoshop's support for the color working space, we want to choose a space that is adequate to accommodate most if not all the colors of our output device, while providing a reasonable view of that color on our monitor.

Unfortunately, the color system used for printing color on paper is the physical opposite of the color system used to emit light on the face of a monitor. With light-emitting devices, the unit creates, and mixes, colors from the three additive color primaries—red, green, and blue. When you add approximately equal parts of red, green, and blue light on a monitor at full intensity, you get "white."

The vibrancy and brightness of these primary colors on a picture tube are usually far greater in those primary colors than they can ever be on the printed page, because the printing process begins with the available "white" light in the viewing environment, and then filters out components of that light to simulate color. The processes are called *additive* (for light-emitting devices) and *subtractive* (for printed products).

When you put pigment on a sheet of paper, superimposing the primary colors of ink (cyan, yellow, magenta) on top of each other, in an ideal world you would get pure black, but in reality, because of impurities in the ink, you get something that approximates deep, yucky brown. (Technical term!) Because pigments subtract light components from the white light in the environment, they reduce its intensity, making it less bright than unfiltered light. Subtractive colorants always reduce the amount of light reflected back at the viewer, and thus it's very hard for the printed page to compete with the bright color on a nice computer monitor. And there we have the classic yin/yang of color—the conflict between the two scientific principles of color reproduction—and another reason we need color management in our lives. The strengths of emitted light on a monitor are the weaknesses of colors on the printed page.

It is common to hear people say that there is *less* color available on the printed page than on a monitor, but that is not necessarily true. If you calculate the *area* occupied by the plot of monitor colors, and compare it to the *area* of colors available on the printed page, the two areas will be approximately equal. But they are *very different.* Where the monitor is strongest in red, green, and blue, the printed page is strongest in yellow, cyan, and magenta, the color complements of monitor colors.

If we want to reproduce the best color possible on the printed page, while still displaying the color in the same images, we must acknowledge and accept the weakness of the monitor relative to the printed page, and vice versa. The compromises we must learn to accept are that there are colors—mostly in the range of cyan to pale green—that we can print, but cannot see on even the best monitor. Likewise, there are colors in the deep blue (you could call it purple) and vibrant green points that we can display on a monitor, but cannot print with the standard four-color ink sets used on ink-jet printers and printing machines.

Making a Colorful Match

Choosing a color working space that is appropriate to the printed page is critically important so that we don't force Photoshop to remap the colors in an image. We want to pick a working space that is not too big (so we don't add colors that are out of the printable range) and not too small (so we don't omit colors needed to accurately represent the image).

The gamut chart in Figure 15.2 and in the color section shows the comparative gamuts of several of Photoshop's color working spaces. Superimposed in yellow is the gamut of standard printing inks on gloss paper (called the SWOP Coated gamut).

Gamma

Gamma is a number, from 1.0 to about 2.5, that describes the curvature of a contrast curve control for a monitor. The Macintosh has traditionally used a gamma of 1.8, which is relatively flat compared to television. Windows PCs use a 2.2 gamma value, which is more contrasty and more saturated. The gamma of Windows is closer to the "natural" appearance of the world, while the 1.8 gamma adopted by the Macintosh is more like the contrast of printing on good paper. If you are working on images destined for television, the World Wide Web, or multimedia, it's better to use a gamma of 2.2. If your destination is the printed page, a gamma of 1.8 to 2.0 may be more appropriate.

Getting to Know RGB Color Working Space

The color working space is, as already mentioned, a plane for holding and handling images in Photoshop that is independent of the monitor. Color working spaces include a variety of oddly-named spaces that usually confound the new visitor. But, we'll work on that…

The RGB color working spaces of Adobe Photoshop include five standard color spaces. Photoshop also has the ability to choose others that that are designed for other working environments or offer special qualities that assist in your work. Each has a combination of characteristics, including its color temperature, gamma, and white point (the phosphor settings for "white"). White is a variable thing in the world of computer-generated color, because the effective "whiteness" of the non-image areas is a key component in getting the color on the screen to match the color that is produced by a printer or a commercial printing press.

sRGB IEC61966-2.1

Of the color spaces available, sRGB (the *s* stands for *standardized*) is the smallest. This means that it puts serious limitations on the colors available in your color palette in Photoshop. The sRGB space, designed by Microsoft and Hewlett-Packard, is well-suited to corporate computer monitors and images destined for viewing on the World Wide Web. sRGB has taken a lot of flack for being destructive to images of large color gamut, and indeed it is. But, if you look at the purpose of sRGB—making images look good on corporate computers—the color space makes more sense and is useful for its intended purpose.

It is, unfortunately, set as the default color working space in Photoshop 6 (as it was in 5), and that is the root of the controversy surrounding it. Adobe allows you to change the setting—but most people don't realize that it is important to do so. Use sRGB as your color working space, or convert images to this space, when developing images strictly for display on the Web or in corporate environments. Otherwise use…

Adobe RGB (1998)

The Adobe RGB (1998) color working space is large enough to accommodate graphic arts images and most scanned images, and allows for good representation on most high-quality monitors. Adobe RGB (1998) has a white point of 6500 K, which is in line with the latest ISO standard (ISO 3664) for color viewing in critical color conditions. Its gamma, a measurement of contrast and saturation, is 2.2. Adobe RGB (1998) is also able to accommodate conversions to CMYK for printing with good results; very little of the CMYK color is clipped or remapped in the process.

Don't confuse the K that crops up in color discussions about white point with K for kilobytes or black (as in CMYK). Here it stands for degrees Kelvin; 6500 K is approximately the "temperature" of outdoor ambient light in the middle of a clear day.

Apple RGB

The original "graphic arts" monitor was the Apple 13-inch RGB monitor. It created an industry, providing color previews to millions of users from 1988 to about 1995, when it was replaced by better and larger monitors. Based on a Sony picture tube, the Apple monitor had good color saturation and a small but reasonable color gamut. The Apple RGB color working space is a good choice for converting images from unknown sources. Almost all the stock photos made between 1988 and 1995 were made with computers and scanners connected to an Apple 13-inch monitor, and though the quality of monitors has improved substantially since then, that monitor still represents the colors of the era. This Apple RGB working space uses 6500 K color temperature for white and a 1.8 gamma, which is relatively flat in appearance.

ColorMatch RGB

The Radius PressView monitor was, for years, the viewing standard of the graphic and visual arts. Almost all professional color work was created on monitors in this class. Now discontinued, the PressView will live on in the form of a color working space that matches its now-famous characteristics.

ColorMatch RGB represents a good gamut of colors, a 1.8 gamma, and a 5000 K white point, which causes some monitors to turn a sickly yellow color. Use this one if it causes the colors on your screen to look good while maintaining a pleasant white. If your monitor turns yellowish, switch to Adobe RGB (1998), as that will deliver a bluer white and a more attractive appearance on many monitors. If you have a PressView, this is an excellent working space for you.

Monitor RGB

This profile sets the color working space to the current monitor profile. Use this working space if other programs in your workflow where you will be viewing the image do not support color management.

Other Color Working Spaces

We are able to choose or load other RGB color working spaces that were the primary spaces in Photoshop 5.0 and 5.5. These appear, along with several dozen others, in the Edit ➔ Color Settings dialog box under Working Spaces RGB. They include:

CIE RGB The International Commission on Illumination (CIE) is an organization of scientists who work with color. CIE standards determine how we measure and describe color in every field of human endeavor. This working space is based on the CIE standard RGB color space, a 2.2 gamma, and 6500 K white point. Its gamut of colors is slightly larger than that of the Apple monitor, and it works almost identically when opening or converting images from older files, those that were created and saved from early versions of Photoshop.

NTSC (1953)   The North American Television Standards Committee established a color gamut and a white point for television in the U.S. that is maintained to this day. Use this color space if you are working on images that will be displayed on television. The gamma is 2.2, and the white point is a very cool-blue Standard Illuminant C.

PAL/SECAM   PAL and SECAM are European and Asian standards for television color and contrast. As with the NTSC setting above, if your work is destined for television outside North America, this setting is appropriate. The gamma is 2.2, and the white point is 6500 K.

SMPTE-C   A movie industry standard, the SMPTE-C standard is compliant with the Society of Motion Picture and Television Engineers standards for motion picture illuminants. It has the same white point as the two television standards, above, and its color temperature is 6500 K.

Wide Gamut RGB   Adobe created this color working space to accommodate images created on the computer, where vibrant greens, bright reds, and cobalt blues are created and must be maintained. This color space is particularly well-suited to work that is destined for an RGB film recorder. The gamma is 2.2, and the white point is a yellowish 5000 K, especially useful to those recording onto "electronic" color transparency films. Wide Gamut may sound attractive to those who believe that more is better, but in fact, too large a color gamut can be damaging to many images. Wide Gamut color remapping will result in strange color shifts in images. Know what you are doing before using this space.

There are numerous RGB spaces for profiles of specific monitors, laptop computers, printers, or working conditions. You can save and load specific profiles from other sources, or you can make your own using Adobe Gamma or a device called a colorimeter, which measures white point, black point, and gamma.

Color Settings

This new version of the program is significantly different than its predecessor and has some new functions for handling color. Photoshop 6 uses ICC color management at all times (even when color management is technically "off"). The settings you select for color handling can make a huge difference in the appearance and reproduction of color.

Choose Edit ➜ Color Settings (Figure 15.3) to access the primary color control window. It has two modes: Standard and Advanced. (The Conversion Options and

Advanced Controls areas shown in the figure are hidden if you uncheck Advanced.) Venture into this environment to take control over color in your world of Adobe Photoshop.

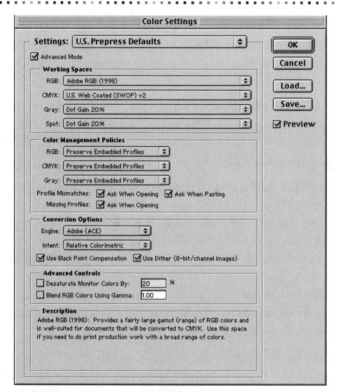

Figure 15.3 *The Color Settings controls*

You should configure color settings prior to opening a document or creating a new document. The Color Settings dialog box controls your color working spaces, your color management policies, and your settings for what should happen when Photoshop opens an image that either has no embedded profile or has one that is different from the current color working space.

First, set your color working space according to the kind of work you do. Choose a setting from the Settings pull-down menu. If you are in doubt, a good place to start is with U.S. Prepress Defaults, which includes the Adobe RGB (1998) color space and typical North American standards for printing color, U.S. Web Coated (SWOP) v2. As mentioned, this is a good space for both RGB and CMYK colors, and will cause little, if any, harm to images handled by the program.

CMYK Working Space

If you plan on converting your image from RGB mode to CMYK, you can choose a color working space for CMYK. If you have a four-color (CMYK) profile for a printer, for example, or a printing press that you normally use, you can set it if it's on the list. If you don't have a custom profile to use, there are several "generic" CMYK profiles you can load. For North America, you can use the SWOP (Specifications for Web Offset Publications) standard profiles. There should be at least two in your system, one for gloss papers and another for uncoated papers. If you are outside North America, choose either Eurostandard (coated or uncoated) or the Japan Standard profiles as appropriate to your location. These CMYK profiles will be used when you convert to CMYK with the Mode ➔ CMYK or Mode ➔ Convert To Profile functions, and the results will be acceptable.

Color Management Policies

Color management policies determine how Photoshop deals with color profiles when opening a document. You can determine how Photoshop deals with documents that have no profiles, or embedded profiles different from the profiles specified in the Color Settings dialog box.

   If we simply reopen a file on the same machine, using the same color working space specified in the Color Settings dialog box, the file will open without interruption. But if we move the file to another machine running Photoshop, or we open an image that came from another machine, Photoshop puts on the brakes, asking, in effect, "Wait. This file is not from around these parts. What should I do with it?"

   Putting the responsibility for controlling how files are opened on the user, Photoshop asks us to set one of the policies for each type of file we might be opening, RGB, CMYK, and Grayscale. Our choices for these policies are:

Off   When set to Off, files with unknown profiles will be opened with color management turned off. This causes Photoshop to behave more like Photoshop 4 (Adobe calls it "pre–color management"), where the monitor's color gamut limits the color available in any image.

Preserve Embedded Profiles   Opening images that already have a color working space profile embedded will retain that space. Any new documents will be created within the current color working space. This is a safe approach to opening files with embedded profiles, as it will allow these images to be opened without making any modification to the color working space of the image. And, after working on the file, it's possible to save the document and retain the embedded profile. When importing color to an RGB or Grayscale document—cutting and pasting an image from another with a different profile document, for example—appearance takes priority over numeric values. When importing color to a CMYK document, numeric values takes priority over appearance.

Convert To Working RGB/CMYK/Grayscale   (This option changes according to the image type.) This will cause mathematic conversion, remapping all the color values in the image to the current color working space. This conversion can cause drastic changes in the color of an image from a color space much smaller or much larger than the current space. For example, if an image is from a stock photo source and shows normal skin tones, let's assume it has an embedded profile for the Apple 13-inch monitor. If we are working in Wide Gamut RGB, opening the image into the current working space will cause the skin tones to shift strongly toward red, making these skin tones appear unacceptably warm. It is preferable to leave the color in its embedded profile space, which will open this image as an Apple RGB color space. Though the gamut of colors is not as great as our current working space, the colors will look good and we will do no harm to the image.

 Whenever Photoshop opens an image into a working space other than the default, it will mark the title bar with an asterisk to indicate that it is not using the default working space.

The Embedded Profile Mismatch Dialog Box

In the Color Settings dialog, there are three Ask When Opening or Pasting check boxes. These determine the behavior of Photoshop 6 when opening an image with no profile, a mismatched profile, or when pasting an image into a Photoshop document. It is a very good idea to check each of these boxes so that you can decide, on a case-by-case basis, how to deal with these variables as they arrive. When you open or paste from a mismatched image, the Embedded Profile Mismatch dialog box (Figure 15.4) will be displayed, displaying the name of the embedded profile. (If the file has no profile at all, the Missing Profile dialog comes up instead; that feature is described in its own section later in this chapter.)

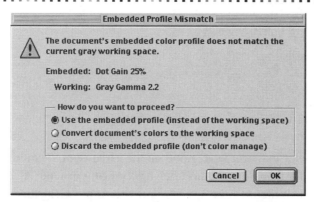

Figure 15.4 *Photoshop can alert you that the image you're opening or pasting from doesn't use your current color profile.*

You certainly do not want Photoshop to assume that importing an Apple RGB image into Wide Gamut RGB space is acceptable! Though it takes a few seconds to make these choices as they occur, the result is a conscious decision, and a skill that can be learned over time.

Of course, there may be circumstances under which you would want all CMYK images with mismatched profiles to be mapped to your current CMYK working space. If this is the case, you can set that CMYK working space in the menu in the Color Settings dialog box, and then uncheck the Profile Mismatches check box to cause this to occur every time an image is opened.

This will also cause RGB images to open into your RGB working space without notice.

Advanced Color Settings

The Color Settings dialog also has an Advanced Mode check box at the top, which will cause the dialog box to grow to include some additional settings called Conversion Options and Advanced Controls. The Conversion Options allow us to set or change the color management "engine" that is used for color conversions. Depending on the options available on your computer, those options range from a selection of two to six or more.

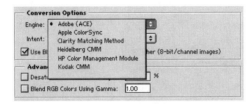

Engine

Adobe has its own color management engine (in the parlance of the industry this is called a CMM, or color management module): Adobe Color Engine (ACE). Other CMMs you might encounter include Apple ColorSync, Apple, Heidelberg, Kodak, Imation, Agfa, X-Rite, and Microsoft.

Which engine you choose depends on your level of sophistication and your understanding of these various CMMs. Each of the companies whose names are reflected in the CMMs suggests that theirs is the superior method for converting color because of the method of polynomial witchcraft they perform on color. Adobe similarly claims that theirs is superior. A good suggestion is to use a CMM that is available in all of the applications you use to manage color. This will ensure that color is not being converted differently between applications. For example, if you use Adobe Photoshop to make some conversions and QuarkXPress (through Apple ColorSync) to make others, then it would be a good idea to set Photoshop to use Apple ColorSync, so that all your conversions are done with the same mathematical "engine."

In reality (and with apologies to the various authors of these CMMs), the net effect of a color management engine is essentially the same. Very, very subtle differences can be discerned by experts on this matter, so it's not worth a lot of worry. You are certainly welcome to try various combinations of engines and rendering intents, and decide for yourself.

Conversions through Rendering Intent

It is the *intent* of this chapter to clarify the settings for color management in Adobe Photoshop 6. Unfortunately, this is the point at which that becomes increasingly difficult.

The ICC has established a set of four "rendering intent" settings under which color conversions can be made. Each has a purpose, and each can be used to maximize the quality of your images for a particular task. Rendering intents cause the color of an image to be modified while it is being moved into a new color space. These modifications can appear as subtle changes or glow-in-the-dark shifts that make color images look very odd. Here we will examine them and identify their purposes.

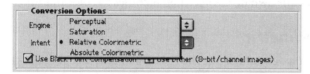

Perceptual

Perceptual is a rendering intent designed to make photos of generalized subjects look "good" when converted to a new color space. The Perceptual rendering intent uses a method of remapping colors that preserves the relationships between colors to maintain a "pleasant" appearance. Though color accuracy will often suffer, the appearance of the image will generally follow the appearance of the original scene. Most photo applications default to Perceptual rendering, and Photoshop does this also. Most people find it pleasing, but read on before making a decision about your imaging policies.

Saturation

Saturation is for business graphics and illustrations made with solid colors. Of the four intents, it is the easiest to understand and the easiest to use. Saturation rendering will result in bright, fully-saturated colors in solid areas, and fairly strong contrast applied to differences in color. Saturation rendering sacrifices color accuracy for sharp contrast and saturation. It simply lives up to its name.

If you convert images from EPS illustration programs like Adobe Illustrator, the Saturation rendering intent will result in a better-looking image after conversion than the other intents. Saturation is best used when converting graphs or financial presentations.

Relative Colorimetric

Relative Colorimetric rendering is a method where color precision is preferred over saturation, resulting in a more accurate conversion of colors into a new color space. Adobe recommends that Relative Colorimetric rendering be used for most color conversions. One of the key components of this rendering intent is its handling of white. Relative Colorimetric rendering moves the white of the image to the white point of the working space, which usually means that, as they say in the ad biz, "whiter whites and brighter brights" in the result than in the original.

For those who use QuarkXPress, this is the default and at present the only rendering intent supported by the program, so working with this setting in Photoshop will match the effect of using color management in QuarkXPress. Other applications, such as Adobe InDesign, are more enlightened when it comes to choices of rendering intent and allow us to make our own decisions when it comes to color modification.

Absolute Colorimetric

This rendering intent is very much like the Relative intent, except that it renders the whites differently. Whites in the source will remain the same in the resulting file. While this sounds obscure, it produces an image that can be used effectively for proofing files that will print on non-white or off-white papers (like newsprint). Absolute Colorimetric is a rendering intent that is designed for those who have a very specific reason for using it; otherwise, avoid it.

Black Point Compensation / Dither

There are two additional settings in the Color Settings dialog under Conversion Options: Use Black Point Compensation and Use Dither (8-Bit/Channel Images). Black Point Compensation is generally left checked, as it is used to maintain saturation of solid black in conversions where the normal behavior of a conversion will desaturate blacks.

An example of this can be seen when converting RGB images to CMYK for print. If we leave this box unchecked and make a conversion (Image ➜ Mode ➜ CMYK), the darkest blacks will often be remapped to the closest color that is within the gamut of the destination profile, which might include an adjustment for dot-gain error or what is called *total ink coverage*. This adjustment will desaturate the solids in order to keep their value below the total ink coverage number, but will result in some washed-out colors where a solid would be better. Black Point Compensation corrects this problem.

The Use Dither check box will cause 16-bit images to be *dithered* when converted to 8-bit images. Dithering is a method of alternating tonal value steps in tiny steps to smooth out tonal shifts. Checking this setting will result in smoother gradations in the converted file. Though the resulting files will likely be larger, the result is worth the price.

Advanced Controls

There are two controls in the color settings window that are new to Photoshop 6: Desaturate Monitor Colors By and Blend RGB Colors Using Gamma. Though recommended for "advanced users only," these settings can have a positive impact on the accuracy of the preview of images on our monitors.

Desaturating Monitor Colors

This option instructs Photoshop to desaturate colors by a specified amount when displayed on the monitor. This option can be helpful when attempting to view the full range of colors in images with color gamuts larger than that of your monitor. An example of this might be viewing on any monitor an image whose color working space is Wide Gamut RGB. Since the gamut in Wide Gamut is larger than any production monitor, this function will simulate the tonality of the image—even though the monitor can't display the actual color beyond the range of its phosphors. Be careful, though—using this feature can cause errors between the displayed color and final output color.

Blending RGB Colors

The Blend RGB Colors Using Gamma setting controls the blending of RGB colors on screen. When the option is selected, RGB colors are blended using a selected curve. The range of values available here is between 1.0, which is linear (it has no effect), and 2.2, which creates a slightly more contrasty image.

When the option is not selected, RGB colors are blended in the document's color space, matching the color display behavior of other applications.

Opening Images with Missing Profiles

When you open an image with a mismatched profile or a file with no profile you can choose from several options.

Missing Profile

A new twist on opening images is the Missing Profile warning in Photoshop 6; it shows itself when an image not containing an embedded profile is opened.

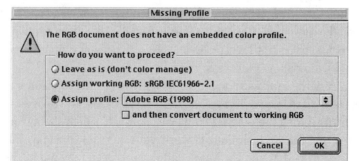

Leave As Is	The image will not be color-managed.
Assign Working RGB	The current RGB working space is assigned to the image.
Assign Profile	The image will be assigned a profile selected from the pop-up menu.

The Assign Profile setting has a secondary check box that will subsequently convert the document to the current working space. This will result in the image taking on the embedded profile of the current working space when it is saved. The net effect of this is to convert the colors to a working space that you think is the correct one for the original image, then assign it to the current working space so its embedded profile will be adequate for the reproduction plans you have.

Passing images through this dialog requires some thought. If you know (or can guess) the source of the image, it is best to assign a profile appropriate to that source. For example, if the image comes from an older stock photo disk, or from a source for which you have a profile, assign an appropriate profile. Converting to the working space after the assignment will cause the current working space profile to be embedded when the image is saved. It does not otherwise change the color in the image.

As an example, say an image is opened from a Digital Stock disc that was created prior to the common use of ICC profiles. Though Digital Stock scanned everything with a calibrated monitor, the images themselves were not embedded with a scanner profile. Later, when ICC profiles became more common, Digital Stock (later acquired by Corbis) posted their profile on the Web; applying that profile now results in the image being adjusted correctly for display.

But what if you don't have the right source profile? It's easy enough to try a few to find a workable solution to your problem. If you assume that the image was scanned and saved on a Macintosh computer using an Apple 13-inch RGB monitor, you can assign the Apple RGB working space to the image. This will usually work.

If you think that the image comes from a Windows PC with a "standard" monitor, try sRGB and the result will probably be good enough. There is not much difference between the color spaces of the Apple 13 and sRGB spaces, and images processed into those spaces will look almost identical.

If, by contrast, the processed image seems flat and lacking in color, it is likely that it came from a larger color space like Adobe RGB (1998); close the image without saving, then reopen it, assigning the Adobe RGB (1998) space. It will probably look much better. Remember that for this technique to work, your monitor must be calibrated (see Chapter 5) and profiled. If not, the image you see on screen may not be the image you'll see in print.

Previewing in CMYK

The world of graphic arts reproduction is changing, and many printing firms are now using a fully color-managed workflow in preparation for printing. Those who do so want you to provide your images to them in RGB color, with embedded working space profiles.

Printers request these files because there is no "generic" CMYK separation that is correct for all different types of paper and ink sets. The separation made for sheet-fed offset on uncoated paper is drastically different than the separation made for Web-fed glossy paper. Printers want control over this conversion.

When an image is destined for the printed page, it is necessary to preview the image before sending the file to the printer. It's also necessary to be able to preview an image in CMYK without making the *conversion* to CMYK. Photoshop 6 has a new control, called Proof Colors, that allows the on-screen preview to simulate a variety of reproduction processes without converting the file to the final color space. This new feature takes the place of Preview In CMYK in earlier versions, and the new version is much more capable. It maintains the same keystroke command, however: Command+Y on MacOS and Ctrl+Y on Windows.

To prepare for and carry out an on-screen proof, first tell Photoshop what kind of proof you want to see. Choose View ➜ Proof Setup (Figure 15.5) to select the type of proof to preview. The top option is for Custom set-ups, which allow essentially any profile to be applied for the proof

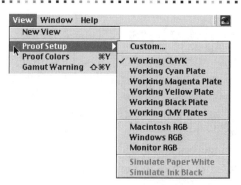

Figure 15.5 *The Proof Setup allows you to assign any profile and rendering intent as the proof destination.*

Once the set-up has been completed, the image on screen can be "proofed" by choosing View ➜ Proof Colors or hitting Cmd/Ctrl+Y. The image will change temporarily to preview in the color space chosen in the Setup window. Options include proofing CMYK, each channel individually, or the CMY colors without black. Three RGB monitor profiles are also available, one for a generic Macintosh monitor, one for a generic Windows monitor, and one for the monitor set as Monitor RGB. Where possible, Photoshop will look to the operating system to get the assigned profile for the monitor for this proofing simulation.

Simulate Paper White and Ink Black

One of the capabilities of Photoshop with regard to proofing is the ability to show the white point of the converted image as a *bright white*, using the monitor's white as the target, or the *paper white*, as measured and calculated in the ICC profile. When working with papers like newsprint and other non-white substrates, the proof can be a better simulation of the actual product if you check the option for Paper White at the bottom of the View ➜ Proof Setup menu. When this is invoked, the image will darken significantly and show a proof that more accurately represents the appearance of the image on the non-white substrate.

Simulating Ink Black in the proof setup will cause the proof to represent the actual measured black of the profile rather than a solid black as dark as the monitor might make it. When this happens, you will see the darkest black from the measured profile, and the image will usually shift away from deep, solid black to a slightly lighter charcoal image. On most images, the differences are very hard to see. Some profiles are able to represent the dark blacks and the paper white with tremendous range, and these will cause less of a shift on the screen during a proof event.

Show Out-of-Gamut Colors

Almost always, there are colors in an image that exceed the color gamut of the reproducing device. These colors are not going to print correctly when converted to CMYK and put on a press. To preview the colors that will not print accurately, you can ask Photoshop to highlight the out-of-gamut areas on screen with a special color by choosing View ➜ Gamut Warning. Usually these colors are very small amounts of relatively unimportant information in an image, but checking is a good idea because the out-of-gamut color might be *the most important* color in the image.

In the Ch15 folder of the *Mastering Photoshop 6* CD, I've included a photo of Venice's gondolas from Photo Disk (`gamwarn1.tif`) that shows color and tonality very nicely on screen. But when Gamut Warning is turned on (`gamwarn2.tif`), the colors that exceed the currently selected CMYK profile are shown in medium gray. These areas, some of them crucial to this particular image, indicate that the colors on the printed sheet will not look as vibrant as the colors in the original. (This gamut-warning image is also presented in the color section, and included in the Ch19 folder on the CD as `Venice.psd`.)

If the image contains a great deal of gray so as to make the gamut warning less distinct, the warning color can be changed in the Transparency & Gamut preferences (see Chapter 5).

For more on viewing and selecting out-of-gamut colors, see Chapter 19, "Making Difficult Selections."

Converting Files

In spite of the color-managed workflow options, many Photoshop practitioners prefer to make their own CMYK conversions. Some printers insist that all files arriving for output be CMYK. To make such conversions, we must set the proper ICC color profile in the Color Settings window, and then make a change of Mode to CMYK. It couldn't be any simpler! But, remember that the quality of a color separation made in Photoshop is dependent of the quality of the CMYK profile.

Converting Profiles

It's possible to convert your color mode and profile by using Image ➜ Mode ➜ Convert To Profile (which replaces the Profile-To-Profile control in Photoshop 5.5). This dialog box allows you to select from RGB, CMYK, and other profile types, and also select the rendering intent for the image you're making. If you choose a profile that requires a change in color mode, Photoshop makes the switch; if you're in an RGB file, for instance, and select a CMYK profile, your file ends up in CMYK mode.

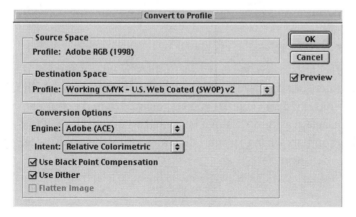

Assigning Profiles

To make the conversion from one profile to another *without changing color mode*, use Image → Mode → Assign Profile. This is helpful if an image was opened with color management turned off, and you want to assign a profile to the image so it can be processed in an ICC-compliant work flow. When working in RGB, only RGB profiles are available in this menu, and only CMYK profiles for those images.

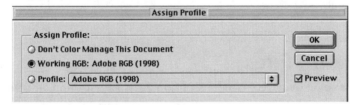

Grayscale Profiles

Converting from color to black and white (also called monochrome or grayscale) in previous versions of Photoshop was less than ideal. Photoshop's luminance-only conversion was seldom optimal. Converting with the Color Mixer made it better, but the ability to use proper grayscale ICC profiles for grayscale conversions makes a better looking image by far.

The image in Figure 15.6 was converted with the 25% Dot Gain Grayscale in Photoshop 6. Notice how nicely the image appears in one color. Conversions using Image → Mode → Grayscale have often been "too mechanical" to have much artistic value, and the methods using the Color Mixer and calculations were too tedious to be effective in production. Using a profile, the conversion not only is correct for the reproduction process, but results in a more pleasing image.

Spot Color Profiles

Spot color profiles are treated like grayscale profiles by Photoshop 6 and are applied in the same way. There are standard profiles loaded by the program, which follow the example of various dot gain values. If you are inclined to make your own profiles, it's a process of printing a gray ramp scale (it is printed automatically by Photoshop if we choose Calibration Bars when printing) then measuring the resulting target patches with a reflective densitometer.

Figure 15.6 *An image converted from color to Grayscale using the Mode* ➜ *Grayscale command*

What you are measuring is *dot area*, which measures the ratio of ink to paper for a selected spot on the printed page. If you read the 50% patch, for example, you will get a value of 73 in typical gloss offset environments. To build a profile, you enter the actual measured values of dot area into a custom dot gain table (Figure 15.7), accessible from the Color Settings dialog box by choosing Custom Dot Gain from either the Gray or Spot pop-up lists in the Working Spaces area. Saving the resulting curve creates an ICC profile.

A custom dot gain table allows you to enter actual grayscale performance curves, which are then used to compensate for the gain you experience. These curves are translated into Grayscale and spot color profiles by Photoshop.

After being created in Photoshop, these profiles are available to any application that supports ICC profiles. Saving a custom profile is done in the Gray or Spot pop-up list in the Working Spaces area of Color Settings—choose Save Gray or Save Spot. The effect of using ICC grayscale profiles on images to be converted for monochrome printing is to create a file that is optimized for reproduction on the measured paper and ink which was used to make the dot area measurements. It is, in essence, a method for matching the image to the printing capabilities of the chosen process.

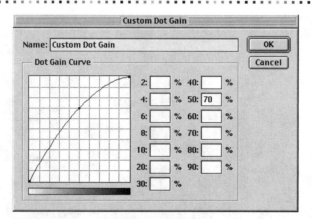

Figure 15.7 *A custom dot gain table*

Printing from Ink-Jet Printers

Once you've completed your image, assigned RGB profiles to it, and converted it or not converted it depending on the circumstances, you can print it. If you are printing to the majority of desktop ink-jet printers, you may not want to convert to CMYK because the printer uses the RGB information to convert the image to CMYK on the fly.

Ink-jet printing results can vary dramatically from model to model because of their different gamuts. If you have the printer's profile, the results will be more predictable. If you don't have the profile of a specific printer, you can improve the results on ink-jet printers by printing the image in RGB and letting the printer software do the conversion on the fly. You can then use the print as a proof to recalibrate your monitor (using Adobe Gamma) to display the image as close to the proof as possible. Save the Adobe Gamma settings to be used specifically for editing images printed on the target printer. Make your adjustments to the image based on the on-screen display and save the image as a separate file, identifying it for the specific printer. This is a funky, trial-and-error way to match the printed image to the monitor, but it works providing you're willing to pull a number of prints and tweak adjustments to get as close a match as possible.

A more accurate and reliable method is to invest in a spectrophotometer and take a reading from the print, then plug the information into a profile writing program and load the profile into the Color Settings dialog box.

The Printing Dialogs

Several dialog boxes offer similar functions for ultimately printing your image. They are Page Setup, Print Options, and Print.

Page Setup

Choose File ➜ Page Setup to determine the paper size, orientation, and scale of the image. The dialog box will include different options depending on your installed printer, sometimes including some of the same options found in the Print Options dialog box.

Print Options

Choose File ➜ Print Options to set up your printing specifications (Figure 15.8). There are several new features in the Photoshop 6 version of this dialog box. For example, the preview image on the left side of the screen displays the image's size in relation to the paper.

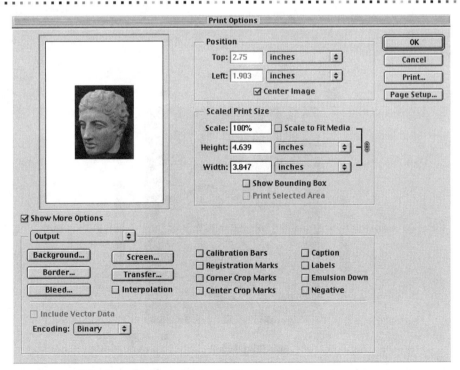

Figure 15.8 The Print Options dialog box

Position specifies the location of the printed image on the current paper size. Scaled Print Size lets you increase or decrease the image while maintaining the image's constrained proportions. Check the Scale To Fit Media box to size the image to fit the paper. Check Show Bounding Box to manually scale and reposition the image by dragging. If you have an active selection, you can then choose to print only that part of the image with the Print Selected Area option.

Check the Show More Options box to expand the dialog box. In the expanded area, a pop-up list offers two sets of settings, Output or Color Management.

Output Options

Some of the Output options are identical to the settings found under File ➜ Page Setup ➜ Adobe Photoshop 6. Some of these options are demonstrated in Figure 15.9.

Background   Choose a color from the Color Picker for the area surrounding the image.

Border   Enter a value from 0.00 to 10.00 points in points, inches, or millimeters to produce a black border around the image.

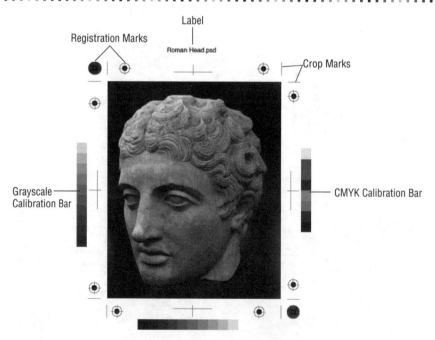

Figure 15.9 *A printed image with various Print Options selected*

Bleed   Enter a value from 0.00 to 0.125 inches to specify the width of the bleed. When printed, crop marks will appear inside rather than outside the image.

Screen   Enter values for screen frequency, angle, and shape for the halftone screens or individual color separations.

Transfer   This function is designed to compensate for poorly calibrated printers. If a printer is printing too dark, for example, adjust the curve to lighten the image to achieve better results.

Interpolation   Check this box to automatically reduce the jagged edges of a low-resolution image by resampling up when printing.

Calibration Bars   Selecting this option produces an 11-step grayscale wedge for measuring dot densities with a densitometer. On CMYK images, a gradient tint bar is printed on each separation.

Registration Marks   These marks, including bull's-eyes and star targets, are used to register color separations.

Crop Marks   Prints crop marks where the page is to be trimmed.

Captions   Prints text entered in the File Info box.

Labels   Prints the file name on images.

Emulsion Down   Prints the emulsion side of the image down so the type is read-able when it is on the back of the film. Most plate burners in the United States use emulsion-down negatives.

Negative   Prints a negative image. Most printers in the United States use negative film to burn plates.

Color Management Options

You can color-manage the image while printing. Let's say that your image is set up with profiles for prepress output to an imagesetter to make color separations, but you're going to print to an ink-jet printer to proof the image. You can temporarily convert the document to a more appropriate profile, like sRGB1e61966-2.1 just before you print. If you're printing to a PostScript printer like a laser printer or imagesetter, you can designate PostScript color management.

Choose a source space: Document uses the current *color* settings as a profile for the printed image, Proof uses the current *proof* settings. Under Print Space, choose a working space from the Profile list. You can also choose a rendering intent.

And of course, click the Print button to print the image.

Print

You can also select the Print dialog box to print the image with File ➔ Print (Figure 15.10). The Print dialog box will be configured differently depending on the printer you have selected. Some of the functions found in the Print Options dialog box may be redundant or irrelevant, like specifying multiple pages and collation. (Photoshop does not support multiple-page documents.)

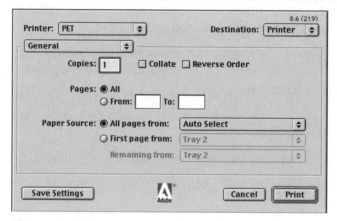

Figure 15.10 *The Print dialog box*

Preflight Checklist

As a final note, I've provided a very general checklist of operations you should perform to ensure accuracy at the printer. These operations are covered in this chapter and throughout *Mastering Photoshop 6*.

1. Calibrate your monitor.

2. Scan the image at the proper resolution.

3. In the Color Settings dialog box, choose the appropriate color profiles for display and printing.

4. Open the image. Duplicate it, crop it, and adjust its color.

5. Edit the image using Photoshop's powerful tools and commands.

6. Duplicate the image again and flatten it.

7. Apply the Unsharp Mask filter.

8. Under File ➜ Page Setup, choose an orientation (portrait or landscape).

9. In the Print Options dialog box, set up the image for printing, choosing print size and position on the page, and attach crop marks, labels, etc.

10. Print the image. This will be a proof.

11. If necessary, recalibrate your monitor and print the image again.

Up Next

Chapter 15 has addressed some rather difficult technical issues. The commands that control color output are extremely important in achieving predictable results on screen and at the printer. I hope this chapter has clarified what color management is all about and that you can apply what you've learned to your images to produce the best possible results.

In Chapter 16, you'll learn how to adjust color and tonality in your images. You'll control the brightness and contrast and learn to eliminate color casts. When you experience how easy it is to transform that lackluster scan into an image with sumptuous colors that leap off the page, you'll never again be satisfied with anything less. And at the end of Chapter 16 is a Hands-On project that will give you the chance to try out methods for adjusting and correcting your color.

Adjusting Tonality and Color

PHOTOSHOP

Chapter 16

For more than any other purpose, Photoshop is used professionally to adjust and correct color. Almost every photograph that finds its way onto your computer—whether it is scanned, copied from a Photo CD, transferred from a digital camera, or downloaded from the Web—will need some color adjustment, from minor tweaking to major surgery. Inferior photographic techniques, like bad lighting, poor focus, or under- and overexposure, are a major cause of color problems in images; however, other variables can significantly degrade color and tonality. The type and quality of the equipment that is used to digitize the image is a factor—an expensive film scanner with a high dynamic range can "see" many more variations of tone than an inexpensive digital camera.

In the process of capturing an image, software interprets the information collected by the scanner or digital camera. The algorithms used to describe the subtle variations of color and assign values to the pixels can vary. Consequently, the color range or *gamut* of each device often differs considerably.

Inevitably, you will use Photoshop's color adjustment features to enhance contrast and remove color casts—two basic operations that compensate for the multitude of variables that can occur during input.

In this chapter, you will learn about:

- Measuring tonality and color
- Making quick adjustments
- Working with levels
- Adjusting curves
- Balancing color
- Mixing channels
- Using Adjustment layers
- Applying the Unsharp Mask filter

Measuring Tonality and Color

When you first open an image, you should scrutinize it carefully to determine what the colors on your monitor represent. Be aware that sometimes the on-screen image doesn't accurately represent the image's actual colors. Be sure to calibrate your monitor using Adobe Gamma or a hardware device to create a "ground zero" before performing any color adjustments (see Chapters 5 and 15).

Look at the image's *histogram* to determine the distribution of tonal values within the image and whether the image has sufficient detail. To view the histogram, choose Image ➜ Histogram.

To more accurately display the actual tonal values within an image, you should avoid using the Image Cache to generate the histogram. Choose Edit ➜ Preferences ➜ Image Cache (Mac) or Memory & Image Cache (Win). Uncheck the Use Cache For Histograms box, quit the program, and then relaunch it. (See Chapter 5 for more on setting memory preferences.)

Histograms

A histogram is a graph composed of lines that show the relative distribution of tonal values within an image. The more lines the graph has, the more tonal values are present in the image. The height of a line displays the relative quantity of pixels of a particular brightness. The taller the line, the more pixels of a particular tonal range the image contains (see the example in Figure 16.1). The histogram looks like a mountain range on some images, because there can be a total of 256 total values represented at one time and the lines are so close together that they create a shape. The dark pixels, or shadows, are represented on the left side of the graph; the light pixels, or highlights, are on the right. The midtonal range is in the center portion of the graph.

When you choose Image ➜ Histogram, the numbers below the graph to the left represent statistical data about the image's tonality. The numbers in the right column indicate values about a specific level or range. To view data about a specific level, place your cursor on the graph and click your mouse. To display data about a range of pixels, click the graph and drag to the left or right to define the range.

Value	Definition
Mean	Average brightness value of all the pixels in the image
Std Dev	(Standard deviation) How widely brightness values vary

Value	Definition
Median	The middle value in the range of brightness values
Pixels	Total number of pixels in the image or selected portion of the image
Level	The specific pixel value between 0 and 255 of the position of the cursor if you place it on the graph
Count	Total number of pixels in the Level
Percentile	Percentage of pixels equal to and darker than the Level
Cache Level	The current image cache setting

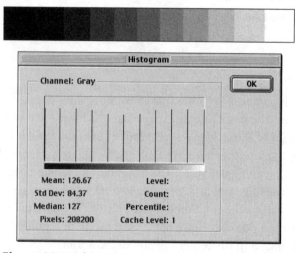

Figure 16.1 *A histogram representing an 11-step grayscale. Notice that there are 11 lines of about the same length, because the amount of each value is equal in the image.*

A histogram can tell us about tonal characteristics of an image. For example, a histogram where tall lines are clustered on the left side of the graph and short lines on the right indicates that the image is dark or *low key*. A histogram where the tall lines cluster on the right side of the graph indicates that the image is light or *high key*. Compare Figures 16.2 and 16.3.

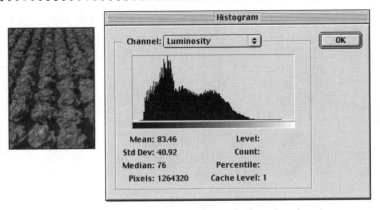

Figure 16.2 *A histogram representing a dark, or low key, image*

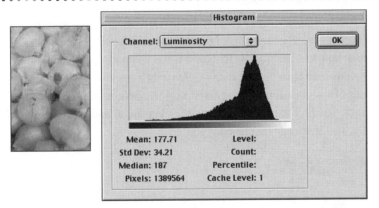

Figure 16.3 *A histogram representing a light, or high key, image*

Histograms can also indicate deficiencies in the image—for example, a histogram devoid of lines on the left and right ends of the graph indicates that most of the pixels are in the midtone range; therefore, the image lacks highlights and shadows and is of poor contrast. A histogram that has gaps in the graph could indicate that there is insufficient detail in the image (see Figure 16.4).

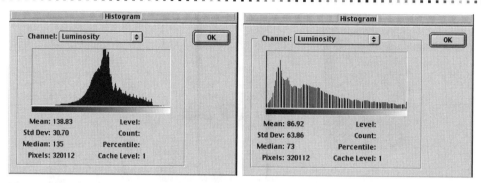

Figure 16.4 *Histograms representing (left) an image with poor contrast and (right) an image with insufficient detail*

The Info Palette

The Info palette enables you to accurately measure the color of a single pixel or determine the average color of a group of pixels. You can use these areas as markers when you make adjustments to the image. To access the Info palette, choose Window → Show Info. By default, the Info palette displays Actual Color and CMYK fields, the x and y coordinates of the position of the cursor, and the height and width of the selection. Place your cursor on the image. As you drag over the image, the numeric values for the pixel under the cursor are displayed.

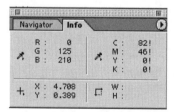

Choosing Palette Options from the Info palette pull-down menu lets you choose from other color spaces for each of the information fields (Figure 16.5). The modes in the Info Options pop-up lists are the following:

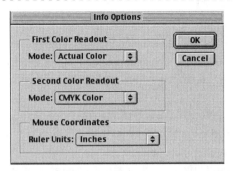

Figure 16.5 *The Info Options dialog box*

Setting	Explanation
Actual Color	Color values of the current mode of the image
Grayscale	Density of black ink that would be deposited if the image were printed in black and white
RGB	Color of the numeric brightness values, from 0 (black) to 255 (white) of each of the red, green, and blue channels
Web Color	RGB hexadecimal equivalents of the sampled color
HSB	Hue, saturation, and brightness values of the sampled color
CMYK	Percentages of cyan, magenta, yellow, and black that would be output to process color separations
Lab	Lightness (L), green–red (a), and blue–yellow (b) values of a CIE Lab color image
Total Ink	Cumulative percentage of ink densities of the combined CMYK separations in a four-color process print
Opacity	Cumulative level of opacity on all of the visible layers of an image

The Eyedropper Tool

When using the Info palette, it is often more accurate to measure a group of pixels than just one in order to get a better idea of the general tonality of a specific area. When you configure the Eyedropper tool to sample an average, the readings in the Info palette, or any other operation that uses the Eyedropper to sample color, will reflect the new configuration.

In the Eyedropper Options bar, choose Point Sample to sample a single pixel. Choose 3 By 3 Average to sample the average color of a 9-pixel square, or a 5 By 5 Average to sample the average color of a 25-pixel square.

You will usually get the best results by averaging a 3×3 square; however, on high-resolution images greater than 400 pixels per inch, you may want to try the 5×5 option.

The Color Sampler Tool

The Color Sampler tool is a way to mark areas of the image for before-and-after comparisons of color adjustments. Prepress professionals will find this tool useful to adjust areas to target CMYK values.

To place a color marker, expand the Eyedropper tool in the Tool palette and choose the Color Sampler. Place the cursor on the image and click your mouse. The cursor leaves a marker and the Info palette expands to display the data for that particular marker, as in Figure 16.6.

Figure 16.6 *The image with Color Sampler markers and the expanded Info palette*

You can sample up to four colors and record the information in the Info palette. To change the color space of a marker, click the arrow next to the Eyedropper icon in the Info palette and drag to the desired color space in the pull-down list shown in Figure 16.6.

To move a marker you've already placed, choose the Color Sampler tool and drag the marker to a new location.

Choose the Color Sampler tool and drag the marker off the image window to delete it. Or choose the Color Sampler tool, press the Option/Alt key, and click the marker.

While a color adjustment is being made to the image, the Info palette displays two numbers for each value, divided by a slash. The number on the left is the numeric value of the sampled color prior to the adjustment, and the number on the right represents the new values of the color after the adjustment. You can compare these values and, with a bit of experience reading these numeric color relations, determine the effect the adjustment will have on the targeted area.

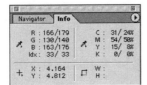

Making Quick Adjustments

They say never sacrifice accuracy for speed. Sometimes, however, it's expedient to use one of Photoshop's semiautomatic operations to perform fast adjustments to correct simple problems. This group of commands can change tonal values in an image quickly but lacks the precision of the high-end adjustment features.

Using the semiautomatic adjustment features hands over the control of how your image looks to the software. Photoshop is not necessarily the best judge of the aesthetic qualities of your image. So use caution when applying these commands. Occasionally, you'll luck out and they'll work just fine. But more often than not, they don't achieve the best possible results.

Brightness/Contrast

Choose Image ➜ Adjust ➜ Brightness/Contrast to perform a global adjustment of brightness or contrast to a selected area or the entire image. The top slider controls how dark or light the image appears, by pushing the pixel values lower when you move the slider to the left, or higher when you move the slider to the right. The slider on the bottom increases or decreases the contrast, by changing the pixel values toward the midtone range when you move the slider to the left, or toward the highlight and shadow ranges when you move the slider to the right. Check the Preview box to see the results.

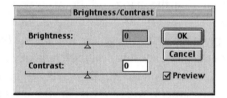

 Be sure that the Preview box, found in all of the adjustment operations, is checked to see the changes to the image before OKing them.

Auto Levels

If you choose Image ➜ Adjust ➜ Auto Levels, Photoshop will make the lightest pixel in each color channel white and the darkest pixel black. It will then distribute all of the other pixels proportionately. By default, the Auto Levels command ignores the lightest and darkest 0.5% extremes when choosing the lightest and darkest colors so as to choose more representative colors. If you use Auto Levels, watch the image carefully, because it can potentially introduce color casts that you will need to eliminate.

You can change the default 0.5% white-point and black-point percentage by choosing Image ➜ Adjust ➜ Levels or Curves. Press the Option/Alt key to display the Options button. Click the button and enter a value from 0% to 9.99% in the Black Clip or White Clip box. Adobe recommends a number between 0.5% and 1% for the least color distortion.

Auto Contrast

Choose Image ➜ Adjust ➜ Auto Contrast to adjust the overall contrast relations in an image. Like Auto Levels, Auto Contrast maps the lightest highlight to white and darkest shadow pixel to black and maintains the color balance. By default, the Auto Contrast command clips the lightest and darkest 0.5% of the light and dark extremes so as to choose more representative colors.

Variations

If you need a little help visualizing what a color adjustment might look like, choose Image ➜ Adjust ➜ Variations. The Variations command displays thumbnails of potential adjustments, like the ones in Figure 16.7, in the color saturation and value of the image, enabling you to visually choose the most appropriate alternative. The two thumbnails at top of the window display the original image, labeled Original, and the current image with adjustments, labeled Current Pick. The circle of thumbnails below shows what the image will look like if you add more of a specific color. The Current Pick thumbnail, which is in the center of the circle, changes as you click any one of the color thumbnails. To undo the addition of a color, click the thumbnail opposite it to introduce its complementary color and neutralize the effect.

You can increase and decrease the amount of color to be added, by moving the Fine/Coarse slider: Fine produces small adjustments, and Coarse produces large ones. You can choose to focus the adjustments on specific areas of tonality by clicking the Highlights, Midtones, or Shadows radio buttons.

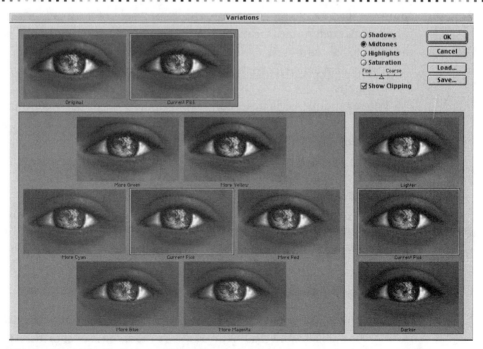

Figure 16.7 The Variations dialog box

Clicking the Saturation radio button transforms the color circle into three thumbnails. Click the left thumbnail to desaturate or the right thumbnail to saturate the image.

The field at the right controls the brightness of the image. Click the top thumbnail to lighten the image and the bottom to darken the image.

As you're using the Variations command, you may notice the proliferation of highly saturated color in the thumbnails. These are gamut warnings, and they're there to enlighten you to the fact that some of the colors may be outside of the range of the current color space, which could result in areas of flat or dithered color. To turn off the gamut warning, uncheck the Show Clipping box.

Working with Levels

The Levels command displays an image histogram, which you use as a visual guide to adjust the image's tonal range. Levels initially gives you three points of adjustment. The black slider on the left of the graph determines the darkest pixel in the shadow areas, which is called the *black point*. The white slider on the right determines the lightest pixel in the highlight area, called the *white point*. Move the black and white sliders to adjust the shadow and highlight extremes, respectively, of the image. The middle or gamma slider determines the median value between the black and white points. Move the slider to the right to decrease the median value, thereby making all values lower than the median darker, or to the left to increase it, making all values higher than the median lighter.

Where Input Levels increase contrast, Output Levels decrease contrast. Move the white slider to the left and the black slider to the right to reduce the range of contrast in an image. You can eliminate the extremes of the highlight and shadow in an image. Printers frequently do this to control ink coverage in preparing files for the press. For example, if the black arrow is moved from 0 to 12, values below 5% (equivalent to a 95% dot value) won't print.

When you perform a Levels adjustment, you are actually reassigning pixel values. For an example, suppose you have a low-contrast image like the prairie dogs in Figure 16.8. Here are the basic steps to increase the contrast in this picture:

1. Open the image in the Ch16 folder on the *Mastering Photoshop 6* CD, Prairie_Dogs.psd.

2. Choose Image ➔ Adjust ➔ Levels. The histogram displays the deficiency in the highlight and shadow areas, where the absence or shortness of lines indicate there are few pixels.

Figure 16.8 *These prairie dogs need more contrast.*

3. Move the white slider toward the center until it is aligned with the lines on the right of the graph, or until the Input Level box on the right reads 180.

4. Move the black slider toward the center until it is aligned with the lines on the left of the graph, or until the Input Level value on the left reads 33.

5. Move the midtone slider to the right to darken the midtone range a little, until the middle Input Level value reads 0.95.

6 Click OK.

7. Choose Image ➔ Adjust ➔ Levels again. The range of pixel values in the histogram has been redistributed to encompass the length of the entire graph. The lines that had a value of 33 now have a value of 0 (black). The lines that had a value of 180 now have a value of 255 (white), and the median midtone has also changed.

Figure 16.9 shows the histogram before and after the correction. Look at the before and after (Figure 16.10) versions of the prairie dogs in the color section to see the difference this makes in your image.

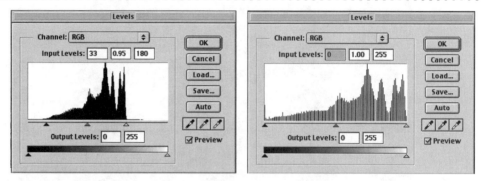

Figure 16.9 *Sample Levels dialogs, before and after adjustment*

Figure 16.10 *The after Prairie Dog image*

Adjusting Channels

If you perform a Levels adjustment on the composite channel, you have only three points of adjustment. If you adjust the Levels of each channel individually, you have 9 points of adjustment in an RGB or Lab color image and 12 points of adjustment on a CMYK image. This triples or quadruples the power of the Levels command; it also can produce weird color combinations. To choose a specific channel in which to work, scroll down the Channel pop-up list in the Levels dialog box. (See the Hands-On section following this chapter to try this operation out.)

When adjusting the levels of individual channels, you may need to reset the Levels adjustment several times before producing the right combination of values. To do so, press the Option/Alt key. The Cancel button becomes the Reset button. Click it to begin again. Note that this cancels all of the operations that you have performed in the dialog box, not just the individual channels. To cancel only the last operation, press Command/Ctrl+Z.

Determining White and Black Points

You can use the Levels command in Threshold mode to locate the highlight and shadow areas of an image. You can then assign specific values to those points to redistribute all of the other pixel values between those values.

Finding the Highlight and Shadow Points

1. Be sure that the composite RGB channel is selected from the Channels palette.

2. Open the Levels dialog box (Image ➜ Adjust ➜ Levels) and check the Preview box.

3. Press the Option/Alt key and slowly drag the white Input Level slider to the left. A high-contrast preview appears. The visible areas of the image are the lightest part of the image.

4. Repeat the process with the black shadow slider, dragging it to the right to identify the darkest areas of the image.

You can assign specific values to the darkest shadow areas and the lightest highlight areas of an image and then redistribute the brightness information based on the light and dark extremes of the image. Prepress professionals frequently determine CMYK values for highlight and shadow areas based on the characteristics of their printing presses. When you determine the white point, you use the lightest printable area of the image that contains detail, not a specular white that when printed will contain no ink. The shadow areas will be the darkest area that contains detail and not an absolute black.

Setting the White Point

1. To set the target ink values, open the image `Dreamcar.psd` from the `Ch16` folder on the CD (see Figure 16.11). Before and after versions of this image are included in the color section.

Figure 16.11 *The Dreamcar before the Levels adjustment*

2. In the Eyedropper Options bar, set the Eyedropper tool to 3 By 3 Average.

3. Choose Image ➜ Adjust ➜ Levels.

4. Double-click the white eyedropper. The Color Picker appears.

5. Enter values for the highlight. Enter these recommended values if you are printing on white paper: 5% cyan, 3% magenta, 3% yellow, and 0% black. The RGB values for this color are 239, 239, 240. The grayscale density is a 6% dot (you can determine the highlight density by the subtracting the Brightness value, B, in the Color Picker from 100).

The RGB values will vary depending on the RGB color space you are working in. I'm working in Adobe RGB (1998) as a color setting (see Chapter 15). The point is, you're going to shoot for about a 4% to 6% neutral gray mix.

6. Locate the lightest area on the image, but not a specular white. In the case of the Dreamcar, it's the rear fender. Click the area to set the highlight.

Setting the Black Point

1. Double-click the black eyedropper. The Color Picker appears.

2. Enter values for the shadow. Enter these recommended values if you are printing on white paper: 74% cyan, 67% magenta, 66% yellow, and 86% black. If you are working in the Adobe RGB (1998) color space, the RGB values for this color are 13, 13, 13. The grayscale density is a 95% dot. (As with the highlight value, you can determine the shadow density by the subtracting the Brightness value, B, in the Color Picker from 100.)

The total ink coverage of all the CMYK values should never exceed 300%. You can try other values of ink depending on the paper, printer, and press you are using. Another frequently used set of values for printing on white stock is 80, 70, 70, 70.

3. Locate the darkest area on the image that still contains detail. In this case, it's the left-front tire. Click your mouse there to set the shadow. Your dream car should now look like Figure 16.12.

The process for determining the white point and black point is the same for both the Levels and Curves operations. I'll discuss Curves just a couple of pages on.

Figure 16.12 *The Dreamcar after adjusting the Levels*

Saving and Loading Levels Settings

Once you've made a correction to the image, you may want to apply it to another image with the same color problems. Let's say you shot a roll of film at the wrong ASA and consequently underexposed all of the images.

You can adjust one image and apply those settings to the entire group. By first saving and then loading the settings.

To save and load a setting:

1. Choose Save from the options on the right side of the Levels dialog.

2. Choose a folder in which to save the settings, name them, and click OK. Click OK again to close the Levels dialog box. Now that you've saved them, you can reload them at any time.

3. To load the settings, choose Load from the options on the right side of the Levels dialog.

4. Locate the folder where the settings were saved and click Open to open the settings.

Adjusting Curves

Curves are Photoshop's most powerful color adjustment tool. Where levels give you the ability to change three to nine points of adjustment, curves enable you to map many more. You can adjust an image's brightness curve to lighten or darken an image, improve its contrast, or even create wild solarization affects.

When you open Image → Adjust Curves, Photoshop displays the Curves dialog box (Figure 16.13).

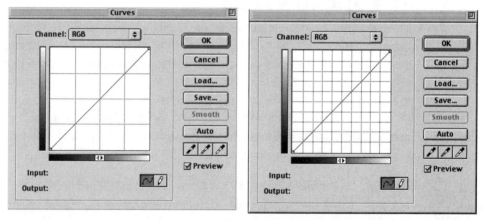

Figure 16.13 *(left) The default Curves dialog box, showing the 16-cell graph. (right) Option/Alt-clicking the grid changes to a 100-cell graph.*

The Graph

By default, the graph is divided into 16 squares each representing 16 brightness levels. Press your Option/Alt key and click the graph to refine the grid into 100 squares, each representing 256 brightness levels for finer adjustment. The horizontal axis of the graph represents the *input* levels, or the colors of the image before the adjustment. The vertical axis represents the *output* levels, or the color of the image after it has been adjusted. By default, for RGB images, dark colors are represented by the lower-left corner and light colors are represented by the upper-right corner of the graph. The diagonal line from bottom-left to top-right represents the brightness levels of the image. Adjustments are made to the image by changing the shape of this line.

Figure 16.14 provides an illustration of the power of curves. The basic photograph (a) is underexposed in the shadows. If you click the center of the diagonal line in the Curves dialog and drag it toward the upper-left, you will lighten the image, as in (b). If you bend it toward the lower-right, you will darken it (c). If you perform either of these operations, you are altering the position of the midtones.

A classic S curve, as shown in (d), will increase the contrast of the image by darkening the shadows and lightening the highlights. A roller-coaster curve (e) pushes the pixel values all over the graph and creates wild solarization effects.

The Brightness Bar

The horizontal brightness bar below the graph represents the direction of the values of the graph. By default, for RGB images, the light values are on the right and the dark values are on the left, but they can be easily switched by clicking the center arrows. If you reverse the graph, the light values will switch to the bottom and left and the dark values to the top and right. If you are working on an RGB or Lab image and you switch the direction of the brightness bar, the numeric input and output values change from a measurement of channel information to ink coverage. This can be useful if you are planning to convert your image to CMYK.

The default Curves dialog box for a CMYK image is reversed from the RGB or Lab image. The brightness bars display dark values on the top and light values on the bottom. The input and output values are in percentage of ink coverage.

Graph Tools

Choose a graph tool in the Curves dialog to edit the brightness curve. The point tool is selected by default. Click the curve to establish anchor points, which can then be moved by dragging them with your mouse. As you drag, you can see the changes to your image if the Preview box is checked.

(a) The unadjusted image

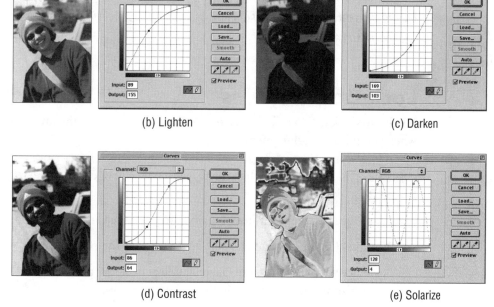

(b) Lighten

(c) Darken

(d) Contrast

(e) Solarize

Figure 16.14 *Examples of curve adjustments.*

The pencil tool lets you draw freeform on the curve by clicking and dragging on it. It performs very much like Photoshop's Pencil tool. If you want to draw a straight line, click once, press the Shift key, and click elsewhere.

Input and Output Values

When you move the cursor over the curve, the input and output values change to reflect its position relative to the horizontal and vertical axes of the graph. You can click a point on the curve and enter new values for that point in these boxes, which will result in bending the curve.

Channels

If you perform a Curves adjustment on the composite channel, you affect all of its channels simultaneously. As with levels, you can work with more precision by adjusting the channels individually. To choose a specific channel in which to work, scroll through the Channel pop-up list in the Curves dialog box.

You can also select a combination of channels by Shift-selecting them in the Channels palette before opening the Curves dialog box.

Lock-Down Curves

It helps to work with a *lock-down curve* so that other colors in the image are unaffected when you make the adjustment.

A lock-down curve stabilizes the curve and prevents it from bending. The brightness values that are affected when manipulating the curve can then be better controlled. To make a lock-down curve, follow these steps:

1. Choose Image ➜ Adjust ➜ Curves to open the Curves dialog box.
2. Press Option/Alt and click the grid to display the 100-cell grid.
3. Place your cursor on the diagonal line at the exact point of intersection of the horizontal and vertical grid lines. Click your mouse.
4. Click each intersection point along the diagonal line, as in Figure 16.15.
5. Choose Red from the Channel pop-up list. Repeat the process.

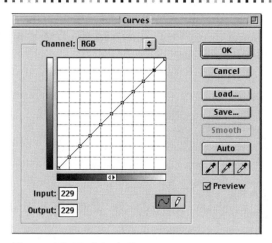

Figure 16.15 *A lock-down curve*

6. Repeat the process for the Green and Blue curves. This way, if you need to lock down a specific channel, the curve will be contained within the file.

7. Choose Save and designate a location for your curve. Name the curve Lockdown_Curve.acv and save the file. You can now load the curve on any RGB document in any channel at any time. A similar file is provided in the Ch16 folder on your CD.

Determining the Position of a Color

You can pinpoint a color and determine its exact location on the curve. You can then place an anchor point and make a precise spot adjustment to that color only.

To determine the location of a color:

1. Open the file Watermelon.psd in the Ch16 folder on the CD.

2. Choose Image ➔ Adjust ➔ Curves to display the Curves dialog box.

3. Choose Channel ➔ Red.

4. Choose Load from the options on the right side of the dialog. Load the lockdown curve you made in the previous section, or load Red_Lockdown_Curve.acv from the CD.

5. Place your cursor on the red center of the watermelon. Press the Option (Mac) or Alt (Win) key and click the mouse. Observe the circle on the graph as you move your cursor (Figure 16.16). Press your Command (Mac) or Ctrl (Win) key and click the mouse to place an anchor point.

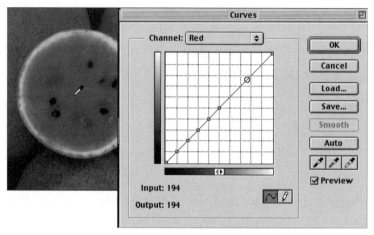

Figure 16.16 *Determining the anchor point*

6. Place your cursor on the anchor point, click your mouse, and drag straight upward until the Output reads 242, as in Figure 16.17. The targeted red in the watermelon intensifies because you've increased its brightness value. All the other colors in the image are left at their original values because you locked them down.

Saving and Loading Curve Settings

As with levels, once you've made a Curves adjustment to the image, you can save the settings and load them to another image:

1. Choose Save from the options on the right side of the Curves dialog box.

2. Choose a folder in which to save the setting, name them, and click OK.

3. To load the settings, choose Load from the options on the right side of the Curves dialog.

4. Locate the folder where the settings were saved and click Open to load the settings.

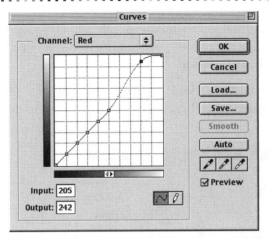

Figure 16.17 *The watermelon with the Curves adjustment*

Balancing Color

After the tonal values have been corrected, you may want to make further adjustments to eliminate the color casts or over- or undersaturation. Color in the image can be balanced using several different methods:

Color Balance is used to change the overall color mix in an image.

Selective Color adjusts the quantities of cyan, magenta, yellow, or black in specific color components.

Levels and Curves enable you adjusts brightness values of individual channels. (See the previous sections in this chapter.)

Hue/Saturation lets you change the basic color characteristics of the image (see Chapter 17).

Replace Color lets you replace the hue, saturation, and brightness of specified areas (see Chapter 17).

Channel Mixer is a method of blending colors from individual channels. (See the section on the Channel Mixer in this chapter.)

Color Balance

Color balance is used to adjust the overall mixture of colors in the image and especially to eliminate color casts. To use the Color Balance command, be sure that the composite channel is targeted in the Channels palette.

1. Choose Image ➜ Adjust ➜ Color Balance; the Color Balance dialog box is displayed. (You can also bring this up with the keyboard shortcut Command/Ctrl+B.)

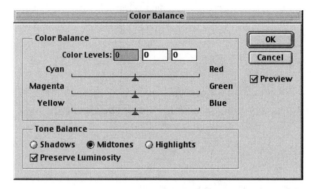

2. Click the Shadows, Midtones, or Highlights radio button to select the tonal range in which you would like to focus your adjustment.

3. Check Preserve Luminosity to maintain the tonal balance of the image and affect only the colors.

4. To increase the amount of a color in an image, drag a slider towards it. To decrease the amount of a color, drag the slider away from it.

Each color slider represents two color opposites. By increasing the amount of a specific color (by moving the slider towards its name), you, in effect, decrease its opposite.

Selective Color

The Selective Color command is designed to adjust CMYK images; however, you can use it on RGB and Lab images too. Selective color lets you determine the amount of cyan, magenta, yellow, and black that will be added to predefined color ranges. This is especially good for prepress professionals who need to control ink densities.

1. Target the composite channel in the Channels palette.

2. Choose Image ➜ Adjust ➜ Selective Color; the Selective Color dialog box appears.

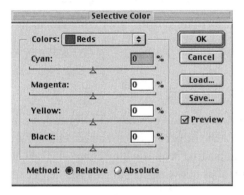

3. From the Colors pop-up list, choose the color range you want to affect. The list shows reds, yellow, greens, cyans, blues, magentas, whites, neutrals, and blacks. Adjust the CMYK sliders to determine how much of each process color the target color will contain. (Some colors may not contain any of the process color, so they will not be affected.)

4. Choose a method.

   Relative changes the existing quantity of process color by a percentage of the total. For example, if you start with a pixel that is 80% cyan and add 10%, 8% is added to the pixel (10% of 80 = 8) for a total of 88% cyan. You cannot adjust specular white with this option, because it contains no color.

   Absolute adds color in absolute values. If, for example, you start with 30% cyan in the pixel and add 10%, you end up with a pixel that is 40% cyan.

5. Drag the sliders to the right to increase the amount of the process color component in the selected color or to the left to decrease it.

The Channel Mixer

The Channel Mixer enables you to adjust the color information of each channel from one control window. You can establish color values on a specific channel as a mixture of any or all of the color channels' brightness values. The Channel Mixer can be used for a variety of purposes, including:

- Creating an optimal grayscale image from an RGB or CMYK file

- Making a high-quality sepia tone from a CMYK or RGB file

- Converting images into alternative color spaces

- Swapping color information from one channel to another

- Making color adjustments to images by altering the color information in a specific channel

- Creating weird-looking stuff

The Channel Mixer does not add or subtract colors per se; it combines values from each channel with those of the target channel. The effect is similar to copying the Red channel, for example, and pasting it on the Blue channel. The Channel Mixer, however, offers much greater control by allowing you to vary the degree of the effect.

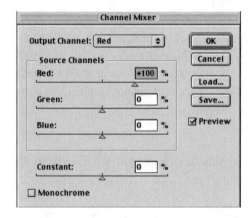

To use the Channel Mixer:

1. Target the composite channel in the Channels palette.

2. Access the window by choosing Image ➜ Adjust ➜ Channel Mixer.

3. Target the channel to be affected by choosing the Output Channel from the pop-up list.

4. Adjust the color sliders to modify the color relations between channels.

Swapping Colors within Channels

You can adjust color information globally on a particular channel or within a selection marquee, so that portions of the image can be quickly altered, corrected, or converted independently while previewing the results.

When you choose a channel by name from the Output Channel pop-up list, the value next to the corresponding Source Channels color slider reads 100%, which represents the total amount of that color in the image. The values can be increased to 200% or decreased to –200%.

The performance of the Channel Mixer depends on the color mode of the image. When working in CMYK, increasing the numeric value of the color cyan or dragging its slider to the right increases the amount of cyan in the Cyan channel. Decreasing the numeric value or dragging to the left subtracts cyan from the channel.

Adjusting the color slider of any other color, such as magenta, while the Cyan channel is targeted, changes the amount of the cyan in the Cyan channel based on the relation between the brightness values of magenta and cyan.

When working in RGB mode, the Channel Mixer performs differently. Increasing the numeric value shifts the selected color toward the color of the selected channel, while decreasing the value shifts the color towards its complement. (As with CMYK, the limits of these changes are 200% and –200%.) You can therefore decrease the value of red if you target the Red channel and move the Red slider to the left, which shifts the color towards cyan—the complement of red on the color wheel. Targeting the Green channel and moving the Green slider to the left shifts the color towards magenta. Targeting the Blue channel and move the Blue slider to the left shifts the color towards yellow.

The Constant slider is like having an independent black or white channel, with an opacity slider added to the targeted color channel to increase or decrease the channel's overall brightness values. Negative values act as a black channel, decreasing the brightness of the target channel. Positive values act as a white channel, increasing the overall brightness of a channel.

Increasing the brightness of a color channel does not necessarily mean that the image will become lighter. It actually adds more of the channel's color to the image. You can demonstrate this by targeting the Blue channel, for example. Move the Constant slider to the right, and any image will turn more blue. Drag it to the left, and it will turn more yellow (the compliment of blue on the color wheel).

Making Optimal Grayscales

Converting a color image directly to a perfect grayscale has been a hit-or-miss process. With the Channel Mixer, you can easily make a perfect grayscale from an RGB or CMYK image, by manual correction and previewing.

When you convert an RGB image to a Grayscale, Photoshop uses an algorithm to convert the brightness values from the 16 million colors in its three color channels into

256 shades of gray in the gray channel. By applying the Channel Mixer to the unconverted RGB file, you can control how the image looks prior to the conversion. By moving the sliders, you can emphasize brightness and contrast within the image.

1. Check the Monochrome box in the Channel Mixer.

2. Adjust each of the color sliders until optimal contrast is achieved.

3. Move the Constant slider to darken or lighten the image.

4. When you're satisfied with the results, click OK.

5. Choose Image ➜ Mode ➜ Grayscale to convert the image.

Using Adjustment Layers

When you apply an adjustment operation like Levels, Curves, Hue/Saturation, or the Channel Mixer to an image, you directly affect the information on a layer or on the Background. The only way to change these operations is to return to them in the History palette, which can have complicated and unexpected results if you've done a lot to the image since. Photoshop's Adjustment layers segregate the mathematical data of the adjustment to a separate layer that can be re-edited at any time during the imaging process. Adjustment layers are very handy indeed, and another element in Photoshop's arsenal that keeps the process dynamic.

Creating an Adjustment Layer

1. Choose Layer ➜ New Adjustment Layer and select the type of Adjustment layer you want from the submenu.

2. The New Layer dialog box appears. Name, color-code, and set the opacity and blending mode of the layer, if desired.

3. The Adjustment dialog appears. Make the adjustment and click OK. The new Adjustment layer appears on the Layers palette.

4. In Photoshop 6, the Adjustment layer has an attached layer mask (as in Figure 16.18), which lets you selectively conceal portions of the adjustment. (See Chapter 20 for more on layer masks.)

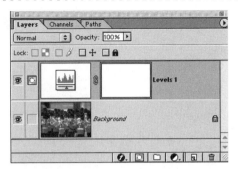

Figure 16.18 *An Adjustment layer, with thumbnails for the adjustment and for a layer mask*

By default, an Adjustment layer will affect all of the layers below it in the Layers stack. You can, however, designate an Adjustment layer to affect *only* the layer immediately below it in the stack. Option/Alt-click the line that separates the Adjustment layer and the layer just below it. The title of the grouped layer becomes underlined, indicating that the two layers are now grouped. You ungroup an Adjustment layer in the same way.

You can also group a layer by clicking the Group With Previous Layer check box in the New Layer dialog box.

Masking Portions of an Adjustment Layer

The ultimate power of Adjustment layers is the ability to selectively apply an adjustment to the image. An Adjustment layer can act as a mask so that you can conceal portions of the effect. To try out this process, display the Layers palette and follow these steps:

1. Open the document in the `Ch16` folder on the CD, `Mr_Parrot.psd`.

2. Choose Layer ➔ New Adjustment Layer ➔ Hue/Saturation.

3. In the Hue/Saturation dialog box, drag the Hue slider to radically alter the color scheme of the image. Click OK.

4. In the Layers palette, target the Adjustment layer.

5. Choose black as a foreground color and white as a background color in the Tool palette by pressing the D key.

6. Choose the Paintbrush. Paint the head of the parrot until its feathers are restored to their original red color. If you make a mistake, paint the mistake out with white.

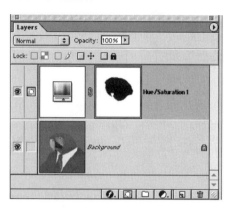

Applying the Unsharp Mask Filter

You might ask what a filter description is doing here in the color adjustment chapter? The answer to the question is, the Unsharp Mask (USM) filter is a contrast-adjustment tool that goes hand-in-hand with color correction, and if used properly, it can further enhance the color relations and contrast of the image and make it really "pop."

USM exaggerates the transition between areas of most contrast while leaving areas of minimum contrast unaffected. It can help increase the contrast of an image and fool the eye into thinking fuzzy areas of the image are in focus.

If It's a Sharpen Filter, Why Is It Called "Unsharp" Mask?

Many of the operations performed in Photoshop today were derived from traditional optical techniques performed in a process camera. Back in the old days before computers, a special mask was cut to protect parts of images when they were being "bumped" or exposed to increase their contrast. This mask would leave important flesh tones and other critical areas unaffected while enhancing the contrast of the most prominent edges to produce the illusion of sharp focus. Since the area within the mask was being protected and the area outside the mask was being sharpened, the term for the process came to be known as an *unsharp mask*. Photoshop essentially performs the same operation, only digitally and with more control and less labor.

To apply the USM, choose Filter ➜ Sharpen ➜ Unsharp Mask (see Figure 16.19). The USM filter has a preview in which you see a thumbnail version of the image. You can reduce or enlarge the preview by clicking the – or + signs. This is helpful if you want to compare the affected preview to the original, unsharpened image. Check the Preview box to see the effect on the image itself.

Figure 16.19 *The Unsharp Mask interface*

You'll have a chance to try Unsharp Masking the image at the end of the following Hands-On section for practice.

To apply the USM, move one of its three sliders:

Amount   By moving the slider or entering a value from 1% to 500%, you determine how much sharpening will be applied. The higher the value, the more the image will be sharpened. Applying only an Amount, however, will not sharpen the image. In order to see the effect, you must also specify a Radius.

Radius   By moving the Radius slider or entering a value, you control the thickness of the sharpened edge. Lower values produce thinner, sharper edges; higher values produce wider edges with more overall sharpening of the entire image.

Threshold   To control the numeric value of adjacent, contrasting pixels, move the Threshold slider. The slider determines how different the pixels must be from the surrounding area before they are considered edge pixels and sharpened. The slider restores smooth areas that acquire texture when the Amount and Radius are applied—the higher the value, the greater the restoration. Too much Threshold will reverse the effect of the USM.

The goal in sharpening an image is to apply as much USM as possible without blowing out areas, shifting colors, creating dark or light halos, or amplifying noise and unwanted detail. These flaws can make the image appear garish or artificial. You can avoid most problems by applying one or more of the following methods.

Small-Dose Technique

USM works better in smaller doses. Apply USM several times with smaller settings, keeping the Amount and Radius lower and the Threshold higher. Sharpen gently several times with the same low settings. Press Cmd/Ctrl+F to reapply the filter with the same values, or reduce the values slightly each time. Keep a close watch on the image as you sharpen it. Sharpen the image until it appears a little too sharp. To see an overall comparison, toggle between the original thumbnail in the History palette (Window ➜ Show History) and the last line of the History list where sharpening was applied.

Flesh-Tone Technique

This technique works particularly well on flesh tones. The problem presented by flesh tones when applying any sharpening filter is the tendency to increase the texture of the skin so that it appears rough or porous. To avoid this problem, apply a larger Amount and smaller Radius. Keeping the Radius low affects only the edge pixels while reducing the sharpening of noise and unwanted detail. Adjust the Threshold to eliminate excess texture in the flesh tones and other areas of low contrast.

Lab-Mode Technique

This method is specially designed to avoid color shifts. In essence, you will be applying your sharpening to the brightness information only. Like RGB mode, Lab mode segregates the image data into three channels. In RGB, however, red, green, and blue channels each contain 256 brightness levels. In Lab mode, the information is divided into an *a* channel (red and green hues), a *b* channel (blue and yellow hues), and an *L* or lightness channel (the brightness information). The L channel is where the USM will be applied.

1. Choose Image ➜ Duplicate to make a copy of your image.

2. Choose Layer ➜ Flatten Image.

3. Use Image ➜ Mode ➜ Lab Color to convert to Lab mode. Don't worry, there is no appreciable loss of color information in this conversion as there is when you convert from RGB to CMYK.

4. Choose Window ➜ Show Channels. Target the Lightness channel by clicking its thumbnail.

5. Click the eye next to the composite Lab channel in the Channels palette so that the full-color image is visible in the image window.

6. Choose Filter ➜ Sharpen ➜ Unsharp Mask.

7. Move the Amount, Radius, and Threshold sliders to produce the desired effect.

Up Next

In the next Hands-On exercise, you'll use several of Photoshop's adjustment features to adjust the tonal range of an image and enhance its colors. You will be surprised at how easy it is to improve the image, and you will never be satisfied with lackluster images again.

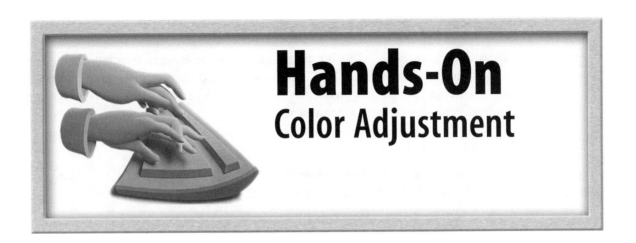

Hands-On
Color Adjustment

O ften, an image needs more than minor color correction. This project will cover a variety of techniques to correct color and tonality, including Levels, Auto Levels, Curves, Color Balance, Adjustment Layers, and Unsharp Masking.

Getting Started

Hide your preferences file before beginning this Hands-On exercise, then restart Photoshop to create a clean version. The "Photoshop's Settings" section in Chapter 5 details how to temporarily reset your preferences to Photoshop's defaults. You can restore your customized, personal settings when you're done.

Once you have launched Photoshop with default preferences, here's how to begin this Hands-On project:

1. Before beginning this particular project, choose Edit ➜ Preferences ➜ Image Cache (Mac) or Memory & Image Cache (Win).

2. Uncheck the Use Cache For Histograms box.

3. Quit Photoshop (Cmd/Ctrl+Q).

4. Relaunch Photoshop again. Launching twice this way is the only way to get factory default settings while getting the Use Cache option the right way; using the cache for histograms when making many levels-type corrections is a sure way to hit your memory limit.

5. Open the file Sonoran_Desert_start.psd (Figure 1) in the Ch16 folder on the CD. To see a color preview of the before and after versions of the image, look at the color section.

6. Save the file to your disk.

Adjusting Levels

1. From the Layers menu, choose New Adjustment Layer ➜ Levels. The layer should name itself Levels 1; click OK.

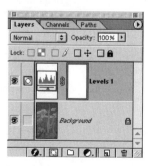

Figure 1 *The start of the Sonoran Desert project*

In the Levels dialog box, notice the histogram: Most of the pixels are clumped into the center, which indicates that the image needs a contrast adjustment. The graph is also devoid of lines in the highlights and shadows. You can increase the overall contrast by spreading the highlight, midtones, and shadows over a broader range of values. We do this by moving the sliders.

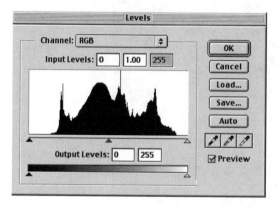

2. Move the White slider toward the center until the output level reads 235. Move the Black slider until it reads 42. The contrast is improved, but we can be more precise. Undo the adjustment by pressing the Option/Alt key and clicking Reset.

3. Choose Red from the Channel pop-up list. Move the sliders toward the center. Drag the shadow Input slider to the right until it just touches the beginning of the "mountain range" on the histogram. The value should read 42. Leave the midtone at 1.00, and adjust the highlight to 198, as in the top of Figure 2.

4. Choose Green from the Channel pop-up list. Move the sliders toward the center. Adjust the Input values to 55, 1.00, and 231.

5. Choose Blue from the Channel pop-up list. Move the sliders toward the center. Adjust the Input values to 15, 1.00, and 236.

6. Click OK.

The reason for adjusting the levels channel by channel is to gain more control over the contrast. Adjusting the highlight, midtone, and shadow areas in each channel will redistribute the pixel values over a broader range and increase contrast in the entire image.

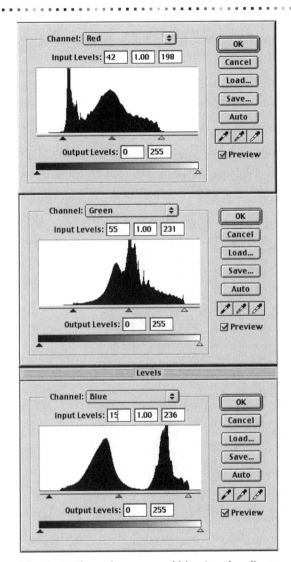

Figure 2 *The red, green, and blue Levels adjustments*

Balancing Color

The image looks a lot brighter but has a yellow color cast. You'll use the Color Balance feature to correct the color cast.

1. Make a new Adjustment layer. This time, choose Layer → New Adjustment Layer → Color Balance.

2. Be sure the Preview box is checked to see the results as you work.

3. Click the Midtone radio button. Move the Magenta–Green slider to +14, and move the Yellow–Blue slider to +13, as in Figure 3. This will reduce the amount of yellow in the image and produce more natural-looking color in the midtones.

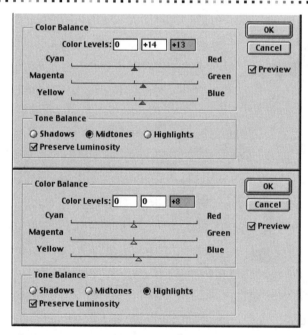

Figure 3 *Color Balance adjustments*

4. Click the Highlight radio button. Move the Yellow–Blue slider to +8. This will produce more neutral colors in the lighter regions of the image.

5. Click OK. The image has lost its yellow cast and the color looks more natural.

6. Press Cmd/Ctrl+S to save the document.

Adjusting Curves

The image is now looking good, having adjusted its contrast and eliminated the color cast, but it would be nice to bring out a little more of the red in the mountains. Curves is by far the most powerful of the color adjustment tools. Curves enables you to be quite specific about the range of color to adjust.

1. Choose Layer ➜ New Adjustment Layer ➜ Curves.

2. Press Option/Alt and click the graph to see the finer grid.

3. Because you want to enhance the reds in the mountains, choose the Red channel.

4. Choose Load and open Red_Lockdown_Curve.acv in the Ch16 folder on the CD.

5. Click and drag over the red rocks; notice that the cursor turns into an eyedropper and a little circle appears that moves up and down the curve. That is the range of the red pixels of the curve that we want to affect. Press Cmd/Ctrl and click the mouse to deposit an anchor point on the highest spot on the curve where the circle moves as you drag.

6. Click the second-highest anchor point on the curve and drag it upward about half of a cell. The mountains become redder (see Figure 4).

7. Click OK.

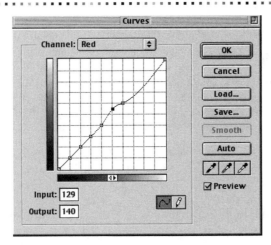

Figure 4 *The Curves adjustment*

Be prudent in the amount you adjust the curve. Too great an adjustment will produce posterization and dithering. It's always a good idea to zoom in on a portion of the affected area and scrutinize it carefully after you've made the adjustment but before you close the dialog box. Press Cmd/Ctrl+spacebar to zoom in and Option/Alt+spacebar to zoom out.

Using Auto Levels

You'll open an image of a cactus wren, select it, and drag and drop it on the new image. Then you'll apply a quick adjustment to it.

1. Open the File Cactus_Wren.psd in the Ch16 folder on the CD (see Figure 5).

Figure 5 *Let's add this wren to the image.*

2. Choose the Magic Wand tool and set the Tolerance to 32.

3. Click the blue background of the image.

4. Choose Select → Inverse to select the prickly pear cactus and the bird.

5. Omit the cactus from the selection by dragging around it with the Lasso tool while holding down the Option (Mac) or Alt (Win) key.

6. Choose the Move tool. Click and drag the selected Wren layer to the Sonoran Desert image and release the mouse. A new layer will be created in the Layers palette.

7. Press Option/Alt and double-click the name of the layer to display the Layer Properties dialog box. Name the layer Wren and click OK.

8. In the Options bar, check Show Bounding Box. Press the Shift key to constrain the proportion of the bird as you drag a corner handle. Drag inward until the bird is a reasonable size for the Sonoran Desert scene, then release the mouse. Double-click to initiate the transformation.

9. Place your cursor inside the marquee. Drag the wren and place it on the top of the large saguaro cactus, as in Figure 6.

Figure 6 *The wren, sized and positioned*

10. With the Wren layer targeted, choose Image ➜ Adjust ➜ Auto Levels. The color of the wren will shift from a muddy brown to a desert yellow.

You can control the color of the wren more precisely if, after you apply Auto Levels, you apply a Color Balance adjustment.

11. Double-click the layer and name it Cactus Wren.

12. Choose File ➜ Save and save the document.

Apply USM

The image is practically complete. Let's see if we can get a little more punch out of it. Because we are going to flatten the image, we should make a copy of it first.

1. To duplicate the image, choose Image ➜ Duplicate.

2. From the Layers palette pull-down menu, choose Flatten Image.

3. Choose Image ➜ Mode ➜ Lab Color to convert the image so as to avoid color shifts when sharpening.

4. Target the Lightness channel in the Channels palette. You should be *viewing* the composite channel in the image window, but only the Lightness channel should be highlighted.

5. Choose Filter ➔ Sharpen ➔ Unsharp Mask. Set the Amount to 69%, the Radius to 4.4 pixels, and the Threshold to 24 levels (see Figure 7).

6. Click OK.

7. Press Cmd/Ctrl+S to save the document.

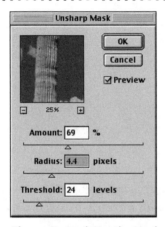

Figure 7 *Applying the Unsharp Mask filter to the image is the final step in enhancing the contrast.*

Up Next

The features covered in Chapter 16 are very important to producing a professional-quality image. Color adjustments give you control over the appearance of your image, and control is really what Photoshop is all about. From the moment you open the image to its final output, you're the boss. You tell Photoshop how you want the image to look by accessing its many tools and operations, and it dutifully performs your command.

In Chapter 16, we covered only a part of Photoshop's color-editing features. Next, we'll look at operations that do more than correct colors—they actually change or map color. These features give you the power to create graphic effects that radically alter the appearance of your images.

Modifying and Mapping Color

PHOTOSHOP

Chapter 17

C olor is one of the most important factors in our visual experience of the world around us. Humans react to color emotionally. Cool, subdued colors can calm our senses, and hot, saturated colors can excite us. Color affects the decisions of our daily lives, like whether we purchase a product or cross the street. It affects our physical and mental space and contributes to our sense of well being.

Since color plays such an important role in our lives, how we use it to communicate ideas is essential to the success of our images. As we have seen, Adobe Photoshop provides numerous ways to apply and adjust color. In addition, we'll explore features in this chapter that can radically alter existing colors in an image—*color-mapping* operations that go beyond brightness and contrast adjustments and simple color fills. They provide the means to alter the basic characteristics of color while maintaining the image's detail. You can use these commands to change the entire color scheme of your image or create eye-popping graphic effects, like vibrant posterizations, high-contrast line art, and textured halftones.

In this chapter, you will learn about:

- Altering the hue and saturation

- Replacing the colors in an image

- Limiting the number of colors in an image

- Producing graphic affects using halftones

Altering Hue and Saturation

Most of the color-mapping operations are found under the Image ➜ Adjust submenu. In Chapter 16, we entered this same menu to access the brightness and contrast operations, like Levels and Curves, and color-correction features, like Color Balance and Selective Color. The Hue/Saturation command lets you alter the basic color characteristics of your image. When you choose Image ➜ Adjust ➜ Hue/Saturation, you are presented with a dialog box with three sliders (Figure 17.1). Each slider *remaps* a different color characteristic.

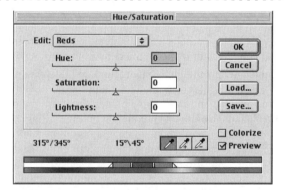

Figure 17.1 *The Hue/Saturation dialog box*

Changing Hue

If you drag the Hue slider to change relative color relations of the image or selection, you can produce some really beautiful and unexpected color combinations. I encourage you to experiment with color images to get a feel for the Hue/Saturation command and to experience its potential. You'll find changing the reality of an everyday landscape into a brilliant Fauvist work of art to be fun and easy. With these tools in hand, after all, who can resist the temptation to transform, with the click of a mouse, a humdrum blue sky to an electric fuchsia and the ordinary green leaves on the trees to bubble-gum pink?

The numeric values you see in the Hue/Saturation dialog box are based on the affected color's position on the color wheel, expressed in degrees. Values in the box reflect the amount of rotation from the original color. Moving the slider to the right, or a positive value, indicates a clockwise rotation of the color wheel. Moving it to the left, to a negative value, indicates a counterclockwise rotation. The color bars at the bottom of the palette are a graphic indicator of how the colors change as you move the Hue slider. By default, the color bars are aligned. The top color bar represents a color wheel that has been cut at the 180-degree point, or blue. As you move the Hue slider, the top color bar remains in place and represents the entire range of colors prior to the change. The bottom color bar is dynamic. It moves as you drag the Hue slider and realigns with the colors on the top bar to reflect the relative change of colors.

Adjusting Hue

The Edit pop-up list at the top of the dialog box enables you to target a specific range of colors to adjust. The colors are divided into basic color ranges of 90 degrees each, including the *overlap* (the amount in which the adjacent colors to the target color on the color wheel are affected). The Master option (the default range) permits the entire spectrum of color to be affected when the Hue, Saturation, or Lightness sliders are moved. The other options perform as follows:

Edit Option	Targets (on the Color Wheel)
Reds	Colors to be affected from 0 to 45 degrees clockwise and 360 to 315 degrees counterclockwise
Yellows	Colors to be affected from 15 to 105 degrees clockwise
Greens	Colors to be affected from 75 to 165 degrees clockwise
Cyans	Colors to be affected from 135 to 225 degrees clockwise
Blues	Colors to be affected from 195 to 285 degrees clockwise
Magentas	Colors to be affected from 255 to 345 degrees clockwise

When you choose a color from the Edit list, you can limit the changes to a specific range of hues. An adjustment slider appears between the two color bars, telling you which colors are being affected and letting you increase or decrease the range of hues to be affected, by dragging left or right in these ways:

- To change the range of color to be affected, drag the dark gray horizontal bar to move the entire adjustment slider.

- To extend the range of color and the amount of overlap, drag the light gray horizontal bars.

- To change the range while leaving the overlap unaffected, drag the white vertical bars.

- To adjust the overlap while leaving the range fixed, drag the white triangles.

The Eyedroppers

The familiar eyedroppers that we saw in the Levels and Curves dialog boxes perform a slightly different function here. Once again, their performance is controlled by the presets made to the Eyedropper tool in the Options bar; choose Point Sample, 3 By 3 Average, or 5 By 5 Average. In the Hue/Saturation dialog box, they are used to pick specific colors to be adjusted. Choose the eyedropper that best suits your purposes.

The Eyedropper samples a pixel or set of pixels, depending on the options selected for the Eyedropper tool in the Options bar.

The Plus Eyedropper lets you add to the sample range by dragging over pixels in the image window.

The Minus Eyedropper lets you subtract from the range by dragging over pixels in the image window.

When you sample a color from an image with an eyedropper, the Edit pop-up list will produce an additional category, titled Reds 2 or Blues 2, for example. The new category includes the 90-degree range of colors of default categories with the specific, sampled hue at its center.

Once you've sampled the color on the image with an eyedropper, drag the Hue, Saturation, or Lightness sliders to affect that color.

Adjusting Saturation

The intensity of the colors in an image can be adjusted in a similar fashion by dragging the Saturation slider. The default saturation value on the center of the slider is 0, which represents the relative saturation of the color as it was scanned. You can move the slider to the right—up to as much as +100%, where the affected colors will be fully saturated, producing intense neon colors—or to the left, to −100% where the colors will be completely desaturated, or gray.

Most of the time your values will fall somewhere between the two extremes. You can enhance a color and make it "pop" by pushing the Saturation slider between +20%

and +40%. On the other hand, if you're interested in muted pastel colors, drag the slider –20% to –40% to the left to diminish the saturation.

You can perform a quick, total desaturation of an image or selection by choosing Image ➜ Adjust ➜ Desaturate. This operation accomplishes the same thing as moving the Saturation slider to –100 in the Hue/Saturation dialog box.

Adjusting Lightness

The brightness values of an image can be edited by moving the Lightness slider. Drag it toward the left to darken the image or selection or to the right to lighten it. The 0 point marks the input lightness value of the image. The extremes are +100% lightness, which produces white, and –100% lightness or black.

If an area of your image is very light and you find that adjusting the Hue and Saturation sliders has no effect on it, darken it a little by dragging the Lightness slider to the left. Then drag the Hue and Saturation sliders. The light areas will begin to change to a color.

Don't like the results of your first try? At any time, you can reset the Hue/Saturation dialog box to the default by pressing the Alt/Option key and clicking the Reset button, or press Command/Ctrl+Z to undo just the last operation.

Colorize

This is where you can create those cool effects that you see in movies like *Schindler's List* or in magazine ads, where the entire image is black-and-white except for one small area that displays a brilliant spot of color. Before a black-and-white image can be colorized, you must change its mode from Grayscale to a mode that supports color, like RGB, CMYK, or Lab. The appearance of the Grayscale image will be unaffected by this conversion.

When you colorize an image or selected area, you convert gray pixels to colored pixels. Gray pixels have RGB values that are all equal. For example, the RGB values for black are red = 0, green = 0, and blue = 0. The RGB value for white is red = 255, green = 255, and blue = 255, and the RGB value for medium gray is red = 127, green = 127, and blue = 127. When you colorize a group of pixels, you shift the red, green, and blue components to disparate values.

When you check the Colorize box, the Hue and Saturation sliders change to represent absolute values instead of relative ones. The default hue that is produced when you check the Colorize box is the current foreground hue. The Hue slider now reads from 0 degrees on the left to 360 degrees on the right, and the current foreground color's position on the color wheel is displayed.

To change the hue, move the slider until you see the color you want or, more precisely, enter its position on the color wheel (in degrees) in the Hue value field. The Saturation slider reads from 0% to 100% and defaults at 25%. Move the slider to the right to increase intensity or to the left to decrease intensity. The default lightness of the pixels remains unchanged, as does the Lightness slider. It continues to display relative values between –100 (black) and +100 (white). By colorizing, you apply color to the image without affecting the lightness relations of the individual pixels, thereby maintaining the image's detail.

Let's go through colorization step by step so you get the hang of how it operates. Open the file `Chili_Peppers.psd` (Figure 17.2) in the Ch17 folder on the *Mastering Photoshop 6* CD.

For this mini-exercise and the one that follows, I've already selected pieces to be colorized onto separate layers. In later projects, you'll combine selecting or sampling with color adjustments.

1. Choose Image ➜ Mode ➜ RGB.

2. When you initially apply colorization, the selection is colored with the foreground color. Click the Default Color icon or press the D key, to restore the foreground color to black and the background color to white.

In fact, the default foreground color, black, is actually pure red hue, 0 degrees on the color wheel, with 0% saturation and 0% brightness.

3. Choose Window ➜ Show Layers and target the layer named Red Chili.

4. Choose Image ➜ Adjust ➜ Hue/Saturation.

5. Click the Colorize box. The chili turns red (the foreground color).

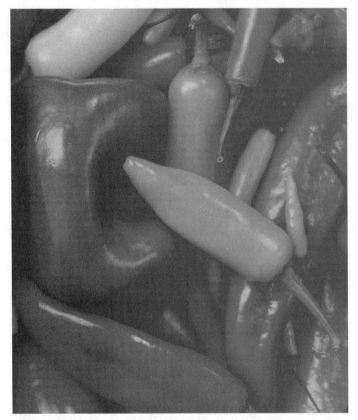

Figure 17.2 *The Grayscale chili peppers*

6. Move the Saturation slider to 60% to increase its intensity. Click OK.

7. Target the Stem layer, and choose Image ➜ Adjust ➜ Hue/Saturation again.

8. Click the Colorize box. The stem turns red.

9. Set the Hue to 90; the stem turns green. Set the Saturation to 20, to decrease its intensity. Set the Lightness to –22. Click OK. (See the result in the color section.)

The Hue/Saturation command can be assigned to an Adjustment layer. You can then make changes to the colors of the image throughout the imaging process. For more about Adjustment layers, see Chapter 16.

Mastering Photoshop 6

Color Gallery

This detail of a pointillist painting by Georges Seurat demonstrates the use of clustered dots to determine color densities. [Chapter 1]

A close-up of a four-color process image, showing the tiny dots that produce color densities [Chapter 1]

The Shape tool made it easy to decorate this watch face. [Chapter 9]

A raster on the left and the same image as a vector graphic on the right [Chapter 3]

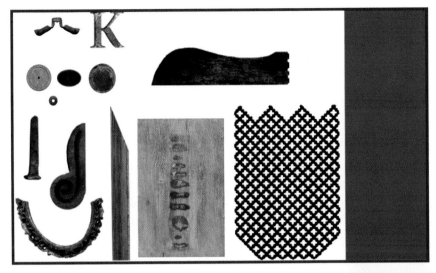

The beginning pieces for the Rex "hands-on" project [Chapter 6]

The finished Rex digital assemblage

David Adix has a particular genius for assembling the most charming and interesting sculptures from stuff that most people would throw away. [Chapter 6 Hands-On]

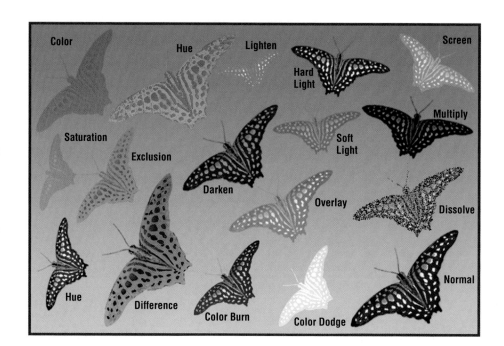

These butterflies show how the same image can be affected by different blending modes. [Chapter 7]

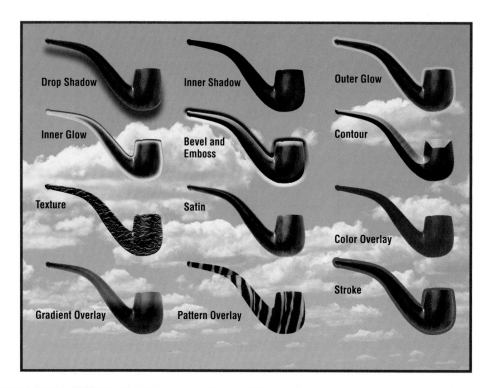

These pipes exemplify how layer styles alter the appearance of an image. [Chapter 7]

Liisa Phillips is a surrealist painter whose art inspired the Amazing Flying Women poster.
[Chapter 8 Hands-On]

The original Amazing Flying Women

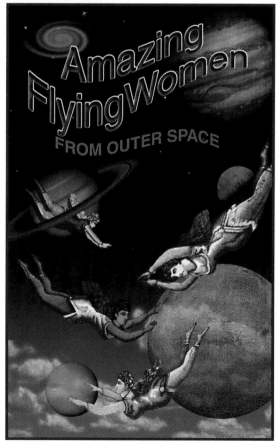

The finished layered image, complete with warped text

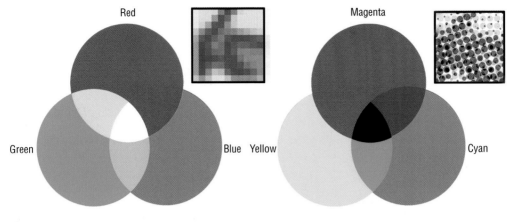

The RGB (left) and CMYK (right) color models [Chapter 10]

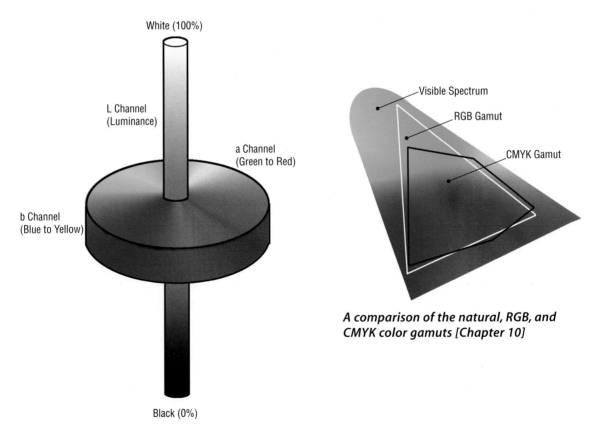

A comparison of the natural, RGB, and CMYK color gamuts [Chapter 10]

The CIE Lab color model [Chapter 10]

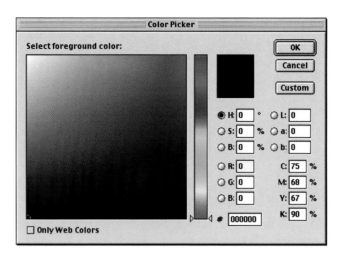

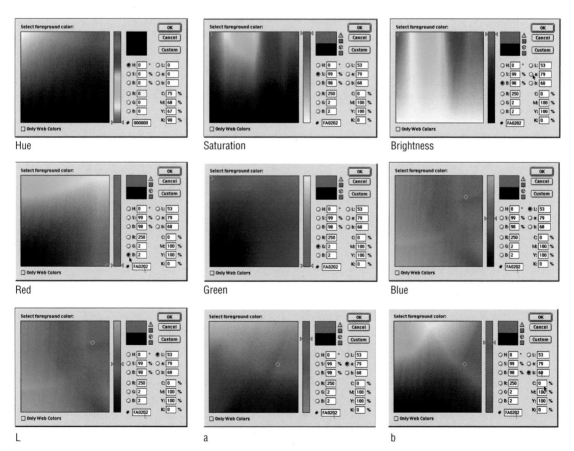

Hue	Saturation	Brightness
Red	Green	Blue
L	a	b

The Color Picker can be configured to display nine different active parameters of color. [Chapter 10]

These photographs have been made to look like paintings by applying color with the painting tools.
[Chapter 10]

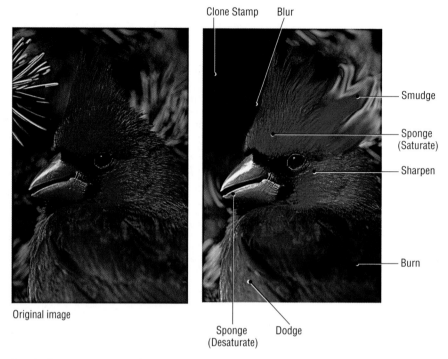

Clone Stamp   Blur

Smudge

Sponge
(Saturate)

Sharpen

Burn

Original image

Sponge
(Desaturate)   Dodge

The "before" cardinal (left) and the same image altered with the editing tools [Chapter 10]

The original barrel cactus photograph, and the Impressionistic version after alterations with the Art History Brush. The version on the right has been altered with Style: Tight Short, Fidelity: 100%, Area: 50 px, and Spacing: 0. [Chapter 10]

If you paint with a snapshot using the History Brush, you can selectively apply portions of the snapshot to the image. (a) shows the original image. In (b), I altered the entire image with the Hue/Saturation command and made a snapshot of it. In (c), I painted the green water from the snapshot onto the image with the History Brush tool. [Chapter 11]

A painted version of the Headville children's book project, including selective application of the Art History Brush tool [Chapter 11 Hands-On]

The original, boring chickens [Chapter 12 Hands-On]

You can change the color of a mask to better reveal the contents of the image.

The completed Chickens in Motion image after it has been masked and filters have been applied

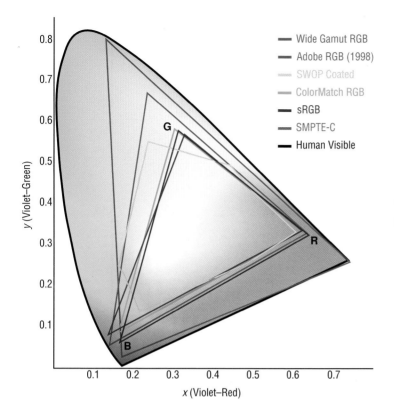

Wide Gamut RGB
Adobe RGB (1998)
SWOP Coated
ColorMatch RGB
sRGB
SMPTE-C
Human Visible

The color gamuts of various color working spaces [Chapter 15]

Compare these prairie dogs before and after adjusting Levels. We've increased the contrast by taking advantage of the full possible range of pixel values. [Chapter 16]

The contrast and color balance of the Dreamcar are much more pleasing after setting the white and black points to account for the color cast. [Chapter 16]

This Sonoran Desert scene becomes more striking when you increase the contrast (using the Levels and Curves dialogs), correct the color, and add a cactus wren. [Chapter 16 Hands-On]

The Image ➜ Adjust ➜ Replace Color function is a combination of two powerful Photoshop operations: the Hue/Saturation command and the Color Range command. [Chapter 17]

Colorizing selectively can make your image hotter. [Chapter 17]

You can open the Dirtbikers file from the CD to manipulate color using Posterize. [Chapter 17]

The RGB image posterized with 2 colors applied to each of the channels

The Grayscale image posterized with 4 shades of gray

The gray shades replaced with colors from the Swatches palette

The original image.
[Chapter 18]

Unsharp Mask applied
to the Blue channel,
Amount 250%, Radius
20, Threshold 2 (dese-
lected background).

Unsharp Mask applied to
the Red, Green, and Blue
channels, Amount 190%,
Radius 30, Threshold 6.
(I used different Fade
amounts and deselected
certain areas to avoid
over-sharpening.)

Gaussian, 20

Uniform, 20

*Some Add
Noise results
[Chapter 18]*

*Gaussian, 20,
Monochromatic*

Original image [Chapter 18]

Find Edges

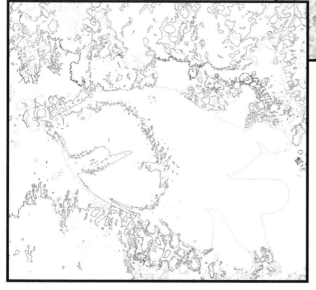

Trace Contour

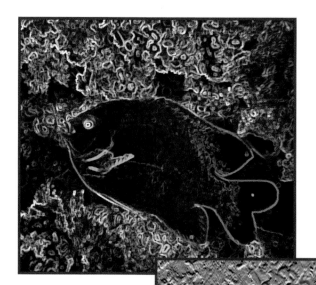

Glowing Edges

The effect of the Emboss filter applied directly to the image (Angle: 33 degrees, Height: 4 pixels, Amount: 360 percent)

The effect of the Emboss filter applied to a duplicate layer and blended in Luminosity mode

Original image [Chapter 18]

Mezzotint, Long Strokes

Color Halftone

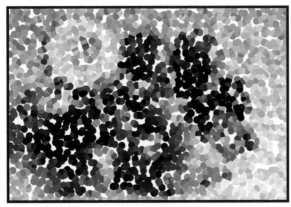

Pointillize

Crystallize

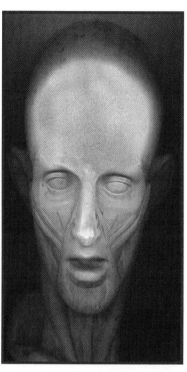

Examples of the
Lighting Effects filter
[Chapter 18]

*The original
image*

*The default light,
expanded and
rotated so that
its source shines
from beneath*

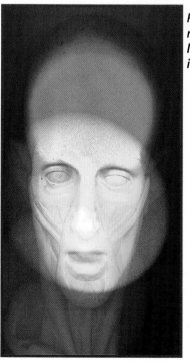

*RGB lights
moved to various
locations on the
image*

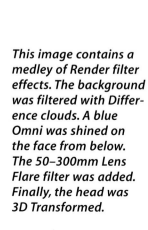

*This image contains a
medley of Render filter
effects. The background
was filtered with Differ-
ence clouds. A blue
Omni was shined on
the face from below.
The 50–300mm Lens
Flare filter was added.
Finally, the head was
3D Transformed.*

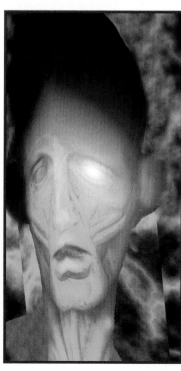

The gray gamut warning marks the colors that are outside the CMYK range.
[Chapter 15 and 19]

The (left) beginning and (right) finished Birdy Condo images demonstrate how layers make your work easier and more interesting. [Chapter 20 Hands-On]

The telephone image altered with an electrifying layer mask [Chapter 20]

The Rhino image (left) before the new layer modes were applied, and (right) with the addition of the two new layers and the change of blending modes. [Chapter 22]

This watercolor demonstrates the power of blending modes. [Chapter 22]

Original image

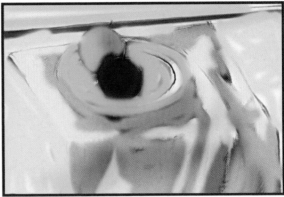

The broadly painted source

Subtract mode at 50% opacity

Multipy mode at 50% opacity

Exclusion mode at 100% opacity

Duotones using various combinations of PANTONE ink colors and brightness curves [Chapter 23]

The Ranch Rock image is made much more dramatic as a Tritone with a small addition of spot color. [Chapter 23 Hands-On]

The spot color overlaid on the samurai's pants [Chapter 23]

The tonal spot color in combination with the knockout and a different PANTONE color produces a different look.

JPEG compression-quality comparisons: (left) Low and (right) Maximum [Chapter 24]

You can create complete Web pages like this, including splices, rollovers, and animations, with Photoshop and its companion program, ImageReady. [Chapter 25 Hands-On]

Matching Colors

You can use the Hue/Saturation feature to sample a color from one image or selection and apply it to another image or selection, thereby perfectly matching the colors. Here's how:

1. Open the file from your CD, in the Ch17 folder, named Colored_Hats.psd.

2. To make it easier to target specific areas of the image, I have separated it into three layers. Target the Pink Hat layer.

3. Choose the Eyedropper tool. In the Options bar, set the Sample Size to 3 By 3 Average.

4. Choose Window ➜ Show Info. In the Info palette pull-down menu, choose Palette Options. For First Color Readout, drag to HSB Color in the submenu. Click OK.

5. Place the cursor on a midtone region of the pink hat. (I chose the area to the left of the word *Bahamas*.) Click your mouse to sample the color as a foreground color. Write down the Hue and Saturation reading in the Info palette; in this case, it's 329 for the Hue and 91 for the Saturation (see Figure 17.3).

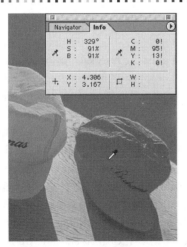

Figure 17.3 *Sampling the color from the pink hat*

6. Target the Yellow Hat layer. Choose Image → Adjust → Hue/Saturation. Be sure the Preview box is checked; check the Colorize box.

7. If you sampled hue 329 as specified in step 5, then it is now the current foreground color. The Hue slider will read 329 when you click the Colorize box. If you did not sample the color, enter 329 in the Hue box and 91 in the Saturation box. (I also adjusted the Lightness slider to +7 to best match the pink hat.) Click OK, and the two hats look as though they came out of the same box. In this way, colors can be matched precisely using the Hue/Saturation command.

Replacing Color

With Photoshop, you can do more than just alter the hue, saturation, and lightness of an image. You can sample a specific range of colors and automatically replace it with a different range of color. This is particularly useful if you need to change a similar color that is scattered throughout an image.

When you choose Image → Adjust → Replace Color (see Figure 17.4), you get a dialog box that is a combination of two powerful Photoshop operations: the Hue/Saturation command and the Color Range command. This dynamic duo can quickly perform miraculous color swapping. The Color Range command makes selections based on colors you sample in the image. (See Chapter 19, "Making Complex Selections," for details on how to use Color Range). The Replace Color dialog box combines this powerful feature with hue, saturation, and lightness controls so that you can precisely sample colors and then instantly replace them. Once again, before you enter the Replace Color dialog box, I recommend that you change the settings on the Eyedropper tool to 3 By 3 Average.

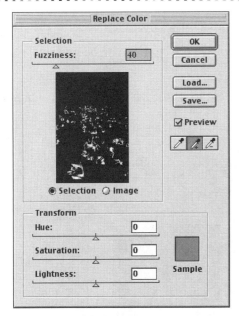

Figure 17.4 *The Replace Color dialog box*

   The default Replace Color dialog box displays a black mask of the image. Be sure the Preview box is checked. Choose an Eyedropper from the Replace Color dialog box, and click the color in the image window that you want to change. The mask reveals white portions that designate where the changes will be made. If you choose the Plus Eyedropper, you click and drag over areas to add colors. If you choose the Minus Eyedropper, you drag over colors and delete them from the replacement. The mask will reflect the changes you make.

Once you've selected the colors to replace, the next step is to move the Hue, Saturation, and Lightness sliders to produce a new range of color. As you drag, the affected colors will change in the image window. If you didn't nail all the areas that you wanted to change when you sampled with the Eyedropper, sample again with the Plus Eyedropper to extend the range, or drag the Fuzziness slider to the right (which may afford you a little more control). If you click the Image radio button under the mask, you'll see the image before the change. You can then compare the "before" version in the Replace Color dialog box to the "after" version in the image window prior to committing to the alteration.

Let's take a crack at replacing colors:

1. From the Ch17 folder on the CD, open the image Desert_Poppies.psd.

2. Choose the Eyedropper tool. (In the Options bar, be sure you've set the Sample Size to 3 By 3 Average.)

3. Choose the Rectangular Marquee and select the area that contains the yellow flowers, as in Figure 17.5.

Figure 17.5 *You can recolor all these poppies with a couple of waves of your mouse.*

4. Choose Image ➜ Adjust ➜ Replace Color.

5. Choose the Plus Eyedropper.

6. Drag over the larger yellow flowers in the foreground of the image to sample the colors. Be careful not to touch the surrounding rock or green plants. The mask changes to include the sampled colors from the flowers.

7. Move the Hue/Saturation sliders to change the colors. I've specified Hue = –85, Saturation = –12, and Lightness = +22 to make the poppies pink.

8. If there are substantial portions of the flowers that are still yellow, drag over the areas with the Plus Eyedropper. If you include too much in the selection,

drag over the unwanted areas with the Minus Eyedropper. If you want to extend the color a little bit, move the Fuzziness slider to the right. Or if you want to decrease it, move the slider to the left.

9. Click the Image radio button to compare before and after versions. When satisfied with the replacement, click OK. If you're not sitting at your monitor right now, check the color section to see the change in these flowers.

Rearranging Colors

Photoshop's color-mapping features enable you to limit the number and range of colors in your image. You can automatically produce higher levels of contrast, convert your images into line art, produce images that resemble serigraphs (silk-screen prints), and change your image from a positive to a negative. With so many available choices as to how to transform your image, no doubt you'll never again be satisfied with just an ordinary photograph. Let's go through them one by one and determine what they do and how they work. They are all found on the bottom rung of the Image ➜ Adjust submenu.

Equalize

You can use this command to alter the contrast of an image. It analyzes the color information in each channel, and maps the darkest pixel it can find to black and the lightest pixel to white. It then evenly distributes the color information between the two extremes. This doesn't mean that the image will contain black or white—only that, in at least one channel, there will be a pixel with a value of 0 and a pixel with a value of 255. It also doesn't mean that the image will be higher contrast, only that the contrast values will be distributed over a larger range. The results can vary depending on the image. See Figure 17.6 for an example of the effect.

Invert

You can use Invert to create negatives because it expertly converts every color in the image to its exact opposite. If you're working on a 256-level Grayscale image, black (0) will become white and white (255) will become black. All other values will also switch; a light gray will become its dark gray counterpart if inverted. For example, if a pixel has a brightness value of 230 (that is, 255 – 25), it will have a value of 25 when converted (0 + 25) (as in the example in Figure 17.7).

Figure 17.6 *(left) Before and (right) after applying the Equalize command*

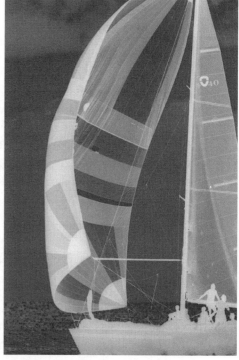

Figure 17.7 *The same image (left) before and (right) after the Invert command.*

Invert works the same way on RGB color images. They are converted channel by channel. However, Invert doesn't produce color film negatives very well, because it omits the colored tint, called an "orange mask," that is found in such negatives. You can use the Invert command and later make a color adjustment with the Color Balance or Variations commands to add an orange tint, but this will require some experimentation.

Because the operation converts the color values of each color channel, the results can vary substantially depending on the image's color mode.

If you invert an alpha channel, the selection it produces will be equal to an inverted selection.

Threshold

When you choose Image ➜ Adjust ➜ Threshold, you map all of your colors to either black or white. The Threshold dialog box displays a histogram of all of the brightness values of your image. You drag the slider to the left or right to determine its midpoint. Values on the right side of the slider are white. As you drag to the left, more pixel values are included on the white side and the image gets increasingly lighter. As you drag to the right, more pixel values are included on the black side and the image gets increasingly darker. Figure 17.8 demonstrates several Threshold midpoints.

Threshold is useful for turning photographs into high-contrast line art, an effect formerly achieved by copying generation after generation of images on a photocopier or by shooting extremely high-contrast film. Threshold has the advantage of being able to determine exactly how much of the image will be black and how much will be white and, therefore, offers far more control than traditional techniques. Threshold is also quite handy for making alpha channels from color channels for use on those seemingly impossible selections, as you will see in Chapter 19.

Posterize

Where Threshold divides an image into two colors, Posterize lets you choose the number of colors in which to divide the image. The problem is you have no direct way of controlling how the colors are mapped. When you choose Image ➜ Adjust ➜ Posterize, you are presented with the Posterize dialog box. You input a Levels value from 2 to 255. Posterize applies the value to each channel of the image, so if you enter 2 while working in an RGB image, you actually produce 8 colors (2^3). These effects can be interesting depending on how many colors you input into the Levels field. By breaking up the image into flat areas of color, with occasional dithering where the edges are

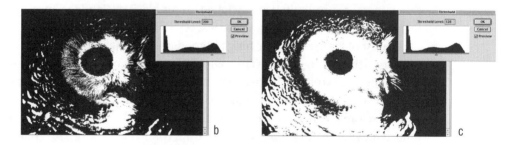

Figure 17.8 *The original image (a) remapped to various Threshold Levels: (b) 85, (c) 128, and (d) 200*

ambiguous, you can achieve a much more graphic appearance to your image. Unfortunately, the results are also unpredictable.

You can, however, use Posterize to determine the number of colors and how they are distributed in your image. The following work-around will give you the ability to create flat areas of color with precision and control. The results can resemble a serigraph effect used on silk-screen posters with bright, vibrant colors.

1. Open the RGB image `Dirtbikers.psd` in the `Ch17` folder on the CD (Figure 17.9). (Several different versions of this image are shown in the color section.)

Figure 17.9 *The original image*

2. Choose Image ➜ Mode ➜ Grayscale, to convert the image to black and white.

3. Choose Image ➜ Adjust ➜ Posterize. Enter a Levels value of 4 (you can actually enter whatever amount you like from 2 to 255, but we'll use 4 for this demo). Click OK. Notice that the image is now divided into four shades of gray: black, dark gray, light gray, and white.

4. Choose Image ➜ Mode ➜ RGB to convert the image back to RGB so it can support the color we are about to apply to it.

5. From the Tool palette, choose the Magic Wand tool. Set the Tolerance to 1 and uncheck the Anti-Aliased and Contiguous options. Click an area of black to select all of the black in the image.

6. Choose Window ➜ Show Swatches. Pick a dark color from the Swatches palette.

7. Press Option+Delete (Mac) or Alt+Backspace (Win) to fill the selected areas with color.

8. Repeat steps 5, 6, 7, and 8 on the areas of dark gray, light gray, and white, choosing a lighter color each time to replace the gray shades.

9. Save the document as `Dirtbikers_posterize.psd`. We'll use it in the Hands-On lesson that follows Chapter 22.

The posterization work-around lets you control the number and placement of the colors in your posterized image.

Creating Digital Halftones

A *halftone* is an image in which ink or toner is transferred to paper, consisting of dots on a grid. The resolution or number of lines per inch (lpi) of a halftone depends on the printer's capabilities. The number of dots on a traditional halftone is finite and depends on the grid's lpi. The tonal densities of an image are determined by the size of the dots—the larger the dot, the more ink is deposited, and the darker the area appears.

Most ink-jet printers, however, produce a *stochastic*, or frequency modulated, dot pattern, in which the tonal density is expressed not by the size but by the number of dots deposited. That's why the resolution claimed by desktop ink-jets (commonly 720 × 1440) is usually higher, though not necessarily better, because the dots are smaller and distributed in a random pattern. When you send an image to a printer, Photoshop, in tandem with the printer driver software, automatically and transparently converts the tonal information contained in pixels into dot density information that the printer's "marking engine" uses to construct your image. Fortunately, you don't have to do any of the math!

Before you begin to create an image for print, you should be aware of the necessary ratio of pixels per inch (ppi) to line screen (lpi) to produce quality halftones; this was covered in Chapter 13.

Photoshop also has built-in tools that let you convert your images to bitmaps and take over the halftoning process before you send your image to the printer. The term *bitmap* is used to describe images that are composed of pixels, each containing one bit of information. That means the pixels are either black or white. When you turn an image into a bitmap, Photoshop simply converts all of the tonal information into a series of black or white elements composed of—you guessed it—pixels. You can then print the bitmap on your laser printer as black-and-white line art or as a fully composited halftone. Even better, you can choose from a variety of bitmap types and patterns to produce specialized graphic effects.

You can't directly convert an RGB, CMYK, or Lab image into a halftone. You must first convert your image into a Grayscale. Bitmapped images do not support layers, alpha channels, filters, or any operations involving color—in fact, about the only things you can do with them are invert them or paint on them with black or white. Because they contain only one bit of information per pixel, the file sizes of Bitmaps are relatively small.

Choose Image ➔ Mode ➔ Bitmap to convert your Grayscale. You are presented with the Bitmap dialog box. Choose a resolution for the Bitmap. The higher the resolution, the smoother the elements that define it will be. If you want a one-to-one ratio with your laser printer, set it to the printer's output resolution (commonly 300, 600, 800, or 1200 dpi). Next, choose a method from the Use pull-down menu.

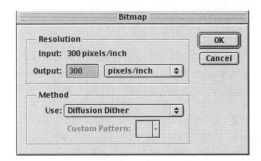

50% Threshold   converts the image to a black-and-white, line art Bitmap with the midpoint at 128. The difference between this function and the Threshold command discussed earlier in the chapter is that the Threshold command works on color and Grayscale images. It converts the image to black and white but retains the bit depth and, hence, the editability of the image. Plus, you can control the mid-point level, which lets you determine what pixels will be converted to white and what pixels will be converted to black. Bitmap images, on the other hand, are extremely limited as far as how they can be edited and what Photoshop operations they support. Another drawback is that 50% Threshold simply converts the image to black and white using the midtone pixels of 127 and 128 as the dividing line. In the bigger scheme of things, you may be better off using the Threshold command.

Pattern Dither applies a preprogrammed, geometric pattern to define the image's tonality. Unfortunately, it produces rather undesirable results, which have a tendency to close up when output to a laser printer.

Diffusion Dither applies a mezzotint pattern to the bitmap. The image is defined by a multitude of stray pixels peppered throughout the image. The effect can pleasantly soften the image but can also darken it. You may want to expose the image to a Levels adjustment to lighten it before you convert it to a Bitmap using the Diffusion Dither option.

Halftone Screen is by far the most useful option of the lot. When you choose Halftone Screen, you are presented with a dialog box. Enter a value for the frequency (lpi), angle of the screen, and dot shape.

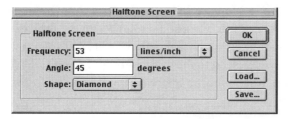

Custom Pattern uses a pattern that you select from the pattern pull-down menu to define the tonality. The results run from really interesting to incredibly ugly. Smaller patterns usually create more desirable effects.

To see variations of the possible results, open the image in the Chapter 17 folder on the CD, `Bridge.psd`. Apply each option in turn. It may be difficult to see some differences at low monitor resolution, or when printed to some printers.

When you view many of these bitmap effects on your monitor at certain sizes, you may see a strangely textured on-screen picture (as in the screen shot in Figure 17.10). This phenomenon is called a *moiré pattern* and is a result of the dot patterns of the image clashing with the matrix of the pixels on your monitor. Don't worry, the image will not print with these moiré patterns. There is not much you can do about this visual noise except to find a different size in which to view the image.

Figure 17.10 *A moiré pattern, caused by the clashing of an image's dot patterns with the matrix of the screen pixels*

Now let's try making a digital halftone using the same image that we posterized earlier.

1. Open the document in the Ch17 folder on the CD, `Dirtbikers.psd`.

2. Choose Image ➜ Mode ➜ Grayscale to convert it from RGB.

3. Choose Image ➜ Mode ➜ Bitmap; the Bitmap dialog box is displayed.

4. For Output resolution, choose 72 pixels/inch. This will produce a fairly coarse dot and is necessary for this demo, but you will want a higher resolution if you are going to print this image professionally.

5. For Method, choose Halftone Screen. For Frequency, enter 15 lines/inch, for Angle, 45 degrees, and for Shape, choose Line. Click OK.

Figure 17.11 shows the end result of this exercise. Save the image to your disk as `Dirtbikers_halftone.psd`.

Figure 17.11 *The outcome of the dirtbike halftone*

Up Next

The color mapping and halftone effects covered in this chapter will extend your ability to manipulate images and produce stunning graphic effects. In Chapter 22, "Overlay Techniques," we will examine the operations that can dramatically combine halftones and posterizations into a vibrantly colored illustration.

Part III, "Mastering Techniques," pushes the Photoshop envelope to the next level to combine images and produce effects for really professional results. The first chapter in Part III—Chapter 18, "Filtering Your Image"—takes you through the incredible world—or should I say, universe—of Photoshop filters. You'll see how this arsenal can turn your image upside down and inside out and produce almost any imaginable effect. Included in Chapter 18 is the centerpiece of the Photoshop 6 upgrade, the exciting, new Liquify feature, which moves pixels as if they were made of clay.

Part III
Mastering Techniques

In This Part

Filtering Your Image

PHOTOSHOP

Chapter 18

A great deal of the "Wow!" factor associated with Photoshop resides in the effects that it can achieve with filters. Filters, like many of Photoshop's other techniques, have their origin in the analog world of photography. A photographer uses filters to correct, adjust, or add lighting effects, and to create or adjust anomalies of perspective. Photoshop's filters take on these tasks and expand them. With filters, you can adjust focus, eliminate unwanted artifacts, alter or create complex selection masks, breath life into less than perfect scans, and apply a range of artistic effects previously unavailable to the traditional photographer. Filters also have the capability to completely destroy anything recognizable in an image and turn it into a mass of swirling colors.

In this chapter, you'll look at the fantastic things that filters can do. You'll learn about:

- Filter basics

- Constructive and destructive filters

- Effects filters

- Filters that render

- Photoshop's amazing new Liquify command

Filter Basics

When it comes down to it, filters are nothing more than mathematical formulae that alter the features of pixels or groups of pixels in specified ways. What can be changed in any individual pixel are its brightness value, saturation, and hue, and its position in relation to other pixels. These changes are limited. What allows for the great variation among filter effects is the way they can alter groups of pixels over a specified range, following specific constraints. Some work subtly; others can be brash and flamboyant. Some effects gain strength when used gently and reapplied; sometimes a filter can be mitigated or softened by fading the effect. The Fade Filter dialog extends the range and usefulness of filters by allowing you to use layer-like blending modes to blend the filter effect back into the original image.

But it is beyond the limits of our space here to delineate every possible effect offered by Photoshop's filters. Rather, some of the most useful ones will be discussed in detail. I encourage you to play and experiment with filters to discover for yourself their vast potential. Keep in mind that when you're working with standard, automated special effects, they are available to every person who uses the software. Some of those effects, if applied generically, are immediately recognizable by anyone who's ever used them. It's a good idea to be aware of what's available, but practice will indicate which techniques have more range of possibility and staying power; creativity will guide the user of filter effects to apply them in unusual or not so obvious ways. Sometimes the most effective special effect is the one that remains invisible.

Activating and Deactivating Filters

By choosing commands from the Filter menu, you can apply your filter of choice to the entire image, or confine it to a selected area. The Filter menu provides a long list of submenus, some of them long in turn. You can add or remove filters from these lists by placing items inside, or deleting them from, the Photoshop application's Plug-Ins folder. If you find you rarely use large groups of filters, you can save Photoshop valuable memory space by removing those from the Plug-Ins folder. If a day comes when you can't get away without applying one, just slip it back into the Plug-Ins folder and it's available once again. Plenty of third-party plug-ins are available for special occasions; they can be treated the same way.

If you hold down Command+Option or Ctrl+Alt when you launch Photoshop, you can specify which plug-ins folder you want to use for that session.

Filter Previews

When you're applying an effect as powerful and image-altering as some filters can be—and certain filters are among Photoshop's most memory-intensive functions—it's good to have some idea of what to expect. Most filters provide a preview inside the dialog box. You can zoom in or out by clicking the + and – buttons, and drag inside the preview box to scroll to the part of the image you wish to preview. Other filters, such as the majority of corrective filters, allow you to preview the effect in the image window itself; just click the Preview box or button. When the blinking bar below the Preview box disappears, the program has finished building the preview. Other filters, such as most in the Distort and Stylize submenus, provide no preview whatsoever. These non-previewable filters are generally among those that consume massive amounts of memory to apply.

Do your experimenting on a lower-resolution version of your image to save computational time. When you get at the effect you want, write down the settings that produce it. Then use those settings to apply the filter to your high-res image.

Fading Filters

Don't like how strong that filter effect comes on? You can mitigate the effect by using the Edit ➜ Fade command. Fade allows you to blend the filter effect in with the original image, just as you would with a separate layer. Fade offers a dialog box containing the same options you see in the Layers palette—that is, you can control Opacity from 1% to 100% and use any of the blending modes (with the exception of Behind and Clear). The Fade command is available immediately after a filter is applied. If you take any other action affecting the image, Fade becomes grayed out in the Edit menu.

In previous versions of Photoshop, Fade lived at the top of the Filter menu, just below Last Filter. It has been moved to the Edit menu, thanks to its enhanced capabilities. In Photoshop 6, Edit ➜ Fade isn't just for filters anymore. Now it can be applied to painting tool and Image ➜ Adjust commands as well.

If you want to reapply a filter with the exact same parameters a second time, simply press Cmd/Ctrl+F and the action of the last filter used is repeated. If you want to apply that same filter again, but you wish to change the options, press Cmd+Opt+F (Mac) or Ctrl+Alt+F (Win). The last-used filter's dialog box appears, allowing you to make changes before reapplying.

Filter Types

Rather than go through the list filter by filter, let's divide them up by what they can do. First, we'll look at the *constructive* filters—those that are used to modify images so they're usable for printing or screen display. *Destructive* filters, on the other hand, are the ones more associated with the aforementioned "Wow!" factor. These are the things that can take your image and turn it inside out. In effect, they displace pixels, more or less radically redistributing image elements. Other filters provide *fine-art effects*, mainly textures and painterly techniques. In addition to these types, there are filters for preparing images for video, for creating a digital watermark, and custom filters that allow you to create your own effects.

Constructive Filters

Four groups of filters provide tools to help improve image quality by changing the focus, or by smoothing transitions within an image. These filters belong to the Filter ➜ Blur, Noise, Sharpen, and Other submenus. These groups are the bread and butter of Photoshop filtering, the workhorses that are put to frequent, day-to-day use.

Some of the constructive filters correspond to and complement one another. For instance, Blur's effect is the opposite of Sharpen; Median acts on an image in exactly the opposite way from Add Noise. In general, the Sharpen filters increase focus and contrast between pixels, while the Blur filters decrease contrast and smooth areas of transition.

Blur Filters

The Blur group of filters contains six filters: Blur, Blur More, Gaussian Blur, Motion Blur, Radial Blur, and Smart Blur. Like their Sharpen counterparts, Blur and Blur More are fully automated. You click, the filter does its job, and that's that—no dialog box, no user input, no control. They diminish contrast, resulting in softer, smoother edges and transitions. Much more powerful than either of these is Gaussian Blur, named for 18th-century German mathematician Carl Friedrich Gauss. Gauss's work with number theory and distribution patterns made him a pioneer of modern mathematics. He is ultimately responsible for the distribution curves employed in the filter that bears his name (he'll crop up again in Photoshop when we get to the Add Noise filter), and he was one heck of a dancer.

But seriously, if you learn to manipulate the niceties of the Gaussian Blur, you'll never need the Blur and Blur More filters. Even with only one variable in its dialog box (Figure 18.1), Gaussian Blur just offers so much more. By entering a number from 0.1 to 250 or by sliding along the Radius slider, you tell Gaussian Blur to apply its softening curve to your intended degree. Lower values produce a slight, subtle blur effect, which can be used to smooth out rough transitions or blotchy areas; higher values can blur the image beyond recognition. Shadow effects can be created by applying this filter to underlying layers. Figure 18.2 shows some of the Gaussian Blur filter's range.

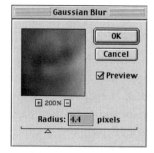

Figure 18.1 *The Gaussian Blur dialog box*

Radically different effects can be achieved with Gaussian Blur depending on whether you're applying it to a selection or freely to an image or layer as a whole. If Gaussian Blur is applied within a selection outline, its effect remains more or less constrained within the selected area. If, on the other hand, you apply it to a layer or to an entire image, the curve is allowed to carry its effect across the full range of the image. Compare the left image in Figure 18.3, where Gaussian Blur is applied within the confines of a selection, to the right image, where the same parameters were used on the entire layer.

The Smart Blur filter (Figure 18.4) is a kind of counterpart to Unsharp Mask in that it applies its blur to the open or continuous areas of an image while retaining edge definition. Like Unsharp Mask, Smart Blur offers the option of defining what it sees as an edge and how far the effect should extend; the Radius and Threshold settings work the same as in Unsharp Mask.

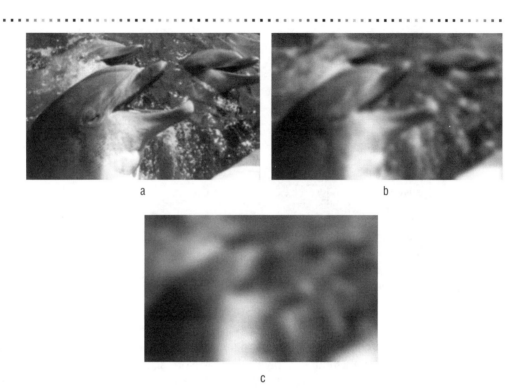

Figure 18.2 *Examples of Gaussian Blur settings: Radius set at (a) 2, (b) 10, and (c) 25*

Figure 18.3 *Gaussian Blur applied to (left) a selection and (right) a layer*

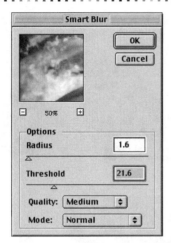

Figure 18.4 *The Mode option in the Smart Blur dialog box allows you to trace edges while blurring.*

The options in the Quality pop-up list control the smoothness of the effect, with the High setting, logically enough, providing the smoothest transitions. The Mode control offers various methods of applying the blur. Normal mode applies the effect, well, normally, as seen in Figure 18.5. The Edge Only and Overlay Edge options trace the edges with white lines. Edge Only shows the edges as white lines against a black background, while Overlay Edge superimposes white edge lines over the visible image. Frankly, though, the Normal mode is most likely the one you'll end up using 99% of the time Smart Blur comes to hand. Other edge-finding filters like Filter ➜ Stylize ➜ Find Edges and Filter ➜ Stylize ➜ Trace Contour allow more control over your image, and more interesting visual effects.

Figure 18.5 *The effect of the Smart Blur filter*

The Blur submenu contains two more filters that apply a blur along motion lines. Filter ➔ Blur ➔ Motion Blur (Figure 18.6) allows you to specify a direction of movement, expressed as an angle in degrees and a distance in pixels. Your image spreads out along a path in a linear distribution in the direction and distance indicated.

Figure 18.6 *The Motion Blur dialog box*

Radial Blur offers a different kind of directional movement in its dialog box. Two Blur Methods are available in this filter: Spin and Zoom. Spin distributes pixels by rotating them around a chosen center point, while Zoom's blur radiates pixels out from the center. The Radial Blur dialog box (Figure 18.7) shows a Blur Center field containing a grid pattern. Click or drag the center point to reposition the starting point of the Spin or Zoom anywhere in your image. Enter an Amount to define how far the blur extends. (Why this slider is named Amount here but named Distance in the Motion Blur filter is a mystery. They both accomplish the same thing.)

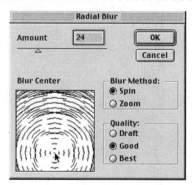

Figure 18.7 *Click in the Blur Center box to position the Spin or Zoom starting point.*

Draft, Good, and Best are offered as options under the Quality button. If Draft is chosen, the effect takes less time to accomplish, but the blur is applied more roughly; Best provides a smoother blur but requires more time and memory capacity. Figure 18.8 compares the effects of the Motion Blur and Radial Blur filters.

a

b

c

Figure 18.8 *The broncobuster: (a) The original image; (b) with Motion Blur applied (Angle −40, Distance 29); (c) with Radial Blur applied (Amount: 8, Method: Spin −40, Quality: Best)*

Try combining filters using the Fade command. Filter ➔ Stylize ➔ Wind used in tandem with the Motion Blur filter can produce an enhanced blast of directional movement. The Radial Blur Spin filter can create interesting concentric patterns when used together with Filter ➔ Distort ➔ Zig Zag. Or try the Radial Blur Zoom option and blend with Filter ➔ Stylize ➔ Extrude.

The look of the blur filters can be more effective if they are gradually faded into a portion of the image as demonstrated in the following exercise using the Motion Blur filter.

1. Open the file in the Ch18 folder on the *Mastering Photoshop 6* CD, Broncbuster.psd.

2. The image is divided into a layer and a Background. Target the Cowboy layer. Choose the Lasso tool. In the Options bar, set the Feather radius to 10 pixels.

3. Make a selection of the back half of the cowboy and the bronco, all the way to the top and left side of the image, as in Figure 18.9.

Figure 18.9 *Select the back of the cowboy and the bronco.*

4. Choose Filter ➔ Blur ➔ Motion Blur. Set the Angle to –45 degrees and the Distance to 44. Click OK. The effect fades into the image (Figure 18.10), producing the look of fast motion while preserving important details.

Figure 18.10 *Selective Motion Blur*

Noise Filters

The next group of filters in the constructive category are found in Filter ➜ Noise. Add Noise, Dust & Scratches, and Median all allow user control; the Despeckle filter is an automated effect that does its work without benefit of a dialog box. Like its "hands-off" counterparts in the Blur and Sharpen submenus, Despeckle's effects are easily surpassed by its more powerful siblings Dust & Scratches and Median. These three filters work in various ways to eliminate noise; Filter ➜ Noise ➜ Add Noise, believe it or not, adds noise to an image.

When you Add Noise to an image, the result is a grittier, grainier look—a bit of texture. Noise can work wonders in helping to smooth tonal transitions; it can help prevent banding in gradations and stair-stepping in your tonal range. In a Grayscale image, noise is added in black, white, and gray grains; in color images, noise is added individually to each color channel, producing natural-looking hues of noise that blend together at random. Figure 18.11 shows the Add Noise dialog box with its three option areas.

Amount   Enter a number from 0.1% to 400% to set a color range for your noise. This controls how far the noise can differ from the existing pixel colors—the higher the number, the greater variation in color of the added noise.

Distribution   Two options are available to define the way noise is distributed across an image. If you click the Uniform button, colors are applied at random throughout the image. Otherwise, Photoshop applies the noise in a Gaussian curve (you were warned that Carl Friedrich would turn up again). Gaussian generally results in a more pronounced effect than Uniform delivers.

Monochromatic Check this box if you wish to distribute noise uniformly across all color channels. If left unchecked, Add Noise applies its effect randomly to each channel separately, resulting in more color variation. Monochromatic ends up producing grayscale noise; if you're working on a Grayscale image, this option has no effect. Take a look at Figure 18.12 for some samples of noise in action. To see variations of noise in color, see the color section.

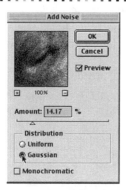

Figure 18.11 *The Add Noise Gaussian option results in more dramatic noise.*

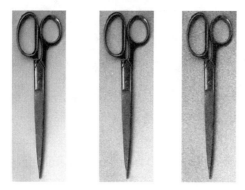

Figure 18.12 *(left) The original image; (center) Add Noise, Uniform, 64; (right) Add Noise, Gaussian, 64*

For practice with the Add Noise filter, open the image `Add_Noise.psd` (the original picture of the woman in the headdress, seen in the color section) from the `Ch18` folder on the CD.

Filter ➜ Noise ➜ Dust & Scratches was created for the purpose of removing those ugly artifacts that are almost unavoidable when scanning old photos. With its by-now familiar Radius and Threshold sliders to help define edges, Dust & Scratches offers a pretty decent tool for eliminating a good deal of the unwanted noise from an image. If you're scanning a batch of old pictures from your grandmother's scrapbook, or you need to use that old team shot from your high school yearbook, Dust & Scratches is a good place to start. It can help a great deal in getting rid of moiré patterns that may appear when scanning printed halftones, but it's not perfect. If you go too far with it, you could end up losing detail along with the unwanted specks. Sometimes a little elbow grease and the old Rubber Stamp tool will be necessary to finish the job. When used in tandem with the Unsharp Mask filter, Dust & Scratches can work wonders.

When you apply the Dust & Scratches filter, it's a good idea to exercise caution. Select a small area of similar texture in which apply the filter. Use the minimum Radius and Threshold you need to achieve results (as in Figure 18.13).

Figure 18.13 *(left) The area selected; (right) the filter applied*

For practice with the Dust & Scratches filter using the old family photograph shown here, open `Dust_and_Scratches.psd` in the `Ch18` folder on the CD.

The closely related Median filter is similar to Dust & Scratches, but its dialog box lacks the Threshold slider. Median's Radius (with a range of 1 through 100) is used to average the colors in an image, pixel by pixel, then apply that average to each pixel. The result is a softened, molded quality almost like a mild posterization. Higher values can destroy image detail, though, so take it easy on this one. Figure 18.14 provides one example of the Median filter at work.

Figure 18.14 *The Median filter with a Radius of 12*

Sharpen Filters

The Sharpen group contains four filters: Sharpen, Sharpen Edges, Sharpen More, and Unsharp Mask. The first three of these are fully automated—that is, the user has no control over their effect. When you click one of these, no dialog box appears. Photoshop simply applies the predefined effect of increasing contrast. Sharpen increases contrast overall; Sharpen More has a stronger effect; and Sharpen Edges focuses on the areas of highest contrast in an image.

Much more powerful than any of these is Unsharp Mask, which we visited in Chapter 16. Unsharp Mask gets its unusual name from an old photographic technique of shooting through a blurred negative as a mask to increase the edge contrast in a film positive. Photoshop's engineers have transformed that arcane bit of low technology into an incredibly useful enhancement tool. Its three-variable dialog box allows for minute adjustments and a very fine level of control. If the other three Sharpen filters were discarded, Photoshop users would still have all the sharpening capability they'd ever need with this one tool.

The Unsharp Mask dialog box (Figure 18.15) appears when you choose Filter ➔ Sharpen ➔ Unsharp Mask. These options appear for your input:

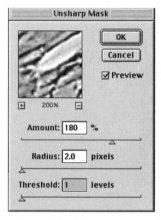

Figure 18.15 *The Unsharp Mask dialog box includes options that are common to many filters.*

Amount   Values from 1% to 500% can be entered to define the degree of sharpening—the higher the value, the greater the effect.

Radius   Defines the thickness (from 0.1 to 250 pixels) of an edge. Lower values produce crisp, sharp edges, while higher values define edges as thicker and generate greater overall contrast throughout an image.

Threshold   Entering a value from 0 to 255 allows Unsharp Mask to determine what's considered an edge. The number indicates the difference in brightness values necessary to recognize an edge. Lower numbers include lots of pixels in the effect; the higher the number, the more exclusive the value.

These three variables work together to do the job of heightening focus and contrast. A little experimentation and practice may be in order to find the right combination of settings to achieve the desired effect. Subtle effects can be produced by keeping the Amount setting under 100%; raising it over 300% can create results that some may consider undesirable. Figure 18.16 demonstrates a very high Amount; the Radius (2.0) and Threshold (1) have been left at their default values.

Figure 18.16 *(left) The original image and (right) Unsharp Masked with Amount set to 500%*

Sometimes repeated applications of a lower Amount setting can produce more desirable results than a single application at a higher setting.

When identifying edges, Unsharp Mask uses the Radius setting as its criteria. The effectiveness of this setting depends entirely upon the resolution of the image. Screen images and Web graphics will require a much lower setting (say, in the 0.5 range) than high-resolution images intended for fine printing (usually nicely sharpened in the 2.0 range.)

Radius values can be set all the way up to 250, but the higher values produce results more suitable for special effects than for day-to-day image correcting. Figure 18.17 compares the effects of different Radius settings, with the Amount fixed at 100% and the Threshold at 1.

Figure 18.17 *Unsharp Masking with a Radius of (left) 2, (middle) 100, and (right) 250*

Raising Threshold values has the effect of increasing the definition of an edge. In other words, higher values require more contrast between pixels to call it an edge; lower values recognize edges between pixels with more similar brightness values. Look at Figure 18.18 to see the results of Unsharp Mask applied with different Threshold values. In these examples, the Amount is set at 250% and the Radius at 2.

Figure 18.18 *Unsharp Masking with a Threshold of (left) 25 and (right) 250*

Another useful function of the Unsharp Mask filter is its application to separate color channels of an image. Muddy scans from lower-end scanners can be greatly improved by applying Unsharp Mask separately to different color channels, especially in the Blue channel. Look at each channel of your color image separately to determine where sharpening is most needed; apply Unsharp Mask and then view the composite to see the results. I've placed three versions of an image in the color section to demonstrate Unsharp Mask effects applied separately to the color channels of an image.

For practice with the Unsharp Mask filter, open the original wall image, which is Unsharp_Mask.psd in the Ch18 folder on the *Mastering Photoshop* 6 CD.

Other Constructive Filters

Some other useful constructive filters reside in the Filter ➜ Other submenu. Filter ➜ Other ➜ Offset (Figure 18.19) is more or less a "Move tool in a box." Input numbers in the Horizontal and Vertical areas to tell Photoshop how far to move a selection. Positive numbers move the image to the right or down; negative numbers move it to the left or up. These same precise moves can be ordered by using the arrow keys in conjunction with the Move tool. The difference is that Offset allows you to determine what happens to the unselected areas by clicking one of its three radio buttons. Set To Background fills the emptied area with the current background color. If the image to be moved is on a layer, then the Set To Background option changes to Set To Transparent and the emptied area will become transparent. Repeat Edge Pixels fills the area with duplicates of the pixels at the edge of the selection, while Wrap Around takes pixels from the opposite side of the selection and duplicates them. These settings reappear frequently in some of the destructive filters we'll see shortly, particularly those in the Filter ➜ Distort and Filter ➜ Stylize submenus.

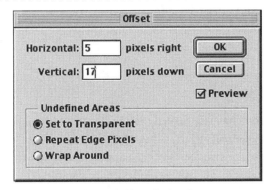

Figure 18.19 *The Offset dialog box*

The Minimum and Maximum filters fulfill functions familiar to anyone who has spent time in a lithography darkroom. In order to make colors in a printed image overlap, or *trap*, printers would change the colors' borders to allow one of the colors (generally the lighter of the two) to spread into the other. When applied to a masking channel, the Minimum filter shrinks the selection. The number you input in the Radius slider is the amount your selection contracts. Maximum does the exact opposite. Input a Radius amount, and the filter expands your selection precisely to that number. This way you can create precise traps mathematically. Masks created using Maximum and Minimum can be used to overlap different colored areas so that just the right amount of trap is created. This prevents dreaded white space from showing where two colors meet during printing.

Filter ➜ Other ➜ High Pass offers a tool for finding and isolating areas of high contrast. On its own, it seems at first glance an awkward and unlikely filter. But when applied to individual color channels or to selection masks, it can help create interesting line effects or imbue unremarkable images with added color. High Pass's Radius slider allows a range from 0.01 to 250 pixels. Lower numbers leave your image a flat, mid-range gray. Higher values let the higher-contrast areas show through in lighter gray. This isn't so great when applied to an image as a whole, but try applying this filter to individual color channels and you have a completely different animal. If you increase contrast by applying High Pass to individual color channels, you end up adding color at either end of the scale.

A line-drawing effect can be achieved by using High Pass in combination with the Threshold command, and then reapplying the image to itself. Figure 18.20 shows how this can be achieved. First, make a duplicate layer of your image, and apply High Pass to the duplicate, using the Radius to find a desirable effect. Choose Image ➜ Adjust ➜ Threshold at the desirable value. Then use the Opacity slider in your Layers palette to blend the line image with your original. Voilá! Line-drawing effect.

Destructive Filters

Now that the constructive filters have displayed their image-correcting prowess, it's time for a little fun. The special effects in the Filter ➜ Distort, Pixelate, and Stylize submenus take your precious pixels and shove them about with wild impunity. With these filters, you can turn images inside out, explode and reassemble them, or boil the life out of them, leaving you with an indigestible goo. Used with care, they can be useful friends; used unwisely, they'll turn on you viciously. These filters are undoubtedly the cool members of the gang; they look good and offer a fun night out, but ultimately they're not quite as responsible as the constructive filters. And some are just plain dumb.

Distort Filters

The common purpose of the filters in the Distort submenu is to transport pixels in your image across specifically defined patterns. For instance, Spherize gives the impression that your image has been wrapped around a ball. Twirl fixes the center point of your image and spirals the pixels around it, clockwise or counterclockwise. Shear offers you an axis along which you can curve or lean your image.

The Distort filters have the distinction of being among the most memory-intensive of any of Photoshop's actions. To save yourself a lot of time watching the progress bar, do your experimenting with these filters on a lower-resolution version of your image. When you arrive at the effect you desire, make notes about the settings that produce the effect, and use those settings to apply the filter to your high-res version.

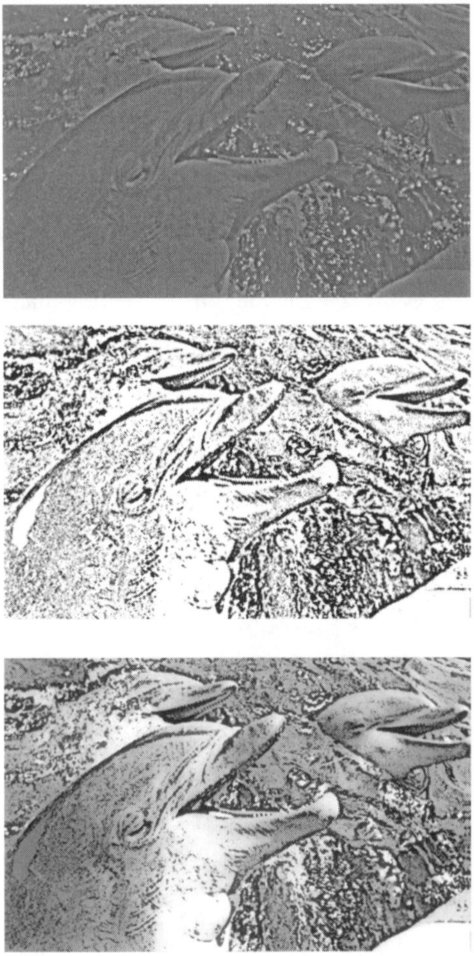

Step 1

Step 2

Step 3

Figure 18.20 *(Step 1) High Pass, Radius 7. (Step 2) Threshold, Level 120. (Step 3) The Opacity slider in the Layers palette adjusted to 50%.*

Filter ➔ Distort ➔ Diffuse Glow seems to be misplaced in this submenu, rather than among its kin, the Stylize filters. It gives the effect of viewing the image through a diffusion filter. You can set the level of Graininess, and define Glow and Clear parameters.

Glass, too, seems to belong elsewhere than with the Distort effects, perhaps among the Texture filters. Its effect approximates viewing your image through a glass lens (defined in the Texture pop-up menu). You also have the option of applying a texture of your own, using the Load Texture dialog. You'll find this option spread out among some of the Effects filters as well. Look for it in Artistic ➜ Rough Pastels and Under-painting, Sketch ➜ Conté Crayon, and especially Texture ➜ Texturizer. These art effects offer a set of textures, but you can apply patterns of your own making by saving them as a grayscale file in Photoshop format.

Ocean Ripple, Ripple, Wave, and Zig Zag all offer methods of introducing degrees of wiggliness into your image. (Some might also include Glass in this group; it applies a rippling effect with the added element of texture.) Of these, Wave is by far the most powerful and the most mysterious. Compare Zig Zag's user-friendly dialog with Wave's scientific control panel (Figure 18.21).

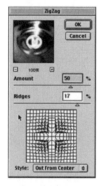 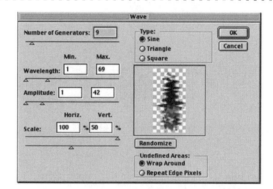

Figure 18.21 *Compare the (left) Zig Zag and (right) Wave dialog boxes.*

The Wave dialog is where some of Photoshop's mathematical underpinnings become most transparent. Too bad they couldn't provide a box with knobs you could twiddle like an old-fashioned synthesizer. You can input the number of wave Genera-tors, define minimum and maximum Wavelength and Amplitude levels, Scale the wave effect horizontally and vertically, and choose between three Types of waves. And when in doubt, just click Randomize; Photoshop will make up its own wave parameters. Figure 18.22 shows some of the effects these filters can accomplish.

For practice with the Distort filter, open up the scissors image on the CD; it's `Distort.psd` in the Ch18 folder.

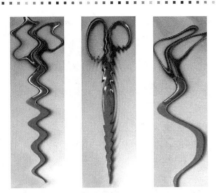

Figure 18.22 *Comparison of filter applications: (left) Ripple, Large; (center) Zig Zag, Pond Ripple; and (right) Wave*

Pinch and Spherize are so closely related, they might even be opposite sides of the same coin. If you apply a negative Amount in the Pinch dialog box, you get a Spherize-like effect; if you go negative in Spherize (Figure 18.23), the result is mighty like a Pinch. The difference is that Pinch maps your pixels onto a rounded cone, while Spherize maps it onto—you guessed it—a sphere. Spherize offers the added option of allowing you to constrain the effect to the horizontal or vertical axis, or both. These two filters don't cancel each other out, though. Compare the effects of each in Figure 18.24.

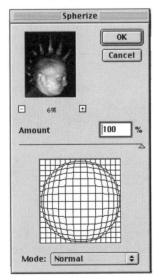

Figure 18.23 *The Spherize dialog box is similar to Pinch, except for the extra Mode (axis) option at the bottom.*

***Figure 18.24** A Pinched image (left) looks almost like the reverse of a Spherized one (right).*

Polar Coordinates (illustrated in Figure 18.25) takes your image at the corners and brings them together to form a circle. Or the reverse: it takes the center and maps it out to the corners. Back in the old days, applying Polar Coordinates Rectangular to Polar was one of the few ways you could get type in a circle in Photoshop. Now that the Type tool offers that capability much more flexibly, Polar Coordinates can go back to what it does best: changing squares into circles.

For practice with the Spherize, Pinch, and Polar Coordinates filters, open `Distort2.psd` (the punk portrait) in the `Ch18` folder on the CD.

Shear, as mentioned above, places your pixels along a curve. When you first open Shear's dialog box, you see a grid with a vertical line down the middle. You can take this vertical and angle it so it leans either way. This is akin to the Skew effect you get in the Transform functions. But if you click anywhere along the line, you can add points that turn the line to a curve. Now your image can distort along that curve in ways that Transform ➜ Skew and Distort can't achieve, as I've done in Figure 18.26. Radio buttons help you designate how the undefined areas will be treated: you can either wrap the image around or have the edge pixels repeat. If you don't like your curve, click the Defaults button and start over.

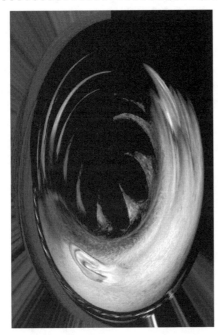

Figure 18.25 *The Polar Coordinates filter applied to the punk*

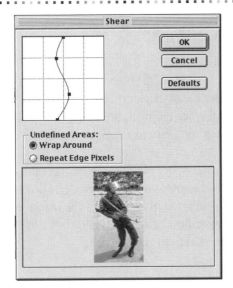

Figure 18.26 *The Shear dialog box*

For practice with the Shear and Twirl filters, open Shear.psd (the soldier photo) from the Ch18 folder on the CD.

The Twirl filter takes your image pixels and rotates them along a spiral. The center of the selection rotates while the edges remain in place. The Twirl dialog (Figure 18.27) offers two directions, expressed in minus and plus degrees, from 1 to 999. Since a circle is 360°, the full application of 999° gives you a spiral with almost three rotations. A positive value maps the spiral in a clockwise direction, while applying a negative number twirls your image counterclockwise.

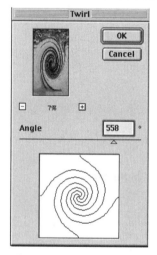

Figure 18.27 *You can Twirl from –999° to 999°.*

Let's not forget about Distort ➜ Displace. This filter is a bit different than others in the Distort submenu. It relies on the use of displacement maps to refigure your image pixels. Like Distort ➜ Wave, Displace retains quite a bit of its hard-science background, making it harder to predict without a lot of experimentation or mathematical know-how.

The Displace filter uses the brightness values in another image, called a *displacement map*, to relocate pixels. If the displacement map is a Grayscale image with a single channel, pixels in the image that align with the black areas of the map are moved to the right and down, depending on your specifications in the dialog box. Pixels that align with the white areas of the map are moved to the left and up.

If the image has two or more channels, as in a Grayscale image with an additional alpha channel or an RGB image, the first channel (Gray for Grayscale and Red for RGB) determines horizontal movement and the second channel (an alpha channel for a Grayscale image or the Green channel for an RGB image) determines vertical movement. The other channels in the image are not used. Areas of the image that align with the black pixels on the first channel are moved to the right, and areas that align with the white pixels are moved to the left. Areas of the image that align with the black pixels on the second channel are displaced down, and the areas that align with white pixels are moved up. Of course, the amount of displacement depends on the specifications you enter in the dialog box.

Suffice to say that you can access Photoshop's provided displacement maps (find them in the Plug-Ins folder in the Photoshop application folder) or create your own. Displace lets you define horizontal and vertical scale, and you get to say how you want undefined areas to be handled. You can also tell Photoshop whether to tile the displacement map or scale it to fit your image.

Pixelate Filters

In general, the Pixelate filters break up and rearrange your image into variously shaped groups of pixels. As I mentioned previously, it would be impossible to fully describe every effect, let alone demonstrate them all visually. I'll just hit the high points here.

Neither Facet nor Fragment offers a dialog box; they simply apply their effects without so much as a by-your-leave. Of the two, Facet has a more pleasing, irregular, sort of hand-colored effect. Color Halftone's controls include a Radius input, and four screen angles boxes. It takes an awful long time to apply this clunky effect, which can be done with more finesse using Filter ➜ Sketch ➜ Halftone Pattern.

Crystallize, Mosaic, and Pointillize all offer a Cell Size slider in their dialog boxes, which allows you to designate how many pixels will be used to create a cell or clump of grouped color. Larger values result in great big groupings of pixels that rob your image of detail. Smaller values can create more interesting artistic effects, mainly by increasing color contrast from cell to cell. The Mezzotint filter offers several ways of adding largely uncontrollable noise to your image, in the form of dots, lines, or strokes. It's like the bullyish big brother of Add Noise without the slider. Mezzotint turns grayscale images black and white; RGB images are reduced to eight colors (red, green, and blue and their opposites cyan, magenta, and yellow) plus black and white. Figure 18.28 shows the effects of some of the Pixelate filters; you can see the same illustration in the color section.

Figure 18.28 *(a) Original image; (b) Mezzotint, Long Strokes; (c) Color Halftone; (d) Pointillize; (e) Crystallize*

Stylize Filters

Some filters in the Stylize submenu deal with the edges of your image in one way or another; others map image pixels into geometric shapes. Solarize is alone in dealing solely with color shifts. Its effect is similar to combining a photographic negative with a positive. All blacks and white become black, grays remain gray, and other colors become their negative equivalent. You have no control over this filter.

Tiles and Extrude are the two Stylize filters that map to shape. Tiles breaks your image up into squares. You can define how many tiles fill a row across your image, how far the tiles can offset from each other, and how the areas between tiles will be filled. But the effect is rather flat; the Texture ➜ Mosaic Tiles filter creates a textured effect (with grouting options) that is much more realistic.

The Extrude filter is similar to Tiles, except that the mapping doesn't stay in two dimensions. The tiles or blocks extend into space. You can make your extruded elements block- or pyramid-shaped, and options are offered for the size and depth of the extruded shapes. In addition, you can decide whether you want incomplete blocks left out, and whether the fronts of square blocks should remain solid or contain image detail. Finally, you can arrange your extruded shapes randomly or arrange them by level. Figure 18.29 presents two sample Extrusions.

Figure 18.29 *The Extrude filter, set to (left) Blocks, Random, Solid Front Faces and (right) Pyramids, Level-based*

Find Edges, Glowing Edges, and Trace Contour all provide ways of getting a color outline of your image. (Remember the technique of using High Pass and Threshold to create line art, and include that method in this repertoire of edge-building tricks.) Find Edges is a no-options effect that draws colored lines around the edges of your image. Glowing Edges does the same, except that you can determine the width, brightness, and smoothness of your edges. Look at the examples in the color section, and notice that Glowing Edges, if left to its defaults, is nothing more than an inverted-color version of Find Edges. Or vice versa: If you want control over Find Edges, just use Glowing Edges instead and then invert the results.

Trace Contour (also demonstrated in the color section) creates colored contours but leaves all non-edge areas white. You can define a threshold above or below which Trace Contour will determine what constitutes an edge. This one seems to require a bit of fading and blending to make it interesting, while Find Edges and Glowing Edge produce a more visually appealing effect.

Diffuse works in a manner similar to the Dissolve brush or blending mode, in that it diffuses the edges of your selection. Due to the similarity, this filter's usefulness is rather limited; you can accomplish more by applying the brush or blending mode to an image. It does have a nice effect on type selections, though.

The Wind filter offers three "strengths" of wind effect: plain old Wind, a Blast of wind, or a Staggeringly strong wind, coming either from left or right. This filter is notoriously time-consuming, so try it on a Grayscale or low-res image for a preview of the effect.

And so we arrive at Emboss, perhaps Stylize's most interesting and entertaining offering. Figure 18.30 shows the Emboss dialog box with its Angle, Height and Amount options. You can input your angle numerically, or slide the circle icon around to find the direction of light Emboss applies. Height is the distance of bas relief you get, whereas Amount specifies the black and white value of edge pixels. Higher values create more contrast, while lowering the value gives the image an overall gray cast.

Figure 18.30 *It's easy to use the Emboss dialog box too frequently.*

Emboss is one of those filters people really like to overuse on its own. Look at magazine ads and you'll recognize this frequently used effect. Its true power comes when applied to layers and blended, when faded back into the original image, or applied individually to color channels. For an effect of color relief, use the Fade command and apply it using the Hue or Luminosity mode. This allows you to retain the colors in your image, while allowing the Emboss effect to reveal itself. To see the effect of the Emboss filter, see Figure 18.31 here and in the color section.

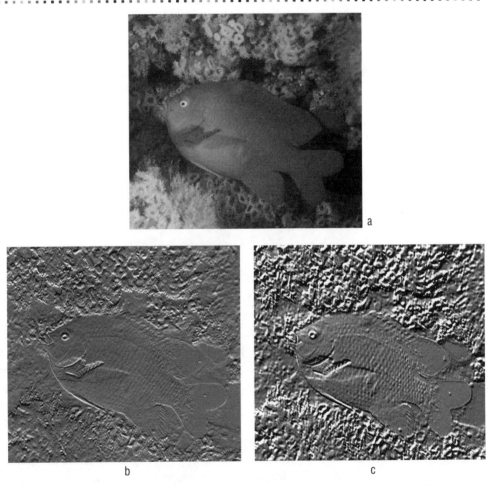

Figure 18.31 *The effect of the Emboss filter, (b) applied directly to the image (Angle: 33 degrees, Height: 4 pixels, Amount: 360 percent), or (c) applied to a duplicate layer and blended in Luminosity mode*

For practice with the Stylize filters, open `Stylize.psd` in the Ch18 folder on the CD to use the original fish art.

Effects Filters

Artistic, Brush Strokes, Sketch, Texture are the four groups of filters once called Gallery Effects. These all approximate different kinds of fine-art, painterly techniques. The Artistic effects attempt to reproduce the effects of traditional art media, such as Water-color, Dry Brush, and Fresco. Brush Strokes turns your image into various styles of color strokes, like Crosshatch and Sprayed Stroke. Sketch filters use your foreground and background colors to replace your image colors while creating textures. If you want to get some of the original color back, just use your handy-dandy Fade command. Its usefulness is not to be underestimated. Finally, Texture applies depth and, well, tex-ture to your image. The Texturizer filter gives you the most play, allowing you to supply and apply your own textures. You can also scale your texture, define Height and Relief values, and determine the direction of light playing across the image. Take a look at Figure 18.32 for a variety of artistic effects.

Artistic, Brush Strokes, Sketch, and Texture filters are not available in Lab, Indexed, or CMYK modes. If you're working in any of those modes, you must convert to RGB before you can apply these effects.

Render Filters

The Filter ➔ Render submenu contains an interesting mix of lighting and texture effects, plus the 3D Transform filter. Clouds and Difference Clouds both reside here; to apply either of these filters to your image, simply choose the command and there you have it. A hazy mixture of foreground and background colors fills your selection. Choose it again, and the cloud pattern changes. Every time you choose this filter, the cloud patterns shift. If you hold down the Option/Alt key while choosing, the colors create a more pronounced effect. Difference Clouds works in the same way as Clouds, but you end up with inverted colors (if you started with blue sky and white clouds, you now get orange sky with black clouds). Apply the filter again and your colors re-invert, back to blue and white.

A simple lighting effect is produced by choosing Filter ➔ Render ➔ Lens Flare. A preview box shows a replica of your image where you can move the pointer to find your flare center. The Brightness slider allows you to adjust brightness from 10% to 300%. Three lens shapes are offered: 50–300mm Zoom, 55mm Prime, and 105mm Prime. The result is a refraction, like light glinted back off a distant object.

Artistic ➔ Palette Knife

Artistic ➔ Plastic Wrap

Artistic ➔ Rough Pastels

Brush Strokes ➔ Sumi-e

Texture ➔ Patchwork

Figure 18.32 *Examples of the "gallery effects" filters.*

Lens Flare and Lighting Effects, a much more powerful lighting tool, operate only on RGB images.

Lighting Effects Filter

The Lighting Effects dialog (Figure 18.33) offers a wide range of options for simulating the play of spot or floodlights over your image. Imagine you're hanging lights in a gallery, shining a flashlight into a dark cave, or driving down a wooded road at night. Any of these lighting situations can be duplicated with these versatile options.

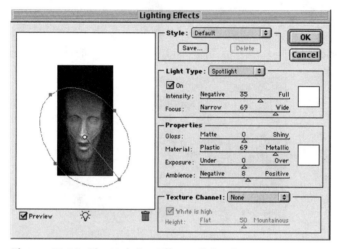

Figure 18.33 *The Lighting Effects dialog box*

First of all, Photoshop provides a wide array of lighting styles in its Style menu. In addition to these preconfigured effects (which can serve as a starting point to add your own touches), the Light Type area allows you to create your own effects, which you can then save to the Style list. You're given options for Intensity and Focus, and you can choose a color for your light effect. You can define properties such as Gloss (Matte or Shiny finish), Material (ranges from Plastic to Metallic), Exposure, and Ambience. A color swatch lets you define the tint of the Ambience, which refers to ambient or overall lighting, separate from the spot or special lighting.

In the Texture Channel section, you can designate one of the channels (red, green, or blue) as a texture map—that is, a grayscale image where the light areas become peaks and dark areas become valleys. If you uncheck the White Is High box, the effect is reversed and the white areas become the valleys. Pick a Height somewhere between Flat and Mountainous, and you're set.

Inside the Preview area, you'll see a lighting footprint that shows you how the light source you've chosen will be applied. If you're working with a Spotlight or Omni, you can grab the handles and change the shape of the light. Clicking the Focus Spot (the end of the preview radius, as shown in Figure 18.33) allows you to change the angle of lighting. You can change the angle but not the shape of a Directional style of light. Keep in mind that the smaller the light footprint, the brighter or more intense the light. As you increase the size of the footprint, the light spreads out and dims accordingly. When you get an effect you like, click the Save button. Photoshop invites you to name your new lighting style, which will then appear in your Style menu.

The dummy in Figure 18.34 (also shown in the color section) demonstrates a few Lighting Effects. `LFX_Dummy.psd` is included in the `Ch18` folder on the CD for you to experiment with lighting effects.

Texture and 3D Filters

Texture Fill, also found in the Filter ➜ Render submenu, is a tool for filling your selection with a previously created texture. Some textures are provided in Photoshop's `\Plug-Ins\Lighting Effects\Textures For Lighting Effects` folder on the Macintosh, or in the `\Plug-Ins\Filters\Texture Fill` directory in Windows. You can also create your own Texture Fill files, by saving any Grayscale image in Photoshop format. When you choose Filter ➜ Render ➜ Texture Fill, you are prompted to find a texture file to apply. Just pick one and go. These fills work just like the ones in Filter ➜ Texture ➜ Texturizer.

3D Transform (Figure 18.35) allows you to map images to three-dimensional shapes: cubes, spheres, and cylinders. In the preview window, you can position and size the shape of your choice. The shape you choose appears as a green wire frame over your image, which you can then manipulate using the tools from the left side of the dialog panel.

The Selection and Direct Selection tools enable you to move the wire frame and alter its size and shape. The Rotate tool lets you apply a rotation; pen tools allow you to add, subtract, or convert points along the path of the wire frame to more exactly fit the shape you desire; and a scaling tool lets you increase or decrease its size. If you arrive at a shape that's impossible for Photoshop to render, the wire frame turns red. The filter's Dolly Camera option magnifies or shrinks the object, as if you were rolling a camera toward or away from it. 3D Transform enables you to work inside the dialog until you're satisfied with what you've set up. Then click OK and let the filter apply itself (Figure 18.36). This toolbox-within-a-filter is also one of the hallmarks of the new Liquify feature.

The original image

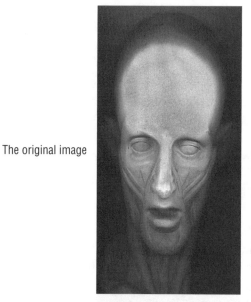

The default light, expanded and rotated so that its source shines from beneath

RGB lights moved to various locations on the image

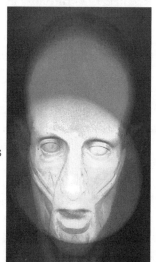

This image contains a medley of Render filter effects. The background was filtered with Difference clouds. A blue Omni was shined on the face from below. The 50–300mm Lens Flare filter was added. Finally, the head was 3D Transformed.

Figure 18.34 *Examples of the Lighting Effects filter*

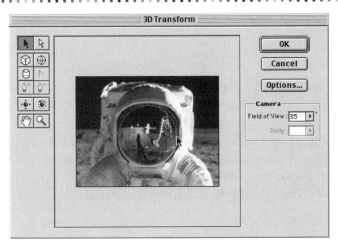

Figure 18.35 *Use the tools at the left to 3D Transform your image.*

Figure 18.36 *Various effects of the 3D Transform filter*

Other Filters

Two filters exist in a category unto themselves, being neither constructive or destructive.

Video

The Video filter has one purpose: to convert the colors of an image for transfer to video tape. This filter is not a color space. It converts your RGB or Lab images to NTSC (North American Television Standards Committee)-compatible colors.

If you continue to work on an image after using the Video filter, you may introduce incompatible colors. A better solution is to close the file, head to the Color Settings, and choose the NTSC RGB color space as your working RGB space. Then reopen the file and OK the profile conversion in the dialog box that appears.

Digimarc

The Digimarc filter lets you embed a digital watermark on your image to protect its copyright. It's particularly useful to professionals who license their work. Code is added to the document as noise and is usually imperceptible to the human eye. The watermark can endure most editing, even filters and file convertion.

To embed a digital watermark:

1. Choose Filter ➜ Digimarc ➜ Embed Watermark.

2. You must first register with Digimarc Corporation to get a creator ID. Click Personalize to launch your browser and access the Digimarc Web site at www.digimarc.com, or call the phone number in the dialog box.

3. Enter the PIN and ID number in the creator ID box. Click OK.

4. In each field, enter information about the image, including the copyright date and usage information.

5. Select a Visibility and Durability value. The more visible the watermark is, the more durable it is.

6. Click OK.

After you've embedded the watermark in an image, test its durability with the Signal Strength meter. Choose Filter ➜ Digimarc ➜ Read Watermark. The meter will tell you under what conditions the watermark will survive a specific intended use.

The Liquify Tool

Photoshop 6's new Liquify command is technically a filter, even though it lives at the bottom of the Image menu. Liquify is, at its heart, a set of painting tools that allow you to distort pixels and transform areas of an image. Imagine using Distort filters on the fly with brushes. You can also mask off areas to protect them from change, or reconstruct unwanted distortions. Liquify will undoubtedly prove to be one of Photoshop 6's most powerful new tools and one of the centerpieces of the program.

Image ➜ Liquify presents a set of transformation tools that you can work with in great detail before actually applying. Get everything exactly the way you want (Liquify has fully functional previewing capabilities), and when you click OK, your whole session of warping/transforming takes effect. Figure 18.37 presents the Liquify dialog panel, complete with all of its tools and submenus.

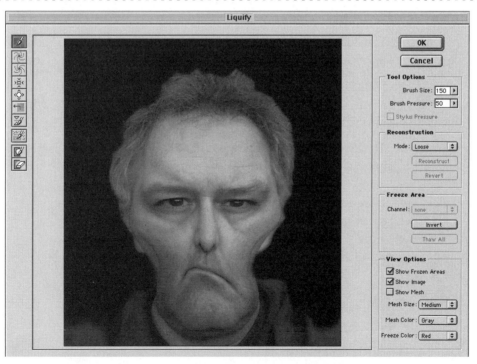

Figure 18.37 *You can Liquify extensively within this "subinterface."*

Liquify makes pixels warp and flow within an image. It contains its own complete set of painting and masking tools, along with a Reconstruct tool that allows you to reverse the distortion. There are several Reconstruct modes, so you can apply a partial or complete reconstruction at will. You can have a mesh grid overlay your image area that shows the amount of warping or reconstruction that's taking place.

Let's first look at the Liquify painting tools (the top seven icons in Figure 18.38), which work somewhat like a set of distortion filters. Instead of individual brushes, you're provided with a Brush Size slider and a Pressure slider. These sliders control the size and opacity of the various tools:

The Warp tool   pushes pixels along as you drag. If you hold the mouse down and drag longer, the effect is enhanced. Short, gentle drags of the mouse can move changes along slowly and precisely.

Twirl Clockwise and Twirl Counterclockwise   rotate pixels. Contrary to the way the Twirl filter works, pixels rotate faster at the edges of the brush than they do at the center.

The Pucker and Bloat tools   squeeze your pixels in or out. Pucker pinches pixels under its drag, and Bloat moves them away from the center of the brush.

Shift Pixels   moves pixels at a 90-degree angle to the way you're moving the brush. Dragging moves pixels to the left of your mouse path, Option/Alt-drag moves pixels to the right.

The Reflect tool   drags along a mirror image of the pixels perpendicular to your brush.

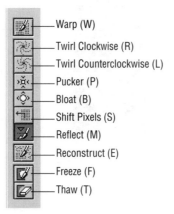

Figure 18.38 *The Liquify tool palette*

Once you've made some distortions, you can use the Reconstruct tool to completely or partially restore your image to its initial state. Masking brushes (the Freeze tool creates a mask, Thaw erases it) allow you to freeze or thaw selected areas of your image—that is, protect them from the transformations underway, or release the protection. You're also able to select an alpha channel to freeze areas.

If you undo an action while transforming in the Liquify display, any mask designating a frozen area will be eliminated. You must re-create or rechoose a mask to keep the area frozen as you proceed.

Now that you've had your way with your image and it's warped all over creation, you're having second thoughts. Can you get it back without canceling the Liquify effect and starting all over again? Sure—that's what the Reconstruct tool is for. But Reconstruct is much more than a History Eraser. The reconstructions you apply can be fodder for further distortions. Look back at Figure 18.37 to see Liquify's Options area, on the right side of the dialog. In the Mode pop-up list of the Reconstruction area, you have several options for regulating the degree and type of reconstruction, ranging from Rigid to Loose. Each one offers a slightly different degree of reconstructing capability. In fact, by the time you get to Loose, you're continuing to distort the image, but at least you're going back the way you came. If you want to reconstruct back to before a certain set of distortions, just click the Revert button in the Reconstruction area, then use the brush to enact your reconstruct.

Among the Reconstruction modes, Displace moves pixels in unfrozen areas to match the displacement of a reference point. This mode can be used to reconstruct the image to a specific point. Amplitwist is used to duplicate the displacement, rotation, or scaling of a reference point. Affine matches displacement, rotation, scaling, and skew of a reference point.

The Freeze Area options give you various ways of protecting segments of your image from distortion. Click to select an alpha channel to apply, or create your own. The View Options area provides options for the way you look at Liquify. Most important of these is the Mesh option. What is at first a regular square grid takes on the shape of the transformations you apply. This can be useful when applying reconstructions, by letting you see how close to square you're able to return.

When you're done, click OK and watch Image ➜ Liquify perform its magic. See Figure 18.39 to see some truly horrifying Liquify transformations. And look inside the `Things_to_Liquify` folder in the `Ch18` folder on the CD for sample files to try out this amazing tool for yourself.

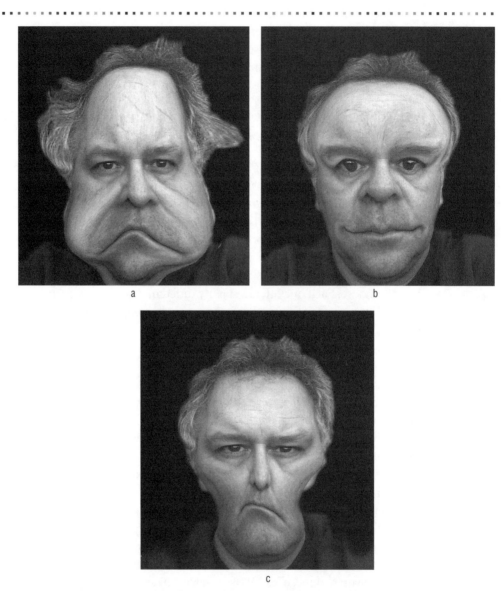

a

b

c

Figure 18.39 *(a) This image was created using the Liquify defaults. (b) I pushed the pixels around and then did partial reconstruction on the chin and eyes. (c) The Liquify tools give you incredible control over the form of your image, though it's easy to get carried away… in which case you can reconstruct any area, as I did with the eyes in this image.*

Up Next

Filters extend Photoshop's capabilities. There's really not a whole lot you *can't* do with them to enhance, texturize, and distort your image. Because there are so many variables in using filters, I encourage you to experiment and have fun applying filters to the images provided on the CD. It can take some time to apply the effects of some filters because they are memory-intensive, so remember to try them out on a low-resolution version of the image first and write down the settings.

Photoshop 6's Liquify tool is probably the most outstanding new feature in this release. Use it to sculpt your images by dragging groups of pixels as if they were clay. You might even increase your popularity by transforming unflattering portrait photographs of your friends (like the one of yours truly on the CD) into really wild caricatures.

The topic of Chapter 19, making difficult selections, is not quite as glamorous as filters but extremely practical and important. You'll learn how to select those really tough areas on images where the distinction between foreground and background is ambiguous, fuzzy, or complicated. You'll use some of the adjustment tools and the Channels palette that you're already familiar with, and Photoshop's improved Extract command to accomplish these seemingly impossible tasks.

Making Difficult Selections

PHOTOSHOP

Chapter 19

n Chapter 6, we covered the basics of selection making. The selection tools provide several manual techniques, like the Marquees and Lasso tools to isolate areas of an image. Photoshop also has a few semiautomatic selection tools like the Magic Wand and the Magnetic Lasso that select pixels based on their brightness or contrast values. The Quick Mask extends selection-making abilities to the painting tools for even more control, and the Pen tool lets you make accurate selections with Bezier curves.

Sometimes, however, areas of an image seem impossible to select due to ambiguous surroundings or complex content. What do you do with these problem images, short of canceling all appointments, turning off the phone, and sitting in front of the computer for the next week, one by one encircling each pixel?

In this chapter, you will learn how to select those really tough areas with a few tools and techniques that, if they don't make these selections easy, at least get the job done with a minimum of effort. You will learn about:

- Working with color range

- Selecting out-of-gamut colors

- Making selections with color channels

- Extracting images

Color Range

The Select ➜ Color Range command is ideal for selecting areas of similar color within the image or a selection outline. We used a similar technique, Image ➜ Adjust ➜ Replace Color, in Chapter 17 to substitute colors. Color Range operates in very much the same way but instead of altering color, it produces an accurate selection marquee of the specified areas of similar color.

This tool really helps you in situations where you have a lot of small areas of similar color situated throughout the image. With so many scattered areas of color, a tedious task can be simplified, as we shall see.

When you choose Select ➜ Color Range, the dialog box (Figure 19.1) presents you with a mask of the image. The Select pull-down menu at the top of the dialog lets you choose a specific color range to sample, and it will automatically select all of the pixels within the range. You can choose to select Reds, Yellows, Blues, Greens, Magentas, Highlights, Midtones, or Shadows, or Out Of Gamut colors.

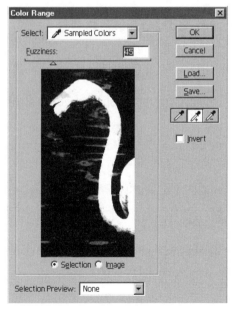

Figure 19.1 *The Color Range dialog box*

If you want more control, however, the best approach to making a selection is to choose the default, Sampled Colors. You use the familiar eyedropper tools to sample the colors you want to select from the image. I recommend that you change the setting in the Eyedropper tool Options bar to 3 By 3 Average. Click in or drag over the image with the Eyedropper to select colors. Drag over the image with the Plus Eyedropper to increase the range of colors selected or with the Minus Eyedropper to decrease the range. The Fuzziness slider also extends the range of selection into adjacent pixels. Check the Invert box to invert the selection.

The radio buttons under the mask lets you view the selection mask on the image as you drag the eyedropper, or adjust the Fuzziness slider to accurately determine the range of the selection. The Selection Preview pull-down menu lets you choose from Grayscale, White Matte, Black Matte, Quick Mask, or None modes in which to view the mask in the image window. These preview modes help you better determine what areas of the image will be selected and what areas will be masked. Choose the most one most appropriate to the tonal or color content of your image. For example, you'll probably choose White Matte if the image is particularly dark, because the mask will be more visible.

Selecting a Sampled Color Range

Let's try selecting part of an image using Color Range.

1. Open the file Alaskans.psd in the Ch19 folder of the CD.

2. In the Tool palette, choose the Eyedropper tool. Change the setting in the Options bar to 3 By 3 Average.

3. Select the top portion of the image with the Rectangular Marquee (see Figure 19.2).

4. Choose Select → Color Range. With the Plus Eyedropper tool, drag over a portion of the sky between the trees. Watch the mask in the Color Range dialog box (Figure 19.3).

5. From the Selection preview, run through the masking options one by one to determine what part of the image will be selected.

6. Move the Fuzziness slider to extend the selection to as much of the sky as possible.

7. Click OK to select the sky.

Figure 19.2 *Select a portion of the image first, then choose Color Range to refine the selection.*

Figure 19.3 *The Color Range dialog box with the mask of the Alaskans*

Depending on the fuzziness and the range of color that was selected, portions of the faces may be included, in which case you'll need to deselect those areas by choosing the Lasso tool, pressing Option/Alt, and encircling them. Think about how much time you saved by using this technique. It certainly would have been labor-intensive to select these areas with the Magic Wand tool, even with the Contiguous option unchecked. Color Range lets you collectively select those colors that are dispersed throughout the image simply by dragging over them.

Selecting Out-of-Gamut Colors

Another unique function of the Color Range command is its ability to isolate unprintable colors. Chapter 15 describes Photoshop's color management features and how you can compensate for out-of-gamut colors. In the Edit ➔ Color Settings dialog box, you can specify a CMYK profile for a device or printing environment that has its own unique CMYK gamut. When you prepare an image for process color printing, the profile affects how the image is converted into CMYK from its working mode (usually RGB). If you choose View ➔ Gamut Warning, Photoshop will display a gray mask that shows you which colors are out of gamut. If you choose View ➔ Proof Setup ➔ Working CMYK (it's Photoshop's default) and then View ➔ Proof Colors, you can preview on-screen how the image will look when printed, before you convert it.

Toggle in and out of Proof Colors by pressing Cmd/Ctrl+Y to compare the CMYK preview to the RGB display.

You'll want to pull the out-of-gamut colors back into the CMYK range before you convert the image, so that you can perform final edits with the knowledge that what you see on screen is as close as possible to what you'll get when you print. But first you'll have to select the out-of-gamut colors, and the method you'll use is buried deep within the Color Range dialog box.

To select and adjust out-of-gamut colors, follow these steps:

1. Open the file Venice.psd in the Ch19 folder on the CD.

2. Make a duplicate of the document (Image ➔ Duplicate). Name the copy Venice_CMYK.psd.

3. Place both images on screen side by side.

4. In the `Venice_CMYK.psd` file, choose Edit ➜ Color Settings. From the CMYK pull-down list, choose U.S. Sheetfed Coated v2 for a CMYK profile. Click OK.

5. Click `Venice.psd.` to activate it. Choose View ➜ Macintosh or Windows RGB to display the original image in RGB mode. You'll keep this image on screen for reference.

6. Activate `Venice_CMYK.psd.` Choose View ➜ Proof Setup ➜ Working CMYK and then View ➜ Proof Colors. Notice the color differences between the two images.

7. Choose Select ➜ Color Range. Choose Out Of Gamut from the bottom of Select pull-down menu (Figure 19.4). The dialog box displays a mask of the out-of-gamut colors.

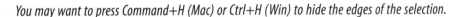

Figure 19.4 *Finding out-of-gamut colors with the Color Range dialog*

8. Click OK. The marquee on the image displays a selection outline.

You may want to press Command+H (Mac) or Ctrl+H (Win) to hide the edges of the selection.

9. Choose View ➜ Gamut Warning. A gray mask covers the out-of-gamut colors within the selection, as in Figure 19.5. (This image, with and without the gamut warning, is also presented in the color section, and in the Ch15 folder on the CD as `gamwarn1.tif` and `gamwarn2.tif`.)

Figure 19.5 *The gamut warning (notice the solid blocks of gray on the gondolas?) marks the colors that are outside the CMYK range.*

10.   Choose Layer ➜ New Adjustment Layer ➜ Hue/Saturation. In the Hue/Saturation dialog box, move the Saturation slider to the left. The gray mask gradually disappears as you include more of the out-of-gamut colors into the CMYK gamut.

11.   You'll notice that the colors in the CMYK gamut are less saturated. You can compensate to a degree, for diminished intensity by experimenting with variations of hue and lightness to produce better results while maintaining the colors within the CMYK gamut. However, you will never achieve the full intensity of the RGB image. (Another way to compensate is to duplicate the layer and use the Multiply blending mode, changing the opacity to suit. See Chapter 22 for more on this.)

12.   When as many of the gray pixels as possible have disappeared as possible and the color looks good, click OK.

Making Selections with Color Channels

An image's color information can be used to make really difficult selections. The differences in the contrast levels of the red, green, and blue channels can often provide a method of isolating portions of the image that would seem impossible to select. You'll use this technique and a combination of Photoshop's painting tools and filters to select images like Figure 19.6, where the background and foreground are complex and almost indistinct. Be warned that this process can be quite labor-intensive, so roll up your sleeves and make it happen.

Figure 19.6 *It's close to impossible to select this model's hair with traditional selection tools, but you can use color channels to do it.*

1. Open the image `Hair_Select.psd` in the `Ch19` folder on the CD.

2. Open the Channels palette (Window ➜ Show Channels, or F7 on the keyboard if you still have it clustered with the Layers palette). Click the Red, Green, and Blue channel thumbnails to display each channel in grayscale in the image window. Determine which channel has the most contrast between the hair on the model and the background. In this case, it's the Red channel.

3. Target the Red channel, and duplicate it by choosing Duplicate Channel from the Channels palette pull-down menu, or by dragging it to the New Channel icon at the bottom of the palette. The channel will be named Red Copy.

4. Choose Image ➜ Adjust ➜ Levels and increase the contrast of the Red Copy channel by dragging the sliders inward. Click OK. I set the Input Levels in this image to 71, 1.00, and 216.

5. Choose Filter ➜ Other ➜ High Pass. The High Pass filter will flatten the colors of the image and make the division between the hair and background even more distinct (see Figure 19.7).

Figure 19.7 *Apply the High Pass filter to make the distinction between the hair and background more distinct.*

6. Choose Image ➜ Adjust ➜ Threshold. This operation will turn all of the pixels either black or white. I set the Threshold value to 123 (Figure 19.8) to maintain the distinction between the hair and the background.

Figure 19.8 *Apply a Threshold adjustment to the duplicate Red channel, to map the pixels to either white or black.*

7. Choose the Paintbrush and block in, with black, the larger areas on the Red Copy channel that you want masked.

8. With a smaller brush, block out the additional areas close to the hair so that the channel resembles Figure 19.9. You may want to view both the Red Copy channel and the RGB image to paint as close as possible to the edge of the hair.

9. When you've finished painting, view the RGB channel and the Red Copy by clicking their eye icons in the Channels palette. With the Lasso tool, select the interior of the model as close to the solid part of her hair as possible, as in Figure 10.

10. Choose Select → Feather and give the selection a 2 px feather radius. Choose white as the foreground color and press Option+Delete or Alt+Backspace to fill the interior of the selection with white. The selection should look like Figure 19.11.

Figure 19.9 *The Red Copy channel should look like this.*

Figure 19.10 *Select the solid area of the hair with the Lasso tool while viewing the RGB and Red Copy channel.*

Figure 19.11 *The finished selection*

11. Open the file from the Ch19 folder on the CD, `Desert.psd`.

12. Click the Hair image. Target the RGB channel. Load the Red Copy channel to select the model.

13. Choose the Move tool and drag the image from the Hair image window onto the Desert image.

14. Some of the colors in the extremities of the model's hair have washed out a little in the process of moving her. To restore those areas, choose the Sponge tool. In the Options bar, choose Saturate.

15. Choose a soft brush and make a few passes on the frizzy areas of hair to intensify those colors.

16. You may also want to carefully erase a few areas at the edge of the model's head with the Eraser tool to give the image a more natural look (as in Figure 19.12).

Figure 19.12 *The finished image*

Extracting Images

Images with fuzzy, complex, or indefinable edges can be pulled from their background. The results may not be as precise as the channels method, but you can, by trial and error, isolate problem edges with much less effort. The Extract command is actually a mini program, complete with a Liquify-like subinterface, that measures subtle differences of the edge of an image by its color and brightness content and then determines how best to isolate the region.

You start the extraction by choosing Image → Extract (Figure 19.13). Define the image's edges, then fill its interior and preview it. You can refine and preview as many times as you like until it contains all of the image and none of the background. You then extract it, which deletes undefined areas and places the image on a transparent layer. In order for the Extract command to work, the image must be on an independent layer rather than the Background.

Because of the radical transformation that Extract produces, you should first duplicate the image or make a snapshot of it.

Edge Highlighter (B)
Fill (G)
Eraser (E)
Eyedropper (I)
Cleanup (C)
Edge Touchup (T)
Zoom (Z)
Hand (H)

Figure 19.13 *The Extract dialog panel*

You specify the following tool options in the dialog panel:

Brush Size   Enter a value or drag the slider to specify the width of the Edge Highlighter tool, which defines the boundary of the image.

Highlight   Choose a color to display the edge boundary that you draw with the Edge tools.

Fill   Choose a color to display the interior fill inside the boundary.

Smart Highlighting   This option helps you keep the highlight on the edge, especially when the edge between the foreground and background is sharp with similar color or texture. To toggle Smart Highlighting on or off while you drag, press the Cmd/Ctrl key.

To Extract an image, open the file Fuzzy_Bear.psd in the Ch19 folder on the CD.

1.   Set the Highlight color to red and the Fill color to blue.

2. Choose a 24 px Brush Size. Select the Edge Highlighter tool and drag along the edge of the bear to highlight the outline of the object you want to extract. Draw the highlight so that it slightly overlaps both the foreground and background regions around the edge, to cover areas where the foreground blends into the background.

3. Use a smaller brush to precisely highlight edges that are more defined, like the area at the top of the bear's head. Use a larger brush to highlight the fuzzy edges of the bear's sides, loosely covering the soft transitions. Don't highlight the bottom of the bear, only the top and sides.

4. If you make a mistake, erase the highlight. Select the Eraser tool from the dialog box, and drag over the highlight. This tool is available when a highlight exists. You can completely erase the highlight by pressing Alt+Backspace or Option+Delete.

To toggle between the highlighter and the eraser while drawing an edge, press the Option or Alt key.

5. To fill the bear, select the Fill tool within the dialog panel (it looks like the regular Paint Bucket). Click inside the outline to fill its interior (see Figure 19.14).

Figure 19.14 *The highlighted and filled fuzzy bear*

If the image is especially intricate or lacks a clear interior, make sure that the highlight covers the entire edge. To highlight the entire object, press Ctrl+Backspace (Win) or Cmd+Delete (Mac), then select Force Foreground. This technique works best with objects that contain tones of a single color.

Viewing the Extraction

Click Preview to view the extracted image. The edges of the bear will be soft, and the area around the bear will be transparent, like the one in Figure 19.15. You can better see the result of the extraction if you view it using the following techniques:

- In the Show menu, switch between previews of the original and extracted images.

Figure 19.15 *The completed bear*

- Use the Display menu to preview the extracted object as a grayscale mask or against a white matte or a black matte. To choose a colored background, choose Other and a color from the Color Picker. To display a transparent background, choose None.

- Select the Show Highlight or Show Fill option to display the object's extraction boundaries or interior.

Refining the Extraction

Several tools let you alter the edges and interior of the extraction, adding areas to the extraction or eliminating unwanted pixels.

The Cleanup Tool

You can edit and refine the extraction with the Cleanup tool, which is only available when you preview the extracted image. The Cleanup tool subtracts opacity. If you make multiple passes, it will have a cumulative effect. Drag over an area to erase to transparency. Press the Option/Alt key while painting with the Cleanup tool to restore opacity.

The Eraser and Fill tools can also be used to edit the Preview. The Eraser restores the edge to transparency. Clicking a filled area with the Fill paint bucket removes the fill.

The Edge Touchup Tool

Use the Edge Touchup tool to edit the extraction boundaries. The tool, which is available when you show the extracted image, sharpens the edges of the extracted image. It has a cumulative effect as you make multiple passes over the edge. If there is no clear edge, the Edge Touchup tool adds opacity to the image or makes the background more transparent.

The Smooth Slider

Drag the Smooth slider or enter a value to help remove stray artifacts in the extraction. When you are finished editing, click Preview again to view the edited extraction. You can edit and preview the extraction as many times as you like until you achieve the results you want.

To apply the final extraction, click OK. All pixels on the layer outside the extracted image are eliminated. If necessary, use the History Brush or the Background Eraser to touch up stray edge pixels and flawed areas.

Up Next

So much of the time you spend working in Photoshop is spent isolating regions of the image that you intend to edit, that many of the tools are devoted exclusively to this purpose. Yet, with all of these tools available, there are still going to be those really stubborn areas that require extraordinary measures. In this chapter, I've presented four more methods that you can rely on: with a sampled Color Range, by finding out-of-gamut colors, via color channels, and using the Extract command. Don't forget that every image presents different problem, and experimentation is always the best way to find the most appropriate method. Any one tool or method from this chapter or Chapter 6 may not be sufficient, in which case you'll want to combine techniques.

In Chapter 20, you'll see that the concept of masking is not only restricted to making selections. It is used to reveal and conceal portions of layers. The advanced layers techniques you'll master will further extend your imaging capabilities. You'll have an opportunity to apply layer masks, clipping groups, matting techniques, and cast shadows to the digital collage in the next Hands-On section.

Advanced Layer Techniques

PHOTOSHOP

Chapter 20

n Chapter 7, I talked about how important layers arc to Photoshop images. I compared a layer to a piece of clear acetate. You learned that you can separate parts of your image onto independent layers in order to maintain a dynamic workflow. You learned how to reshuffle layers in the stack so as to reposition their plane of depth in the picture, and how to link layers or create layer sets in order to organize your work. We changed a layer's opacity to be able to "see through" it, experimented with blending modes to dramatically alter the color relationships of layers, and applied cool special effects like drop shadows and bevels.

In this chapter, we'll explore more of Photoshop's layer capabilities and look at techniques that empower you to combine visual elements in unique and rather surprising ways. You will learn about:

- Creating layer masks

- Grouping layers

- Seamless compositing

- Casting shadows

Layer Masks

Photoshop relies on masks to perform many of its most powerful operations. I discussed masking in Chapter 6 as a way to isolate a part of an image, which you do when you make a selection. In Chapter 12, we worked with Quick Masks to extend the power of selecting to the painting tools. In the same chapter, we looked at ways to store selections as alpha channels so that they could be used at any time during the editing process. Selections, alpha channels, and Quick Masks all work to the same ends: to protect an isolated region from the application of a tool or operation. Layer masks are a little different. Instead of protecting an area of the image from an operation, they conceal it from view.

When you adjust the Opacity controls on the Layers palette, you change the transparency of the entire layer so that the content of layers beneath it in the stack will be visible. But when you apply a layer mask to an image, you control the transparency of a particular part of the layer.

You make a layer mask by choosing Layer ➜ Add Layer Mask ➜ Reveal All or Hide All. A thumbnail appears in the Layers palette to the right of the targeted layer's thumbnail. When you click the layer mask thumbnail, it displays a double border to indicate that it is ready for editing.

Reveal All   The mask thumbnail appears white and begins by *revealing all* of the layer. As you paint with black, you conceal portions of the targeted layer.

Hide All   The mask thumbnail appears black and begins by *hiding all* of the layer. As you paint with white, you reveal portions of the layer.

On a layer mask, white always represents the parts of the image that can be seen. Black represents parts of the image that are concealed, and gray represents areas that can be partially seen.

Making Layer Masks

To understand how layer masks work, you'll use one to conceal a portion of the rings of a planet. You'll create the illusion that the rings wrap behind the planet. To practice creating a layer mask, follow these steps:

1. Open the file Ringed_Planet.psd in the Ch20 folder on the *Mastering Photoshop 6* CD (Figure 20.1).

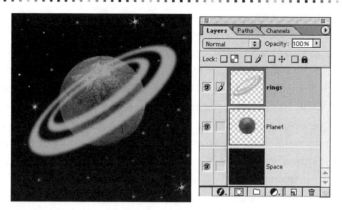

Figure 20.1 *The ringed planet and its layers*

2. The image is composed of three layers: a Planet and the Rings on a starry back-drop called Space. Target the Rings layer.

3. Choose Layer ➜ Layer Mask ➜ Reveal All. In the Layers palette, next to the Rings layer, you'll see a layer mask thumbnail. It's targeted by default.

4. Choose black as a foreground color. Choose the Paintbrush and paint the top portion of the rings. As you paint, the rings disappear.

To save time, instead of painting on a layer mask, you can select an area and Fill it with black or white to conceal or reveal that portion of the mask.

5. Be careful to paint right up to the edge of the planet but not on the portion of the rings that extend outside the planet, as in Figure 20.2. If you paint too much of the rings out, choose white as a foreground color and restore the ring by painting out the layer mask.

As the rings recede behind the planet, they should darken slightly. You will use the layer mask to create this effect by partially concealing the back-most portion of the rings.

1. Choose the Airbrush tool.

2. In the Options bar, set the Pressure to 15.

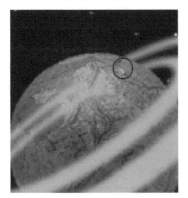

Figure 20.2 *Paint right up to the edges of the planet*

3. Paint the portions of the rings immediately to the left and right of the planet, to partially conceal them. Hold the airbrush in place slightly longer at the back to darken the rings a little more, and drag faster as you move forward (see Figure 20.3).

Figure 20.3 *Darkening the back part of the rings*

To get an idea of how the layer mask looks, press the Option/Alt key and click the layer mask icon in the Layers palette to display it in the image window (Figure 20.4). The mask is composed of areas of black (which conceals completely), gray, and white (where the rings are completely visible).

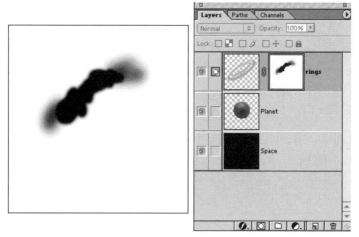

Figure 20.4 *The layer mask, displaying the black, white, and gray areas*

Layer Mask Controls

Once you've created a layer mask, you can control it in the following ways.

Activating and Deactivating a Layer Mask   Press the Shift key and click the layer mask to turn it on or off, or choose Layer ➜ Enable or Disable Layer Mask.

Viewing a Layer Mask   Press the Option/Alt key and click the mask thumbnail to view the layer mask in the image window.

Making a Selection from a Layer Mask   Press Cmd/Ctrl and click the layer mask to generate a selection outline.

Moving a Layer's Mask and Contents   Click between the two thumbnails to reveal or conceal the link icon. When the two thumbnails are linked, and you drag on the image with the Move tool, both the image on the layer and layer mask move as a unit. When the link is not visible, only the content of the targeted thumbnail will move.

Removing a Layer Mask   Choose Layer → Remove Layer Mask → Discard or Apply. Discard removes the layer mask and does not apply the effect. Apply removes the layer mask and applies the effect directly to the pixels of the layer.

Clipping Groups

When you group layers together, you can perform some very interesting graphic tricks. You can literally "tattoo" one image on to the other. With the help of layer masks, layer opacity, and blending modes, you can mold and model the image into superbly realistic forms.

In order to join two layers into a clipping group, the image on the bottom layer must be surrounded by transparency. The layer that will be clipped will appear one step higher in the stack. When a layer is clipped, it fills the shape of the image on the layer below it, in other words, the bottom layer acts as a mask to clip the layer immediately above it.

To try out clipping groups, you'll clip two layers together to create an "electric" telephone. Then you'll use blending modes and a layer mask to enhance the affect.

1. Open the file in the Chapter 20 folder on the CD, `Electric_Telephone.psd`. The image is separated into three layers: the topmost is the Lightning layer, the middle is the Telephone, and the bottom is the black Background (see Figure 20.5).

Figure 20.5 *The beginning Electric Telephone image is composed of three layers.*

2. To create a clipping group, press the Option/Alt key and click between the Lightning and Telephone layers (see Figure 20.6).

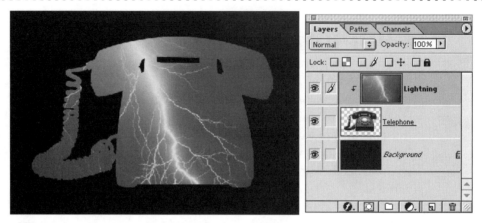

Figure 20.6 *After Option/Alt-clicking between layers, the Lightning layer is shown as a clipping group to the Telephone layer.*

3. You may want to adjust the color relations to see more of the features of the telephone. Choose Hard Light from the pop-up menu at the top of the Layers palette.

4. You can also add a layer mask to subtly model the telephone. With the Lightning layer targeted, choose Layer ➜ Add Layer Mask ➜ Reveal All.

5. Be sure that the layer mask is targeted. Choose black as a foreground color. Choose the Paintbrush and set its opacity in the Options bar to 20%. Choose a soft brush from the Brush panel. Paint on the telephone in various places to diminish the effect of the lightning and enhance the phone's three-dimensionality. If necessary, paint multiple passes to achieve the effect shown in Figure 20.7. (Look at the telephone in the color section to see what happens to your telephone when a bolt of lightning hits a power line!)

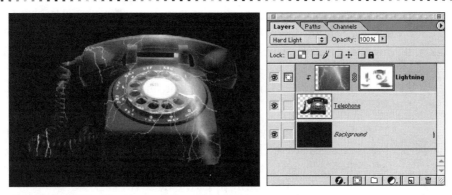

Figure 20.7 *The final image altered with a layer mask*

Seamless Compositing

You often see advertisements in glossy magazines that you know have been "Photo-shopped." The non sequitur, neo-surreal images are a dead give-away, and sometimes they are amazingly clever. The image may have a brilliant concept, dazzling colors, and a truly dynamic composition and be perfect in every way—except for a few out-of-place pixels. It is unfortunate when a great work of commercial art is just short of perfection, especially when Photoshop has built-in bandages to cover every possible boo-boo.

Matting is the key to clean composites. When you select an image, the anti-alias programmed into the selection tool selects edge pixels. When you drag the selection onto another image, the stowaway edge pixels can't be seen until they reach their destination. When you see them, it's usually a row of one or two pixels that are significantly darker or lighter than the color behind them, as in Figure 20.8.

Figure 20.8 *Edge pixels selected and carried over from another document*

You can easily eliminate unwanted edge pixels using Photoshop's matting functions. The matting functions eliminate those nasty little fellows and blend your image into the layers beneath it. There are three ways to matte an image, and if your edge pixels are particularly stubborn, there's a work-around that does the job every time.

In order to matte an image, it must be on an independent layer surrounded by transparency.

Defringe   Choose Layer ➜ Matting ➜ Defringe, and enter a value in the dialog box that is displayed. This is a very effective method of eliminating the off-color edge pixels selected by the anti-alias. Defringe replaces the color of the edge pixels with the colors of the nearby pixels on the layer.

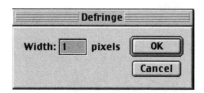

Remove White or Black Matte   Choose Layer ➜ Matting ➜ Remove White Matte or Remove Black Matte to replace the colored edge pixels with gray pixels. This is helpful if you are moving selection with a colored background to a white or black background.

If none of these operations works to your satisfaction—and sometimes you just can't eliminate enough of that edge—here's a neat work-around:

1. Select the image pixels on the layer by pressing the Cmd/Ctrl key and clicking the thumbnail.

2. Choose Select ➜ Modify ➜ Contract. Enter the amount to Contract the selection. View the edge close up to see how far into the image the marquee has contracted. Undo and enter different values if necessary.

3. Choose Select ➜ Inverse.

4. Choose Select ➜ Feather, and feather the selection 1 pixel.

5. Press your Delete key (Mac) or Backspace key (Win) to delete the edge.

Casting Shadows

In Chapter 7, we looked at how to create realistic drop shadows using Photoshop's built-in layer styles. *Cast* shadows present a set of completely different problems. The difference between the two shadows is that a drop shadow is quite simply a gray, semi-transparent, soft-edged duplicate of the image from which it is dropped. A cast shadow has all the qualities of a drop shadow, except that it is distorted by the direction of light and the terrain on which it rests. Using layers, you can create a very convincing cast shadow and blend it perfectly into its surroundings.

The sun is low and our skier is racing downhill, but without a shadow. Let's make one.

1. Open the Skier.psd file in the Ch20 folder on the CD. The image is composed of two layers named Skier and Snow (Figure 20.9).

Figure 20.9 *The shadowless skier*

2. Duplicate the Skier layer by dragging it to the New Layer icon. Double-click the new layer to display the Layer Properties dialog box. Name the layer Shadow.

3. Check the Transparency lock. Choose black as a foreground color and press Option+Delete (Mac) or Alt+Backspace (Win) to fill the contents of the layer with black. Uncheck the Transparency lock.

4. Drag the Shadow layer between the Skier layer and the Snow layer (Figure 20.10).

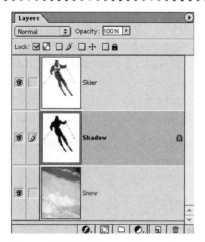

Figure 20.10 *The stacking order of the layers in the Layers palette*

5. Choose Edit ➜ Transform ➜ Distort. Distort the marquee so that the contents of the shadow layer appears to lie on the ground, as in Figure 20.11. You may have to play with this a little to get it to look convincing. When you're satisfied, commit your transform by pressing the Return or Enter key.

Figure 20.11 *Distort the cast shadow so it appears to lie on the ground.*

6. Choose Filter ➜ Blur ➜ Gaussian Blur. Drag the slider to 2.3 to soften the edges of the shadow. Click OK.

7. Move the Opacity slider on the Shadow layer to 40% to make it transparent, as you can see in Figure 20.12.

Figure 20.12 *The skier with the cast shadow set to 40% opacity*

8. The shadow looks convincing except for its color. Choose Image ➜ Adjust ➜ Hue/Saturation; check the Colorize box. Move the Lightness slider to +22, Saturation to 76, and Hue to 222 to match the color of the shadows on the snow.

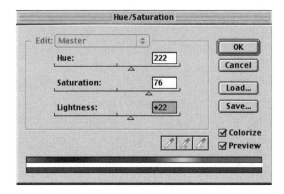

Up Next

The techniques covered in this chapter give you an idea of how layers can be used to combine images. You have more control because you can selectively determine the color and shape relations of images separated to layers. You'll find layer masks and clipping groups to be invaluable to developing your compositions because of the precision with which you can reveal or hide image content. Another plus is that, unlike alpha channels, layer masks require very little real estate on your hard disk.

In the Hands-On tutorial that follows, you'll have a chance to apply many of the layer skills I've talked about in this chapter and in Chapter 7.

Hands-On
Advanced Layers

Now try out some of the advanced layer techniques on a project. You'll make layer masks, clipping groups, and a drop shadow, and you'll apply matting to clean up edge pixels on portions of the image.

In the Ch20 folder on the CD, open the file Birdy_Condo_start.psd. Save the image to your disk. To view the starting and completed (Birdy_Condo_end.tif) versions of the Birdy Condo, see Figure 1 (which is also presented in the color section).

Figure 1 *The (left) beginning and (right) finished Birdy Condo*

Quit Photoshop and hide your preferences file before beginning this hands-on exercise. Then relaunch Photoshop to create a clean version. The "Photoshop's Settings" section in Chapter 5 details how to temporarily reset your preferences to Photoshop defaults. You can restore your customized personal settings when you're done.

Placing the Parrot in a Window

The image has been divided into five layers and a background. You'll start by creating a layer mask to place the parrot in a window of the condo.

1. Target the Parrot layer.

2. Choose Layer ➔ Add Layer Mask ➔ Reveal All.

3. Choose the Paintbrush, and a hard-edged brush from the Options bar. Choose black as a foreground color. With the layer mask targeted, carefully paint out the background and portions of the parrot to give the appearance that the parrot is partially inside the window, as in Figure 2. Figure 3 shows the Parrot layer mask.

Figure 2 With the layer mask targeted, paint out the background to give the appearance that the parrot is partially inside the building.

Figure 3 *The Parrot layer mask*

Placing the Crane in the Window

You'll place the crane in the window using a layer mask but with a different technique for concealing the background.

1. Target the Crane layer.

2. Choose the Magic Wand tool. Set the Tolerance to 32. Click the blue rectangle to select it.

3. Choose Select ➔ Inverse.

4. Choose Layer ➔ Add Layer Mask ➔ Hide All. The bird disappears, but you can see the selection marquee.

5. In the Tool palette, choose white as the foreground color.

6. Press Option+Delete or Alt+Backspace to fill the selected area on the mask and reveal the bird.

7. Deselect. Choose the Paintbrush and black paint; on the layer mask, paint out the lower-right portion of the crane so it appears to be partially in the window.

8. To enhance the effect, target the Crane layer thumbnail and pass over it with the Burn tool to darken the bottom edge of the crane.

Casting the Penguins' Shadow

1. Target the Penguins layer. From the Layers palette pull-down menu, choose Duplicate Layer; name the layer Shadow.

2. Check the Transparency lock. Choose black as the foreground color and press Option+Delete (Mac) or Alt+Backspace (Win) to fill the contents of the layer with black. Uncheck the Transparency lock.

3. Drag the Shadow layer beneath the Penguin layer.

4. Choose Edit ➜ Transform ➜ Distort. Distort the marquee so that the contents of the Shadow layer appears to lie on the ground, as in Figure 4. You may have to play with this a little to get it to look convincing. When you're satisfied, press the Return/Enter key.

5. Choose Filter ➜ Blur ➜ Gaussian Blur. Drag the slider to 2.6 to soften the edges of the shadow. Click OK.

6. Move the Opacity slider on the shadow layer to 40% to make it more realistic.

You can use this same shadow technique to create shadows for the flamingo and the crane.

Figure 4 *Distorting the Penguins' shadow*

Matting and Placing the Flamingo

1. Open the file Flamingo.psd.

2. Choose the Magnetic Lasso tool. Drag around the edge of the flamingo, as in Figure 5, until you've selected it.

Figure 5 *Selecting the flamingo with the Magnetic Lasso*

3 Choose the Move tool and drag the flamingo onto the Birdy Condo image.

4. The flamingo is too large; let's reduce its size by 50%. Still using the Move tool, check Show Bounding Box in the Options bar. Place your cursor on the upper-left corner of the bounding box, click and drag inward a little bit, and release the mouse. The Options bar now changes to allow you to input numeric values for the transformation.

5. Click the link icon between the Width and Height fields to constrain the proportion of the flamingo. Enter 50% in the Width field. Click the check mark on the Options bar to confirm the transformation.

6. Move the flamingo so that its neck aligns with the second row of windows, in the center window (the eighth from either the left or right side).

7. Choose Layer ➔ Matting ➔ Defringe to eliminate the edge pixels. Enter **2 px** in the dialog box and click OK.

8. Choose the Eraser tool and erase the bottom part of the flamingo so that it looks as though its neck is sticking out of the window (see Figure 6).

9. To enhance the effect, use the Burn tool to darken the bottom part of the flamingo's neck.

Figure 6 *Placing the defringed flamingo*

Creating a Clipping Group for the Gulls

The easiest and most flexible method of placing the gulls in the sky is to create a clipping group with the Sky layer.

1. Target the Sky layer.

2. Place your cursor between the Sky layer and the Gull layer. Press Option/Alt and click your mouse. The Gull layer is now clipped to the Sky layer, taking its shape.

3. Target the Gull layer. Choose the Move tool; drag the Gull layer inside the clip until you are satisfied with its position.

4. Save the image.

Up Next

I hope this Hands-on project has helped you understand how to use Photoshop's advanced layers functions. I recommend that you use layer masks and clipping groups techniques whenever possible as a streamlined way to manage your layered images.

The next chapter, "Automating the Process," focuses on Actions. Many of the techniques we have learned for manipulating images can be recorded as you perform them, stored in a palette, and then played back. In essence, you can write a script and, with the touch of a key, apply the operation to another image, greatly accelerating your workflow.

Automating
the Process

PHOTOSHOP

Chapter 21

When working in Photoshop, you often repeat tasks. For example, if you publish a lot of work on the Web, you may regularly convert files from RGB to Indexed color before you save them as GIFs. Here's another: Let's say you want to place all of the images in a file on a single document to make a contact sheet for comparison. Opening, sizing, and pasting the images can be tedious, time-consuming work.

Building a Web site is a lot of work. Wouldn't it be nice if there was some way to accomplish this by simply pressing a button? This chapter is about Photoshop's magic buttons called Actions and Automation. These operations can greatly accelerate your workflow and automatically perform tedious and repetitious tasks. You can perform most Actions and automations to single or multiple documents and you can save them and store them for later use.

You'll learn how to:

- Set up an Action

- Apply Actions to a batch of images

- Create contact sheets, picture packages, and a Web photo gallery

- Create Droplets

Creating and Applying Actions

When a multimillion-dollar Hollywood movie is produced, everybody involved in the production, including the director, actors, and cinematographer, follows a script. A script is simply a written dialog and set of directions. Just like the movies, computers also use scripts. Unlike actors, however, computers never ad-lib; they follow the script to the letter! When you record an Action, you are actually writing a script that tells the software what sequence of operations to perform. Fortunately, recording a script for Photoshop is a lot easier than writing a script for a movie.

Any single operation or sequence of operations can be programmed into an Action, with the exception of the some of manual tools like the Airbrush and Paintbrush tools. You can program an Action to select the Paintbrush, but you can't make an Action to paint with it. Neither can the zoom tools, window commands, and view commands be recorded. The tools from which you can record an Action are: the Marquees, Polygon, Lasso, Magic Wand, Crop, Slice, Magic Eraser, Gradient, Paint Bucket, Type, Shape, Line, Note, Eyedropper, and Color Sampler. You can record many of the menu commands, but you can't make an Action out of program preference changes.

Before you record an Action, envision the end product first. Try to imagine what you want the image to look like. Then ask yourself what processes need to be applied in order to accomplish that end.

As you will see, Actions are flexible. You can create a sequence of Actions and then apply a single Action from the sequence to your image. Or you can apply the same Action with different settings to the image.

The Actions Palette

Actions are recorded and played in the Actions palette, shown with its pull-down menu in Figure 21.1. Choose Window ➔ Show Actions to access the palette. When you first open the palette, you see a "set" called Default Actions. A *set* is simply a folder where groups of Actions are stored. All Actions must be contained within a set.

Expand the Default Actions by clicking the triangle next to its name. You see a list of Actions that Adobe includes with Photoshop. Actions are applied to the image in sequence from top to bottom. When a check mark appears in the Item On/Off box (the first column on the left side of the palette) next to its name, the Action or set will be applied to the image when played. If unchecked, the Action will be skipped. By checking or unchecking the boxes, you can determine which Actions will be applied in a sequence. When the Dialog On/Off box (the second column of the Actions palette) is checked, the Action will stop running and display a dialog box so that you can change the settings.

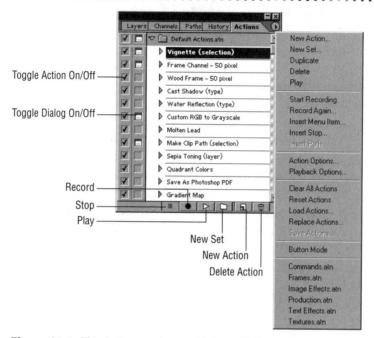

Figure 21.1 *The Actions palette with its pull-down menu*

The pull-down menu provides commands to save, load, duplicate, and create new Actions and sets. Button mode (new to Photoshop 6) displays a button interface on the Actions palette. Click the Action's name to run it. The bottom section of the Actions pull-down menu provides tons of additional default Actions. Click an Action to load it in the Actions palette. Experiment with these default Actions to get to know their capabilities.

Actions can be nested within other Actions; you'll notice that the Actions inside the Default Actions set have, in turn, substeps. These are also Actions, but for clarity, I'll refer to these "sub-Actions" as opera-tions within an Action.

Applying an Action Step by Step

In order to better understand Actions, it might be beneficial to run one of the Default Actions to see how the Actions palette applies commands to the image.

1. Open the Toddler.psd file in the Ch21 folder on the *Mastering Photoshop 6* CD. Duplicate the file (Image ➜ Duplicate) and save it to your disk.

2. Choose the Elliptical Marquee. Place your cursor on the center of the image. Press the Option/Alt key and drag to generate an elliptical selection from a center point (see Figure 21.2).

Figure 21.2 *The toddler selected*

3. Expand the Default Actions set. Target the Vignette action.

4. Expand the Vignette Action. You can see the sequence of operations contained within the Action (see Figure 21.3).

5. We will use the default settings, so click each of the Dialog On/Off icons in the second column on the left, to turn them off.

6. Target the Vignette Action and click the triangular Play button at the bottom of the Actions palette. When the Action has finished running, the image should look like Figure 21.4.

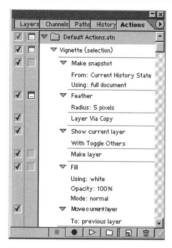

Figure 21.3 *The Vignette Action and its operations*

Figure 21.4 *The Vignette operations applied to the image*

Making an Action

Of course, you can make your own Actions and apply them to one or more images. You can name, color-code, and specify a function key for an Action so all you have to do is press the key to apply it. We'll go through making an Action step by step as we perform a tonal adjustment, eliminate moiré patterns, convert, and colorize an image. We'll work on two images cut from old yearbook.

1. Open the file Becky_1964.psd from the Ch21 folder on the CD.

2. Choose Window ➜ Show Actions. From the pull-down menu, choose New Set. Name the set Yearbook Photos.

3. From the pull-down menu, choose New Action. In the dialog box, name the Action Becky. From the Function Key menu, choose F2. Click Record. The Record button on the Actions palette turns red.

4. Choose Image ➜ Adjust Levels. Drag the black shadow slider until the value in the box reads 10. Drag the white highlight slider to 189 and the gray midtone slider to 1.34. Click OK.

5. Choose Filter ➜ Blur ➜ Gaussian Blur; set the Radius to 1.0 to eliminate the moiré pattern.

6. Choose Filter ➜ Sharpen ➜ Unsharp Mask and set the following values: Amount: 66%, Radius: 3.4 pixels, Threshold: 2 levels.

7. Choose Image ➜ Mode ➜ RGB Color to convert the image so that it supports color.

8. Choose Image ➜ Adjust ➜ Hue/Saturation and check Colorize. Enter 239 for the Hue, 12 for the Saturation, and 0 for the Lightness. Click OK.

9. Click the Stop Recording button. The Actions palette should look like Figure 21.5, and the image should look like the "after" version in Figure 21.6. We'll use this recorded set throughout this chapter.

Exercise caution when recording. Remember that almost anything you do is being recorded. If the image does not appear the way you want it to or if you if you make a mistake, stop recording, drag the Action to the trash, and rerecord it.

Figure 21.5 *The Actions palette with the Yearbook Photos set and the Becky operations*

Figure 21.6 *The Becky 1964 yearbook image (left) before and (right) after the Yearbook Photos set was applied*

Applying Actions to Another Image

Obviously, the main purpose of Actions is to repeat a command or series of commands. But because the settings often need to be readjusted to achieve good results on a different image, you can stop the Action during the process of applying it. In this exercise, you'll apply the Actions recorded in the preceding section and you'll change some of the settings as the action is playing.

1. Open Becky_1965.psd from the Ch21 folder on the CD.

2. In the Actions palette, click the icons in the second column next to Levels, Gaussian Blur, and Unsharp Mask to turn on the Dialog On/Off icons, so the Action will pause and present the operation's dialog box. You can make the necessary changes to accommodate the different image and then continue to run the action.

3. Target the Becky Action and press the F2 key. The Play button turns red.

4. As the action runs, enter new values in the dialog boxes as they appear. Levels: 15 for the shadow and 220 for the highlight; Gaussian Blur: 0.8; and Unsharp Mask: Amount: 47%, Radius: 2.9 pixels, Threshold: 4 levels. Click OK in each box. The new settings are applied and the Action continues to run. The Convert Mode and Hue/Saturation operations are applied without interruption. The image will look like Figure 21.7.

Figure 21.7 *The Becky 1965 image, (left) before and (right) after the Becky Actions have been applied*

Inserting a Stop

You can stop the Action so that you can perform a task that is not recordable, like painting a stroke with the paint brush for example. To insert a stop:

1. Select the Action or operation where you want to insert the stop. The stop will be inserted at the end of that Action or operation.

2. Choose Insert Stop from the Actions palette pull-down menu.

3. Type a message in the dialog box that appears. Check the Allow Continue box if you want a dialog box to appear that lets you choose to stop or continue. Click OK.

Undoing an Action

Since an Action is a sequence of operations, choosing Edit ➜ Undo or pressing Command/Ctrl+Z will not undo the Action, but only the last operation in the sequence. Instead, press Cmd+Option+Z (Mac) or Ctrl+Alt+Z (Win) as many times as necessary to step backwards through the operations. You can also undo the Actions that were recorded in the History palette. Click the state in the History palette just above the first recorded state of the Action.

Saving and Loading an Action

Once you've compiled a series of operations into an Action, you'll want to save the Action to your disk. From the Actions pull-down palette, choose Save Actions. Then choose a destination on the disk. Its always a wise idea to add extension .atn to the Action to anticipate platform problems and to identify the file as an Action. To load an Action, choose Load Action from the pull-down palette and locate the file where you saved it.

Controlling the Speed of an Action

The Playback Options dialog box (from the Actions palette pull-down menu) lets you control how fast an Action is played. Choosing Accelerated plays the Action as quickly as possible. Step By Step waits until the Action is finished and the image redrawn before playing the next Action. Pause lets you enter a number in seconds between Actions.

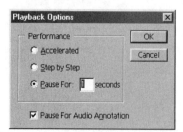

Editing, Moving, and Discarding an Action

You can edit the settings of an operation within an Action when it's not running by double-clicking its name in the Actions palette. Its dialog box appears so you can change the settings. The next time you run the Action, the new settings will be applied.

Actions can be repositioned in the stack. The Action's position in the stack can greatly affect the final outcome of the image. To reposition an Action, click and drag it within the Actions palette; release the mouse when it's positioned in the desired location.

To discard an Action, drag it to the trash icon in the Actions palette.

Inserting Unrecordable Commands

Some menu items that are unrecordable as Actions can be inserted at the end of an Action. To insert a menu item:

1. Target an Action in the Actions palette by clicking it.

2. Choose Insert Menu Item from the Actions palette pull-down menu.

3. With the Insert Menu Item dialog box displayed, choose a command from the menu at the top of the screen.

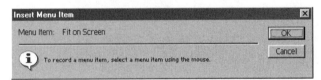

Automation Operations

So far we've applied Actions to images manually. Hmmmm! Manual automation? Sounds like an oxymoron, doesn't it? Wouldn't it be really cool if we could apply Actions automatically while we were away from the computer, maybe strolling in the park or dining out? "Why would he mention it if it couldn't be done?" you might be asking yourself right now. Yes, it can be done. There are several ways to do it, and most of them are easy.

Batch Processing

You can apply an Action to multiple files within a folder by choosing File ➜ Automate ➜ Batch; the Batch dialog box is shown in Figure 21.8. This formidable-looking dialog lets you apply a set, a group of Actions, or a single Action. You can batch-process a group of images within a folder or from a different source, like a digital camera or scanner with a document feeder. You can then automatically save the images within the folder, or save them to new folders leaving the originals unchanged.

Your scanner or digital camera may need an Acquire plug-in to support batch-processing.

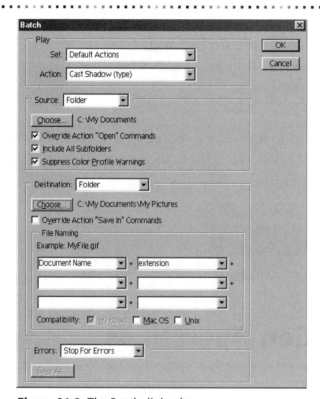

Figure 21.8 *The Batch dialog box*

For better performance batch-processing images, go to the History palette. Decrease the number of saved History states and uncheck the Automatically Create First Snapshot box.

To batch-process a group of images, choose File ➔ Automate ➔ Batch. Under Play, choose the set and Action that you want to run from the pop-up lists. Then choose your input method from the Source list:

Import applies the images on a scanner or digital camera.

Opened Files plays the Action on open files.

Folder runs the Action on all of the images within a selected folder. Click Choose to locate and select the folder, and check the following options as desired.

Override Action "Open" Commands ignores any Open commands that are part of the Action to ensure that the images are opened from specified folder.

Include All Subfolders affects the contents of any folders within the selected folder.

Suppress Color Profile Warnings turns off the color policy and profile mismatch messages.

Choose destination options for the batch-processed files from the Destination pop-up list.

None leaves the files open without saving changes (unless the action included a Save command).

Save And Close saves the files in the source folder.

Folder specifies a new location for the batched processed files. Click Choose to locate and select the folder.

Override Action "Save In" Commands ignores Save As commands that are part of the action to ensure that the specified files are saved to the destination folder.

 The Batch command always saves the files in the same format as the original. To create a batch-process that saves files in a new format, record the Save As or Save A Copy command. Designate a location within the Action, followed by the Close command. In the Batch dialog box, choose None for the Destination.

File Naming

File naming is available if you selected a folder as the destination. You can determine how batch-processed files will be named and their platform compatibility.

Choose from pop-up menus or type into the fields to create file naming conventions. You can determine the naming convention for the document name, identification number or letter, date, and file extension. The fields let you change the order and formatting of the filenames. For File Name Compatibility, choose Windows, MacOS, and/or Unix.

Error Processing

You can choose an option for error processing from the Errors pop-up menu: Stop For Errors pauses the operation until you OK the error message. Log Errors To File records the error in the file. The error message appears after the process is complete. Click Save As and name the error file.

Creating and Using Droplets

A Droplet is a mini application that sits on the desktop. You can apply an Action by dragging a file or folder onto the Droplet's icon.

The Create Droplet dialog box is quite similar to the Batch dialog box. To create a Droplet from an Action, choose File → Automate → Create Droplet (Figure 21.9).

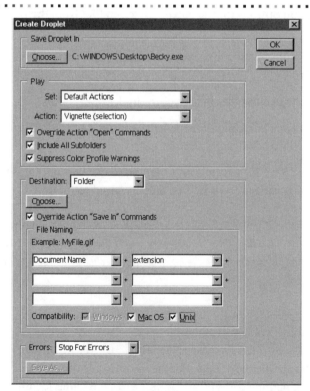

Figure 21.9 *The Create Droplet dialog box*

Under Save Droplet In, click Choose. Determine a location for the Droplet. Choose a set and an Action from pop-up menus. Set the Play and Destination options for the Droplet (these options are the same as the Source and Destination settings described in the earlier section "Batch Processing").

File Naming

File naming is available if you select a folder as the destination. Determine how batch-processed files will be named and their platform compatibility. Choose from pop-up menus or type into the fields to create file-naming conventions. Determine naming conventions for the document's name, identification number or letter, date, and file extension. The fields let you change the order and formatting of the filenames. For File Name Compatibility, choose Windows, MacOS, and/or Unix.

Using a Droplet to Apply an Action

Let's make a Droplet from the Becky Action we recorded in the previous section, "Making an Action," and apply it to an image.

1. Choose File ➜ Automate ➜ Create Droplet.

2. In the Create Droplet dialog box, do the following: Click the Choose button and choose the Desktop of your computer. For Set, choose Yearbook Photos; for Action, choose Becky.

3. Check Override Open Commands, Include All Subfolders, and Suppress Color Profile Warnings.

4. For Destination, choose Folder. Click Choose and determine a location for the image.

5. Leave the default file names, and the Stop for Errors default.

6. Click OK and the Droplet will appear on the desktop.

7. On your desktop, open the Ch21 folder on the CD. Drag the icon of the Vicky.psd image onto Droplet icon.

8. The adjustments for this photograph will be different than the ones recorded in the Action. As the Levels, Gaussian Blur, and Unsharp Mask dialog boxes appear, make adjustments to improve the image.

9. Open the image in the destination folder to observe the changes to the image. Your image should look better, perhaps something like Figure 21.10.

Figure 21.10 *Vicky (left) before and (right) after being dragged to the Droplet*

Other Automation Commands

The File ➜ Automate commands are a group of Actions consolidated into a dialog box. You can configure options that vary the outcome of the image. Some of the Automations convert files to other formats or construct files into contact sheets.

Conditional Mode Change

You can change the color mode of a document while in an Action by recording File ➜ Automate ➜ Conditional Mode Change. Choose the modes that you need changed, or click All to choose any mode. If your Action encounters a file in an unchecked mode, it will leave that file unchanged. Then choose a target mode to which the document will be changed. Click OK. The advantage of Conditional Mode Change (over, say, the Image ➜ Mode submenu) is that this command allows your Action to avoid any error messages that occur when an image is required to be in a specific color mode, or is already in the desired mode.

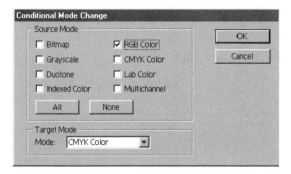

Contact Sheet II

This command produces a new document of thumbnail previews on a single sheet from the files in a folder. Choose File ➜ Automate ➜ Contact Sheet II to display the Contact Sheet dialog box (Figure 21.11). Choose a source folder from which to make the document, and specify a width, height, resolution, and mode for the document. In the Thumbnails field, Place determines whether the sequence of files will be placed horizontally or vertically. Choose the number of columns and rows. Check the box if you want to add the file's name as a caption although the images will be somewhat smaller. You can also choose a font and a size for the caption. The graphic on the right side of the dialog box displays the layout of the contact sheet.

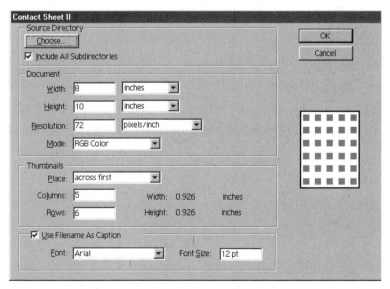

Figure 21.11 *The Contact Sheet II dialog box*

I've provided a folder of images on the CD so you can try out making a contact sheet.

1. Choose File ➜ Automate ➜ Contact Sheet II.

2. Click Choose. On the CD in the Ch21 folder, click the Contact_Sheet folder, then click Choose.

3. In the Contact Sheet II dialog box, use these settings:

Width	8
Height	10
Resolution	72
Mode	Grayscale
Place	Across first
Columns	3
Rows	3

4. Check the Use Filename As Caption box. For Font, use Helvetica; enter Font Size: 11.

5. Click OK… and wait! This process can take a while. But eventually, an image that looks like Figure 21.12 will appear on screen.

Fit Image

This command will fit an image to a specified width or height without changing its aspect ratio. Keep in mind that this will resample the image, changing the amount of data in the image.

Multi-Page PDF To PSD

Use this command to convert the pages of an Adobe Acrobat PDF document into separate Photoshop files.

Figure 21.12 *The contact sheet*

Picture Package

The Picture Package command creates a document with multiple copies of an active image on a single page. This feature is used to assemble a sheet of multiple copies of one image, the kind you might receive from a portrait studio, for example. The Picture Package dialog box (Figure 21.13) lets you choose an image from a file or an open image on the desktop. Choose from a list of layout options and a resolution and mode for the new document. The graphic on the right side of the dialog box displays the layout of the picture package.

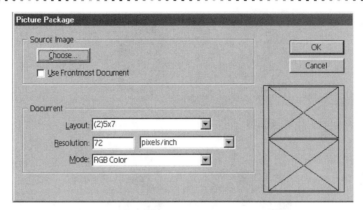

Figure 21.13 *The Picture Package dialog box*

Web Photo Gallery

The Web Photo Gallery command simplifies Web publication of your images by automatically creating a Web site. The site contains an HTML document, an index page,
individual JPEG image pages, and hyperlinks. Photoshop generates the code and the
source files.

To create a Web site, choose File ➜ Automate ➜ Web Photo Gallery. A dialog box
(Figure 21.14) is displayed that features Web site options.

Styles   Choose from Simple, Table, Vertical Frame, or Horizontal Frame styles.
The graphic on the right of the dialog box displays the layout.

Options   Define banners, thumbnails, images, and colors to be used in the site.
The graphic on the right side of the dialog box displays the options for each of the
styles.

Files   Choose Source to designate the folder where the images are contained.
Choose Destination to determine the location of the new folder containing the
HTML document and all the supporting images.

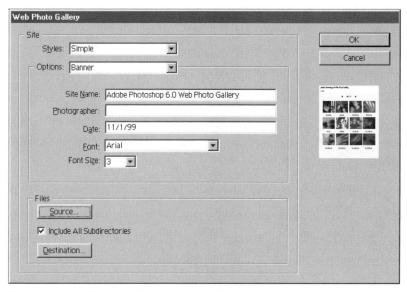

Figure 21.14 *The Web Photo Gallery dialog box*

Up Next

I hope you'll take advantage of Actions and the Automate submenu because they are indeed some of the most powerful components of Photoshop 6. Automating tasks helps you save time and money by making your workflow more efficient. Key commands for often-repeated tasks can be programmed and executed with the touch of a button. Tedious processes that formerly required a great deal of time can now be performed from the Automate menu in a matter of seconds. You can even instantaneously develop your own custom Web gallery to display your images.

In Chapter 22, we'll take a look at two more powerful operations. These are the compositing techniques that overlay images with precision control. I think you'll find these operations quite useful.

Overlay Techniques

PHOTOSHOP

Chapter 22

One of Adobe Photoshop's greatest strengths is its ability to combine images. In Chapters 7 and 20 you mastered the power of compositing with layers. Image parts separated to layers can effectively be superimposed on each other. In addition, images from multiple sources can be collaged together and precisely tuned with layer masks and clipping groups. We saw in Chapter 6 and Chapter 19 that, like layers, alpha channels can also be combined. The process of combining images from multiple sources takes many forms and is one of Photoshop's most useful features. In this chapter, we're going to look at industrial-strength image compositing.

You will learn how to:

- Superimpose images to enhance their quality

- Create artistic effects by applying images

- Use calculations to combine complex selections

Layer-Based Compositing

Imagine, if you will, that you have two different transparencies on a light table, one on top of another. When you look at them through a magnifying loupe, you see the effect of combined colors on the two superimposed images. Opposite colors like reds and greens may cancel each other and produce areas of dark gray, while colors that are closer to each other on the color wheel, like reds and yellows, may tend to produce richer, more saturated oranges.

Now imagine that you have duplicates of the *same* transparency on the light table, and you are able to "sandwich in" filters that produce a variety of color relations between the two superimposed images. In Photoshop, these are the *blending modes,* and you apply them to an image in the Layers palette. The blending modes, which are described in Appendix C and illustrated in the color section, can be used to enhance color on an image. When you superimpose one layer on another, you can apply a layer effect to alter the color relations and then precisely control result by adjusting the opacity of the layer.

To demonstrate this effect, open the file `Rhinocerose.psd` (from the Ch22 folder on the *Mastering Photoshop 6* CD). Notice that the image is divided into two layers. The rhino appears flat compared to the Background it was pasted into, and if you make the Rose layer visible, you'll see that the rose could be a lot more intense.

1. (Just in case you made it visible in that paragraph, start out with the Rose layer hidden!) Choose the Freeform Pen tool, check Magnetic, and select the rhinoceros. The Magnetic Pen will most likely not make a perfect selection, so you'll need to add to and subtract from the selection with the Lasso tool or the Quick Mask.

2. Choose Layer ➜ New ➜ Layer Via Copy to copy the rhino to a new layer. Name the new layer Rhino.

3. Target the new layer and choose Hard Light from the mode pull-down menu. It looks more saturated but a little too dark.

4. Drag the Opacity slider to 63% to diminish the effect. A big improvement!

5. We'll now enhance the rose. Click the Rose layer's eye icon.

6. Drag the Rose layer to the New Layer icon to duplicate it.

7. Choose Multiply from the mode menu, and reduce the opacity to 80%.

The image appears much richer, as you can see in the examples printed in the color section. The colors in the targeted areas are more saturated and have better contrast. You can experiment with creating additional layers and applying different blend modes at varying degrees of opacity to the vary effect.

Excluding Colors

You can use Photoshop's Layer Style dialog box (Figure 22.1) to exclude colors in the image. Advanced Blending lets you exclude targeted information in a specific channel. With the exclusion sliders, you can omit colors of a specific brightness value. To demonstrate how these sliders work, open the file Heavenly_Roses.psd (Figure 22.2) from the Ch22 folder on the CD.

1. The image is divided into a layer and a Background. Double-click the Rose layer, to display the Layer Style dialog box.

2. First, uncheck all of the Channels boxes. The image of the roses disappears. Now check the red (R) box only. The channel information from the red channel appears and affects the underlying layer. The red channel appears to contain most of the detail of the red rose.

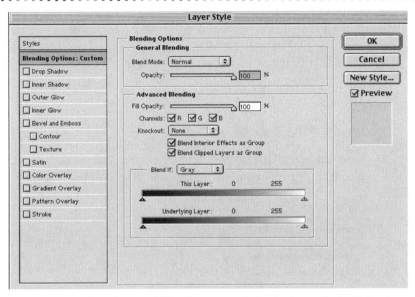

Figure 22.1 *The Advanced Blending controls in the Layer Style dialog box*

Figure 22.2 *The Heavenly Roses image*

 If you were to look at the information of the rose layer in the Channels palette, you would see that the red channel contains most of the detail of the red rose and more pixels with higher brightness values.

3. Check the green box and uncheck the red and blue boxes. Notice that there is more detail on the green rose when the green box is checked. The same is true for the blue rose.

4. Check all of the boxes to display the roses in full color.

You will now use the exclusion sliders to omit pixels of a specific brightness value within each channel.

1. Make sure Blend If is set to Gray.

2. Move the black This Layer slider to the right until the shadow value reads 90. The darker pixels in the roses disappear, as seen in Figure 22.3.

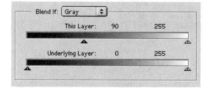

Figure 22.3 *The image with the channel options set to Gray and the black exclusion slider set to 90.*

3. Press the Option/Alt key and click Reset. In the Blend If pull-down menu, choose Red. Move the black This Layer slider to the right, again until it reads 90. The dark pixels on the green and blue rose disappear, but all of the pixels on the red layer remain.

4. Press the Option/Alt key and click Reset. Now move the white slider to the left, until the highlight value reads 96. The red rose completely disappears.

If you use exclusion sliders to omit pixels of a specific brightness range from the layer, you force colors to disappear. This can produce harsh color transitions and jagged edges. You can diminish the effect by adjusting the Fuzziness, which softens the transition. Here's how: Press Option/Alt and click Reset. This time, press the Option/Alt key as you drag the *left half* of the white slider to the left. The effect on the red rose produces a softer edge, as in Figure 22.4.

Figure 22.4 *Softer transitions result by pressing the Option or Alt key while dragging half of a slider.*

Channel-Based Compositing

Adobe once counted channel-based compositing to be among its most powerful features. Now it is, to a certain extent, redundant with new extensive layer compositing techniques. However, additional modes can be applied that, even in this latest version of Photoshop, have not been added to the Layers palette. Photoshop's two channel-based compositing techniques are the Apply Image command and the Calculations command.

Apply Image

The Apply Image command applies a source image to the target image. To use Apply Image, both images have to be open on the desktop. The images must be the exact same physical size and resolution.

First, let's have a look at the Apply Image dialog box to understand what its commands do. To access it, choose Image ➜ Apply Image.

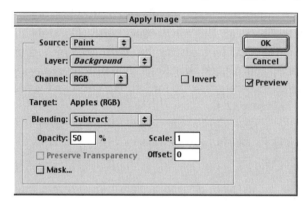

Source   This is the image that is applied, or overlaid. Choose the desired image from the pop-up list.

Layer   The pop-up lists all of the layers and the Background in the source image. You can overlay all the layers if you choose Merged.

Channel   Select the channels you apply to the image from this list. If you choose the composite channel (RGB, CMYK, etc.), the entire channel will be mixed.

Invert   Check the box to invert the contents of the selected channel. Pixels that are black will be applied as if they are white and vice versa.

Target   This the image that is active on the desktop. The target lists the channel(s) and layers that the image will be applied to.

Blending   The pop-up list displays fourteen blending modes in which the color will be applied (see Appendix C for a description of each mode).

Opacity   Enter the opacity of the mode.

Preserve Transparency   This check box leaves transparent areas on a layer unaffected.

Mask   Checking this option masks off a part of the source image. When you choose Mask, the Apply Image dialog box expands. From the menus, choose an image and a layer. Choose a color channel or alpha channel or an active selection on the source image to isolate the application of the affect.

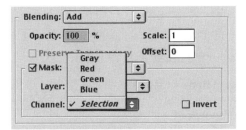

Scale and Offset   If you choose either the Add or Subtract modes, you can enter values for scale and offset. These values are used in the calculation to determine the brightness values of the superimposed pixels. See Appendix C, "Blending Modes."

The Apply Image command can produce some beautiful artistic effects. You can vary the results by choosing different settings. We'll start with a sepia watercolor by artist Andrew Rush. We'll apply a broadly painted version of the image and mitigate the effect by adjusting the blending modes and the opacity.

1.   Open the file on the Ch22 folder on the CD, Apples.psd (Figure 22.5). For this exercise, refer to the full-color versions of this image included in the color section.

Figure 22.5 *Play with this sepia-toned watercolor by applying various blending modes.*

2. Choose Image ➔ Duplicate to make a copy of the image. Name the new image `Paint`.

3. With the painting tools, color the image with broad strokes.

4. Click the `Apples.psd` image to make it active.

The image that is active will become the Target image.

5. Choose Image ➔ Apply Image. Enter the following, then click OK:

Source	`Paint`
Layer	Background
Channel	RGB
Blending	Subtract
Opacity	50%

6. Try different combinations of modes, channels, and opacities to produce vastly different results.

Apply Image can also be used to produce interesting overlay graphic effects. In Chapter 17, we created a posterization and a halftone from the same image. You can combine two types of images together to produce a strong posterized halftone effect.

1. Open the images `Listerpstr.psd` and `Listerbmp.psd` in the Ch22 folder on the CD.

2. Activate `Listerbmp.psd` and choose Image ➔ Mode ➔ Grayscale to convert the bitmapped image to a grayscale.

Channel-based compositing techniques do not work on Bitmap images. It is therefore necessary to convert their mode.

3. Click `Listerpstr.psd` to activate it.

4. Choose Image ➔ Apply Image. Enter the following and click OK (see Figure 22.6 to see the before and after results.):

Source	`Listerbmp.psd`
Layer	Background
Channel	Gray
Blending	Add
Opacity	40%

5. Try different combinations of modes, channels and opacities to produce different results.

(a)   (b)   (c)

Figure 22.6 *(a) A posterized image, (b) a halftone, and (c) the halftone applied to the posterized image*

Calculations

Despite the complexity of its dialog box, the Calculations command actually performs a rather simple operation—it creates only one channel. Image ➜ Calculations works exclusively to combine two source channels into a new channel. You can composite channels on an existing image, or create an entirely new image. The Calculations command has three purposes: to create a new Grayscale image, or to combine two masks into a single alpha channel or active selection.

Like Apply Image, the images must be the exact same height, width, and resolution. When you go to Image ➜ Calculations, you see the Calculations dialog box (Figure 22.7).

It's quite similar to the Apply Image dialog box; the only difference is the additional Source. The source areas let you choose two channels to combine.

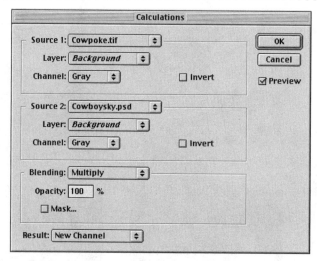

Figure 22.7 *The Calculations dialog box*

Let's combine a couple of alpha channels to see how the Calculations command works.

1. From the Ch22 folder on the CD, open the document Cowpoke.psd (Figure 22.8).

2. Look at the Channels palette. Alpha 1 is a channel of the circle surrounding the cowboy; Alpha 2 is the outline of the cowboy. You are going to combine the two channels into a third.

3. Choose Image → Calculations. Enter the following:

Source 1	Cowpoke.psd
Channel	Alpha 1
Source 2	Cowpoke.psd
Channel	Alpha 2
Blending	Difference
Result	New Channel

Figure 22.8 *The cowpoke image and its Channels palette*

4. Click OK and Alpha 3 is created that combines the Alpha 1 and Alpha 2 (see Figure 22.9).

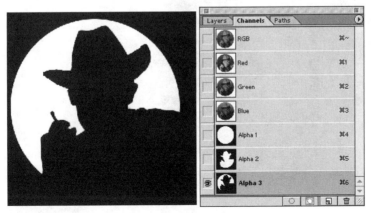

Figure 22.9 *The new combined alpha channel*

5. You can also use the Calculations command to blend channels from two source documents and create a new grayscale document. Open the file Cowboy_Sky.psd from the Ch22 folder on the CD. Then click Cowpoke.psd to reactivate it.

6. Choose Image ➜ Calculations. Enter the following:

Source 1	Cowpoke.psd
Channel	Gray
Source 2	Cowboy_Sky.psd
Channel	Blue
Blending	Darken
Result	New Document

7. Click OK. A new document is created combining the composite gray channel of the Cowpoke.psd document and the blue channel from the Cowboy_Sky.psd document (see Figure 22.10).

Figure 22.10 *This image was created by using Calculations to combine the Gray channel of the cowpoke with the Blue channel of the cowboy sky.*

Calculations are complex, to say the least, and as always there are several work-arounds that perform the same operations. Mastering Calculations, however, gives you the skills you need to quickly combine channels, and that can extend your selection making capabilities.

Up Next

The features covered in Chapter 22 are helpful in a variety of ways. When working on layers, you can enhance colors by applying blending modes to duplicate layers in the stack. And you can eliminate unwanted pixels with the exclusion sliders. The channel operations are more indirect, but you'll find them useful when combining images and alpha channels.

Up to now, most of the printing capabilities we've been talking about have to do with process inks, cyan, magenta, yellow, and black. Next, in Chapter 23, we'll look at Duotones and spot color; two operations that enable you to apply custom inks to your image. Then, in a Hands-On session, you'll get a chance to convert a black and white photograph into a Duotone and apply a rich spot color to a logo.

Duotones and
Spot Color

PHOTOSHOP

Chapter 23

The majority of images printed from Photoshop are printed in process colors. Printing presses use cyan, magenta, yellow, and black ink spread on individual metal or plastic plates and impressed onto paper to print color images. Ink-jet printers deposit ink from cartridges containing the CMYK colors. From time to time, the occasion arises when you need to create images using custom color ink systems, either for a specific look or for reasons of economy. Photoshop has two functions that are designed to prepare images for printing using custom colors: Duotones and spot colors. These systems depend on color information found in the Channels palette.

In this chapter, you'll discover:

- The nature of Duotones

- How to make Duotones, Tritones, and Quadtones work

- How to create spot color channels

- Printing Duotones and spot color

Why Use Duotones?

Duotones are a source of disagreement around the printing presses. Some press professionals call them a waste of two-color press time. Others claim they can turn otherwise lackluster halftones into subtle works of art. Duotones, and their siblings Tritones and Quadtones, print Grayscale images using two (or three or four) separate inks. Usually, the inks are colored, but occasionally a Duotone will surface using two black plates. Proponents claim two blacks can attain a richness and depth out of reach of the simple halftone; critics say it's just one black plate too many. They may never reach an agreement.

No such controversy exists over the use of spot colors. Pressroom shelves are lined with tubs of premixed and mixable inks, and now with six- and eight-color presses becoming more and more common, combinations of four-color process, spot colors, and/or varnishes are being used with greater frequency. Photoshop's spot color channels provide a tool for creating and separating spot colors for printing.

Both Duotones and spot color involve the concept of putting ink on paper from the outset, so even though they're dealt with by Photoshop in entirely different ways, they appear together in this chapter. And you'll have a chance to try them out for yourself. Then you can decide where you come down on the Duotone question.

What Are Duotones?

When a Grayscale digital image is converted to a halftone and printed with black ink on paper, the shades of gray that you created on your computer are represented by the size and concentration of dots. The black ink is still black, no matter what size you make the dot. It just can't quite represent all 256 levels of gray found in the Grayscale image.

Duotones can help you achieve a wider tonal range in a Grayscale image by using more than one shade of ink to fill in the gaps. You can enhance the detail and texture in an image. If you're printing a two-color book with halftones, adding the second color to the photographs can add an elegant touch. Duotones using a dark and a metallic ink can have an opaque, antique quality, while lighter pastel shades might approximate a hand-tinted look, as you can see in the saguaro cactus images included in the color section.

Duotones present one potential problem. Because several inks are being superimposed on one another, it is possible to generate too much ink. If the distribution of ink is not dealt with properly, it could saturate the paper and fill in the spaces between the fine halftone dots. That's why Photoshop's Duotone mode features a Curves palette right in its dialog box, so that you can adjust each ink level individually... but we'll get to that in a minute.

Working with Duotones

Suppose you start with a color photo you've scanned. Open your RGB image, then look in the Image ➔ Mode submenu. You'll see that the Duotone mode is grayed out, unavailable as an option. In order to convert an image to Duotone mode, you have to convert to Grayscale first. Wait! Before you do that, it's best to first correct tonal and color values using Levels, Curves, or the other adjustment features discussed in Chapter 16. Get that image exactly where you want it before you reduce it down to a single channel. In fact, take a look at your color channels individually. You may find something there you like (the Green channel in an RGB image may contain a convincing microcosm of the whole, for example). Even better, use the Channel Mixer to get the perfect Grayscale image. Once you're happy with it, go ahead and choose Image ➔ Mode ➔ Grayscale. Then if you want to do any further tweaking, do it while you're in Grayscale mode. *Then* choose Image ➔ Mode ➔ Duotone (Figure 23.1). Now you're in Duotone country.

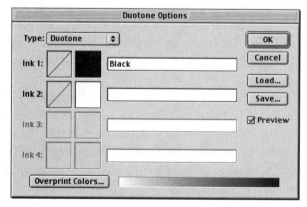

Figure 23.1 *Correct the tonality and color values* before *accessing the Duotone Options dialog box.*

The Duotone Options dialog box lets you choose a Type—that is, the number of inks you want to use, up to four. Monotones are just colored halftones, Duotones use two inks, Tritones three, and Quadtones... you guessed it. You can set curves and choose colors individually for each ink. Click the color box to bring up the Color Picker. If you want to use printing ink colors, click Custom. There you can view a wide variety of swatch books to choose your ink colors. (See the section in Chapter 10 on custom colors.) Check with your printer for the availability of inks.

If you plan to import the Duotone into a page-layout document, keep an eye on the names of your inks. Make sure the Duotone ink has the exact same name as the one in the other application's color dialog. You can always come back to the Duotone Options dialog and change the ink name if you have to.

By default, the Ink 1 color is designated Black. If you choose any Type other than Monotone, the new ink color(s) are empty (white) by default.

To choose an ink, click the swatch and the Custom Colors dialog box is displayed. The default book is PANTONE Coated (as in Figure 23.2). Choose an ink color from the list, and click OK. Define additional inks in the same way. The color bar at the bottom of the dialog box displays the range from dark to light of the color mix you've specified. The image window also has a live preview. When you specify colors, the image displays the changes on screen.

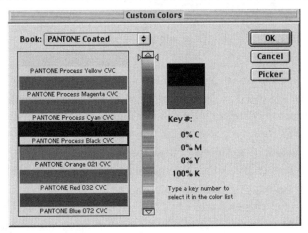

Figure 23.2 *Choosing the color of your Duotone ink*

When you define ink colors for Duotones, Tritones, and Quadtones, make sure your darkest ink is at the top and lightest at the bottom. When Duotone images print, the inks go down in the order they appear in the dialog box. Allowing the darker inks to print first provides for a uniform color range from shadows to highlights.

Duotone Curves

Duotone curves let you control the density of each ink in the highlights, midtones, and shadows. Click any of the curve thumbnails to display the corresponding Duotone Curve dialog box (Figure 23.3). When you first convert a file to Duotone mode, the curves are straight by default.

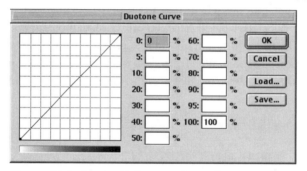

Figure 23.3 *Setting the curve of your Duotone ink*

Here you can adjust the curve to define ink coverage for that color. If you leave the curve straight, Photoshop will distribute the ink evenly across the entire tonal range of the image. If all of your curves on a Duotone are straight, you'll end up with a dark, muddy mess. It's best to apply colors to suit the needs of the image in question; generally, you'll want the darkest inks densest in the shadows, somewhat lighter inks in the midtones, and the lightest colors enhancing the highlights.

You have two ways of adjusting the curves using the Duotone Curve dialog. Either input numeric settings for ink percentages by typing in the boxes provided, or drag inside the curve's grid to adjust the curve directly. Like the Curves dialog box we encountered in Chapter 16, the grid's horizontal axis expresses the gradations from white (highlights) on the left to black (shadows) on the right. The vertical axis maps ink density, increasing as you go up. Click anywhere on the line and drag up or down to add or subtract ink in that part of the curve. As you adjust the curve, the numbers change accordingly in the percentage boxes. Inversely, when you type numbers in the percentage boxes, the curve adjusts itself to match. The lower-left of the grid box controls the highlights; diagonally across at the upper-right is where the shadows are adjusted. The first curve shown in Figure 23.4 retains color in the shadow areas, while reducing the amount of ink to be printed in the highlights. The second curve concentrates ink in the midtones and highlights, while the third presents just the highlights. The final illustration is the Duotone Options box showing all three curves.

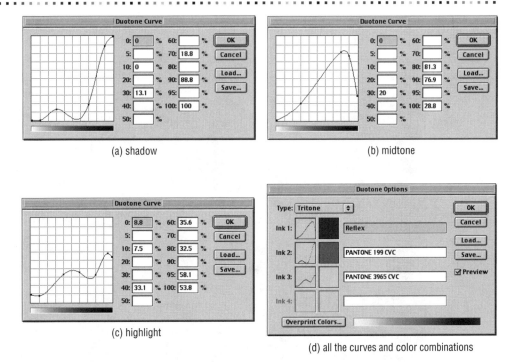

(a) shadow

(b) midtone

(c) highlight

(d) all the curves and color combinations

Figure 23.4 *Duotone curves for (a) shadow, (b) midtone, and (c) highlight inks. Figure (d) shows all the curves and color combinations.*

You can save the curves you create in the Duotone Curve dialog by clicking the Save button; the program prompts you to choose where to save the curve file. Likewise, you can load curves you've already created by clicking Load and opening an earlier adjustment. The "master" Save and Load buttons in the Duotone Options dialog will allow you to save or load a *complete set* of curves, inks, and overprint colors.

Photoshop provides several sample settings for Duotones, Tritones, and Quad-tones that you can use to see how these options work. Use them as a starting point for experimentation and adventure.

Let's load some Duotone curves.

1. Open the file in the Ch23 folder on the CD, Cactus_Forest.psd (Figure 23.5).

2. Choose Image ➜ Mode ➜ Duotone. For type, choose Duotone. The Duotone Options dialog box is displayed.

3. Click Load. These curves are located in the Photoshop 6.0\Presets\Duotones\Duotones\PANTONE Duotones folder; choose one of the Duotone presets in that folder. Click Load to load the curves and OK to apply the settings.

Figure 23.5 *The Cactus Forest image*

4. If you wish to make changes to your settings, try different inks, or tweak the curves, just go back to Image ➜ Mode ➜ Duotone, and your previous settings reappear with the Duotone Options dialog. Make the changes you desire and click OK.

Multichannel Mode

If you look in the Channels palette of a Duotone image, you see only one channel, labeled Duotone, Tritone, or Quadtone. Where are the channels representing the inks you've chosen? Photoshop creates Duotones by applying the various curves you've defined to an image composed of one channel. If you care to view the channels independently, you have to convert the image to Multichannel mode (Image ➜ Mode ➜ Multichannel). In Figure 23.6, you see the Channels palette with the Tritone channel and, next to it, the *same image's* palette with the three Tritone channels listed separately in order, according to the ink color names. The image has been split into three channels. There is no composite view of a Duotone, Tritone, or Quadtone in Multichannel mode. If you make any changes or adjustments in this mode, you will not be able to return to Duotone mode. You can print directly from Multichannel, and you will get two, three, or four separated prints called *color separations,* one for each color.

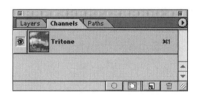
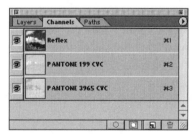

Figure 23.6 *The Channels palette of the same Tritone image, in (left) Duotone mode and (right) Multichannel mode*

Overprint Colors

Overprint colors are two or more unscreened inks that are printed one on top of the other. The order of how the inks are laid down can affect the final outcome. The Overprint Colors dialog box displays a chart that shows how different pairs of colors (or groups of three or four) will blend when printing. If you click any of the color swatches, the Color Picker comes up and allows you to replace the color. The new overprint colors will be applied to the image but only affect how the image appears on screen. These settings don't affect how the image prints; use Overprint Colors to help you *predict* how colors will look when printed. Let me remind you that you should only use this function on a calibrated monitor.

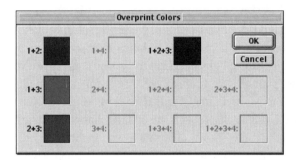

Using Spot Color Channels

Spot colors are additional inks used in a print job other than black or process colors. Each spot color requires a plate of its own, and the inks can be overprinted on top of the Grayscale or CMYK image or independently. Spot colors are printed in the order in which they appear in the Channels palette, from top to bottom. Spot color channels are totally independent of the color mode of the image; that is, the spot colors are not blended with the other channels in a Grayscale, RGB, or CMYK image. Spot color channels are also independent of layers—you cannot apply spot colors to individual layers.

Here are some of the likes and dislikes of spot color:

- Spot color channels are like layers in that they are independent of and separate from the Background image.

- Spot color channels are unlike layers in that they cannot be merged with the rest of the image and still remain as spot colors.

- Spot color channels are like color channels in that they exist only in the Channels palette.

- Spot color channels are unlike color channels because, by default, they print separately from the rest of the image.

Creating Spot Colors

1. Open the image Musashi.psd (Figure 23.7) in the Ch23 folder on the CD. Save it to your disk.

Figure 23.7 *The Musashi samurai image*

2. Choose Window ➜ Show Channels to display the Channels palette. Load Alpha 1, which is a selection of the samurai's pants, by dragging it to the Load Channel icon.

3. From the Channels palette pull-down menu, choose New Spot Channel. Your selection fills with red the default spot color and becomes the new spot color channel, and the New Spot Channel dialog box appears.

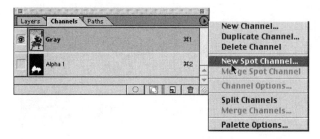

4. By default, the spot color is red. Click the color swatch to bring up the Color Picker. Choose Custom Colors and choose a premixed ink like a PANTONE ink. The spot color channel will be named automatically with the name of the selected ink.

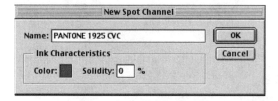

5. Choose your Solidity (I've included a sidebar on the difference between solidity and opacity) and click OK.

When your new spot color channel has been created, it resides in the Channels palette just below the separate channels of the color mode you're working in (see Figure 23.8). In a Grayscale image, Spot Color 1 follows Black; in an RGB image, Spot follows Blue. You cannot move spot color channels up above the regular color mode channels, unless you convert your image to the Multichannel mode. Likewise, alpha channels follow spot color channels in the pecking order. You can rearrange the order of your spot color channels all you want, but you can't put alpha channels above them unless you are in Multichannel mode. As with Duotone mode, spot color channels print in the order in which they're listed in the Channels palette.

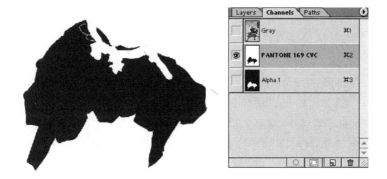

Figure 23.8 *The spot color channel of the samurai's pants*

Solidity vs. Opacity

Entering a value in the Solidity box lets you control the viewing density of the spot color channel. The Solidity control is for visual reference only. It's there to help you visualize what an ink may look like when printed in a tint value from 0% to 100%. Solidity is not to be confused with Opacity. Opacity effects the amount of color applied to an image with the paint tools, or the transparency of an image on a layer. Solidity is a visual reference, and does not affect the image unless you merge the spot colors with the other color channels. It then applies the tint value of the color to the image and is no longer a spot color.

If you want the spot color ink to print as a tint, you have to create a gray (instead of black) selection in the spot color channel. Spot color inks always print full intensity unless your selection mask in the spot color channel itself contains a gradation or tint. (See the samurai figure in the color section to view the spot color channel and how it will produce a solid ink color over the image when printed.) Printing inks are transparent. When printed over the image, the spot color will mix with colors underneath it.

Viewing Spot Colors

If you're viewing the image in the composite view, and your spot channel is active, the foreground color becomes the channel's spot color, with white as the background color. The foreground color swatch, however, will appear black, white, or a shade of gray depending on the brightness of the selected color. If you're viewing the spot color channel independently of the composite, the foreground color is black and the background color white. You can edit a spot color channel exactly as you would an alpha channel: use painting tools, selection tools, filters, type, placed artwork, etc., to impose the image you want to print.

Special rules apply to type in spot color channels. In fact, in Photoshop 6, type behaves in spot channels the way that type used to, before Adobe made it editable. In other words, when you apply type to a spot color channel, the text shows up as a selection outline on the channel; you then fill it. Once you deselect it, it's no longer editable except in the ways you would normally edit a selection.

Knocking Out Spot Colors

If you don't want your spot color to overprint another spot color or a part of the underlying image, you can create a *knockout*. A knockout prevents ink from printing on part of an image so the spot color can print directly on the paper. Thus, no blending of ink colors occurs in the desired area. Activate the channel that you want to knock out. Choose Select ➜ Load Selection, and load the spot color channel in question. Choose Select ➜ Modify ➜ Expand (or Contract) to adjust the fit of the knockout. (See the Hands-On section that follows this chapter to try this.) You can create a trap at this point by slightly enlarging or reducing the selection outline to allow a small outline of both inks to overprint. This way, no white space appears between two colors when the job is printed. Once you have your selection adjusted to fit, press Delete (Mac) or Backspace (Win) to eliminate the underlying image. Now the spot color can print unimpeded.

You can also select a portion of the image, copy it, and then attribute a spot color to it using its tonal qualities. We will use this technique on the Musashi image to create a different spot color affect. Here's how to create a spot color from a tonal area on the image with a knock out:

1. Open the image Musashi.psd again in the Ch23 folder on the CD. Save it to your disk as Musashi_knockout.psd.

2. Choose Window ➜ Show Channels to display the Channels palette. Load Alpha 1 by dragging it to the Load Channel icon, to select the bottom portion of the samurai's costume.

3. Choose Edit ➜ Copy to copy the image to the clipboard.

4. From the Channels pull-down menu, choose New Spot Channel Your selection fills with red and becomes the new spot color channel.

5. Click the color swatch in the dialog box and choose a PANTONE color. Click OK.

6. Target the spot color channel, hold down the Command (Mac) or Ctrl (Win) key, and click the channel to load it as a selection.

7. Choose Edit ➜ Paste Into to paste the image into the selection (Figure 23.9).

8. Be sure white is the background color. Target the RGB channel. Press the Delete or Backspace key to create the knockout. Your image should look like the illustration in the color section.

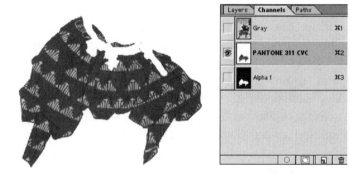

Figure 23.9 *The spot color channel after pasting the image into the selection*

Other Uses for Spot Color

Spot color channels can be used to create varnish plates and dies as well as color plates. Varnishes are simply unpigmented inks. Apply them to highlight areas of an image or to coat the image with a glossy surface. Dies are shaped forms used to cut paper. Remember those birthday cards that have an oval hole cut that reveals George Washington's face on the dollar concealed within? Die-cutting. Precise shapes can be created by using spot color channels; those shapes can then be printed as negatives, which are then used to create the die.

Printing Duotones and Spot Color

Printing Duotones and spot colors presents its own set of challenges. For one thing, in this book, the Duotones and Tritones were created using two or three custom color inks. But the color sections of the book are printed using four-color process. So the Tritones had to be converted to CMYK before printing. The custom colors convert to their CMYK equivalents, and generally this results in darker, less distinct colors than premixed inks provide.

If you want to import your Duotone into another application, you'll have to save it in EPS format. Only EPS preserves Duotone mode's color information properly. If you save it in another format, the additional curves simply won't be recognized; only Ink 1 ends up printing.

A special problem common to Duotones and spot color jobs is the difficulty in proofing. Most color proofers convert everything to CMYK when printing; custom ink colors simply aren't recognized. If you have Duotones composed of say, black and magenta, things will work out fine. But a proofing device can't recognize, say, PANTONE 185 unless it can read CMYK equivalents. You have to fake it out either by renaming the colors (and then you don't get a true color proof) or by converting to CMYK (same result). This is part of the reason some printers are loath to work with Duotones; they feel as though they're working blind, since no real accurate proof is available to guide them.

The problem is similar but not quite as worrisome with spot colors. When you print a job with spot colors on your printer, a composite is printed, and the spot color channels print out separately afterwards. Once again, proofs can be created, but only by compromising the integrity of the color channels. When you choose Merge Spot Channel from the Channels palette menu, the spot color is converted to your image's color mode and blended in with the other channels. The spot color channel is then eliminated. You end up with a composite image incorporating your spot colors. It's important to have your spot colors in the right order before making this step. Different Solidity settings can produce different results when merging. Layered images flatten during this procedure. And once again, you run the risk of altering the color matching, since the CMYK inks reproduce colors differently than premixed inks will. If you want a composite CMYK proof of your spot color image, always duplicate the file first. Print the duplicate image to your ink-jet or other proofing device and print the separations to an imagesetter or laser printer from the spot color original.

If you plan on importing an image with spot color channels into another application, you must save it in Photoshop's DCS 2.0 format. This is the only format that will allow other applications to recognize the individual spot color channels.

Up Next

Duotones and spot colors extend your printing capabilities because you can configure documents to print custom colors such as PANTONE. You can convert your ordinary black and white photos into richly toned images that have more atmosphere and depth. Spot color images that print in just a few colors of ink can be prepared in Photoshop with the necessary traps to assure a quality print job.

Remember the reservations and caveats of the press pros, then go ahead and do Duotones anyway. They can have a cool, subtle beauty unattainable by other means. You'll see how to get there as you try out the following Hands-On project.

Hands-On
Duotones and
Spot Color

We will convert this image of a rock at Rancho Linda Vista in Oracle, Arizona, by photographer Boyd Nicholl into a Tritone to enhance the drama of the image, create depth, and bring out the details. Then we will place the Rancho Linda Vista logo on the image as a spot color. The image will be used as a postcard.

Getting Started

Hide your preferences file before beginning this Hands-On exercise, then restart Photoshop to create a clean version. The "Photoshop's Settings" section in Chapter 5 details how to temporarily reset your preferences to Photoshop's defaults. You can restore your customized, personal settings when you're done.

Once you have launched Photoshop with default preferences, here's how to begin the Hands-On project:

1. Insert the *Mastering Photoshop 6* CD in the CD-ROM drive.

2. Choose File ➔ Open; select and open the image in the Ch23 folder on the CD, Ranch_Rock_start.psd (Figure 1).

Full-color versions of the beginning and final stages of this project are included in the color section. To follow along on screen, you can preview the finished image by opening Ranch_Rock_end.tif *from the* Ch23 *folder on the CD.*

Figure 1 *Ranch Rock*

3. Save the file to your disk as `Storm_Rock_tri.psd`.

4. Choose Image ➔ Mode ➔ Duotone.

5. From Type, choose Tritone.

6. Click the top color swatch. The Color Picker appears. Choose Custom Color. As a Book, choose PANTONE Coated. Type **2727** on the keypad or scroll down the list and find Pantone 2727 CVC (it's a rich blue color).

7. Click the second color swatch. On your keypad, enter **349** to designate PANTONE 349 CVC, a dark green for the midtones. Click OK.

8. Click the third color swatch. Click in the middle of the slider. Move the slider until you find PANTONE 459 CVC. Click OK.

Adjusting Curves

Now we'll adjust the curves of each color to precisely control the distribution of ink in the highlights, midtones, and shadows.

1. Start with the shadows: Click the curves swatch of PANTONE 2727 to display the Duotone Curves dialog box. The values in the next few steps are shown in Figure 2; clear any presets from fields that aren't listed here.

2. In the Percentage fields, enter the following values:

Field	Value
0%	Enter 6.9% to reduce the size of the halftone dot and, hence, the density of color in the highlight areas.
20%	Enter 8.8% to reduce the size of the halftone dot in the midtone areas.
70%	Enter 81.3% to assure that no area on the image is totally covered with ink.
100%	Set to 95% to insure that that there is not too much ink coverage in the shadows.

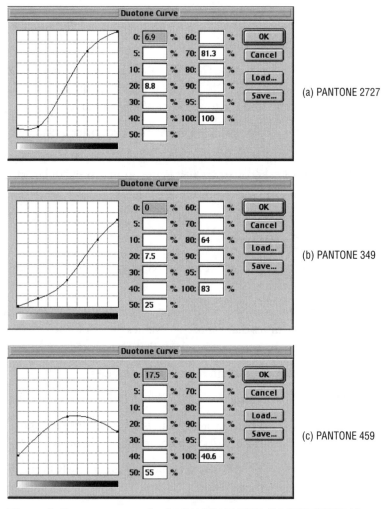

Figure 2 *Duotone curves for (a) PANTONE 2727, (b) PANTONE 349, and (c) PANTONE 459*

3. For PANTONE 349, enter the following values to distribute the color in the midtone range:

Field	Value
0%	Enter 0 to distribute the ink into the lightest areas of the image.

Field	Value
20%	Enter 7.5% to reduce the size of midtone dot in the highlight areas and produce a subtle tint.
50%	Enter 25% to reduce the distribution of green in the midtones.
80%	Enter 64% to reduce the amount of green in the lighter shadow areas.
100%	Enter 83% to reduce the amount of green in the darker shadow areas like the sky.

4. For PANTONE 459, enter the following values. When you click OK, your Duotone Options dialog should look like Figure 3.

Field	Value
0%	Enter 17.5% to assure that the lightest areas of the image contain a moderate amount of the lightest color, to provide a subtle warm tint to the grassy areas and the rock.
50%	Enter 55% to increase the amount of the light colored ink in the midtones, to provide a warm tint to the grassy areas.
100%	Enter 40.6% to ensure that there will be no coverage of this ink in the shadow areas.

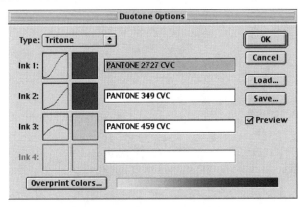

Figure 3 *After setting the Duotone curves*

Adding the Logo

The logo is on an independent layer. We want to add a little spot of color to the image to enhance the logo for an elegant touch.

1. Choose Window ➜ Show Layers.

2. Make the RLV Logo layer visible. Target it. Notice that it is hard to see because it is displayed against the grassy area of the desert.

3. Choose the Magic Wand tool and click outside of the diamond shape to select the transparent pixels surrounding the logo. Choose Select ➜ Inverse to select the logo.

We now need to create a type of trap called a *choke*. The spot color needs to be contracted slightly so that it will not overprint onto the desert grasses if the press should wobble during printing. If the *edge* of the spot color aligns on the *middle* of black outline of the logo, that will prevent this from happening. The selection for spot color, therefore, needs to be slightly smaller than the diamond-shaped outline.

4. Choose Select ➜ Modify ➜ Contract. Enter 2 pixels.

5. Target the Background in the Layers palette. Be sure white is the background color. Press the Delete/Backspace key to create the choked knockout (see Figure 4).

Figure 4 *The knockout*

6. With the selection still active, reveal the Channels palette. The Tritone channel is the only channel in the palette.

7. From the palette pull-down menu, choose New Spot Channel. Set the Solidity to 0 so you can see how the spot color will print.

 Since printing inks are transparent, the combination of the logo's Duotone colors, PANTONE 2727 and 349, produces a very dark color. When the lighter color of the diamond, PANTONE 1635, is overprinted, the logo will become even darker. On the white knockout, however, PANTONE 1635 will appear at full strength.

8. Click the color swatch to reveal the custom color list. Choose a PANTONE color to overlay on top of the logo (I used PANTONE 1635).

9 Click OK in both dialog boxes. See Figure 5, and its version in the color section, to view the final Duotone with the spot color.

Figure 5 *The Duotone with the spot color logo*

Converting to Multichannel

In order to be able to see the content of the separated channels, it's a good idea to convert the image to Multichannel mode. You can look at the channels to get a better understanding of how Duotones and spot colors distribute ink when they are printed.

1. Choose Image ➜ Mode ➜ Multichannel. In the Channels palette, the three Tritone channels are separated and named for their PANTONE colors, and the one spot color channel is at the bottom of the list.

2. Go to Edit ➜ Preferences ➜ Color Channels In Color.

3. Click the eye icon of each channel, one at a time, to observe the densities of each color as it will be printed on paper.

4. If you have a printer, print the document and see how the colors are separated.

Up Next

In Chapter 24 (which begins Part IV), we leave the ink, paper, solvents, and presses behind us and enter the cutting-edge universe of World Wide Web publishing. Photoshop is the ultimate tool for laying out your Web pages, with its dynamic interface, powerful editing tools, and keen ability to move and shuffle items on layers. Photoshop's upgrades have steadily included more and more Web tools with each version. Photoshop 6 and its bundle buddy, Adobe ImageReady 3, make an awesome Web authoring duet.

Part IV

Photoshop 6 for the Web

Designing for the Web
with Photoshop

PHOTOSHOP

Chapter 24

The Web is the world's most recent and dynamic publishing phenomenon. It gives you instant access to an enormous amount of information and entertainment. The Web is like having at your fingertips a several-million-volume encyclopedia that is revised hourly with the latest information. It is also the world's largest department store, stock exchange, post office, and sex shop.

In addition to being able to access information, you can also publish your ideas and images instantaneously on the Web. What a boon to the Immediate Gratification Generation! When designing a Web site, you must rely on software that provides the power to produce quality images that make your Web site visually strong. As I'm sure you've realized by now, Adobe Photoshop is the premier software for manipulating images. With built-in tools, operations, and filters, you can create amazing one-of-a-kind images that transform your site from the ho-hum to the all-out impressive.

In this chapter, we'll talk about:

- Designing page elements

- Making a margin style and wallpaper background

- Creating a typographic heading

- Optimizing images

- Using Photoshop as a layout tool

- Using layers to set up an animation

Why Design Web Sites with Photoshop?

Photoshop supports numerous image formats, which makes it ideal for importing scans and graphics from sources such as Photo CDs, digital cameras, and video captures. Once an image has been edited, it can easily be saved or exported to a Web-compatible image format such as JPEG, GIF, or PNG. You can take advantage of the unique characteristics of each format including file size, progressive rendering, transparency, and compression.

Photoshop's user-friendly Layers palette is ideal for separating portions of an image so that they can remain editable throughout the creative process. This empowers designers to lay out entire Web sites within Photoshop, and then use the elements created on the layers. The original files remain intact and can be modified as necessary. The Layers palette is also quite useful for creating and organizing simple animation sequences. These layer stacks are saved and re-opened in programs like Adobe ImageReady and LiveMotion, that have the capability of generating animated images. (Chapter 25 tells you how to take advantage of ImageReady.)

Designing Page Elements in Photoshop

Photoshop's unique interface make it the software of choice for laying out and developing Web elements. I'm going to demonstrate how to build a variety of popular Web graphics. Follow the exercises in this chapter to become accustomed to designing for the Web using Photoshop.

Creating a Margin-Style Background

A margin-style background is a common visual element that helps unify the design of a simple Web page. It serves as a visual compass because it fills the entire vertical depth of the document no matter how tall it may be. Furthermore, a margin can help establish the ordered division of information by separating the background into vertical blocks. It is also a perfect way to infuse the page with interest and character by adding a splash of color or texture.

A margin background is simply a pattern that is configured so that the image repeats vertically but not horizontally. Because all Web backgrounds tile from the left topmost corner into the available space, we have to ensure that we create a strip long enough that the tile doesn't appear to repeat along the horizontal axis.

To create a margin-style background:

1. Choose File ➜ New.

2. Name the file `Margin`.

 Don't worry about the `gif`, `jpg`, *or* `png` *extension at this point. Because the default Saving Files preferences is Append File Extension, Photoshop will automatically add the extension when the document is saved.*

3. Enter a width of **1070** pixels and a height of **36** pixels (Figure 24.1).

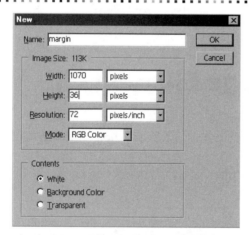

Figure 24.1 *The New Document dialog box*

4. Set the resolution to 72 pixels per inch.

5. Choose RGB Color for the Mode.

6. Under Contents, choose White.

7. Click OK.

Now, fill a portion of the file with color. To do so:

1. Click the Rectangular Marquee tool to display its settings in the Options bar.

2. Choose Fixed Size from the Style pull-down menu; enter **72 px** (1 inch) for the width and **36 px** (0.5 inch) for the height.

3. Click the image in the top-left corner of the document.

The width of 1070 pixels in this image ensures that the image will not repeat at resolutions of 1024×768 or lower. However, at higher resolutions, you run the risk of having the image repeat. For this reason, some Web designers prefer to set their margin background widths to 1280.

4. Click a dark color of your choice, from the Web-safe palette or Color Picker, as a foreground color.

5. Press Option+Delete (Mac) or Alt+Backspace (Win) to fill the marquee with the foreground color.

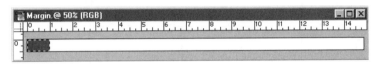

6. Choose Select ➜ Inverse to select the portion of the image that was not colored.

Choosing a Web-Compatible Color

There are three ways to choose colors that are Web-compatible:

- Choose Window ➜ Show Swatches. From the pull-down menu in the upper-right corner of the palette, choose Web Hues.aco, Web Safe Colors.aco, or Web Spectrum.aco. Any of these color palettes display the 216 Web-safe colors; the palettes consist of the same colors organized differently. If you hover your cursor over any color in the palette, its hexadecimal name will be displayed.

- You can click the foreground color in the Tool palette to reveal the Color Picker and check the Only Web Colors box. Move the slider on the color bar to scroll through the hexadecimal hues and then pick a color from the color field.

- Choose Window ➜ Show Colors. From the pull-down menu in the upper-right corner of the Color palette, choose Web Color Sliders. Drag the sliders to pick a color.

7. Choose a light color from the Web-safe palette and fill the selection.

8. To add a design to the left margin, choose Select ➜ Inverse to reselect the left portion of the image.

9. Choose the Paintbrush tool, choose a brush from the Options bar, and use a different color to paint a design within the selection. Experiment with several colors and brushes until you are satisfied with the results.

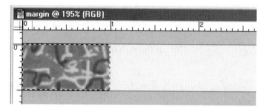

You can now choose what to do with the file:

- Save the file in native Photoshop format, layers intact, for future use or modification in Photoshop (always recommended!) or to import into ImageReady for processing.

- Save the file to a Web format (see "The Save For Web Feature" later in the chapter).

Once the file is optimized, you can load it into your HTML editor as part of your Web page. When the image is loaded as a background, it will repeat vertically as a pattern and appear to be a continuous design down the depth of the page (see Figure 24.2).

Creating a Seamless Background Pattern

An alternative to the margin-style background is a background repeating tile, also referred to as *wallpaper*. In most cases, you will want the pattern to be subtle so as to not compete with the information that floats on top of it.

Wallpaper patterns were the first wave of background graphics. You've probably seen lots of them, in all kinds of styles. They're problematic for a number of reasons, including the fact that if they're too dark or busy, they'll interfere with readability. They're also demanding on the designer—it takes a bit of skill if you're making them completely by hand.

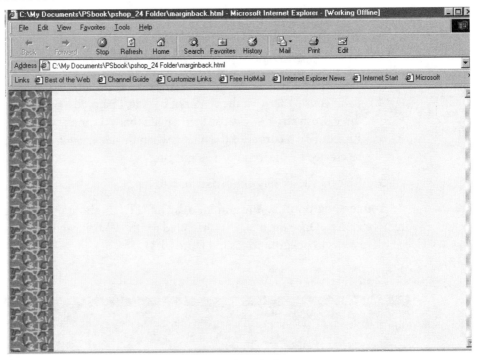

Figure 24.2 *The margin-style background in the browser*

However, if you design them properly, seamless backgrounds can create an extremely attractive look for your site. The following are some general guidelines to use when creating tiles:

- Individual tiles should be at least 50 pixels by 50 pixels.

- Work to ensure that tiles appear seamless.

- Avoid repeating a small tile with a single image.

- Always ensure that you do *not* interlace background graphics.

Follow along as I create a tile using Photoshop 6.

1. Create a new file (File ➔ New, or Cmd/Ctrl+N). Name the file Seamlessback. I'm making my image 50 pixels by 50 pixels, RGB, 72 pixels per inch. I set my background to white.

2. Now select any one of the painting tools. You can choose to use a brush, create geometric shapes—whatever you'd like to try. For this example, I chose the brush with a soft setting.

3. Now choose a color. Since I'm going to create a floral wallpaper pattern, I selected yellow.

4. Paint your pattern. In the center of my tile, I painted a flower by simply using three brush strokes Because I anticipate that this image will tile, I put a partial stroke in each corner of the tile, so when the tiles match up, a small flower will be created by the four corners meeting.

5. Save the file as `Seamless.psd` for later use.

You can now optimize the graphic as a GIF (I'll talk about optimizing a little later in this chapter). Once the image is formatted for the Web, it can be placed into an HTML page as a background (as in Figure 24.3).

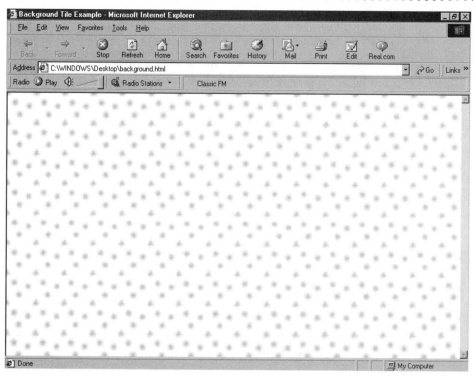

Figure 24.3 *The tile background in a Web page*

Creating a Typographic Header

Photoshop's Type tool includes features that facilitate the creation of sophisticated type-based graphics. Features include:

- Fully editable character-based type

- A type interface that allows for the selection, editing, colorization, and manual repositioning of type directly on the image

- Vertical text generation

- Text warping

- Layer Style operations that enables you to jazz up your text with cool graphic enhancements

In this exercise, you'll create a header using the Type tool.

1. Choose File ➜ New. Name the file Header.

2. Enter a width of **400** pixels and a height of **100** pixels. Set the resolution to **72** pixels per inch. Choose RGB Color for the Mode. Since this text will be centered on a white background on the Web page, choose White for Contents.

3. Click OK.

4. Now, you'll add the type. Choose the Type tool. The Options bar offers the available type options.

5. Choose a color (I chose green), a type size (I chose 100 pt), and a font (I used Fritz Quadrada).

6. Type the words **CyberBeetle**.

There are two ways set color for type. You can set the foreground color in the Color Picker, Color palette, or Swatches palette before launching the Type tool, or click the color swatch in the Options bar either before or after the type has been generated.

7. With the Type layer targeted, choose Layer ➔ Layer Style ➔ Drop Shadow.

8. Use the Drop Shadow dialog to configure the drop shadow.

9. I also used an Inner Shadow. You can apply whatever layer effects you like. Because the text will be rasterized before it is placed on a Web page, it will appear just the way you create it.

You can now save the file in native Photoshop format so that you'll have it for later modification. You'll want to optimize using the techniques discussed later in this chapter for use in a Web page.

Optimizing Your Images

When it comes to optimizing Web graphics with Photoshop, you have several options. First, you can use the built-in Save For Web feature, which many Web designers opt to do. Or you can choose to optimize in ImageReady (covered in Chapter 25), which also contains many similar features to the Save For Web dialog. Another choice is to optimize by hand, using Indexed color mode. You can no longer export your files as GIF89a, however. That function has been absorbed into the Save For Web feature. You can save as JPEG, CompuServe GIF (GIF86a), and PNG, but ultimately Save For Web gives you the most choices, the best previews, and the best information.

Using the Save For Web feature or employing ImageReady to help you out actually puts some excellent power tools into your hands. Without them, you'll have to rely on testing and experience in order to make the best decisions.

Web File Formats

Images need to be saved in one of several formats in order to be read by browsers. JPEG, PNG, and GIF formats and their variations are briefly described here. Look in Appendix B, "File Formats," for more detailed descriptions.

JPEG (Joint Photographic Experts Group)

JPEG is a lossy compression format. It supports 24-bit color and is use to preserve the tonal variations in photographs. JPEG compresses file size by selectively discarding data. A higher quality setting results in less data being discarded. Low JPEG settings result in blocky areas within the image and a profusion of artifacts. JPEG compression can degrade sharp detail in images and is not recommended for image with type or solid areas of color. See Figure 24.4 (here and in the color section) for a comparison of JPEG settings.

Figure 24.4 *JPEG compression-quality comparisons: (left) Low and (right) Maximum*

Each time you save the file as a JPEG, you discard more data. To avoid progressive deterioration, you should save JPEG files from the original image, not from a previously saved JPEG.

The JPEG Options Dialog Box

If you use the JPEG Options dialog box (File ➜ Save As ➜ JPEG) to save an image, you can specify characteristics of the JPEG.

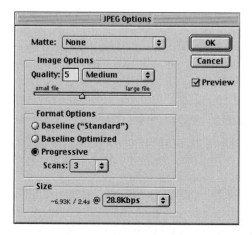

The JPEG format does not support transparency. When you save an image as a JPEG, transparency is replaced by the *matte* color. Use the background color of the Web page as the matte color to simulate transparency. Choose Matte to select a color for the background of an image that is on a transparent layer. The color will fill the areas where there are transparent pixels when the image is seen on the browser. If your image is going to be displayed over a pattern or multiple colors, save it as a transparent GIF.

In the Image Options field, enter a quality value from 0 to 10, or choose Low Medium, High, or Maximum from the pull-down menu.

Choose a format option by clicking the radio buttons.

Baseline ("Standard") displays the image after it has downloaded.

Baseline Optimized displays the image form top to bottom as it downloads.

Progressive allows you to specify 3, 4, or 5 scans. These have the effect of progressively displaying low-resolution versions of the image as it is downloading. Use this option to hold your viewer's attention while the image loads.

PNG-8 and PNG-24 (Portable Network Graphic)

The PNG-8 format is similar to GIF 8-bit color. It uses 256 colors, supports transparency, and is lossless, but is not supported by older browsers. PNG-24 is an excellent format because it combines the attributes of JPEG and GIF in lossless compression. It supports 24-bit color and is fine for saving photographs to the Web because it preserves tonality. Like GIF, PNG-24 preserves the sharp detail found in line art, logos, and type. It also supports transparency and matting.

Another great feature of the PNG-24 format is that it supports *multilevel* transparency, in which you can preserve up to 256 levels of transparency to blend the edges of an image smoothly into a background color. This seems like the dream format doesn't it? The only (minor) drawback is that versions of the major browsers from 1999 and earlier don't support it; it takes a while before the latest browsers are used by the majority of Web users. Take this into consideration when deciding to use the PNG formats.

GIF (Graphics Interchange Format)

The GIF format is used primarily for saving images with solid areas of color and sharp edges, like line art, logos, or illustrations with type. It is also the format for saving animations produced in ImageReady.

Unlike JPEG, the GIF format uses lossless compression. Yet because GIF files are 256 colors or fewer, optimizing an original 24-bit image as an 8-bit GIF can degrade the image. You can create lossy GIFs, which produce much smaller files but sometimes produce artifacts similar to those found in JPEG images. You can control the number of colors in a GIF image and adjust the dithering options to simulate the effect of blending. There are two ways to save a file as a GIF. Choose File ➜ Save As ➜ Compuserve GIF. The Indexed Color dialog box appears where you can optimize the image. (See "Indexed Color" later in the chapter.) The second method is the Save For Web option.

The Save For Web Feature

With Photoshop version 5.5 came a very special feature that has helped Web designers optimize their graphics with ease: the Save For Web command. Photoshop 6 has improved this powerful operation.

I'm going to describe the Save For Web feature here for your convenience, and also step you through optimization by hand. In Chapter 25, you can read more about ImageReady, which has many of the same features in its File ➜ Save Optimized dialog box.

Figure 24.5 shows the Save For Web dialog box. It behaves very much like a plug-in application, with full features all contained within the dialog box itself.

The Save For Web dialog contains the following tab options:

Original   shows the image in its original state.

Optimized   shows the image with whatever Web optimization features you select.

2-Up   displays the original image next to the optimized image.

4-Up   provides a look at the original image with three possible optimization results.

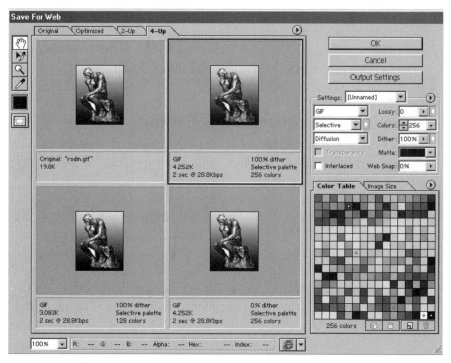

Figure 24.5 *The Save For Web dialog, a "subinterface"*

The Preview menu is accessible from the small arrow on the right of the image window. It has several options, including the ability to simulate what a graphic will look like on different computers. This feature allows you to make cross-platform decisions about your Web graphics. It also displays several different baud rates. Choose one to determine the amount of time your image will take to download. The value is displayed below the image window.

The right side of the Save For Web dialog box offers numerous file format and color controls, including:

Settings   This option provides a pop-up menu of preconfigured settings for saving images as GIFs, JPEGs, and PNGs.

Optimized File Format   This option provides a pop-up menu of possible file formats, including GIF, JPEG, and PNG.

Color Reduction Algorithm   This option is available for GIFs. In most cases, you'll want to select Web.

Dithering Algorithm   Standard dithering options are provided for the GIF format. Work with these to see which gives you the best results.

Lossy   This option allows you to create lossy GIFs. Quality will be sacrificed, but file size can be reduced.

Colors   This pop-up menu allows you to specify the exact number of colors you'd like to include in your image.

Transparency   This option produces transparency if you are saving the image as a GIF image and the image is on a transparent layer.

Dither   If you have a dithering algorithm selected, this slider allows you to precisely control the amount of dithering that occurs in the image.

Web Snap   If you are using a color palette other than the 216 Web-safe colors, this slider allows you to adjust the number of colors that snap to the Web palette.

Interlaced   Select this option if you want your image to be rendered progressively.

Color Table   The color table allows you to see the exact colors being used in the optimized image. Colors with dots in the center are Web-safe colors. The arrow to the right above the color table displays a menu that allows you to select, sort, lock, shift, save, and load colors.

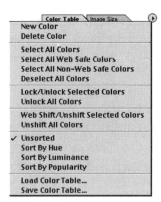

Image Size   This palette allows you to change the physical dimensions of the image you are saving.

The annotations under the image(s) denote the format type, file size, the download time on a selected modem, plus the various characteristics of a selected group of settings. Click the arrow at the top of the tabbed display to choose additional options for the display and annotations.

As it turns out, the images in this chapter so far can be saved as GIFs, because they use few colors. I recommend working with the Save For Web, trying different values to achieve the best results.

When working with the Save For Web dialog, it's good to remember that the variations you apply to an image will not influence your original image. Instead, the image is saved as a new file. You can save your choices by using the Save Settings feature if you like a particular way that a combination of options worked for you.

I like to use the 4-Up option to display as many possible options at once. This way, I can compare settings and results. The goal is to get the perfect balance of good-looking graphics and low file weight.

Now let's go through the by-hand optimization process so you can effectively optimize your graphics to retain their good looks yet weigh little for fast load times. I'll step through the same graphic, once with a solid background and once preserving transparency; however, you can use the general process defined here to optimize your GIF and JPEG images.

Be sure to visit Chapter 25 to learn how to use ImageReady for optimizing graphics.

Indexed Color

Before an image is saved, you can reduce the number of colors and thus its file size by changing its mode from RGB to Indexed color. Converting the file to Indexed color will substantially reduce the number of colors in the document. By reducing the number of colors, you reduce the file size without reducing the image quality. See the practice steps in the next section ("Exporting to GIF") to learn how to convert your image to Indexed.

If the image you're working with naturally lends itself to transparency, you can save the image as a transparent GIF in the Save For Web dialog box. Images containing transparency need to be on layers surrounded by a transparent area. Since Indexed color does not support layers, leave the image in RGB mode until you optimize it in the Save For Web option. You can reduce the number of colors there.

Exporting to GIF

GIF (Graphics Interchange Format) is a common format used to optimize and export graphic files to the Web. We'll save the same image to GIF format using Save For Web, first with an opaque and then with a transparent background.

1. Open the file in the Ch24 folder on the CD, `Beetle.psd`.

2. Choose Image → Mode → Indexed Color. The Indexed Color dialog box appears (Figure 24.6).

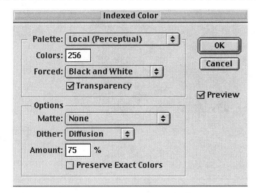

Figure 24.6 *The Indexed Color dialog*

3. For Palette, choose Local (Perceptual).

4. You can change the number in the Color field to reduce the number of colors in the document and the document's file size. Enter 64 in the number field. Observe the preview of the image, whose quality does not change significantly.

5. Dithering can help blend the areas of color together and help the image look less posterized. In this instance, choose Diffusion Dither to see the result.

The file must have the proper extension (`.gif`, `.jpg`, or `.png`, for instance) for an HTML file to read it correctly.

6. Choose File → Save For Web (see Figure 24.7). Click the 4-Up tab. The dialog box displays the original in the upper left and three additional images.

7. Choose GIF from the pop-up menu. Notice that the color table displays the 64 colors that were designated in the Indexed Color dialog box.

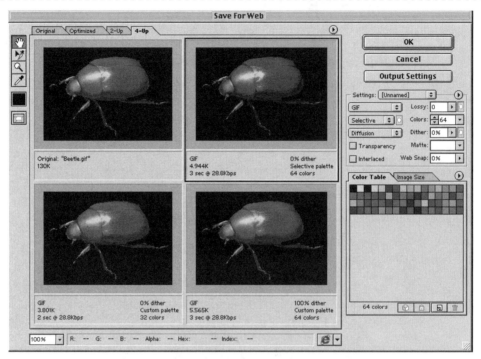

Figure 24.7 *Save For Web with the GIF option selected, displaying the color table*

8. Click the top-right image. You will configure this image first.

9. Under Settings you can choose a preset format; under the Optimized File For-
    mat menu, choose GIF. For Color Reduction Algorithm, choose Adaptive. For
    Color, scroll down the list trying different options to achieve the best possible
    image with the fewest number of colors.

10. Click the other images and try different settings to compare the results.

11. Click the best image and click OK. Name the image and choose a location in
    the Save File dialog box.

Creating a Transparency Mask

The streamlined features in File ➜ Save For Web have replaced the GIF89a Export of
former versions as the method of creating transparent GIF images. In order to create

transparency on an optimized Web image, the image must be on a layer surrounded by transparency. Let's use the same image, but this time we'll knock out its background.

1. Open the file in the Ch24 folder on the CD, `Beetle.psd`.

2. Choose the Magic Wand tool. Set the Tolerance to 16 and click the black background to select it.

3. Choose Select ➜ Inverse to select the beetle.

4. Choose Layer ➜ New ➜ Layer Via Copy, to isolate a copy of the beetle on a separate layer.

5. Click off the eye icon on the Background.

6. Choose File ➜ Save For Web (see Figure 24.8). Choose GIF from the pop-up list. Notice the Transparency option is active and the image is displayed on a checkerboard indicating transparency.

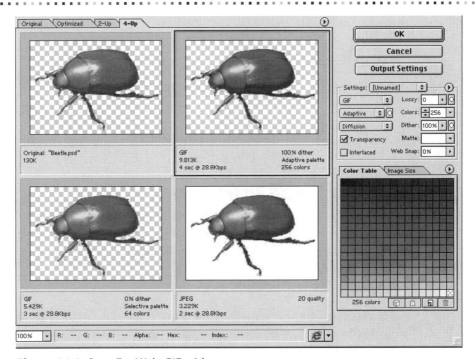

Figure 24.8 *Save For Web, GIF with transparency*

7. Choose 4-Up.

8. Optimize the image as you did the opaque GIF. Try different settings on each image to compare the results.

9. Click the best image and click OK. Name the image and choose a location in the Save File dialog box.

Saving the Image as an HTML File

If you click the Output Settings button in the Save For Web dialog box (Figure 24.9), you see a rather confusing set of commands. These settings are for specifying file-saving preferences for Web images, including HTML documents, background images, and images that have been sliced.

Preference Settings

Select a preference setting from the Settings pop-up list at the top of the dialog box, to specify how the file will be saved:

Setting	Description
Default	Photoshop's default settings
Background	Settings for background tiles
Include GoLive Code	Configures the image for export into Adobe GoLive
Custom	Any variations to the above settings will be saved as custom settings.

Setting File Saving Preferences

You can set four categories of options in the Output Settings dialog box. Choose a category from the pop-up list (HTML, Saving Files, Slice Naming, or Background), or click Prev or Next to switch from one category to the next.

Saving Files

File Naming   Choose items from menus or enter values or test for saving Web images. Items include preferences for saving the document's name, slice name if the image has been cut into slices, rollover state if the image contains a rollover created in ImageReady, file creation date, slice number, punctuation, and file extension. You can reconfigure the filenames for example, using a different abbreviation to name the file.

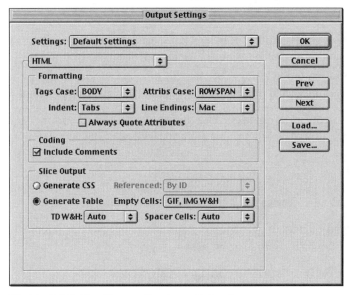

Figure 24.9 *The Output Settings dialog box*

Filename Compatibility   Select one or more options to make the file name compatible with compatible with Windows, Macintosh, and Unix platforms.

Copy Background Image When Saving   Check this box to preserve the background settings of an image that is being used a background.

Put Images In Folder   This option consolidates sliced images into a separate folder (not the folder with the HTML document) when saving.

Include Copyright   Check to include copyright information with the image. You add copyright information for an image in the Image Info dialog box.

HTML

Tags Case   Select the case for HTML tags: uppercase, initial cap, or all lowercase.

Attributes Case   Select the tag attribute case: uppercase, initial cap, second initial cap, or all lowercase.

Indent   Determine a means for code indention: use the authoring software's default tab settings, a specific number of spaces, or no indention.

Line Endings   Select a platform for line ending compatibility: Mac, Windows, or Unix.

Always Quote Attributes   This option places quotation marks around all tag attributes. This option is necessary for compatibility with some early browsers. It is not recommended to always quote attributes. Quotation marks are used when necessary to comply with most browsers, even if this option is deselected.

Coding: Include Comments   Use this option to embed comments into the HTML code.

Slice Output

Generate CSS   creates cascading style sheets for slices.

Referenced   refers to how the cascading style sheet will be referenced in the HTML code: by ID, inline, or by class.

Generate Table   aligns sliced images in an HTML table.

Empty Cells   indicates how to fill empty table data cells (slices without content):

- Select GIF, IMG W&H to use a one-pixel spacer GIF with width and height in the IMG tag.

- Select GIF, TD W&H to use a one-pixel spacer GIF with width and height in the TD tag.

- Select NoWrap, TD W&H codes a non-standard NoWrap attribute on the table data and place width and height in the TD tags.

TD W&H   determines when to place width and height attributes for table data: Always, Never, or Auto (recommended).

Spacer Cells   says when to place a row and a column of empty spacers around the table: Always, Never, or Auto (recommended). Spacer cells align slice boundaries in tables where slice borders do not line up to prevent the table from breaking apart in some browsers.

Slices

You can set naming HTML conventions for slices by entering text or choosing from the menu items. This will configure the code to specific or universal browser compatibility.

Like many of Photoshop's dialog boxes, the Output Settings dialog box lets you save and load settings.

Background

To designate the characteristics of a background, choose the Background preference category. You can specify the following configurations.

- To designate the current image as a background, choose View As Background.

- To a designate background to be used with the current image, click View As Image. Click the Choose button and locate the image to be used.

- To specify a solid color that will be displayed while the image is downloading or through areas of transparency, click the color box and choose a color.

Slicing Images

A group of small images will download more efficiently in a browser than one large image. You *slice* a Web image in order to divide it into smaller files to accelerate download time.

Slicing is the process of cutting an image into pieces, saving the individual parts as image files, and writing an HTML document that reassembles the slices in screen. This is done to increase the efficiency of displaying the images on the browser by decreasing the download time.

Although ImageReady has supported slicing, it is new to Photoshop 6. You can slice the image with the Slice tool in the Tool palette, then save the sliced image in the Save For Web dialog box. The individual slices are saved as separate files, and an HTML document with table code is written that reassembles them on the browser. You can select a slice with the Select Slice tool either from the Tool palette or within the Save For Web dialog box. The slice can be repositioned, or different options can be designated for the slice.

To slice an image, choose the Slice tool from the Tool palette. Click the mouse and drag the cursor where you want the slice.

Slices can only butt up against each other or butt up against the top, bottom, or sides of the image. You cannot cut a slice out of the center of the image unless it is adjacent to other slices.

By default, when you choose the Slice tool, you see that the image is really one slice. The number 1 appears in the upper-left corner of the slice. Each time you create a slice, a new sequential number is assigned it (see Figure 24.10).

When you're satisfied with your slice arrangement, save the image using the Save For Web option. You can select an individual slice by choosing the Slice Select tool. If desired, you can optimize the slices individually or, if no slices are selected, as a group. For more on slicing, see Chapter 25.

Figure 24.10 *An image divided into slices*

Making Thumbnails from Images

Web sites often contain small *thumbnail* images that are used as a link to a page containing a larger version of the image. This is particularly useful in Web sites that display a lot of images, such as art galleries or photography sites. Site visitors can get an idea of the images they like, and click only on those thumbnails of the images where they would like to see more detail.

Photoshop has an automated function that will allow you to open a file of images and build a digital contact sheet. The images from that sheet can then be selected and saved for use as thumbnails. The original image will remain unaffected.

Making the Contact Sheet

To make the contact sheet:

1. Choose File ➜ Automate ➜ Contact Sheet II.

2. Choose a size for the sheet. The size will depend on how many images you want to fit on the sheet (Figure 24.11).

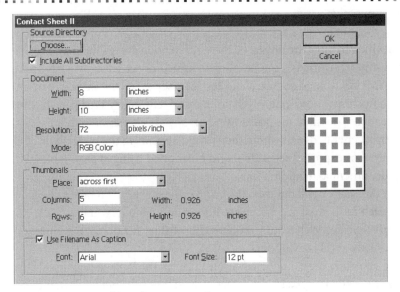

Figure 24.11 *Making the contact sheet*

3. Choose a Source folder.

4. Choose the number of columns and rows. The number of images you have in the folder will determine the maximum size of your thumbnail. In this case, there are 30 images, so there will be 5 columns and 6 rows.

5. Click OK.

The thumbnails can each be copied to a new document, cropped, and saved to Web-compatible formats for publication.

When making thumbnails, you'll sometimes want to grab a close-up of the image rather than the full image. For instance, if your large image is a standing figure, you might want the thumbnail to be only a detail of the figure's head. Of course, you'll have to do this by hand, but it's an effective choice. Choose a close-up that is visually interesting and will entice the visitor to click the thumbnail to see the full image.

Using Photoshop as a Layout Tool

A Web page consists of two primary elements: those that are code-based, such as HTML type, tables, and frames; and graphic elements (e.g., display text, images, and animations) that are created in a graphics program such as Photoshop.

Laying out a Web page in HTML is problematic. With no visible, active matrix upon which to view the results of the written code except the final browser, positioning text or importing images can be a hit-or-miss process. Designers have to toggle between the HTML text-based software and the browser to see the work in progress.

Photoshop is used extensively to design preliminary Web page layouts. The Layers palette makes possible the positioning of graphic elements so that the designer can develop a general idea of where they would appear on the page. Various elements are then saved or exported separately, and positioned using HTML tables with the Photoshop document as a guide.

In this section, I'll describe the basic process. Then, I'll take a closer look at how to make each individual graphic using Photoshop. Finally, you'll get a chance to use Photoshop's Save For Web feature, and use Photoshop for preparing animations in ImageReady and LiveMotion.

To accommodate the varied resolutions on the Web, very conservative Web designers use the 640×480 pixels-per-screen rule. If you subtract from that the parts of a browser that eat up space, such as the menus and scroll bar, you're left with a safe area of 585×295 pixels to work with. However, developers are designing for other resolutions these days—dimensions that are often dictated by what their statistics report about the resolutions of their audiences' browsers.

Create a file with the dimensions best suited to your audience's needs. Creating a new layer for each element ensures that you have optimum control of that element. I'm going to give the step-by-step instructions for creating a basic, layered Web page layout in Photoshop 6.

1. With your new image active, choose Layer ➜ New ➜ Layer.

2. Select your background color using the Eyedropper tool and Color palette, which you can open by selecting Window ➜ Show Color.

3. Fill the layer with the proposed browser-safe color selection you want by choosing Edit ➜ Fill. Make sure you select Foreground and uncheck the Transparency box in the Fill dialog box.

4. Create a new layer, following the directions in step 1.

To this layer, you can add a background pattern if you'd like. Save the pattern image in the native Photoshop format as `Background.psd`. Then:

1. Open your background file.

2. Choose Select ➜ All.

3. Choose Edit ➜ Define Pattern.

4. Move to your new layer on the workspace.

5. Choose Edit ➜ Fill ➜ Pattern. Choose the pattern from the pull-down list and let your image fill the layer.

To add a text header:

1. Select the Type tool from the Tool palette, and click your canvas.

2. Choose your typeface, size, leading, and spacing. In most cases, you'll want to be sure that you've selected Crisp as an anti-alias option, because that has proved to work best on Web graphics.

3. Click OK.

4. Place the text where desired by using the Move tool.

Continue creating layers and adding elements as you want.

After you have a page design with which you are satisfied, save it as a Photoshop file (choose File ➜ Save ➜ *name*`.psd`). I like to do this so that I can keep the layers intact, enabling me to come back later and make any necessary adjustments to the fonts, colors, and positions of my elements.

You can now use this layout not only to make adjustments to the design, but actually to generate the individual graphics for the Web page by cutting or copying and pasting each element individually and saving it using the Save For Web feature or other available export options.

Consider that the elements on a Web page should relate to one another aesthetically. This is best achieved by managing their color, proportional, and spatial relationships within Photoshop.

Using Photoshop to Prepare Animations

Because Photoshop's Layers palette allows you to successively stack one transparent layer on top of another in sequence, it serves as a very effective cell animation program.

You can target an image on one layer, copy the layer and apply a small increment of a filter, movement, or other operation. Copy the layer again and apply the operation one more time. Continue this process until the animation is complete. Incidentally, you can record the duplicate layer function and the operation into an action, and quickly automate your task.

Here is a step-by-step example of preparing a Photoshop animation.

1. Open the `Heart_anim.psd` image in the Ch24 folder on the CD. In my document, the Heart image has been separated from its background and named Layer 1.

2. Go to Window ➜ Show Actions.

3. From the Actions palette pull-down menu, choose New Set. Name the set Animation.

4. From the Actions palette pull-down menu, choose New Action. I named mine Heart Beat. Assign the F2 key as a key command. Click Record and OK.

5. Drag Layer 1 to the New Layer icon to duplicate it.

6. Choose Filter ➜ Distort ➜ Spherize. Set the Amount to 20% and the Mode to Normal.

7. Stop recording.

8. Target Layer 1. Run the action by pressing the F2 key. A new layer is created called Layer 1 Copy. On the new layer, the heart appears to have grown a little.

9. Each time targeting the new layer, repeat the action four more times by pressing the F2 key. The heart will grow a little bit each time as each new layer is created. Name each layer with a sequential numeric value from 1 to 5 (as in Figure 24.12) so that when you do the animation in ImageReady, you'll have no problem keeping them organized.

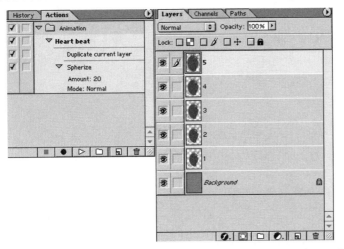

Figure 24.12 *The Heart Beat action and the Layers palette after the animation has been completed*

The animation file is complete. Save it as a Photoshop file named `Beating_Heart.psd`, layers intact. In order to create the beating heart animation and convert the file to animated GIF format, you'll import it into ImageReady (I'll show you how in Chapter 25).

Up Next

In this chapter, you've not only learned image-editing basics, but you've applied several professional techniques, including Web page layout and preparation for Web animations. You know how to create all types of files for the Web just by having gone through these stepped exercises.

Be sure to polish your skills by using Adobe ImageReady in Chapter 25 to expertly optimize the images you've created here. You'll also be able to easily create backgrounds, splice graphics, and batch-process graphics. Animation is a special feature of Image-Ready, which makes it not only a sensible tool, but a fun one, too!

Working with ImageReady

PHOTOSHOP

Chapter 25

n Chapter 24, you examined Adobe Photoshop in the context of Web design. Photoshop has always been a formidable tool, and version 6 has many features that are appropriate for Web-related tasks.

Of course, along with the features offered by Photoshop came a significant learning curve. Adobe, recognizing early on the need for streamlined, Web-specific software, introduced ImageReady to provide powerful tools to the Web designer. Not only does ImageReady help you create Web graphics, but actually output HTML where necessary. What's more, it is fairly easy to learn and an excellent starting place for newcomers.

This chapter is intended to cover the cool stuff ImageReady can do. It will take you through several step-by-step processes so that you can begin creating, optimizing, and adding interactivity to images and animations for the Web.

In this chapter, you will read about:

- Graphic optimization

- Coordinating images and Web backgrounds

- Slicing graphics

- Creating image maps and rollovers

- Creating an animation

The Development of ImageReady

About the same time ImageReady was introduced, Adobe introduced ImageStyler. As Web designers and Adobe looked more to Photoshop to handle the brunt of work, ImageReady and ImageStyler were both re-examined. Unwilling to let go of the power of ImageReady, Adobe decided to keep the program, but package it *along* with Photoshop, providing maximum power to Web designers.

ImageStyler also was put back on the drawing board and re-emerged as a brand new product with the addition of motion graphics support. This new program is known as LiveMotion; it is in and of itself worthy of a complete book, so I only mention it here and focus instead on ImageReady, which ships with Photoshop. However, experienced designers among you will appreciate the advanced Web support available in LiveMotion. I highly encourage you to check it out.

To learn about LiveMotion, visit the Adobe Web site: `www.adobe.com/products/livemotion/`.

ImageReady offers several exciting features, including built-in, intelligent graphic optimization. The software offers support for a variety of file types, and gives you extensive information on graphic files, such as how long they'll take to download at a variety of speeds and how they compare to the original file size. ImageReady allows the novice optimizer to create fast-loading, good-looking graphics with little knowledge, and places powerful tools into the hands of experienced Web graphic designers who want to combine the software's intelligence with their refined eye and experience.

You can use ImageReady to create backgrounds and complex graphics that require slicing. In both instances, ImageReady offers you the option to save to graphic formats but also to HTML files, which you can use as an entire Web page or then export into a Web authoring program like Adobe GoLive. Another powerful feature of ImageReady is the ability to add special effects to graphics.

Any time you want to tap into the power of integration and open ImageReady from within Photoshop, simply use the Jump To option, found on the File menu or as the bottom button on the Tool palette.

ImageReady and Photoshop

When you open ImageReady 3, your first observation may very well be that it looks a lot like Photoshop, and indeed it performs in very much the same way. It contains many of the same tools, filters, commands, and palettes of its bigger, older, sibling. ImageReady's strength is its ability to prepare files for the Web, an ability it shares, in part, with Photoshop's Save For Web option. However, it also provides the additional capability of creating sophisticated sliced graphics, rollovers, image maps, and animations.

The primary difference is that it in place of the extensive printing features of Photoshop, ImageReady has numerous powerful operations for Web file preparation. Instead of print-specific adjustments, color settings, and gamut tools, there are (among others) the Image Map tool, default browser preview, and the Slice, Rollover, Image Map, Animation, and Optimize palettes. Another major difference is Photoshop's ability to save a document to many different formats including those that support printing and desktop publishing, video, and the Web. ImageReady, on the other hand, is designed to save optimized files exclusively to Web formats—GIF, JPEG, PNG—and the Photoshop format, PSD.

 If you use the Export Original command, you can save in BMP, PCX, TGA, TIF, and PXR formats and you can save an animation as a QuickTime movie.

Optimizing Graphics

I'll begin by taking a look at how ImageReady started out, as a graphic optimization program. You'll recognize a lot of ImageReady 3's interface as being similar to Photoshop 6. What's more, you'll also see how the Save For Web feature in Photoshop is very similar to the technology available for image optimization in ImageReady.

Several important features of ImageReady's optimization capabilities include:

Live Preview   Whenever you are working on a file in ImageReady, you can automatically see changes based on file type and optimization choices (Figure 25.1).

Choice of File Types   ImageReady supports GIF, JPEG, PNG, and PSD. Depending upon the file, and your needs, you can adjust accordingly.

User-Level Control   While ImageReady gives you immediate optimization choices, advanced users can use options to customize their graphic output.

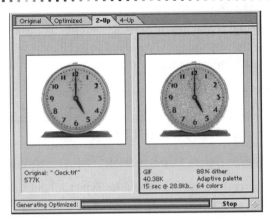

Figure 25.1 *Live preview allows you to see changes in a file as you make changes within the Optimize window. The Generating Optimized bar indicates the progress of each edit.*

While you don't really need a working knowledge of optimization to use ImageReady, you will no doubt be empowered by understanding the basic rules of thumb when it comes to optimization:

- Use GIFs when working with line art, flat color, and few colors.
- Use JPEGs for photographs and for art with many colors, shadows, and light gradations.
- PNGs are useful for broad application, but they are not supported by all browsers.

With this basic knowledge, we can get right down to optimizing our files.

Getting Information About File Sizes

ImageReady provides information regarding the file size of your images. All of these are available in the two drop-down menus built right into the image window. You can display different information in each of these windows.

1. Select one of the tabs in the image window.

2. Choose one of the options: Original, Optimized, 2-Up, and 4-Up. I like to set this option to 2-Up, which gives a comparison between original file size and current file specifications.

3. Choose information from the arrows at the bottom of the menu. The first arrow indicates the size in which you are viewing the image. The second two arrows offer additional information, including the image's type, file size, and the possible speeds at which it will be downloaded.

Working with GIFs

This popular Web graphic format is also the most widely supported. You can get very small file sizes when you create and optimize GIFs using ImageReady.

Start by creating a simple design, and then optimizing it as a GIF.

1. In ImageReady, select File → New.

2. Set the size of the file to **350** pixels in width and **155** pixels in height. Be sure the Contents radio button is set to White. Click OK.

3. From the Swatches palette, select a dark color for your foreground.

4. From the Tool palette, choose the Type tool; the Type tool options will appear along the Options bar, which is identical to that of Photoshop's Type tool.

5. Select the font face you'd like to use. I chose Hobo, 60 point. I set the color to our foreground color selection. My Anti-Aliasing option is set to Crisp. Choose whichever option provides the smoothest, least-jagged results for your typeface.

6. Be sure the Original tab is selected in the image window. Click the image and enter the word **CyberJunky** in the image window. The type will be set in your new image. You can use the Move tool to adjust the location of your type.

7. As in Photoshop, you can warp text and add layer styles to the image. I applied a Bulge with a 50% Bend, an Inner Shadow, and a Drop Shadow.

The layer styles are accessed by clicking the layer effects icon at the bottom of the Layers palette. When you target an effect in the Layers palette, the Layer Options palette switches to present the effect's options.

8. Click the 2-Up tab in the window to compare ImageReady's optimized version of the graphic with the original, as in Figure 25.2. For my graphic, the results are very good! This simple header is only 18 KB and will take 4 seconds to download on a 56.6 Kbps modem.

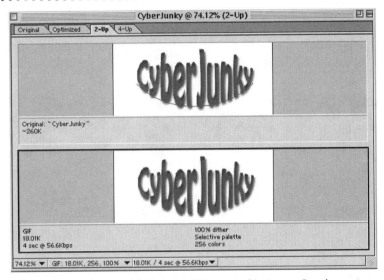

Figure 25.2 *The graphic header GIF created in ImageReady as compared to the original image. Note the extreme difference in file size.*

9. To save as an optimized GIF, select File ➜ Save Optimized As. The Save As dialog will appear. Choose the location where you'd like to save your file, and name the file. Click Save.

If you'd like to optimize a pre-existing graphic, such as clip or spot art, that is appropriate for GIF, follow these steps:

1. Open the file Leaf.psd in the Ch25 folder on the CD.

2. This time, click the 4-Up tab to display four versions of the image. Click the second image. Choose Window ➜ Show Optimized to display the Optimize palette.

3. In the Settings pop-up list, choose GIF 128 Dithered. Compare the optimized version to the original. The original's size is approximately 209 KB compared

to the optimized version of about 50 KB (see Figure 25.3). In this particular image, there is not a great variation in quality but the file size has been substantially reduced.

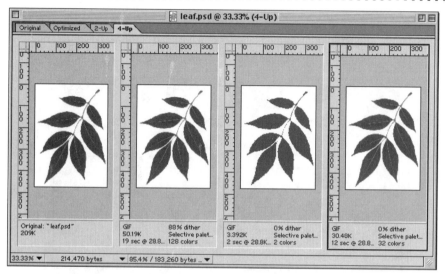

Figure 25.3 *The original leaf is on the left at 209K. The second image displays the GIF 128 Dithered auto setting. The third image has been reduced to 2 colors, and at the far right it's 32 colors, optimized to look its best and maintain detail with minimum file size.*

4. Click the third image. In the Optimize palette, reduce the number of colors to 2. Typically, this will be too few colors for most images, but it's a good idea to get a feel for how the image would look at the lowest possible compression of only 3 KB.

5. On the fourth image, bring the color number to 32, which gives you a great look but even better compression at about 30 KB than you had at the auto setting.

6. Save the GIF following the instructions in step 9 above.

You can now make additional selections for your GIF, such as interlacing or transparency using the Optimize palette settings. Interlacing allows the GIF image to appear progressively on the page, and transparency is discussed below in the "Transparency and Matting" section.

Working with JPEGs

For photographs and any image with significant amounts of gradations in light or shadow, JPEG is the file format of choice for best look and compression. You can optimize an image as a JPEG to produce the best results for your photographs.

1. In ImageReady, open the file Face_Paint.psd in the Ch25 folder on the CD.

2. When the file is open, go to the Optimize palette and choose JPEG from the file format pull-down menu.

3. Click the 2-Up tab on the image.

4. View the image using Maximum, High, Medium, and Low JPEG settings in the Optimize palette. Try to find the setting that gives you the best quality and compression without causing blotchy spots (known as artifacts) on the image (Figure 25.4).

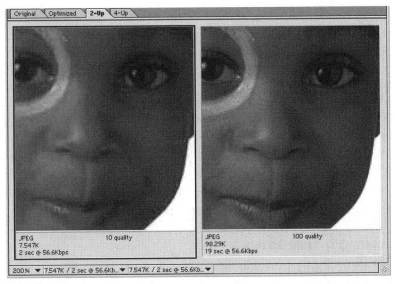

Figure 25.4 *The extremes of JPEG settings. Notice the deterioration and artifacts in the image on the left, set to JPEG Low to produce a file size of only 7.5 KB at the expense of image quality. The image on the right maintains quality, at 98 KB, set to JPEG High 100.*

You can make further, custom adjustments by using the Quality slider bar. For example, if the quality at medium setting (30) is fine, but low setting (10) is showing artifacts, try moving the slider to a setting of 20 and seeing how the image's look and size add up.

5.   Save the image by choosing File ➜ Save Optimized. Determine the file location and name, then click Save.

Making these kinds of decisions are the heart-and-soul of image optimization for the Web. It's always a balance of good looks and quick load times, and always based within the context of the page with which you are working.

To progressively render a JPEG, check the Progressive box. This enables supporting browsers to display the image incrementally.

Transparency and Matting

If you'd like an image to appear seamless against a patterned or solid background, you either have to make an image transparent, or matte the image on the background color. This technique is especially important to use whenever your image isn't a rectangle.

There are unique challenges with transparency and matting. Transparency is only supported in the GIF or PNG formats, and getting a transparency to look good with solid edges is a bit of a challenge. Matting, while allowing you to get a solid, flat color in GIF, PNG, or JPEG, sometimes will save the matte color as a slightly different color than your HTML-based background.

Some of these troublesome issues are addressed by ImageReady, but to get truly effective transparencies and matted files takes time and practice, as well as good sense. You'll want to be sure to use transparency only when absolutely necessary, and try to keep your colors Web-safe and consistent for best results.

Creating a Transparent GIF

The idea here is to have the edges of a shape blend with the background design of a page. In order to get that soft edge, anti-aliasing is used. However, this causes a potential halo effect, which is troublesome. Transparency in ImageReady is layer-based—in other words, the transparent areas that surround an area of a layer will be transparent in the browser.

To create transparency in a GIF in ImageReady:

1.   Open the file in the Ch25 folder on the CD, Piggy.psd.

2. Choose the Magic Wand tool. Set the Tolerance to 32. Click the white background area of the image.

3. Choose Select ➜ Inverse and then Layer ➜ New ➜ Via Copy. Name the new layer Piggy.

4. Target the Piggy layer and conceal the Background layer. Expand the Optimize palette by clicking the arrows on the tab. Choose GIF from the pull-down menu, and check the Transparency box.

5. From the Matte menu, choose None.

6. Play with the number of colors to produce the best-looking image at the lowest cost in kilobytes.

7. Choose File ➜ Save Optimized to save the image. You can now display the image in the browser (as in Figure 25.5) against any background.

If you have a solid background on your Web page, you can matte your image to match the background color of your page. When you save a file as a GIF, matting places a thin edge of pixels of the color you choose around your image so that its appearance on your Web page is seamless. When you save a matted image as a JPEG, it fills the transparent part of the image with the matte color. To matte an image against a background color:

1. Reopen the piggy file and follow steps 2 through 4 above.

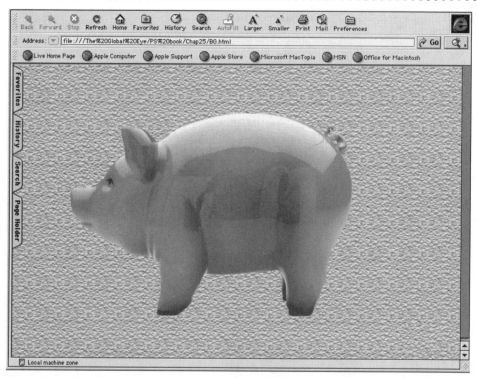

Figure 25.5 *The piggy saved as a transparent GIF and displayed on a pattered background in Internet Explorer*

2. In the Optimize palette, click the arrow next to the Matte swatch and choose a color from the pull-down list.

3. If you choose GIF, PNG-8, or PNG-24 from the format list and check the Transparency box, you'll see a small area around the image display the edge of the matte color. If you choose JPEG, the transparent area on the layer will change to the matte color.

ImageReady will place a thin matte behind your shape. The edges of the shape will be well-blended with the background, creating a smooth, appealing look (Figure 25.6).

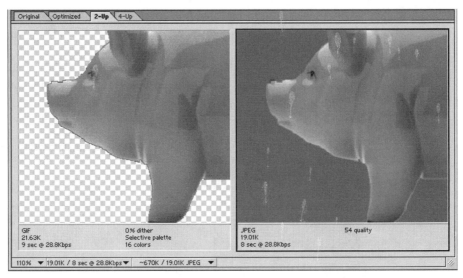

Figure 25.6 *Detail of the piggy with the Matte option (left) as a GIF and (right) as a JPEG*

Creating Background Images

Now that I've introduced optimization methods, transparency and matting techniques, it's time to create graphic backgrounds.

As you'll recall from Chapter 24, it's important to keep in mind that all backgrounds tile into the entire available space of the browser. This means that whether you have a 50×50 pixel tile or a 1280×50 tile, the browser systematically adds the tile from left to right, top to bottom until the entire space is filled. Because of this, you have to anticipate the repetition that will occur.

Wallpaper Tiles

Wallpaper tiles are those tiles that are repeated to create a pattern effect along the background of your Web page. When done well, they can be downright stunning. Lots of people run into trouble with wallpaper tiles, as they create images that are too dominant and don't blend into the whole of the design. Another common problem has to do with contrast: Text has to be easy to read no matter the background. As a result, soft, blended designs are often most effective.

ImageReady has some tools that help you create tiled backgrounds. You'll use ImageReady to make a simple, textured tile.

1. Select File ➜ New. I made my tile 50×50 pixels and clicked the Transparency radio button.

2. Choose a color from the Swatches palette and fill the tile with the color. Typically, a lighter color will give you best results if you want to use dark text, and a very dark color will provide the contrast necessary with light text.

3. Go to Filter ➜ Texture ➜ Texturizer. The Texturizer dialog will open.

4. Select a texture. I chose Sandstone for this example.

5. You can adjust the texture using the Scaling and Relief slide bars. You can also modify the light direction using the Light Dir drop-down menu; I set mine to Top. Checking the Invert box will invert the texture; I left it unchecked.

6. Click OK. Click the Optimized tab and see if the size of your tile is acceptable (it should be very small, around 2 KB). If it is, go ahead and save the file. If you'd like to try other optimization techniques such as described earlier in the chapter, feel free to experiment. The tile looks like this:

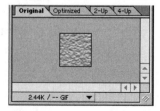

7. Choose File → Output Settings → Background. The Output Settings dialog appears (Figure 25.7). Click the View As Background radio button. Click OK.

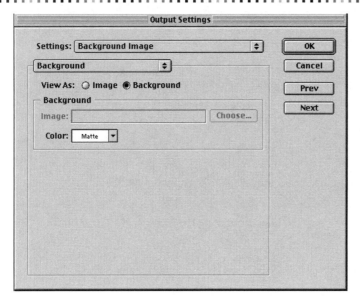

Figure 25.7 *The Output Settings dialog box*

8. Select File → Save Optimized. Name your file. The Format pop-up list provides the following options:

    HTML File   saves an HTML file with the images written into the code.

    HTML And Images   saves an HTML file with the images written into the code and a separate folder of the image or slices.

    Images Only   saves only the image or slices.

    Choose HTML And Images to create a document and files that are Web-ready. ImageReady will generate the image in a separate folder as well as the HTML file. You can now view your HTML file in the browser of your choice to see how the background looks (Figure 25.8).

You can also import this file into Adobe GoLive or any other HTML editor as a background. Once you do this, you can edit the page and test to see whether the contrast between your text and background is sufficient.

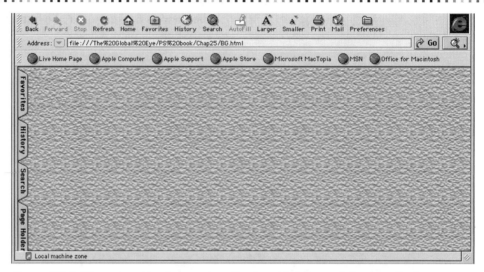

Figure 25.8 *The pattern background as displayed in Microsoft Internet Explorer*

The Tile Maker

ImageReady has a built-in tile maker that can help smooth out some problems that can be encountered when creating continuous, or seamless, background images. One such problem is that if each tile's edge is slightly different, those edges will show where the tile repeats. The effect is somewhat disturbing!

To correct or avoid this problem:

1. Open or create the continuous background image.

2. Select Filter ➜ Other ➜ Tile Maker. The Tile Maker dialog will appear.

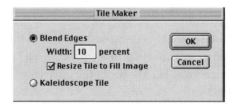

3. Click the Blend Edges radio button. You can select the amount of pixels for blending; I've left it at the default of 10. I've also left the Resize Tile to Fill Image option checked. This expands the file where necessary to make the blending as seamless as possible.

4. Click OK.

5. Optimize and save your file.

You can now view your file within an HTML page or import it into GoLive to begin designing your page. The result is a smoother, more attractive background.

Kaleidoscopic Tiles

When you're working to make your background tile seamless, you might have noticed the Kaleidoscope Tile option in the Tile Maker dialog. This is a very cool background effect with endless design possibilities!

To create a kaleidoscope background:

1. Open or create an image. You can start with the textured tile just developed in the previous section.

2. Select Filter ➜ Other ➜ Tile Maker. When the Tile Maker dialog appears, Click the Kaleidoscope Tile option.

3. Click OK. You now have a kaleidoscope tile.

4. Once done with the kaleidoscopic effect, you can blend the edges of the tile. Select the Tile Maker filter again and blend the edges of the image for smooth results.

You can use a wide range of effects and source images before applying the kaleidoscope effect.

Slicing Graphics

Another powerful feature of ImageReady is the ability to create and slice graphics, and then have ImageReady export the slices as well as the HTML code to make them work. Slicing is particularly helpful when you have an image on a Web page that is particularly large. The rationale is that the smaller, simple, or static portions of an image can be better optimized. The result is an all-around faster-loading page because instead of one large, heavy graphic, you have several smaller graphics.

To slice a complex graphic:

1. Open the image Bio_Web_Site.psd, in the Ch25 folder on the CD, in ImageReady.

2. Make sure the rulers and guides are turned on by selecting them from the View menu.

3. Drag guides along the design to isolate the sidebar. In my example, the guides are isolating the photo of the orangutan image and other important areas. Note how I paid little attention to where I sliced the other portions of the graphic (Figure 25.9). The reason is that ImageReady will worry about how to make this fit together in the best possible way! You don't have to be concerned with that—your job is to isolate the complex or active area in as simple a fashion as possible.

Figure 25.9 *The image to be sliced, with guides in place*

4. Under Slices, choose Create Slices from Guides.

5. Select File ➔ Save Optimized. When the Save As dialog appears, select HTML And Images from the Save As Type drop-down menu, and All Slices from the Slice menu. Click Save. Your image should now look like Figure 25.10.

Figure 25.10 *After slicing, ImageReady numbers the slices.*

 You can make a slice into a link to connect it to another Web page or URL. Click the slice you want to make into a link. Activate the Slice palette (choose Window ➔ Show Slice or, if the palette is visible, click the Slice tab). Enter the Name of the slice and the URL.

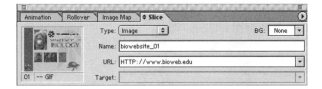

ImageReady will now save the separate images as well as the HTML necessary to lay them out properly.

To view the results, open the HTML file in your browser, and you'll see that Image-Ready maintained the integrity of your design while optimizing the sliced images in the best fashion possible

Creating Image Maps

An *image map* is an area of an image that links the site visitor to another Web page or URL. You can set up multiple areas in the image called hotspots. Slices let you define only rectangular areas as links. Image maps let you define circular, polygonal, or rectangular regions.

To define an image map as a region of the entire image, use the Image Map tools:

1. Choose one of the Image Map tools from the Tool palette.

2. Drag over the area you want to make into an image map.

3. Click the Image Map tab to display the Image Map palette.

4. Name the image map and assign a URL to it. Now when visitors click that area of the image (like the beetle in Figure 25.11), their browser will transport them to that URL.

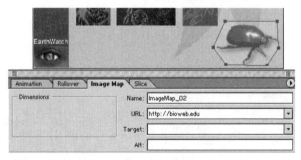

Figure 25.11 *An image map defined by the Polygon Image Map tool and the Image Map palette*

You can also make a layer-based image map.

1. In the Layers palette, target the layer you want to make into an image map.

2. Click the Layer menu and choose New Layer Based Image Map Area.

3. Click the Image Map tab to display the Image Map palette.

4. Name the image map and enter a URL.

Creating a GIF Animation

Another very attractive aspect of ImageReady is that you can create layer-based animations. In Chapter 24, we created the Beating Heart document; now, in ImageReady, we'll give it life.

1. In ImageReady, open the `Beating_Heart.psd` file you saved in Chapter 24 (or open the copy I've provided in the Ch25 folder on the CD). The Layers palette shows five layers and the Background, displaying the eye icons next to only the Background and Layer 1.

2. Choose Window ➜ Show Animation. The frame in the Animation palette displays the visible portions of the image (see Figure 25.12).

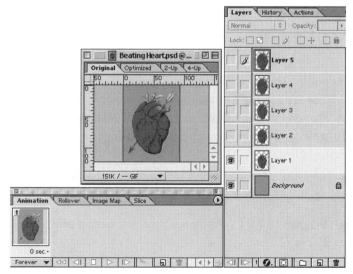

Figure 25.12 *The image, the Layers palette, and the Animation palette displaying the visible portion of the image*

Each frame in ImageReady's Animation palette displays the current visible layers. You create an animated sequence by making a new frame and then making visible only those layers that you want to appear in that frame.

3. Click the Duplicate Current Frame icon to insert a frame in the Animation palette or choose New Frame from the palette pull-down menu. Click off the eye icon for Layer 1 and click it on next to Layer 2. Leave the eye next to the Background on.

4. Repeat the process, adding new frames for Layers 3, 4, and 5. Your Animation palette should look like Figure 25.13.

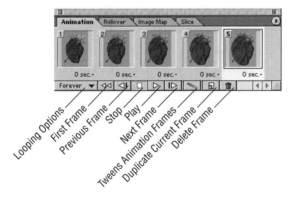

Figure 25.13 *The Animation palette with the first half of the animation*

5. At this point you may want to see the result. Click the Play button to see the first half of the beating heart animation. The heart expands and suddenly contracts. The second part of the animation will create a smooth contraction. We create the second half of the animation by using the same layers but in reverse order.

6. Click the Duplicate Current Frame button and make the contents of Layer 4 and the Background visible.

7. Repeat the process for Layers 3 and 2; the Animation palette should look like Figure 25.14.

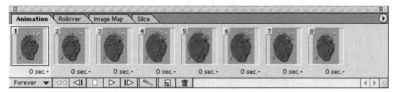

Figure 25.14 *The Animation palette with the completed animation*

8. In order to create a smoothly animated sequence, we want each frame to appear for the same amount of time. To set the speed between each frame, select all the frames by choosing Select All Frames from the Animation palette pull-down menu. Choose the arrow on the lower right of each frame and choose a time to set a uniform delay for each frame (or choose a duration for each frame individually).

9. You'll want to set up the iterations of the animation. This means how many times it loops. Forever is only appropriate when the animation keeps looping in a constant motion; this is best for slower, more subtle animations. Setting the animation to Once may be appropriate if the animation is particularly large and detailed. You can also set the animation to loop to a custom number of turns, which is usually my choice for Web animations.

To add a smooth transition between points on an animation, use the Tween option from the Animation palette drop-down menu. Tweening, or "in betweening," will automatically add a blur so that a smooth transition occurs between frames.

10. To view your animation, simply click the Play button at the bottom of the Animation palette. The animation will cycle in the originating file. At this point, you can stop the animation and make any adjustments to it you feel are necessary.

11. Once you're happy with your animation, save it as a GIF by choosing File ➜ Save Optimized, naming the file, and clicking Save.

Creating Rollovers

A *rollover* is a mini animation that is implemented by the behavior of your mouse. It's intended to add interactivity to your Web page. Like animations, rollovers depend on layers for their behavior. You designate a rollover on an image by changing the visibility of a layer's content.

To create a rollover, you should slice your image so that the portion that contains the rollover is independent from the rest of the image.

1. In ImageReady, open the file `Bio_rollover.psd` from the `Ch25` folder on the CD. To simplify the process I have merged all of the layers in the document except the ones are needed for the rollover.

2. Choose the Slice tool and drag a rectangle over the lower-right corner of the image to slice the beetle. Other slices will also be displayed. The beetle is the slice we want, so click it with the Slice Select tool, accessible by expanding the Slice tool in the Tool palette. It will be numbered Slice 03, as you see in Figure 25.15.

Figure 25.15 *The Sliced document*

3. Choose Window ➜ Show Rollover to display the Rollover palette, which contains Slice 03. This rollover state is named Normal and will be what is displayed prior to implementing a rollover.

4. Click the New Rollover State icon. This state is named Over and will be the image that is displayed when the mouse is placed on the Beetle slice.

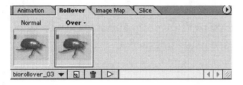

5. Click *off* the eye next to the Legs layer, and click *on* the eye next to the Legs 2 layer.

6. To see the rollover, click the Preview button in the Rollover palette. Place your cursor in Slice 03 in the image window. The legs move.

7. Now, when you move your cursor off of the slice, the image is restored to the Normal state.

You can program other states into a rollover and create additional rollover frames. Click the arrow next to the Over state to reveal the rollover options. Choose from the list of mouse behaviors.

Normal The image doesn't change; this is the default or nonanimated state.

Over The state changes when the mouse is hovered over the image or slice.

Down The state changes when the mouse is clicked and held down in the area.

Click The state changes when the mouse is clicked and released over the area.

Out The state changes when the mouse is moved off the area.

Up The state changes when the mouse is released within the area.

Custom This option lets you enter a custom behavior. You must write JavaScript code and add it to the HTML file in order for this to work.

None The state does not change.

8. When the rollover is complete, you can optimize the image slice by slice. Choose the Select Slice tool from the Tool palette. Click the individual slices one by one and optimize them individually with the Options palette.

9. Save the entire page as an HTML document. Choose File ➜ Save Optimized ➜ HTML And Images.

Up Next

Photoshop gives you limitless power to edit images and lay out your Web page. ImageReady enhances Web production by implementing rollovers, animations, image maps, and slices. These applications work neatly in tandem to prepare images for publication to the Web.

The Hands-On section up next will give you an opportunity to practice the layout features that we've discussed in Photoshop and then use ImageReady to create the extras that make a Web page really interactive.

Hands-On
Web Design and ImageReady

I n this Hands-On project, you'll lay out a Web site in Photoshop and use ImageReady to prepare the files for publication. The project is intended to take you through the Web features of ImageReady, but you will also use some of the image editing commands covered in previous chapters. The goal of this project is to use Photoshop and ImageReady to assemble a little home page for New Yawk City.

To see the finished version of the exercise, see the example in the color section or open New_Yawk_end.tif in the Ch25 folder on the CD.

Getting Started

Quit Photoshop and hide your preferences file before beginning this hands on exercise. Then relaunch Photoshop to create a clean version. The "Photoshop Settings" section in Chapter 5 details how to temporarily reset your preferences to Photoshop defaults. You can restore your customized personal settings when you're done.

To create a new Photoshop 6 document, choose File ➜ New within Photoshop. Name it New_Yawk.psd and save it to your disk. Enter the values shown in Figure 1.

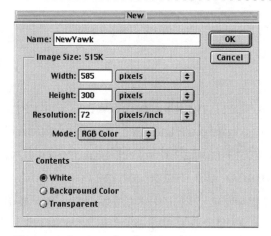

Figure 1 *Settings for the new document*

These pixel dimensions are for display on a browser seen on a 13" monitor. If you want to prepare the image for display on a 17" monitor, then make the image at least 780 pixels wide.

Creating a Background

Since we're going to slice the image in ImageReady, we don't have to worry about creating a seamless background. We'll fill the document with a color and then apply a filter to it.

1. Choose Window ➜ Show Swatches. From the Swatches palette pull-down menu, choose Web Safe Colors.ACO.

The Web Safe Colors swatches let you choose from the 216 colors that are displayed uniformly on the World Wide Web.

2. Choose a sky blue swatch from the Color palette for the foreground color.

3. Select Filter ➔ Render ➔ Clouds. Click OK.

Pressing the Option/Alt key as you apply the clouds filter produces clouds with more contrast.

4. Press Command/Ctrl+F to produce a different set of clouds. Repeat the command until you get the exact set of clouds that you want.

Adding King Kong and Other Elements

1. Open the file `King_Kong.psd` in the `Ch25` folder on the CD.

2. Choose the Move tool. Drag the King Kong image to the New Yawk image. Name the new layer that is created Kong 1.

3. Repeat the process for `Empire_State.psd` (name its layer Empire) and the `Logo.psd` document (which you will name Logo1).

4. Position the elements as shown in Figure 2. Be sure that the Kong 1 layer is below the Empire layer in the layer stack.

5. Press Command/Ctrl+S to save the document.

Figure 2 *The image with King Kong, the Empire State Building, and the logo placed*

Entering the Type

1. Choose the Type tool. I used 72-point Impact for the font, but if you don't have it, use a bold typeface. In the Type tool's Character palette, set the Leading to Auto. Type the words **New Yawk** (return) **New Yawk**.

2. Highlight the *N* in New. Choose a rich blue from the Web Safe Colors. I chose #0000FF. Repeat the process on the other *N* and the two *Y*s.

If you hover your mouse over a swatch, the color's hexadecimal name will be displayed.

3. Color the rest of the characters a bright red from the Web Safe Colors. I chose #FF0033.

4. Click the Commit button (the check mark icon) in the Options bar to initiate the type.

5. Double-click the Type layer to display the Layer Style dialog box.

6. Check Drop Shadow and use the defaults.

7. Click the word Stroke in the Styles list. Enter **3 px** for the width.

8. Click the color swatch. The Color Picker appears. Check Web Colors Only and choose a dark blue for the stroke. Click OK twice.

9. Target the Logo layer and center the logo under the type, as in Figure 3.

Figure 3 *After creating the type*

Recording an Action for the Animation

When we open the file in ImageReady were going to bring it to life with an animation. We'll create the necessary layers in Photoshop.

1. Target the Kong 1 layer.

2. Choose Window ➔ Show Actions.

3. Choose Clear All Actions from the Actions palette pull-down menu.

4. Choose New Set. The New Set dialog box appears. Name the set Enter Kong.

5. Choose New Action from the palette menu. In the dialog box that appears, name the action Kong Up to identify it. For function key, choose F2. Click the Record button.

6. Drag the Kong 1 layer to the New Layer icon to duplicate it.

7. Choose Filter ➔ Other ➔ Offset. Under Vertical, enter 20. For Undefined Areas, choose Set To Transparent. Click OK.

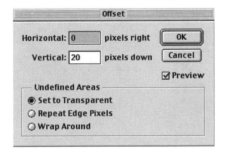

8. Click the Stop button in the Actions palette.

9. Press the F2 key five times. You should have a total of seven Kong layers—the first two, plus the five additional layers, as shown in Figure 4, each with Kong's head lower on the screen.

Figure 4 *The image after the Action has been applied seven times*

10. It is important to number the layers to keep them organized. Press Option/Alt and click each new layer in the stack to label it. The bottom layer should be Kong 1, the next highest in the stack Kong 2, etc.; the top layer will be Kong 7, as in Figure 5.

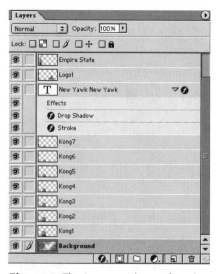

Figure 5 *The Layers palette after the actions have been recorded—note the names and numbering of the new layers.*

Jumping to ImageReady

We'll now open the document in ImageReady and slice it into smaller, more manageable pieces. We'll then create an animation from the multiple layers we made with the action. We'll create a rollover and an image map. Finally, we'll save the all the elements as an HTML document for publication to the Web.

1. Click the Jump To icon in the Tool palette. ImageReady launches and the New Yawk image appears.

2. Choose the Slice tool. Drag rectangles with the tool to divide the image into four slices, as shown in Figure 6. Exact boundaries aren't important here; your goal is to isolate Kong in one slice and the apple logo in another. But lining up those boundaries will reduce the number of slices as much as possible.

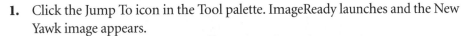

Figure 6 *The sliced image (with only the Kong 1 layer visible)*

If need be, you can readjust or reposition the slices by dragging their edges with the Slice Select tool.

Animating King Kong

ImageReady can create layer-based animations. We'll use the Kong layers we created with Actions.

1. In the Layers palette, display the eye icons next to the all the layers *except* Kong layers 1 through 7.

2. Choose Window ➜ Show Animation. The frame in the Animation palette displays the visible portions of the image. The notorious ape should be out of the picture (see Figure 7).

Figure 7 *The image and the Animation palette displaying the visible portion of the image*

Remember, each frame in the Animation palette in ImageReady displays the current visible layers. You create an animated sequence by making a new frame and then making visible only those layers that you want to appear in the frame.

3. Choose the Duplicate Frame icon to insert a frame in the Animation palette. Click the eye icon in the Layers palette next to Kong 7. (Kong 7 is our ape at the lowest point of his famous ascent; you can just see the top of his head.) Leave the eye next to all other layers off.

4. Repeat the process, adding new frames for Kong 6, 5, 4, 3, 2, and 1 and changing the layer visibility for each. When completed, your Animation palette should look like Figure 8.

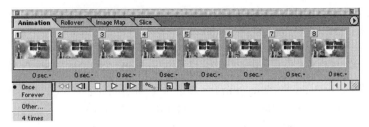

Figure 8 *The Animation palette displaying all the needed frames*

5. Kong is climbing pretty fast. We want to slow him down a bit. For smooth flow, each frame should appear for the same amount of time. To set the delay time between each frame, select all the frames by choosing Select All Frames from the Animation palette pull-down menu. Click the arrow on the lower right of the first frame and choose 0.2 sec.

6. You'll want to set the *iterations* of the animation, meaning how many times it loops. Forever is only appropriate when the animation keeps looping in a constant motion. Setting the animation to Once may be appropriate for an animation like this one. From the Looping Options menu, choose Once.

Creating a Rollover

Like animations, rollovers depend on layers for their behavior. You designate a rollover on an image by changing the visibility of a layer's content. We'll create a rollover to change the color of the Big Apple logo and also trigger King Kong's climb.

Unfortunately when you have an animation and a rollover in the same document, the rollover acts as a trigger to begin the animation. The two operations cannot exist in the same document independently of each other. You should design your Web page with this in mind.

First, we'll need to create a second rollover state from an existing layer; then we'll assign a behavior to it.

1. Drag the Logo layer to the New Layer icon to duplicate it. Name the new layer Logo 2.

2. Choose Image ➜ Adjust ➜ Hue/Saturation. Adjust the Hue and Saturation sliders to alter the color of Logo 2 (I chose a purple). Click OK.

3. Conceal Logo 2 but display the original logo and the rest of the document.

4. Click the Animation tab, then click frame 1.

5. Choose the Slice Select tool. Click the slice that contains the logo. Click the tab to display the Rollover palette. The first rollover state is called Normal.

6. Click the New State icon in the Rollover palette. Make Logo 2 visible and conceal Logo 1, and keep Over (the default) as a behavior. This means when you move your mouse on the logo, the new state will appear.

7. To preview the rollover, click the Preview button. Place your mouse on the Big Apple logo. The apple turns red briefly, and King Kong ascends the Empire State Building. When you remove the mouse, the apple turns green again and once again the ape climbs.

In trying variations on this feature, combining different rollover states with animations, I have found that their behaviors are erratic and difficult to control. If you are looking for a more predictable solution, it might be better to limit your interactivity choices to either an animation or a rollover within the same document.

8. Click the Stop button after you've previewed the rollover.

Creating an Image Map

An image map defines an area on the image that will be interactive. We'll make the New Yawk New Yawk text a link to a URL.

1. Choose the Image Map tool. Draw a rectangle around the New Yawk New Yawk characters.

2. Click the Image Map tab and name the image map New Yawk.

3. Enter the URL, http://www.NYC.gov (see Figure 9).

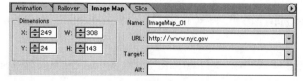

Figure 9 *Identifying the image map*

Previewing the Page

Before saving the optimized file, it's a good idea to look at it in your browser and test the animation, rollover, and image map. Choose File ➜ Preview In and choose a browser from the submenu. The preview displays the Web page and the source code for the document, as shown in Figure 10. When the image opens, the animation will run. Place your mouse on the logo; the animation will run again and the apple will change color. Click the type and, if you are connected to the Internet, you will be transported to NYC.gov.

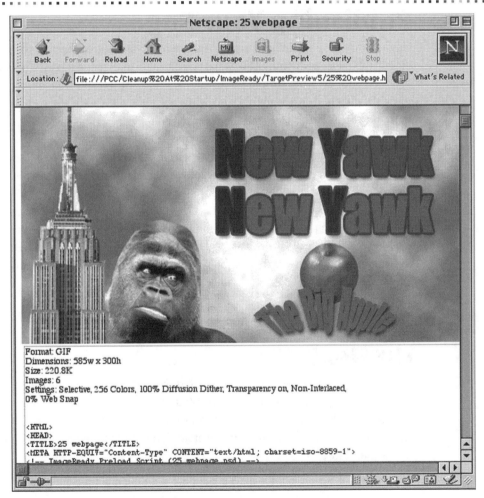

Figure 10 *The New Yawk Web page previewed in Netscape Navigator*

Saving the File as a Web Page

When the image is complete, you can optimize it slice by slice. Choose the Select Slice tool from the Tool palette. Click the slices one by one and optimize them individually with the Options palette.

Save the entire page as an HTML document: choose File ➜ Save Optimized ➜ HTML And Images. The slices and animation will be divided into separate images and inserted into an image folder. It's important not to remove the images from the folder, as the HTML code refers to these images within the folder hierarchy.

Publishing Your Page

Having brought your images to life, you are ready to publish them to the Web. For a sliced Web page, with straightforward cell animation, Photoshop and ImageReady are good tools for creating simple publications. Photoshop 6 and ImageReady 3 have seen some significant improvements, and with each new release these two programs become more powerful, better integrated, and easier to use.

For more complex animations, you may want to try Macromedia Flash or Adobe LiveMotion. To generate and manage larger, more sophisticated Web sites, you'll find what you need in programs such as Adobe GoLive, Macromedia Dreamweaver, or Microsoft FrontPage.

Many professional Web designers still prefer to assemble their Web pages in HTML code. They claim the code is cleaner than that generated by WYSIWYG (what you see is what you get) editors. I recommend that you at least learn basic HTML code so that you can understand the structure of Web pages and troubleshoot any problems that may be a result of too-complex code or code that is not universally compatible with all current browsers.

Up Next

Adobe Photoshop is the most sophisticated image editing software on the market today. *Mastering Photoshop 6* has attempted to teach you how to use its many features to your best advantage. Knowing the tools that are available to you is the first step in mastering the art of digital imaging. But applying these tools creatively to your images is your ultimate goal.

Much of what we see published today in print, on CD, or on the Web has been touched by Photoshop. When you see an image with dazzling effects that really turns you on, try to envision how it may have been created. What were the artist's sources for images? How did he or she generate the concept? What tools and techniques were employed to arrive at this end? Practice some of these techniques on your own images. Soon, you'll be creating new combinations of techniques and developing your own personal style. You have the tools that empower you to transform your dreams into tangible visual reality. With Adobe Photoshop 6, if you can imagine it, you can make it happen.

Appendices

In This Part

Tool Descriptions

PHOTOSHOP

Appendix A

Photoshop's tools are found on the Tool palette (Figure A.1). Some tools are grouped into sets, such as the Blur, Sharpen, and Smudge tools, and only one of the tools from a group appears on the Tool palette.

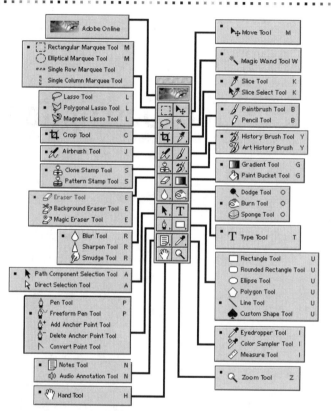

Figure A.1 *Adobe Photoshop 6 Tools*

To choose a tool, click its icon on the Tool palette. To select a tool that is not currently displayed, press and hold down the mouse button over the tool that appears in the same position in the Tool palette, and select the tool from the pop-up list.

To select a tool quickly, press its shortcut key (the shortcut letter or Shift plus the letter, depending on your preference settings). For grouped sets of tools, pressing the shortcut key repeatedly cycles through the tools in the group.

This appendix describes the tools in Photoshop's Tool palette, in alphabetical order. For each tool, you will find a brief description of its function and usage, as well as a list of its options and the other tools that share its position in the Tool palette.

Some tools are exclusive to a specific part of the program: the Extract dialog, the Liquify dialog, or ImageReady. These tools are included in this list, with a note about where they're used.

Add Anchor Point

Function   Adds anchor points to existing paths.

Usage   Click the Add Anchor Point tool or press P, then click the path. You can add anchor points to the middle of a segment, but you can only add segments to the endpoints of an open path.

Shares Position with   Pen, Freeform Pen, Delete Anchor Point, and Convert Point.

See   Chapter 9 for more information.

Airbrush

Function   Sprays color, simulating painting with an airbrush.

Usage   Click the Airbrush tool or press J, then click and drag to spray a pattern of color. If you drag slowly or stop dragging and just hold down the mouse button, the color will build up in that area. To create a straight spray, click where you want it to begin, hold down the Shift key, and click where you want it to end.

Options   Brush, Mode, and Pressure, plus Size, Pressure, and Color under Brush Dynamics.

See   Chapter 10 for more information.

Art History Brush

Function   Uses the history state or snapshot that you specify as its source data, as well as the options you set, to paint with different colors and styles.

Usage   Click the Art History Brush tool or press Y, click the column next to a state or snapshot in the History palette, and drag in the image. When you paint with the Art History Brush, color is deposited rapidly in several directions.

Options   Brush, Mode, Opacity, Style, Fidelity, Area, and Spacing, plus Size and Opacity under Brush Dynamics.

Shares Position with   History Brush.

See   Chapter 10 for more information.

Audio Annotation

Function   Adds an audio annotation to an image (requires a microphone attached to the computer).

Usage   Click the Audio Annotation tool or press N, then click where you want the audio annotation icon (a speaker icon) to appear. Record the message, using the Record, and Stop buttons in the dialog box that appears. To play back the audio annotation, double-click the speaker icon.

Options   Author, Color, and Clear All.

Shares Position with   Notes.

See   Chapter 2 for more information.

Background Eraser

Function   Erases the background elements in an image, making the pixels on the layer transparent.

Usage   Click the Background Eraser tool or press E, then drag through an area to erase it.

Options   Brush, Limits, Tolerance, Protect Foreground Color, and Sampling, plus Size and Tolerance under Brush Dynamics.

Shares Position with   Eraser and Magic Eraser.

See   Chapter 10 for more information.

Bloat

Function   Expands an area in all directions simultaneously. (Found in the Liquify dialog box.)

Usage   Place your cursor over an area, click and hold the mouse. Drag to affect adjacent areas.

Options   Brush Size, Brush Pressure, and Stylus Pressure. Holding down the Option/Alt key reverses the effect.

See   Chapter 18 for more information.

Blur

Function   Softens an area by decreasing the relative contrast of adjacent pixels.

Usage   Click the Blur tool or press R, then drag through an area to blur it.

Options   Brush, Mode, Pressure, and Use All Layers, plus Size and Pressure under Brush Dynamics.

Shares Position with   Sharpen and Smudge.

See   Chapter 10 for more information.

Burn

Function   Darkens an area by lowering the brightness values of pixels.

Usage   Click the Burn tool or press O, and drag over the portion of the image you wish to darken.

Options   Brush, Range, and Exposure, plus Size and Pressure under Brush Dynamics.

Shares Position with   Dodge and Sponge.

See   Chapter 10 for more information.

Cleanup

Function   Makes the extraction mask transparent or semitransparent or restores opacity to the mask. (Found in the Extract dialog box.)

Usage   You must be in preview mode to use the Cleanup tool. Click and drag over the area that you want to make transparent. To restore opacity press the Option/Alt key while dragging.

Options   Brush Size and Brush Pressure.

See   Chapter 19 for more information.

Clone Stamp

Function   Copies (samples) an area of an image and paints with the sample.

Usage   Click the Clone Stamp tool or press S, place the pointer over the area to sample, hold down the Option/Alt key, and click. Release and reposition the cursor where you want to paint, then drag over the area to paint with the sample.

Options   Brush, Mode, Opacity, Aligned, and Use All Layers, plus Size and Opacity under Brush Dynamics.

Shares Position with   Pattern Stamp.

See   Chapter 10 for more information.

Color Sampler

Function   Marks areas of an image for before-and-after comparisons of color adjustments.

Usage   Click the Color Sampler tool or press I, place the cursor on the area to sample, and click. The cursor leaves a marker, and the Info palette expands to display the data for that particular marker. You can sample up to four colors and record the information in the Info palette.

Options   Sample Size and Clear.

Shares Position with   Eyedropper and Measure.

See   Chapter 16 for more information.

Convert Point

Function   In a path, changes a corner point to a curve or a curve to a corner point.

Usage   Click the Convert Point tool or press P, click an anchor point, drag out the direction handles until the desired curve is achieved, and release the mouse button.

Shares Position with   Pen, Freeform Pen, Add Anchor Point, and Delete Anchor Point.

See   Chapter 9 for more information.

Crop

Function   Crops an image to a selected area.

Usage   Click the Crop tool or press C, drag through an area in the image to define the bounding box, then click the Commit (check mark) button in the Options bar or press the Return or Enter key. You can also double-click inside the cropping area to commit your crop. To adjust the crop before committing it, drag the bounding box handles, move the bounding box by placing the cursor inside its boundaries and dragging, or move the mouse just outside any of the corner selection handles until the cursor changes to the curved rotation icon and rotate the crop.

Options   Width, Height, Resolution, Front Image, Clear, Color, Opacity, Delete, Hide, Perspective, and Shield Cropped Area.

See   Chapter 13 for more information.

Custom Shape

Function   Generates custom shapes.

Usage   Click the Custom Shape tool or press U, choose a shape from the Options bar Shape menu, click in the image, and drag until the shape is the size and proportion you want. To draw from the center of the shape, hold down the Option/Alt key as you drag.

Options   Shape Layer, Work Path, Filled Region, Add, Subtract, Intersect, Exclude, Shape, Width, Height, Mode, Opacity, and Style, plus Unconstrained, Defined Properties, Defined Size, Fixed Size, and From Center under Custom Shape Options.

Shares Position with   Rectangle, Rounded Rectangle, Ellipse, Polygon, and Line.

See   Chapter 9 for more information.

Delete Anchor Point

Function   Removes anchor points from existing paths.

Usage   Click the Delete Anchor Point tool or press P, then click the anchor point you want to remove. The two segments connected by the point join into one.

Shares Position with   Pen, Freeform Pen, Add Anchor Point, and Convert Point.

See   Chapter 9 for more information.

Direct Selection

Function   Selects and moves individual anchor points and segments in a path.

Usage   Click the Direct Selection tool or press A, click a segment or anchor point to select it, and drag. Dragging an anchor point repositions it. Dragging a segment reshapes it.

Shares Position with   Path Component Selection.

See   Chapter 9 for more information.

Dodge

Function   Lightens specific areas of an image by increasing the brightness values of pixels.

Usage   Click the Dodge tool or press O, then drag over the area you wish to lighten.

Options   Brush, Range, and Exposure, plus Size and Pressure under Brush Dynamics.

Shares Position with   Burn and Sponge.

See   Chapter 10 for more information.

Edge Touchup

Function   Cleans the edges of an extracted area. (Found in the Extract dialog box.)

Usage   You must be in Preview mode to use the Edge Touchup tool. Click and drag over the edge of the extraction. Press Command+Option/Ctrl+Alt and drag to change the position of the edge.

Options   Brush Size and Brush Pressure (press a number from 1 to 0 to change pressure).

See   Chapter 19 for more information.

Ellipse

Function   Draws a circular or elliptical shape.

Usage   Click the tool or press U, click in the image, and drag to size the ellipse. To constrain the shape to a circle, hold down the Shift key as you drag. To draw from the center of the shape, hold down the Option/Alt key as you drag.

Options   Add, Subtract, Intersect, Exclude, Unconstrained, Circle, Fixed Size, Proportional, and From Center.

Shares Position with   Rectangle, Rounded Rectangle, Polygon, Line, and Custom Shape.

See   Chapter 9 for more information.

Elliptical Marquee

Function   Selects elliptical or circular portions of an image.

Usage   Click the Elliptical Marquee tool or press M, click in the image, and drag in any direction to produce an elliptical or circular selection. To constrain the selection area to a circle, hold down the Shift key as you drag. To originate the marquee from its center, place your cursor in the center of the area and hold down the Option/Alt key as you drag.

Options New Selection, Add To Selection, Subtract From Selection, Intersect Selection, Feather, Anti-Aliased, Width, Height, and Style (Constrained Aspect, Fixed Size, Normal).

Shares Position with Rectangular Marquee, Single Row Marquee, and Single Column Marquee.

See Chapter 6 for more information.

Eraser

Function When working on the Background, replaces the area with the background color. When erasing to a layer, replaces the layer content with transparency (or background color if Transparency is Locked).

Usage Click the Eraser tool or press E, then drag over the area you wish to remove.

Options Brush, Mode, Opacity, Wet Edge, and Erase to History, plus Size and Opacity under Brush Dynamics.

Shares Position with Background Eraser and Magic Eraser.

See Chapter 10 for more information.

Eyedropper

Function Specifies the foreground or background color by sampling directly from an image.

Usage Click the Eyedropper tool or press I, then click or drag in the image to select a foreground color. To sample a background color, hold down the Option/Alt key as you click.

Options Sample Size.

Shares Position with Color Sampler and Measure.

See Chapters 10 and 16 for more information.

Freeform Pen

Function   Draws a freeform line that converts itself to a path when the mouse is released.

Usage   Click the Freeform Pen tool or press P, place the cursor in the image, click, and drag to draw a path. When you release the mouse, the path is produced.

Options   Add, Subtract, Intersect, Exclude, Auto Add/Delete, Rubber Band, Curve Fit, and Magnetic.

Shares Position with   Pen, Add Anchor Point, Convert Point, and Delete Anchor Point.

See   Chapter 9 for more information.

Freeze

Function   Protects areas of the image from the effects of the Liquify tools and commands. (Found in the Liquify dialog box.)

Usage   Click or click and drag the mouse to deposit masking color.

Options   Brush Size, Brush Pressure, and Color.

See   Chapter 18 for more information.

Gradient

Function   Blends multiple colors into each other or into transparency over a specified distance.

Usage   Click the Gradient tool or press G, click the image where you want the gradient to start, and drag in the desired direction. Release the mouse where you want the gradient to end. You will fill a selection if one is active, or the entire Background or layer if no selection is active.

Options   Linear Gradient, Radial Gradient, Angle Gradient, Reflected Gradient, Diamond Gradient, Gradient Editor, Mode, Opacity, Transparency, Reverse, and Dither.

Shares Position with   Paint Bucket.

See   Chapter 10 for more information.

Hand

Function   Pans across the image when the image exceeds the size of the image window.

Usage   Click the Hand tool or press H, click the image, and drag to move the image around.

See   Chapter 4 for more information.

Highlighter

Function   Highlights the edges of an area to be extracted. (Found in the Extract dialog box.)

Usage   Click and drag around the edges of the area to be extracted.

Options   Brush Size, Color, Smart Highlighting, Show/Conceal Highlight.

See   Chapter 19 for more information.

History Brush

Function   Restores a portion of an image to a former state.

Usage   Click the History Brush tool or press Y, click the column next to a state or snapshot in the History palette, and drag in the image.

Options   Brush, Mode, and Opacity, plus Size and Opacity under Brush Dynamics.

Shares Position with   Art History Brush.

See   Chapters 10 and 11 for more information.

Image Map

Function   Defines areas on the image to make interactive. (Found in ImageReady only.)

Usage   Click and drag to define a rectangle or ellipse. Click and release to deposit a point. Move the mouse to define a side. Click to establish the next point.

Options   Rectangle, Ellipse, Polygon, and Image Map Selection tools.

See   Chapter 25 for more information.

Lasso

Function   Makes a freeform selection.

Usage   Click the Lasso tool or press L, click the edge of the area you want to select, and drag to surround the area with the selection border. Close the marquee by dragging the cursor to the starting point, or release the mouse to close the selection with a straight line.

Options   New Selection, Add To Selection, Subtract From Selection, Intersect With Selection, Feather, and Anti-Aliased.

Shares Position with   Polygonal Lasso and Magnetic Lasso.

See   Chapter 6 for more information.

Line

Function   Draws a line.

Usage   Click the Line tool or press U and drag in the image to create a line. To draw in only multiples of 45-degree angles, hold down the Shift key as you drag.

Options   Add To, Subtract From, Intersect With, Exclude Overlapping Area, and Weight, plus Arrowheads: Start, End, Width, Length, and Concavity.

Shares Position with   Rectangle, Rounded Rectangle, Ellipse, Polygon, and Custom Shape.

See   Chapter 9 for more information.

Magic Eraser

Function   Erases all pixels of the color similar to the selected color. When working on the Background, replaces the area with the background color. When erasing to a layer, replaces the layer content with transparency (or background color if Transparency is Locked).

Usage   Click the Magic Eraser tool or press E, then click an area in the image that contains the color you want to erase. All similar colors in the image will be erased.

Options   Tolerance, Anti-Aliased, Contiguous, Use All Layers, and Opacity.

Shares Position with   Eraser and Background Eraser.

See   Chapter 10 for more information.

Magic Wand

Function   Selects areas of an image that are similar in color.

Usage   Click the Magic Wand tool or press W, place your cursor on the area to be selected, and click. Adjacent pixels of similar color will be included in the selection.

Options   New Selection, Add To Selection, Subtract From Selection, Intersect With Selection, Tolerance, Anti-Aliased, Contiguous, and Use All Layers.

See   Chapter 6 for more information.

Magnetic Lasso

Function   Makes selections based on the contrast values of pixels.

Usage   Click the Magnetic Lasso tool or press L, click in the image, and drag. The Magnetic Lasso deposits a path that is attracted to areas of the most contrast. Release the mouse, and the path becomes a selection.

Options   New Selection, Add To Selection, Subtract From Selection, Intersect With Selection, Feather, Anti-Aliased, Width, Edge Contrast, Frequency, and Stylus Pressure.

Shares Position with   Lasso and Polygonal Lasso.

See   Chapter 6 for more information.

Measure

Function   Measures the distance between two points.

Usage   Click the Measure tool or press I and drag from the starting point to the ending point. To measure in only multiples of 45-degree angles, hold down the Shift key as you drag. The distance between the two points appears in the Info palette.

Shares Position with   Eyedropper and Color Sampler.

See   Chapter 14 for more information.

Move

Function   Moves, rotates, or scales a layered element or a selected element.

Usage   Click the Move tool or press M, then drag the element to move or transform it. To constrain proportions in transformation operations, press the Shift key as you drag. To make a copy of the element instead of moving it, hold down the Option/Alt key as you drag.

Options   Auto Select Layer, Show Bounding Box, and Alignment and Distribution.

See   Chapter 13 for more information.

Notes

Function   Adds textual notes to an image.

Usage   Click the Notes tool or press N, click in the area where you want the note icon to appear, and type your note in the window that appears. After you've entered the text, click the close button (in the upper-left corner) in the note window. To read the note, double-click the note icon.

Options   Author, Font, Size, Color, and Clear All.

Shares Position with   Audio Annotation.

See   Chapter 2 for more information.

Paint Bucket

Function   Fills an area with color.

Usage   Click the Paint Bucket tool or press G, place your cursor on the area you want to fill, and click.

Options   Fill, Mode, Opacity, Tolerance, Contiguous, Anti-Aliased, Use All Layers, and Pattern.

Shares Position with   Gradient.

See   Chapter 10 for more information.

Paintbrush

Function   Applies strokes of color.

Usage   Click the Paintbrush tool or press B, click in the image, and drag to apply the selected color. To create a straight stroke, click where you want it to begin, hold down the Shift key, and click where you want it to end.

Options   Brush, Mode, Opacity, and Wet Edges, plus Size, Opacity, and Color under Brush Dynamics.

Shares Position with   Pencil.

See   Chapter 10 for more information.

Path Component Selection

Function   Selects and moves the path as a unit.

Usage   Click the Path Component Selection tool or press A, then click to select all of the anchor points and segments of a path. To reposition a path, drag it with the Path Component Selection tool. To duplicate a path, drag and drop it with the Path Component Selection tool while holding down the Option/Alt key. To add paths to a selection, hold down the Shift key and click the paths to add.

Options Show Bounding Box, Add, Subtract, Intersect, Exclude, Combine, Align, and Distribute.

Shares Position with Direct Selection.

See Chapter 9 for more information.

Pattern Stamp

Function Paints an area with a repeating pattern.

Usage Click the Pattern Stamp tool or press S, select a pattern from the Options bar, and click and drag to paint with the pattern.

Options Brush, Mode, Opacity, Pattern, and Aligned, plus Size and Opacity under Brush Dynamics.

Shares Position with Clone Stamp.

See Chapter 10 for more information.

Pen

Function Draws straight lines or smooth curves.

Usage Click the Pen tool or press P. To draw a straight path, click to place the first anchor point, release the mouse button, then continue to click and release. To draw a curve, click and drag. Without releasing the mouse button, drag the handle to form the curve. To finish drawing an open path, click the Pen tool or hold down the Command/Ctrl key and click outside the path. To create a closed path (a shape), place the cursor over the first anchor point and click.

Options Add To, Subtract From, Intersect With, Exclude Overlapping Areas, Auto Add/Delete, and Rubber Band.

Shares Position with Freeform Pen, Add Anchor Point, Convert Point, and Delete Anchor Point.

See Chapter 9 for more information.

Pencil

Function   Produces an aliased or hard-edged stroke.

Usage   Click the Pencil tool or press B, click in the image, and drag to create the stroke. To create a straight stroke, click where you want it to begin, hold down the Shift key, and click where you want it to end.

Options   Brush, Mode, Opacity, and Auto-Erase.

Shares Position with   Paintbrush.

See   Chapter 10 for more information.

Polygon

Function   Draws a polygonal shape.

Usage   Click the Polygon tool or press U, click in the image, and drag until the shape is the size and proportion you want. To draw from the center of the shape, hold down the Option/Alt key as you drag.

Options   Add To, Subtract From, Intersect With, Exclude Overlapping Area, and Sides, plus Radius, Smooth Corners, Indents Sides By, and Smooth Indents under Polygon Options.

Shares Position with   Rectangle, Rounded Rectangle, Ellipse, Line, and Custom Shape.

See   Chapter 9 for more information.

Polygonal Lasso

Function   Creates straight-edged selection borders.

Usage   Click the Polygonal Lasso tool or press L, then click and release the mouse. Reposition the mouse to the next corner of the polygon, and click and release again. Repeat the process until the area is surrounded. Close the marquee by clicking the starting point again.

Options New Selection, Add To Selection, Subtract From Selection, Intersect With Selection, Feather, and Anti-Aliased.

Shares Position with Lasso and Magnetic Lasso.

See Chapter 6 for more information.

Pucker

Function Contracts an area in all directions simultaneously. (Found in the Liquify dialog box.)

Usage Place your cursor over an area, click and hold the mouse. Drag to affect adjacent areas. Press the Option/Alt key to reverse the effect.

Options Brush Size, Brush Pressure, and Stylus Pressure.

See Chapter 18 for more information.

Reconstruct

Function Restores portions of the image that have been Liquified. (Found in the Liquify dialog box.)

Usage Place your cursor over an area click and hold the mouse. Drag to affect adjacent areas.

Options Brush Size, Brush Pressure, and Stylus Pressure.

See Chapter 18 for more information.

Rectangle

Function Draws a rectangular shape.

Usage Click the Rectangle tool or press U, click in the image, and drag to size the rectangle. To constrain the shape to a square, hold down the Shift key as you drag. To draw from the center of the shape, hold down the Option/Alt key as you drag.

Options   Add To, Subtract From, Intersect, and Exclude Overlapping Shape Area, plus Unconstrained, Square, Fixed Size, Proportional, From Center, and Snap To Pixels under Rectangle Options.

Shares Position with   Rounded Rectangle, Ellipse, Polygon, Line, and Custom Shape.

See   Chapter 9 for more information.

Rectangular Marquee

Function   Selects rectangular or square portions of an image.

Usage   Click the Rectangular Marquee tool or press M, click in the image, and drag in any direction to select a rectangular area. To constrain the selection area to a square, hold down the Shift key as you drag. To originate the marquee from its center, place your cursor in the center of the area and hold down the Option/Alt key as you drag.

Options   New Selection, Add To Selection, Subtract From Selection, Intersect With Selection, Feather, Anti-Aliased, and Style, plus Width and Height if Constrained Aspect Ratio or Fixed Size are chosen as the Style.

Shares Position with   Elliptical Marquee, Single Column Marquee, and Single Row Marquee.

See   Chapter 6 for more information.

Reflect

Function   Moves the center areas to the outside edge of the brush as you drag. (Found in the Liquify dialog box.)

Usage   Click and drag.

Options   Brush Size, Brush Pressure, and Stylus Pressure.

See   Chapter 18 for more information.

Rounded Rectangle

Function   Draws a rectangular shape with rounded corners.

Usage   Click the Rounded Rectangle tool or press U, click in the image, and drag to size the rectangle. To constrain the shape to a square, hold down the Shift key as you drag. To draw from the center of the shape, hold down the Option/Alt key as you drag.

Options   Add To, Subtract From, Intersect, Exclude Overlapping Area, and Radius, plus Unconstrained, Square, Fixed Size, Proportional, From Center, and Snap To Pixels in the Rounded Rectangle Options.

Shares Position with   Rectangle, Ellipse, Polygon, Line, and Custom Shape.

See   Chapter 9 for more information.

Sharpen

Function   Increases the relative contrast values of adjacent pixels, creating the effect of a sharper focus.

Usage   Click the Sharpen tool or press R, then drag over an area to sharpen it. As you drag over an area, the pixels randomly change color. The more you drag, the more diverse the colors of the adjacent pixels become.

Options   Brush, Mode, Pressure, and Use All Layers, plus Size and Pressure under Brush Dynamics.

Shares Position with   Blur and Smudge.

See   Chapter 10 for more information.

Shift Pixels

Function   Moves pixels perpendicular to the direction of the movement of the mouse. (Found in the Liquify dialog box.)

Usage   Click and drag to the left to shift pixels down, to the right to shift pixels up, upward to shift them to the right, or downward to shift them to the left. Pressing the Option/Alt key reverses the direction of the shift.

Options   Brush Size, Brush Pressure, and Stylus Pressure.

See   Chapter 18 for more information.

Single Column Marquee

Function   Selects a single vertical column of pixels.

Usage   Click the Single Column Marquee tool or press M, then click in the image. A selection marquee appears around a single column of adjacent pixels that runs vertically across the entire image.

Options   New Selection, Add To Selection, Subtract From Selection, Intersect With Selection, and Feather.

Shares Position with   Rectangular Marquee, Elliptical Marquee, and Single Row Marquee.

See   Chapter 6 for more information.

Single Row Marquee

Function   Selects a single horizontal row of pixels.

Usage   Click the Single Row Marquee tool or press M, then click in the image. A selection marquee appears around a single, continuous row of adjacent pixels that runs horizontally across the entire image.

Options   New Selection, Add To Selection, Subtract From Selection, Intersect With Selection, and Feather.

Shares Position with   Rectangular Marquee, Elliptical Marquee, and Single Column Marquee.

See   Chapter 6 for more information.

Slice

Function   Divides an image into slices, which can be saved as individual files.

Usage   Click the Slice tool or press K, then click and drag over the area that you want to make a slice. To constrain the slice to square, hold down the Shift key as you drag. To draw the slice from the center, hold down the Option/Alt key as you drag.

Options   Normal, Constrained Aspect Ratio, and Fixed Size, plus Height, Width, Show Slice Numbers, and Line Color when Constrained Aspect Ratio or Fixed Size are selected.

Shares Position with   Slice Select.

See   Chapter 24 for more information.

Slice Select

Function   Selects a slice in the image.

Usage   Click the Slice Select tool or press K, then click the slice you wish to select. You can add slices to the selection by Shift-clicking.

Options   Bring To Front, Bring Forward, Send Backward, Send To Back, Promote To User Slice, plus a Slice Options button that opens a dialog box with options for setting Slice Type, Name, URL, Target, Message Text, Alt Tag, and Dimensions.

Shares Position with   Slice.

See   Chapter 24 for more information.

Smudge

Function   Moves one area of color into another while blending and mixing the colors as they are moved, simulating charcoal or pastel effects.

Usage   Click the Smudge tool or press R, then drag to paint with the tool.

Options   Brush, Mode, Pressure, Use All Layers, and Finger Painting, plus Size and Pressure under Brush Dynamics.

Shares Position with   Blur and Sharpen.

See   Chapter 10 for more information.

Sponge

Function   Enhances or diminishes color intensity by changing the saturation or levels of gray.

Usage   Click the Sponge tool or press O, then drag through the area that you wish to affect.

Options   Brush, Saturate, Desaturate, and Pressure, plus Size and Pressure under Brush Dynamics.

Shares Position with   Dodge and Burn.

See   Chapter 10 for more information.

Thaw

Function   Unfreezes areas that have been frozen. (Found in the Liquify dialog box.)

Usage   Click or click and drag.

Options   Brush Size, Brush Pressure, and Stylus Pressure.

See   Chapter 18 for more information.

Twirl

Function   Spins pixels in a clockwise or counterclockwise motion. (Found in the Liquify dialog box.)

Usage   Click or click and drag to affect the pixels. The longer the tool is held in position, the greater the effect.

Options   Brush Size, Brush Pressure, Clockwise, and Counterclockwise Rotation.

See   Chapter 18 for more information.

Type

Function　Creates type generated from installed fonts.

Usage　Click the Type tool or press T, click the point in the image where you want the text to appear, and enter the text from the keyboard. When you enter type in Photoshop using the Type tool, a new layer is automatically created.

Options　Type Mask, Horizontal Orientation, Vertical Orientation, Font, Style, Size, Anti-Aliasing Method, Left Align, Center Align, Right Align, Color, Warp Text, and Show Character and Paragraph Palettes.

See　Chapter 8 for more information.

Warp

Function　Pushes pixels forward as you drag. (Found in the Liquify dialog box.)

Usage　Click and drag.

Options　Brush Size, Brush Pressure, and Stylus Pressure.

See　Chapter 18 for more information.

Zoom

Function　Enlarges or reduces the size of the displayed image.

Usage　Click the tool or press Z, then click the area you want to enlarge. Each time you click, the zoom increases, to a maximum view magnification of 1600%. To reduce the size of the displayed image, click with the Option/Alt key held down. (The tool will have a minus sign to indicate that it is in reduction mode.) To restore the display to 100% view, double-click the Zoom tool.

Options　Resize Window To Fit, Ignore Palettes, Actual Pixels, Fit On Screen, and Print Size.

See　Chapter 4 for more information.

File Formats

PHOTOSHOP

Appendix B

Photoshop 6 can open and save image files in a variety of file formats. The number of supported file formats can be further extended with the addition of the plug-ins that attach to the Import and Export submenus.

File Compression Methods

Because graphics files are usually quite large, most graphic file formats use compression to reduce the size of the file when it is saved. There are two categories of compression: lossy and lossless.

Lossy compression schemes create smaller files but can affect image quality. When decompressed, the image produced is not identical to the original. Usually, colors have been blended, averaged, or estimated in the decompressed version.

Lossless compression schemes preserve image detail. When the image is decompressed, it is identical to the original version.

Some image file formats have compression methods built in, so that when you save a file, the compression is handled automatically. Other formats, such as JPEG and TIFF, have optional compression that you control through a dialog box when you save the file. Photoshop supports the following types of compression:

CCITT (International Telegraph and Telekeyed Consultative Committee) is a lossless compression technique for black-and-white PDF and PostScript images.

JPEG (Joint Photographic Experts Group) is a lossy compression method used for JPEG, PDF, and PostScript formats. It is typically used to prepare files for the Web or to archive images to read-only media.

LZW (Lempel Ziv Welch) is a lossless compression method supported by TIFF, PDF, GIF, EPS, and DCS formats. It is typically used to prepare files for the Web or for use in desktop-publishing programs.

RLE (Run Length Encoding) is a lossless compression method supported by TIFF and Photoshop formats.

ZIP is a lossless compression method supported by PDF files.

Supported Image File Formats

Photoshop 6 supports the following file formats:

BMP	DCS 1.0 and 2.0	EPS	Filmstrip
GIF	IFF	JPEG	Kodak ICC Photo CD
PCX	PDF	Photoshop 2.0	PICT
PICT Resource	PIXAR	PNG	PSD
Raw	Scitex CT	TGA	TIFF

These file formats and the Photoshop options for them are described in the following sections.

BMP (Microsoft Bitmap Format)

BMP is the native format for Microsoft Paint, the generic graphics program included with Windows. BMP supports 16 million colors and RLE compression. You can open and save BMP files in RGB, Indexed, Grayscale, and Bitmap color modes.

DCS 1.0 and 2.0 (Desktop Color Separation)

The DCS format, also known as a Five-File EPS, is designed to separate the cyan, magenta, yellow, and black color information. You may want to save a file in this format to use in a desktop-publishing program like QuarkXPress, Adobe PageMaker, or Adobe InDesign. Before saving to this format, convert the color mode to CMYK.

The DCS formats create five files, one for each of the four process color channels and a separate file as a low-resolution composite preview to be placed in the desktop publishing program. You can print the low-res image from the desktop publishing application as a proof. This saves processing time and streamlines workflow. When you ultimately print to film, the four process-color files are used to create the high-resolution version output. The preview and the separated files must all remain in the same folder.

You can choose to save a file in DCS 1.0 or DCS 2.0 format. DCS 2.0 also supports grayscale images with spot color. Both formats allow you to save four separate files that contain the separated cyan, magenta, yellow, and black color channels, as well as one image that is placed in your desktop-publishing program.

In the DCS Format dialog box, which appears when you choose to save an image in DCS 1.0 or 2.0 format, you can choose the type of DCS composite you want to use for the file. The other options in this dialog box are Preview, Encoding, Include Halftone Screen, and Include Transfer Function, which offer the same settings as are available for EPS files (described in the next section).

EPS (Encapsulated PostScript)

EPS files are generated by PostScript illustration programs such as Illustrator, Free-Hand, and CorelDRAW. You can open and save EPS files in CMYK, RGB, Lab, Indexed, Grayscale, Duotone, and Bitmap color modes. EPS does not support alpha channels, but it does support clipping paths.

When you *open* an EPS file in Photoshop, it becomes rasterized (Photoshop converts the vector art into pixels). Photoshop displays the Rasterize Generic EPS dialog box, which lets you specify the size and resolution of the image, and the mode to which you want it converted. Because the vector image is resolution-independent, you can specify any dimension without compromising its quality. You can also choose the Anti-Alias option, which will slightly blur the pixels between vector objects when they are rendered.

When you open a vector EPS file in Photoshop, areas that contain no information—the white pasteboard in the illustration program—become transparent.

You can *place* an EPS image in an existing Photoshop document by choosing File → Place. The image is displayed on a separate layer and can be sized, rotated, or positioned. If the vector image contains an imported raster image that has been placed into it, you should enter the resolution of the imported image and leave the suggested dimensions unchanged to maintain the quality of the imported image.

You may want to save your document as an EPS file when you intend to use it in a desktop-publishing program like QuarkXPress or an illustration program like Adobe Illustrator, particularly if you plan to print it on a PostScript printer. When you save your file in EPS format, it is saved in two parts: the PostScript code and the on-screen preview. In the EPS Options dialog box, which appears when you choose to save a file in EPS format, you can set the following options:

Preview   For Macintosh platforms, your choices are 1-bit Macintosh for a black-and-white preview (the smallest file), 8-bit Macintosh for a 256-color PIC preview, or a Macintosh JPEG for a 24-bit color preview with JPEG compression. For Windows platforms or Macintosh-to-Windows transfers, you can save the preview as a 1-bit (black-and-white) or 8-bit (256-color) TIFF.

Encoding   Your choices are Binary, ASCII, or JPEG. When saving the image for use in an illustration or desktop-publishing program, select Binary, sometimes called Huffman Encoding, which compresses the file. Some programs and older printers do not recognize binary encoding, in which case you'll need to save the document in ASCII encoding, which produces a larger file. Choose JPEG if you want to use this compression method to compress the file. (See the "File Compression Methods" section earlier in this appendix for more information about JPEG compression.)

Include Halftone Screen   You can include a halftone screen in the EPS document if you saved one in Page Setup.

Include Transfer Function   This option controls the brightness and contrast settings on your printer (selected in the Page Setup).

PostScript Color Management   Choose this option if you are printing to a PostScript Level 2 or 3 printer. It embeds a color management profile in the EPS document.

Include Vector Data   If there are unrendered type layers on an image, check this box to preserve them.

Image Interpolation   Check this box to include the interpolation method in the file should it be scaled in a destination program.

Filmstrip (QuickTime Movies)

Filmstrips that have been saved as QuickTime movies in Adobe Premiere can be edited frame by frame in Photoshop (each frame can be edited individually or as a group). When you open the file in Photoshop, each frame is separated by a gray bar, with the frame number appearing on the right and the time code appearing on the left. Filmstrip only works with RGB images.

When you are working with a Filmstrip file in Photoshop, do not change its size or add canvas to it. Resizing will prevent you from saving the changes to Filmstrip mode.

GIF (Graphics Interchange Format)

The primary GIF format, also called GIF87a, supports 256 colors but does not support transparency or animation. (GIF89a, the later GIF version, does support transparency and animation.) GIF format uses LZW compression. Before saving to this format, convert the color mode to Indexed to reduce the number of colors and the file size.

IFF (Amiga Graphic File Format)

Graphics files generated by the Amiga (a personal graphic arts workstation introduced in the 1980s by Commodore Computer) still exist. Photoshop lets you open and save these file in IFF (Interchange File Format). You can open and save IFF files in RGB, Indexed, Grayscale, and Bitmap color modes.

JPEG (Joint Photographic Experts Group)

JPEG format is primarily used for two purposes: to compress files and to save files for use on the Web. You can open and save JPEG files in RGB, CMYK, and Grayscale color modes.

As explained earlier in this appendix, JPEG is a lossy compression mode, which means that it loses information to make the file smaller. The amount of data that is lost depends on the settings you choose when you save a file in JPEG format.

 Avoid opening a JEPG file, editing it, and saving it back to the JPEG format. Photoshop recompresses the image each time you save it, and therefore the quality will diminish with each open-and-save cycle. A better approach is to work in the native Photoshop format (PSD) until the image is complete. Archive the final version to a read-only CD as a JPEG at maximum quality to get the most compression with a minimum of quality loss.

When you choose to save a file in JPEG format, the JPEG Options dialog box appears. This dialog box is divided into three sections:

Image Options   This section offers either a drop-down list or a slider for choosing a compression setting. The list includes Low, Medium, High, and Maximum settings. The slider offers 13 numerical settings. The more the file is compressed, the less space it consumes on your hard disk and the lower its quality.

Format Options   The three radio buttons control how the image downloads to a Web browser. The Baseline Standard setting displays the image all at once, only when all of the data has been received from the modem into RAM. (If the image is large, the site visitor may need to wait quite some time to see anything on the screen.) The Baseline Optimized setting loads the image in strips, from top to bottom, as the data is received. The Progressive setting gradually resolves the image as it loads, depending on the number of scans you choose. You can choose three, four, or five scans.

Size   The numbers at the bottom of the dialog box display the file size and the download time. For comparison, you can choose a modem speed from the drop-down list to recalculate the information for the speed selected.

Kodak ICC Photo CD

You can open ICC (International Color Consortium) Photo CD format images in Photoshop. However, Photoshop does not save to the Photo CD format.

When you open images directly from a Kodak Photo CD, you are presented with a dialog box that shows a preview of the image. This dialog box also contains a drop-down list with five options for setting the height and width of the image in pixels. These images have a resolution of 72 pixels per inch. The smallest option, 192×128, is a little over 2.5×1.75 inches and is 72 KB. The largest, 3072×4028, is just over 42.5×55.9 inches and is 18 MB. A Pro version of the Photo CD contains one additional image size of 6144×4096 pixels.

The Source and Destination buttons in the Kodak ICC Photo CD dialog box let you choose an ICC color profile in which to open your image. The Image Info button shows information about the image on the Photo CD.

PCX (PC Paintbrush Format)

PCX is the native format for PC Paintbrush, the Windows paint program. PCX supports 24-bit color. You can open and save PCX in RGB, Indexed, Grayscale, and Bitmap color modes.

PDF (Portable Document Format)

PDF is the format Adobe Acrobat uses to produce cross-platform, electronic documents for on-screen viewing. You can save both raster and vector art to PDF format. PDF files look like electronic versions of desktop-published documents, complete with formatted text and graphics. They are ideal for transport over the Internet because their file sizes are relatively small. In order to view PDF files, you need a copy of Acrobat Reader, which Adobe distributes for free.

When you open, in Photoshop, a PDF file saved from an application like Adobe Illustrator or Adobe Acrobat, it becomes rasterized. You can edit PDF documents in Photoshop and browse through page thumbnails (provided that the previews were originally saved with the document). PDF supports RGB, CMYK, Indexed, Grayscale, Lab, and Bitmap color modes.

Photoshop 2.0

Photoshop 2.0 format is backward-compatible with Photoshop versions 2.0 and 2.5, which do not support layers. Saving an image in Photoshop 2.0 format eliminates its layers and other attributes of later versions of the program. Before converting a file to Photoshop 2.0 format, you may want to duplicate it or rename the file when you save it.

PICT (Macintosh Picture)

PICT is the native Macintosh image format. This format has been used extensively in desktop-publishing applications and for transferring files across platforms. PICT can support bitmaps and object-oriented images. PICT can compress files and works particularly well on images with large areas of color, such as black and white alpha channels.

You can open and save PICT files in RGB (with one alpha channel), Indexed, Grayscale, and Bitmap (without alpha channels) color modes. You can save grayscale images in bit depths of 2, 4, and 8 bits. RGB images can be saved in 16 or 32 bits.

If you have QuickTime installed on your Macintosh, you can choose between four JPEG compression levels. However, if you want to compress your file this way, it is better to save it as a JPEG, unless you need backward-compatibility with an older Macintosh system.

PICT Resource (Special Macintosh Format)

PICT Resource files are special Macintosh files. You can import a PICT Resource file into Photoshop, and you can save a file in PICT Resource format. PICT Resource format can support RGB (with one alpha channel), Indexed, Grayscale, and Bitmap (without alpha channels) color modes.

To open a PICT Resource image, choose File → Import → PICT Resource and select the Scrapbook file in the System folder. When the PICT Resource dialog box appears, choose Preview to browse forward or backward in the Scrapbook. When you locate and select the PICT Resource file you wish to open, click OK.

One reason to save a file in PICT Resource format is to create a custom splash screen for your Macintosh. The resource fork of your MacOS system file contains the splash screen image that welcomes you when you boot up your Macintosh. You can save an image in PICT Resource format to the System folder to create your own splash screen to greet you every time you launch your computer. To save an image as a splash screen, follow these steps.

1. Create an image at the pixel dimensions of your monitor (see the Monitors information in the Display Control Panel for these dimensions).

2. Choose Image → Image Size and make sure that the resolution is set to 72 ppi.

3. Choose File → Save → Format PICT Resource. Name the image **StartupScreen** and save it to your System folder.

4. In the PICT Resource dialog box, enter the name **SCRN**. Select None for compression and click OK.

PIXAR (3-D Animation Workstation Format)

PIXAR is the 3-D animation workstation used to create feature-length animated movies (like *Toy Story* and *Dinosaur*). Photoshop can open images saved to PIXAR format and save images for use on a PIXAR workstation. PIXAR format supports RGB and Grayscale color modes (with one alpha channel).

PNG (Portable Network Graphic)

The PNG format supports transparency and 16 million colors. Older Web browsers, such as previous versions of Netscape Navigator and Internet Explorer, do not support PNG-formatted images, although the most recent versions do.

PNG supports RGB and Grayscale color modes (with one alpha channel). When you choose to save a file in PNG format, you are presented with the PNG Options dialog box. In this dialog box, you can choose Adam 7 to interlace the file, so that the image will resolve in increasing detail as it is loaded into the browser. You can also choose to compress the image using the following filters:

- The None option uses no filter compression and is recommended for grayscale and bitmap images.

- The Sub filter compresses images with horizontal patterns or gradients.

- The Up filter compresses images with vertical patterns or gradients.

- The Average filter compresses low-level noise by averaging the RGB values of adjacent pixels.

- The Paeth filter compresses low-level noise by reassigning the color values of adjacent areas.

- The Adaptive option applies the most appropriate filter to the image.

Adobe recommends that you choose the Adaptive option if you are unsure of which filter to apply.

PSD (Photoshop Format)

PSD is the native Photoshop format. It supports all of the capabilities that the program has to offer. Photoshop opens and saves PSD files more quickly than files in other formats. PSD is backward-compatible with Photoshop versions 3, 4, 5, and 5.5. This means that you can open a Photoshop 6 document in Photoshop 3 (although you will lose some of the attributes that the earlier version does not support, like the ability to run Actions, create spot color channels, use vector-based shapes and type, among all of the other cool features supported by the Photoshop 6).

Photoshop's native format is now compatible with several other programs in varying degrees. Adobe AfterEffects and Adobe ImageReady will open a layered PSD file. Corel's Painter and PHOTO-PAINT and Jasc's Paint Shop Pro can import PSD files with layers. Adobe Illustrator gives you the option of converting layers to objects. Macromedia FreeHand can open Photoshop files and supports layers to a limited extent. Adobe InDesign can place Photoshop files; however, it does not support Photoshop layers.

Adobe PageMaker and QuarkXPress are the last holdouts of professional mainstream publishing software that don't open or place native Photoshop files. To use an image in a PSD file in Quark, you will need to flatten it (eliminate its layers) and convert it to TIFF, EPS, or another compatible format.

 It's a good idea to check your destination application and version for the degree of compatibility.

Raw Format

Images generated on mainframe computers cannot be saved in any of the common image formats that are used for publishing. The Raw format is used to transfer files of unknown origin between platforms and applications. It is stripped-down binary code that describes color information about each pixel.

You can open and save Raw files in CMYK, RGB, and Grayscale color modes with alpha channels and multichannel; and in Indexed, Lab, and Duotone color modes without alpha channels.

When you open a Raw document, the Raw dialog box appears, which allows you to assign some values that control how the image information will be structured. Fill in the Raw dialog box fields as follows:

- In the Width and Height fields, enter the dimensions of the document. (Swap reverses width and height.)

- In the Count field, enter the number of color channels in the image. For example, if the image is CMYK, enter a value of 4.

- In the Depth field, enter the number of bits per channel.

- For the Byte Order, choose PC or Mac for 16-bit images.

The Interleaved check box controls the sequence in which the color information is described. The pixels are described in bytes in a particular order. Checking the Interleaved box describes the color information pixel by pixel. For example, for an RGB image, the code sequentially describes the red, green, and blue values of each pixel are at a time. If the Interleaved box is unchecked, the code describes the information channel by channel. In the case of an RGB image, the code first describes all of the red, then the green, and then the blue values of the entire document in sequence.

The Header field indicates how much information in the header that Photoshop can ignore. The Retain Header When Saving option tells Photoshop to retain the header information in the code if its value is greater than zero.

You can click the Guess button to have Photoshop guess at the values of the information, but you need to know either the width or height or the header information.

You might want to save a file as a Raw document to prepare it for a mainframe or another type of computer that doesn't support other common formats. When you choose to save a file in Raw format, the Raw Options dialog box appears. In the File Type field, enter the four-character code, such as TIFF or PICT, if you are using the file on a Macintosh. For the File Creator setting, use the default 8BIM code for Photoshop. In the Header field, enter the size of the header in bytes. For the Save Channels In setting, choose Interleaved Order or Non-interleaved Order.

Scitex CT

Scitex CT format saves files for use on the Scitex continuous-tone, color-processing computer and image-scanning systems. It is used primarily for high-end image processing for full-color output to film color separations. This format supports RGB, CMYK, and Grayscale color modes with no alpha channels.

TGA (Targa)

TGA, or Targa, format is designed for MS-DOS color applications running with a TrueVision video board for compositing images onto live video. Targa supports 32-bit RGB, Indexed, and Grayscale color modes.

TIFF (Tagged Image File Format)

TIFF format is a standard for images that will be placed in desktop-publishing programs. It can be neatly transported across platforms and compressed to reduce file size.

You can open and save TIFF files in RGB, CMYK (with alpha channels), Grayscale, Lab, Indexed, and Bitmap (without alpha channels) color modes. TIFF format can support a total of 24 channels in a document. If you want to reduce the file size, choose Save A Copy, select TIFF as the format, and check the Exclude Alpha Channels box.

When you save an image in TIFF format, the TIFF Options dialog box appears. This dialog box offers two options:

Byte Order   Choose Mac or PC, depending on the platform you are working on or to prepare a file to work on a different platform.

LZW Compression   Choose this option to compress the file using the LZW compression method, so that it takes up less space on the disk. (See the "File Compression Methods" section earlier in this appendix for more information about LZW compression.)

Note that many service bureaus request that you do not choose LZW compression when saving a file for placement in a desktop-publishing program if you are going to print it on a high-resolution imagesetter. A TIFF image that has been compressed with LZW compression takes longer to process and print. It also can cause errors in older raster image processors.

Blending Modes

PHOTOSHOP

Appendix C

he blending mode you select for a painting or image-editing tool or command controls how the color you are applying with the tool blends with the existing color in the area where you are working. The Mode menu on the Options bar (and repeated at the top of the Layers palette and within the Fill, Apply Image, and Calculations commands) offers these 20 blending modes.

Mode	Description
Add	Available in the Apply Image and Calculations dialog boxes. Adds the brightness value of each pixel in the source image to the aligned pixel in the target image, divides the difference by the scale, then adds the offset value. The Add mode lightens the image. Here's the formula: $(\text{Target} + \text{Source}) \div \text{Scale} + \text{Offset} = \text{Brightness value}$
Behind	Available only with the painting tools. Applies the action of the selected tool to just the transparent portion of the layer (provided that the Preserve Transparency setting is not in effect).
Clear	Fills an area or draws a line (created with the Line tool, Paint Bucket, Fill command, or Stroke command) with transparent pixels.
Color	Blends the color being applied with the original color, using the original color's luminance value and the applied color's hue and saturation values (so the original levels of gray are maintained).
Color Burn	Darkens the original color to reflect the color being applied with the selected tool.
Color Dodge	Brightens the original color to reflect the color being applied with the selected tool.
Darken	Colors the area affected by the selected tool with the darkest color (either the original color or the color being applied by the selected tool).

Difference | Blends the original and applied colors by subtracting the color values of the one that is less bright from those of the brighter color.

Dissolve | "Dissolves" the applied color into the original color by replacing the pixels with either the original color or the color being applied, based on the opacity of the pixels in the area. (Opacity is set using the Opacity slider on the Options bar.)

Exclusion | Works much like the Difference mode, but the resulting contrast is not as great.

Hard Light | Produces an effect similar to casting a glaring light on the area affected by the selected tool. Depending on the color applied, this mode either lightens or darkens the area. Applying a color that is less than 50% gray lightens the affected area, as with the Screen mode. Applying a color that is more than 50% gray darkens the area, as with the Multiply mode.

Hue | Blends the colors using the original color's luminance and saturation values and the applied color's hue value.

Lighten | Colors the area affected by the selected tool with the lightest color (either the original color or the color being applied by the selected tool).

Luminosity | Blends the colors using the original color's hue and saturation values and the applied color's luminance value.

Multiply | Blends the colors by multiplying the values of the original color by those of the applied color, producing a darker color.

Normal | Applies the color used by the selected tool to the affected area, which is the default mode. This mode appears as Threshold for Bitmaps and Indexed color images.

Overlay | Overlays the original color with the applied color, blending to produce a lighter color (like the Screen mode) or a darker color (like the Multiply mode), depending on the original color.

Saturation | Blends the colors using the original color's hue and luminance values and the applied color's saturation value.

Screen	Blends the colors by multiplying the inverse values of the original color by the applied color, producing a lighter color.
Soft Light	Produces an effect similar to bathing the affected area in a soft light. Depending on the color applied, this mode either lightens or darkens the area. Applying a color that is less than 50% gray lightens the affected area, as with the Color Dodge mode. Applying a color that is more than 50% gray darkens the area, as with the Color Burn mode.
Subtract	Available in the Apply Image and Calculations dialog boxes. Subtracts the brightness value of each pixel in the source image from the aligned pixel in the target image, divides the difference by the scale, then adds the offset value. The Subtract mode darkens the image. Here's the formula: (Target – Source) ÷ Scale + Offset = Brightness value
Threshold	Applies the color used by the selected tool to the affected area, which is the default mode for Bitmaps or Indexed color images. This mode appears as Normal for other types of images.

Quick Keys

PHOTOSHOP

Appendix D

Photoshop 6 offers keyboard shortcuts for many program operations. This appendix lists the more commonly used shortcuts, organized as follows:

- Display

- Document

- Tools

- Scrolling

- Image editing

- Type

- Layers

- Filmstrip editing

Many of Photoshop's commands are the same as ImageReady's. Key commands that are exclusive to either program are noted.

Display

Table D.1 Quick Keys for Display Operations

ACTION	MACINTOSH	WINDOWS
Set default colors	D	D
Set display mode options	F	F
Issue Jump To command	Shift+Cmd+M	Shift+Ctrl+M
Switch to Quick Mask/Standard mode	Q	Q
Switch background and foreground color	X	X
Zoom in	Cmd++	Ctrl++
Zoom out	Cmd+-	Ctrl+-
Show/hide open palettes, Tool palette, and Options bar	Tab	Tab
Show/hide open palettes and Options bar	Shift+Tab	Shift+Tab
Show Preferences dialog box	Cmd+K	Ctrl+K
Show Reset Preferences dialog box	Hold down Shift+Cmd+ Option at launch	Hold down Shift+ Ctrl+Alt at launch
Show Layers/Path/Channels palette cluster	F7	F7
Fit on screen	Cmd+0	Ctrl+0
Show actual pixels	Cmd+Option+0	Ctrl+Alt+0
Show Paint/Swatches/Styles palette cluster	F6	F6
Show proof colors (Photoshop)	Cmd+Y	Ctrl+Y
Toggle standard/precise cursor	Caps Lock	Caps Lock
Launch browser for preview (ImageReady)	Cmd+Option+P	Ctrl+Alt+P
Show rulers	Cmd+R	Ctrl+R
Snap/unsnap to guides	Cmd+;	Ctrl+;
Lock/unlock guides	Cmd+Option+;	Ctrl+Alt+;

Document

Table D.2 Quick Keys for Document Operations

ACTION	MACINTOSH	WINDOWS
New	Cmd+N	Ctrl+N
Open	Cmd+O	Ctrl+O
Open As	NA	Ctrl+Alt+O
Close	Cmd+W	Ctrl+W
Close All	Shift+Cmd+W	Shift+Ctrl+W
Print	Cmd+P	Ctrl+P
Print Options	Cmd+Option+P	Ctrl+Alt+P
Page Setup	Shift+Cmd+P	Shift+Ctrl+P
Quit	Cmd+Q	Ctrl+Q
Save file	Cmd+S	Ctrl+S
Save Optimized (ImageReady)	Cmd+Option+S	Ctrl+Alt+S
Save Optimized As (ImageReady)	Shift+Cmd+Option+S	Shift+Ctrl+Alt+S
Save For Web (Photoshop)	Shift+Cmd+Option+S	Shift+Ctrl+Alt+S
File (Mac) / Image (Win) Info (ImageReady)	Shift+Cmd+K	Shift+Ctrl+K
Help Contents	Cmd+?	Ctrl+?

Tools

Table D.3 Quick Keys for Tools

TOOL	KEY
Rectangular Marquee/Elliptical Marquee/Single Column Marquee/Single Row Marquee	M
Lasso/Polygonal Lasso/Magnetic Lasso	L
Crop	C
Airbrush	J

Table D.3 Quick Keys for Tools (*continued*)

Tool	Key
Clone Stamp/Pattern Stamp	S
Eraser/Background Eraser/Magic Eraser	E
Blur/Sharpen/Smudge	R
Path Component Selection/Direct Selection	A
Pen/Freeform Pen/Add Anchor Point/Convert Point/Delete Anchor Point	P
Notes/Audio Annotation	N
Hand	H
Move	V
Magic Wand	W
Slice/Slice Select	K
Paintbrush/Pencil	B
History Brush/Art History Brush	Y
Gradient/Paint Bucket	G
Dodge/Burn/Sponge	O
Type	T
Rectangle/Rounded Rectangle/Ellipse/Polygon/Line/Custom Shape	U
Eyedropper/Color Sampler/Measure	I
Zoom	Z

Scrolling

Table D.4 Quick Keys for Scrolling

Action	Macintosh	Windows
Scroll up	Control+K	PgUp
Scroll up slightly	Shift+Control+K	Shift+PgUp
Scroll down	Control+L	PgDn

Table D.4 Quick Keys for Scrolling (*continued*)

ACTION	MACINTOSH	WINDOWS
Scroll down slightly	Shift+Control+L	Shift+PgDn
Scroll left	Cmd+Control+K	Ctrl+PgUp
Scroll left slightly	Shift+Cmd+Control+K	Shift+Ctrl+PgUp
Scroll right	Cmd+Control+L	Ctrl+PgDn
Scroll right slightly	Shift+Cmd+Control+L	Shift+Ctrl+PgDn

Image Editing

Table D.5 Quick Keys for Image Editing

ACTION	MACINTOSH	WINDOWS
Undo	Cmd+Z	Ctrl+Z
Redo	Shift+Cmd+Z	Shift+Ctrl+Z
Deselect/reselect	Cmd+D	Ctrl+D
Select all	Cmd+A	Ctrl+A
Inverse selection	Shift+Cmd+I	Shift+Ctrl+I
Hide selection edges	Cmd+H	Ctrl+H
Copy to Clipboard	Cmd+C	Ctrl+C
Copy merged layers	Shift+Cmd+C	Shift+Ctrl+C
Paste	Cmd+V	Ctrl+V
Paste into selection	Shift+Cmd+V	Shift+Ctrl+V
Cancel operation	Cmd+period	Esc
Step forward	Shift+Cmd+Z	Shift+Ctrl+Z
Step backward	Cmd+Option+Z	Ctrl+Alt+Z
Feather	Cmd+Option+D	Ctrl+Alt+D
Free transform	Cmd+T	Ctrl+T

Table D.5 Quick Keys for Image Editing (*continued*)

Action	Macintosh	Windows
Transform again	Shift+Cmd+T	Shift+Ctrl+T
Extract (Photoshop)	Cmd+Option+X	Ctrl+Alt+X
Liquify	Shift+Cmd+X	Shift+Ctrl+X
Show Color Settings dialog box (Photoshop)	Shift+Cmd+K	Shift+Ctrl+K
Show Fill dialog box	Shift+Delete	Shift+Backspace
Fill with the foreground color	Option+Delete	Alt+Backspace
Apply foreground color fill to areas with pixels	Shift+Option+Delete	Shift+Alt+Backspace
Fill with background color	Cmd+Delete	Ctrl+Backspace
Apply background color fill to areas with pixels	Shift+Cmd+Delete	Shift+Ctrl+Backspace
Reapply filter	Cmd+F	Ctrl+F
Reapply filter with changed options	Cmd+Option+F	Ctrl+Alt+F
Fade	Shift+Cmd+F	Shift+Ctrl+F
Add to selection with selection tool	Shift-drag	Shift-drag
Subtract from selection with selection tool	Option-drag	Alt-drag
Duplicate selection with selection tool	Cmd+Option-drag	Ctrl+Alt-drag
Duplicate selection with the Move tool	Option-drag	Alt-drag
Change opacity of selected painting tool	Type a number between 0 and 100	Type a number between 0 and 100

Type

Table D.6 Quick Keys for Type Operations

Action	Macintosh	Windows
Increase selected type size in 2-point increments	Shift+Cmd+>	Shift+Ctrl+>
Decrease selected type size in 2-point increments	Shift+Cmd+<	Shift+Ctrl+<
Increase selected type size in 10-point increments	Shift+Cmd+Option+>	Shift+Ctrl+Alt+>

Table D.6 Quick Keys for Type Operations (*continued*)

ACTION	MACINTOSH	WINDOWS
Decrease selected type size in 10-point increments	Shift+Cmd+Option+<	Shift+Ctrl+Alt+<
Increase selected type tracking/kerning in 20–em space increments	Option+→	Shift+Alt+→
Decrease selected type tracking/kerning in 20–em space increments	Option+←	Alt+←
Increase selected type tracking/kerning in 100–em space increments	Cmd+Option+→	Ctrl+Alt+→
Decrease selected type tracking/kerning in 100–em space increments	Cmd+Option+←	Alt+Ctrl←
Increase selected type baseline shift in 2-point increments	Shift+Option+↑	Shift+Alt+↑
Decrease selected type baseline shift in 2-point increments	Shift+Option+↓	Shift+Alt+↓
Increase selected type baseline shift in 10-point increments	Shift+Option+↑	Shift+Alt+↑
Decrease selected type baseline shift in 10-point increments	Shift+Cmd+Option+↓	Shift+Ctrl+Alt+↓

Layers

Table D.7 Quick Keys for Layer Operations

ACTION	MACINTOSH	WINDOWS
Bring layer to front	Shift+Cmd+]	Shift+Ctrl+]
Bring layer forward	Cmd+]	Ctrl+]
Send layer backward	Cmd+[	Ctrl+[
Send layer to back	Shift+Cmd+[	Shift+Ctrl+[
Make new layer	Shift+Cmd+N	Shift+Ctrl+N

Table D.7 Quick Keys for Layer Operations (*continued*)

ACTION	MACINTOSH	WINDOWS
Make new layer via copy	Cmd+J	Ctrl+J
Make new layer via cut	Shift+Cmd+J	Shift+Ctrl+J
Group layer with previous	Cmd+G	Ctrl+G
Ungroup	Shift+Cmd+G	Shift+Ctrl+G
Merge layers down	Cmd+E	Ctrl+E
Merge visible layers	Shift+Cmd+E	Shift+Ctrl+E
Select contents of layer	Cmd-click layer	Ctrl-click layer

Filmstrip Editing

Table D.8 Quick Keys for Filmstrip Editing

ACTION	MACINTOSH	WINDOWS
Scroll up one frame	Shift+PgUp	Shift+PgUp
Scroll down one frame	Shift+PgDn	Shift+PgDn
Move a selection one frame up	Shift+↑	Shift+↑
Move a selection one frame down	Shift+↓	Shift+↓
Clone a selection up or down	Shift+Option	Shift+Alt

PHOTOSHOP

Glossary

Action

A Photoshop script that automates a single operation or a sequence of operations. Photoshop comes with default Actions, and you can create and save custom Actions to a file. When you need a particular Action or Action sequence, you can play it and apply its operations to any image by pressing a function key.

Actions palette

The Photoshop palette that contains controls for recording and playing back Actions.

additive primary colors

Red, green, and blue, which are used to create all other colors when direct, or transmitted, light is used (for example, on a computer monitor). When pure red, green, and blue are superimposed on one another, they create white.

Adjustment layer

In Photoshop, a separate layer containing the mathematical data for an adjustment operation applied to an image. You can re-edit the Adjustment layer at any time during the imaging process.

Adobe Gamma calibration package

A package that includes Adobe Gamma software, the Gamma Wizard, and ICC (International Color Consortium) color profiles for some RGB devices. You can use the Gamma software to calibrate your monitor.

alpha channel

An 8-bit, grayscale representation of an image. Alpha channels are selections that have been stored for later use. The values of gray can represent tonality, color, opacity, or semitransparency. Image formats that support alpha channels include Photoshop (PSD), Photoshop 2.0, Photoshop PDF, PICT, Pict Resource, Pixar, Raw, Targa, TIFF, and Photoshop DCS 2.0.

anti-alias

A process that adds a 2- or 3-pixel border around an edge that blends into the adjacent color to create a small transition zone. Without the anti-alias, an image would look stairstepped, without smooth transitions between colors. The width of an anti-alias is determined by the resolution of the image; you have no control over its size.

artifact

An unintentional image element produced in error by an imaging device or inaccurate software. Dirty optics are one common reason for artifacts.

aspect ratio

The height-to-width ratio of a selection or an image.

Background

In Photoshop, the area behind layers. The contents of all layers float on top of the Background. Unlike a layer, the Background is opaque and cannot support transparency. If the document contains more than one layer, the Background is always at the bottom of the stack and cannot be moved and placed in a higher position. When new layers are added to the document, their content always appears in front of the Background.

baseline

An imaginary line on which the bottom of most textual characters are placed. Some characters, such as *g* and *y*, have descenders that extend below the baseline.

baseline shift

The movement of the baseline of a character horizontally or vertically from its default starting position. Unlike leading, which affects all of the characters in a paragraph, baseline shift affects individual characters.

batch Action

An Action that will be applied to all of the images in a folder automatically, also known as *batch processing*. You can batch-process a group of images within a folder or from a different source, such as a digital camera or scanner with a document feeder.

Bezier curves

Lines and shapes composed of mathematically defined points and segments. Bezier curves are used in vector graphics.

bit depth

Refers to the amount of information per color channel. Photoshop can read images with 16 bits of information per channel, such as a 48-bit RGB or a 64-bit CMYK color image. Even though images with higher bit depths contain more color information, they are displayed on the monitor at the bit-depth capability of the computer's video card, which is 24 bits in most cases.

Bitmap mode

A Photoshop mode that displays and converts images that are composed of pixels, each containing 1 bit of information. The pixels are either black or white. Bitmap images are used to create line art and digital halftones. Bitmap image file sizes are smaller than Grayscale images, which contain 8 bits per pixel, or color images, which contain 24 bits per pixel. Bitmapped images do not support layers, alpha channels, filters, or any operations involving color.

black point

The darkest pixel in the shadow areas of an image. In Photoshop, you can set this point in the Levels and Curves dialog boxes.

blending mode

A preprogrammed color formula that determines how the pixels in an image are affected by painting or image-editing operations. In Photoshop, the Mode menu on the Options bar offers a choice of 19 blending modes.

brightness
The relative lightness or darkness of a color, measured from 0 to 100 percent. Brightness is also referred to as *value*.

burn
A technique used by photographers in the darkroom to underexpose or darken areas of an image. Photoshop's Burn tool darkens by lowering the brightness values of pixels as you move the tool over the image.

calibrated monitor
The foundation from which all other color settings are determined. You can use a calibration device or the Adobe Gamma calibration package to calibrate your monitor.

calibration bars
The grayscale or color indicators that appear on printed output. When you print a CMYK color separation, the calibration bars appear only on the black plate. On a color image, the calibration bars are the color swatches printed at the sides of the image.

canvas
In Photoshop, the surface on which your image resides.

Channel Mixer
A Photoshop feature that allows you to adjust the color information of each channel. You can establish color values on a specific channel as a mixture of any or all of the color channels' brightness values.

channel
Analogous to a plate in the printing process, the foundation of an image. Some image types have only one channel, while other types have several channels. An image can have up to 16 channels. See also *color channels*.

Channels palette
The Photoshop palette that allows you to work with an image's color information, or channels, and create alpha channels.

Character palette
The Photoshop palette that contains settings for type, such as size, tracking, kerning, and leading.

chroma
See *saturation*.

CIE (Commission Internationale de l'Eclairage)
An international organization of scientists who work with matters relating to color and lighting. The organization is also called the International Commission on Illumination.

clipping group
Layers grouped together to create effects. In order to join two layers into a clipping group, the image on the bottom layer must be surrounded by transparency. When a layer is clipped, it fills the shape of the image on the layer below it, so that it acts as a mask to clip the layer immediately above it.

clipping path

A path designed to be used as a mask in other applications. In Photoshop, the Clipping Paths option in the Paths palette menu allows you to create a path that will knock out the area outside the path when it is opened in another program. The interior portion of the path will be displayed, and the area outside the path will be transparent.

cloning

In Photoshop and other image editing programs, a feature that allows you to copy a part of an image and use that copy to replace another part of the image. Cloning is accomplished with the Clone Stamp and Pattern Stamp tools.

CMYK

The colors used in process printing. Each color plate contains tiny dots of cyan, magenta, yellow, or black (CMYK). The densities of the colored dots on each plate influence the surrounding colors when the eye mixes them together.

CMYK color mode

A color mode that produces a full range of color by printing tiny dots of cyan, magenta, yellow, and black ink. Because the colored dots are so small, the eye mixes them together. The relative densities of groups of colored dots produce variations in color and tonality. CMYK is referred to as a *subtractive* color system.

CMYK image

A four-channel image containing a cyan, magenta, yellow, and black channel. A CMYK image is generally used to print color separations.

color channels

Color information from an image. The number of color channels depends on the image's color mode. For example, Photoshop configures the information for an RGB image into three color channels, for the red, green, and blue components, plus a composite RGB channel, which displays the entire image in full color. The computer processes the information in each channel as an independent grayscale image. Each pixel is assigned a specific numeric gray value, where black equals 0 and white equals 255. Each color channel is actually an 8-bit grayscale image that supports 256 shades of gray.

color correction

Changing the colors of pixels in an image—including adjusting brightness, contrast, mid-level grays, hue, and saturation—to achieve optimum printed results.

color depth

Refers to the number of shades an imaging device can capture at once. The more bits there are per pixel, the more hues you can represent. The most common color depth, 8 bits per color, can produce 256 shades of each hue.

color management module (CMM)

The color management engine used by software to convert colors. The Adobe engine is ACE (Adobe Color Engine). Others you might encounter include Agfa, Apple ColorSync, Apple, Heidelberg, Imation, Kodak, Microsoft, and X-Rite.

color management policies

Policies that determine how Photoshop deals with color profiles when opening RGB, CMYK, or Grayscale files.

color mapping

Operations that can radically alter existing colors in an image. Color mapping provides the means to alter the basic characteristics of color while maintaining the image's detail.

color mode or model

A system of displaying or printing color. Photoshop supports the HSB color model and RGB, CMYK, Lab, Indexed, Duotone, Grayscale, Multichannel, and Bitmap color modes.

color separation

An image that has been separated into the four process colors: cyan, magenta, yellow, and black (CMYK). The image is then printed on four separate plates, one for each of the process colors.

color space

The colors produced by a specific device, such as a printer or monitor. Photoshop 6 allows you to edit and store an image with a color space other than that of your monitor. The image is embedded with an ICC (International Color Consortium) profile that describes the working color space. The image can then move from one computer to another with its profile, and it can be displayed on two different monitors and appear the same.

colorize

To convert gray pixels to colored pixels. Before a black-and-white image can be colorized in Photoshop, you must change its mode from Grayscale to a mode that supports color (RGB, CMYK, or Lab). By colorizing, you apply color to the image without affecting the lightness relationships of the individual pixels, thereby maintaining the image's detail.

continuous-tone image

An image containing gradient tones from black to white.

contrast

The tonal gradation between the highlights, midtones, and shadows in an image.

crop marks

The marks that are printed near the edges of an image to indicate where the image is to be trimmed.

crop
To select part of an image and discard the unselected areas.

Curves
A Photoshop color-adjustment tool that allows you to lighten, darken, add contrast, and solarize images.

densitometer
An instrument used by print shops and service bureaus to measure the tonal density of printed halftones.

density range
The range from the smallest highlight dot a press can print to the largest shadow dot it can print.

density
The ability of an object to stop or absorb light. The less the light is reflected or transmitted by an object, the higher its density.

digitizer board
A special-purpose computer card that transforms video signals into image data. Image sources for this technology include television signals and the output from VCRs and traditional analog video cameras. Digitizer video boards are also called *frame grabbers*, because they receive the frames sent by the video image sources.

distort
To stretch a selection along either of its axes. Unlike skewing, distortion is not restricted to a single border at a time.

dither
A method of distributing pixels to extend the visual range of color on screen, such as producing the effect of shades of gray on a black-and-white display or more colors on an 8-bit color display. By making adjacent pixels different colors, dithering gives the illusion of a third color.

dodge
A technique used by photographers in the darkroom to overexpose or lighten specific areas of an image. In Photoshop, the Dodge tool performs a similar function by increasing the brightness values of pixels as you paint with it.

dot gain
A phenomenon in printing that causes dots to print larger due to the absorbency of the paper they are printed on. Dot gain creates darker tones or colors. Dot gain is reflected in an increase in the density of light reflected by an image.

dots per inch (dpi)
The measurement of the number of dots produced by a printer that define the tonal elements of a halftone dot or stochastic screen. The dpi determines the resolution of printed output.

Droplet

A mini-application that contains Actions. A Droplet can sit on the desktop or be saved to a disk file. You can apply an operation to a file or group of files by dragging the file or folder onto the Droplet's icon.

drum scanner

A type of scanner that uses a spinning drum. The image is taped to a drum that spins very rapidly while the scanner's sensors record its color and tonality information.

Duotone

An image that uses two inks. Duotone can add a wider tonal range in a grayscale image by using more than one shade of ink to fill in the gaps. Duotone curves let you control the density of each ink in the highlights, midtones, and shadows. Photoshop creates Duotones by applying the various curves you've defined to a single image.

Duotone mode

A Photoshop mode that displays Duotones, which are images that have been separated into two spot colors. Duotone mode supports Tritones (images with three colors) and Quadtones (images with four colors). The Duotone color information is contained on one color channel. Photoshop displays a preview that is an RGB simulation of the ink combinations.

emulsion

The photosensitive layer on a piece of film or paper.

equalization

A technique for distributing image data across a greater range of pixel values. Typical equalization techniques include gamma correction and adaptive histogram equalization.

fade-out rate

The rate at which the Photoshop Paintbrush and Airbrush tools fade out as you paint with them to simulate an actual brush stroke.

feather

A process that creates a gradual transition between the inside and the outside of image borders. When you apply an effect to a feathered selection, it diminishes and becomes more transparent, producing a softening or blurring effect. Feathering gradually blends colored pixels into each other and eliminates hard edges. Feathering differs from anti-aliasing in that you can determine the size of the soft edge in pixels.

feather edge

The area along the border of a selection that is partially affected by changes you make to the selection.

fill

To paint a selected area with a gray shade, a color, or a pattern.

Fill layer

A Photoshop 6 method for filling an area. Fill layers combine the action of the Fill command with the flexibility of layers. You can create Fill layers with colors, gradients, or patterns.

filter

A software method for applying effects to images. With filters, you can adjust focus, eliminate unwanted artifacts, alter or create complex selection masks, and apply a wide range of artistic effects.

flatbed scanner

A type of scanner that reads a line of an image at a time, recording it as a series of samples, or pixels, by bouncing light off the area it needs to digitize. The scanner directs the bounced light to a series of detectors that convert color and intensity into digital levels.

floating selection

In Photoshop, a selection that has been moved or pasted on an image or converted to a floating selection using the Float command in the Select menu. The selection floats above the pixels in the underlying image until it is deselected, and it can be moved without affecting the underlying image.

font

The style or appearance of a complete set of characters. The four main categories of fonts are serif, sans serif, cursive, and display or decorative.

font obliqueness

Refers to whether the characters in a font lean, as does italic style type.

font weight

Refers to the thickness or heaviness of characters in a font.

frame grabber

See *digitizer board*.

full-color image

An image that uses 24-bit color. A full-color image uses three 8-bit primary color channels—for red, green, and blue—each containing 256 colors. These three channels produce a potential of 16.7 million colors ($256^3 = 16,777,216$). Photorealistic images that consist of smooth gradations and subtle tonal variations require full color to be properly displayed.

gamma

A measurement of contrast and saturation for a monitor. Gamma values range from 1.0 to about 2.5. The Macintosh has traditionally used a gamma of 1.8, which is relatively flat compared to television. Windows PCs use a 2.2 gamma value, which has more contrast and is more saturated.

gamut

The range of viewable and printable colors for a particular color model, such as RGB (used for monitors) or CMYK (used for printing). When a color cannot be displayed or printed, Photoshop can warn you that the color is "out of gamut." In terms of color working spaces, the gamut of a monitor is a triangular space with its corners in the red, green, and blue areas of an industry-standard color gamut chart. The gamut chart plots the device's available colors compared to the gamut of colors humans can see.

GIF87a and GIF89a

The Graphics Interchange Formats, used for Web applications and for saving animations produced in ImageReady. GIF is a *lossless-compression* format that compresses the image through reduction of the available colors. GIF87a does not support transparency. GIF89a is used to omit the visibility of selected colors on a Web browser.

gradient

Variations of color that subtly blend into one another. Photoshop gradients blend multiple colors into each other or into transparency over a specified distance.

gradient fill

A fill that displays a gradual transition from the foreground color to the background color. In Photoshop, gradient fills are added with the Gradient tool.

gray-component replacement (GCR)

An operation that removes a mixture of cyan, magenta, and yellow, and replaces them with black. GCR is generally more extreme and uses more black than undercolor removal (UCR).

Grayscale image

An image that use an 8-bit system, in which any pixel can be one of 256 shades of gray. Each pixel contains 8 bits of information. Each bit can either be on (black) or off (white), which produces 256 possible combinations.

Grayscale mode

A Photoshop color mode that displays black-and-white images. A grayscale image is composed of one channel consisting of up to 256 levels of gray, with 8 bits of color information per pixel. Each pixel has a brightness value between 0 (black) to 255 (white). Grayscale pixels may also be measured in percentages of black ink, from 0 percent (white) to 100 percent (black). When color images are converted to Grayscale mode, their hue and saturation information is discarded and their brightness (or luminosity) values remain.

grid

In Photoshop, a series of equally spaced horizontal and vertical lines that create a visual matrix. A grid helps you see the global relations between aligned elements on a page. Grids do not print.

GUI (graphical user interface)

A software program's way of interacting with users. The GUI (pronounced "gooey") of Photoshop lets you perform virtual operations that mimic real-world tasks like painting, compositing, or filtering.

guide

In Photoshop, a horizontal or vertical line that can be positioned anywhere on the image's surface. Guides do not print.

halftone

The reproduction of a continuous-tone image, which is made by using a screen that breaks the image into various size dots. The resolution, or number of lines per inch (lpi), of a halftone depends on the printer's capabilities. The tonal densities of an image are determined by the size of the dots. The larger the dot, the more ink deposited, and the darker the area appears. When you send an image to a printer, Photoshop, in tandem with the printer driver software, automatically converts the tonal information contained in pixels into dot-density information that the printer uses to construct the image.

halftone screen

Refers to the dot density of a printed image, measured in lines per inch (lpi). A halftone screen, also called screen frequency, is a grid of dots.

highlight

The lightest part of an image, represented on a digital image by pixels with high numeric values or on a halftone by the smallest dots or the absence of dots.

histogram

A graph of the brightness values of an image. The more lines the histogram has, the more tonal values are present in the image. The length of a line represents the relative quantity of pixels of a particular brightness. The taller the line, the more pixels of a particular tonal range the image will contain. Histograms are displayed in Photoshop's Levels and Threshold dialog boxes.

History palette

The Photoshop palette that records all of the changes that you make to an image during a session, as a series of individual states. You can use the History palette to revert to former versions of an image and to create special effects. The History palette also works in conjunction with the History Brush and Art History Brush tools.

hotspot

In an image map, an area that links to another Web page or URL.

HSB color model

A color model that uses hue, saturation, and brightness characteristics to define each color.

HTML (HyperText Markup Language)

The programming language used to create Web pages.

hue

The color of light that is reflected from an opaque object or transmitted through a transparent one. Hue in Photoshop is measured by its position on a color wheel, from 0 to 360 degrees.

ICC

See *International Color Consortium*.

image caching

A mechanism that accelerates screen redrawing during the editing process.

image link
A link on a Web page activated by clicking an image.

image map
An image on a Web page that has multiple links to another Web page or URL. Each link is called a hotspot. Image maps let you define circular, polygonal, or rectangular areas as links.

image size
The physical size and resolution of an image. The size of an image specifies the exact number of pixels that compose a picture.

ImageReady
A companion program to Photoshop, used to create Web graphics.

Indexed color image
A single-channel image, with 8 bits of color information per pixel. The index is a color lookup table containing up to 256 colors.

Indexed color mode
A color mode that uses a maximum of 256 colors to display full-color images. When you convert an image color to Indexed mode, Photoshop stores the color information as a color lookup table. You can then use a specific palette to display the image to match the colors as closely as possible to the original. Because it contains fewer colors, Indexed color mode creates smaller file sizes than the other color modes produce.

Info palette
The Photoshop palette that shows information about the current image. By default, the Info palette displays Actual Color and CMYK fields, the X and Y coordinates of the position of the cursor, and the height and width of the selection. This palette can display values in many different modes, including Web, HSB, Lab, Total Ink, and Opacity.

interlacing
A technique used to display a GIF image progressively on a Web page.

International Color Consortium (ICC)
An organization that sets standards for color management systems and components.

interpolation
In Photoshop, the setting for how the program resamples, or sizes, images.

inverse
In Photoshop, to reverse the selection; that is, to change the selected area to the portion that you did not select with a selection tool.

invert
To remap the brightness values of a channel to its opposite value. When you invert a channel, the white pixels with a value of 255 become black with a value of 0. Dark gray pixels in the channel with a value of 20, for example, will be remapped to a value of 235.

JPEG (Joint Photographic Experts Group)

A *lossy-compression* file format that supports 24-bit color and is used to preserve the tonal variations in photographs. JPEG compresses file size by selectively discarding data. JPEG compression can degrade sharp detail in images and is not recommended for images with type or solid areas of color. JPEG does not support transparency. When you save an image as a JPEG, transparency is replaced by the matte color. (See also *matting*.)

kerning

The space between two individual characters in text.

knockout

An area that prevents ink from printing on part of an image, so that the spot color can print directly on the paper. Knockouts keep a spot color from overprinting another spot color or a portion of the underlying image.

Lab color mode

A color mode that is device-independent. Lab color consists of three channels: a luminance or lightness channel (L), a green–red component (a), and a blue–yellow component (b). Lab can be used to adjust an image's luminance and color independently of each other.

labels

A Photoshop printing option that prints the document and channel name on the image.

layer

A software feature that allows you to isolate image elements so that you can work on each one individually. You can also rearrange the positions of layers, allowing parts of an image to appear in front of other parts. Earlier versions of Photoshop supported 99 layers; Photoshop 6 supports an unlimited number.

layer mask

A mask that conceals an area from view. When you apply a layer mask to an image, you control the transparency of a particular part of the layer.

Layers palette

The Photoshop palette that contains controls for working with layers, including creating and deleting layers, reordering layers, merging layers, and many other layer-related functions.

layer set

A Photoshop 6 layer-management tool. Layer sets let you consolidate contiguous layers into a folder on the Layers palette. By highlighting the folder, you can apply certain operations to the layers as a group. For example, the layers in a layer set can be can simultaneously hidden, displayed, moved, or repositioned.

layer styles

Predefined Photoshop 6 effects (called layer effects in Photoshop 5), such as drop shadows, neon glowing edges, and deep embossing. Layer styles apply their effects to the edges of the layer. Because they may be translucent or soft-edged, the colors of the underlying layer can be seen through the effects.

leading

The typographic term to describe vertical spacing between lines, measured from baseline to baseline.

Levels

A Photoshop tool that allows you to adjust an image's tonal range. When you perform a Levels adjustment, you are actually reassigning pixel values.

ligature

A set of two characters that is designed to replace certain character combinations, such as fl and fi, to avoid spacing conflicts.

linear gradient

A gradient that is projected from one point to another in a straight line.

lines per inch (lpi)

A measurement of the resolution of a halftone screen.

Liquify

A Photoshop 6 feature that allows you to distort pixels and transform areas of an image using a special set of distortion and transformation tools.

lossless compression

An image-compression scheme that preserves image detail. When the image is decompressed, it is identical to the original version.

lossy compression

An image-compression scheme that creates smaller files but can affect image quality. When decompressed, the image produced is not identical to the original. Usually, colors have been blended, averaged, or estimated in the decompressed version.

lpi

See *lines per inch*.

margin-style background

A background that is configured so that the image repeats vertically but not horizontally. This type of background appears as a continuous design down the depth of the page. It is a common visual element that helps unify the design of a Web page.

mask

An element that isolates and protects portions of an image. A masked area is not affected by image editing such as color changes or applied filters. Masks are stored as 8-bit grayscale channels and can be edited with Photoshop tools.

matting

Filling or blending transparent pixels with a matte color. Matting can be used with GIF, PNG, and JPEG files. It is typically used to set transparent image areas to the background color of a Web page.

midtone

A tonal range of brightness values located approximately halfway between white and black.

moiré pattern

An undesirable pattern in color printing, resulting from incorrect screen angles of overprinting halftones. Moiré patterns can be minimized with the use of proper screen angles.

monitor profile

A description of a monitor's characteristics used by Photoshop to display images correctly on that monitor. One way to create a monitor profile is to make a visual calibration of your monitor using Adobe Gamma and then save the resulting information as a color profile.

monitor resolution

The number of pixels that occupy a linear inch of your monitor screen. The resolution for most Macintosh RGB monitors is 72 ppi. Most Windows VGA monitors have a resolution of 96 ppi.

monospaced type

Type in which all of the characters are the same horizontal width.

Multichannel mode

A Photoshop mode that allows you to view the spot-color channels in color separations. The number of channels in a Multichannel document depends on the number of channels in the source image before it was converted. Each channel in a Multichannel document contains 256 levels of gray. Multichannel mode will convert RGB to cyan, magenta, and yellow spot color channels, and CMYK into CMYK spot color channels.

Navigator palette

The Photoshop palette that shows a map of the current image displayed as a thumbnail. It indicates the exact location of what appears in the image window relative to the entire image and provides features for scrolling and zooming.

noise

In an image, pixels with randomly distributed color values. Noise is primarily a result of digitizing technology. Noise in digital photographs tends to be the product of low-light conditions.

NTSC (North American Television Standards Committee) system

The video standard for television used in North and South America and many Asian countries.

object-oriented software

Vector-based illustration applications (such as Adobe Illustrator, Macromedia FreeHand, and CorelDRAW) and page-layout programs (such as QuarkXPress, Adobe PageMaker, and Adobe InDesign). Vector-based illustration software is appropriate for creating graphics such as charts, graphs, maps, cartoons, architectural plans, and other images that require hard edges and smooth blends. Vector-based page-layout software is suitable for creating books, pamphlets, brochures, flyers, and other documents that combine images and text. Photoshop is raster-based software, rather than vector-based illustration software; it does not print object-oriented graphics as vectors.

one-quarter tone

A tonal value located approximately halfway between the highlight and midtone.

optimization

In Photoshop and ImageReady, features that put images in the best possible form for Web applications, such as the file format, color-reduction method, and matting settings. In Photoshop, optimization settings are available in the Save For Web dialog box. In ImageReady, these settings are on the Optimize palette.

Optimize palette

The ImageReady palette that contains controls for optimizing images for Web applications.

Options bar

In Photoshop, the area that contains settings for tools. When you select a tool in the Tool palette, the Options bar changes to reflect the options available for the selected tool.

overprint colors

Two or more unscreened inks that are printed one on top of the other.

PAL (Phase Alternation Line) system

The video standard for television used in Western Europe, Australia, Japan, and other countries.

PANTONE

A brand name of spot color inks. The PANTONE Matching System is a group of inks used to print spot colors. PANTONE inks are solid colors used to print solid or tinted areas. The PANTONE system is recognized all over the world.

Paragraph palette

The Photoshop palette that contains settings that apply to entire text paragraphs, such as alignment and hyphenation.

path

A vector object that mathematically defines a specific area on an image. Vector objects are composed of anchor points and line segments known as *Bezier curves*. Paths enable you to create straight lines and curves with precision. If a path's two endpoints are joined, it encloses a shape. A path can be filled with color, stroked with an outline, or stored in the Paths palette or the Shape library for later use. A path also can be converted into a selection.

Paths palette

The Photoshop palette that contains controls for working paths, including creating deleting paths, filling paths, stroking paths, and saving work paths.

perspective

In Photoshop, a transformation that squeezes or stretches one edge of a selection, slanting the two adjacent sides either in or out. This produces an image that mimics the way you perceive a picture slanted at a distance.

pixel

An individual square of colored light, which is the smallest editable unit in a digital image. The pixels (short for *picture elements*) in a digital image are usually so small that, when seen, the colors blend into what appears to be a *continuous-tone* image.

pixels per inch (ppi)

The number of pixels that can be displayed per inch, usually used to refer to pixel resolution from a scanned image or on a monitor.

plug-in

A modular mini program or filter, usually developed by a third-party vendor, that adds functions to Photoshop.

PNG-8

A *lossless-compression* file format that supports 256 colors and transparency. PNG-8 is not supported by older Web browsers.

PNG-24

A lossless file format that supports 24-bit color, transparency, and matting. PNG-24 combines the attributes of JPEG and GIF. PNG-24 is not supported by older Web browsers.

point

A measurement system for type. There are traditionally about 72 points in 1 inch.

ppi

See *pixels per inch*.

preferences

In Photoshop, settings that affect the appearance and behavior of the program, which are stored in the Preferences file.

Preset Manager

A library of palettes that can be used by Photoshop. As you add or delete items from the palettes, the currently loaded palette in the Preset Manager displays the changes. You can save the new palette and load any of the palettes on the system.

printer resolution

The number of dots that can be printed per linear inch, measured in dots per inch (dpi). These dots compose larger halftone dots on a halftone screen or stochastic (random pattern) dots on an ink-jet printer.

process color

The four color pigments used in color printing: cyan, magenta, yellow, and black (CMYK).

progressive JPEG file

A file that displays a low-resolution version of the image while the full image is downloading.

Proof Colors

A Photoshop 6 control that allows the on-screen preview to simulate a variety of reproduction processes without converting the file to the final color space. This feature takes the place of the Preview in CMYK feature in earlier Photoshop versions.

Quadtone

An image that has been separated into four spot colors.

Quick Mask mode

A Photoshop mode that allows you to edit a selection as a mask. This mode provides an efficient method of making a temporary mask using the paint tools. Quick Masks can be converted into selections or stored as alpha channels in the Channels palette for later use.

radial gradient

A gradient that is projected from a center point outward in all directions.

random access memory (RAM)

The part of the computer's memory that stores information temporarily while the computer is on.

raster image processor (RIP)

Software on a computer or a device inside an imagesetter or PostScript printer that interprets a vector curve by connecting a series of straight-line segments.

raster image

An image that consists of a grid of pixels. Raster images are also called *bitmaps*. The file sizes of raster images are usually quite large compared to other types of computer-generated documents, because information needs to be stored for every pixel in the entire document. See also *raster-based software*.

raster-based software

Photoshop and other programs that create raster images. Raster-based software is best suited for editing, manipulating, and compositing scanned images, images from digital cameras and Photo CDs, continuous-tone photographs, realistic illustrations, and other graphics that require subtle blends, soft edges, shadow effects, and artistic filter effects like impressionist or watercolor.

rasterize

To convert vector information into pixel-based information. For example, you can rasterize type so that you can apply filters and other effects that do not work on vector-based type. Rasterized type cannot be edited as individual characters and appears at the same resolution as the document.

red eye

An effect from flash photography that appears to make a person's eyes glow red.

registration mark

A mark that appears on a printed image, generally for color separations, to help in aligning the printing plates.

rendering intents

Settings established by the International Color Consortium (ICC) under which color conversions can be made. Rendering intents cause the color of an image to be modified while it is being moved into a new color space. The four rendering intents are Perceptual, Saturation, Relative Colorimetric, and Absolute Colorimetric.

resample

To change the size or resolution of an image. Resampling down discards pixel information in an image; resampling up adds pixel information through interpolation.

resolution

The number of units that occupy a linear inch of an image, measured in pixels per inch (ppi) on an image or monitor or dots per inch (dpi) on a printer. The resolution of an image determines how large it will appear and how the pixels are distributed over its length and width. Resolution also determines the amount of detail that an image contains. High resolutions produce better quality but larger image file sizes. Resolution can also refer to the number of bits per pixel.

resolution-independent image

An image that automatically conforms to the highest resolution of the output device on which it is printed.

RGB color mode

A color mode that represents the three colors—red, green, and blue—used by devices such as scanners or monitors to display color. Each range of color is separated into three separate entities called *color channels*. Each color channel can produce 256 different values, for a total of 16,777,216 possible colors in the entire RGB gamut. RGB is referred to as an *additive* color model. Each pixel contains three brightness values for red, green, and blue that range from 0 (black) to 255. When all three values are at the maximum, the effect is complete white. Colors with low brightness values are dark; colors with high brightness values are light.

RGB image

A three-channel image that contains a red, green, and blue channel.

rollover

A mini animation that is activated by mouse behavior. Rollovers add interactivity to Web page. Rollovers depend on layers for their behavior. You designate a rollover on an image by changing the visibility of a layer's content.

saturation

The intensity of a color. Saturation, or *chroma*, is determined by the percentage of the hue in proportion to gray, from 0 to 100 percent. Zero percent saturation means that the color is entirely gray.

scanner

An electronic device that digitizes and converts photographs, slides, paper images, or other two-dimensional images into pixels.

scratch disk

An area of memory that Photoshop uses as a source of virtual memory to process images when the program requires more memory than the allocated amount.

screen angles

The angles at which the halftone screens are placed in relation to one another.

screen frequency

The density of dots on the halftone screen, commonly measured in lines per inch (lpi). Also known as *screen ruling*.

SECAM (Sequential Color and Memory) system
A video standard for television used in some European and Asian countries.

shadow
The darkest part of an image, represented on a digital image by pixels with low numeric values or on a halftone by the smallest or absence of dots.

skew
To slant a selection along one axis, either vertical or horizontal. The degree of slant affects how pitched the final image appears.

slice
To cut an image into pieces, saving the individual parts as image files and writing an HTML document that reassembles the slices on the screen. Slicing increases the efficiency of displaying images with a Web browser by decreasing the download time. Slices also allow you to define rectangular areas as links to other Web pages or URLs.

SMPTE-C
A movie industry standard, compliant with the Society of Motion Picture and Television Engineers standards for motion picture illuminants.

snapshot
In Photoshop, a saved image state. By default, when the image is opened, the History palette displays a snapshot of the image as it appeared when it was last saved. You can save the current image to a snapshot to preserve that state.

sort proof
An on-screen document that appears as close as possible to what the image will look like if printed to a specific device. Image formats that allows you to embed a sort proof profile in the saved document are Photoshop EPS, Photoshop PDF, and Photoshop DCS 1.0 and 2.0.

splash screen
A screen that appears when you first load a program. For example, the default Photoshop 6 splash screen indicates the components that are loading and program-specific data, such as the registered owner's name and the program's serial number.

spot color
Ink used in a print job in addition to black or process colors. Each spot color requires a plate of its own. Spot colors are printed in the order in which they appear in the Channels palette. Spot color channels are independent of the color mode of the image, which means that they are not blended with the other channels in a Grayscale, RGB, or CMYK image. Spot color channels are also independent of layers, which means that you cannot apply spot colors to individual layers. Image formats that support spot color are Photoshop (PSD), Photoshop PDF, TIFF, and Photoshop DCS 2.0.

sRGB color space
A color space designed for corporate computer monitors and images intended for Web applications. sRGB is the default color working space in Photoshop 6 but other color spaces are available.

state

In Photoshop's History palette, a stored version of an image. Each time you perform an operation, the History palette produces a state with the name of the operation or tool that was used. The higher the state appears in the stack, the earlier in the process the state was made.

stroking

Outlining a selection border with a color. In Photoshop, strokes can vary in width and relative position on the selection border.

subtractive primary colors

Cyan, magenta, and yellow, which are the printing inks that theoretically absorb all color and produce black. Because pigments subtract light components from the white light in the environment, they reduce its intensity, making it less bright than unfiltered light. Subtractive colorants reduce the amount of light reflected back at the viewer.

tolerance

A parameter of the Magic Wand and Paint Bucket tools that specifies the color range of the pixels to be selected.

Tool palette

In Photoshop, the area that contains icons for tools, also called the Toolbox. Some of the tool icons expand to provide access to tools that are not visible, bringing the entire number of tools to 50, plus paint swatches, Quick Mask icons, view modes, and the Jump To command. The Tool palette is a floating palette that you can move or hide.

tool tip

A GUI identifier that appears when you hover your cursor over a screen element and wait a few seconds. For example, Photoshop includes tool tips for the tools on the Tool palette, as well as for many of its operations accessible from other palettes, Options bar, dialog boxes, and windows.

tracking

The global space between selected groups of characters in text.

transparency scanner

A type of scanner that passes light through the emulsions on a piece of negative film or a color slide. A transparency scanner's dynamic range determines its ability to distinguish color variations.

trap

A technique used in preparing images for printing color separations. Misalignments or shifting during printing can result in gaps in images. A trap is an overlap that prevents such gaps from appearing along the edges of objects in an image.

Tritone

An image that has been separated into three spot colors.

tweening

From "in betweening," a method for adding transitions between frames in animations.

undercolor removal (UCR)
The process of reducing the cyan, magenta, and yellow inks from the darkest neutral shadow areas in an image and replacing them with black.

unsharp mask (USM)
A mask that exaggerates the transition between areas of most contrast, while leaving areas of minimum contrast unaffected. It can help increase the contrast of an image and fool the eye into thinking fuzzy areas of the image are in focus.

value
See *brightness*.

vector graphics
Images that are composed of lines and objects that define their shapes. The objects created in vector-based software are made from *Bezier curves*, which are composed of mathematically defined points and segments. Vector images take up less space on a disk than raster images of comparable dimensions. See also *object-oriented software*.

virtual memory
The memory space that is separate from the main memory (physical random access memory, or RAM) in a computer, such as hard disk space. Virtual memory helps to increase the amount of memory available to work on large documents.

wallpaper tiles
A background that is configured so that the image is displayed as repeating tiles.

Web colors
Colors that are browser-safe, meaning that all Web browsers can display them uniformly. Photoshop's Web-Safe Colors feature lets you choose colors that will not radically change when viewed on other monitors of the same quality and calibration as the one on which you are working.

white point
The lightest pixel in the highlight area of an image. In Photoshop, you can set this point in the Levels and Curves dialog boxes.

work path
In Photoshop, a temporary element that records changes as you draw new sections of a path.

Index

Note to the Reader: Throughout this index **boldfaced** page numbers indicate primary discussions of a topic. *Italicized* page numbers indicate illustrations.

G

H

Y

Z

What's on the CD-ROM

The CD-ROM included with this book is packed with files and accessories you can use.

Chapter Files

The supplemental files on the CD include the images and documents used to perform the step-by-step operations and Hands-On modules described throughout the book.

Sample Images

A gallery of Photoshop files shows you examples of the kinds of things you can create with this outstanding program!

Plug-ins and Demos

We've included some of the hottest Photoshop plug-ins and related programs for you to try out.

→ **Eye Candy** Eye Candy is a collection of 23 special-effects filters for use with Photoshop and other graphics programs.

→ **PhotoImpact** PhotoImpact gives you the necessary tools to create and edit compelling Web graphics and complete HTML pages.

→ **Xenofex** Energize your graphics projects quickly and easily with Xenofex, a collection of 16 inspirational special effects.

→ **3D Words** 3D Words enables you to create three-dimensional text designs in Adobe Illustrator (version 7 or later).

→ **Hot Text** Create three-dimensional text for your designs in Photoshop with Hot Text.

→ **Dizzy** You can add 3D models to your Photoshop and Illustrator graphics with Dizzy. Mac version only.

→ **Photo/Graphic Edges** Add edges and special effects to images with Photo/Graphic Edges.

→ **Paint Shop Pro Demo** With more than 75 special effects, Paint Shop Pro provides you with essential tools to design, create, and enhance Web graphics and digital images.